De/Colonizing the Subject

Sidonie Smith and Julia Watson, editors

De/Colonizing the Subject

The Politics of Gender in Women's Autobiography

University of Minnesota Press/Minneapolis

Chapter 6, "The Margin at the Center: on *Testimonio* (Testimonial Narrative)," first appeared in *Modern Fiction Studies,* vol. 35, no.1 (Spring 1989), copyright 1989 by Purdue Research Foundation, West Lafayette, IN 47907, reprinted with permission; portions of chapter 11, "The Changing Moral Discourse of Nineteenth-Century African American Women's Autobiography: Harriet Jacobs and Elizabeth Keckley," also appeared in *Slavery in the Americas,* ed. Wolfgang Binder, copyright Verlag Königshausen & Neumann, Würzburg, 1991, by permission; chapter 14, "The Subject of Memoirs: *The Woman Warrior*'s Technology of Ideographic Selfhood," also appeared in Lee Quinby, *Freedom, Foucault, and the Subject,* copyright 1991 by Lee Quinby, reprinted with the permission of Northeastern University Press.

Library of Congress Cataloging-in-Publication Data

De/colonizing the subject: the politics of gender in women's autobiography/ Sidonie Smith and Julia Watson, editors.
p. cm.
Includes bibliographical references and index.
ISBN 0-8166-1991-3 (alk. paper). — ISBN 0-8166-1992-1 (pbk.)
1. Women's studies—Biographical method. 2. Autobiography—Women authors—History and criticism. I. Smith, Sidonie. II. Watson, Julia.
HQ1185.D4 1992
305.42'092'2–dc20   91–30498
                                                                                              CIP

Published by the University of Minnesota Press
2037 University Avenue Southeast, Minneapolis, MN 55414
Printed in the United States of America on acid-free paper

The University of Minnesota is an
equal-opportunity educator and employer.

To Evan Orion and Tony

CONTENTS

ACKNOWLEDGMENTS

The intellectual and professional debts for this collection are many and varied. The project grew out of four Modern Language Association Special Sessions on aspects of women's autobiography organized by Julia Watson between 1984 and 1988. Encouragement for those sessions came particularly from Renée Riese Hubert. Among the panelists who aided in the book's inception were Sara Speidel, Barbara Harlow, Mary G. Mason, Celeste Schenck, and Bella Brodzki, as well as contributors Caren Kaplan, Shirley Geok-lin Lim, Nancy Paxton, and Janet Varner Gunn. To Bella we owe an unusual debt, for she was instrumental in bringing us together and mapping out issues involved in collaborative work.

Thanks are also due to Nancy K. Miller, who not only believed in the original idea for the project but also proposed the subtitle, and to Janet Braun Reinitz, Lee Quinby, and Mary Louise Pratt for vital encouragement over its long evolution. Rebecca Hogan, editor of *a/b: Auto/Biography Studies,* and members of that publication's editorial board have also made generous suggestions.

Several conferences in the last five years have provided a necessary forum for debate, exchange, and intellectual connections with the growing community of feminist scholars fascinated by autobiographical practices, most notably the 1986 conference on women's autobiography and biography held by the Center for Research on Women at Stanford University and the 1989 conference on autobiography hosted by the University of Southern Maine. The recent outpouring of reprinted and original publications of women's autobiographical writings, particularly by small presses, continues to convince us, as it has others, of the vitality and the centrality of the issues addressed in these essays. Finally, the responsiveness of our students over the years has sustained our commitment to broadening the scope of what is understood by, and what is read as, "women's autobiography."

We acknowledge also the support of Biodun Iginla, our editor at the University of Minnesota Press, who responded eagerly to our proposed collection and who consistently encouraged us as the project grew. Readers Shirley Neuman, Tom Conley, and Margo Culley offered perceptive critiques of the collection as a whole and of individual contributions. Meg Aerol, Mary Byers, and Kathy Wolter of the Press guided us skillfully through the final preparation and production of the volume. And we extend special thanks to all the contributors for their patience, their cooperation in rewriting to our exacting standards, and their enthusiasm and vision, which in turn sharpened our sense of the collection.

Partial support for planning, revision, and preparation came also from the University of Montana Office of Research, the National Endowment for the Humanitites, and the University at Binghamton.

Finally, as ever, we acknowledge the support and tolerance of our families and the love and humor of our sons, to whom this collection is dedicated.

Introduction

De/Colonization and the Politics of Discourse in Women's Autobiographical Practices

Julia Watson and Sidonie Smith

> *Is [autobiography] the model for imperializing the consciousness of colonized peoples, replacing their collective potential for resistance with a cult of individuality and even loneliness? Or is it a medium of resistance and counterdiscourse, the legitimate space for producing that excess which throws doubt on the coherence and power of an exclusive historiography?*
>
> Doris Sommer, "'Not Just a Personal Story':
> Women's *Testimonios* and the Plural Self"[1]

The Colonial Subject

Decolonization, of course, refers literally to the actual political processes set in motion in various geographical locations before and during this century. Colonies established under European domination achieved independent statehood, sometimes through peaceful and sometimes through violent struggle. But decolonization remains a problematic notion, a potential disenchantment. Colonial relationships persist today—in Northern Ireland, on the Left Bank in Israel, in South Africa, in many other parts of the world. Indigenous colonialisms characterize the relationships among peoples in many countries. Moreover, as communication networks shuttle information instantly around the globe and multinational corporations reorganize the flow of labor, capital, and control across national borders, a process of neocolonization seems to render the earlier achievement of autonomous nationhood almost irrelevant to the circulation of goods, money, and culture.

Yet if we must constantly probe the reach, contradictory strategies, and contested achievements of *decolonization,* we must also probe the reach of the term *colonization.* So widespread has become the practice of weaving the word *colonization* through various critiques

xiii

of the subject of Western humanism and the politics of representation that the word now seems to signify a universalized descriptor of subjectivity. From a Foucauldian theoretical perspective all "I"s are sites where generalized operations of power press ineluctably on the subject. From a Lacanian perspective everyone is subjected to and "colonized" by the Law of the Father. In the vogue of a materialist postmodernity, all "I"s, subject to the cultural field of multiple determinations, are colon-I-zed through irresistible interpellations. In the midst of this theoretical quagmire, Gayatri Spivak's provocative query, "Can the subaltern speak?" would need to be opened out.[2] Can any subject speak? Or is every subject "spoken for" and thus "colonized" by processes constitutive of "the human condition," from the psychological and biological to the economic, political, and discursive?

We have difficulty with such a comprehensive invocation of the concept of colonization, and for a variety of reasons. If decolonization holds out the promise of a change in subjects, so universalized a notion of colonization forecloses that possibility. Because no one can escape the realm of "the subjected," because decolonization remains a utopian dream, no one set of political actions assumes legitimacy, efficacy, or a prompt utility. The colonized subject is effectively stripped of agency.

Furthermore, however compelling and sophisticated this critique of the subject may be, it is a central instance of the universalizing agenda of Western theorizing that erases the subject's heterogeneity as well as its agency. This agenda has become increasingly apparent in feminist theories that hypostasize a universally colonized "woman," universally subjected to "patriarchal" oppression. As theorists such as bell hooks, Elizabeth V. Spellman, and Spivak, among others, insist, privileging the oppression of gender over and above other oppressions effectively erases the complex and often contradictory positionings of the subject. The axes of the subject's identifications and experiences are multiple, because locations in gender, class, race, ethnicity, and sexuality complicate one another, and not merely additively, as Spellman so effectively argues.[3] Nor do different vectors of identification and experience overlap neatly or entirely. One cannot easily sever, separate out, or subsume under one another the strands of multiple determinations. For instance, colonial regimes needed and global economies continue to need "classes" as well as "races" in order to achieve their goals. And class identifications call particular women to specific psychological and cultural itineraries that may collide and/or converge with itineraries of race and nation.

Nor can one be oblivious to the precise location in which the subject is situated. Attention to specific locations leads Spivak to insist that "the situation of the subject(s) of post-modern neo-colonialism must be rigorously distinguished from the situation of immigrants, who are still caught in some way within structures of 'colonial' subject-production; and, especially, from the historical problem of ethnic oppression on First World soil."[4]

Moreover, just as there are various colonialisms or systems of domination operative historically, there are various patriarchies operative historically, not one universal "patriarchy." There are various positions of men to patriarchy, not just an equivalence among them. As Carolyn Kay Steedman emphasizes in her analysis of the autobiographical storytelling of her working-class mother, her father was neither the patriarch of Lacan's Law of the Father nor the uncontested and powerful figure at the center of socioeconomic, political, and cultural regimes; he was, like her mother, an outlaw.[5] As there are various positions of specific men (for instance, those enjoying the benefits of hegemonic power, those suffering under the domination of others) to colonial environments, there are differences in the relationships of specific women to those men. Thus domination has different meanings and implications for the "wife," "daughter," and "independent woman" of the colonizer and for the "wife," "daughter," and "independent woman" of the colonized.

Insistence on an undifferentiated (read normatively white) global "sisterhood" of oppressed women empties the subject of all its "colorfulness"[6] by "colonizing under the sign of the same those differences that might otherwise call that totalizing concept into question."[7] Since there are always, as Chandra Talpade Mohanty reminds us, "*political* implications of *analytic* strategies and principles,"[8] we need to resist the tendency of Western theorizing to install another colonial regime, albeit now a discursive regime that works to contain "colorfulness" inside a Western theoretical territory.

Finally, as scholars of colonialism and imperialism have argued recently, the avant garde taking up of the terms *colonization* and *decolonization* by "First World" theorists intent on dislodging the certitudes of the old subject of Western humanism does an injustice to, effectively occludes, very real colonial practices in specific geographical locations and historical periods.

Although the universally colonized "woman" might be a limiting concept, a concept of colonization too carefully circumscribed, too narrowly applied to specific historical processes and geographical venues, has its limitations. Certainly the work of historians, sociologists, political theorists, anthropologists, and literary critics must be grounded in the locales and temporalities of specific colonial, postcolonial, and neocolonial experiences. But there has been more colonizing going on in the world than that which took place under the obvious colonial authorities, say, the British Raj or the French and British Protectorates. And there have been, as cultural critics point out, colonies within colonies, oppressions within oppressions. While attention to specific colonial regimes helps us resist certain totalizing tendencies in our theories, thinking broadly of the constitutive nature of subjectivity and precisely of the differential deployments of gendered subjectivity helps us tease out complex and entangled strands of oppression and domination. To this end, for instance, feminist theorists have sometimes invoked theories of gendered subjectivity, sometimes histories of gendered social practices and behaviors, to critique postcolonial theorizing that maintains a masculinist bias by failing to factor issues of gender and sexuality into discussions of colonialist discourses and colonial practices.

It is not the accumulative intent of this collection of essays to argue the universalized colonization of the human subject or the universalized colonization of "woman." On the other hand, only some of the essays focus on autobiographical writing in specific locations of colonialism—in colonial Kenya, India, Indochina/Vietnam. Our selection of essays takes as a guiding definition the one used by Chandra Talpade Mohanty when she argues that "however sophisticated or problematical its use as an explanatory construct, colonization almost invariably implies a relation of structural domination, and a suppression—often violent—of the heterogeneity of the subject(s) in question."[9] And so, other essays open out the discussion of colonial practices and decolonizing strategies by looking at autobiographical subjects in such diverse contexts as postreservation Native American culture, the Australian outback, pre- and postbellum American slavery, and compressed urban environments in Western countries.

The subject in question is called variously *the colonial subject, the dominated object,* and *the marginalized subject.* Acknowledging the significant distinctions among these phrases, we note here that, for the sake of brevity, we will use throughout our discussion the phrase *the colonial subject.* We note also that the writing/language that emanates from the position of the colonial subject is variously called the *discourse of the margins, minority discourse,* and *postcolonial discourse.* Whatever the label, that subject and that writing emanate from what Abdul R. JanMohamed and David Lloyd call a position of damage, one in which "the cultural formations, languages, the diverse modes of identity of the 'minoritized peoples' are irreversibly affected, if not eradicated, by the effects of their material deracination from the historically developed social and economic structures in terms of which alone they 'made sense.'"[10] And so the essays in this collection, in their different ways, ask what autobiographical processes are set in motion when this subject struggles toward voice, history, and a future.

The Autobiographical Subject

The very notion of "autobiography" itself requires at least three perspectival adjustments. The first involves historicizing Western practices. Although the genres of life writing in the West emerge in Antiquity, the term *autobiography* is a post-Enlightenment coinage. Yet the word and the practice invoke a particular genealogy, resonant ideology, and discursive imperative. Powering and defining centers, margins, boundaries, and grounds of action in the West, traditional "autobiography" has been implicated in a specific notion of "selfhood." This Enlightenment "self," ontologically identical to other "I"s, sees its destiny in a teleological narrative enshrining the "individual" and "his" uniqueness.[11] Autobiography also entwines the definition of the human being in a web of privileged characteristics. Despite their myriad differences, of place, time, histories, economies, cultural identifications, all "I"s are rational, agentive, unitary. Thus the "I" becomes "Man," putatively a marker of the universal human subject whose essence remains outside the vagaries of history, effectually what Spivak has termed the "straight white Christian man of property,"[12] whose identity is deeply embedded in a specific history of privilege.

Since Western autobiography rests upon the shared belief in a commonsense identification of one individual with another, all "I"s are potentially interesting autobiographers. And yet, not all are "I"s. Where Western eyes see Man as a unique individual rather than a member of a collectivity, of race or nation, of sex or sexual preference, Western eyes see the colonized as an amorphous, generalized collectivity. The colonized "other" disappears into an anonymous, opaque collectivity of undifferentiated bodies. In this way, argues Rey Chow, "Man (hence Europe) . . . hails the world into being . . . in such a way as to mark [the non-European world] off from European consciousness or universality."[13] Moreover, heterogeneous "others" are collapsed and fashioned into an essentialized "other" whose "I" has no access to a privatized but privileged individuality.[14]

Thus the politics of this "I" have been the politics of centripetal consolidation and centrifugal domination. The cultural dominance of the West effectively enables this "Man" to *"make a meaning stick,"*[15] to make *his* meaning stick. The impact of this epistemological franchise on the matter of meaning has ramifications for the perpetuation of relations of dominance. As Deborah Cameron argues, "Meaning can be deployed to sustain domination" in that "it can *reify* domination by presenting as eternal and natural what is in fact historical and transitory."[16] Erasing historical contingency in service to a universalized humanism, the Man without history contains and silences the heterogeneity of subject peoples.

Western autobiography colludes in this cultural mythmaking. One of the narratives that brings this Man into being, it functions as an exclusionary genre against which the utterances of other subjects are measured and misread. While inviting all subjects to participate in its practices, it provides the constraining template or the generic "law" against which those subjects and their diverse forms of self-narrative are judged and found wanting. In order to unstick both this Man and his meanings, we need to adjust, to reframe, our understanding of both traditional and countertraditional autobiographical practices.

The second adjustment requires that we consider the flexibilities of generic boundaries. In fact, we need to consider, with Ralph Cohen, how "classifications," including generic ones, "are empirical, not logical"; how "they are historical assumptions constructed by authors, audiences, and critics in order to serve communicative and aesthetic purposes."[17] And, we would add, political purposes. If that is so, autobiographical writing is at this historical moment a "genre of choice," for authors, audiences, and critics. Autobiographical writing surrounds us, but the more it surrounds us, the more it defies generic stabilization, the more its laws are broken, the more it drifts toward other practices, the more formerly "out-law" practices drift into its domain.[18] While popular practitioners carry on the old autobiographical tradition, other practitioners play with forms that challenge us to recognize their experiments in subjectivity and account for their exclusion from "high" literature.

The third adjustment will require more time to accomplish. What has been designated as Western autobiography is only one form of "life writing." There are other modes of life story telling, both oral and written, to be recognized, other genealogies of life story telling to be chronicled, other explorations of traditions, current and past, to be factored into the making and unmaking of autobiographical subjects in a global environment.[19]

Alternative and Diverse Autobiographical Practices

Decolonization is always a multidimensional process rather than a homogeneous achievement. And it involves the deformation/reformation of identity. That is why we have chosen to foreground the slash in the word *de/colonization*. The slash symbolizes the exchange between the processes of colonization and decolonization and the issues inherent in the process of neocolonization. Given the colonial, postcolonial, and neocolonial locales in which a writer produces an autobiographical text, what then does the speaker make of the auto-biographical "I"? And what strategies drive, what meanings emerge from, what uses define her autobiographical project?

The autobiographical occasion (whether performance or text) be-comes a site on which cultural ideologies intersect and dissect one another, in contradiction, consonance, and adjacency. Thus the site is rife with diverse potentials, some of which we would like to suggest here, some of which the essays that follow explore in more detail. Take the mimetic potential of autobiographical practice. On the one hand, the very taking-up-of-the-autobiographical transports the colo-nial subject into the territory of the "universal" subject and thus promises a culturally empowered subjectivity. Participation in, through re/presentation of, privileged narratives can secure cultural recognition for the subject. On the other hand, entry into the territory of traditional autobiography implicates the speaker in a potentially recuperative per-formance, one that might reproduce and re/present the colonizer's figure in negation.[20] For to write "autobiography" is partially to enter into the contractual and discursive domain of universal "Man," whom Rey Chow calls the "dominating subject."[21] Entering the terrain of autobiography, the colonized subject can get stuck in "*his* meaning." The processes of self-decolonization may get bogged down as the autobiographical subject reframes herself through neocolonizing metaphors.

Yet autobiographical practices can be productive in that process as the subject, articulating problems of identity and identification, strug-gles against coercive calls to a "universal humanity."[22] For the margina-lized woman, autobiographical language may serve as a coinage that purchases entry into the social and discursive economy.[23] To enter into language is to press back against total inscription in dominating struc-tures, against the disarticulation of that spectral other that Chow calls the "dominated object."[24] Precisely because she is subject to "incom-mensurable solicitations and heterogeneous social practices,"[25] the autobiographical speaker can resist the processes of negation. Deploy-ing autobiographical practices that go against the grain, she may con-stitute an "I" that becomes a place of creative and, by implication, political intervention. "The colonized," argue Chandra T. Mohanty and Satya P. Mohanty, "are not just the object of the colonizer's discourses, but the agents of a conflicted history, inhabiting and transforming a complex social and cultural world."[26] If, with Judith Butler, we think of agency as "located within the possibility of a variation on th[e] repetition" of certain "rule-bound discourse[s],"[27] and if we think of discourses of identity as heterogeneous even in their seeming hegemony, then we make a space in autobiographical practices for the agency of the autobiographical subject.

In this space too the autobiographical speaker may authorize an alternative way of knowing, filtered through what Barbara Harlow describes as specific "conditions of observation"[28] and others refer to as "experience." Averring the integrity of her perspective on identity, experience, and politics, the autobiographical subject may offer up what Nancy Hartsock calls a "standpoint epistemology": "an account of the world as seen from the margins, an account which can expose the falseness of the view from the top and can transform the margins as well as the center . . . an account of the world which treats our perspectives not as subjugated or disruptive knowledges, but as primary and constitutive of a different world."[29] Thus both self-representation and self-presentation have the potential to intervene in the comfortable alignments of power relationships, relationships "controlled by conditioned ways of seeing."[30] They also have the potential to celebrate through countervalorization another way of seeing, one unsanctioned, even unsuspected, in the dominant cultural surround. And with shifts in vision can follow social change, even creations of new worlds, since, as Arif Dirlik argues, "culture is not only a way of seeing the world, but also a way of making and changing it."[31]

Also in this alternative space, narrative itineraries may take different paths. For the colonial subject, the process of coming to writing is an articulation *through* interrogation, a charting of the conditions that have historically placed her identity under erasure. Consequently, her narratives do not necessarily fall into a privatized itinerary, the journey toward something, the personal struggle toward God, the entry into society of the *Bildungsroman,* the confessional mode, and the like. Such Western modes both define and collusively maintain the narrow range of narrative paradigms, holding the politicized dimension of identity and self, as of cultural consciousness, in abeyance. Such modes secure the "individual" rather than the collective character of self-representation. Yet even if the colonial subject does mime certain traditional patterns, she does so with a difference. She thus exposes their gaps and incongruities, wrenches their meanings, calls their authority into question,[32] for "illegitimate" speakers have a way of exposing the instability of forms.

As many of the essays acknowledge, the colonial subject inhabits a politicized rather than privatized space of narrative. Political realities cannot be evaded in the constitution of identity. In fact, attention to them can become a source of subversive power, as Harlow claims in her essay on women's prison writings: "In the same way that institutions of power . . . are subverted by the demand on the part of dispossessed groups for an access to history, power, and resources, so too are the narrative paradigms and their textual authority being transformed by the historical and literary articulation of those demands."[33] Attention to the politics of identity can also become a source of hybrid forms, what Kaplan calls "out-law" genres, and what others in this volume explore as counterhegemonic narratives: ideographic selfhood, ethnography, collective self-storytelling.

As a process and a product of decolonization, autobiographical writing has the potential to "transform spectators crushed with their inessentiality into privileged actors," to foster "the veritable creation of new [wo]men," to quote, with a shift in emphasis, the revolutionary Frantz Fanon.[34] Thus autobiographical performances, drawing upon exogenous and indigenous cultural practices, signal the heterogeneity of the subject and her narrative itinerary. In resistance to the panoptic figuration of an anonymous object unified as cultural representative, the autobiographical speaker may "dissolve," as David Lloyd suggests, "the canonical form of Man back into the different bodies which it has sought to absorb."[35] But the power of cultural forms to recolonize peoples cannot be underestimated. All of which is to suggest that the relationship of the colonial subject to autobiographical inscription is indeed troubled.

The Essays

We offer here our contribution to the debates about autobiographical practices, politics, and gender in the global environment. We have tried to gather essays that range broadly around the world, from North to South, from America to Africa to Australia. There are essays on women in historically colonial, transitional, and currently postcolonial environments; essays from various borders of marginality; essays on women writing from diverse class positions; essays exploring the authors' positions in systems of oppression and their impact on the relationship between the author and the essay's subject; essays exploring the complicities of authors in colonizing practices. From multiple perspectives we hope through this volume to investigate the heteronomous meanings of the "colonial subject" and to explore autobiography as a potential site of decolonization.

We do not claim to present here a representative sampling of women's autobiographies of colonization and decolonization, nor do we claim to offer a "history" of such autobiographical practices. We believe no definitive history could be collected and written at this time. Both the parameters of colonization and the texts of women's coming to voice are in flux, with narratives still being "discovered" and produced, reprinted and translated, and otherwise brought into circulation. Nor can "academic" women necessarily measure the power of an autobiography to "speak" to readers either within a culture or transnationally. Our selections need to be understood as in every sense exemplary, and clustered in some areas at the expense of others.

For example, the Indian subcontinent, with its history of British colonization, is the only area of Asia explored in depth here. Yet the autobiographical practices discussed—of British women under the Raj, of Kamala Das, of Indira Gandhi as semiotic sign—offer illuminating instances of the numerous and complex ways that women's self-representational practices both display and interrogate moments of this specific colonial heritage. British women in mid-nineteenth-century India, as Nancy Paxton shows, both participate in the Empire's colonization of the bodies and subjectivity of the Indian populace and experience their own marginality within a gendered society that places them in proximity to, and sometimes in communication with, the silences of Indian women. By exploring the conjunction of technologies of gender and of imperialism in these texts, Paxton discovers points of exposure, those textual moments in which the constitution of the imperial "I" confronts the destabilizing impacts of embodiedness. Shirley Geok-lin Lim discusses how Kamala Das explores the cultural imperatives that have defined her as a silent, dutiful postcolonial daughter. The insufficiency of available cultural discourses for Das to write her embodied sensuality leads her to unavoidably transgressive self-assertion. Lim explores how this negotiation of Indian female sexuality involves Das in an epistemological confrontation with patriarchal society. Gita Rajan discusses Indira Gandhi as a semiotic text of postliberation India to be deciphered against Western cultural modes of subjectivity. In Gandhi's self-presentation, the subaltern is figured; but over successive historical moments, she both ensnares and undoes her subaltern status. Reading Gandhi, Rajan rereads both her own culture and the influential Indian critic, Gayatri Spivak, in order to rewrite the possibility of agency as/for Indian women. In this triangulated reflection on Indian de/colonization, Paxton, Lim, and Rajan are not primarily interested in defining colonizers and colonized, but in observing the operations that complicate distinctions between colonizer and colonized. In each case politics operates as a move from a private, unwritten history to an articulation that can become transformative, and, in the rare case of Indira Gandhi, formative as collective political history.

The task of representing the range and specificity of women's identities in the United States and North America has been daunting. We have made choices and left gaps for others to fill. The most notable gap is in Chicana autobiography, where both a first-person literature by such writers as Cherríe Moraga, Gloria Anzaldúa, and Sandra Cisneros and critical work by such emerging literary critics as Ramón Saldívar and Sonia Saldívar thrives in book-length works that cannot be glossed briefly. But an exploration of how the appropriation of Chicano culture can be read through its cookbooks is mapped in Anne Goldman's essay. Recipes for exoticization, hybridization, and normalization can be found in the remaking of Mexican food for mainstream American consumption, as can recipes for the distortion and erasure of indigenous cultures. As Goldman suggests, the Western reader has to begin by reading the effacement that the practices of the dominant culture have exercised upon ethnic identities in the name of authenticating them. But she also proposes, in her subsequent reading of the cookbook narratives of Cleofas Jaramillo and Fabiola Cabeza de Baca, how the colonized subject can resist cultural appropriation through her own authenticating of autobiographical recipes. Debra A. Castillo also explores how indigenous North American culture is literally colonized and its collective autobiographical inscription effaced. Tracing the migration of identity and the Western claim to ownership of the apparatuses of identity in Rosario Castellanos's autobiographical writing, Castillo marks the disruption of language between a Mexican child of Spanish descent and her Indian nursemaid, who cannot lay claim to identity in verbal terms but is only the "ashes without a face" of centuries of colonization.

Other essays look to the problem of the subject in the African American community. In his essay on the narratives of ex-slaves, William L. Andrews focuses on the difference in discursive strategies employed by Harriet Jacobs, who, writing prior to the Civil War, invokes the moral discourse of true womanhood, and Elizabeth Keckley, who, writing just a few crucial years later, employs the discourse of economic materialism. This difference speaks not just of a historical shift in the formation of the African American woman's cultural identity, but also of the variety and specificity of responses to oppression and of the bind of needing both to internalize and to resist/rewrite discursive strategies as the condition of writing the female subject into literary identity. Andrews points up the instability of borders separating colonization and decolonization, and refocuses our attention from a unitary agenda of liberation to the problematic of the subject speaking the master's discourse if she is to speak at all.

In a similar vein, Claudine Raynaud considers Zora Neale Hurston's *Dust Tracks on a Road* as a discursively manipulated text. Hurston's autobiography was, if not colonized, censored by both her editor and herself as they struggled in the margins of the draft over the kind of subject that would be acceptable to her predominantly white audience. Working with previously unexamined manuscripts, Raynaud notes editorial excisions and interpolations in various hands and considers both their origins and the resulting differences in voices of a text that has been read as Hurston's "authoritative" autobiography. If Raynaud looks for the "noise" in the margins of the drafts of Hurston's text, Françoise Lionnet theorizes the relationship between noise and the resistance of *métissage*. If autobiographical texts are reams of pages to be inscribed and excised, they are also voices—many voices in tension and in play. In examining the autobiographical writings of Jamaican-born American resident Michelle Cliff, Lionnet focuses on the patois of native dialect and the metaphors of mangoes and maroons in order to foreground Cliff's strategies for writing the narrative of difference through the inimical discourse of standard English and First World autobiographical paradigms.

Native American ethnicities may also be read against the dominating culture's penchant for stereotyping and classifying. The essays by Janice Gould and Greg Sarris are autobiographical essays about autobiography. Each writer insists on framing "autobiography" as a problematical model of storytelling that not only silences Native Americans but fails to account for differently told and differently heard stories. Gould explores the dilemma of being fixed through racist categorizations and the uncertainties of cultural identification she confronts as a Maidu mixed-blood. Yet, she identifies herself with a large and growing group of mixed-blood Native American writers who tell stories of difficult negotiations of cultural mixing, loss of homeland and tribal family, locations in urban landscapes where the particulars of difference are neither seen nor prized. Sarris's autobiographical account of Mabel McKay's appearance before a class of literature students at Stanford University is a double narrative of McKay's unmaking of fictions of identity and her making, in a basket, of a figure of collective self-reference that is concretely located yet resistant to conventional Western modes of interpretation. Refusing to be contained in the lecture hall of the "mainline" institution, McKay unsettles her audience and challenges Sarris himself by telling stories that defy their understanding and classifying.

In another look at indigenous peoples, Kateryna Olijnyk Longley discusses the autobiographical narratives of aboriginal women in Australia whose identities are culturally under erasure and yet specifically oral, generational, and tribal. For Aborigines, as for many Native Americans, coming to writing and autobiographical inscription coincided with or resulted from oppression and genocidal acculturations. As Longley suggests, Aboriginal stories thus allude to an empowered past irretrievable outside collective narrative and a resulting sense of identity caught between flux and flight.

There is assuredly much in European autobiography to lure us: for instance, the engendering of the imperial subject in First World autobiography or the complexities of historical consciousness and the tensions of ethnicities and nationalisms in an increasingly "unified" Europe. We choose, however, to look at texts in which European women are placed in specific colonial locations. Marguerite Duras's best-seller *The Lover,* as Suzanne Chester argues, positions the problems of de/colonization precisely at the slash. In this veiled autobiography personal history is written by and read through French colonial domination of Southeast Asia. The interplay of its subject's complex positionings with respect to gender, class, and race creates a tension of discourses through which oppressor and oppressed constantly change places. For European women in colonial locations, identity becomes a nomadic fiction. In discussing the autobiographical narratives of Isak Dinesen and Beryl Markham, two white women writing of life in colonial Kenya, Sidonie Smith explores the relationship of gender to the narrative politics that emerge in a specific colonial environment. However divergent their narrative strategies, both Markham and Dinesen make and remake themselves as "African." Between Africa as the maternal goddess in Dinesen's nostalgic dream and Africa as the wild space of Markham's masculinist adventuring, different metaphorical scenarios play out the complicities and resistances of "colonial" narrative practices.

The two essays on texts by Middle Eastern women explore the representation of childhood in part to foreground identity formation through practices of postcolonial education. Both discussions gesture toward the diversity of identity formations, ethnic heritages, and political configurations "orientalized" under the sign of the Middle East.

In recovering the serialized autobiography of Egyptian feminist and educator Nabawiyya Musa from archives in Cairo, Margot Badran discovers a model of middle-class Egyptian "feminism" antinomial to the privileged and Europeanized feminism of Huda Sha'rawi, the only other precontemporary Egyptian woman autobiographer extensively discussed in the West to date. Badran reads a self-decolonizing strategy in Musa's refusal of a model childhood, and insistence on a childhood characterized by a series of rebellions that prepared her to oppose the Egyptian ideology of colonial womanhood in championing educational reforms. During a Palestinian winter, Janet Varner Gunn writes autobiographically of discovering her impatience with the imperialist presumption underlying Western idealization of the individual. In this setting she reads the reification of romantic individualism idealized in Annie Dillard's *An American Childhood* against the unromantic realities of childhood and the "conscientization" of identity in the autobiography of Palestinian "terrorist" Leila Khaled. Gunn explores how Khaled's education prepares her to question individualist values and to redefine identity as collective, history as mission, and education as practice. Reframing her own poetics of experience as a politics, Gunn asks if Western autobiographical writings, including her own, can avoid being acts of expropriation.

The essays by Lee Quinby, John Beverley, Caren Kaplan, and Carole Boyce Davies, in different ways, theorize the collection's focus on women's autobiography, inquiring into claims about subject formation that make such writing both persuasive and suspect. These mappings of the territorialization and transgression of autobiographical theory offer a mirror for reading these essays against First World accounts of autobiography and its canon. Quinby uses *The Woman Warrior* to develop a Foucauldian analysis of how the female subject of autobiography is formed at the intersection of two discourses of power, the systems of alliance and sexuality, that are deployed to maintain the daughter's silence and marginalization. Quinby argues for reading Kingston's narrative as memoirs, promoting the new subjectivity of ideographic selfhood, rather than as autobiography, because she considers autobiography's totalizing and normalizing of the subject to be implicated in modern power structures. In an influential essay published three years ago and reprinted here with a new postscript, John Beverley discusses *testimonio* as an embryonic form of collective autobiographical witnessing that gives voice to the struggles of oppressed peoples against neo- and postcolonial exploitation. *Testimonio* has to be seen, Beverley argues, as an alternative to autobiography, an essentially conservative humanistic mode. A narrative urge to communicate the personal as political becomes, in *testimonio,* an affirmation of the marginalized speaking subject and her experience of the real. In *I, Rigoberta Menchú* Beverley finds conscious resistance to "a humanist ideology of the literary." The subject of *testimonio* narrates more than she authors, in the Western sense, her subalternity, and thus destabilizes the reader's world.

Caren Kaplan both builds on and resituates Beverley's analysis of *testimonio* as a form of antihumanistic, collective witnessing in her notion of out-law genres of autobiography. She sees as problematic autobiography's fixation on stable—read nationally identified—subjects at a time when identities are nomadic, national borders are being redefined, and the parameters invoked in naming women's differences are shown to be part of the instrumentality for maintaining those differences. Kaplan proposes, in this transitional surround, reframing autobiographical practice through "out-law" genres. Refusing to contain collaborative life stories in traditional autobiographical frameworks, Carole Boyce Davies discusses the ways in which this "crossover genre" becomes a form for the empowerment of women formerly silenced. Elaborating the degree and the form of editorial intervention in three forms of collaborative life story telling, she considers the complex dynamic between the speaking subject and the "interpreter" in projects that transform oral histories into written texts.

Finally, Julia Watson considers "sexual decolonization" as a notion within Western feminism that appears problematic when read in the context of neocolonial and postcolonial women's writing. Generally invoked in critiques of a universalized patriarchy, sexual decolonization requires an oppositional framework that reifies sexual difference. But autobiographies both lesbian and feminist have now begun to critique oppositional notions of gender for their complicity in maintaining heterosexist hegemony. In Audre Lorde's biomythography, Adrienne Rich's irreducibly split self-representation, and Jo Spence's photo-therapy, Watson finds autobiographical practices that deconstruct hierarchical sexual difference while contesting sexual identity as a sufficient index of colonized status.

These introductory remarks suggest one way of putting the essays in this volume in dialogue with one another, both within and across geopolitical boundaries. They also suggest possible ways to stimulate debate around the key concepts we have been addressing in this introduction, around the terms *colonization, decolonization, authorship, authenticity, agency, subjectivity, individuality, location, resistance, collusion.* But our intent here is not to fix the relationships among essays so much as to provoke connections. Individual readers will make and remake this dialogue to fit their different interests.

We do want, however, to call into question Western literary practices and theorizing. It does us no good, it does literary practice no good, to take up critical definitions, typologies, reading practices, and thematics forged in the West through the engagement with canonical Western texts and to read texts from various global locations through those lenses. Different texts from different locales require us to develop different theories and practices of reading, what we might call "standpoint" reading practices. Such practices call all of us, positioned specifically in our own locales, both to engage the autobiographical practices of colonial subjects and to critique our own points of observation.[36]

Finally, we note that the people contributing essays to this volume write in various locations throughout the world—in Australia, the Middle East, various "states" in the United States. While this volume issues from the "West" and primarily from people in its academies, a number of the contributors have come from various geographical and geopolitically marked places, from India, Malaysia, the Caribbean, Mauritius. Thus, despite the location of production, we hope that the volume signifies a collectivity of people working in a global environment, positioned in different personal and theoretical locations. We hope, then, that we gesture toward what Kaplan calls "transnational" perspectives rather than enshrining neo-imperialist scriptures on the politics of autobiographical practices. We have worked to resist an easy and imperialist universalization of experience in order to recognize, salute, and give validity to positions of difference and to affinities rather than prescriptive identifications. We do not want to appropriate in a too-easy gesture of imperial identification, or to romanticize in a fantasy of feminist homogeneity, or to silence by a telescoping act of interpretation the multiple and specific voices of the autobiographical texts invoked in these essays.

Notes

1. Doris Sommer, "'Not Just a Personal Story': Women's *Testimonios* and the Plural Self," in *Life/Lines: Theorizing Women's Autobiography,* ed. Bella Brodzki and Celeste Schenck (Ithaca, N.Y.: Cornell University Press, 1988), 111.

2. Gayatri Chakravorty Spivak, *"Can the Subaltern Speak? Speculations on Widow Sacrifice,"* in *Marxism and the Interpretation of Culture,* ed. Cary Nelson and Lawrence Grossberg (Urbana: University of Illinois Press, 1988), 271–313. This provocative essay has generated various contestatory theoretical stances on the "voice" of the subaltern.

3. Elizabeth V. Spellman, *Inessential Woman: Problems of Exclusion in Feminist Thought* (Boston: Beacon, 1988); see especially chapter 5.

4. Gayatri Chakravorty Spivak, "The Political Economy of Women as Seen by a Literary Critic," in *Coming to Terms: Feminism, Theory, Politics,* ed. Elizabeth Weed (New York: Routledge, 1989), 226.

5. Carolyn Kay Steedman, *Landscape for a Good Woman: A Story of Two Lives* (New Brunswick N.J.: Rutgers University Press, 1987), 65–82.

6. For a provocative analysis of the struggle of "the universal human subject" with all the "colorful" around it, see Peter Stallybrass and Allon White, *The Politics and Poetics of Transgression* (Ithaca, N.Y.: Cornell University Press, 1986), 199.

7. Judith Butler, *Gender Trouble: Feminism and the Subversion of Identity* (New York: Routledge, 1990), 13.

8. Chandra Talpade Mohanty, "Under Western Eyes: Feminist Scholarship and Colonial Discourses," *Boundary* 2, 12 (1984): 336. See also Ketu H. Katrak, "Decolonizing Culture: Toward a Theory for Postcolonial Women's Texts," *Modern Fiction Studies* 35 (Spring 1989): 158–60.

9. Mohanty, "Under Western Eyes," 336.

10. Abdul R. JanMohamed and David Lloyd, "Introduction," *Cultural Critique* 6 (Spring 1987): 8–9.

11. David Lloyd argues that the concept of a universal human subject soliciting common identification "inaugurates a universal history of development which always contains the realization of individual autonomy within a narrative so exclusive that it becomes the legitimation of an irreducible heteronomy," with the result that "the path by which social identity is formed is the one which leads back from differentiation to identification with an imperial Man whose destiny is always the same." "Genet's Genealogy: European Minorities and the Ends of the Canon, *Cultural Critique* 6 (Spring 1987): 85.

12. Gayatri Chakravorty Spivak, *Harper's Magazine* (September 1989), 52.

13. Rey Chow, "'It's you and not me': Domination and 'Othering' in Theorizing the 'Third World,'" in *Coming to Terms: Feminism, Theory, Politics,* ed. Elizabeth Weed (New York: Routledge, 1989), 158.

14. As JanMohamed and Lloyd argue, "Minority individuals are always treated and forced to experience themselves generically." "Introduction," 10.

15. John B. Thompson, *Studies in the Theory of Ideology* (Cambridge: Polity, 1984), 132. Deborah Cameron quotes this passage in her comparative analysis of various feminist language theories, "What Is the Nature of Women's Oppression in Language?" *Oxford Literary Review* 8 (1986): 84.

16. Cameron, "What Is the Nature," 83.

17. Ralph Cohen, "History and Genre," *New Literary History* 17 (Winter 1986): 210.

18. See Marjorie Perloff, "Introduction," in *Postmodern Genres,* ed. Marjorie Perloff (Norman: University of Oklahoma Press, 1988), 7.

19. On Arabic autobiographical traditions see, for instance, Leila Ahmed, "Between Two Worlds: The Formation of a Turn-of-the-Century Egyptian Feminist," in *Life/Lines: Theorizing Women's Autobiography,* ed. Bella Brodzki and Celeste Schenck (Ithaca, N.Y.: Cornell University Press, 1988), 154. On traditions of life writing in Japan, see Chizuko Yonamine, "'Self' in a Tenth-Century Japanese Autobiography" (Paper presented at the conference "New Approaches to Biography: Challenges from Critical Theory," University of Southern California, 19–21 October 1990).

20. See Abdul R. JanMohamed, "Negating the Negation as a Form of Affirmation in Minority Discourse: The Construction of Richard Wright as Subject," *Cultural Critique* 7 (Fall 1987): 246–47.

21. Chow, "'It's you,'" 157.

22. "The most crucial aspect of resisting the hegemony," suggest JanMohamed, "consists in struggling against its attempt to form one's subjectivity, for it is through the construction of the minority subject that the dominant culture can elicit the individual's own help in his/her oppression." JanMohamed, 246–47.

23. For a discussion of the relation between hegemonic domination and human agency, see Benita Parry, "Problems in Current Theories of Colonial Discourse," *Oxford Literary Review* 9 (1987): 27–58. Parry suggests that certain strands of deconstructive practice that take their cues from Derridean deconstruction produce "a theory assigning an absolute power to the hegemonic discourse in constituting and disarticulating the native." Thus from one point of view, the subaltern does not, cannot, "talk back" to the "metropolis." Critiquing Spivak's theory, Parry suggests that "the story of colonialism which she reconstructs is of an interactive process where the European agent in consolidating the imperialist Sovereign Self, induces the native to collude in its own subject(ed) formation as other and voiceless. Thus while protesting at the obliteration of the native's subject position in the text of imperialism, Spivak in her project gives no speaking part to the colonized" (p. 35).

24. Chow, "'It's you,'" 157.

25. Parry, "Problems in Current Theories," 43–44.

26. Chandra T. Mohanty and Satya P. Mohanty, "Contradictions of Colonialism," *Women's Review of Books* 7 (March 1990), 19.

27. "To understand identity as a *practice,* and as a signifying practice," suggests Butler, "is to understand culturally intelligible subjects as the resulting effect of a rule-bound discourse that inserts itself in the pervasive and mundane signifying acts of linguistic life." *Gender Trouble,* 145. See also Paul Smith, who argues that "a person is not simply an *actor* who follows ideological scripts, but is also an *agent* who reads them in order to insert him/herself into them—or not." *Discerning the Subject* (Minneapolis: University of Minnesota Press, 1988), xxxiv-xxxv.

28. Barbara Harlow, "Introduction," in *The Colonial Harem,* Malek Alloula (Minneapolis: University of Minnesota Press, 1986), xxii.

29. Nancy Hartsock, "Foucault on Power: A Theory for Women?" in *Feminism/Postmodernism,* ed. Linda J. Nicholson (New York: Routledge, 1990), 171.

30. Arif Dirlik, "Culturalism as Hegemonic Ideology and Liberating Practice," *Cultural Critique* 6 (Spring 1987): 14.

31. Dirlik, "Culturalism as Hegemonic Ideology," 14. "Recalling culture in its double meaning," suggests Dirlik, "both as a 'way of seeing' and as a way of making the world, returns the historical subject (or agent) to his dialectical temporality which, Jameson has suggested, decenters him from his privileged position in history . . . in other words, there is the possibility of a truly liberating practice which can exist only as a possibility and which must take as its premise the denial of a center to the social process and of a predestined direction to history" (p. 49).

32. Homi Bhabha, "Of Mimicry and Man: The Ambivalence of Colonial Discourse," *October* 28 (1984): 125–33. See also Parry's critique of Bhabha's concept of mimicry/hybridity. She argues that, unlike Spivak, Bhabha makes a space for the articulation of the subaltern or minoritized speaker: "A narrative which delivers the colonized from its discursive status as the illegitimate and refractory foil of Europe, into a position of 'hybridity' from which it is able to circumvent, challenge and refuse colonial authority, has no place for a totalizing notion of epistemic violence. Nor does the conflictual economy of the colonialist text allow for the unimpeded operation of discursive aggression." "Problems in Current Theories," 42.

33. Barbara Harlow, "From the Women's Prison: Third World Women's Narratives of Prison," *Feminist Studies* 12 (Fall 1986): 502–3.

34. Frantz Fanon, *The Wretched of the Earth* (New York: Grove, 1963), 36.

35. Lloyd, "Genet's Genealogy," 185.

36. Spivak warns that academic scholars must engage the texts of the other through knowledge of the language of the other. "Political Economy," 228.

PART I

Autobiographical Identities and Cultural Interventions

Chapter 1

Collaboration and the Ordering Imperative in Life Story Production

Carole Boyce Davies

> *Soon it was clear that the testimonies would not sit neatly into an introductory section. They refused to become supporting evidence of predetermined factors. They threatened to take over the entire project and they would not behave. . . . So, in the end we gave up trying to trim them and silence them and we decided to change the nature of the entire project.*
>
> Sistren, *Lionheart Gal: Life Stories of Jamaican Women*[1]

The primary theoretical question posed in identifying life stories, orally narrated and transferred to print, is the problem of authority and control over the text. As distinct from written autobiography, where there is the assumption of a single, *writing* author and specific authorial control, the life story is first narrated orally and then presented in writing. In effect, then, two texts are active: the oral and the written. But in the process of writing the life, the oral text is displaced. At the same time, because of the collaborative process involved, the autobiographical "I," with its authority, is replaced by a less stable "we." The mediating or intervening presence between the two processes—oral narration and writing—is an editor or collector who often becomes, but is not necessarily always, the writer. So issues of orality and writing, editors and speaking subjects, are all implicated. The central and motivating question for this essay, then, is, What are the implications of editorial intervention and ordering processes in the textual production of a life story?

For the purposes of this essay, it is important to delineate some of the modes of life story telling/writing that have appeared so far.[2] Formally, the most accessible type of life story is the extended autobiographical narrative. It is usually a detailed story, narrated at intervals

3

to an interviewer and then subsequently produced chronologically by the writer. Examples include Winnie Mandela's *Part of My Soul Went with Him,* edited by Anne Benjamin; *Nisa: The Life and Words of a !Kung Woman,* edited by Marjorie Shostak; and *Poppie Nongena: One Woman's Struggle against Apartheid,* edited by Elsa Joubert.[3] These narratives tend to be closest to the given autobiographical format as an extended, linear, chronological reconstruction of a life. Yet, on close scrutiny, they are manipulated chronologies, constructed and ordered to meet the very narrow conventions of published autobiography.

The formal and ideological technicalities of this type of collaboration have been explored by Albert Stone in "Two Recreate One: The Act of Collaboration in Recent Black Autobiography, Ossie Guffy, Nate Shaw, Malcolm X."[4] For Stone, *The Autobiography of Malcolm X,* written by Alex Haley, is the most successful of this type of dually authored text and hence a theoretical model for studying this form. In Stone's model, two persons make the process and "neither subject nor scribe is famous in that particular role." Further, "*what* has happened in this life is more immediately compelling than *how* it is being communicated and *by whom.*"[5] The strength of the writer then rests on the ability to re-create the words and voice of the subject.

The proliferation of collections of women's oral histories and life stories has inaugurated a careful examination of collection processes and of the formal features of these texts and their contexts. These collections challenge Stone's model of dual collaboration, which implies only two participants. Instead, they necessitate the identification of the *collective life story* as a second mode of life story telling that moves beyond the sense of a *dually authored* text to a *multiply articulated* text. This model of the collective life story advances much of the discussion of oral history by examining issues of narrative process. Examples of this model include Sistren's *Lionheart Gal: Life Stories of Jamaican Women; Hard Times Cotton Mill Girls,* edited by Victoria Byerly; *Old Wives' Tales: Life-Stories from Ibibioland,* edited by Iris Andreski; *Life Histories of African Women,* edited by Patricia W. Romero; *Silenced,* edited by Makeda Silvera; *Khul Khaal: Five Egyptian Women Tell Their Stories,* edited by Nayra Atiya; and *Brazilian Women Speak: Contemporary Life Stories,* edited by Daphne Patai.[6] These narratives can be read as individual stories (corresponding more in length to the short story), or they can be read collectively as one story refracted through multiple lives, lives that share a common experience.

In this particular form of life story telling, the editor is often positioned in an activist, working relationship with a variety of women.
Out of this experience of struggle and shared political purpose come
these stories. The women whose stories are told seem to share a
commitment to making their stories public. In all of these collections,
the editors describe an ongoing process of struggle over issues that
led to the need to document their collective experiences.

In a third mode, individual life experiences are interspersed in
various ways in an extended discursive interaction with the editorial
voice. The lives of women become illustrations of explicitly defined
ideological positions. As well, they tell anecdotally of different life
experiences at different times. Or they may be interviews, or "case
histories," or snapshots of lives that illustrate specific issues. Awa
Thiam's *Black Sisters, Speak Out* is a good example, as are Lesley
Lawson's *Working Women: A Portrait of South Africa's Black Women
Workers,* Julie Frederikse's *South Africa: A Different Kind of War,* and
Diana Russell's *Lives of Courage.*[7] These life experiences are often
incorporated in larger "scholarly" texts for the overtly practical purpose of meeting academic publishing demands or for political reasons,
such as advancing a cause or challenging a pattern of domination. In
the Thiam text, the case of women's oppression and silence is the
issue. In the others, resistance to apartheid and the exploitation of
women's labor are motivating factors.

At the furthest end of this type of life presentation is the interview
or conversation model, which I hesitate to identify separately as a
fourth mode primarily because all the other forms are based on the
interview. Fatima Mernissi's *Doing Daily Battle* is an excellent example
of published interviews.[8] Yet, this interview/conversation form offers
the most direct challenge to life story as a single, linear narration.
Essentially, all oral life story collections are initiated as interviews.
But in this mode of life story production, there is an unabashed presentation of the interview as an antiphonal, contrapuntal discourse.
Interviewer questions; speaker responds. The total effect is produced
once the reader puts together the various pieces of the life. The interviewer as writer, we trust, presents the material in a format as faithful
as possible to the actual interviewing process. Ann Oakley, in a
chapter titled "Interviewing Women: A Contradiction in Terms," nevertheless cautions against such a format, defining the social science
interview itself as a "masculine paradigm."[9] For her it is a process that
objectifies the interviewee and renders her as source, constructs her
as passive. It is a one-way process in which the interviewer "elicits
and receives but does not give information." Oakley suggests, instead,

a nonhierarchical approach that eschews prescribed format and goes for friendship, shared work, responsibility, and space for the interviewee to "ask back." Mernissi, in her introduction, identifies some of the implications of her interviews, her attempts to preserve the "relaxed, often confusing, way in which many of the interviewed relate time sequences and events."[10] But often the classic interview format of brief question and encouraged extended response persists. Nevertheless, the overarching project with which Mernissi as Arab feminist identifies is the liberation of female discourse.

The unifying formal feature of these three categories of life story production is that they are all collaborative. Yet, there are degrees of collaboration and editorial intervention. In the case of the first form, the narrative seems written to fit the conventional autobiographical format in terms of chronology and other conventions. It is still a doubly authored text, with the editor's voice and the storyteller's voice together making the narrative. The second and third forms are choral or plural in mode. These "multiple lives" as single text are, for me, more expansive than the first mode. They challenge many of the generic expectations of autobiography. They are, as well, subversions of the definition of "author."

Consideration of the forms of lifestories forces a rethinking of traditional autobiographical theory. In particular, thinking autobiography through life story puts into question the notion of standard autobiography as extended, linear narrative, and invites instead more complex approaches to text, discourse, author, and narrative. Therefore, I propose in this essay to explore the following: (1) the role of editor-subject relations; (2) race, gender, class, and "trust" in the creation of these texts; and (3) the oral narrative contract and the ordering imperative. In exploring these issues, I will refer to expressed and implicit editorial practices and to commentary by scholars engaged in collecting and presenting life stories.

An important preliminary consideration is the loaded question of literariness. Many of these stories were collected as oral history, for anthropological purposes (Andreski, Shostak), historical or sociological purposes (Gordon, Thiam), or political or economic purposes (Mandela, Byerly). In other words, they were never intended to be introduced to the public as "works of literature." Yet, the theoretical issues raised by editors of life stories in these multidisciplinary venues bear striking resemblance to the theoretical issues raised about autobiography among literary critics. Perhaps this is so because autobiography has always been of interest to people coming from diverse disciplines, and because it has always proliferated in its forms. The proliferation of categories identified by Olney is perhaps best invoked here. Olney, in "Autobiography: An Anatomy and a Taxonomy," argues for open and multiple definitions, for the sense of the form as one still defining and redefining itself, and thus places it squarely in current postmodernist discussions.[11]

While we interrogate the implications of life stories for what they contribute to autobiographical theory, it is for me profoundly important to define them as a separate literary genre. The critically defining feature is that they blur the boundaries between orality and writing. I define them as a *crossover genre* that challenges the oral/written separations and unites these forms as they maintain their distinct textualities. We can see women's life stories, then, as a contemporary form, made possible by certain technological advances: relatively easier access to communication and transportation. They are all women's personal stories, told and presented through female agency. They share with male self-stories the human impulse to define, shape, and order a life. Yet, the collection activity and/or the giving of value to women's stories has its impetus in the recent feminist movement, which provides the space and the need to hear women's voices. They also come out of oral history projects designed to let peasants and working-class people speak. The closest that mainstream autobiographical theory comes in allowing space for women's voices is in the "collaborative autobiography" that Stone identifies in the essentially male bonding between Alex Haley and Malcolm X. More recently, Philippe Lejeune, in a chapter titled "The Autobiography of Those Who Do Not Write," has approached this issue and come to some conclusions similar to mine.[12] Lejeune seems to come close to arguing for the life story as an independent form as such, but he locates it within autobiography (as the chapter's title suggests). He says, for example, that writing "negotiates between the model's supply and the public's demand . . . a kind of floating writing, an autobiographical form with no subject to ground it, but which, on the contrary, grounds in its role as subject the one who is responsible for it or the one to whom the responsibility is given."[13] The "scandal" implied in the shifting authority of the text comes at the level of the *signature*. Lejeune also identifies the class factors involved, in which the person writing invariably belongs to the ruling classes and is linked to institutions such as publishing, newspapers, universities, and museums.

However, Lejeune invests more control in the individual writer than I am willing to concede. I am guided less by victimization of the storyteller/subject than by an approach that is at least collective/collaborative or one that asserts that the storyteller often exercises control of the narrative. Further, the storyteller's approach is one that sees stories as existing in multiple forms, not necessarily locked into writing as a finite form in the way we see it in the academy. The *author* of a specific text then is not necessarily the *writer.* Trinh T. Minh-ha offers thoughtful commentary on the various ways of seeing writing, authorship, and storytelling once we destabilize the authority of the *written text.*[14] Further, a number of African women who have done research in African villages report that rural women repeatedly assert that the one thing they appreciate from their interviewers is that they can speak and write the language of those in power and therefore can relay their stories to those who need to hear them.[15]

In the process of finding a way to see these lifestories I am guided by these identified positions as well as by recent theoretical advances in women's autobiography that leave some space for the noncanonical.[16] I am also influenced by current discourses on postcoloniality that open a desired theoretical and ideological space for the creation of new forms and new identities. Black women's creative expression seems always to reside in that aesthetic and creative, often conflicted, space where boundaries and identities of various forms are continually transgressed.

Editor-Subject Relations

The role of the editor in women's life stories is best defined tentatively as that of facilitator. Yet, the editor is engaged in a process that by definition makes her occupy a range of positions: collector, transcriber, translator, writer of the narrated story. This process is articulated by Anne Benjamin, who, in her introduction to *Part of My Soul Went with Him,* says:

> This is not an autobiography in the conventional sense. The restrictions placed on her activities by the government and her daily involvement in the liberation movement make it impossible for Winnie Mandela to sit down and write a book. . . . Winnie Mandela granted me the privilege of conducting lengthy tape-recorded interviews with her over a considerable period of time.[17]

While *Part of My Soul Went with Him* is published as a single, extended narrative that follows the male paradigm or the "celebrity autobiography format," it is nevertheless collaborative storytelling. It is simultaneously the people's story of their collective surge to freedom, the woman's (Winnie's) story of struggle over subordination, and

Benjamin's biography of Winnie. If we assert gender as one of the primary alliances for this telling of Winnie Mandela's story, then one of the roles of the female as editor is to ensure that the woman's story is not obliterated. And given the context of the narrative, we do get some glimpses of Winnie, the woman. It is nevertheless a "self" contained by a larger struggle that comes through here, or, as I have shown elsewhere, a "self" synonymous with struggle.[18] The structure of the book itself mirrors this pattern. The narrative is framed by the editorial note and introduction, then a tribute by Bishop Mana Buthelezi, president of the South African Council of Churches. It closes with letters from Nelson to Winnie and finally the South African Freedom Charter, copies of banning orders, petitions, and conditions under which she could visit her husband.

Part of My Soul Went with Him is a multiauthored text. Throughout the narrative there are italicized glosses and clarifying statements added by the editor. The editor describes her many conversations with Winnie and admits to being unable to have her see the project before it went into print. The sense of editorial positioning is further complicated by the presence of Mary Benson, a friend of the family, political ally, and biographer of Nelson Mandela. It exists in that hybrid status between biography and autobiography, and therefore is more fully defined as a collaborative life story.

In another version of collaborative life story, Marjorie Shostak, in her introduction to *Nisa*, states that her mode was to establish a shared gender context with the women of the community by presenting herself as girl-woman wanting to learn how to be a woman in *!Kung* culture, thus setting the terms for the narration that followed. Since Shostak's subject, Nisa, was not a celebrity figure with a specific public relations agenda, her approach seemed to allow the narrator to develop her life as she chose. In this way we get much of Nisa's self-inventiveness:

> One woman—Nisa—impressed me more than the others with
> her ability to describe her experiences. I was struck by her
> gift as a storyteller; she chose her words carefully, infused her
> stories with drama, and covered a wide range of experience.[19]

Nisa's active choosing of Shostak as her amanuensis can easily be elided if we persistently construct the narrator as victim of the editor's manipulations. It becomes very clear as we read the introduction and the narrative that Nisa knew about Shostak's work and technically interviewed Shostak in order to give her the story. But this was not without conflict. For example, the epilogue describes Shostak's attempts to get Nisa's permission to publish this version of her life. Nisa concurs with the changing of names for anonymity but, in the midst of the discussion, recounts a dream in which she felt herself drowning in a well. We can read this alternatively as an acknowledgment of the loss of a self to the fictionalizing of her life or a donation of her "self" to the project. It is the same link that is often made between autobiography and self-immolation. Nisa narrates, but Shostak carries on a number of editing processes: interviewing, listening, taping, transcribing, translating, writing, ordering. In more recent work, Shostak has identified some of the unanswered questions in writing down oral narratives.[20] Three voices make the narrative, she admits: those of Nisa, Shostak the anthropologist, and Marjorie, a young American woman experiencing another culture. Clearly *Nisa* is as well a multiauthored text.

The most extremely problematic of this group of texts is Joubert's rendition of *Poppie Nongena,* which is based on a number of intermittent narrations by Poppie. In the English version, Joubert's introduction, which should clarify the context of the story, is absent. A foreword by Alan Paton closes by saying: "One is left with two overriding impressions. One is the courage of this woman in her never ending struggle to live under the cruelty of the laws. The other is the art of the woman who tells her story.[21] The blurb on the back cover of the book identifies the process, but transfers it to another genre—the novel:

> This novel is based on the actual life story of a black woman living in the Cape area of South Africa today. Only her name, Poppie Rachel Nongena, born Matati, is invented. Poppie went to Elsa Joubert for advice after the 1960's Cape Town Riots against apartheid and revealed—over several years of taped conversations—her extraordinary story, which remains in Joubert's retelling remarkably true in tone and detail to the firsthand account.

The entire text, although produced through a collaborative process, is attributed to Joubert as *the author.* There is no editorial discussion or recognition of Poppie's creativity in the process. Once the project is complete, Poppie as narrator of her own life has become effectively erased.[22]

The narratives that become extended recountings of a single life (as is this one) seem to be written to meet a commercial demand. Editorial ordering is deliberate, although attempts are made to be faithful to the *voice* and *words* (Stone's distinctions) of the narrator.

These three extended narrative forms are identified to show a variety of editorial processes and a range of possible collaborations or expropriations.

In the texts that are collections of life stories, editorial positions are often more definite but, paradoxically, more self-erasing. Editors describe a certain deliberateness in their method as it relates to maintaining an exchange of information, having the life stories develop collectively, keeping open the possibility of revisions of the text. Makeda Silvera, who edited *Silenced,* describes her process:

> At the end of each interview, I took home the tapes, transcribed and then edited them. I then took the transcribed tapes back to the women, who read them over and sometimes suggested changes. Then I took them home and re-typed them and gave them back to be read a final time. . . . If there were anxieties about parts of the interview, we talked it over and came to some amicable agreement. . . . I remember one woman being quite concerned about what she had said on tape about her family. She feared they might read the book and get angry with her. Upon reading the manuscript, she felt that she had the power to change everything she wanted, and she did change it.[23]

Many collectors with collaborative politics similar to Silvera's describe a long process, with some stories coming easier than others.

Unlike Silvera, Victoria Byerly, editor of *Hard Times Cotton Mill Girls,* does not provide an introduction in which she explains her process; however, she does offer a rather detailed version of her process when she gives oral presentations about her work. She generally makes these presentations with Katie Cannon, a black woman scholar and colleague who helped facilitate Byerly's entrée into the southern community of black women represented in the text. Byerly and Cannon together effect a type of re-oralizing of the editorial process.

Nevertheless, the editorial role is intrinsically one of ordering and selecting. Nayra Atiya's approach in *Khul Khaal* fits the pattern. All the women who told Atiya their stories did so in Arabic. She translated the stories, trying to keep the sequences of events as they were told to her, and cutting as little as possible: "Throughout, I made an effort to convey in English the style of the storyteller, the spirit in which each story was told and the drama which makes up the fabric of each of these lives."[24]

Daphne Patai provides the most detailed analysis of the conflicted nature of the editorial process in her chapter titled "Constructing a Self." Patai raises questions about insider-outsider relationships, time, access, language, and some of the processes she struggled to destabilize in her interviewing and writing:

> That is why I have opted, instead, for a more speaker-centered approach: I listened to what was said and, by noting repetition, emphasis, and the features selected by—and therefore evidently important to—the speaker, developed a sense of what mattered to her. This then became the basis of my selection and organization from the dozens and sometimes hundreds of pages of transcripts that resulted from each interview. In addition, I have tried to interfere as little as possible with the stories' own rhythms, and have confined contextual information to the notes.[25]

Once the editorial process is closely scrutinized, it reveals how the editor becomes co-maker of the text. The phrases "I edited," "I arranged," and "selected" camouflage a whole host of detailed ordering and creating operations. As in the oral literary tradition, the subject nevertheless resists complete framing, only telling as much as needs to be told for each particular production.

The Oral Narrative Contract and the Ordering Imperative

The oral narrative contract in life story telling turns on the concept of "trust." All of the collectors identified building "trust" as the critical ingredient in having the stories told at all. Affiliations or disjunctions of gender, class, nationality, language, and shared politics seem to be the primary facilitators of, or interferences in, the collaborative life story telling process. The extent to which the editor shares common identity locations with the narrator determines the extent of full articulation of an autobiographical "we" rather than the "I." There are some collections in which identities converge or in which certain identifications are absent. But, clearly, the ones in which at least three of these factors are present provide the more revelatory narration. The narrator, for her part, is often also conflicted. As Doris Sommer says:

> The narrator often strains between affirming her singularity and denying it in favor of the first-person plural. "I" is the part that represents "we"; at least this is the conscious assumption made in the face of the Westernizing temptation to slide from the metonymy of the communal to the metaphor of a single subject that replaces the contiguous and more collective sign.[26]

In the oral narrative process "trust" is often fostered when the editor supplies features of her own life story. The narrating takes place then in a context of plural identity and shared story. In the written version, however, it seems, this oral life narrating contract is often violated. Rarely is the collector's story a part of the narrative. At the point of writing, then, the dominant-subordinate relationships are enforced and the editor becomes a detached, sometimes clinical, orderer or even exploiter of the life stories for anthropological ends, research data, raw material, or the like. Writing another person's life can become an act of power and control.

In this particular process, then, the authority of the written text and male autobiographical conventions remain in place. Ideas raised in Shari Benstock's examination of textual peripheralities become important in this context. Benstock argues importantly that the marginalia speak more tellingly to the understanding of the entire text:

> Prefaces, afterwords, and footnotes are thus obvious append-
> ages that comment on and participate in the principal text that
> engenders them; they call into question the whole notion of
> margin, border, boundary, edge, and the layers and infoldings
> of the text; they put into relief the question, What constitutes
> a "text"?[27]

It must be made clear that the editorial positions, introductions, self-reflections on the process are legitimate parts of these life story collections. A renewed understanding of the role of the editor in the narrative process therefore reveals itself. The editor can play a dominant role given the racial politics or class politics (historically resonant) involved in, or imposed upon, white women/black women or intelligentsia/peasant woman collaborations. Or, alternatively, the editor can be a scribe, subjected to the demands of narrator.

So, the interpretive, editorial position must remain an area of close scrutiny as it relates to the transmission of the collective voice. Ordering impulses that reside at the root of male autobiography and that are allied with individualism and colonial or patriarchal authority often remain intact. These are also subject to the marketing expectations of publishers and reader requirements.

A few responses to the editorial imperatives are instructive. Bonnie G. Smith, in *Confessions of a Concierge*, experimented with a three-part structure in presenting one life story: (1) an introductory theoretical overview, (2) the use of Mme Lucie's voice/words while reordering her narrative chronologically, and (3) the imitation of the order of Mme Lucie's memory and the order of observations made about her by witnesses, including dialogue and flashbacks as they actually occurred.[28] In a telephone conversation in October 1989, Smith told me that she came to the conclusion that there was no authentic way of capturing oral discourse. In the "true" account, Mme Lucie frequently "distorts . . . normal, historical time by interjecting feelings, stretching moments that are important to her, breaking her narrative."[29] Yet Smith stated that in the first part she used chronology and "actually pieced together from the higgledy-piggledy order" in which she told her story. Unfortunately, what Smith and other editors define as disorder represents specific oral narrative strategies that she, as editor, herself recognized in process.

Honor Ford-Smith, editor of the Jamaican group Sistren's collection called *Lionheart Gal,* the result of an overtly collaborative process, describes the oral/written discursive strategy she used with Sistren as talking through the stories, interviewing, recording, discussing, examining, fleshing out. Yet the sense of ordering remains present:

> I searched for a throughline for each story and then discussed
> it with each woman. If she agreed, we then talked some more
> to add detail and to conclude the problem we had focused on.
> Afterwards I *reordered* the material in a first draft and then
> went over it again in a third phase of interviewing and discus-
> sion, questioning for more detail and for reflection.[30]

Some of the editorial strategies adopted come close to open-ended interpretation between oral and written text. They are aspects of a discursive process that do not end with the text in print. In Ford-Smith's words: "Each finished testimony still remains to be discussed as fully as it deserves within the group."[31] A similar choral pattern is observed in *Black Sisters, Speak Out,* in which the entire text is a combination of voices, including that of Thiam (as an educated and vocal member of that community) as a kind of sister-interpreter.

Clearly, the ideological orientation of the editor is a critical issue in collaborative storytelling, as dominant-inferior relationships cannot elicit group stories. Instead, one gets one side of the dialogue, the implied contract of oral discourse left uncompleted.

Gender, Class, and Orality in Life Storytelling

The discourse of the oral life story is open-ended and conversational. The process begins naturally once the formulaic entrée is provided, usually by one woman telling some feature of her own story. It is thus characteristic of what Barbara Bate calls "women's talk." For Bate, women's talk manifests four important elements: a recognition of the value of the communication process, an awareness of multiple perspectives, a search for identification with others, and delight in creativity. Ultimately, women's talk works toward cooperative goals as the speakers affirm human connection while recognizing differences that emerge. Identifying women as "rational speakers," Bate suggests that women "examin[e] alternatives for talk in environments which often mute their voices or ignore their words."[32]

Patricia Meyer Spacks identifies another form of women's talk as gossip, and is particularly interested in the way that gossip provides a context for "finding new ways to think about perplexities of narrative and voice and subject."[33] "Serious" gossip, proposes Spacks, "takes place in private, at leisure, in a context of trust. . . . Its participants use talk about others to reflect about themselves, to express wonder and uncertainty and locate certainties, to enlarge their knowledge of one another."[34] Gossip as women's talk thus enables the silenced to articulate personal subjectivity and communal interdependency.

In its aesthetic features and political implications, the life story shares similarities with Bate's women's talk and Spacks's serious gossip. Oral life story clearly exists in that same liminal space between the public and the private, between oral and written discourses. In its intertextuality, its open-ended, dialogic form, then, the oral life story form functions explicitly to facilitate empowerment for women who historically have been silenced, whose words are not accepted as having legitimacy in the realm of accepted public discourse where formal autobiography resides. Life stories, viewed against this backdrop, are another of those sublimated women's articulations.

Nancy Fraser asserts that there are central, hegemonic discursive areas—the academy, parliament, media.[35] These are public spaces that set boundaries on public discourse. Thus they privatize and depoliticize certain matters by making them familial and private. Issues such as wife battering and rape are sanctioned and discussed only in specific contexts. Often these are relegated to the arena of women's speech. My reading reveals that many of these often unspeakable issues become the subject of life stories and thus become public.

Reflecting on her interviewing process, for example, Victoria Byerly notes that the narrator often becomes conscious of the personal epic as she tells the story.[36] Often this occasion is the first time that she has engaged in a dialogue with the world and become a proactive subject in her own life. By narrating her story, then, she enters history, names themes for the future, and seizes the authority of the teller of experience. The public space of discourse therefore becomes a contested space as she violates the established boundaries between silence and speech to reflect on experience, put shape and meaning to it. We might parallel slave narratives—often silenced in favor of the slave master's journals—which, when orally narrated and subsequently written, became authentic documents of lived experience. Life stories then become one facet of the public discourse of silenced groups that begin to find ways to engage in their history as subjects, to set themes of collective epic.

The facilitator of this oral discourse can be called, as Walter Ong suggests, the interpreter. This interpreter makes visible those women who are hidden by everyday lives and ordinariness, allows their verbal utterances some permanence. Ong provides a most significant understanding of the terms of the editor/interpreter vis-à-vis the intertextuality of oral discourse:

> The world of oral utterance is typically one of discourse, in which one utterance gives rise to another, that to still another and so on. Meaning is negotiated in the discursive process. . . . Your actual response makes it possible for me to find out for myself and to make clear in my counter-response what my fuller meaning was or can be. Oral discourse thus commonly interprets itself as it proceeds. It negotiates meaning out of meaning.[37]

Writing down an oral discourse makes of it autonomous discourse by "stringing it out indefinitely in time and space," and allowing it to resume interaction when someone reads the text. Then the interpretive/editorial function is to make of the reader something analogous to the listener in spoken discourse.

Oral theorists have been almost unanimous in holding that there is no way to transfer an oral text to written form and maintain its integrity. But recent examinations of orality and literacy, informed by poststructuralist understandings of textualities, are beginning to question the incompatibility of oral and written modes of literary expression. Instead, they are interrogating our scriptocentric expectations. In their introduction to *Discourse and Its Disguises,* Karin Barber and P. F. de Moraes Farias assert:

> Our scriptocentrism may blind us to the most fundamental constitutive principles of the text's literariness. [A more interesting way of looking at text is to see it as] utterance or as a species of social action: the capacity of the text to activate spheres beyond the confines of its own textuality, and be implicated in social and political action.[38]

Yet, if there is a shared gender or race context, all of the interpreters noted above exist in a class relationship to their subjects, who are often poor, working women, living difficult lives. To mitigate class differences, I would argue, is to recognize and articulate the possible interferences and ways of surmounting them. For me, the most satisfying of texts are the ones that begin with some awareness of the varying levels of differences between women and the areas of common ground.

Conclusion

If we agree with Gloria Anzaldúa that boundaries are sites of contestations, then life stories are boundary-breaking texts.[39] Collaboratively told and written by women, they exist in oppositional relationship to autobiography as it is defined now. They present a multileveled relationship to discourse. Close examination reveals, for example, stories that expose while they camouflage, stories that negotiate public and private space, challenge and retreat, open up some issues and silence others. Gaps and spaces in narration, we know, point to texts in process.

Black women's texts often contest established boundaries, offer alternative interpretations, create new public discourses, challenge hegemonic definitions of discourse. There is, necessarily, as well for black women an oppositional relationship to those in power: the range of experts, including feminist theorists and "interpreters." This is perhaps the final import of oral life stories that expand the boundaries of the genre, create something new, and thereby redefine received, canonical notions of autobiography.

Notes

1. Sistren, *Lionheart Gal: Life Stories of Jamaican Women,* ed. Honor Ford-Smith (London: Women's Press, 1986), xxvii.

2. This study is part of a much longer project on the theoretical implications of the life story for autobiographical theory and the ways in which black women tell their lives.

3. Winnie Mandela, *Part of My Soul Went with Him,* ed. Anne Benjamin (New York: W. W. Norton, 1984); Marjorie Shostak, *Nisa: The Life and Words of a !Kung Woman* (Cambridge, Mass: Harvard University Press, 1981); Elsa Joubert, *Poppie Nongena: One Woman's Struggle against Apartheid* (New York: Henry Holt, 1980).

4. Albert E. Stone, *Autobiographical Occasions and Original Acts: Versions of American Identity from Henry Adams to Nate Shaw* (Philadelphia: University of Pennsylvania Press, 1982), 231–64; see also Patricia Meyer Spacks, *Gossip* (New York: Alfred A. Knopf, 1985), 4, 5.

5. Stone, *Autobiographical Occasions,* 234.

6. Sistren, *Lionheart Gal;* Victoria Byerly, ed., *Hard Times Cotton Mill Girls: Personal Histories of Womanhood and Poverty in the South* (New York: ILR, 1986); Iris

Andreski, ed., *Old Wives' Tales: Life-Stories from Ibibioland* (New York: Schocken, 1970); Patricia W. Romero, ed., *Life Histories of African Women* (Atlantic Highlands, N.J.: Ashfield, 1988); Makeda Silvera, ed., *Silenced* (Toronto: Williams-Wallace, 1983); Nayra Atiya, ed., *Khul Khaal: Five Egyptian Women Tell Their Stories* (London: Virago, 1988); Daphne Patai, ed., *Brazilian Women Speak: Contemporary Life Stories* (New Brunswick, N.J.: Rutgers University Press, 1988).

7. Awa Thiam, *Black Sisters, Speak Out: Feminism and Oppression in Black Africa,* trans. Dorothy Blair (London: Pluto, 1986); Lesley Lawson, *Working Women: A Portrait of South Africa's Black Women Workers* (Johannesburg: Ravan, 1985); Julie Frederikse, *South Africa: A Different Kind of War* (London: Beacon, 1986); Diana E. H. Russell, *Lives of Courage: Women for a New South Africa* (New York: Basic Books, 1989).

8. Fatima Mernissi, *Doing Daily Battle: Interviews with Moroccan Women* (London: Women's Press, 1984).

9. Ann Oakley, "Interviewing Women: A Contradiction in Terms," in *Doing Feminist Research,* ed. H. Roberts (London: Routledge & Kegan Paul, 1981), 30–61.

10. Mernissi, *Doing Daily Battle,* 20.

11. James Olney, "Autobiography: An Anatomy and a Taxonomy," *Neohelicon* 13, 1 (1986): 57–82.

12. Philippe Lejeune, "The Autobiography of Those Who Do Not Write," in *On Autobiography,* trans. Paul John Eakin (Minneapolis: Univ. of Minnesota Press, 1989), 185–215. Lejeune's work was brought to my attention by Paul John Eakin at a 1989 conference on autobiography at the University at Binghamton, at which I presented this paper. I read the subsequently published text and found many of his ideas clarifying and supportive of some of the directions my work was taking.

13. Ibid., 189.

14. Trinh-T. Minh-ha, *Woman, Native, Other: Writing Postcoloniality and Feminism* (Bloomington: Indiana University Press, 1989), 6–44.

15. This was expressed by Omolara Ogundipe-Leslie (Nigeria) and Pat McFadden (Lesotho, S. Africa) in various conference discussions and informal communications, in particular at the "Decentering Discourses Conference" at the University at Binghamton.

16. See the Personal Narratives Group, ed., *Interpreting Women's Lives: Feminist Theory and Personal Narratives* (Bloomington: Indiana University Press, 1989); this recent volume is a valuable contribution to the discussion of gender and autobiographical theory.

17. Mandela, *Part of My Soul,* 7.

18. Carole Boyce Davies, "Private Selves and Public Spaces: Autobiography and the African Woman Writer," in *Crisscrossing Boundaries in African Literatures, 1986,* ed. Ken Harrow, Jonathan Ngate, and Clarissa Zimra (Washington, D.C.: Three Continents, 1991), 109–27.

19. Shostak, *Nisa,* 7.

20. Shostak, "What the Wind Won't Take Away—The Genesis of *Nisa: The Life of a !Kung Woman,*" in *Interpreting Women's Lives: Feminist Theory and Personal Narratives,* ed. The Personal Narratives Group (Bloomington: Indiana University Press, 1989), 228–39.

21. Joubert, *Poppie Nongena,* 3.

22. Anne McClintock, in "Dismantling the Master's House: The Family and Resistance in *Poppie Nongena*" (forthcoming), examines some of these questions and locates this erasure of Poppie within the power politics of South African apartheid, which renders Black women triply removed from the sources of power in that society.

23. Silvera, *Silenced,* 20.

24. Atiya, *Khul Khaal,* xxviii.

25. Patai, *Brazilian Women Speak,* 10.

26. Doris Sommer. "'Not Just a Personal Story': Women's *Testimonios* and the Plural Self," in *Life/Lines: Theorizing Women's Autobiography,* ed. Bella Brodzki and Celeste Schenck (Ithaca, N.Y.: Cornell University Press, 1988), 123.

27. Shari Benstock, "At the Margin of Discourse: Footnotes in the Fictional Text," *PMLA* 98 (January-May 1983): 220.

28. Bonnie G. Smith, *Confessions of a Concierge* (New Haven, Conn.: Yale University Press, 1985), xviii.

29. Ibid., xvii-xviii.

30. Sistren, *Lionheart Gal,* xxviii.

31. Ibid., xxx.

32. Barbara Bate, "Themes and Perspectives in Women's Talk," in *Women Communicating: Studies of Women's Talk* (Norwood, N.J.: Ablex, 1988), 312.

33. Spacks, *Gossip,* 4.

34. Ibid., 5.

35. Nancy Fraser, "Talking about Women's Needs" (Paper presented at the University at Binghamton, 21 April 1988).

36. Victoria Byerly with Kate Cannon, oral presentation, Cornell University, 6 October 1987.

37. Walter J. Ong, S. J., "Text as Interpretation: Mark and After" in *Oral Tradition in Literature: Interpretation in Context,* ed. John Miles Foley (Columbia: University of Missouri Press, 1986), 148.

38. Karin Barber and P. F. de Moraes Farias, eds., *Discourse and Its Disguises: The Interpretation of African Oral Texts* (Birmingham, U.K.: Birmingham University, Centre of West African Studies, 1989), 3.

39. Gloria Anzaldúa, *Borderlands/La Frontera* (San Francisco: Spinsters/Aunt Lute, 1987).

Chapter 2

"What I'm Talking about When I'm Talking about My Baskets"
Conversations with Mabel McKay

Greg Sarris

Early one February morning in 1987, I helped Mabel McKay load a long glass case containing samples of her basketry into the back of my car.[1] I remember the year because I was about to take my qualifying exams at Stanford. I was anxious to finish my course work so I could begin writing Mabel's life story, my proposed dissertation. Over the years I had driven Mabel to countless museum openings honoring her work and to several colleges and universities, where she talked about her art as a weaver and Pomo Indian dreamer, that is, as a prophet and medicine woman.

I wanted my Stanford colleagues to hear her, all those people—advisers and friends—who had suggestions for writing the stories Mabel had been telling me about her life for as long as I could remember. But I also wanted them to see me with her. I wanted them to see me as an Indian, someone positioned as an insider who understood Mabel in ways they could not. I am of mixed-blood heritage (Pomo-Coast Miwok and Filipino on my father's side; Jewish, German, and Irish on my mother's) and light skinned. Because of my skin color and the academic training I shared with colleagues, I wondered if they considered the vast differences between their world(s) and the one I know as an Indian with Mabel.

As we drove south from Rumsey, where Mabel was living at the time, she warned me that she would not talk about spiritual matters to the Stanford students. "Only my baskets," she said with a playful laugh. "I'll demonstrate for them. Did you bring my bowl and the roots?"

"Yes, I packed them in back," I said.

She set her black patent leather purse squarely, resolutely, on her knees. At seven o'clock in the morning she was impeccable: wide awake, effortlessly present. She wore a purple print dress and over it a modish down jacket. Her square glasses below a shock of permed and tinted black hair suggested something of an old schoolmarm. People are often caught off guard by her appearance; they imagine a traditional American Indian woman differently. They do not catch at first her adamant jaw and down-turned mouth, or the playful eyes. They do not see Mabel until she begins talking, answering their questions.

I wondered if she was angry just then, if she thought maybe I had committed her to others in inappropriate ways. I knew she could get angry if I said something she did not like. She would either confront me directly or wait and catch me off guard to teach me a lesson. She was particularly adept at the latter, bamboozling me in ways I least expected. And she always seemed to know what I was up to, what I was thinking.

So I explained again, just to relieve my own angst, how I told the professor that she would talk only about things she felt like talking about. His class had been reading American Indian literature, including the so-called myths and folktales and various autobiographies of individuals from different tribes. Since it was winter, and since Mabel will tell creation stories only in winter, I thought she might want to tell some of the old stories.

"I'm going to talk about my baskets," she said, opening her purse and rummaging for a cigarette. "I'm going to demonstrate."

The professor met us in the parking lot. He was tall; he wore a navy blue blazer and khaki slacks. I noticed a turquoise ring on his finger as he extended his hand to Mabel. He led Mabel around the parked cars, toward the quad. I followed, carrying the glass case containing Mabel's baskets. I glanced at the feather baskets and miniatures, Mabel's specialties, and then at the red flicker feather sunbasket, a shallow basket about four inches in diameter, used for poisoning people. "My mother-in-law was blinded by one of those," Mabel once said. "But not this one. This one is just for show, but it has rules, stories, too."

I overheard the professor telling Mabel how he had informed his students about her. Mabel stopped, dropped her cigarette, and exhaled a cloud of smoke. She said to him, "That's nice."

As we entered the large lecture hall, I heard the ten o'clock bell. Among the nearly two hundred students were several faculty. I spotted a famous poet on the side near the front. She was sitting forward, gazing intently at Mabel.

I set the basket case on the long table in front of the audience. Then, opening the plastic K-mart shopping bag that I had carried on top of the case, I pulled out Mabel's bundle of sedge roots, her awl, and a Tupperware bowl. I went to fill the bowl with water. When I came back, the professor was introducing Mabel, who was standing off to the side smoking a cigarette. I wondered about the smoking laws.

"She is the last of her tribe. Once her tribe numbered about six hundred people. They were the Cache Creek Pomo and they lived east of Clear Lake, just a little over a hundred miles from here. She is, therefore, the last to speak the language of her people. Imagine, if you were the last person to speak English. Mabel is also a dreamer. She has dreams and visions that tell her how to weave her baskets and help with her doctoring. She is a doctor, a medicine woman, just like the woman we saw in the film, *The Sucking Doctor*. In fact, Essie Parrish and Mabel were good friends. Mabel claims she saw Essie— that they were communicating in dreams, seeing each other—before they actually met in person. Mabel has rules that govern her life. She has to pray before she does anything. I've talked to you about this before. She was raised by her grandmother in the old way. Early on her people understood that she was given the power to doctor and to weave by spirit. As I've also said to you, she is a world-renowned basket weaver. She has baskets in the Smithsonian and in many other museums in this country and in Europe. So we are honored today to have this important woman talk to us about her life and work."

The professor turned to Mabel, who was holding the burning butt of her cigarette between her thumb and forefinger. She seemed to be asking what to do with this butt. I took it from her, and rubbed it out in the chalk trough.

I sat at the end of the table. Mabel stood before her chair, untying the bundle of sedge roots. I knew her audience was anxious, particularly after the long introduction, and not used to this extended period of silence. Mabel placed several strands of the blond-colored sedge in the water and sat down. She pulled the bowl to her, reached for her awl, and then from her purse on the floor found a bundle wrapped

in Kleenex. Slowly, she pulled away the tissues and revealed the beginnings of a basket. She examined the work in her hands, tapped the
roots in the water with her middle finger, then looked up, over her
glasses, to the audience.

"Okay, now anybody got any questions?"

The students and faculty were still, unmoving. The professor bit
his nails.

I had seen Mabel's antics before. Once, when she spoke before the
Stanford medical school staff and faculty, she prayed and sang a song,
then talked, trancelike, about the dictates of the spirits and her work
as a medicine woman. She had been talking for some time when she
stopped suddenly, looked out to her audience, and asked, "Now who
can tell me what I just said?" The large, mostly male audience was
stunned. "Ain't nobody got a word for me?" she asked finally and
laughed. "I thought you wanted to know about healers." Another time,
when she was speaking before a museum crowd, she merely told a
story about how a certain basket in one of the display cases told its
weaver that it would take one human life each year as sacrifice unless
it was fed water once a month. "It's true, whether you believe it or
not," Mabel said, and then stepped off the stage.

Mabel tapped the roots in the bowl again, and then, as if just finding
what she wanted, lifted one of the strands from the water. She held
the strand between her teeth as she picked up the basket she had
begun and the awl. She opened a hole in the coil with her awl and
then took the sedge root from her mouth and made the first loop.
She looped again, and again.

"Does anyone have any questions?" the professor asked, urging the
audience to come forth.

Mabel glanced at the crowd occasionally. She was tapping in the
water again, looking for another strand.

Finally, a hand. I sighed with relief. At the rate things were going,
I thought Mabel might weave before the crowd for the entire fifty
minutes, which was not what I wanted.

Mabel acknowledged a woman, who rose and asked what Mabel
was using to weave her basket. "Roots," Mabel said. "It all starts from
the beginning with roots. How the basket makes itself. Like two people
meeting." She turned to me. "Now what you call this roots in English?"

"Sedge," I said, and then repeated for the woman standing near
the back of the lecture hall.

"Then for the color part, this red color part," Mabel said, holding
up the small work in her hand, "I use redbud. Got to pick it right
time of year. It has songs, prayers, rules to it, too."

"But what is that thing in your hand?"

"Oh, this awl?"

"Yes."

"I poke the holes with it, make the spaces when I do the coiled baskets. Is that all?" Mabel asked, chuckling to herself.

The woman sat down and Mabel resumed her weaving.

The professor, fearing continued silence, stepped forward. "Mabel," he said, "you are a traditional weaver, which means you only weave the designs the spirit tells you. Do you want to say something about that?"

Mabel set her awl on the table. "Yes," she said. "Traditional weaver only weave the designs the spirit tells you. So what you want to know?"

"I meant could you tell us something about that."

"Well, some modern weavers and the white people, they just weaves whatever they like, their own idea. Their baskets don't have rules, stories, the history. Oh, sometimes they just sees something, maybe in a book or museum, and they copy, do it to their own idea. But that is dangerous thing, not respectful. Could get trouble that way. These things," she said, holding up the basket in one hand, "is living, is living."

She picked up her awl, then stopped suddenly. She looked at the professor, still standing where he had posed his question. "Now who can tell me what I mean 'is living'?"

A student stood up. "Do you mean your basket is living?" he asked.

"Uh-huh," Mabel answered. "Do you know what that means?"

"Does it breathe?"

Mabel laughed out loud. "That's cute," she said, "'Does it breathe.'"

"Does it talk?" The student, who wore a tie-dyed shirt, shifted impatiently.

"Yeah, it talk all right."

"What does it say?"

"Oh, about things. Depend what kind of basket, what it's talking to." She paused, then continued. "You got to hear it, but how YOU going to hear it?"

I thought of the basket Mabel had given her late friend Essie Parrish thirty years ago. In a trance Essie saw the basket dripping sweat at the time of a future plague.

The student sat down.

"What I'm talking about when I'm talking about my baskets is my life, the stories, the rules, how this things is living, what they do to you." Mabel held the basket toward the audience again. The long, loose willow rod, the basket's foundation, bobbed in the open air. The professor stepped backward to the blackboard behind Mabel. "Now who can tell me what I am meaning here?"

Mabel lowered the basket and began weaving. The renowned poet raised her hand. Mabel nodded her acknowledgment.

"Mabel, are you saying the spirit is like a muse that . . . "

"Well, sometimes spirit is amusing, I suppose."

I interjected in an attempt to cover Mabel's apparent misunderstanding. "What I think she meant, Mabel, is whether or not the spirit talks to you, whether it inspires you."

"Oh," Mabel said, as if just informed she would have coffee with lunch. She began weaving.

Another student raised her hand. "Can you see the spirit?" she asked, and quickly sat down.

"Yeah, sometimes. You want to know what it looks like now?"

The young woman, red-faced by this time, did not respond.

"Sometimes you don't even know what you are seeing, so how YOU going to know?"

Another student: "How did you learn to weave? Who taught you? Your grandmother? We heard you were raised by your grandmother."

"No, spirit teach me, since I was small child."

The student, a tall African American woman, was persistent. "You mean you didn't see your grandmother weave, she didn't teach you how to do it? What about the designs?"

"Yes, I seen her. She show me some things, where to dig the roots where we living that time, get the redbud, like that. But I got to do what I know. Spirit is saying. My grandmother, she a great weaving woman. My mother, she a weaving woman, too. But lots to their weaving. Lots to this weaving here." Mabel looked down at her work and made one more loop.

The student, who looked perplexed, sat down. A long period of silence followed and then Mabel told a story.

"See, what it happened, this woman had dream. This woman I'm talking about was dreaming [in preparation for a life as medicine woman]. Woman, over there, let's see, by Ukiah someplace. Well, how it happened, she weave this design. But it attracts the snakes. A design singing snakes.

"But even yet this woman did not believe. She doubted, want to have normal life. Well, this feather basket she weave, it's small, I guess. Because one day it disappeared. She say to herself, 'How come my basket, it's not here?' She leave it there in shack where they was living.

"Then it happened, her sister go crazy-like. Say she going to live with snakes. Dreaming of the snakes all the time. Then how it happened, I don't know. But she disappeared. They seen her tracks to the mountain up there, but she is gone. The tracks, they just stop, people says. She disappeared. I don't know.

"So, this woman, she start crying, then she go down, get sick so she can't even talk. She blind. But she seeing something. Only she don't know it. She can't talk, tell about it. Something not working in her.

"We knowed because that time they called in Doctor, that north man, and he pray. He seen this: sister was taken by snakes. She is snake now, I guess, living with them up on that mountain. And this sick lady, she seeing this in her dream. She even seen where this basket it is.

"It's in snake's body. That's how it happened. Snake come for it and swallow it. Then with that woman's basket and song, it got her sister.

"Well, this woman, she tell us this after, how she seen her sister and the basket. I don't know. But that man, he seen it, too. I remember. I was just young woman yet. Anyway, what it happened this woman had to start singing her songs to get her sister back. And the sister, she come back, too, come walking from out in the brush, and she's carrying that basket. It's full of songs, for that woman's work on this earth."

A young man in the front row now stood up. "Maybe the sister just played a game on her sister and took the basket," he said.

"Why a sister want to do that?" Mabel responded, chuckling.

"Did the woman really turn into a snake?" the student asked, nonplussed.

"Well, I suppose so."

"What happened, I mean what did she do?" he continued from his seat.

"I don't know. I'm not a snake," Mabel answered. "But one time, it happened to me my grandfather give me rattlesnake song in MY dream. 'This snakes going to be your helpers' he is saying. Then I seen them, in my house, in closet, bathtub when it's hot, all over. Then I say, 'Grandfather, this is modern times, you better take that song out of me. People around here don't understand things like that. They might call animal control place.

"Anyhow, I guess that's why, this lady when she get ready to die she give me this basket. She knew me that time. She tells me to keep her basket alive, so it would take none of her children. So I bless it, do its rule every month."

Mabel put down her awl and leaned over, looking into her glass case. "It's this one, right here," she said, pointing. "She said I would use it one day. I don't know."

Mabel finished talking. I asked if people wanted to see the baskets on their way out of class. I glimpsed the small feather basket that I had assumed was made by Mabel. It was upside down, its underside, or outside, an intricate zigzagging pattern of yellow-gold and metallic blue-green feathers. The breast of a meadowlark, the head of a mallard.

One woman, obviously a teacher or professor from another university, came by and moved around to the back of the table, where Mabel was tying up her bundle of roots with a twist tie. "Mabel," she said, bending over as if to have a private conversation with Mabel, "I've been right all along. I'm working with this Navajo woman who is a weaver. She weaves blankets and my notion is that the blankets are autobiography."

Mabel looked confused. I figured it was the word *autobiography.* She dropped her bundle into the plastic K-mart bag on the floor.

"I mean her life. As if the blanket is her life."

"Might be. Some Indians are that way. Turn into things."

The woman looked embarrassed. She saw I was listening. Still, she pushed on. "No, Mabel. I mean the blanket represents her life; it represents her stories, just as you talk about your baskets. The blanket is a story, like a book."

"Oh, it is?" Mabel asked. "I don't know. Did I say that?" Mabel placed her basket on the table. "Each thing is living, talking. You got to know rule. I don't know this lady you are talking about. But if she's living, if that blanket deal is living, how do you know what it is? Are you that lady?" Mabel was serious, adamant. Then at once she burst into laughter. "Just checking," she laughed.

The African American woman who had asked if Mabel's grandmother had taught her to weave came around then. She had been watching Mabel with the first woman. Mabel began wrapping the unfinished basket in Kleenex. She stopped and looked up.

"Mabel," the young woman said. "I feel . . . I mean, will anything happen to me if I look in that glass case, at the baskets?"

"It already has," Mabel said. "Thank you for asking."

Mabel finished wrapping her basket and secured the tissues to it with a rubber band. She dropped the awl in the K-mart bag, then opened her purse and carefully placed her basket inside. She told me

to feed a plant with the water in her bowl. A few people lingered
with the professor, looking at the baskets.

"I need a smoke," Mabel said, snapping her purse shut and pushing
herself away from the table.

Somewhere beyond Berkeley and Albany we stopped off at a Denny's
for lunch. I wanted to ask Mabel about the story regarding the woman
who gave her the basket, the woman whose sister followed snakes. I
had not heard the story before, and it surprised me; somehow, after
thirty years of listening to Mabel, and after taking notes on stories,
some of which I had heard hundreds of times, this one I had missed.
I wanted to know just what she was doing at that point in her life.
How young was she? Did she believe it?

I didn't ask then. I knew she was talked out and hungry. She was
enjoying a fried chicken dinner and salad.

I thought of the students and faculty we left at Stanford. What they
experienced I had seen before. As always, Mabel was predictable in
that she was unpredictable; she was uncanny, inverting the subject-
object dichotomy established by the professor's presentation of her
as a relic, a representative of a prelapsarian past, from whom students
and others could extract information. As a result, she halted, or at
least momentarily interrupted, in her encounter with the crowd, the
projection of meaning, which, after all, is not too unlike the projection
of a knife or bullet in the way it can silence opposition. She located
the past in the present, exposing what made for the differences
between her life and worldview and that of her interlocutors, never
allowing in the encounter her self or life to be appropriated or seen
other than it is for all its complexity and difference. If, as Arnold
Krupat notes, "the [Euro-American] movement westward was achieved
not only with the power of the sword but of the pen as well," then
Mabel McKay is a one-woman holdout.[2]

Mabel has been hounded by art historians, curators, private collectors, linguists, anthropologists, folklorists, and biographers for as
long as she can remember. Yet, as one anthropologist once said to
me, "she is impossible to crack. I can't follow her." Perhaps this man
experienced with Mabel what Vincent Crapanzano calls "epistemological vertigo" in the face of an Other.[3] Mabel's experience, her sense
of the world, is not only different, however. Presented with authority,
it will not yield to her interlocutor's cultural presuppositions and the
power associated with those presuppositions. Mabel's dynamic, her
talk, whether a story, a response to a question, or an observation, not

only makes for an instance of culture contact but calls up the story of that contact in terms of its power relations.

Mabel told the professor that her baskets were living. At that moment she was calling attention to different cultural notions of what constitutes life and material objects and the relationship between them and the weaver. But she was also interrogating him to "tell me what I mean," thereby revealing his culture-specific knowledge and how it shapes his interpretive endeavors in particular ways. When Mabel said the basket was alive, she meant the basket was alive. The professor would have to have begun by taking that statement at the literal level, thereby beginning to see the difference between his world and hers. His subjectivity was exposed, and he was asked, in his encounter with Mabel, to be accountable for it. The same thing happened when the student asked about the influence of Mabel's grandmother. The student assumed some distinction between acquisition of the craft of basketry through the grandmother's demonstration and the young girl's imitation and maturation into the craft through a spiritual engagement with the process.

Mabel's response to the teacher working with a Navajo weaver unveiled another strategy of appropriation. In the face of difference, the teacher created a new category to account for or explain the difference. Thus she reads Navajo rugs as autobiography. Autobiography, as it is understood in the Western tradition, presupposes a culture-specific sense of self and certain expectations for its readers. Whether or not the Navajo weaver was even attempting to represent her life in her rugs is unclear. And if she was, would it be a self familiar to that constructed in the tradition of autobiography as the teacher knows it?

The Navajo weaver's relationship to her rugs, like Mabel's relationship to her baskets, is understood and experienced in ways that are personal and particular to her culture and history and, I imagine, not literate in a Western or Euro-American sense. But, again, can we know anything about this different relationship or sense of self if the teacher simply named what she encountered without exploring her definitions as they met with those of the Navajo weaver? The act of naming— or, in this case, appropriation—cuts a wide swath. It silences or obscures not only the individual subject and the distinct qualities of her voice and life, alone or in contact with the teacher, but the power dynamic that enables one party to name another in the first place. The teacher, and her readers, risk the danger of forgetting that, as Mabel pointed out, the teacher is not the Navajo weaver.

I have seen other so-called Pomo informants interact with interested outsiders. I have known women who made up stories for anthropologists, collected meager stipends for their stories, and laughed afterward. One of the women said to me: "Our stories, like our lives, are living. Might as well give white man your leg or arm. No matter what he gets, he just does with it how he likes. Like our land." Another Pomo woman, Essie Parrish, told me that she never lied, but that she gave pieces of this and that. "What they asked for," she said. "How they [anthropologists] going to see the tree when they are only looking at a leaf?" These Pomo women, in interaction with non-Pomo people, close down discouse, either fabricating information or presenting information in certain ways. But Mabel does something quite different. By exposing what makes for the differences between her life and worldview and that of her interlocutors, she continually opens discourse with others. She provokes exchange, providing the opportunity for people to see and talk about different worldviews as they emerge in shared moments.

For a long time I tried to figure out a way to write Mabel's autobiography. I was, after all, positioned as a reader of Mabel's life, since I would write, or make sense of her, for others. What about the problems of language? What about narrative format, specifically, Mabel's disjointed, nonchronological presentations? What about myself as a listener?

I remember once before when I thought I had all the answers. I was home after my first trip away at college. We had just returned from a school where Mabel was demonstrating her basket weaving. It had been a long drive, and, as I remember, it was quite late when we finally arrived home. I was sitting, having a cup of coffee, and laughing about the dumb questions people had asked Mabel. "I could write your book," I said then. "I know more about you and our way of life than those university idiots." She was opening the glass case that was in front of her on the kitchen table. I watched as she took out a miniature basket. Without a word, she stood up and pinned the basket and some ribbon to my shirt. "Think about that," she said.

Of course, that afternoon in Denny's I was still struggling with the need to make sense of Mabel's life. At least, at that time I was still feeling I needed to know the parts, so, if only in my head, I might create a coherent chronology, her life from beginning to end.

"Mabel," I said, "I never heard that story about the woman who went blind, about the woman and the basket."

She had finished eating and was sipping her coffee. She put down her cup. "Oh, that," she said, suddenly reminded.

"How old were you when that happened?"

"What?" She was lighting a cigarette.

"When you knew that woman, when that problem with the basket happened."

"Lots of problems," Mabel answered, beginning to laugh. She exhaled her first puff of smoke, raising her chin, as if pointing above us. She seemed interested in talking. She was laughing about something.

"Well, I mean when did you first meet the woman? Was it in Ukiah?"

"No. I think it was Middletown. I don't remember. I don't know. Someplace, anyway."

"Well, I mean for your book. You want me to do your book. Remember, I have talked to you about how to do it. I need to get all the people and places you know . . ."

"I know lots," Mabel interjected, tapping her cigarette in the ashtray.

"Were you a young woman?"

She ignored my question, or seemed to. She took a puff off her cigarette. "See, when that lady going to die, she give me that basket. She say it's talking, that basket. Talks all the time. I use it one day, she is saying. Come handy. So I feed it, take it with me and that way I keep her family from troubles. One day, some woman there, from that lady's people, she will want to know. Then I give it up. Now it's working with me. Now I seen what that woman is saying."

"Oh, you mean the way . . ."

"What am I saying now?"

"Oh, you mean the way you used it today in the class, to tell the story?"

Mabel looked at me and rubbed out her cigarette. She was serious, admonishing. "How you going to write my book?" she asked, or repeated. "I'm demonstrating." Then she burst into laughter. "If it was snake, it bite you," she laughed.

I felt bamboozled, stupid. She was right. I couldn't see what was right in front of me. I thought about others, my colleagues in particular, and about Mabel. But I took myself and Mabel for granted. I was not Mabel, even if I was an insider, an Indian. It was not just because of my mixed-blood heritage and fair skin. There were other things: generation, gender, my university education. I still harbored notions that such things as a chronology of Mabel's life and an index of all the people and places she knew would give me an understanding of her separate from my interaction with her. Did she sense as much just then? Was I stopped deliberately?

I thought of a story. It was about a cult of women bear doctors who shared a cave along Cache Creek in Lake County. Bear doctors put on the hide and head of the grizzly bear and, with certain songs, assumed great powers. They could hunt and search for acorns and other foods in distant places. They could travel at great speeds. They killed enemies. Mostly you heard about men bear doctors. But Mabel said these were women. They were women from many different neighboring bands and tribes. They watched other women and chose their members carefully. No one knew which women belonged to this cult. Any woman might have bear power.

One morning, quite early, a man was on his way to fish. He came upon his wife, who was kneeling by the water. He stopped and hid behind a rock so he could see what she was doing. She was washing a bear skin. He did not believe what he saw. So he followed and found the cave she entered. He did not return home that evening. For the next year, pieces of that man, first a finger or an eye, then an arm bone or a tooth, appeared near his village. The people thought it was him, that he had been ripped apart by human bears, but they could never positively identify him. So there was never a funeral. He made the mistake of not believing she was a bear and following her, Mabel said. He did not respect her.

Stories Mabel tells come back and forth with my own. They become mine, too. The story about the woman and the basket both implicated me and was about me. Like the woman in the story, I wanted my life—say, my work with Mabel—to be normal, different and separate from what I was experiencing with her. Certainly, I felt an internal struggle between my acquired notion of autobiography, closely associated with my academic training, and Mabel's sense of how a life story or life stories are meaningful. But I was blinded when I yielded to the former, unable to see. Just as the woman could not speak about what she saw, I could not write about Mabel. For Mabel, a life did not and could not exist in a vacuum, as an object, anymore than a basket or a story could. This was an idea I had in Denny's that day.

I thought of the yellow-gold and blue-green feathers, the zigzagging design of the basket. It was our story, about me and Mabel together. It was about the writing of "her book," not just about her or me, but a story intricately woven, of different materials, as in any good basket. And the lesson, in turn, became the story for a paper.

"You got big ideas," Mabel said just then. "Like everybody has ideas. Like them people who going to read what you write about us."

She laughed, then checked that the bill was paid, and slid around so she could get out of the booth. "Think of your basket," she said.

"Now let's go before something else starts demonstrating." She started laughing again. She was shaking so hard she couldn't move. "Maybe, it will start amusing."

Notes

1. This chapter is drawn from tapes and memories of conversations with Mabel McKay in February 1987.

2. Arnold Krupat, *For Those Who Come After* (Berkeley: University of California Press, 1985), 33–34.

3. Vincent Crapanzano, "The Life History in Anthropological Field Work," *Anthropology and Humanism Quarterly* 2 (1977): 5.

Chapter 3

"Rubbing a Paragraph with a Soft Cloth"?
Muted Voices and Editorial Constraints in *Dust Tracks on a Road*

Claudine Raynaud

It is like going out in the morning, or in the springtime to pick flowers. You pick and you wander till suddenly you find that the light is gone and the flowers are withered in your hand. Then, you say that you must run back home. But you have wandered into a place and the gates are closed. There is no more sharp sunlight. Gray meadows are all about you where blooms only the asphodel. You look back through the immutable gates to where the sun still shines on the flowered fields with nostalgic longing, but God pointed man's toes in one direction. One is surprised by the passage of time and the distance travelled, but one may not go back.

(MS, folder 13, 66)

This passage might serve to epitomize Zora Neale Hurston's outlook on writing her life story in 1941, at a moment when, as Robert Hemenway observes, "she was written out" (*ZNH*, 275).[1] Weaving the inexorable passing of time into the governing metaphor of *Dust Tracks on a Road,* she wrote about life as a journey. The passage embodies Hurston's feelings about her literary career and about her station in life. In 1941, she was fifty and had produced three novels, *Jonah's Gourd Vine* (1934), *Their Eyes Were Watching God* (1937), *Moses, Man of the Mountain* (1939), and two books of folklore, *Mules and Men* (1935) and *Tell My Horse* (1938).[2] Although she did not die until 1960, Hurston would write only one more novel, *Seraph on the Suwanee* (1948).[3] The above passage tells of death and of the impossibility of recovering the paradise of childhood or the happy moments of bygone times. It speaks of irreversible exile in an inhospitable underworld. It should have appeared on pages 70–71 of the published version of Hurston's autobiography, but readers of *Dust Tracks on a Road* will look for it in vain, because it was deleted from the manuscript.[4] In a section in which Hurston was describing to the reader the genesis of her creative imagination, the melancholy of this passage was jarring in its juxtaposition to the lighter-hearted childhood memories of her storytelling talents. Yet it did express metaphorically that she had reached a point in her life where her ability to create fiction had been sapped of its vital energy, and self-reflexively commented on her autobiographical venture.

Readers of the printed text seldom contemplate that they might be treading in a mine field of excisions, deletions, changes—sometimes willed by the author, other times imposed by the editor(s). Although Hemenway's 1984 edition and his analysis of the autobiography should lead any reader to distrust the published text, Hurston's critics have failed to address the unreliability of the printed version.[5] Yet is it not vital, when dealing with an autobiographical text, to check the original manuscript against the published version?[6] In an elusive text, where Hurston hides rather than unveils, the first draft might be precisely the place where self-construction is less embroiled in tactics of delusion. Analyzing the published version, critic Nellie McKay discusses the strategies displayed by Hurston to cope with the "powerlessness and vulnerability of the racial self."[7] A study of the omitted sections emphasizes the complexity of her resistance to the white publishing world, and the ways in which she eventually complied. It stresses how the creation of her fictive self is not solely a self-conscious textual strategy, but also a product of her historical position as a black female writer. It restores from the original text a more accurate, if still extremely puzzling, portrait of Hurston.

Françoise Lionnet's reading of the autobiography as "autoethnography" centers, as did my earlier essay, "Autobiography as a 'Lying' Session," on the creation of the self in folklore, while placing the narrative within a broader philosophical framework.[8] But the voices of the excised passages displace the emphasis from folklore. Rather, they converge to create a persona that contrasts with the overall casting of the book. In those excised passages Hurston's biting irony, her vibrant denunciations, her sharp political opinions create other layers that complicate the reading of her text as auto-ethno-graphy. To the voices of the Eatonville girl who was exemplifying the lore and the anthropologist who was studying it must be added these polemical voices.

Elizabeth Fox-Genovese, aware of the crucial issue of audience and of the racial, sexual, and class tensions operating within texts, has pointed out the recurrent tension at the heart of black women's autobiographies between "the autobiographer's intuitive sense of [herself] and [her] attitude towards [her] probable readers."[9] Hurston's "sense of self" can be better specified by examining the differences between the published text and the manuscript. If, to borrow Hurston's metaphor, she was making a statue for herself, the excised passages could be seen as many invisible cracks in this mirror of self finally presented to the Other(s). For the most part these cracks act as positive loci of resistance to the editors' wishes for an ideal autobiographical self; they can be read as pockets of resistance to the form, to the final ideal product. Once restored, the deleted passages project a self closer to Hurston's initial response to the autobiographical exercise. Ultimately, Hurston censored or condensed many of them in compliance with publishing rules.[10] Thus the printed text is the result of a mediation, an unequal dialogue with her publisher in response to the projected audience.[11]

The History of the Manuscript

Hurston wrote *Dust Tracks on a Road* from late spring 1941 until mid-July of that year. She spent more than a year on revisions; *Dust Tracks* was published in late November 1942. The full manuscript of *Dust Tracks* is kept in folders 10 to 15 of the James Weldon Johnson Collection at the Beinecke Library at Yale University. It bears the notice, "Parts of this manuscript were not used in the final composition of the book for publisher's reasons," a commentary that shifts the responsibility for major corrections onto the publisher.[12] Hurston must have finally agreed to the changes, yet in reading the manuscript one cannot think of Hurston as simply a collaborator with her white readers. In Hurston's case, one needs to assess how the subject's agency can be salvaged within an environment that did not recognize the black woman as subject. Hurston's manuscript reveals, in one of her metaphors, how much she sharpened her oyster knife in her text, only to be left begrudgingly with a blunt blade.[13] The Hurston thus rescued shows more extreme contradictions, sharper contrasts, more edifyingly unsettling stories, more pronounced angles of self-portraiture. If she eventually "[rubbed] a paragraph with a soft cloth," a metaphor that brings to the foreground her numerous jobs as a house servant, much was lost in the process.[14]

The Beinecke document of *Dust Tracks* consists of a series of autographed chapters and of typed chapters that correspond to the chapters of the published text, apart from notable omissions of up to ten pages of the typescript. For instance, pages 141–50 of the manuscript (folder 13, box I) would have appeared on page 140 of the chapter "Backstage and Railroad" and told the frightening story of Johnnie the murderer, brother of Miss M—, Hurston's protector in the Gilbert and Sullivan repertory company for which she worked eighteen months as a wardrobe attendant before she enrolled at Morgan Academy in September 1917. The first part of the document, the autographed chapters in folder 10, comprises a chapter titled "The Inside Light—Being a Salute to Friendship" (no. 1);[15] chapter 9 "School Again" (no. 2); chapter 14 "Love" (no. 3); an unpublished chapter titled "Concert" (no. 4); "My People! My People!" (no. 5); and two untitled pieces (nos. 6 and 7) that were subsequently typed and constitute the chapter "Seeing the World as It Is," reprinted in Hemenway's edition. This chapter would have been chapter 14 of the original text. The last page of the manuscript shows that Hurston finished the draft on July 5, 1941. The second part of the document, a typescript of the whole text, is kept in folders 11 to 15. Although one might have thought that the autographed chapters were the only ones to differ significantly from the final version, the typescript, when compared with the printed text, also presents considerable changes. Certain passages are crossed out; others have been omitted without having been explicitly crossed out; still others bear marginal comments or are corrected in Hurston's hand.

The editors of *Dust Tracks* were Mr. Bertram Lippincott and Ms. Tay Honoff.[16] Just as she called her patron, Mrs. Rufus Osgood Mason, "Godmother," Hurston refers to Bertram Lippincott as "Colonel":

> So you see why that editor is *Colonel* to me. When the Negroes in the South name a white man a colonel, it means CLASS. Something like a monarch, only bigger and better. And when the colored population in the South confer a title, the white people recognize it because the Negroes are never wrong. They may flatter an ordinary bossman by calling him "Cap'n" but when they say "Colonel," "General" and "Governor" they are recognizing something internal. It is there, and it is accepted because it can be seen. (*DT,* 212)

Bertram Lippincott is also mentioned in the list of friends in the original chapter on friendship, which did not make it to the final version: "There are so many others, Colonel and Mrs. Bert Lippincott, . . ." (*DT,* 313). The manuscript also makes clear that the Colonel is Bertram Lippincott. On page 245 of the manuscript "Mr. Bertram Lippincott" is crossed out and replaced by "One of the editors." His name is also crossed out on page 247 of the typescript and replaced by "that editor" (folder 15). It is not always clear who, Bertram Lippincott or Tay Honoff, is doing the editing; some of the marginal comments seem to prove that in some instances Hurston must have offered to effect some of the changes. But it is undeniable that *Dust Tracks* was crucially altered by the process of editing.[17]

The Problematic Nature of Editorial Intervention

Hemenway's 1984 edition of *Dust Tracks on a Road* establishes the instability of the published version, as he chose to publish the typed version that is kept in folder 11.[18] Assessing the impact of the alterations, Hemenway has stressed how the excision of Hurston's opinions on international politics in what was to be the last chapter of the book, the omission of a whole chapter titled "Concert," and the numerous stylistic corrections have given us a very different autobiography from the one Hurston may have intended.[19] Yet the manuscript has been excised beyond what is available to the reader of the 1984 edition. I will address only some of the changes that can be listed between the original manuscript and the published version, for an exhaustive listing would be tantamount to establishing a new edition of *Dust Tracks*.[20] I want here to offer representative examples of the changes and to address the possible significance of those changes.

Among the problems faced by a researcher who compares manuscript and published version are those of identifying obvious editorial intrusions and considering the extent to which Hurston was anticipating her editor's demands. In effect, the autobiographical text enters into a dialogue with its own assumptions. Certain pages are clearly marked by the editors, such as the chapter titled "Seeing the World as It Is," in which Hurston's remarks about Japan and her anti-American statement on the eve of Pearl Harbor are labeled as "irrelevant" to her autobiography.[21] Some passages that were excised for fear of libel suits bear the remark "libel?" in the margin, as on page 192 (folder 11), where Hurston tells the story of Logan, who went to jail for beating his wife in a fight over a hog head.[22] Pages 138–40 of the manuscript twice bear the libel comment.[23]

The motivations behind the excisions can only be hypothesized based on the content of the deleted sections. Working backward to recover the genesis of writing means exploring the relationship at work between Hurston's text and her publisher's requests. This power relationship, fraught with racial, sexual, and class tensions, is rendered more complex by Hurston's own ambivalent identity. Hurston is both, but not always simultaneously, the Eatonville girl and the writer-anthropologist. This doubleness results in a plurality of voices that are themselves shaped by readers' expectations.[24] Thus the manuscript unveils a Zora more deeply embroiled in her integrationist compromises. It spells, writ large, the "bundle of sham and tinsel, honest metal and sincerity that cannot be untangled" that made up Zora Neale Hurston (*DT,* 347).[25]

Alterations of Language

At the level of minor alterations, the correction of grammatical errors and the stylistic changes work toward eliminating the presence of black dialect in passages where Zora, as the writer of the autobiography, must display her command of correct English. As a southerner, Hurston is "proud to have the map of Dixie on [her] tongue" (*DT,* 134). Yet the original text reveals a conflict between southern accent and black dialect and correct English spelling and pronunciation as imposed by the publishing world. The manuscript reveals an effort to force Hurston's language away from the quality of oral speech into the polished, acceptable form of written language. For instance, Hurston's word was "wrassle," not "wrestle." Hemenway quotes Hurston telling Mrs. Mason: "I shall wrassle me up a future or die trying" (*ZNH,* 160). But in the published version "wrassle" becomes "wrestle," phonetic transcription displaced by correct spelling: "The very next day Mr. Johns came in and announced that they had a bear up at Keith's theater, and they needed somebody to wrestle with him" (*DT,* 161). Hurston also has to spell the word correctly when it is part of the dialogue between Logan and Mr. Johns: "Git me a little bitty baby bear, Mr. Johns, 'bout three months old. Dats de kind of bear I wants to wrestle wid. Yassuh!" (*DT,* 162). The orality of the word, including the accent, gives way to standard spelling, not only in reported speech, where the author should have control over the speech of others, but also in dialogue that reproduces Logan's accent.[26] The excision of Hurston's misspellings—"sumptious" instead of "sumptuous"—and her grammatical "errors" ("Mrs. Meyer, who was the moving spirit in founding the college and who is still a trustee, did noble [instead of nobly] by me in getting me in"; *DT,* 171) show how language is emptied of voice.[27] Speech (*parole*) recedes before language (*langage*), the conventional graphic and grammatical English with which readers can identify.[28] Hurston's "errors" foreground her double and conflicting identity as both Barnard scholar and Eatonville girl; her characters might have been allowed to speak like that, but she no longer was.

Beyond this taming of southern speech, close attention to the letter discloses humorous oppositions. Whereas Hurston had originally talked about her teacher "[liquifying [*sic*]] the imortal [*sic*] grains of Coleridge," the published version reads "he liquefied the immortal brains of Coleridge" (*DT,* 147). It seems that Hurston had intended to use an image from black rural life, the distillation of grains to produce gin or corn liquor; the reader is left with the vision of an English teacher reducing Coleridge's immortal brains to pulp, to the delight of her black student. And yet distillation and poetry go hand in hand in black American poetry, the former the ideal metaphor for the latter. For Gwendolyn Brooks, for instance, "Poetry is life distilled."[29] Audre Lorde similarly defines poetry as "a revelatory distillation of experience."[30] The instability of the word is also brought to light by other instances of slippages or printer's errors. "Bountiful" in the manuscript becomes "beautiful" in the published text (*DT,* 150), "prowess" becomes "powers" (*DT,* 161). Both noticeably weaken the language's vibrancy.

Hurston's text is the site of an encounter between different speech genres: on the one hand, proper, grammatical, standard English; on the other, the "words" of folklore, black idiom, an authentic black voice.[31] The constant interaction between the two voices sometimes leads to friction, sometimes to subversion of proper English by the aural/oral, rural black voice. To go back to Hurston's handwriting on the page and recover the "errors" of the first draft is to retrace her struggle to sort out these two speech genres, a struggle neutralized in the published version, where each "voice" falls into its respective place. Hurston's "speakerly text," one defined by Henry Louis Gates, Jr., as the third term beyond the opposition between "a profoundly lyrical, densely metaphorical, quasi-musical, privileged black oral tradition" and "a received but not yet fully appropriated standard English literary tradition," is undermined by the publisher's desire for a readerly text.[32] The speakerly can be seen as the ideal representation of the Eatonville folk voice as it struggles with the impositions of the readerly; that is, the editorial voice and the persona of the accomplished writer that justifies the writing of the autobiography.

Altered Voices: The Erotic Voice

One of Hurston's most powerful voices, the erotic, was also excised from the published text. Propriety ruled out the explicitly sexual, especially in the 1940s, and even more so when uttered by a woman. Erotically inflected folklore is consequently "cleaned up," stripped of what Hurston might have herself called the "juicy bits." Although, for the most part, the text's excisions expose the sexist attitudes prevalent and reinforced by the folklore, the racial politics of these erasures of her sexuality are ironically acknowledged in the original text. In order to illustrate U.S. imperialism and American refusal to admit that Japanese intervention in Asia parallels the imperialistic stance of the

United States on the American continent, Hurston quotes the following dialogue:

> We [the Americans] are like the southern planter's bride when he kissed her the first time.
> "Darling," she fretted, "do niggers hug and kiss like this?"
> "Why, I reckon they do, honey. Fact is, I'm sure of it. Why do you ask?"
> "You go right out and kill the last one of 'em tomorrow morning. Things like this is much too good for niggers." (*DT,* Appendix, 340–41)

Now available in the 1984 edition of the chapter titled "Seeing the World as It Is," this passage did not appear in the original printed text. It illustrates Hurston's craft at its best. In one single bold stroke, she denounces racism in the South and the sexual exploitation of black women by white men ("Fact is, I'm sure of it"). The dialogue serves as a metaphor for the brutal imperialism that would be seen in World War II, and any kind of imperialism, at that. The excision of this passage exemplifies the censorship of the explicitly sexual throughout the text. The sexual, in this case as an illustration of the political, had to be deleted, an editorial gesture that parallels the wish for the eradication of the black race uttered by the southern white bride, who wanted to keep to her race and herself the pleasures of kissing.

In the 1940s the practice of censorship dictated that folklore collections not contain explicitly sexual material, and a celebration of sexual pleasure in black male-female relationships might have been too much for a white audience.[33] In the draft of *Dust Tracks,* a group of black men talking on a store porch engaged in exchanges that had to be censored for the prudish.[34] After a sexist remark by one of the men on the store porch—"To save my soul, I can't see what you fooled with her for. I'd just as soon pick up a old tin can out off the trash pile" (*DT,* 63)—the following passage was excised:

> The other one stroked his chin and said, "On de average, I'd say de same thing. But last night, I had de feeling dat anything hot and hollow would do. Just like Uncle Bud." One afternoon my oldest brother was on the store porch with the men. He was proudly stroking two or three hairs on his top lip. A married man in his late twenties was giving him some advice about growing a big, thick mustache [*sic*]. I went on inside. When I was coming out, I heard something about getting his finger wet from a woman and wiping it on his lip. Best mustache-grower [*sic*] God ever made. They all grew theirs that way. It was a good thing my brother let them

know so he could be told the inside secret. I emerged from
the door and the porch fell silent. Later on, I asked my
brother what they were talking about, and he slapped me all
over the place. (MS, folder 11, 59A–B)

The excised passage shows how a young girl is excluded from sexual
knowledge to which the older male members of her family are privy.
Conversely, the published version emphasizes her understanding of
adult double entendre: "It did not take me long to know what was
meant when a girl was spoken of as 'ruint' or 'bigged'" (*DT*, 62). The
store porch is ultimately described as the stage of male culture and
initiation on which women cannot set foot. Folk culture, as reported
by Hurston, ironically retells the creation of sexual differences by
making Adam owe part of his outward signs of manhood to Eve; his
moustache is Eve's pubic hair.[35] Ironically, only later, as an anthropologist, will Hurston discover the manly secret from which she was
excluded as a young girl.[36] The female anthropologist crosses the
boundaries between male and female sexual knowledge, which the
"Eatonville waif" had been denied. The disclosure of the secret in
the autobiographical text is a breaking of several taboos. A woman's
voice speaks the sexual, contrary to the rules of male-dominated discourse on the store porch. Zora Neale Hurston as a black anthropologist exposes folk knowledge and its questioning of gender relations
through humor and wit. Finally, as a black female anthropologist, she
tells the hidden tale of male and female adolescent initiation within
her community.[37]

Her celebration of Polk County and the black men felling trees,
working in phosphate mines, laying railroad tracks, and picking
oranges ends with the evocation of the jook houses and the love
between black men and women (*DT*, 179–85). While this passage is
replete with work songs, sections of a song that praises the eroticism
of the female body and contextualizes Hurston's views on love between
black men and women have been excised:

> Evalina! Make your dress a little longer, hark!
>
> Oh Evalina! Make your dress a little longer, hark!
>
> I see your thighs—
>
> Lawd, Lawd, I see your thighs! (MS, folder 14, 193)[38]

Similarly, the excised second line of the song that follows the lyrical
prose passage about men in Polk County makes the sexual meaning
of the first line explicit. The text reads: "I got up this morning, and

I knowed I didn't want it, / Yea! Polk County!" (*DT*, 181). The line that has been erased makes the reference explicit: "'cause I slept last night with my hands all on it" (MS, folder 14, 194). Obviously, the voice behind these songs is male. The epitome of the genre, a song titled "Uncle Bud," could not be performed, according to Hurston, in front of respectable ladies.[39] Thus Hurston, the female folklorist, transgresses the distinction between respectable lady and "jook" woman (i.e., woman of ill repute) by quoting these lines. In the world of the jook joint, sexuality and profanity can be uttered by a woman. Because she speaks the sexual within the black community in spite of the puritanism of the projected audience, Hurston problematizes what could otherwise be construed as sexist songs.

Hurston made the relationship between song-making and lovemaking explicit in an earlier (1934) text:

> Likewise love-making is a biological necessity the world over and an art among Negroes. So that a man or a woman who is proficient sees no reason why the fact should not be moot. He swaggers. She struts hippily about. *Songs are built on the power to charm beneath the bed-clothes.*[40] (emphasis mine)

Yet Hurston's autobiographical text could not live up to the claim she makes about black men and women talking openly about sexuality. Deletions veil her sexual voice. Bawdy language and erotic evocations have been erased because they might offend. Folklore has been censored. Considering how black Americans are stereotyped, a plausible explanation for these deletions is that their inclusion would contribute to a vision of the black American denounced by Zora Neale Hurston in her article "What White Publishers Won't Print":

> Until [the fact that we have things in common] is thoroughly established in respect to Negroes in America, as well as of other minorities, it will remain impossible for the majority to conceive of a Negro experiencing a deep and abiding love and not just the passion of sex.[41]

Could Hurston run the risk of being constantly reconstructed as the lewd, loose black woman of the racist/sexist stereotypes? Or did she simply fall victim to the still prevailing censorship of profane language?

Altered Voices: The Black Woman's Voice

Hurston's unself-consciousness, her "bodaciousness," is counterbalanced by a denunciation, at times blatant, at other times under the cover of humor, of how, as a black woman, she was subjected to an inextricable mixture of racism and sexism rendered even more complex by power relationships.[42] A section of four pages in folder 13 has been omitted because it exposes the mixture of racism and sexism of the male members of the households in which the young Hurston was employed as a maid.[43] Hurston worked for Mrs. Moncrief, who was bedridden and had a small child. Her unscrupulous husband, Hurston writes, took to the habit of "waylaying her," going so far as to ask her to elope with him to Canada.[44] She eventually decided to tell Mrs. Moncrief about her husband's intentions, but the woman responded:

> "You have nothing to cry about, Zora. You haven't been lying here for three years with somebody hoping to find you dead every morning. You don't know what it means for every girl who comes in hailing distance to be mixed up in your life. You don't know what it means to give birth to a child for your husband and find that your health is gone the day the baby is born and for him not to care what becomes of the baby or you either. God! Why wouldn't he leave *you* alone?" (Box I, folder 13, 120–21)

Hurston realized too late that she should not have told Mrs. Moncrief. The man's absolute lack of morality and his disdain for black women is made evident in Hurston's reconstruction of his speech, added on the back of the page:

> "I am not the kind of man to be worried with so much responsibilities. Never should have let myself get married in the first place. All I need is a young, full-of-feelings girl to sleep with and enjoy life. I always did keep me a colored girl. My last one moved off to Chicago and left me without [end of over]. I want a colored girl and I'm giving you the preference." (MS, folder 13, 122).

Such exposure of sexual, racial, and class tensions and prejudices would assuredly have cost the book the Anisfield-Wolf Award for the improvement of race relations.[45] Yet, the deletion of this passage contributes to the confusion about Hurston's autobiographical persona. Assuredly, the voice here is not the compromising voice so often heard throughout the published autobiography. Moreover, such a passage documents the continuity of the oppression of black women and the tensions in their relations to their white mistresses already exposed in the slave narrative. Harriet Jacobs's *Incidents in the Life of a Slave Girl,* for example, brilliantly exposes the difficult and hitherto seldom addressed issue of the plight of black women under slavery.[46] She records in her narrative how she resisted and fled the advances of her master, Dr. Flint, and had to fight the suspicion and the jealousy of her mistress. From slavery to domestic labor, the situation of a young black female in a white household has always been a threatened and a cruel one.

Another omitted passage describes how Hurston was subjected to sexism. While working as a wardrobe attendant, she found herself turned into a laughingstock by the baritone of the company, who tricked her into a corner of a train coach, talked to her, and then shouted so that the others could hear: "Porter! A flock of hand towels and a seven o'clock call!" (MS, folder 13, 134). In her comment, Hurston tones down her humiliation and tries to describe the situation "objectively":

> **Nearly everybody burst out laughing. I couldn't see what for. I knew the joke was on me somehow, but I didn't know what it was. I sat there blank-faced and that made them laugh more. Miss M— did not laugh. She called called [*sic*] me and told me to sit down by her and not to listen to dirty cracks. Finally she let me know what the joke was. Then** I jumped up and told him to stop trying to run the hog over me. That set everybody off **again.** (MS, folder 13, 134–35; material in boldface corresponds to deletions)

In the published version the joke has been excised, and the reader is left to conjecture about its actual content.[47] She concludes the same chapter with a depiction of the repertory theater company as a symbol of the melting pot and of harmony among the races. The passage, however, contains a denunciation of verbal racism mixed with sexism in the mouth of Miss M—, who up to now had seemed to act as Hurston's protectress:

> With all branches of Anglo-Saxon, Irish, three Jews and one Negro together in a huddle, and all friendly, there were a lot of racial gags. Everybody was so sure that nobody hesitated to pull them. It was all taken in good part. Naturally, all of the Negro gags were pulled on me. There were enough of the others to divide things up. For instance, one night, Miss M— cut her eyes in my direction slyly, began to talk about, blondes, brunettes and *burnt-ettes*. (MS, folder 13, 153–54; emphasis mine)[48]

Characteristically, Hurston again tones down the impact of the racial slur by adding: "But the whole experience on that job gave me an approach to racial understanding" (MS, folder 13, 154). In the examples of "gags" or "cracks," as she calls them, Hurston is derided as a black woman working in a subservient position. The reader cannot help but read these supposedly humorous situations as Hurston's effort to expose racist and sexist attitudes. She does insist, after all, on the fact that she was the only black person in the company.

A long episode that should have appeared at the top of page 124 in the chapter "Backstage and Railroad" has been excised and, with it, the circumstances that led to Zora's dismissal from her early job as a maid (MS, folder 13, 116–19).[49] The final version emphasizes the antagonism between an old black nurse and the young Zora, who, hired as an upstairs maid, ends up playing with the children and not doing the housework. The manuscript details the reasons for the loss of her job. In fact, after the incident described in the published text, Zora was kept on a little while, another maid was hired, and she made peace with Aunt Cally: "Cally talked to me then, and gave me a piece of pie" (MS, folder 13, 117). Zora's a posteriori explanation for her final abrupt dismissal is that the husband was jealous of his wife's freedom:

> Years later when I had seen more, I concluded that he was
> jealous of his wife. He was not one of those pretty men, and
> she was a beautiful thing, much younger than he was. I do
> not think that she ever did anything wrong, but he felt inse-
> cure. If she had to be around to keep up with the children,
> she had her hands full. There was much less danger of her
> wandering off. Cally was in his confidence. (MS, folder 13, 118)

The omission is again crucial, for it highlights sexism within a white household, whereas the published text leaves the reader to understand that hierarchy and competition between two black women as well as the cross-racial link between the black nurse and the white man she had brought up led to Zora's dismissal. In the manuscript the solidarity among women, black and white, is brought to the foreground and contrasted to the defensive despotism of the male head of the household.

Altered Voices: Voices of Excess

Hurston's extreme statements of love or derision directed toward other people have also been deleted, her voices of excess subdued. For instance, Rosa Brown, a student at Morgan College, is qualified in the manuscript as "the most luscious piece of gal meat in all colored Baltimore" (*DT,* 150). This statement is left out of the published text. So is an anecdote about the wife of a U.S. president told by White House correspondent Frederick William Wile. The woman, Hurston writes, "had been quite the grande dame when she was First Lady." "Why, she was so glad when that man proposed to her that she fell out of bed," Wile is quoted as saying (*DT,* 159). Ironically, the suppressed story of the First Lady would have appeared after the passage in which Hurston explains how she was the ideal confidante to all those Washington politicians and journalists who came to her for a manicure. "Now, I know that my discretion really didn't matter," she writes. "They were relieving their pent-up feelings where it could do no harm" (*DT,* 159). In the autobiography, however, her disclosure of the story could do some harm; it is eventually crossed out.

In the manuscript, this iconoclastic Zora is balanced by another ostentatiously self-effacing one. In "Concert," Hurston apologizes to Alain Locke, who had written the concert's program notes, for a faux pas she made the night of the premiere.[50] Her oversensitive and girlish request for forgiveness deflates the image of the strong, self-confident theater producer, the savior of authentic black folklore and creativity. She seems also to view *Dust Tracks* as the ideal occasion to acquit herself of her debts by celebrating those people who had helped her. The manuscript version of the chapter titled "Two Women in Particular" is a long list of Hurston's friends, starting with Mrs. Mason, Hurston's patron. Hurston exclaims: "I owe her and owe her and owe her!" (*DT,* Appendix, 309). In the manuscript, her relationship to Fannie Hurst brings to her mind an episode in which Hurst had Hurston dress as an Asian princess to avoid racial segregation. That anecdote is omitted in the final version, which focuses more on how Hurst fulfilled Hurston's wishes.[51] The overall tone is one of overenthusiastic gratitude, as Hurston unfolds the scroll of her benefactors, saviors, and helpers. Hurston uses autobiographical writing to acknowledge debts, debts one feels she might have preferred not to have incurred. One may wonder what motivated the deletion of the voice of honey-dripping gratitude. The omission of certain stories that might have led to libel suits against the publisher is understandable; so is the silencing of the political and the erotic. But why were Zora's lists of thank-yous, her autobiographical text as *"reconnaissance de dettes,"* kept to bare minimum? Might it be because the litany of names too blatantly exposed the system of patronage and its exploitation of a young black woman's creative talent?

Altered Voices: The Political Voice

Hurston's opinions on politics have also been deleted. The silencing of Hurston's political opinions on European and American imperialism as well as domestic politics suggests that the publisher had in mind a strict notion of the thematic content of an autobiography. A female author's opinions on international politics fell outside the scope of autobiographical expectations.[52] Yet the political opinions that have been erased might offer a positive counterpoint to the ambiguous attitude on race that emerges in the published text. In the chapter titled "Religion," Hurston charts her doubts about religious faith. She believes that "even in his religion man carried himself along" (*DT*, 275); to prove her point, she describes how military might and evangelical missions have always gone hand in hand, citing the apostle Paul and Emperor Constantine as examples. In 1941, on the eve of America's involvement in the war, she asks similar questions about her country's future: "Will military might determine the dominant religion of tomorrow?" (MS, folder 15, 311).

A long satirical passage that rather heavy-handedly describes Roosevelt's abrupt and fictitious conversion to the cult of Father Divine has been deleted (MS, folder 15, 311–14).[53] As the followers of Father Divine gave up their mortal names to take up spiritual names, Hurston imagines the new government turned into Divinites who pay lip service to the charismatic black leader:[54]

> Then, we might hear the former Franklin D. Roosevelt addressed as Sincere Determination. Eleanor would be Divine Eternal Commutation [*Commution* is crossed out]. Celestial Bountiful Tribulations would be Sister Frances Perkins. Harry Hopkins, Angelic Saintly Shadow. His Vocal Honor, La Guardia, would be known as Always Sounding Trumpet, and on his evident good works in his nursery, Harold Ickes would be bound to win the title of Fruitful Love Abounding. (MS, folder 15, 312)[55]

American politics is rewritten as a huge banquet offered and presided over by Father Divine—the cult leader famous for offering splendid free meals to his followers:

> The Senate Chamber would be something to see. All of the seats in the center taken out and a long table loaded down with baked hams, turkeys, cakes and pies all ready for the legislative session to begin. With Father Divine at the head and Sincere Determination at the foot, slicing ham and turkey for the saints, there might not be much peace, but the laws

would be truly wonderful. The saints would not overeat,
either; what with being forced to raise their hands and cry
"Peace!" every time Father Divine spoke and "it's truly wonderful" every time Sincere Determination uttered a sound,
their eating would be negligible. (MS, folder 15, 312–13)

Franklin Delano Roosevelt, renamed Sincere Determination, is at
the foot of the table. Contemporary racial politics are inverted, but
Hurston is still in keeping with reality: Father Divine had a number
of rich white followers. Her description of the relations among the
different political institutions is a wry attack on Roosevelt's politics at
the time of World War II. The words "Peace" and "It's truly wonderful," with which Father Divine punctuated his sermons, must be
replaced within the highly emotional climate of the year preceding
the government's decision to go to war, a decision made inevitable
after the December 1941 Japanese attack on Pearl Harbor.[56] The scene
is both a strident and uncompromising critique of the government
and a religious satire. It reminds the reader of the caricatures the
younger Hurston used to draw when she was a wardrobe attendant
(*DT,* 138–39). After the United States had entered the war, such mockery would have appeared crudely out of place. Even if the country
had not gone to war, one wonders whether such irreverence toward
the president could be tolerated in the autobiography. One senses in
this type of writing the journalistic Hurston of the 1945 essay, "Crazy
for This Democracy," in which she openly and sarcastically questions
Roosevelt's version of democracy.[57]

In another omitted section, dealing with Bahamian politics, race
and politics are linked. The candidate, whom she names Botts
"because it is not his name," rejected his color and subsequently lost
the 1935 local elections:

People remembered things about Barrister Botts they otherwise would have forgotten. Poor people down on the waterfront remembered that, though he went for a great man now,
his mother had stood down the waterfront night after night,
selling fried fish to send him to England to be educated. His
father was living and prosperous. He was in business, and a
member of the House, but long years ago he had divorced
Botts' mother for a woman of lighter skin. But the mother had
seen him through the Inner Temple. He had come back, not
full of gratitude for the sacrifices she had made, but scornful
of her black skin and all that she stood for. People said that
he paid her ten shillings ($2.50) a week to stay away from his
house. (MS, folder 14, 212–13)

The episode is a complex narrative of color politics in Nassau. The reader is struck, however, by Hurston's compassion for the mother. In a more personal passage, she tells how she wondered about this woman's behavior:

> I was down on the wharf when the boats returned. I wanted to see the behavior of the old woman who had been divorced by her husband for being too black after he gained a certain amount of success. The same woman who had been barred from her son's home for the same reason, after she had felt that no labor was too humble for her to do to put him through law school in London to come home to her as a barrister. She was not there. I wondered if she was off somewhere trying to rustle up a tuppence or two, or merely that she did not want to look on his dear face when his pretentions had met his realities. She had her bitter moments, but after all, she was his mother. (MS, folder 14, 215)

In the pathos of this scene, Hurston foregrounds the personal toll of internalized racism on the black mother.

Hurston's opinions in the manuscript are not limited to domestic and Caribbean politics; she also criticizes the colonial ventures of the European powers, refusing to see cruelty and warring instincts as the sole attribute of African kings. For instance, at one point the published version reads:

> You see, the Kings of Dahomey were truly great and mighty and a lot of skulls were bound to come out of their ambitions. While it looked awesome and splendid to him and to his warriors, the sight must have been most grewsome and crude to Western eyes. (*DT*, 199)

The manuscript version carries on: "Imagine a Palace of Hindu or Zulu skulls in London! Or Javanese skulls in The Hague!" (MS, folder 14, 219), but these comments have been deleted in the published version. Hurston explicitly voices an opinion on European colonialism in "Seeing the World as It Is." Commenting on the prevailing pro-European sentiment in the United States during World War II, and highlighting the racism that underlies it, she writes:

> All around me, bitter tears are being shed over the fate of Holland, Belgium, France, and England. I must confess to being a little dry around the eyes. I hear people shaking with shudders at the thought of Germany collecting taxes in Holland. I have not heard a word against Holland collecting one twelfth of poor people's wages in Asia. Hitler's crime is that he is

doing a thing like that to *his own kind*. That is international cannibalism and should be stopped. (*DT,* 342; emphasis mine)

In the manuscript she had added ironically: "What happens to the Balinese is unimportant I take it" (MS, folder 10, no. 7, 7), a sentence that has been crossed out in the typed version.[58] Hurston had added in ink on the back of the page of the typed version the following personal remark: "That makes the ruling family in Holland very rich, as they should be. What happens to the poor Javanese and Balinese is unimportant I take it" (folder 11, typed version). These sentences have also been deleted.[59]

Hurston saw colonialism as an extension of slavery:

The idea of human slavery is so deeply ground in that the pink-toes can't get it out of their system. It has just been decided to move the slave quarters away from the house. It would be a fine thing if on leaving office, the blond brother could point with pride to the fact that his administration had done away with group-profit at the expense of others. I know well that it has never happened before, but it could happen, couldn't it? (*DT,* 343)

Colonialism is slavery's new name, and she makes the analogy quite plain in another passage in which she stages an imaginary dialogue between herself and the white male descendant of a slave owner, one that disenchantedly concludes with a reflection about the omnipresence of human injustice:

If I reminded him that his old folks acheived [*sic*] their wealth, leisure and culture at the expense of my ancestors' lives and blood, he would not fall out on the sidewalk in a fit of remorse. He would look into my face to see if I were blind. If he were not too hurried, he might take time to ask me if I thought the principle of slavery had disappeared from the earth. Did not nations still hold colonies? The process of one man living at the expense of another is no longer called slavery. All enlightened people have agreed on that. It is now called the sources of raw material. If he were in a big hurry, he might merely ask: "Who *is* just?" and like Pilate pass on without waiting for an answer. (MS, folder 11, 193)

In light of Hurston's critique of colonialism, it would be tempting to view her relationship to her editors as one between "colonized" and "colonizers." Yet to invoke the term *colonize* in analyzing the power relationships between men and women in their political, economic, *and* sexual dimensions implies that women are a territory to be conquered within the framework of a settler mentality, a highly problematic geopolitical metaphor.[60] Hurston's relationship to her editors must be read within the framework of racial, sexual, and class power relationships.

Altered Structure/Altered Meaning

Omissions also alter the overall composition of Hurston's text. The most important structural change is the reduction of a whole chapter titled "Concert" (folder 10, no. 4) to two pages in the published version (*DT,* 194–95, 206–8). Hall Johnson, the most famous choral director in the United States in the 1920s, first rejected Hurston's offer to perform dances and songs from black folklore. He later accepted, only to back out eventually in a cavalier manner. The manuscript version details Hurston's frustration not only with Hall Johnson, but with his singers, who ridiculed her West Indian dancers. It celebrates her joy and her sense of achievement; it also reveals an explosive bitterness at failing to be recognized as the innovator of this type of music and dance. She dispiritedly comments: "My name is never mentioned, of course." The Zora of the manuscript is bitter, acrimonious, combative; she sets the record straight and reclaims her due share of fame. The Zora of the published version is milder, better mannered, more elusive. She even goes so far as to contradict herself: "I am not upset by the fact that others have made something out of the things I pointed out" (*DT,* 208). Her antagonism toward Hall Johnson and her deep resentment, squarely spelled out in the manuscript, are laconically summarized: "After trying to vainly interest others, I introduced Bahaman songs and dances to a New York audience at the Golden Theater, and both the songs and the dances took on" (*DT,* 194).[61] The published text silences her anger at Hall Johnson, who unashamedly plagiarized her show in his "Run Little Chillun." She writes: "Hall Johnson took my group to appear with his singers at the Lewisohn Stadium that summer and built his 'Run Lil' Chillun' around them and the religious scene from my concert, 'From Sun to Sin'" (*DT,* 194).[62]

In the published version the equilibrium between the "Research" and "Books and Things" chapters and the chapter titled "Concert" is lost, making Zora's field trips and her literary and academic achievements appear more important than her career as a producer. She is also denied the occasion of staging a moment of intense personal gratification.[63] In the manuscript version she introduces the chapter with a disclaimer: "I am not a singer, a dancer, nor even a musician. I was, therefore, seeking no reputation in either field." The final remark suggests that she knew she could have been a successful concert producer. Indeed, the concert proved that she was capable of dramatizing her research on her own initiative. She strongly believed work songs were not only to be collected, but should be heard and staged in their original context. Thus "Concert" is a direct outcome of "Research." Illustrating what must be done out of research, it bridges the gap between the academic world and popular entertainment.[64]

In order to understand better Hurston's compliance with editorial queries, one must bear in mind that she was already constrained as a folklorist by the system of patronage. Her patron, Mrs. Mason, literally owned the material that Hurston collected on her different field trips. In a contract signed on December 8, 1927, she made sure that Hurston "[returned] and [laid] before her all the said information, data, transcripts of music, etc. which she shall have obtained."[65] She also prohibited Hurston from publishing. Hemenway states:

> The reason for the prohibition against Zora's publishing her own fiction is difficult to determine. Since information about Mrs. Mason is sparse, we cannot know the extent of her commitment to scholarly, as opposed to popular, publication. We do know that Mrs. Mason interfered editorially with her protégés, and clearly, one reason for the restriction was to insure her editorial control over a person with a well established reputation for independence. The ban against publication became a lever for her to govern her young folklorist. (*ZNH,* 113)

This situation of dependence made Hurston doubly sensitive to the compromise she had to make as a black novelist in an editorial world dominated by the white establishment. She said in 1944: "Rather than get across all the things that you want to say you must compromise and work within the limitations [of those people] who have the final authority in deciding whether or not a book shall be printed."[66] The disappearance of "Concert," which covers three years of her life, from the final version of *Dust Tracks* echoes Hurston's dependence on her patron, Mrs. Mason, who was opposed to Hurston's using material collected under her patronage for "theatrical purposes." An agreement signed in 1932 ended with the admonition: "In all that you do, Zora, remember that it is vital to your people that you should not rob your books which must stand as lasting monument in order to further a commercial venture."[67] In effect, Hurston was robbed of the possibility of using black folklore for a mass audience. With "Concert" reduced to a few paragraphs, her autobiographical writing was also deprived of the triumphant expression of her desire to dramatize her folk on the stage. The reader must rest content with the textual dramatization of the folk voice in the autobiography, *Mules and Men, Tell My Horse,* and in her novels and short fiction, not to speak of her plays.

Editorial intervention appears most blunt when a whole chapter has been deleted, but its efforts to clarify chronology also shift meaning.[68] The editor reintroduces logical order and continuity at the expense of initial spontaneous writing. In the case of Hurston's autobiography, such intrusive editorial reordering obscured the specific link between the concepts of race and familial relations, which might throw some light on the complexity of Hurston's response to violence. An episode depicting the relationship between Hurston's parents is now part of chapter 2, "My Folks," whereas it originally appeared in chapter 12, "My People! My People!" dedicated to the question of race. Hurston's digression about domestic violence within her family occurs when she wants to contrast two kinds of black Americans: those who push ahead and those who are content with their plight. Her mother typifies the desire for self-improvement, the will to fight; her father, resignation. She depicts one of their fights, detailing her father's defeat in front of her mother:

> But everytime Mama cornered him with her tongue he would
> seize a chair and threaten to wring it over Mama's head. She'd
> keep right on asking him questions about his doings and then
> answering them herself until Papa slammed out of the house.
> He would put the chair down and ease on out like he had
> been whipped all over with peach hickories. But if I made a
> mistake of letting out a giggle, I was going to catch it good
> and proper. I think that this was his way of asserting his lord-
> ship over his home, and denying himself that he had been
> worsted by a woman. Probably he hated to admit to himself,
> that not only did she worst him always in a battle of wits, but
> that he did not have the nerve to console himself in a mascu-
> line way by beating her. I saw this conflict between what
> Papa wanted for his family and what Mama wanted him to
> want, going on from my earliest remembrance. It was not too
> clear, but mixed up somehow with the other things that con-
> fused me about what Negroes were supposed to be. (MS,
> folder 10, no. 5)[69]

It is telling that Hurston should trace her confusion about racial identity back to her parents, and to an aborted fight between them. Not only do they embody two antinomic attitudes of determination (the mother) and resignation (the father), they are also engaged in a war of the sexes, where manhood can be asserted only through physical violence directed against women, and where being outwitted verbally by a woman is ultimate defeat.

This passage has been truncated in the final version; Hurston's comments and analysis have been crossed out and replaced with a simple mention of a fight within the chronological progression. The racial and the sexual are conflated in Hurston's mind, since she felt compelled to include a narrative of violence within the family when she had given herself the task of talking about conflicting positions among black Americans. To the editor, it was a blatant "digression." For the reader on the lookout for an explanation of Hurston's ambivalence about race and self, it is a precious piece of information. Her father's attitude is understandable only within the context of racial violence. Racial oppression is conceptualized through family violence, as if the one necessarily led to the other. If one chooses to focus on Hurston's psychological makeup, her obsessive remembrance of this painful episode might point to her priorities. The personal, the familial, came before the racial. Thus the reshaping of the text to fit chronological progression from childhood to adulthood erases the psychological implications of Hurston's "tangents."

Conclusion

A comparison of manuscript and published versions of *Dust Tracks* retraces the process of Hurston's gradual submission to the control of the white publishing world; conversely, the first draft brings to light a freer, but not uncontradictory, "authorial" voice. In terms of literary history, that unequal dialogue finds its source in slave narratives, collaborative autobiographies, as-told-to narratives. The slave's story did not belong to him/her. Most American slave narratives were sponsored by northern white abolitionists and contained authenticating documents, letters, and prefaces, evidence that the slave told a true story and that he or she was a person of high moral standards. Robert Stepto argues that these documents function as voices and that they enter into a dialogic relationship with the actual text of the slave's life story:

> These documents—and voices—may not always be smoothly integrated with the former slave's tale but they are nevertheless part of the narrative. Their primary function is, of course, to authenticate the former slave's account; in doing so, they are at least partially responsible for the narrative's acceptance as historical evidence. However, in literary terms, the documents collectively create something close to a *dialogue*—of forms as well as voices.[70] (emphasis mine)

The narrators were further constrained by the genre that required little or, at best, no deviation from a set formula. Slave narrative had to fit a stereotypical narrative pattern. Thus the slave narrator had little control over his or her self-image, which had been repeatedly reshaped by the abolitionists' expectations. Speaking more generally about African American literature, Robert Stepto summarizes as follows this battle for authorial control, which acquires increased urgency in black autobiography:

> In Afro-American letters, for example, while there are notable exceptions, the battle for authorial control has been more of a race ritual than a case of patricide. Author has been pitted against author, primarily to reenact the 18th and 19th century struggles between author and guarantor. The competition has rarely been between artist and artist for control of an image, line, or trope; rather, it has been between artist and authenticator (editor, publisher, guarantor, patron) for control of a fiction—usually the idea of history or of the artist's personal history—that exists outside the artist's text and functions primarily as an antagonistic force with regard to this text's imaginative properties.[71]

Within the black tradition of access to writing and to publication, the relationship between the editors and the author reenacts the race ritual established by the "dialogue" between the authenticating documents and the text of the slave narrative. The black author's relationship to earlier texts in the same tradition cannot follow the model of anxiety of authorship described by Harold Bloom. Diachronically, the ambiguity central to *Dust Tracks on a Road* can thus be construed as a trace of the duality of voices (the subject's and the scribe's) that shaped the black slave narrative and collaborative autobiographies. The black American autobiographical text is both the stakes and the product of a racial ritual, repeating, at a historical remove, the relationship that united the black slave and the white abolitionist as guarantor of the authenticity of the slave's life story. The editor (the publisher, the guarantor, the patron) carries on, acting as authenticator; he or she actively competes with the author for control over the production of the text. The resulting unequal dialogue mirrors the racial, sexual, and class tensions of society at large, the Jim Crow laws, the status of women, and especially black women, in the United States of the 1940s.

In *Dust Tracks* the transition from handwritten version to typed version and finally to the printed text illustrates a gradual slippage from an original intent to the final acceptance of a public self/text mediated by editorial pressure. Editorial intervention and Hurston's awareness that she had to fit a certain mold in order to please shape the text, which becomes the site of a complex interaction between author and editor, between writer and audience. In the case of *Dust Tracks on a Road,* the editor guarantees the readability of autobiographical fiction for a primarily white audience. The incidence of his control on the production of a fiction of the self is such that the question of the authenticity of Hurston's rendering of her life story is indeterminable. Closer study of the manuscript's editorial queries reveals that editorial and publishing constraints create a central undecidability. As the text is reshaped in answer to those queries, the author's response to the editorial voice undermines the autobiographical gesture of self-construction, already problematic in Hurston's case since she did not want to write her autobiography.[72] The reader is left with a text informed more by external expectations and restraints than by a self-assured "authorial" voice.

Editorial intrusion and Hurston's responding self-consciousness assuredly lead the reader to construct a self that is less self-confident and more reverent than the Zora Neale Hurston of the original version. But beyond that taming of the tone and self, the manuscript crudely unveils the mechanisms of the creation of a fiction: an obsequiously grateful and overpolite Hurston is balanced by an occasionally biting and playfully irreverent Zora. Zora Neale Hurston might be, in her words, "rubbing a paragraph with a soft cloth," or she might have been asked to do so, editorial constraints *obligent*. At times arguably apposite, the polishing of language happened for the most part at the expense of speech. While the autobiographer was thus being constructed, the autobiographed remained "wrassling" as a trace in her characters' speeches. The erasure of the political and the erotic voice can be understood only within the historical and sociocultural context of the period. Thanks to Hurston's bequest, the twentieth-century reader can now rescue a more self-affirming Hurston as well as a text that does not shy away from speaking the sexual and exposing the political.

Notes

1. A longer version of this study will be included in my forthcoming book-length study of African American women's autobiographies. I am using throughout this essay Robert E. Hemenway's edition of *Dust Tracks on a Road* (Urbana: University of Illinois Press, 1984), hereafter cited in parentheses as *DT.* Hemenway's biography, *Zora Neale Hurston: A Literary Biography* (Urbana: University of Illinois Press, 1986), will be cited

as *ZNH*. Material from the manuscript that remains unpublished is cited as MS, with accompanying folder number.

2. Hemenway concurs with Cheryl Wall's finding that Hurston was born on January 7, 1891. Hurston often changed her birth date. She cited 1898, 1899, 1900, 1901, 1903, and 1910 in various public documents (*DT,* xi).

3. Hemenway writes that "she gave up fiction almost entirely to write essays for white magazines, and her journalism reflected the editorial lessons learned in the writing of her autobiography" (*ZNH,* 288). She wrote differently depending on whether she was addressing a black or a white audience. Four of those articles—"The 'Pet' Negro System" (1943), "My Most Humiliating Jim Crow Experience" (1944), and "Crazy for This Democracy" (1945)—are reprinted in Alice Walker, ed., *I Love Myself: A Zora Neale Hurston Reader* (Old Westbury, N.Y.: Feminist Press, 1979), 150–69.

4. This essay is an extension of a paper I gave at the New Orleans MLA Conference in 1988. At Robert Hemenway's suggestion I first went to Yale to look at the manuscript in 1985 with a grant from Rackham Graduate School at the University of Michigan. A self-funded research trip to the Beinecke Rare Book and Manuscript Library in January 1990 helped me complete part of my research. A two-month Fulbright Research Fellowship granted by the French-American Commission in Paris provided additional funding in August and September 1990. I am extremely grateful to Lucy Ann Hurston, spokesperson for the Hurston heirs, and to the Yale Collection of American Literature, Beinecke Rare Book and Manuscript Library, James Weldon Johnson Collection, Yale University, for permission to quote from the Beinecke manuscript. I also wish to thank Robert Hemenway for his support and generosity, and Henry Louis Gates, Jr., for his appreciation of my work. Folklorist and writer Stetson Kennedy has been a thoughtful commentator on my work and a generous correspondent.

5. See chapter 11 of *ZNH,* 271–88.

6. In the afterword to her anthology, Alice Walker quotes a student who says, "You have to read the chapters Zora left out of her autobiography." *I Love Myself,* 308.

7. Nellie Y. McKay, "Race, Gender, and Cultural Context in Zora Neale Hurston's *Dust Tracks on a Road,*" in *Life/Lines: Theorizing Women's Autobiography,* ed. Bella Brodzki and Celeste Schenck (Ithaca, N.Y.: Cornell University Press, 1988), 181. McKay's statement, for instance, that "if the text lacks self-disclosure and bombards us with factual inaccuracies, its absence of bombast and arrogance, for one of Hurston's standing, is also quite remarkable," is considerably qualified by an analysis of editorial excisions (p. 188).

8. Françoise Lionnet, "Autoethnography: The An-Archic Style of *Dust Tracks on a Road,*" in *Autobiographical Voices: Race, Gender, Self-Portraiture* (Ithaca, N.Y.: Cornell University Press, 1989), 97–129; Claudine Raynaud, "Autobiography as a 'Lying' Session: Zora Neale Hurston's *Dust Tracks on a Road,*" in *Studies in Black American Literature,* vol. 3, ed. Joe Weixlmann and Houston Baker (Greenwood, Fla.: Penkevill, 1988), 110–38.

9. Elizabeth Fox-Genovese, "To Write My Self: The Autobiographies of Afro-American Women," in *Feminist Issues in Literary Scholarship,* ed. Shari Benstock (Bloomington: Indiana University Press, 1987), 169; idem, "My Statue, My Self: Autobiographical Writings of Afro-American Women," in *The Private Self: Theory and Practice of Women's Autobiographical Writing,* ed. Shari Benstock (Chapel Hill: University of North Carolina Press, 1988), 63–90.

10. The mention of libel on page 138 of the manuscript (folder 13) seems to be written in Hurston's hand.

11. Fox-Genovese emphasizes that, like Jacobs, Hurston expected her reader to be white: "So I give you all my right hand of fellowship and love. . . . In my eyesight, you

lose nothing by not looking just like me. . . . Let us all be kissing friends" (*DT,* 286). "To Write My Self," 174.

12. The date of Hurston's bequest of the manuscript is 14 January 1942. The full dedication reads: "To the James Weldon Johnson Memorial Collection of Negro Arts and Letters at Yale University, through the efforts of Carl van Vechten to enrich it" (folder 10, box I, front page of MS).

13. Hurston claims: "No, I do not weep at the world—I am too busy sharpening my oyster knife." "How It Feels to Be Colored Me," in Walker, *I Love Myself,* 153.

14. Quoted by Hemenway (*DT,* xxxiv).

15. In the published version this chapter corresponds to chapter 13, "Two Women in Particular," in which Hurston discusses her relationships with Fannie Hurst and Ethel Waters.

16. Robert Hemenway, letter to the author, 28 August 1989.

17. It is worth noting that in black English "editing" means "telling off," or "putting in one's place." As a young maid, Zora is told by Aunt Cally how to put on her apron. She writes, "I took the apron and put it on with quite a bit of editing by Sister Cally" (*DT,* 119).

18. Chapter 12, "My People, My People!" was written in Port-au-Prince, Haiti, on 2 July 1937, and seems to have been first intended as a separate piece. It differs substantially from the autographed chapter that bears this title. The following chapter, "The Inside Light—Being a Salute to Friendship"—is a transcription of the autographed manuscript kept in folder 10 (no. 1); it was written just before the book went to the publisher (20 July 1941). "Seeing the World as It Is" is the reproduction of a typed chapter that corresponds to nos. 6 and 7 of the autographed version kept in folder 10. According to Hemenway, this last chapter was obviously written prior to 7 December 1941, and could not have been published after the attack on Pearl Harbor because of its denunciation of America's attitude toward Japan. Hemenway dates these chapters in his introduction to the appendix (*DT,* 287–89).

19. Hemenway contends that "the manuscript of *Dust Tracks* reveals that the book's inconsistency also results from Hurston's uncertainty over what her editors and white audience expected, a fact proven by those portions which never made it from manuscript to galleys, and which, if they had, would have given us quite a different autobiography" (*ZNH,* 287).

20. This work would require extensive annotation and listing and a careful examination of Hurston's correspondence. Professor Henry Louis Gates, Jr., told me in personal correspondence (24 May 1990) that a new edition is being prepared by Harper and Row, with an introduction by Maya Angelou.

21. The full annotation reads: "suggest eliminating international opinions as irrelevant to autobiography." It appears on the last page of the typescript in folder 11. The manuscript that corresponds to this text is kept in folder 10 (nos. 6 and 7).

22. The passage should have appeared at the top of page 162 of the published version. After Logan's first repartee in the dialogue—"Git me a little bitty baby bear, Mr. Johns, 'bout three months old. Dats de kind of bear I wants to wrestle wid. Yassuh!"—the excised passage reads: "The mental picture of a big, long-armed, awkward six-footer like Logan wrestling with a tiny cub was too much for the shop. Dignity of every sort went out of the window. The bear cycle took on. Everday, important men, high in life, came in with suggestions on the wrestle. It kept up until Logan furnished them with another laugh by getting into jail over the weekend for beating his wife about a hog-head. He thought she had given a pimp the 'ears offen dat head' and found out after he was in jail that it had no ears when he bought it. Mr. Johns went down

and persuaded the judge to let Logan go, and then Logan in a burst of good will offered to give the judge the hog-head—still uncooked. The judge chased Logan out of the court, and that hog-head became a classic around the shop" (MS, folder 14, 172–73). The excised passage tells the story of how a man is ridiculed for having beaten his wife, whom he had wrongfully suspected of being unfaithful. The butt of the joke is, however, a black man in a presumably white court system.

23. This passage, which was excised because of possibly libelous content, should have appeared on page 139 of the text before the passage starting with "When the run came to an end." It is a satirical description of the new company manager of the repertory company. Here is an excerpt from the incriminating passage: "Somehow, he struck everybody wrong from the start. The baritone who was always quick on the draw said he looked like he had been soaked in greasy dish-water and had not been wiped off. Even Miss M—who seldom 'cracked'—said he reminded her of the left-overs from the stock yards. His trousers sagged at the knees, so I named him Old Bustle-Knees. His name was Smith, but he became knows [sic] on the quiet as 'B. K.'" (MS, folder 13, 138).

24. Trinh T. Minh-ha defines the complex interaction of writing, gender, and race relations as follows: "As the focal point of cultural consciousness and social change, writing weaves into language the complex relations of a subject caught between the problems of race and gender and the practice of literature as the very place where social alienation is thwarted differently according to each specific context." *Woman, Native, Other: Writing Postcoloniality and Feminism* (Bloomington: Indiana University Press, 1989), 6.

25. The article "The 'Pet' Negro System" was actually drafted as part of the autobiography (folder 10, no. 5). It was published in *American Mercury* 56 (May 1943): 593–600, and was condensed and reprinted in *Negro Digest* 1 (June 1943): 37–40. See Walker, *I Love Myself,* 156–63. As she did for her fiction, Hurston used and reused previously written material.

26. The struggle between "wrassle" and "wrestle" illustrates perfectly Bakhtin's theory of the word as the locus of social conflict: "Each word . . . is the little arena for the clash and the criss-crossing of differently oriented social accents. A word in the mouth of a particular individual is the product of the living interaction of social forces." Quoted by Michael Holquist in *Mikhail Bakhtin* (Cambridge, Mass: Harvard University Press, 1984), 220.

27. The process here at work seems to be opposed to that of collaborative autobiographies, where the reader must hear a voice, according to Albert E. Stone: "Most collaborative autobiographies deliberately simulate an oral performance by the subject. The reader almost always *hears* a voice." "Two Recreate One: The Act of Collaboration in Recent Black Autobiography, Ossie Guffy, Nate Shaw, Malcolm X," in *Autobiographical Occasions and Original Acts: Versions of American Identity from Henry Adams to Nate Shaw* (Philadelphia: University of Pennsylvania Press, 1982), 234.

28. Here are some further instances of that editorial process. Compare "Their looks drag them one way and their brain another" (MS, folder 10, no. 5) with "Their looks and charm interfere with their brain-work" (*DT,* 152); "I couldn't say for not knowing" (MS) to "I can't be sure" (*DT,* 264).

29. Brian Lanker, *I Dream a World: Portraits of Black Women Who Changed America* (New York: Stewart, Tabori & Chang, 1989), 43. The full quotation reads: "In writing poetry, you're interested in condensation. So you try to put all of a particular impression or inspiration on a page. You distill." Brooks's vision of poetry is celebrated in Maria K. Mootry and Gary Smith, eds., *A Life Distilled: Gwendolyn Brooks, Her Poetry and*

Fiction (Urbana: University of Illinois Press, 1987). Similarly, Hurston uses a culinary metaphor to describe folklore: "Folklore is the boiled down juice of human living." The Library of Congress, Federal Writers' Project, American Guide, Negro Writers Unit, page 1 of the manuscript.

30. Audre Lorde, *Sister Outsider: Essays and Speeches* (Trumansburg, N.Y.: Crossing, 1987), 37.

31. According to Henry Louis Gates, Jr., this represents the second pole of preoccupation of black authors as it emerged at the turn of the century. The first pole of the debate, "the value of the representation, of the reality imitated in the text," had been established by the end of the Civil War. See *The Signifying Monkey: A Theory of African-American Literature* (New York: Oxford University Press, 1988), 172.

32. Gates, *The Signifying Monkey*, 174. The critic is obviously building his terminology on Roland Barthes's typological opposition between the readerly and the writerly. The writerly is "Ce qui peut être aujourd'hui écrit (ré-écrit). . . . En face du texte scriptible s'établit sa contrevaleur, sa valeur négative, réactive: ce qui peut être lu mais non écrit: le lisible. Nous appelons classique tout texte lisible." *S/Z* (Paris: Seuil, 1970), 10. The reader of the writerly text is an active producer, whereas the reader of the readerly text is a consumer. Gates's own definition of the speakerly links it to the textual reproduction of voice (*effet d'oralité*): "a rhetorical strategy . . . designed to represent an oral literary tradition, designed to emulate the phonetic, grammatical, and lexical patterns of actual speech and produce an 'illusion of oral narration'" (p. 180).

33. This censorship of the text is a reflection of a more prevalent censorship that extended to social codes. In a September 1990 letter, Florida folklorist and writer Stetson Kennedy told me, "This matter of sex among blacks was not just a taboo of printed words; it extended into society as a whole, so that blacks, as contradistinguished from whites, were not expected to display physical affection toward one another in presence of whites (no hand-holding, hugging, embracing, kissing)."

34. Kennedy recalls that a collection called *Lilies* was sent back by the Florida post office as "unmailable material." Conversation with the author, August 1990. Until recently, pornographic songs collected on the Federal Writers' Project could not be printed and were stored at the Library of Congress in the Archives of American Folklore Collection under a special file labeled "Delta."

35. The passage carries on: "He and my second brother, John, were in secret session upstairs in their room. I went on down and crept back to listen and heard John asking how old the woman had to be? It seemed that Bob was not sure. He had forgotten to ask. But it was evident that some great discovery had been made, and they were both most eager to grow big, manly moustaches. It was still mysterious to me. I was out of college and doing research in Anthropology before I heard all about it. Then I heard that a man's moustache was given by a woman anyway. It seems that Adam came to feel that his face needed more decoration than it had. Eve, obligingly, took a spot of hair from where she had no particular use for it—it didn't show anyway, and slapped it across Adam's mouth, and it grew there. So what Bob was being told, was regular knowledge that he was supposed to get when he approached manhood. Just as I learned at puberty that a girl is supposed to catch water-beetles and let one bite her on each breast if she wants a full bosom. There is another way, of course. You could let a boy—anywhere from sixteen to sixty—do what boys call 'steal a feel' on you, but of course that would not be nice. Almost as having a baby, and not being married" (MS, folder 11, 59A–B).

36. This role reversal is interesting. For the most part, it was because of her knowledge of the folklore that the anthropologist could be a good scholar. Having grown up in Eatonville, Hurston had privileged access to the lore.

37. Another deletion on page 18 of *Dust Tracks* alludes plainly to her father's promiscuity and to her father's sex (MS, folder 11, 14).

38. In June 1938 Hurston was acting as supervisor of the Negro Unit of the Florida Project, which was headed by Carita Dogget Corse. The song would have been included in "The Florida Negro," a collection of stories and songs compiled by Hurston before the Florida Federal Writers' Project as well as slave narratives collected by the Florida Federal Writers' Project staff. It is printed on page 3 of the manuscript kept at the Library of Congress: "Oh Angeline, Oh Angeline / Oh Angeline that great great gal of mine / And when she walks, and when she walks / And when she walks she rocks and reels behind / You feel her legs, you feel her legs / You feel her legs and you want to feel her thighs / You feel her thighs, you feel her thighs / You feel her thighs and then you fade away and die." The song is quoted by Hemenway (*ZNH*, 253).

39. In the 1939 recordings kept at the Archives of American Folklore, Hurston sings the work song "Mobile," which is included in the autobiography (*DT,* 180–81). She also sings "Uncle Bud," a jook song that she says could not be sung in front of respectable ladies; only jook women could hear it, and she heard it. The song goes as follows: "Uncle Bud's a man, a man like this / He can't get a woman, he's gotta use his fist / Uncle Bud (five times) / I'm going out of town, gonna hurry back / Uncle Bud has got something I sure do like / Uncle Bud (five times) / Little Cat-Feet got a little bit of kitten / Gotta work that tail that can't stop shitting." Some of the stanzas are scatological and explicit about race relations; others are extremely direct about Uncle Bud's sexual prowess. One feels that Hurston knew more verses, but she stopped singing and declared that she could not recall them to the interviewer, Herbert Halpert. Some of the cleaner verses of the song are reprinted on page 4 of the WPA Federal Writers' Project manuscript of the "Florida Negro": "Uncle Bud is a man, a man in full / His back is strong like a Jersey bull (refrain) / Uncle Bud's got cotton ain't got no squares / Uncle Bud's gal ain't got no hair." Stetson Kennedy has sent me a version of the song in which the line reads, "His nuts hang low like a Georgy bull"; he writes: "No one entertained any notion of including anything risqué or sexually explicit in the Guide, it being unthinkable for any publication sponsored by the Federal government. This was true not only of matters sexual, but style itself was dictated by the Guidebook style manual and precedents established by the early works of the project." Personal correspondence, September 1990.

40. Zora Neale Hurston, "Characteristics of Negro Expression," in *The Sanctified Church: The Folklore Writings of Zora Neale Hurston* (Berkeley, Calif.: Twetle Island, 1981), 61.

41. In Walker, *I Love Myself,* 171.

42. Fox-Genovese asserts: "Hurston should be understood as a woman who was, so far as her self-representation was concerned, primarily concerned with a 'self' unconstrained by gender." "To Write My Self," 173. The restoration of those passages problematizes this vision of Hurston's self-projection.

43. Hemenway mentions that she left her employment as a maid several times because of such pressures, but does not document it: "She did not act humble and she refused to entertain the advances of her male employers" (*ZNH*, 17).

44. One senses that the word encapsulates Hurston's resistance to male advances. The term also comes up later in the episode with the baritone. She writes: "He *waylaid* me down the coach aisle way from Mis M— and told me I looked like a nice girl and wanted to help me out" (MS, folder 13, 134; emphasis mine).

45. Hurston is acutely aware of class distinction. She writes: "Finally, I got over being timid of his being the boss and just told him not to bother me" (MS, folder 13, 120).

46. Harriet Jacobs, *Incidents in the Life of a Slave Girl,* ed. Jean Fagan Yellin (Cambridge, Mass.: Harvard University Press, 1987; originally published in 1861).

47. In the printed version, Hurston is reduced to the role of mediator-messenger, representing the motion of desire, yet being refused a subjectivity and a sexuality of her own (*DT,* 137).

48. In the margin, Hurston notes that the passage had been left in by the typist by mistake.

49. The whole passage, omitted because it incriminated a well-known Boston family, also illustrates Hurston's sexual humiliation (see MS, folder 13, 140–51).

50. Hemenway explains that the relationship between Zora Neale Hurston and Alain Locke was not always smooth: "She resented his editorial responsibilities, perhaps because he was there as a representative of Mrs. Mason, serving as a talent scout for her, and in Zora's case Mrs. Mason made clear from the start that she should consult with him" (*ZNH,* 131).

51. Hemenway notes that her characterization of her relationship with Fannie Hurst differs somewhat from the published version (*DT,* 288).

52. Tzvetan Todorov speaks of "horizon d'attente" when it comes to the readers of genres: "C'est parce que les genres existent comme une institution qu'ils fonctionnent comme des 'horizons d'attente' pour les lecteurs et des 'modèles d'écritures' pour les auteurs. . . . Chaque époque a son propre système de genres, qui est en rapport avec l'idéologie dominante, etc." *Les Genres du discours* (Paris: Seuil, 1978), 50–51.

53. George Baker, alias God or Father Divine, was a southern evangelist preacher who in the 1930s invested himself with a social mission in the face of the depression and quickly prospered. His disciples, known collectively as the Peace Mission, organized a network of cooperatives dedicated to racial equality.

54. A wealthy follower of Father Divine, Mrs. Mary Sheldon Lyon, took the name of "Peace Dove"; Father Divine's second wife, a young blond white woman, was renamed "Mother Divine in the Second Body."

55. The politicians mentioned by Hurston are Frances Perkins, secretary of labor, member of the Roosevelt government since 1933; Harold L. Hopkins, secretary of commerce since 1933; and Fiorello H. La Guardia, mayor of New York and head of the Office of Civilian Defense (OCD) in 1941. Mrs. Roosevelt was at the head of the Voluntary Participation Committee, a branch of the OCD, at the same time. In his autobiography, *White House Witness 1942–1945* (Garden City, N.Y.: Doubleday, 1975), Jonathan Daniels notes the confusion of the OCD under Mrs. Roosevelt and Fiorello La Guardia, director of the agency; both of them left after the attack on Pearl Harbor.

56. See Charles Austin Beard, *President Roosevelt and the Coming of the War, 1941* (New Haven, Conn.: Yale University Press, 1948). In the second half of his book Beard questions Roosevelt's antiwar stance.

57. See Walker, *I Love Myself,* 165–68.

58. The passage, from "He is a bandit" to "that is what he is doing," is handwritten at the back of page 7 of the manuscript.

59. Stetson Kennedy also points out letters written by Hurston to the *Saturday Evening Post* "urging that she be sent on a Third World tour to interview Nehru et al., and to urge the US to stop propping up European empire remnants in the Third World, and support liberation movements." Personal correspondence with the author, September 1990.

60. The metaphor also obscures the differences between Third World women from colonized countries or ex-colonies and First World women. Furthermore, it diffuses the politics at work between First World powers, including First World women, and the

inhabitants of both sexes of their ex-colonies. What would that mean for Indian, Balinese, Javanese, Moroccan, Algerian, and Tunisian women, for instance? Are they doubly colonized subjects? "Decolonization" has generally been followed by a period of neo-colonialism; ultimate independence has never come about in the global economic order.

61. See also *DT,* 207.

62. Hemenway comments on Hurston's rage at Hall Johnson: "[Hurston] claimed that he deliberately sabotaged the arrangement, then stole some of the material for adaptation in *Run Little Chillun.* Indeed, the ending of Johnson's play was staged exactly as Zora had staged the finale of *The Great Day*" (*ZNH,* 178).

63. Hemenway states: "*The Great Day* was an unqualified success. . . . It received good reviews, and the *Herald Tribune* hoped it would become a regular show. Sterling Brown remembers traveling from Washington to see it and being impressed with the reception" (*ZNH,* 181).

64. Typically, Hurston claims to have influenced both black songs and research into black folklore, since Katharine Dunham went off to Jamaica to collect dances, preceding Hurston there on her 1936 trip.

65. Contract between Mrs. Mason and Zora Neale Hurston, 8 December 1987 (Alain Locke Papers, Moorland-Spingarn Research Center, Howard University Library) (*ZNH,* 110). For a full development of Hurston's relationship to Mrs. Mason, see *ZNH,* 104–35.

66. "Zora Neale Hurston Reveals Key to Her Literary Success," *New York Amsterdam News,* 18 November 1944 (Moorland-Spingarn Research Center, Howard University Library), quoted by Hemenway (*ZNH,* 287).

67. Letter of agreement between Mrs. Mason and Zora Neale Hurston, 20 January 1932 (Alain Locke Papers, Moorland-Spingarn Research Center, Howard University Library), quoted by Hemenway (*ZNH,* 182–83).

68. Such editorial reshuffling was present in the slave narrative. Lucius Matlack's introduction to Henri Bibb's *Narrative of the Life and Adventures of Henri Bibb, an American Slave* reads: "The work of preparation . . . was that of orthography and punctuation merely, an arrangement of the chapters, and a table of contents—little more than falls to the lot of publishers generally." Quoted in Robert B. Stepto, *From behind the Veil,* (Urbana, Ill.: University of Illinois Press, 1979), 9.

69. The published version reads: "Every time Mama cornered him about his doings he used to threaten to wring a chair over her head. She never even took notice of the threat to answer. She just went right on asking questions about his doings and then answering them herself until Papa slammed out of the house looking like he had been whipped all over with peach hickories. But I had better not let out a giggle at such times, or it would be just too bad" (*DT,* 25–26). Readers of *Their Eyes Were Watching God* might recognize in this passage a biographical echo of Joe Starks's defeat and death. In the autobiography, Hurston's feminism is located here, in this episode, and in the exposure and then the erasure of her father's sex (*DT,* 18).

70. Stepto, *From behind the Veil,* 3–4.

71. Ibid., 45.

72. Hurston wrote that "[she] did not want to write it at all, because it is too hard to reveal one's inner self." Letter from Zora Neale Hurston to Hamilton Holt, 1 February 1943 (Hurston Collection, Rare Books and Manuscripts, University of Florida Library), quoted by Hemenway (*ZNH,* 278).

Chapter 4

A Politics of Experience
Leila Khaled's *My People Shall Live: The Autobiography of a Revolutionary*

Janet Varner Gunn

This essay is about trying to understand something. Understanding anything requires, first of all, the desire to understand. (More on this desire later.) Second, it requires acknowledgment of the distance that stands between the seeker of understanding and the thing she wants to figure out. The distance between Leila Khaled's life and my own is the distance of at least one world, maybe two. She has been described as "the world's most celebrated aerial terrorist."[1] I am a middle-aged American academic, currently living, as I begin this essay, in a bourgeois East Jerusalem neighborhood. Up to now, in the winter of 1990, this neighborhood shows little effect of the popular uprising, the Palestinian Intifada, which began more than two years ago.

To plant Leila Khaled's book in the middle of current theorizing about autobiography could invite charges of critical terrorism. It was written, after all, by a left-of-center Palestinian revolutionary who played a major role in the hijacking of two planes, a TWA flight in 1969 and an El Al flight in 1970, both at the height of the fadayeen terrorist activity following the Arab-Israeli war of 1967. Khaled ends her book one year before the Black September operation at the Olympic Games in Munich. Although that operation was work of a political faction other than Khaled's, it was fueled by the same anger.

What, then, am I to make of this piece of writing, I and it so far from home? Better to chart the distance, I want to start out in more familiar territory with Annie Dillard's autobiography, *An American Childhood*. Its Pittsburgh setting is seventy-five miles due west of my own hometown. Her book about growing up in Western Pennsylvania is the kind of autobiography I had wanted more than anything to write in the summer of 1974, when my then-husband and I moved with our five-year-old son to North Carolina from Chicago, where I had gone for graduate work and then lived for the next seventeen years. Leaving the flat plain of the Midwest, I suddenly found myself again in the Back Country, with its low mountains chaining down through the Alleghenies to the Carolina Piedmont. I continued to live there until I came back to Jerusalem, this city among other hills that I had first encountered on a research leave four years ago.

Annie Dillard's memories are set into that Back Country landscape, and she begins her book with the following passage:

> When everything else has gone from my brain—the President's name, the state capitals, the neighborhoods where I lived, and then my own name and what it was on earth I sought, and then at length the faces of my friends, and finally the faces of my family—when all this has dissolved, what will be left, I believe, is topology: the dreaming memory of land as it lay this way and that.[2]

This topophilia and the fact that Dillard's memories begin at about the same age and year as Leila Khaled's—the former in 1950 at age five, the latter in 1948 at age four—form the similarities between the two stories. Beyond that, their autobiographies divide along the fault line between two worlds. The differences set each in bolder relief and measure the distance the First World autobiography theorist must cross to see from the other side. Looking at Annie Dillard's "poetics of experience"[3] from where I now sit in East Jerusalem, and then looking from its (and, until three years ago, my) America to Leila Khaled's politics of experience, this is how I will cross and recross the distance that separates me from Dillard's "homeland" as well as from Khaled's. But I need each of them in order to see the other. Seeing (or noticing), in fact, is the point. For Annie Dillard, it is a matter of so "tuning [her] own gauges" that she will notice just enough: "Too much noticing and I was too self-conscious to live. . . . Too little noticing, though— I would risk much to avoid this—and I would miss the whole show" (p. 155). Her earliest memory is about watching her infant hands discover the boundaries of herself at the "complex incurve of her skin." And at sixteen, where she ends the account of her childhood, she can no longer remember how to forget herself: "Now I was in my own way; I myself was a dark object I could not ignore" (p. 224).

For Leila Khaled, the point is not so much seeing as being seen, not so much noticing as being noticed. It was during six days in her mid-twenties, not at an extended moment in infancy, that she experienced her identity. It was when, as a result of three plane hijackings in one day (6 September 1970), the Palestinians "for the first time in modern history . . . were on the centre stage." Notice of her identity was taken not at the boundaries of her own skin, but on the front pages of the world press when, she says, "we became a people for a whole week."[4] What accounts for the weight these women give, respectively, to seeing and being seen or, better, to noticing and being noticed? For Dillard, noticing (or remembering) is her "life's work" against loss. Without her vigilant seeing, the past would swallow her up in its "blank cave." "The growing size of that blank and ever darkening past frightened me," she writes. "It loomed beside me like a hole in the air and battened on scraps of my life I failed to claim" (p. 130).

While noticing enough may require a lifetime's dedication to fine-tuning, being noticed comes automatically (and often embarrassingly) within the "interior life" Annie Dillard inhabits. That life, she says, "is often stupid." Blinded and deafened by "egoism," the interior life "fancies that the western wind blows on the Self, and leaves fall at the feet of the Self for a reason, and people are watching" (p. 20). Nonetheless, her placement in the world is secure, even if it results from her own observation: "I saw us as if from above [herself and her friends as they "paced out" their "ritual evenings"], even then, even as I stood in place living out my childhood and knowing it, aware of myself as if from above and behind, skinny and exultant on the street" (p. 123).

Seeing herself and seeing enough—these are what it means to have her childhood. As long as she can keep herself in focus, it is not important what she sees. In themselves, things have no interest; "instead things were interesting as long as you had attention to give them." It is the interior life that has reality, not what is outside, although "from time to time" it is important to "seize the actual world" in order to exercise the imagination, joining her "mind and skin" in order to live at her "own edge" (p. 79).

She admits that it is through books that she has contact with the "actual, historical, moral world," especially books such as *The Diary of Anne Frank,* which offered her a "secret hope" that life on the "surface" could somehow match the "exultation" of life underneath. This surface life, "where history is still taking place," "could be found and joined," she writes, "like the Resistance" (p. 183).

Somehow and somewhere, the actual could be as real as the imagined, but only if one could come awake, jump on the "spinning globe" (a later equivalent of "wedging one's feet downward"), and "remember everything, everything, against loss" (pp. 243, 183).

While devoting her life to remembering everything against the possibility of loss, Dillard admits, however, to knowing nothing about it: "As for loss, as for parting, as for bidding farewell, so long, thanks, to love or a land or a time—what did I know of parting, of grieving, mourning, loss?" (p. 171).

Khaled, on the other hand, knows everything about loss and, within the first paragraph of her account, must relinquish hold on all clear memories but one of the childhood territory to which Dillard devotes an entire book. Khaled refuses, however, to give way to a remembrance of things past that lingers, like Dillard's, lovingly and in slow motion on evocative detail. The actual territory of childhood appears only momentarily at the beginning of the book's second line: "I can see the area where I played as a small child." The line ends, however, with the house she cannot remember except for the staircase. And in the very next line, she is "taken away":

> I come from the city of Haifa, but I remember little of my birthplace. I can see the area where I played as a small child, but of our house, I can only remember the staircase. I was taken away when I was four, not to see Haifa again for many years. (p. 21)

Suddenly, the camera pulls back. From the initial little scene on the ground, it moves far above and far away to a panoramic shot from an airplane:

> Finally I saw my city twenty-one years later, on August 29, 1969, when Comrade Salim Issawi and I expropriated an imperialist plane and returned to Palestine to pay homage to our occupied country and to show that we had not abandoned our homeland. (p. 21)

Khaled shifts not only location, but style and tone: from the staircase, where she speaks in a quiet and (more or less) personal voice, to the sky, where she announces as though from a loudspeaker her official return to the "homeland," an ideological space that swallows up any cozy sense of house and home. The triumphal anger in the last line of her paragraph totally eclipses any of the nostalgia that may have lingered in the first lines: "Ironically, the Israeli enemy, powerless, escorted us with his French and American planes." From "child" to "terrorist" in the blink of an eye.

For Khaled, it is not to capture an otherwise disappearing past that she writes. Not the cave of private memory but the stage of public performance must be filled; not the recovery of the past but the envisioning and revisioning of the future must be undertaken as her life's work. Not to notice, but to be noticed. Her agenda, in fact, must be a collective one, the agenda of a woman as well as the agenda of an exiled Palestinian, both gender and politics.

Until the massive defeat by Israel in June of 1967, an earlier generation of Palestinians was generally captive to nostalgia, lamenting the losses of twenty years earlier when their land was taken away, living in a state of shock and bound to a dead past. It is that nostalgic memory of the past that Leila Khaled so vigorously rejects. Like Muslim women in general, the Palestinians "were not allowed [or did not allow themselves] a future. They only grew old."[5]

Not only did they lack a sense of a future, they also—again, like traditional Muslim women—virtually lacked visibility. What the English anthropologist Michael Gilsenan has written about village women in North Lebanon might translate into a description of Palestinian political culture before 1967:

> Women, when they walk down such a path [in the village streets], are in the literal sense of the word visible. But they are not "seen." That is to say, the path itself has zones of open and closed. Men walk down the middle, women cling to the sides and walk fast. Neither gives any sign of seeing the other at all. The women are socially and for all practical purposes invisible. They must be.[6]

Invisible, without a future, and only growing old: these factors define the context out of which Leila Khaled writes her story. *My People Shall Live* is an autobiography of conscientization, a process that involves both a coming to an awareness of the past that has shaped her reality and a designing of a future that can transform that reality.[7] It was the June 1967 defeat (after which Khaled "felt catatonic for a month") that transformed debilitating nostalgia for a "golden past" into revolutionary action toward the future. "Our defeat was indeed our salvation," Khaled writes, "our means of regeneration and renewal" (p. 41). History had now to be reshaped by means of revolutionary activity, not quietly relived under the olive tree.

The Western reader is far more at home, as I have said, with an autobiography such as Annie Dillard's. Its announced subject surely signals familiar autobiographical territory. Since Rousseau's *Confessions,* childhood has been a trope in Western autobiography. Childhood is, after all, where it all begins, and those early years deserve close scrutiny and detailed exposition. In a passage to which I have already referred, Dillard records her earliest memory in a slow-motion close-up: "An infant watches her hands and feels them move. Gradually she fixes her own boundaries at the complex incurve rim of her skin. Later she touches one palm to another and tries for a game to distinguish each hand's sensation of feeling and being felt." "What is a house but a bigger skin," she concludes by asking, "and a neighborhood map but the world's skin ever expanding?" (p. 44). Khaled's title issues another kind of announcement. *My People Shall Live* will embed her ("my") personal story in the life of her people, already going beyond the conventional first-person singular of traditional Western autobiography. And the title's tense stretches toward the future, not the more recognizably autobiographical past.

From the perspective of Palestinian exile, Dillard's world is a star system away, its "skin" a metaphor for an imperial infantilism that recognizes no boundaries between self and other. A projection of one's most intimate sense of touch, the world that spells home for Dillard's American infant exists for Khaled's Palestinian woman as territory occupied by strangers. *Homeland* gives ironic expression to violated boundaries and expropriated land as well as to a steadfastness that has increased under occupation.

Like her view of Haifa from the hijacked plane, much of Khaled's writing must strike the Western reader as miles up in the air. It is lacking in the concrete detail and the arresting image we have long associated with good writing. Her book reads like a manifesto and lacks self-reflexivity. Khaled's story goes along uninterrupted by any self-conscious probing into the nature of her enterprise: no laments about lost time, no reflections on selfhood, no formulations about self/world distinctions; no embarrassment about shifting from family squabbles to political history; no compunctions about long quotes from factional publications.

And, most astonishing of all, Khaled's writing registers no equivocation about the authority of her own position, standing as she does (and must know that she does) at some distance from mainstream PLO ideology as well as from the Western readership on which she no doubt counts.[8] With all this, *My People Shall Live* raises important questions about First World assumptions regarding the genre of autobiography, for example, assumptions about the importance of child-hood as well as what continues to be taken for granted about the personal and its distinction from the political. Khaled's autobiograph-ical practice problematizes these assumptions as part of its collective agenda of conscientization. It is a story that goes "beyond the veil" of such assumptions as well as a story meant to achieve the visibility as a daughter that has heretofore been accorded only to sons. At the same time, it is a story about finding a voice and a stage by a culture that had been silenced and rendered invisible for three decades.

No personal journey of recovery, autobiography in Khaled's hands is a form of resistance literature that aims toward social and political transformation. Far from holding on to a time and place that would otherwise be swallowed up in the blank cave of oblivion, the Third World autobiographer must reenvision the past in order to uncover those myths of powerlessness that the subordinate culture (women, natives) has introjected from what Paulo Freire calls the "director society." Only when these structures of domination and dependency have been exposed can the autobiography project move from (again, Freire) "cultural action" to "cultural revolution," from denostalgizing the past to generating a future: "Underdeveloped people live by fate," Khaled writes, they look with nostalgia to a "golden past."[9] "My people and I suffer these debilities, but we are also living in the ongoing process of history and are trying to determine our future rather than bind ourselves to a dead past" (p. 41).

It is from the hijacked plane, miles above the under-staircase refuge of childhood, that Leila finds herself part of that "ongoing process of history." She overcomes nostalgia through what Freire calls "structural perception" without which people "attribute the . . . facts and situa-tions in their lives either to some superreality or to something within themselves."[10] Khaled moves from traditional nostalgia to revolution-ary autobiographical activity in the course of relocating her private life in the arena of political activism and transforming herself from a daughter into a "warrior": "I knew that I had a role to play: I realized that my historic mission was as a warrior in the inevitable battle between oppressors and oppressed, exploiters and exploited. I decided to become a revolutionary in order to liberate my people and myself" (p. 22).

From the time Khaled was taken away from her home in Haifa at age four, she was burdened, she says, "by the adult problems of life and death, right and wrong" (p. 28). But it was in the years between eight and twelve that she came of age in the world of social and political reality. While Annie Dillard was discovering the social world in dancing school, Leila Khaled was learning about the effects of structural poverty and class discrimination in nearby refugee camps. She records her personal memories (of a violent winter storm, a bad cold, a collection taken up by classmates to buy a new dress for a camp girl) not only, like Annie, in the context of her neighborhood—in this case, the battlefield of civil war—but against the backdrop of international alliances intended to ensure an uninterrupted flow of Arab oil to the West and to protect U.S. strategic interests in the Middle East. The line between the personal and political gets increasingly smudged, if it was ever there in the first place.

While Dillard was looking for "beauty bare of import" (and finding it, interestingly, in fragments of Middle Eastern poetry), Khaled could escape the import of nothing. Even the activities of her cat, Sarah, were emblematic of the larger political world. When Sarah returned after a long absence, she wrote, "I felt that if the cat could find her way back to me after one year, I would be able to find my way back to a liberated Palestine" (p. 38). She was ten years old at the time and, since three years before, the dates of Palestinian "betrayal," as her mother called them, were more "vital and integral" to her life than her own birthday, uncelebrated since leaving Haifa and not to be observed until her return. Those dates of betrayal, drilled into her by her mother when the seven-year-old Leila stayed away from a protest demonstration against the "Zionist occupation of Palestine," were the signing of the Balfour Declaration in 1917, the United Nations partition of Palestine in 1947, and the establishment of the state of Israel in 1948.

Other anniversaries will become just as vital, for example, the death of the revolutionary Ché Guevara and the subsequent birth of the Popular Front for the Liberation of Palestine. It is not only that the personal has been relocated in the political; the events that for Annie Dillard exist only as "rumors from beyond the horizon skin's rim" are for Leila Khaled the very furniture of her world. When, in her freshman year at the American University in Beirut, she is called up before the dean, an American woman, for having broken the rule against distributing political leaflets on campus, it is not disingenuousness that prompts Leila's response: "Palestine is not politics to me."

While it was her mother who brought her on political line in 1951, it was this same mother she had to get around when fourteen-year-old Leila became a candidate for membership in the Arab Nationalist Movement. Now that the civil war in Lebanon was over, her mother thought that "the girls should stay at home and leave politics to men."

Eighteen years later, Khaled recounts a prison visit paid her in Damascus by "four ladies of upperclass appearance" who brought her a bouquet of flowers in tribute to the El Al hijacking she had directed. She "looked at them in contempt," she writes, "and asked if their bouquet was a fitting tribute to a living revolutionary who had accomplished her mission." When the ladies expressed their reservations about her operation, suggesting that it might "eclipse" a recent terrorist attempt on the part of an Israeli to burn down Jerusalem's al-Aksa mosque, "an action which was gaining sympathy for the Arabs," Leila told the women she was striving for a "unity of the anti-imperialist forces," not a "unity based on religious bigotry." The women "walked out in a huff," she noted, "never to return to amuse me with their feminine slave passions and fashions" (pp. 153–54). The rhetorical violence she employs in describing this visit communicates something more than overreaction. Although unweighty in the aftermath of a plane hijacking, the event proves a measure of the distance that remains between her generation and what she sees as the false consciousness of her mother's. To dismantle this consciousness requires action of their own, not the sympathy of the world that might or might not result from terrorist action on the part of their enemies. It will be her mother and her mother's generation that Leila will have to continue fighting. But it will also be a fight against her male comrades who, when she sneaked out in her pajamas to attend a Nationalist Movement meeting, "blasted her for violating Arab decorum and polite womanly behaviour" (p. 51).

When she was undergoing plastic surgery in preparation for the second hijacking operation, she was recognized by a man who was visiting his wife and new baby daughter in the same hospital. On her discharge, Khaled gave the "new daughter a necklace made of bullets and wished her a long, long revolutionary career" (p. 181).

By this time, Leila, too, has become a "new daughter." Toward the end of her book, Khaled returns to the view above Haifa, this time composing a meditation in which Palestine becomes her "true Mother," and calling on all mothers to be patient for their daughters' return. The homeland to which she pays abstract homage in the opening paragraph now becomes her partner in a love affair: "As we approached the land of my birth," she writes, "it seemed that my love and I were racing towards each other for an eternal embrace" (pp. 138–39). She continues with a passage that, like many contemporary Palestinian poems, employs an older tradition of Arab love poetry to address the political themes of exile and return:

Oh my homeland! My love, my only love! I shall revolt
against thine enemies, all enemies. I shall make bombs from
the atoms of my body and weave a new Palestine from the
fabric of my soul. With all my power and the power of my
sisters, we shall convert our existence into bombs to redeem
the land, the coast, the mountain. (pp. 146–47)

The land that must be "redeemed" with lives converted into weapons stands at a seemingly immeasurable distance from the "dreaming
memory of land" that opens Annie Dillard's autobiography. It is a
distance not only geographical, but rhetorical. While Khaled's passage
about her Palestine is militant and even, to the Western ear, histrionic,
Dillard's seems elegaic. I quote Dillard's opening lines once again:

When everything else has gone from my brain—the President's name, the state capitals, the neighborhoods where I
lived, and then my own name and what it was on earth I
sought, and then at length the faces of my friends, and finally
the faces of my family—when all this has dissolved, what will
be left, I believe, is topology: the dreaming memory of land
as it lay this way and that. (p. 3)

Both Dillard and Khaled love the topology that has shaped and
continues to define their respective lives. And both, in the face of
feared or experienced losses, return to the land to anchor their experience. But here, again, their worlds divide. The disappearance of
Dillard's "all this" (the outside world) will accompany the natural
process of growing old. Khaled's world disappears not from memory
loss (or from the failure to notice enough), but as a result of war and
the policy of her enemy—villages destroyed, trees uprooted, little girls
forced into exile.

More important than the actual difference in geopolitical location,
but, surely, as a result of that difference, Annie Dillard's autobiography
can assume the ongoingness of the world out there even though she
lives a life that continues unaffiliated with it. Suggesting a national
report, the title of her autobiography turns out to be apt. She does,
in fact, portray an American (or U.S.) childhood, a childhood very
much like my own, removed from the poverty around her and oblivious, except through books, of the cost for such a childhood that
much of the rest of the world has had to bear.

While Annie Dillard writes out of a culture that has a voice, Leila
Khaled writes out of a culture of silence. It is not that her people are
mute; it is rather that their voices cannot penetrate the raptness of
attention that an Annie Dillard must pay to staying the flood of oblivion

and to creating an original and ever wakeful relation to the Emersonian universe. Is it surprising that the voice in Khaled's autobiography seems often to come through a loudspeaker?

It is the envisioning of things future, not the remembering of things past, that is at issue in Third World autobiographies such as Leila Khaled's: to perform on the stage of history, not to reenter the cave of memory. The Western autobiographical tradition has been defined in large part by those whose place on that stage has been secure. That they are members of the "director society" is no accident.

I began this essay by saying that understanding requires, first of all, the desire to understand. Let me end the essay by turning to my own autobiography as a way of accounting for my interest in Leila Khaled and my desire to understand a world whose strangeness and distance have diminished but certainly have not disappeared.

In 1982, I published *Autobiography: Toward a Poetics of Experience,* in which I developed a theory of autobiography as a form of survival literature. Autobiography, I wrote, displays a "fundamental gesture of resistance to mutilation." In 1986, I decided to spend a university research leave in Israel as my just reward for having survived a divorce: I would join the survivors of this century's most overt and systematic genocidal mutilation to begin a book on Holocaust autobiography.

I began the 1986–87 research year knowing little more about Palestinians than most Americans did before the Intifada—as terrorists who specialized in plane hijackings. I recognized no faces other than that of the unshaven Yassir Arafat. I had never heard of Leila Khaled. But I ended that year by editing a report on the uprooting of thousands of olive trees in a West Bank village. By then, I had made my way across the Green Line, which divides Israel from the West Bank, to visit Palestinian villages and camps whose residents were living under far less than benign occupation. Although I did not abandon my Holocaust research, I put it on the shelf for another time. The Palestinian Intifada began some five months after I returned to my university in North Carolina.

It is now nearly two months into the third year of the Intifada, and, having resigned from my university, I am back in Jerusalem. For the past year and a half, I have been volunteering with a Palestinian human rights organization and writing a first-person account of a Palestinian camp family, one of whose teenage sons was shot three weeks after I arrived. My earlier interest in theory has found new expression in practice.

It is out of these personal and political contexts that I have written this essay on Leila Khaled. Moreover, I have used her autobiography as the occasion to think once again about the genre I tried to define nine years ago, before coming to the Middle East.

When I defined autobiography as "resistance to mutilation," I meant resistance to loss or to what Marcel Proust called *temps perdu*. But I also wanted to communicate something more immediate and embodied, like the phantom limb phenomenon that the amputee often continues to experience. To feel the "presence" of the amputated limb, I argued, was the result of neither self-delusion nor denial but instead the result of the self's prior commitment to a world of motion and locomotion, an interhuman world to which the self insists on belonging, despite mutilation. Autobiography, I argued, is rehabilitative activity, a learning of how to walk again. More fundamental than the body's readjustments to the prosthesis or crutch, walking again requires a new sense of the ground, a trust that the ground will hold up and not give way.

But what happens when it is the ground itself that gets lost, not simply a leg to stand (and walk) on?[11] What if it is one's world that disappears? This was the profound experience I wanted to explore the first time I came to Jerusalem to begin a book on Holocaust autobiography. It was nothing less than their world that a people lost in that genocidal mutilation. How were they able to survive that loss? Israel must hold the secret, I thought. The establishment of the state must itself have been a display of resistance and of recovered trust in the ground.

The adherence to motion defined for me what I called the autobiographical impulse. Acknowledgment of a fiduciary ground that holds the self in place, recovery of that ground after it has been lost: these were the activities (human, cultural, even religious) that defined autobiography. I had not read Leila Khaled's autobiography when I was formulating my ideas about Jewish loss and recovery. Nor had I known about the Palestinian experience when I developed a theory of autobiography based on adherence to a world of walking despite amputation. Leila Khaled's story begins when she was forced out of Haifa to make way for the new state of Israel. She continues in exile to this day. "I did not leave Haifa of my own free wish," she writes. "The decision was not made by my family but by a people who should have known better—a persecuted and hunted race who in turn became my persecutors and hunters of my brethren" (p. 24).

Looking back, I realize that the poetics of experience that I developed nine years ago ignored the incipient possibility of trespassing into territory whose boundaries remain invisible to the ones intent on recovering lost ground. That ground is not only phenomenological; like the repertoire of memory, it is historical and political. (Only unlived or dead space is empty, what the early Zionists called "a land without people.") Unchecked by a sense of what is out of bounds, the impulse toward being can become a form of expropriation.

I concluded back then that "the self which autobiography performs is the self who forgets as well as remembers, the self who dies as well as lives. It is the self that comes up against its limits, most especially the limits of the other by virtue of which and only in relation to which the self knows who and where it is.[12] I would want now to underscore those limits of mortality as well as the limit of the other(s). But Khaled's autobiography highlights another set of limits that, in fact, delegitimate the self. Some of these limits are imposed from the outside by geo-political circumstances, but just as important are the limits that have been internalized and have rendered a people voiceless. Because of these introjected structures of domination, it is not enough to recover an individual past.

Third World autobiography must perform a collective experience. It differs in two respects from mainstream Western autobiography, both male and female. First, it involves an unmasking or what I have called a denostalgizing of the past; second, it orients itself toward a liberated society in the future. In the first respect, it is a form of resistance literature;[13] in the second, it is a form of utopian literature. Providing the context for this form of autobiographical practice is the history of colonialism and those introjected forms of oppression that continue long after a people has gained its independence. It is those introjections that must be unmasked before the past can be rendered autobiographically useful. This requires a collective understanding that not only the oppressive past but the very memory of that past has been informed by false consciousness.

Not quite a generation before Dillard's, I was getting ready to go off to college, caring nothing about the out-of-work miners in my hometown, knowing nothing about the world's oppressed, eager to extend the rim of my own skin. And not more than a month before beginning this essay, I was writing about a day I had spent on a beach near Tel Aviv on the one-year anniversary of my return to Jerusalem. I had described the drive from East Jerusalem to Tel Aviv, which had taken only an hour but had covered, and covered up, centuries. Faster than the speed of sound, we had gone from antique hillsides outside Jerusalem to the prefab industrial buildings near Tel Aviv. The acres of Jewish settlements had made palpable the most recent twenty years of occupation.

I had been reminded of other times and places when we arrived first in the town and then at the beach. Herzliyya reminded me of Sarasota, Florida, a transplant of America into the Middle East. "Was my personal story, the story I was writing alongside the story of the refugee camp family I had come to know, as unnatural a transplant?" I wondered. "Was it, too, a means of muting other voices and superimposing myself on a landscape that belonged to others?"

The beach was another of those large, undefined spaces like the Outer Banks off the coast of North Carolina where I had felt agoraphobic some ten years earlier. I wrote, too, about the deserted mosque and the only two Palestinians to be seen among the Israelis and Westerners on the beach. They were two boys who were clearing it of garbage. I had spoken to them when we left and learned they were from Nablus, easily two hours away, through territory that is especially hostile these days. I ended the account with the following paragraph:

> Herzliyya beach was a time capsule for me, overcrowded with forty years of my own history: sunbathing at the public pool in Western Pennsylvania, living among the palmettos and banyon trees in Florida, hyperventilating on the empty dunes of Okracoke, and, less than a week ago, being led by the children through the dense warrens of Deheishe Refugee Camp.

But it is the final line of my account that continues to worry me: "I am wondering if I, too, am expropriating Palestine to construct my own sense of place." I wrote about autobiographical imperialism in my 1982 book and used Wordsworth's leech-gatherer poem to illustrate both the autobiographer's temptation to impose herself on the world and how, by virtue of the leech gatherer's "resolution and independence," the poet is saved from the solipsistic madness that can follow on ignoring the boundary between self and other. At that time, I was concerned for the sanity and self-determination of the poet. Now, however, I am concerned for the rights of the leech gatherer. Autobiographical activity must resist mutilation without, at the same time, mutilating. Justice is at stake.

I end this essay on the politics of experience with some questions I cannot answer but also cannot ignore: Is autobiography, theory as well as practice, an unavoidable act of expropriation? Is some form of interpretive colonization inevitable in the writing or in the reading of autobiography? Along with desire and the acknowledgment of distance, do these questions have to be factored into any possibility of understanding an autobiographical practice so far from home?

Notes

1. See David Hirst, *The Gun and the Olive Branch: The Roots of Violence in the Middle East* (London: Macdonald, 1983), 303.

2. Annie Dillard, *An American Childhood* (New York: Harper & Row, 1987), 3. Page numbers of subsequent quotations from this book will appear in parentheses in the text.

3. The phrase is from the subtitle of my book, *Autobiography: Toward a Poetics of Experience* (Philadelphia: University of Pennsylvania Press, 1982). I will be returning to the theory developed in this book at the end of this essay.

4. Leila Khaled, *My People Shall Live: The Autobiography of a Revolutionary* (London: Hodder & Stoughton, 1973), 214. Page numbers of subsequent quotations from this book will appear in parentheses in the text.

5. See Fatima Mernissi, *Beyond the Veil: Male-Female Dynamics in Modern Muslim Society* (Bloomington: Indiana University Press, 1987), xii.

6. Michael Gilsenan, *Recognizing Islam: Religion and Society in the Modern Arab World* (New York: Pantheon, 1982), 172.

7. For a discussion of "conscientization," see Paulo Freire, "Cultural Action and Conscientization," in *The Politics of Education: Culture, Power and Liberation* (South Hadley, Mass.: Bergin & Garvey, 1985).

8. Dr. George Habash's Popular Front for the Liberation of Palestine stands to the left of Yassir Arafat's more politically mainstream Fatah faction within the currently united Palestine Liberation Organization.

9. An incident fifteen years after the family's exile to Lebanon illustrates the nostalgia that Khaled's autobiographical project must repudiate. It was a family reunion across the barbed wire at Jerusalem's Mendelbaum Gate, which still divided Israel from Jordan in 1963. Paralyzed, Leila's father was unable to go. The meeting, she writes, was a nightmare of barbed wire: "When grandmother saw mother, she presumed her son must have died and she collapsed. My aunts, my cousins, and mother carried on a teary dialogue for about an hour. Little or nothing was said beyond conveying greetings and fleeting reminiscences. We were all drenched with tears. We looked at each other wondering whether reunion would ever be possible; no one could utter a coherent sentence; we parted infuriated at the Zionist overlord" (p. 76).

10. Freire, "Cultural Action and Conscientization," 75.

11. See Oliver Sacks, *A Leg to Stand On* (New York: Summit, 1984). Sacks describes the phenomenological loss I am trying to communicate in his account of a fall that incapacitated him for a period of time.

12. Gunn, *Autobiography*, 147.

13. See Barbara Harlow, *Resistance Literature* (New York: Methuen, 1987), xvi. My debt to Harlow's study goes beyond the use of her term for the writing that has grown out of the struggle for liberation by colonized people under the domination of Western Europe and North America. I read her book just as I was nervously getting under way on this essay and found both courage and inspiration to keep at it. I hope that my own work demonstrates, as does hers, that "this literature, like the resistance and national

liberation movements which it reflects and in which it can be said to participate, not only demands recognition of its independent status and existence as literary production, but as such also presents a serious challenge to the codes and canons of both the theory and the practice of literature and its criticism as these have been developed in the West" (p. xvi).

Chapter 5

The Problem of Being "Indian": One Mixed-Blood's Dilemma

Janice Gould

A mile or so from the University of California in Berkeley, two huge granite grinding stones stand embedded in a hillside overlooking San Francisco Bay. There is a grand view of Mt. Tamalpais to the northwest and of Suisun Bay to the north. These are desecrated places, their meanings disappeared beneath the litter of broken beer bottles and scrawled graffiti.[1] Long ago, not so long, but far enough back that I imagine the earth still retained its energy of being, Indian women worked on these rocks, crushing acorns gathered from the large oak trees that once grew on the hillsides. Over much of California grinding acorns was a daily task, as acorns were a staple food for many California natives. The rocks are a testimony to the years of labor, pocked as they are with depressions made or enlarged by hand-held stone manos. Women sang on those rocks, songs connected to the labor, in a tongue long since forgotten. Their feet rested on the uneven surface of the rock, warming in the sun. Their hands were busy shelling, sifting, creating nourishment. That is how I imagine it in my almost native imagination. My mind and heart give back to me those rocks, those women and their songs.

It is obvious that there is not a university in this country that is not built on what was once native land. We should reflect on this over and over, and understand this fact as one fundamental point about the relationship of Indians to academia. I lived nearly all my life in Berkeley, and I have hiked in canyons behind the university and stood on the hillcrests looking out over the bay to the Pacific Ocean. As kids, we wondered how the area must have looked to the explorer de Anza because that is how we were taught to see and to think in school, through the eyes of the conquistadores. It was only later, trying to create for myself what no textbook gave me, that I wondered how it must have appeared to the people who inhabited this land, this place we call California. It was important for me to do this because I am a member of the Konkow tribe (in native dialect, *koyomk'auwi*). This tribe—subsumed under the name Maidu—lived in the northern part of the Sierra Nevada range, in its foothills, and out into the Central Valley. The history of my people was not in any textbook I ever read. Perhaps this is because the Maidu were not "Mission Indians." History did not touch the Maidu; they were swallowed up, and so erased without a chapter, somewhere between the Gold Rush and the construction of the railroads.

When I was a kid my mother told us, "You are French, Irish, English, and Indian." We always said it that way, too, in that order. Being part Indian was a source of pride to us because we understood how unique it must be in a world so populated by white folk. And we were warned by my mother always to be proud, always to hold our heads up and never to let anyone make us feel ashamed of being Indian. Pride and shame were involved with our Indianness in an extraordinarily self-defining way. What it meant to be Indian, however, was problematic. Did we live in a wigwam? asked the kids at school. No. Did our mother wear a buckskin dress? No. And didn't we always say "Ugh!" and "How!"? No. But still we were Indian. What kind of Indian? Konkow. Konkow is a stupid name. What kind of Indian is that? We did not answer. We would not say. Somehow the questions silenced the responses.

I give you this brief and personal history to introduce myself and to set the groundwork for some of the issues I wish to address. Although I am a Ph.D. student in American studies, I am not a teacher. I assume that I have been asked to participate in this volume because I have been studying contemporary American Indian literature. I assume that it is hoped I can make a contribution representative of the Native woman's viewpoint. This is a dilemma for me. Because I am a mixed-blood, I do not feel competent to speak for full-bloods. Because I am an urban and middle-class Indian, I cannot speak for Indians who have lived most of their lives on reservations. I was brought up in the city of Berkeley, California, and never went to Indian School. As a California Indian, I believe I have been formed by a unique and little-known history that adds to my complexity. I have been taught no specific Maidu cultural traditions; none, to my knowledge, were retained by my family. None of my living relatives speaks *koyomk'auwi.* What family I had on my mother's side were scattered, the girls coming to the city to be housemaids, the boys finding jobs in the mountains. The more I look at it, the more unique I feel, even for an urban Indian mixed-blood. So how do I know I'm Indian? With all that I lack, what has informed me of my Indian identity? And what right have I to that identity, to that quarter-blood self who was enjoined to be proud and never ashamed of my Indian blood? And why does that quarter-blood self insist on speaking, insist on its Indianness, in spite of its doubts and fears? And what have any of these questions to do with feminism, identity, or autobiography?

With the word *feminist* I mean someone engaged in the critique of patriarchy who desires, and in some way works for, the liberation of all women from patriarchal oppression. I agree with Cherríe Moraga, who has said that one goal of feminism must be "the obliteration of that system [capitalist and patriarchal] which violently discriminates against people on the basis of sex, color, place of origin, etc."[2] Moraga has also said that women of color must be seen not as "'objects' of inquiry [but as] active participants in the definition of themselves."[3] I may question what in myself constitutes "Indianness," but I have no doubt as to my status as a woman of color.

Perhaps it can be said that one of the goals of racism is to fix people in a racial category based on what we are taught to perceive as color. More frequently in the past than now, the Euro-American slotted people into color categories: white, red, black, yellow, and brown. These colors were a racial code. I have not found the folk mythology that connects human blood to racial type, but certainly that sort of thinking exists to this day, and informs one's claim, especially to being Indian, on the basis of blood quantum. It seems that people thought that the blood in our veins determined the differences in the races and that somehow race was manifested in some variation of these colors. The details of hair type, shape of eyes, and even skull size were added to support the variation in and separation of the races as if on some empirically scientific basis. We know, of course, that the point of these categorizations was to allow the Euro-American male to congratulate himself on his superiority over non-Euro-Americans.

Be that as it may, we are left with a legacy that allows us to speak of Euro-Americans as whites and African Americans as blacks. We say, "a white woman I work with" or "a black woman I know." But we do not say "a red (or yellow or brown) woman I know," because this has somehow lost favor, as James Clifton has pointed out.[4] We imagine that color coding the rest of us is somehow racist. Instead, we tend to speak of reds, yellows, and browns as Native Americans, Asians, and Hispanics.

Now, there are some of us going around who cannot easily be located in one of these color (read ethnic/racial) categories. For example, I am sometimes perceived as Hispanic, sometimes as Asian. My first experience of racism as a child, in fact, had to do with a stupid misperception. A little girl called me a "dirty Jap." My mother had taught us never to say mean words like "nigger," "spick," or "Jap," nor to think that way. She said that white people who used such words were prejudiced against others. They thought they were superior because they were white. So, thanks to that little girl, I understood that I was not seen as white by everyone. But that she hated me for the wrong reason, for thinking that I was Japanese instead of Indian, made my response to her racism more difficult.

Recently, something similar occurred to me. It lacked the viciousness of that little girl's hatred, but it smacked of similar ignorance. I was in an office in the English Department at my university, the University of New Mexico. The secretary, I could tell, was observing me. After a moment she asked, "Are you Asian?" "No," I answered, "I'm not." I hesitated, then decided to help the lady out. "I'm part Indian," I said. "Oh," she replied, "you *are* Asian. You people came over from China thousands of years ago!" Thus I was both corrected and informed about my origins. And maybe the lady felt better knowing she hadn't made a mistake. Somehow I became both more Indian and less Indian in this conversation. I was rendered invisible not only because of this woman's initial misperception of me (which, given my complexion, hair color, and physical stature, but more essentially given the fact of racism, was an understandable misperception), but also through the forced disappearance of my claim to Indianness, which is a quintessentially Indian experience.

What do I mean by this? I mean that it is not extraordinary for an Indian to feel that she is ignored solely on the basis of being Indian. This is somewhat the case for Mohawk writer Beth Brant, a light-skinned half-breed who gave a reading a few years ago in Marin County. After her reading a white woman came up to her and said, "I don't see why you go on about being a half-breed. You look white enough!" This was another way of saying Brant did not look Indian enough. Her Indianness was erased.

What should be our response to this? I don't know. Louise Erdrich is a mixed-blood Chippewa writer, and I've heard that her response to someone who says, "Funny, you don't look Indian," is "Funny, you don't look rude!" I know my worst fear is to have some person come up to me and say, "So, you aren't really an Indian after all!" Some Indians can laugh off such remarks, but we do look for ways to say to the person, No, you're wrong.

Joseph Bruchac has edited a wonderful book of interviews with Indian writers called *Survival This Way*. In one interview, Peter Blue Cloud and Joe Bruchac, who are both mixed-bloods, discuss this problem. Bruchac says, "Sometimes people don't understand how a person of mixed-blood could call themselves Indian." Blue Cloud responds, "They wouldn't understand even if you explained it. . . . The fact is that we adopted a lot of non-Indians in the old days. But when we adopted someone they entered the clan, they became *us*." Later, Bruchac comments, I've heard traditional people say that it's not our way to exclude someone. It's not our way to leave people out."[5]

This is different, however, from the practice of white people who have joined the "wannabe" tribe. They want to be Indians. Clifton points out that there was a 75 percent increase in the Indian population (that is, in people identifying themselves as Indian) in the United States between 1970 and 1980. He argues that this leap in population has been caused, in part, by the lax definition of Indianness. He claims, as well, that there is a perceived economic advantage in being Indian because of monies made available to Indians through government agencies.[6] Perhaps this is true. I had a friend at Berkeley who knew she had a Cherokee in the family tree. This woman was an older student, divorced, with kids to support. She was a white woman with red hair and light eyes. In terms of blood quantum, I don't think she could claim to be more than one-sixteenth Cherokee. But she got a Graduate Minority Fellowship. On the records, our department looked like it had two Indian graduate students. And isn't this good for affirmative action? My friend admitted, however, that she had never identified as Indian before this, and clearly she had never been perceived as "other." Nevertheless, this Indian identification allowed my friend to begin to say things like, "I feel that the earth is our mother," and to attribute that idea to being Indian.

I'm glad that she seems to feel this relationship with the earth. But is this feeling an attribute of being Indian? My mother taught us kids to love and respect the earth from the time we were little. She never called it the Indian way. It seemed to be her way. Without a living cultural system available to lodge these values in, it is hard to know whether these are Indian beliefs or not. I wish I could claim my love of the earth, and other values, as Indian, as Maidu, with absolute certainty. But for a mixed-blood like myself, that is not possible.

Louise Erdrich has said:

> One of the characteristics of being a mixed blood is searching. You look back and say, "Who am I from?" You must question. You must make certain choices. You're able to. And it's a blessing and it's a curse. All of our searches involve trying to discover where we are from.[7]

This quest for identity can be seen in such novels as *Ceremony,* by Laguna writer Leslie Marmon Silko, and *House Made of Dawn,* by Kiowa writer M. Scott Momaday. These authors set their novels around the dilemma of being mixed-blood in traditional communities, and create complex mixed-blood heroes. Louise Erdrich, in her three novels, *Love Medicine, The Beet Queen,* and *Tracks,* explores varieties of mixed-blood experience over a period of decades in rural and small-town America. Similarly, James Welch, in *Winter in the Blood,* locates his protagonist in a rural and small-town setting but adds a surreal quality to his mixed-blood's life. Michael Dorris creates a female mixed-blood protagonist in his novel *A Yellow Raft in Blue Water,* an important work because of how it imaginatively explores African/Native American female identity.[8] One could cite many more mixed-blood authors, poets, and story writers, such as Joy Harjo, Linda Hogan, Gerald Vizenor, Vickie Sears, Paula Gunn Allen, Chrystos, Ai, and Wendy Rose. Often the issue of being mixed-blood is the topic of a poem or story, as in Paula Gunn Allen's poem "Dear World," in which the blood disease lupus symbolizes the mixed-blood dilemma of blood attacking itself.[9] In Linda Hogan's poem "The Truth Is," the narrator speaks of her two hands, one dark and one light, and how they raise the question "about who loved who / and who killed who."[10] Sometimes the difficulties of mixed identity reside in the background of a piece, more embedded in the text, as in Wendy Rose's poem "Julia," about a deformed Native American woman whose body, after her death, is billed as "The Lion Woman" and displayed in a circus sideshow.[11]

Someday, perhaps, American Indian literature will come to be thought of as truly important to academia. If that happens, and this literature is finally included in every English department and American studies curriculum across this country, it will be essential to understand that these novels, poems, essays, and plays are often the product of mixed-blood writers who feel varying degrees of identification as

Indian. I think it is necessary to remember that many of us see our literature as coming out of a kind of colonial experience, rather than as simply another kind of American experience. Finally, we must bear in mind that there are in this country enormous numbers of mixed-bloods, not only of Native American ancestry. There are varieties of mixed-blood experience lived by the students we have now and by the students we will have in the future. Mixed-bloodedness will be an issue of profound interest to many of them. They will look for ways to explore their complexity through literature. So the voices of mixed-blood Asian, African American, Hispanic and Indian writers must be elicited, listened to, consulted, and considered in a global perspective. We will be prodded to challenge concepts of acculturation and assimilation, of race and ethnicity. We will be asked to examine in a more thorough, radical, and frightening way this legacy of racism. We may not even be able to consider issues of gender and class before we explore this troubling thing we call race. I believe that facing these issues is some of the most vital work ahead for feminist educators and scholars.

Notes

1. I consciously use the word *disappeared* for political reasons. I mean it to be read in the same sense in which it is currently being used in such places as Guatemala, Argentina, Chile, and El Salvador.

2. Cherríe Moraga, speech made to women's studies graduates, University of California, Berkeley, 25 May 1989, 3.

3. Moraga, speech, 5.

4. James A. Clifton, *Being and Becoming Indian: Biographical Studies of North American Frontiers* (Chicago: Dorsey, 1989), 11.

5. Joseph Bruchac, *Survival This Way* (Tucson: Sun Tracks and the University of Arizona, 1987), 36–37.

6. Clifton, *Being and Becoming Indian*, 16.

7. Quoted in Bruchac, *Survival This Way*, 83.

8. Leslie Marmon Silko, *Ceremony* (New York: Viking Penguin, 1977); M. Scott Momaday, *House Made of Dawn* (New York: Harper & Row, 1966); Louise Erdrich, *Love Medicine* (New York: Holt, Rinehart & Winston, 1984); idem, *The Beet Queen* (New York: Henry Holt, 1986); idem, *Tracks* (New York, Henry Holt, 1988); Michael Dorris, *A Yellow Raft in Blue Water* (New York: Henry Holt, 1987).

9. Paula Gunn Allen, *Skins and Bones* (Albuquerque, N.M.: West End, 1988), 56.

10. Linda Hogan, *Seeing Through the Sun* (Amherst: University of Massachussetts Press, 1985), 4.

11. Wendy Rose, *That's What She Said,* ed. Rayna Green (Bloomington: Indiana University Press, 1984), 212.

PART II

Theorizing the Politics of Form

Chapter 6

The Margin at the Center
On *Testimonio* (Testimonial Narrative)

John Beverley

> *The deformed Caliban—enslaved, robbed of his island, and trained to speak by Prospero—rebukes him thus: "You taught me language and my profit on't / Is, I know how to curse."*
>
> Roberto Fenández Retamar, "Caliban"[1]

Do social struggles give rise to new forms of literature, or is it more a question of the adequacy of their representation in existing narrative forms such as the short story and the novel, as in, for example, Gayatri Spivak's articulations of the stories of the Bengali writer Mahasweta Devi or Fredric Jameson's notion of national allegory in Third World writing?[2] What happens when, as in the case of Western Europe since the Renaissance, there has been a complicity between the rise of "literature" as a secular institution and the development of forms of colonial and imperialist oppression against which many of these struggles are directed? Are there experiences in the world today that would be betrayed or misrepresented by the forms of literature as we know it?

Raymond Williams formulates a similar question in relation to British working-class writing:

> Very few if any of us could write at all if certain forms were not available. And then we may be lucky, we may find forms which correspond to our experience. But take the case of the nineteenth century working-class writers, who wanted to write about their working lives. The most popular form was the novel, but though they had marvelous material that could

91

go into the novel very few of them managed to write good or any novels. Instead they wrote marvelous autobiographies. Why? Because the form coming down through the religious tradition was of a witness confessing the story of his life, or there was the defence speech at a trial when a man tells the judge who he is and what he had done, or of course other kinds of speech. These oral forms were more accessible forms centered on "I," on the single person. . . . The novel with its quite different narrative forms was virtually impenetrable to working-class writers for three or four generations, and there are still many problems in using the received forms for what is, in the end, very different material. Indeed the forms of working-class consciousness are bound to be different from the literary forms of another class, and it is a long struggle to find new and adequate forms.[3]

Let me set the frame of the discussion a bit differently than Williams does. In the period of what Marx describes as the primitive accumulation in Western Europe—say 1400 to 1650, which is also the age of the formation of the great colonial empires—there appears or reappears, under the impetus of humanism, a series of literary forms: the essay; the short story, or *novela ejemplar;* the picaresque novel; the various kinds of Petrarchan lyric, including the sonnet; the autobiography; and the secular theater. These forms, as ideological practices, are also a *means* of these developments (in the sense that they contribute to the creation of the subject form of "European Man"). By the same token, then, we should expect an age such as our own— also one of transition or the potential for transition from one mode of production to another—to experience the emergence of new forms of cultural and literary expression that embody, in more or less thematically explicit and formally articulated ways, the social forces contending for power in the world today. I have in mind here, by analogy to the role of the bourgeoisie in the transition from feudalism to capitalism, not only the struggle of working people everywhere against exploitation, but also in contingent ways movements of ethnic or national liberation, the women's liberation movement, poor and oppressed peoples' organizations of all types, the gay rights movement, the peace movement, ecological activism, and the like. One of these new forms in embryo, I will argue, is the kind of narrative text that in Latin American Spanish has come to be called *testimonio.*

By *testimonio* I mean a novel or novella-length narrative in book or pamphlet (that is, printed as opposed to acoustic) form, told in the first person by a narrator who is also the real protagonist or witness of the events he or she recounts, and whose unit of narration is usually a "life" or a significant life experience. *Testimonio* may include, but is not subsumed under, any of the following textual categories, some of which are conventionally considered literature, others not: autobiography, autobiographical novel, oral history, memoir, confession, diary, interview, eyewitness report, life history, *novela-testimonio,* nonfiction novel, or "factographic" literature. I will deal in particular with the distinctions among *testimonio,* life history, autobiography, and the all-encompassing term "documentary fiction."[4] However, because *testimonio* is by nature a protean and demotic form not yet subject to legislation by a normative literary establishment, any attempt to specify a generic definition for it, as I do here, should be considered at best provisional, and at worst repressive.

As Williams suggests, *testimonio*-like texts have existed for a long time at the margin of literature, representing in particular those subjects—the child, the "native," the woman, the insane, the criminal, the proletarian—excluded from authorized representation when it was a question of speaking and writing for themselves rather than being spoken for. But for practical purposes we can say that *testimonio* coalesced as a new narrative genre in the 1960s and further developed in close relation to the movements for national liberation and the generalized cultural radicalism of that decade. *Testimonio* is implicitly or explicitly a component of what Barbara Harlow has called "resistance literature."[5] In Latin America, where *testimonio* has enjoyed an especially rich development, it was sanctioned as a genre or mode by two related developments: the 1970 decision of Cuba's Casa de las Américas to begin awarding a prize in this category in its annual literary contest, and the reception in the late 1960s of Truman Capote's *In Cold Blood* (1965) and Miguel Barnet's *Autobiography of a Runaway Slave/Biografía de un cimarrón* (1967).[6]

But the roots of *testimonio* go back to the importance in previous Latin American literature of a series of nonfictional narrative texts, such as the colonial *cronicas* and "national" essay (*Facundo, Os sertoes*), the war diaries (*diarios de campaña*) of, for example, Bolivar or Martí, or the romantic biography, a key genre of Latin American liberalism. This tradition combined with the wide popularity of the sort of anthropological or sociological life history composed out of tape-recorded narratives developed by academic social scientists such as Oscar Lewis or Ricardo Pozas in the 1950s.[7] *Testimonio* also drew on—in my opinion much more crucially—the sort of direct-participant account, usually presented without any literary or academic aspirations whatever (although often with political ones), represented by books such as Ché Guevara's *Reminiscences of the Cuban Revolutionary*

War (1959), one of the defining texts of 1960s leftist sensibility throughout the Americas. The success of Ché's account (with its corresponding manual, *Guerrilla Warfare*) inspired in Cuba a series of direct-participant *testimonios* by combatants in the 26 of July Movement and later in the campaigns against the counterrevolutionary bands in the Escambray mountains and at the Bay of Pigs. In a related way (in some cases directly), there begins to emerge throughout the Third World, and in very close connection to the spread of armed struggle movements and the Vietnam War, a literature of personal witness and involvement designed to make the cause of these movements known to the outside world, to attract recruits, to reflect on successes or failures of the struggle, and so on.[8]

The word *testimonio* translates literally as "testimony," as in the act of testifying or bearing witness in a legal or religious sense. This connotation is important because it distinguishes *testimonio* from recorded participant narrative, as in the case of "oral history." In oral history it is the intentionality of the recorder—usually a social scientist—that is dominant, and the resulting text is in some sense "data." In *testimonio,* by contrast, it is the intentionality of the narrator that is paramount. The situation of narration in *testimonio* has to involve an urgency to communicate, a problem of repression, poverty, subalternity, imprisonment, struggle for survival, implicated in the act of narration itself. The position of the reader of *testimonio* is akin to that of a jury member in a courtroom. Unlike the novel, *testimonio* promises by definition to be primarily concerned with sincerity rather than literariness. This relates *testimonio* to generic 1960s ideology and the practice of "speaking bitterness," to use the term popularized in the Chinese Cultural Revolution, evident, for example, in the consciousness-raising sessions of the women's liberation movement, Fanon's theory of decolonization, the pedagogy of Paolo Freire (one of the richest sources of testimonial material has been in the interaction of intellectuals, peasants, and working people in literacy campaigns), and Laingian and, in a very different way, Lacanian psychotherapies. *Testimonio,* in other words, is an instance of the New Left and feminist slogan, "The personal is the political."[9]

Because in many cases the narrator is someone who is either functionally illiterate or, if literate, not a professional writer, the production of a *testimonio* generally involves the tape-recording and then the transcription and editing of an oral account by an interlocutor who is an intellectual, often a journalist or a writer. (To use the Russian formalist term, *testimonio* is a sort of *skaz,* a literary simulacrum of oral narrative.) The nature of the intervention of this gathering and editing function is one of the more hotly debated theoretical points in the discussion of the genre, and I will come back to it. What needs to be noted here is that the assumed lack of writing ability or skill on the part of the narrator of the *testimonio,* even in those cases where the story is written instead of narrated orally, also contributes to the "truth-effect" the form generates.

The situation of narration in the *testimonio* suggests an affinity with the picaresque novel, particularly with that sense of the picaresque that sees the hero's act of telling his or her life as yet another picaresque act. But *testimonio,* even where it approximates in content a kind of neopicaresque, as it does quite often, is a basically different narrative mode. It is not, to begin with, fiction. We are meant to experience both the speaker and the situations and events recounted as real. The "legal" connotation implicit in its convention implies a pledge of honesty on the part of the narrator that the listener/reader is bound to respect.[10]

Moreover, *testimonio* is concerned not so much with the life of a "problematic hero"—the term Georg Lukács uses to describe the nature of the hero of the bourgeois novel[11]—as with a problematic collective social situation in which the narrator lives. The situation of the narrator in *testimonio* is one that must be representative of a social class or group. In the picaresque novel, by contrast, a collective social predicament, such as unemployment and marginalization, is experienced and narrated as a personal destiny. The "I" that speaks to us in the picaresque or first-person novel is in general the mark of a difference, an antagonist to the community, in the picaresque the *Ich-form* (Hans Robert Jauss's term[12]) of the self-made man: hence the picaresque's cynicism about human nature, its rendering of lower-class types as comic, as opposed to the egalitarian reader-character relation implied by both the novel and *testimonio.* The narrator in *testimonio,* on the other hand, speaks for, or in the name of, a community or group, approximating in this way the symbolic function of the epic hero, without at the same time assuming the epic hero's hierarchical and patriarchal status. René Jara speaks of an "epicidad cotidiana," an everyday epicality, in *testimonio.*[13] Another way of putting this would be to define *testimonio* as a nonfictional, popular-democratic form of epic narrative.

By way of example, here is the opening of *I, Rigoberta Menchú,* a well-known *testimonio* by a Guatemalan Indian woman:

> My name is Rigoberta Menchú. I'm 23 years old. This is my testimony. I didn't learn it from a book and I didn't learn it alone. I'd like to stress that it's not only my life, it's also the

testimony of my people. It's hard for me to remember everything that's happened to me in my life since there have been
many bad times but, yes, moments of joy as well. The important thing is that what has happened to me has happened to
many other people also: My story is the story of all poor Guatemalans. My personal experience is the reality of a whole
people.[14]

Rigoberta Menchú was and is an activist on behalf of her community,
the Quiché-speaking Indians of the western highlands of Guatemala,
and so this statement of principles is perhaps a little more explicit
than is usual in a *testimonio*. But the metonymic function of the
narrative voice it declares is latent in the form, is part of its narrative
convention, even in those cases when the narrator is, for example, a
drug addict or criminal. *Testimonio* is a fundamentally democratic and
egalitarian form of narrative in the sense that it implies that any life
so narrated can have a kind of representational value. Each individual
testimonio evokes an absent polyphony of other voices, other possible
lives and experiences. Thus, one common formal variation on the
classic first-person singular *testimonio* is the polyphonic *testimonio,*
made up of accounts by different participants in the same event.

What *testimonio* does have in common with the picaresque and
with autobiography, however, is the powerful textual affirmation of
the speaking subject. This should be evident in the passage from *I,
Rigoberta Menchú* quoted above. The dominant formal aspect of the
testimonio is the voice that speaks to the reader in the form of an "I"
that demands to be recognized, that wants or needs to stake a claim
on our attention. This presence of the voice, which we are meant to
experience as the voice of a real rather than a fictional person, is the
mark of a desire not to be silenced or defeated, a desire to impose
oneself on an institution of power, such as literature, from the position
of the excluded or the marginal. Jameson has spoken of the way in
which *testimonio* produces a "new anonymity," a form of selfhood
distinct from the "overripe subjectivity" of the modernist *Bildungsroman.*[15] But this way of thinking about *testimonio* runs the risk of
conceding to the subjects of *testimonio* only the "facelessness" that
is already theirs in the dominant culture. One should note rather the
insistence on and affirmation of the individual subject evident in such
titles as *I, Rigoberta Menchú* (even more strongly in the Spanish—*Me
llamo Rigoberta Menchú y así, me nació la conciencia), Juan the
Chamula (Juan Peréz Jolote), Let Me Speak! Testimony of Domitila,
a Woman of the Bolivian Mines (Si me permiten hablar), Doris Tijerino: Inside the Nicaraguan Revolution ("Somos millones . . .": La*

vida de Doris María).[16] Rather than a "decentered" subjectivity, which, in the current Koreanization of the world economy, is almost synonymous with cheap labor, *testimonio* constitutes an affirmation of the individual self in a collective mode.[17]

In a related way, *testimonio* implies a challenge to the loss of the authority of orality in the context of processes of cultural modernization that privilege literacy and literature as norms of expression. It allows the entry into literature of persons who would normally, in those societies where literature is a form of class privilege, be excluded from direct literary expression, persons who have had to be "represented" by professional writers. There is a great difference between having someone like Rigoberta Menchú tell the story of her people and having that story told, however well, by someone like, say, the Nobel Prize-winning Guatemalan novelist Miguel Angel Asturias.[18]

Testimonio involves a sort of erasure of the function, and thus also of the textual presence, of the "author," which by contrast is so central in all major forms of bourgeois writing since the Renaissance, so much so that our very notions of literature and the literary are bound up with notions of the author, or, at least, of an authorial intention. In Miguel Barnet's phrase, the author has been replaced in *testimonio* by the function of a "compiler" (*compilador*) or "activator" (*gestante*), somewhat on the model of the film producer.[19] There seems implicit in this situation both a challenge and an alternative to the patriarchal and elitist function the author plays in class and sexually and racially divided societies: in particular, a relief from the figure of the "great writer" or writer as cultural hero that is so much a part of the ideology of literary modernism.

The erasure of authorial presence in the *testimonio*, together with its nonfictional character, makes possible a different kind of complicity—might we call it fraternal/sororal?—between narrator and reader than is possible in the novel, which, as Lukács has demonstrated, obligates an ironic distancing on the part of both novelist and reader from the fate of the protagonist. Eliana Rivero, writing about *La montaña es algo más que una inmensa estepa verde*, a *testimonio* by the Sandinista guerrilla comandante Omar Cabezas (published in English as *Fire from the Mountain*),[20] notes that "the act of speaking faithfully recorded on the tape, transcribed and then 'written' remains in the *testimonio* punctuated by a repeated series of interlocutive and conversational markers . . . which constantly put the reader on alert: 'True? Are you following me? OK? So . . .'" She concludes that the *testimonio* is a "snail-like discourse (*discurso encaracolado*) which turns on itself and which in the process totally deautomatizes the reaction of the reader, whose complicity it invites through the medium of his or her counterpart in the text, the direct interlocutor."[21]

Just as *testimonio* implies a new kind of relation between narrator and reader, the contradictions of sex, class, race, and age that frame the narrative's production can also reproduce themselves in the relation of the narrator to this direct interlocutor. This is especially so when, as in *I, Rigoberta Menchú,* the narrator is someone who requires an interlocutor with a different ethnic and class background in order first to elicit the oral account, then to give it textual form as a *testimonio,* and finally to see to its publication and distribution. (In cases where *testimonios* are more directly a part of political or social activism—for example, in the use of *testimonio* in liberation theology-based community dialogues or as a kind of cadre literature internal to leftist or nationalist groups—these editorial functions are often handled directly by the party or movement in question, constituting then not only a new literary form but also new, noncommodified forms of literary production and distribution.)

I do not want to minimize the nature of these contradictions; among other things, they represent the possibility for a depoliticized articulation of the *testimonio* as a sort of *costumbrismo* of the subaltern or for the smothering of a genuine popular voice by well-intentioned but repressive (Stalinist, feminist, humanist, and so on) notions of political "correctness" or pertinence. But there is another way of looking at them. It is a truism that successful revolutionary movements in the colonial and postcolonial world have generally involved a union of working-class—or, to use the more inclusive term, popular—forces with a radicalized intelligentsia, drawn partly from formally educated sections of the peasantry and working class but also from the petty bourgeoisie and déclassé bourgeois or oligarchic strata that have become imbued with socialist ideas, organizational forms, culture, and so on. (Lenin was among the first to theorize this phenomenon in *What Is to Be Done?*) In this context, the relation of narrator and compiler in the production of a *testimonio* can function as an ideological figure or *ideologeme* for the possibility of union of a radicalized intelligentsia and the poor and working classes of a country. To put this another way, *testimonio* gives voice in literature to a previously "voiceless," anonymous, collective popular-democratic subject, the *pueblo* or "people," but in such a way that the intellectual or professional, usually of bourgeois or petty bourgeois background, is interpellated as being part of, and dependent on, the "people" without at the same time losing his or her identity as an intellectual. In other words, *testimonio* is not a form of liberal guilt. It suggests as an appropriate ethical and political response more the possibility of solidarity than of charity.[22]

The audience for *testimonio,* either in the immediate national or local context or in metropolitan cultural centers, remains largely that reading public that in presocialist societies is still a partially gender- and class-limited social formation, even in the "advanced" capitalist democracies. The complicity a *testimonio* establishes with its readers involves their identification—by engaging their sense of ethics and justice—with a popular cause normally distant, not to say alien, from their immediate experience. *Testimonio* in this sense has been important in maintaining and developing the practice of international human rights and solidarity movements. It is also a way of putting on the agenda, within a given country, problems of poverty and oppression, for example, in rural areas that are not normally visible in the dominant forms of representation.

The compiler of Rigoberta Menchú's *testimonio,* Elisabeth Burgos-Debray, was a Venezuelan social scientist living in Paris at the time she met Menchú, with all that implies about contradictions between metropolis and periphery, high culture and low culture, dominant and emergent social formations, dominant and subaltern languages. Her account of the relationship she developed with Rigoberta Menchú in the course of doing the *testimonio* forms the preface to the book, constituting a sort of *testimonio* about the production of a *testimonio.* One of the problems the two women encountered is that Menchú had to speak to Burgos-Debray in Spanish, the language for her of the *ladinos* or mestizos who oppressed her people, which she had just and very imperfectly learned (the conflict in Guatemala between Spanish and indigenous languages is in fact one of the themes of her narrative). In preparing the text, Burgos-Debray had to decide then what to correct and what not to correct in Menchú's recorded speech. She left in, for example, repetitions and digressions that she considered characteristic of oral narrative. On the other hand, she notes that she decided "to correct the gender mistakes which inevitably occur when someone has just learned to speak a foreign language. It would have been artificial to leave them uncorrected and it would have made Rigoberta look 'picturesque,' which is the last thing I wanted."[23]

One could speak here, in a way familiar from the dialectic of master and slave or colonizer and colonized, of the interlocutor manipulating or exploiting the material the informant provides to suit her own cosmopolitan political, intellectual, and aesthetic predilections. K. Millet makes the following argument, for example, about the *testimonio* of an indigenous woman, *Los sueños de Lucinda Nahuelhual,* compiled by the Chilean feminist activist Sonia Montecino Aguirre:

> *Los sueños de Lucinda Nahuelhual* is not a narrative about a Mapuche Indian woman, but rather it is a textualizing of Ms. Sonia Montecino Aguirre and her political sympathies. From the moment of the narrative's inception, the figure of "the other," Lucinda Nahuelhual, is only that, a figure, an empty signifier, a narration constructed on the significance of Ms. Aguirre's own political agenda. . . . the idea of "elevating" the Mapuche woman, Lucinda, to the status of a signifier of an urban feminist movement where power is maintained primarily within the hands of "enlightened" women from the hegemony requires that the indigenous woman accept a position of loss in order to signify meaning to her audience of "sisters."[24]

Because I have not read *Los sueños,* I cannot comment on the specifics of Millet's critique. But although it is true that there are possibilities of distortion and misrepresentation involved in *testimonio,* the argument here seems to reject the possibility of any textual representation of an "other" as such (all signifiers are "empty" unless and until they signify something for somebody) in favor of something like a (liberal?) notion of the irreducible particularity of the individual. In a situation such as that of Chile today, politically the question would seem not so much one of the *differences* in the social situations of the direct narrator and the interlocutor, but rather one of the possibility of their articulation together in a common program or front that *at the same time* would advance women's rights and the rights of the indigenous groups, without subordinating one to the other.

In the creation of the testimonial text, control of representation does not flow only one way, as Millet's argument implies: someone like Rigoberta Menchú is also in a sense exploiting her interlocutor in order to have her story reach and influence an international audience, something that as an activist for her community she sees in quite utilitarian terms as a political task. Moreover, editorial power does not belong to the compiler alone. Menchú, worrying, correctly, that there are some ways in which her account could be used against her or her people (for example, by academic specialists advising counterinsurgency programs such as the CIA set up in Guatemala), notes that there are certain things—her Nahuatl name, for example—she will not speak of: "I'm still keeping my Indian identity a secret. I'm still keeping secret what I think no-one should know. Not even anthropologists or intellectuals, no matter how many books they have, can find out all our secrets."[25] Although Burgos-Debray does the final selection and shaping of the text, the individual narrative units are wholly composed by Menchú and, as such, depend on her skills and intentionality as a narrator. An example of this may be found in the excruciating detail she uses (in chapters 24 and 27) to describe the torture and murder of her mother and brother by the Guatemalan army, detail that gives the episodes a hallucinatory and symbolic intensity different from the matter-of-fact narration one expects from *testimonio*. One could say this is a kind of testimonial expressionism, or "magic realism."

Perhaps something like Mao's notion of "contradictions among the people" (as opposed to contradictions between "the people" as a whole and imperialism, as in the case of the war against Japanese occupation) expresses the nature of the narrator/compiler/reader relations in the *testimonio*, in the sense that there are deep and inescapable contradictions involved in these relations, contradictions that can be resolved only on the level of general structural change both on national and global levels. But there is also a sense of sisterhood and mutuality in the struggle against a common system of oppression. *Testimonio* is not, in other words, a reenactment of the anthropological function of the colonial or subaltern "native informant," about which Spivak, among others, has written. Hence, although one of the sources and models of the *testimonio* is undoubtedly the ethnographic "life history," it is not reducible to that category (nor, as noted above, to oral history).[26]

One fact that is evident in the passage from *I, Rigoberta Menchú* under discussion is that the presence of a "real" popular voice in the *testimonio* is in part at least an illusion. Obviously, we are dealing here, as in any discursive medium, with an effect that has been produced, in the case of a *testimonio* by both the direct narrator—using devices of an oral storytelling tradition—and the compiler, who, according to norms of literary form and expression, makes a text out of the material. Although it is easy to deconstruct this illusion, it is also necessary to insist on its presence to understand the *testimonio*'s peculiar aesthetic-ideological power. Elzbieta Sklodowska, developing a point about the textual nature of *testimonio* that can be connected with the argument made above by Millet, cautions that

> it would be naive to assume a direct homology between text and history. The discourse of a witness cannot be a reflection of his or her experience, but rather a refraction determined by the vicissitudes of memory, intention, ideology. The intention and the ideology of the author-editor further superimposes the original text, creating more ambiguities, silences, and absences

in the process of selecting and editing the material in a way consonant with norms of literary form. Thus, although the *testimonio* uses a series of devices to gain a sense of veracity and authenticity—among them the point of view of the first-person witness-narrator—the play between fiction and history reappears inexorably as a problem.[27]

What is at stake, however, is the particular nature of the "reality effect" of the *testimonio,* not simply the difference between (any) text and reality. What is important about *testimonio* is that it produces if not the real then certainly a sensation of *experiencing the real* that has determinate effects on the reader that are different from those produced by even the most realist or "documentary" fiction. "More than an interpretation of reality," notes Jara in a useful corrective to Sklodowska's point, the *testimonio* is "a trace of the real, of that history which, as such, is inexpressible."[28]

Sklodowska is right about the interplay between real and imaginary in *testimonio.* But to subsume *testimonio* under the category of literary fictionality is to deprive it of its power to engage the reader in the ways I have indicated here, to make of it simply another form of literature, as good as, but certainly no better than and not basically different from, what is already the case. This seems to me a formalist and, at least in effect, a politically liberal response to *testimonio,* which tolerates or encourages its incorporation into the academically sanctioned field of literature at the expense of its moral and political urgency.[29] What has to be understood, however, is precisely how *testimonio* puts into question the existing institution of literature as an ideological apparatus of alienation and domination at the same time that it constitutes itself as a new form of literature.

Having said this much, however, I now need to distinguish *testimonio* from (1) that central form of nonfictional first-person narrative that is autobiography and cognate forms of personal narrative, such as memoirs, diaries, confessions, and reminiscences; and (2) Barbara Foley's articulation of the category of "documentary fiction" in *Telling the Truth.*[30] I will consider autobiography first, with the proviso that some of the forms of "documentary fiction" Foley considers are autobiographical or pseudoautobiographical. The dividing line is not always exact, but the following might represent the general case. Even in nineteenth-century memoirs of women or ex-slaves (that is, texts in which the narrator writes clearly from a position of subalternity), there is often implicit an ideology of individualism in the very convention of the autobiographical form, an ideology built on the notion of a coherent, self-evident, self-conscious, commanding subject who appropriates literature precisely as a means of "self-expression" and who in turn constructs textually for the reader the liberal imaginary of a unique, "free," autonomous ego as the natural form of being and public achievement. By contrast, as I have suggested, in *testimonio* the narrative "I" has the status of what linguists call a shifter—a linguistic function that can be assumed indiscriminately by anyone. Recalling Rigoberta Menchú's narrative proposition, the meaning of her *testimonio* lies not in its uniqueness but in its ability to stand for the experience of her community as a whole. Because the authorial function has been erased or mitigated, the relationship between authorship and forms of individual and hierarchical power in bourgeois society has also changed. *Testimonio* represents an affirmation of the individual subject, even of individual growth and transformation, but in connection with a group or class situation marked by marginalization, oppression, and struggle. If it loses this connection, it ceases to be *testimonio* and becomes autobiography, that is, an account of, and also a means of access to, middle- or upper-class status, a sort of documentary *Bildungsroman*. If Rigoberta Menchú had become a "writer" instead of remaining as she has a member of, and an activist for, her ethnic community, her narration would have been an autobiography. By contrast, even where the subject is a person "of the left," as, for example, in Agnes Smedley's *Daughter of the Earth,* Leon Trotsky's *My Life,* or Pablo Neruda's *Memoirs,* autobiography and autobiographical novel are essentially conservative modes in the sense that they imply that individual triumph over circumstances is possible in spite of "obstacles." Autobiography produces in the reader—who, generally speaking, is already either middle- or upper-class or expecting to be a part of those classes—the specular effect of confirming and authorizing his or (less so) her situation of relative social privilege. *Testimonio,* by contrast, even in the case of *testimonio* from the political right, such as Armando Valladares's prison memoir, *Against All Hope* or Solzhenitsyn's *Gulag,* always signifies the need for a general social change in which the stability of the reader's world must be brought into question.[31]

As such, *testimonio* offers one kind of answer to the problem of women's access to literature. Sidonie Smith has argued that every woman who writes finally interrogates the ideology of gender that lies behind the engendering of self in forms such as the novel or autobiography.[32] She alludes to the notion that the institution of literature itself is phallocentric. On the other hand, repressing the desire for power in order to avoid complicity with domination is a form of female self-effacement sanctioned by the patriarchy. How do we find forms of expression that break out of this double bind? Many of the best-known *testimonios* are in the voices of women, yet, because of the narrative situation I have identified, *testimonio* does not produce textually an essentialized "woman's experience." It is a (self-conscious) instance of what Spivak has advocated as "tactical essentialism" in feminist political practice.[33]

I am generally sympathetic with the project Barbara Foley has staked out in *Telling the Truth*. In particular, her deconstruction of what she calls "the fact/fiction distinction" and her emphasis on the inevitable historicity of literary categories are useful for conceptualizing some aspects of the *testimonio,* including its peculiar truth-claim on the reader. What Foley is not doing in *Telling the Truth,* however, is producing an account of testimonial narrative as such. Although some of the texts she discusses in her chapter on African American narrative are *testimonios* in the sense outlined here, Foley herself prefers to deal with them through the somewhat different category of the documentary novel. But this is to make of *testimonio* one of the mutations the novel has undergone in the course of its (European) evolution from the Renaissance on, whereas I have wanted to suggest here that it implies a radical break (as in the structuralist notion of *coupure*) with the novel and with literary fictionality as such. In other words, *the testimonio is not a form of the novel.* It cannot be adequately theorized, therefore, by the sort of argument Foley develops, which is, nonetheless, very useful for understanding certain forms of fiction and fictionalized autobiography that depend on the semiotic intensification of a reality effect.[34]

If the novel is a closed and private form in the sense that both the story and the subject end with the end of the text, defining that auto-referential self-sufficiency that is the basis of formalist reading practices, the *testimonio* exhibits by contrast what Jara calls a "public intimacy" (*intimidad pública*) in which the boundary between public and private spheres of life essential in all forms of bourgeois culture and law is transgressed.[35] The narrator in *testimonio* is a real person who continues living and acting in a real social history that also continues. *Testimonio* can never in this sense create the illusion of that textual in-itselfness that has been the basis of literary formalism, nor can it be adequately analyzed in these terms. It is, to use Umberto Eco's slogan, an "open work" that implies the importance and power of literature as a form of social action but also its radical insufficiency.

In principle, *testimonio* appears therefore as an extraliterary or even antiliterary form of discourse. That, paradoxically, is precisely the basis of both its aesthetic and political appeal. As Foley suggests, in literary history the intensification of a narrative or representational reality effect is generally associated with the contestation of the dominant system and its forms of cultural idealization and legitimation. This was certainly the case of the picaresque novel and *Don Quixote* in relation to the novels of chivalry in the Spanish Renaissance. What happens, however, when something like *testimonio* is appropriated by "litera- ture"? Does this involve a neutralization of *testimonio's* peculiar aes- thetic effect, which depends, as we have seen, precisely on its status outside accepted literary forms and norms? In relation to these ques- tions and the discussion of Foley above, I need finally to distinguish *testimonio* from testimonial novel. Miguel Barnet calls his *Autobiog- raphy of a Runaway Slave* a "testimonial novel" (*novela testimonio*), even though the story is nonfictional.[36] In so doing, he emphasizes how the material of an ethnographic "life history" can be made into a literary form. But I would rather reserve the term *testimonial novel* (or Capote's "nonfiction novel") for those narrative texts in which an "author" in the conventional sense has either invented a *testimonio*like story or, as in the case of *In Cold Blood* or *Woman at Point Zero* (or Barnet's own later work, *Canción de Rachel*), extensively reworked, with explicitly literary goals (greater figurative density, tighter narrative form, elimination of digressions and interruptions, and so on), a testimonial account that is no longer present except in its simulacrum. If the picaresque novel was the pseudoautobiography of the lower-class individual (thus inverting a "learned" humanist form into a pseudopopular one), we might observe in recent literature (1) novels that are in fact pseudo*testimonios,* inverting a form that grows out of subaltern experience into one that is middle-brow (an example might be the Mexican novel *Las aventuras, desaventuras, y sueños de Adonis García: El vampiro de la Colonia Roma,* by Luis Zapata, which purports to be the *testimonio* of a homosexual pros- titute); (2) a growing concern on the part of contemporary novelists to produce something like a testimonial "voice" in their fiction, with variable political intentions (for example, Mario Vargas Llosa's *The Story of Mayta* on the right, Manlio Argueta's *One Day of Life* on the left); and (3) a series of ambiguous forms located between the novel and *testimonio* as such; examples include *Woman at Point Zero* and the very intriguing novel/memoir of the Cultural Revolution, Yang Jiang's *A Cadre School Life,* which is a *testimonio* rendered in the mold of a narrative genre of classical Chinese literature.

But if the *testimonio* comes into being necessarily at the margin of the historically given institution of literature, it is also clear that it is becoming a new postfictional form of literature, with significant cultural and political repercussions. To return to our starting point: if the novel had a special relationship with humanism and the rise of the European bourgeoisie, *testimonio* is by contrast a new form of narrative literature in which we can at the same time witness and be a part of the emerging culture of an international proletarian/popular-democratic subject in its period of ascendancy. But it would be in the spirit of *testimonio* itself to end on a more skeptical note: literature, even where it is infused with a popular-democratic form and content, as in the case of *testimonio,* is not itself a popular-democratic cultural form, and (*pace* Gramsci) it is an open question as to whether it can ever be. How much of a favor do we do *testimonio* by positing, as here, that it has become a new form of literature or by making it an alternative reading to the canon (one track of the Stanford Western culture requirement now includes *I, Rigoberta Menchú*)? Perhaps such moves preempt or occlude a vision of an emergent popular-democratic culture that is no longer based on the institutions of humanism and literature.

Postscript

I want to take up briefly the question of the relation of, to use Caren Kaplan's phrase, "out-law genres" such as *testimonio* to the sort of authority represented by this collection itself or by the inclusion noted above of *I, Rigoberta Menchú* in the Stanford undergraduate humanities curriculum, which itself has become a central issue in the current debates about "political correctness" and "multiculturalism" in the university.[37] Autobiography is a literary construct. I make the case in this essay that *testimonio* is a "politically correct" alternative to autobiography in that, among other things, as (usually) a textual representation of actual speech, it implies a challenge to the loss of the authority of orality in the context of processes of cultural modernization that privilege literacy and literature as norms of expression. What is phallic—in the Lacanian sense—about the institution of literature, it seems to me, is the need for it to be engendered by an authorizing signifier of inscription (which gives "permission to write"). If this is true, then nothing much in the way of decolonization is accomplished by shifting that signifier to the clitoris or vagina, women's experience, the anima, or whatever: there is no *écriture féminine* (though there is certainly women's writing).

The persistence of orality (in women's culture, in the culture of colonized and/or proletarianized subjects) might be seen in these terms as a form of conscious and active resistance to writing and literacy, not just as an effect of ethnic or gender discrimination, poverty, or underdevelopment. *I, Rigoberta Menchú* begins with a strategic disavowal of both literature and the liberal concept of the authority of private experience ("My name is Rigoberta Menchú. I'm 23 years old. This is my testimony. I didn't learn it from a book, and I didn't learn it alone."), and several passages in the narrative explicitly counterpose book learning to direct experience, or attack the presence in the Indian communities of undoubtedly well-intentioned school-teachers, arguing that they represent an agency of forced acculturation by the landowners and the Guatemalan state. For example:

> When children reach ten years old [in our village], that's the moment when their parents and the village leaders talk to them again. . . . It's also when they remind them that our ancestors were dishonored by the White Man, by colonization. But they don't tell them the way it's written down in books, because the majority of Indians can't read or write, and don't even know that they have their own texts. No, they learn it through oral recommendations, the way it has been handed down through the generations.[38]

> I had a lot of ideas but I knew I couldn't express them all. I wanted to read or write Spanish. I told my father this, that I wanted to learn to read. Perhaps things were different if you could learn to read. My father said, "Who will teach you? You have to find out by yourself, because I can't help you. I know of no schools and I have no money for them anyway." I told him that if he talked to the priests, perhaps they'd give me a scholarship. But my father said he didn't agree with that idea because I was trying to leave the community, to go far away, and find out what was best for me. He said: "You'll forget about our common heritage." . . . My father was very suspicious of schools and all that sort of thing. He gave as an example the fact that many of my cousins had learned to read and write but they hadn't been of use to the community. They try to move away and feel different when they can read and write.[39]

> When teachers come into the villages, they bring with them the ideas of capitalism and getting on in life. They try and impose these ideas on us. I remember that in my village there were two teachers for a while and they began teaching the people, but the children told their parents everything they were being taught at school and the parents said: 'We don't want our children to become like *ladinos* [in Guatemala a

Spanish-speaking white or mestizo]." And they made the teachers leave. . . . For the Indian, it is better not to study than to
become like *ladinos.*[40]

The cultural genealogy of Menchú's position involves in part the
Spanish practice during the conquest of segregating the children of
the Indian aristocracy from their families in order to teach them both
the Spanish language and Christian doctrine. Walter Mignolo has
observed of this practice that it

> shows that literacy is not instilled without violence. The vio-
> lence, however, is not located in the fact that the youngsters
> have been assembled and enclosed day and night. It comes,
> rather, from the interdiction of having conversations with their
> parents, particularly with their mothers. In a primary oral
> society, in which virtually all knowledge is transmitted by
> means of conversation, the preservation of oral contact was
> contradictory with the effort to teach how to read and write.
> Forbidding conversations with the mother meant, basically,
> depriving the children of the living culture imbedded in the
> language and preserved and transmitted in speech.[41]

But it is not that Menchú does not value literacy or formal education
at all, or that she romanticizes orality as an essential expression of her
own subalternity as both a woman ("conversations with the mother")
and an Indian (just as I don't mean to romanticize *testimonio* here as
the essential literary form of the subaltern). Part of the oedipal struggle
with her parents recounted in her story involves her desire and eventual success as a teenager to first memorize and then learn to read
passages from the Bible in order to become a Catholic lay catechist—
an experience that obviously inflects her own practice as a narrator
in producing her *testimonio* (which also required her to learn
Spanish).[42]

It is rather, as these passages suggest, that she does not accept
literacy and book learning, or the narrative of cultural and linguistic
modernization they entail, as adequate or *normative* cultural modes.
She is conscious, among other things, of the holistic relation between
the individualization produced by the curriculum and disciplinary
practices of the government schools and the attempts to impose on
her community an agrarian reform based on private ownership of
parcels (as opposed to its own tradition of communal ownership and
sharing of resources). That is why she remains a testimonial narrator
rather than becoming an "author"—a subject position that in fact
would, as in Richard Rodriguez's *Hunger of Memory,* imply a self-

imposed separation from her community and culture of birth (and a loss or change of name and identity). As Doris Sommer has shown, even in the act of addressing us through the literary artifice of the *testimonio*—which is built on the convention of truth telling and openness—Menchú is also consciously withholding information from her metropolitan readers, on the grounds that it could be used against her and her people by academically trained or advised counterinsurgency specialists.[43] She is aware, in other words, of something we may have forgotten since the Vietnam War: the complicity of the university in cultural (and sometimes actual) genocide.

I suggested above that Menchú's descriptions of the torture and murder of her brother and mother by the Guatemalan army represented a sort of testimonial "magic realism" because of their intensity of detail and affect. I have been criticized on this point for seeming, from the privileged position of the First World literary intellectual, to aestheticize something that more properly should be dealt with as an ethical, legal, and political matter.[44] But I'm not sure that these two things—how Menchú works as a narrator and the implications for solidarity practice of the reception of her narrative—can be separated. As noted, Menchú does not construct her narrative only from an oral, "non-Western" model of story telling, but also from her experience as a lay catechist (which involves the "Book of books" of Western culture, so to speak). It is the function of a lay catechist to dramatize and allegorize the biblical stories she narrates in order to provoke discussion among the congregation about their contemporary relevance. To recall the Aristotelian distinction of history and poetry, *I, Rigoberta Menchú* is not only a *history* in the sense of a chronology of particulars; it also aspires to be *exemplary* in its specificity ("My story is the story of all poor Guatemalans. My personal experience is the reality of a whole people."). Yet against the traditional dichotomy of logos and body, universal and particular, something of the experience of the body itself inheres in *testimonio*. In her harrowing descriptions of torture and brutality, Menchú is trying to enact for the reader the force of the genocidal violence that destroyed not only members of her immediate family, but also whole communities of her people. By the same token, Menchú's evocation of Mayan community life and traditions, which some anthropologists have found idealized and unrepresentative of the real conditions of life and consciousness of contemporary Guatemalan Indians,[45] must be seen, like any ideological project, as in part realistic, in part heuristic or utopian. Her *testimonio* represents an "ascribed" or possible consciousness, which seeks to interpellate around the communal values that it celebrates a broad movement of Indian and peasant resistance and an international solidarity network to support it.

It would be yet another version of the "native informant" of classical anthropology to grant testimonial narrators such as Rigoberta Menchú only the possibility of being "witnesses" (for the prosecution or the defense), and not that of constructing narratives with their own epic or historical authority. That would be a way of saying that the subaltern can of course speak, but only through the institutionally sanctioned authority—itself dependent on and implicated in colonialism and imperialism—of the journalist or ethnographer, who alone has the power to decide what counts in the narrator's "raw material" and to turn it into literature (or "evidence"). The opposition of the four different modes of narration that make up the text of Richard Price's reconstruction of the social history of the Dutch slave colony of Suriname in the eighteenth century, *Alabi's World*—oral-historical *testimonios* of runaway slaves, administrative reports by colonial authorities, diaries of missionaries, and the historian's own "mediating" discourse—also enacts the different forms of racial and class conflict in that society and our own, and in turn their respective forms of cultural legitimation and agency.[46] *Testimonios* such as *I, Rigoberta Menchú* are not only *representations* of new forms of subaltern resistance and struggle but also models and even *means* for these. In the context of the Western academy they are almost literally "foreign agents"—which is perhaps why *I, Rigoberta Menchú* has become a central focus for the neoconservative assault on multicultural education.

We could say that Menchú uses the *testimonio* as a kind of literary autobiography without subscribing to a humanist ideology of the literary. This may be one way of answering Gayatri Spivak's question in "Can the Subaltern Speak?"—no, not as such (because "the subaltern is the name of the place which is so displaced . . . that to have it speak is like Godot arriving on a bus").[47] But the testimonial narrator, like Rigoberta Menchú, is not the subaltern as such either, rather, she is something more like an "organic intellectual" of the subaltern who speaks to the hegemony by means of a metonymy of self in the name and in the place of it. *Testimonio* is located at the intersection of the cultural forms of bourgeois humanism, such as literature and the printed book, engendered by the academy and spread by colonialism and imperialism, and subaltern cultural practices. It is not an authentic expression of the subaltern (whatever that might be), but it is not (or should not be) easily assimilable to, or retrievable and teachable as, literature/autobiography, either.

Notes

An earlier version of this article appeared in Spanish as "Anatomía del testimonio," *Revista de crítica literaria latinoamericana* (Lima, Peru) 25 (1987): 7–16; it also appeared as a chapter in my book, *Del Lazarillo al Sandinismo: Estudios sobre la función ideologica de la literatura española e hispanoamericana* (Minneapolis: Institute for the Study of Ideologies and Literature, 1987). An English version appeared in *Modern Fiction Studies* 35 (Spring 1989): 11–28. My thanks to Gayatri Spivak for the lesson of her example.

1. Roberto Fernández Retamar, *"Caliban" and Other Essays,* trans. Edward Baker (Minneapolis: University of Minnesota Press, 1989).

2. See Gayatri Chakravorty Spivak, *In Other Worlds* (New York: Methuen, 1987); Fredric Jameson, "Third World Literature in the Era of Multinational Capitalism," *Social Text* 15 (1986): 65–88; Ahmed Aijaz, "Jameson's Rhetoric of Otherness and the 'National Allegory,'" *Social Text* 17 (1987): 3–27; and Jameson's rejoinder to Aijaz in the same issue of *Social Text.*

3. Raymond Williams, "The Writer: Commitment and Alignment," *Marxism Today* 24 (June 1980): 25.

4. I will touch on Barbara Foley's work later. *Testimonio* is difficult to classify according to standard bibliographic categories. To what section of a library or a bookstore does a *testimonio* belong? Under whose name is a *testimonio* to be listed in a card catalog or data base? How should it be reviewed, as fiction or nonfiction?

5. Barbara Harlow, *Resistance Literature* (New York: Methuen, 1987). Harlow is more attentive than Spivak or Jameson to the ways in which the social transformations produced by liberation struggles also transform or problematize the institution and existing forms of narrative literature itself.

6. The definition of *testimonio* in the rules of the Casa de las Américas contest is as follows: "Testimonies must document some aspect of Latin American or Caribbean reality from a direct source. A direct source is understood as knowledge of the facts by the author or his or her compilation of narratives or evidence obtained from the individuals involved or qualified witnesses. In both cases reliable documentation, written or graphic, is indispensable. The form is at the author's discretion, but literary quality is also indispensable." On the Latin American reception of *In Cold Blood,* see Ariel Dorfman, "La última novela de Capote: ¿Un nuevo género literario?" *Anales de la Universidad de Chile* 124 (1966): 97–117.

7. Pozas and Lewis were actually reviving a form that had been initiated in the 1930s by University of Chicago anthropologists and had then fallen into disuse during the period of academic McCarthyism during the Cold War.

8. Thus there are Palestinian, Angolan, Vietnamese, Irish, Brazilian, South African, Argentinian, Nicaraguan, and other such testimonial literatures. On guerrilla *testimonio,* see Harlow, *Resistance Literature;* Juan Duchesne, "Las narraciones guerrilleras: configuración de un sujeto épico de nuevo tipo," in *Testimonio y literatura,* ed. René Jara and Hernán Vidal (Minneapolis: Institute for the Study of Ideologies and Literature, 1986), 137–85.

9. One of the most important protagonists of the *testimonio* has been the North American socialist-feminist poet Margaret Randall, who played a major role in developing the form in Cuba in the 1970s and then in Nicaragua after 1979, where she conducted a series of workshops to train people to collect their own experience and begin building a popular history written by themselves. She is the author of a handbook on how to make a *testimonio: Testimonios: A Guide to Oral History* (Toronto: Participatory Research Group, 1985). Her own testimonial work available in English includes *Cuban*

Women Now (Toronto: Women's Press, 1974) *Doris Tijerino: Inside the Nicaraguan Revolution* (Vancouver: New Star, 1978), *Sandino's Daughters* (Vancouver: New Star, 1981), *Christians in the Nicaraguan Revolution* (Vancouver: New Star, 1983), *Risking a Somersault in the Air: Conversations with Nicaraguan Writers* (San Francisco: Solidarity, 1985), and *Women Brave in the Face of Danger* (Trumansberg, N.Y.: Crossing, 1987).

10. The reception of *testimonio* thus has something to do with a revulsion for fiction and the fictive as such, with its "postmodern" estrangement.

11. Georg Lukács, *The Theory of the Novel,* trans. Anna Bostock (Cambridge: MIT Press, 1971).

12. Hans Robert Jauss, "Ursprung und Bedeutung der Ichform im *Lazarillo de Tormes,*" *Romanische Jahrbuch* 10 (1959): 297–300.

13. René Jara, "Prólogo," in *Testimonio y Literatura,* ed. René Jara and Hernán Vidal (Minneapolis: Institute for the Study of Ideologies and Literature, 1986), 2.

14. Rigoberta Menchú, with Elisabeth Burgos-Debray, *I, Rigoberta Menchú: An Indian Woman in Guatemala,* trans. Ann White (London: Verso, 1984), 1.

15. See his idea of a postbourgeois "*collective subject,* decentered but not schizophrenic . . . which emerges in certain forms of storytelling that can be found in the third-world literature, in testimonial literature, in gossip and rumors, and in things of this kind. It is storytelling that is neither personal in the modernist sense, nor depersonalized in the pathological sense of the schizophrenic text." Quoted in Anders Stephanson, "Regarding Postmodernism: A Conversation with Fredric Jameson," *Social Text* 17 (1987): 45.

16. Ricardo Pozas, *Juan the Chamula: An Ethnological Recreation of the Life of a Mexican Indian,* trans. Lysander Kemp (Berkeley: University of California Press, 1962); Domitila B. De Chungara and Moema Viezzer, *Let Me Speak! Testimony of Domitila, a Woman of the Bolivian Mines,* trans. Victoria Ortiz (New York: Monthly Review Press, 1979); Randall, *Doris Tijerino.*

17. The most dramatic instance of this affirmation of the self that I know of occurs in the Egyptian testimonial novel written by Nawal al-Saadawi, *Woman at Point Zero,* trans. Sherif Hatata (London: Zed, 1983). The narrator is Firdaus, a young prostitute who is about to be executed for murdering her pimp. Her interlocutor is the Egyptian feminist writer Nawal al-Saadawi, who was at the time working in the prison as a psychiatrist. Firdaus begins by addressing this person, who represents, albeit in benevolent form, the repressive power of both the state and the institution of literature, as follows: "Let me speak! Do not interrupt me! I have no time to listen to you. They are coming to take me at six o'clock this evening" (p. 11). Barbara Harlow notes that al-Saadawi was herself imprisoned by the Sadat regime for feminist activities some years later and wrote an account of her experience in *Memoirs from the Women's Prison. Resistance Literature,* 139–40.

18. A kind of anti*testimonio,* for example, is Richard Rodriguez's *Hunger of Memory* (Boston: D. R. Godine, 1981), which is precisely a *Bildungsroman* of the access to English-language literacy—and thence to middle-class status—by a Chicano from a working-class background. Because one of its themes is opposition to official bilingualism, it has become a popular text for neoconservative initiatives in education. Paradoxically, it is also used frequently in English writing classes by persons who would otherwise probably not identify with neoconservatism to indoctrinate students into the ideology of "good writing."

19. See Miguel Barnet, "La novela-testimonio: Socioliteratura," in *La fuente viva* (Havana: Editorial Letras Cubanas, 1983), 12–42.

20. Omar Cabezas, *Fire from the Mountain,* trans. Kathleen Weaver (New York: Crown, 1985).

21. Eliana Rivero, "Testimonios y conversaciones como discurso literario: Cuba y Nicaragua," in *Literature and Contemporary Revolutionary Culture,* ed. Hernán Vidal (Minneapolis: Society for the Study of Contemporary Hispanic and Lusophone Revolutionary Literatures, 1984–85), 218–28. Cabezas recorded himself and edited the transcript, acting as his own interlocutor.

22. *Testimonio* in this sense is uniquely situated to represent the components of what Sandinista theoreticians Roger Burbach and Orlando Nuñez have called the "Third Force" in their potential linkage with working-class issues and movements: that is, middle-class intellectuals and sections of the petty bourgeoisie; marginalized social sectors; and what have come to be known as "new social movements" (religious *comunidades de base,* feminist groups, ecology organizations, human rights groups, and so on). *Fire in the Americas: Forging a Revolutionary Agenda* (London: Verso, 1987).

23. Menchú, *I, Rigoberta Menchú,* xx-xxi.

24. K. Millet, "Framing the Narrative: The Dreams of Lucinda Nahuelhaul," in *Poetica de la Población marginal: Sensibilidades determinantes,* ed. James Romano (Minneapolis: Prisma Institute, 1987), 425, 427.

25. Menchú, *I, Rigoberta Menchú,* 247.

26. See Gayatri Chakravorty Spivak, "Can the Subaltern Speak?" in *Marxism and the Interpretation of Culture,* ed. Cary Nelson and Lawrence Grossberg (Urbana: University of Illinois Press, 1981), 271–313.

27. Elzbieta Sklodowska, "La forma testimonial y la novelística de Miguel Barnet," *Revista/Review Interamericana* 12, 3 (1982): 379.

28. Jara, "Prólogo," 2.

29. This seems in particular the outcome of Roberto González Echevarría's influential discussion of Miguel Barnet's *Autobiography of a Runaway Slave,* trans. Jocasta Innes (New York: Pantheon, 1968). "Biografia de un cimmarón and the Novel of the Cuban Revolution," in *The Voice of the Masters: Writing and Authority in Modern Latin American Literature* (Austin: University of Texas Press, 1985), 110–24.

30. Barbara Foley, *Telling the Truth: The Theory and Practice of Documentary Fiction* (Ithaca, N.Y.: Cornell University Press, 1986).

31. I have perhaps overstated here the distinction between *testimonio* and autobiography. I am aware, for example, of the existence in slave narratives, certain forms of women's writing, and in working-class, black, latino, and gay literature in the United States, of something that might be called "popular" autobiography, somewhere between autobiography—as I characterize it here—and *testimonio* as such. Moreover, in Latin American writing autobiography often has a direct political resonance. See Sylvia Molloy, "At Face Value: Autobiographical Writing in Spanish America," *Dispositio* 24–26 (1985): 1–18.

32. Sidonie Smith, "On Women's Autobiography" (Paper delivered at the Stanford Conference on Autobiography, April 1986).

33. See, for example, Spivak, *In Other Worlds,* 209ff.; see also her critique of post-structuralist notions of the subject in "Can the Subaltern Speak?"

34. Foley claims that the documentary novel "locates itself near the border between factual discourse and fictive discourse, *but does not propose an eradication of that border.* Rather, it purports to represent reality by means of agreed-upon conceptions of fictionality, while grafting onto its fictive pact some kind of additional claim to empirical validation." *Telling the Truth,* 25; emphasis mine.

35. Jara, "Prólogo," 3.

36. See Barnet, "La novela-testimonio."

37. See, for example, Dinesh D'Souza, "Travels with Rigoberta," in *Illiberal Education* (New York: Free Press, 1991). There has been considerable discussion of *testimonio,* decolonization, and women's liberation lately, so these remarks should be taken as provisional. For a more extensive discussion, see my "'Through All Things Modern': Second Thoughts on Testimonio," *Boundary* 2, 18, 2 (1991).

38. Menchú, *I, Rigoberta Menchú,* 13.

39. Ibid., 89.

40. Ibid., 205.

41. Walter Mignolo, "Literacy and Colonization: The New World Experience," in *1492–1992: Re/Discovering Colonial Writing,* ed. R. Jara and N. Spadaccini (Minneapolis: Prisma Institute, 1989), 67.

42. Mignolo distinguishes the practices of the colonial and neocolonial state from the contemporary literacy campaigns instituted, for example, by the Cuban and Nicaraguan revolutions based on the methods of Paolo Freire's "pedagogy of the oppressed," which he sees as a means of empowerment of the subaltern.

43. Doris Sommer, "Sin secretos," in "La voz del otro: Testimonio, subalternidad y verdad narrative," special issue, ed. John Beverley and Hugo Achugar, *Revista de crítica literaria latinoamericana* 36 (1992): 135–54.

44. See, for example, Robert Carr, "Re(-)presentando el testimonio: Notas sobre el cruce divisorio primer mundo/tercer mundo," in "La voz del otro: Testimonio, subalternidad y verdad narrativa," special issue, ed. John Beverley and Hugo Achugar, *Revista de crítica literaria latinoamericana* 36 (1992): 78.

45. See, for example, David Stoll, "'The Land No Longer Gives': Land Reform in Nebaj, Guatemala," *Cultural Survival Quarterly* 14, 4 (1990): 4–9; and his talk (subsequently revised) "*I, Rigoberta Menchú* and Human Rights Reporting in Guatemala" (Presented at the Western Humanities Institute Conference on "Political Correctness" and Cultural Studies at the University of California, Berkeley, 20 October 1990).

46. Richard Price, *Alabi's World* (Baltimore: Johns Hopkins University Press, 1990).

47. Gayatri Chakravorty Spivak, "On the Politics of the Subaltern" (interview with Howard Winant), *Socialist Review* 90 (July-September 1990): 91.

Chapter 7

Resisting Autobiography
Out-Law Genres and Transnational Feminist
Subjects

Caren Kaplan

Like most literary genres in the West, autobiography has a specific history of debatable origins, ambiguous parameters, and disputed subject matter. Most contemporary discourse around autobiography centers on the problematic nature of generic definition. It can be argued, however, that autobiography has only just reached its most stable and valued moment in the course of this history. Autobiography's peripatetic fortune in the marketplace of literary value differs, nevertheless, from that of other Western literary genres in that its "troubles" seem to define it. That autobiography now *appears* to be as entrenched as the novel, for example, in the canon of Western literature does not erase marked signs of tension in the critical discourse.

In the United States, emerging transdisciplinary fields such as women's, ethnic, and American studies have provided feminist readings of autobiographical traditions and definitions. As feminist theories have entered the debates around autobiography, the questions of generic definition and tradition have shifted in order to challenge primarily masculine conventions and canons. Critics have established alternative canons of Western autobiography that include African American slave narratives, diaries, captivity narratives, abolitionist and suffragist personal records, labor activists' accounts, oral histories of immigration and exile, and modernist fiction, among other forms. As the genre has expanded to include various media, autobiography criticism has had to become literate in photography, film, video, photocopy, music, textiles, and numerous other technologies. Yet, the popularity of the *concept* of autobiography in contemporary studies and practices of Western culture does not obviate the troubling legacy of this complicated genre.

In this essay I would like to question whether or not autobiography is recoverable as a feminist writing strategy in the context of transnational affiliations among women. If Western autobiography criticism is itself a form of colonial discourse, does Western feminist autobiography criticism continue postcolonial forms of cultural domination? Are there reading and writing strategies that historicize and deconstruct mythologies of nationalism and individualism? What kind of postcolonial writing and reading strategies intersect with feminist concerns to create transnational feminist subjects?

Utilizing the term *transnational* links the questions I am raising here about genre and gender to a world-system of emergent cultural production. The term *global feminism* has been co-opted in many cases into part of a neo-imperialist project that constructs Western agendas and subjects *for* women in non-Western locations. Chandra Talpade Mohanty's analysis of the function of the "global" in some Western feminist theories reveals a process of dehistoricization in which "politics and ideology as self-conscious struggles and choices get written out."[1] To avoid the construction of monolithic categories such as "Women of the World" or "Third World Women" or "First World Women," an antiracist and anti-imperialist feminism must articulate differences in power and location as accurately as possible. It must also find intersections and common ground; but they will not be utopian or necessarily comfortable alliances. New terms are needed to express the possibilities for links and affiliations, as well as differences, among women who inhabit different locations. Transnational feminist activism is one possibility. I would argue that this mode of affiliation occurs in many academic and nonacademic contexts and that its histories and present existence often remain to be read.

The Law of Genre

In his essay "The Law of Genre," Jacques Derrida suggests that the institution of literature (in collusion with its siblings in Western humanism—philosophy, history, and so on) works a particularly duplicitous arrangement. The "law of genre" is based on a "counterlaw"; that is, the possibility of genre limits is always already undermined by the impossibility of maintaining those very limits. Yet the law of genre asserts that "genres are not to be mixed":

> As soon as the word "genre" is sounded, as soon as it is heard, as soon as one attempts to conceive it, a limit is drawn. And when a limit is established, norms and interdictions are not far behind: "Do," "Do not" says "genre," the word "genre," the figure, the voice, or the law of genre. . . . Thus, as soon as genre announces itself, one must respect a norm, one must not cross a line of demarcation, one must not risk impurity, anomaly or monstrosity.[2]

A brief glance at the history of autobiography criticism in the West confirms Derrida's thesis. Although genre criticism frequently consists of continual definition and redefinition, most autobiography criticism appears to be engaged in a vigorous effort to stabilize and fix generic boundaries. For example, in the essay that James Olney claims "begins" the contemporary study of autobiography theory, Georges Gusdorf describes autobiography as "a solidly established literary genre, its history traceable in a series of masterpieces from the *Confessions* of St. Augustine to Gide's *Si le grain ne meurt,* with Rousseau's *Confessions,* Goethe's *Dichtung und Wahrheit,* Chateaubriand's *Mémoires d'outre tombe,* and Newman's *Apologia* in between."[3] Critics adjust the canon according to their scholarly interests, yet the common denominator of contemporary autobiography criticism remains the preoccupation with "conditions and limits." Autobiography, in fact, engenders a critical anxiety that may be peculiar to mid- to late-twentieth-century Western concerns. In 1956 Gusdorf claimed that autobiography could be contained, yet the introduction to Olney's 1980 anthology, *Autobiography: Essays Theoretical and Critical,* is marked by signs of uncertainty. "Autobiography," Olney writes, "produces more questions than answers, more doubts by far (even of its existence) than certainties."[4]

The placement of Gusdorf's essay at the head of Olney's anthology of autobiography criticism signifies the influence of Gusdorf in the field. Gusdorf's views on the cultural specificity of autobiographical writing must be read with an awareness of his position of authority in the production of genre criticism. Part of Gusdorf's effort to circumscribe (and canonize) autobiography includes drawing a limit at the borders of Western culture:

> Autobiography is not to be found outside of our cultural area; one would say that it expresses a concern peculiar to Western

man; a concern that has been of good use in his systematic conquest of the universe and that he has communicated to men of other cultures; but those men will thereby have been annexed by a sort of intellectual colonizing to a mentality that was not their own.[5]

Gusdorf is not the only Western literary critic to claim that only Westerners can write autobiography. Roy Pascal, writing in 1960, claims that autobiography is "a distinctive product of Western, post-Romantic civilization, and only in modern times has it spread to other civilizations."[6] Pascal's attempts to fix the national and cultural borders of autobiography are challenged by his own consideration of the sixteenth-century memoirs of Babur, the Turkish founder of the Mogul dynasty in India. Pascal writes:

> It is beyond my scope to suggest why autobiography does not come into being outside Europe, and the existence of such a work as Babur's memoirs of the sixteenth century, which would occupy a significant place in the history of autobiography had it belonged to Europe, makes one hesitate to generalise. But there remains no doubt that autobiography is essentially European.[7]

If Pascal did not find Babur's memoirs enough of a challenge to his theory of the genre, another critic did not have trouble accommodating the sixteenth-century mogul's writings to *his* history of the genre. Georg Misch readily included Babur on a list of "self-portraits of kings" who present themselves as "ordinary human beings of flesh and blood" in "portraits striking in their freshness of coloring."[8] Misch's monumental *Geschichte der Autobiographie,* published in 1907, begins with prehistoric Babylonia and Assyria and aimed to conclude with the late nineteenth century. Without disputing Misch's orientalism, the absence of any consideration of non-European texts or concepts of self-representation in most Western autobiography criticism in the postwar period piques interest in Misch's version of the history of autobiography. A consideration of why the boundaries of the genre are drawn in ever-narrowing circles of cultural specificity throughout the twentieth century must be reserved for a more detailed treatment elsewhere.

Recent feminist autobiography criticism has begun to reevaluate Gusdorf's generic conditions and limits. Leila Ahmed has critiqued the Gusdorf school of autobiography criticism by examining the tradition of autobiography in Islamic-Arabic letters. Ahmed distinguishes between the classical autobiographies "of rulers, religious-mystic auto-

biographies, and the autobiographical accounts of scholars" and modern Arabic autobiography in order to pose questions of historical
continuity and change in the aftermath of European colonialism.[9]
Another refutation of the Eurocentric origin of autobiography can be
found in Domna Stanton's reference to the "introspective writings"
of Japanese women in the Heian period.[10] Stanton and Ahmed read
contemporary autobiography criticism through the lens of gender in
order to see beyond the national and ethnic borders constituted by
at least two generations of Western critics.

Adopting Derrida's version of genre production in the service of
autobiography criticism poses both limits and possibilities. The limits
of Western literary structures are abundantly obvious in the powerful
elisions, co-optations, and experiments that constitute cultural margins. As counterlaw, or *out-law,* such productions often break most
obvious rules of genre. Locating out-law genres enables a deconstruction of the "master" genres, revealing the power dynamics embedded
in literary production, distribution, and reception.

Out-law genres in autobiographical discourse at the present moment
mix two conventionally "unmixable" elements—autobiography criticism and autobiography as thing itself. Thus, in all the cultural productions that I will discuss, critical accountability is implicitly or
explicitly a primary subject. These emerging out-law genres require
more collaborative procedures that are more closely attuned to the
power differences among participants in the process of producing the
text. Thus, instead of a discourse of individual authorship, we find a
discourse of situation; a "politics of location."[11]

I will examine a number of versions of the discourse of situation:
expansions or revolutions of generic boundaries that rework and challenge conventional notions of critic and author (including prison memoir, testimonial literature, ethnographic writing, "biomythography,"
"cultural autobiography," and "regulative psychobiography"). I juxtapose these alternative genres not as a comprehensive list or complete
map of global literary production that refers to the "autobiographical"
tradition, but as an indication of a variety of reading and writing
strategies in operation as the law of genre intersects with contemporary postcolonial, transnational conditions.

Resistance Literature: Women's Prison Memoirs as Out-Law Genre

Barbara Harlow uses the term "resistance literature" to describe a
body of writing that has been marginalized in literary studies: writing

marked by geopolitical situation.[12] As a global phenomenon, resistance literature is created out of political conflicts between Western imperialism and non-Western indigenous resistance movements. Resistance literature, therefore, breaks many of elite literature's laws: it is comparative but not always linked to a national language; it is overtly political, sometimes anonymous, always pressuring the boundaries of established genres.

In her essay "From the Women's Prison: Third World Women's Narratives of Prison," Harlow articulates a set of social relations that may merge with Western feminist concerns even while they may be constituted in opposition to certain aspects of Western feminism. Rather than adapting Western concepts of "feminism," "autobiography," and "individuality" to a non-Western culturally specific use, the incarcerated women writers whom Harlow discusses are producing alternate genres. Reading this cultural production as outside or oppositional to mainstream autobiography, Harlow locates "the emergence of a new literary corpus out of contemporary conditions in the Third World of political and social repression":[13]

> Women's prison writings from the Third World present a two-fold challenge to Western theoretical developments, both literary critical and feminist. What may seem to be incidental as the common feature among them, that they are written by women in the Third World and deal with the experience of prison, is in fact potentially constructive of a discursive category. Generically, these writings defy traditional categories and distinctions and combine fictional forms with documentary record. Furthermore, the women's collective experience and political development that they describe emerges out of their position within a set of social relations giving rise to a secular ideology, one not based on bonds of gender, race, or ethnicity—which may be shared by men and may not be shared by all women.[14]

The critique of Western feminism enacted in Harlow's account of the emergence of a literary genre parallels her critique of narrative structure. Harlow argues that the same process is at work *in narrative* as in social structure:

> In the same way that institutions of power . . . are subverted by the demand on the part of dispossessed groups for an access to history, power, and resources, so too are the narrative paradigms and their textual authority being transformed by the historical and literary articulation of those demands.[15]

The institution of literature—its production, distribution, and reception—changes through this form of class struggle. One form of subversion can be identified as the deconstruction of the individual bourgeois author (the sacred subject of autobiographical narrative) and the contruction of a collective authorial entity—a kind of collective consciousness that "authorizes" and validates the identity of the individual writer. As Harlow explains in *Resistance Literature:* "The prison memoirs of political detainees are not written for the sake of a 'book of own's own,' rather they are collective documents, testimonies written by individuals to their common struggle."[16]

Harlow is careful to differentiate, within the genre of prison writing itself, a specific category of writers who "did not simply 'discover' their writing selves while in prison, but rather were incarcerated because they wrote."[17] This group of writers necessarily views writing as a political act that links their individual experience of incarceration with larger social movements and actions. Given that many prisons refuse writing materials or disallow writing entirely for political prisoners, the act of writing itself resists the rationale of the prison and the state power it represents.

The choice of autobiography as a genre by women in nonmetropolitan or non-Western prisons will necessarily change the narrative structure itself to reflect what Harlow calls "secular critical consciousness."[18] The prison writing of Third World women does not automatically conform to conventional genre specifications, but "it does . . . propose alternative parameters for the definition and articulation of literary conventions."[19] Harlow names Bessie Head, Nawal al-Saadawi, Akhtar Baluch, Domitila Barrios de Chungara, Ruth First, and Raymonda Tawil as writers whose works constitute an emerging genre that challenges and reworks dominant social structures.

There is an implicit critique of many categories of Western feminism in Harlow's discussion of Third World women's prison memoirs. Yet, Harlow's theory of resistance literature as a component of social change aids the delineation of transnational feminisms. For example, Harlow asserts that the texts she discusses rewrite "the social order to include a vision of new relational possibilities which transcribe ethnic, class, and racial divisions as well as family ties."[20] This view of Third World women's writing as dynamic and synthetic unravels the polar opposition between Western feminism and non-Western women. Harlow deconstructs the gender-specific modernity of Western feminism as well as the monolithic, antimodern nationalism of non-Western women to propose transnational affiliations among liberation movements. Reading women's prison writing as resistance literature provides "new modes of affiliation" based on the "material conditions of people themselves."[21]

The critical consciousness produced by the reworking of a conventional genre such as autobiography in a specific relocation such as the experience of detainment creates genre destabilization. The essential categories of autobiography, especially as adopted by Western feminism in the last twenty years—the revelation of individuality, the chronological unfolding of a life, reflections and confessions, the recovery and assertion of suppressed identity—are utilized, reworked, and even abandoned. The primacy of the individual author whose mind is separate and unique is especially moribund in the context of Harlow's "women's prison." Ultimately, we read the rejection of purely aesthetic categories in favor of a worldly, politicized framework for narrative and cultural production in the texts that Harlow highlights in her work.

Once the author has been deconstructed in postcolonial and neocolonial contexts, the question remains how to situate the critic and, especially, the figure combining and managing the functions of translator, editor, and collaborator in the production of particular kinds of "autobiographical" discourse emerging from non-Western locations. The testimony of non-Western women that arrives in the West in book form requires new strategies of reading cultural production *as* transnational activity. Treating the "author" of the "testimonial" as an authentic, singular voice without acknowledging the mediations of the editors and market demands of publishing can result in new forms of exoticization and racism. The nature of the relationship between author and critic in the instance of testimonial writing is never simple or nonpolitical, and must always be charted.

Testimonial Literature and the Question of Authenticity

Testimonial literature, because it usually takes the form of first-person narrative elicited or transcribed and edited by another person, participates in a particularly delicate realm of collaboration. Like many emerging genres, *testimonio* (as this form of writing is called in Latin American contexts) has an out-law and an "in-law" function. As an out-law genre, testimonial literature is a form of "resistance literature"; it expresses transitional material relations in neo- and postcolonial societies and disrupts mainstream literary conventions. Testimonial literature highlights the possibilities for solidarity and affiliations among critics, interviewers, translators, and the subject who "speaks."

As an in-law genre, *testimonio* may refer to colonial values of nostalgia and exoticization, values that operate via a discourse of "truth" and "authenticity."

Several recent considerations of testimonial literature emphasize the problematic nature of genre and politics in the production and reception of the emerging form. In his essay, "The Margin at the Center: on *Testimonio* (Testimonial Narrative)," John Beverley maps the parameters of *testimonio* discourse, focusing on the material conditions that produce this form of expression as well as the ways in which these conditions limit and expand possible reception. Arguing that literary forms that developed in the period of colonial expansion do not merely reflect social relations, but act as agents in the formation of hegemony, Beverley views testimonial literature as part of the struggle to resist and subvert the colonial discourse of literature. Thus, *testimonio* challenges the hallowed categories of singular authorship, literary aesthetics, and the elite cultural construction of "masterpieces." "*Testimonio*," Beverley writes, "is a fundamentally democratic and egalitarian form of narrative in the sense that it implies that *any* life so narrated can have a kind of representational value."[22]

Among the many important characteristics that Beverley cites as inherent to *testimonio,* the collectivization of authorship and the reassertion of orality against the dominance of writing in the culture of literature refer most directly to the question of autobiographical form. As an "extraliterary" or "antiliterary form of discourse," *testimonio* replaces the "author" with two aspects of an authorial function: the "speaker" who tells the story and the "listener" who compiles and writes the narrative that is published. This heavily mediated process of collaboration points to the heart of testimonial literature's problematic critical reception, for the ideal vision of the "subaltern" brought to the realm of public discourse via the efforts of a transparent medium cannot be maintained. Even as *testimonio* avoids the documentary "truth-value" of the category of "oral history" by highlighting the relationship between "editor" or "facilitator" and "subject" or "speaker," the question of power remains. Do such *testimonios* as *I, Rigoberta Menchú* or *Let Me Speak! Testimony of Domitila, a Woman of the Bolivian Mines* constitute collective action or appropriation?

In a provocative essay, "Re(-)presenting Testimonial: Notes on Crossing the First World/Third World Divides," Robert Carr emphasizes the problem of *testimonio*'s reception in North America. Questioning the consumption of texts that purport to represent Third World women, Carr situates testimonial literature in a global marketplace, where "Otherized communities and their worlds" come into public discourse as already exploited, serving as pretexts for the "accumulation of knowledge and power."[23] The construction of the "I" in *testimonio,* in this reading, erases critical differences between the parties that are brought into contact through the production of literature, posing a "full, transhistorical, and transparent reality" in which the *testimonio* stands as "the voice of all indigenous Americans throughout history."[24] It is impossible, therefore, to *read* testimonial literature in the West outside the influence of capital and colonial discourse. Carr chooses to differentiate among kinds of testimonial projects, searching for moments of resistance and affiliation in non-Western women's modes of expression that work against the no-win choice between commodification and erasure.

The differences between Carr's and Beverley's critical considerations of testimonial literature are more in degree than in kind. Beverley acknowledges the effects of editorial "intervention" and the appropriative tendencies of First World readers. Carr critiques the process of cross-cultural "translation" inherent to the production of testimonial literature from an "overarching concern" with "international and intercultural alliances."[25] Both critics contribute to our understanding of the difficulties of deviating from dominant genres such as autobiography when the cultures of literacy, national literatures and languages, and publication work to valorize and promote textual commodification. The politics of location will determine what instances of narrative production may be read as resistant in either content or form at specific historical moments. In this view, how we read *testimonio* (and how diverse "we" are) holds as much power as the question of how this genre is produced.

Testimonio read as out-law genre provides a powerful critique of the colonial discourse inherent to Western feminist discussions of identity politics in autobiography. Doris Sommer's essay on *testimonio* and the concerns of feminist autobiography, " 'Not Just a Personal Story': Women's *Testimonios* and the Plural Self," does not just contrast the singular "I" of conventional Western autobiography to the collective "I" of *testimonio.* Reading *I, Rigoberta Menchú* and *Let Me Speak! Testimony of Domitila, a Woman of the Bolivian Mines* as exemplary testimonial productions, requiring the collaboration of testifier, interviewer, and, sometimes, translator, Sommer emphasizes the difference between autobiographical and testimonial strategies of identification:

> The testimonial "I" does not invite us to identify with it. We are too different, and there is no pretense here of universal or essential human experience. . . . The singular represents the

plural not because it replaces or subsumes the group but because the speaker is a distinguishable part of the whole.[26]

Thus, testimonial literature, by the very nature of its mode of production, calls attention to a process that is more often muted or invisible in autobiographical writing. Sommer's emphasis on *testimonio* as a mode of production works against a mystification of the oral to reveal points of contradiction and congruity in women's writing. When Sommer reads written testimonials as models of "experimental syncretism,"[27] she joins Beverley and Carr in critiquing the romanticization and commodification of transnational cultural artifacts. As Sommer argues:

> The phenomenon of a collective subject of the testimonial is, then, hardly the result of personal preference on the part of the writer who testifies. It is a translation of a hegemonic autobiographical pose into a colonized language that does not equate identity with individuality. It is thus a reminder that life continues at the margins of Western discourse, and continues to disturb and to challenge it.[28]

The destabilizing effect of testimony comes through reading as well as through writing; that is, our responsibility as critics lies in opening the categories so that the process of collaboration extends to reception. Refusing to read testimonial writing by poor and imprisoned women *only* as autobiography links resistance literature to resistance criticism. The possibility of transnational feminist cultural production requires affiliations among prison memoir, life writing, political testimonial, autobiography, and ethnography. Each category is provisional and different in relation to specific struggles and locations. Learning to read the differences will engender the possibility of strategic similarities.

Ethnography and the Question of Authorship

Ethnographic writing shares issues of authorship and power with testimonial writing and the other forms considered here. All potential out-law genres are highly mediated. These genres are produced within the matrix of colonial and postcolonial discourses that discipline the humanities. Reading ethnographic writing as an out-law genre challenges the traditional hierarchy of objective scientist and native informant in mainstream anthropology and demystifies the "literary" classics of the field. Linking ethnography to the issues raised by prison memoir and testimonial literature deconstructs the nostaligia for perfect rapport between the fieldworker and the "Other."

The recent publication of a set of books that "read" the activity of "writing culture," drawing on the various interpretive strategies available to the literary critic (especially poststructuralist theories), has politicized the poetics of anthropology.[29] As a result, the role of the ethnographer as reader and writer has been destabilized and retheorized even as the position and subjectivity of the informant have come to be renegotiated.[30]

As part of this process of destabilization and renegotiation, the gender of the subjects of anthropology has come to matter. Deborah Gordon describes ethnographic writing as one location of emerging transnational feminist discourses:

> Women who claim some relationship to feminism and women's movements as well as decolonization are creating new kinds of ethnographic subjectivity linking indigenous and feminist ethnography. This is what attention to ethnographic form should be about—insights and knowledge into global relations among people diversely located and vying for power.[31]

Questions of power and the legacies of colonialism in ethnography as a written mode of production must be raised in texts that chart the encounters of Western and non-Western women. Kamala Visweswaran suggests that the first-person narrative is a logical form to convey the dilemmas and solutions of cross-cultural interaction, even as this mode leads to narratives of "imperfect rapport" that construct and support colonial discourse.[32] Visweswaran suggests that there is an entire genre of "confessional" first-person accounts written by Western women that has been ignored or rejected by conventional and experimental anthropologists, a genre that constitutes an important element in colonial discourse. To dismiss this literature as "too subjective" or "confessional" or even literarily uninteresting is to miss the political and cultural issues raised by the encounters between Western and non-Western women. Visweswaran explains: "Questions of positionality more often than not confront female rather than male fieldworkers, and the female ethnographer is more likely to be faced with a decision over which world she enters."[33]

Both Kamala Visweswaran and Roger Keesing raise the issues of who speaks and under what conditions. Visweswaran asserts that "a feminist anthropologist cannot assume the willingness of women to talk."[34] In his study of the construction of "autobiography" by both ethnographer and indigenous subject, Keesing argues that scrupulous attention to the micropolitics of the "elicitation situation," the context of interviewer and interviewee, raises critical questions about how women's subjectivity is formed, reported, and interpreted: "What constraints are imposed on what women will say about their lives and cultures by male ideological and political hegemony? How do ethnographers get caught up in this process?"[35] Keesing summarizes his argument:

> (a) Neither "muteness" nor articulate accounts of self and society represent a direct reflection of "women's status" or the role of women in a society; rather (b) what women can and will say is a product of specific historical circumstances; and (c) emerges in a specific micropolitical context both of male-female relations and of the ethnographic encounter itself; therefore, that (d) whatever texts derive from such an encounter (whether rich and coherent or limited and incoherent, whether ostensibly "autobiographical" or not) must be interpreted in terms of these historical circumstances and micropolitics, which inextricably include the ethnographer her/himself; (e) that such texts cannot be uncritically taken either to represent "autobiography" or to constitute normative accounts of culture and society—the texts never "speak for themselves"; and finally (f) that lack of success in eliciting rich accounts of self and society from women cannot be taken as evidence that they are ultimately unable, because of life experience and societal role, to give such accounts; "muteness" must always be historically and contextually situated, and bracketed with doubt.[36]

While Keesing's concept of autobiography, with its Western notions of chronological time and psychosociological life stages, may limit the usefulness of some of his information, his examination of the political dynamics of communication in the era of postcolonialism raises important questions. Ethnography as autobiographical out-law genre, like testimonial writing, requires radical revisions of notions of individual authorship and authenticity. For the subject of ethnographic writing to circulate in transnational culture as "author," essentialist mythologies of identity and authorship must be challenged and bracketed in favor of reading strategies that acknowledge the complexities of power in the production of life writing from nonmetropolitan, non-Western locations. The stakes in developing nonexploitative political alliances between women from different parts of the world to produce documents that empower the subjects of ethnographic writing are very high. Feminists who are alert to power dynamics in identity politics will find in resistance literature and out-law genres useful models of multiracial, multinational, multiethnic, and polysexual struggle.

Biomythography: Lesbian Identities and Literary Production

One location of the struggle for multiple identification strategies in the field of late-twentieth-century Western culture is the cultural revolution of politicized sexual preference characterized by gay and lesbian liberation. In an effort to identify effective methods of representation that counter damaging stereotypes, some lesbian and gay writers have utilized autobiographical forms to varying extents, from conventionally celebratory to experimental forms. The construction of a political entity that can agitate for change in Western democratic social structures requires the support of cultural institutions such as literature. The construction of sexual identity and the creation of literary genres are linked by necessity in the process of cultural production.

In one of the most intellectually engaging essays on autobiography to come out of feminist criticism in recent years, Biddy Martin writes that "much recent lesbian writing is autobiographical, often taking the form of autobiographical essay and coming-out stories."[37] To conclude that the categories involved in such a statement are total, "airtight" packages, Martin cautions, would be false. One must ask "what a lesbian life is, what autobiography is, and what the relation between them could possibly be."[38] Martin states that the connection of two such powerful terms as *lesbian* and *autobiography* may produce particular misreadings:

> Their combination brings out the most conventional interpretation in each, for the *lesbian* in front of *autobiography* reinforces conventional assumptions of the transparency of autobiographical writing. And the *autobiography* that follows *lesbian* suggests that sexual identity not only modifies but essentially defines a life, providing it with predictable content and an identity possessing continuity and universality.[39]

Martin's discussion of the troubling aspects of autobiography frames a powerful contextualization of feminist identity politics. To critique the "truth value" of certain kinds of coming-out narratives, Martin examines recent autobiographical writings that "work against self-evidently homogeneous conceptions of identity, writings in which lesbianism comes to figure as something other than a 'totalizing self-identification' and to be located on other than exclusively psychological grounds."[40] Martin urges readings of lesbian life stories that start from the standpoint of multiplicity, using the material experience of the construction of sexuality to add to reflections on race, gender, and other crucial distinctions. Pointing to the writing of lesbian women of color in anthologies such as *This Bridge Called My Back,* Martin writes:

> Lesbianism ceases to be an identity with predictable contents, to constitute a total political and self-identification, and yet it figures no less centrally for that shift. It remains a position from which to speak, to organize, to act politically, but it ceases to be the exclusive and continuous ground of identity or politics. Indeed it works to unsettle rather than to consolidate the boundaries around identity, not to dissolve them altogether but to open them to the fluidities and heterogeneities that make their renegotiation possible. At the same time that such autobiographical writing enacts a critique of both sexuality and race as "essential" and totalizing identifications, it also acknowledges the political and psychological importance, indeed the pleasures, too, of at least partial or provisional identifications, homes, and communities. In so doing, it remains faithful to the irreducibly complex and paradoxical status of identity in feminist politics and autobiographical writing.[41]

This deconstruction of conventional assumptions of identity and genre can be found, as well, in Katie King's recent work on contemporary sexualities and debates about cultural production. In her essay, "Audre Lorde's Lacquered Layerings: The Lesbian Bar as a Site of Literary Production," King highlights Lorde's term "biomythography" for her autobiographical memoir, *Zami,* as naming "a variety of generic strategies in the construction of gay and lesbian identity in the USA."[42] "Biomythography," King suggests, is "a writing down of our meanings of identity . . . with the materials of our lives."[43] The generic strategy of biomythography focuses on the process as well as the materials of autobiographical narrative without insisting on any one rule or form. As King writes:

> The generic strategies of the biomythography of lesbian and gay history currently include historical monograph and book, polemical critique, film and video and slide show, oral history, review essay, introspective analysis, academic/polemical anthology, novel and poem and short story, and undoubtedly others as well.[44]

The discussions of expanded genres and multiple identities found in King's and Martin's critical framing of lesbian texts suggest compelling models for transnational feminist cultural production. Biomythography as out-law genre requires a recognition of "layers of meanings, layers of histories, layers of readings and rereadings through webs of power-charged codes."[45] In this particularized sense, "difference" becomes a material reality that can be charted. As King writes in another essay: "This doesn't mean that gay people have no interests in common: we do. But our coalitions and identities are in flux and appropriately so."[46] Making "maps" of changing affiliations and coalitions is part of the "work" of biomythography as text. The bridging of disparate and shifting concerns and identities raised in biomythography echoes the political affiliations forged through the coalition work that engenders transnational feminisms. The critique ·of identity politics (and the forms of autobiography that are attached to modern Western structures of identity) requires the reformulation of authorship and selfhood found in emerging out-law genres.

Rewriting Home: The Coalition Politics of Cultural Autobiography

Traditionally, Western autobiographical writing has participated in the literary construction of "home"; a process of generalizing the particular, fabricating a narrative space of familiarity, and crafting a narrative that links the individual to the universal. The homogenizing influence of autobiography genres identifies similarities; reading an autobiography involves assimilating or consenting to the values and worldview of the writer. Out-law genres renegotiate the relationship between personal identity and the world, between personal and social history. Here, narrative inventions are tied to a struggle for cultural survival rather than purely aesthetic experimentation or individual expression.

A concern with the "rapid disintegration of black folk experience" leads bell hooks to life writing and the complicated process of reworking the autobiographical genre.[47] In her essay "Writing Autobiography," hooks uses the genre to preserve and transmit experiences of black southern life. Autobiography, she argues, can counter some of the damaging effects of capitalism and middle-class cultural domination. Remembering experiences nonsynchronous with dominant culture, hooks contends, is the activity of cultural and personal survival.

Writing autobiography as a record of the individual self is not a trouble-free procedure for hooks. She begins by describing the blocks and troubles she had with the process and the form:

To me, telling the story of my growing up years was intimately connected with the longing to kill the self I was without really having to die. I wanted to kill that self in writing. Once that self was gone—out of my life forever—I could more

easily become the me of me. . . . Until I began to try and
write an autobiography, I thought that it would be a simple
task this telling of one's story. And yet I tried year after year,
never writing more than a few pages.[48]

To write a record of her life that connects to collective black experience, hooks finds that her illusions about autobiography and the
relationship between writing and the past must be dismantled. Once
she begins to give herself permission to allow for the fictional nature
of memory, the process of recall begins to shape itself into a narrative.
The autobiography becomes a "place," a safe location to keep crucial,
culturally specific memories: "Remembering was part of a cycle of
reunion, a joining of fragments, 'the bits and pieces of my heart' that
the narrative made whole again."[49]

The joining of fragments in hooks's autobiographical process does
not result in a seamless accommodation of generic rules. Rather, the
process of delineating a narrative space for the coexistence of disparate
parts underscores a productive tension between homogeneity and
difference. In her essay "Coalition Politics," Bernice Johnson Reagon
argues that a distinction has to be made between "home" and "coalition"; a difference between the safety net of similarity and familiarity
and the difficult but necessary terrain of diversity and unfamiliarity.[50]
Writing a life story as both an affirmation of "home" and a declaration
of affiliation through coalition work requires alternative versions of
self, community, and identity, versions that may be read in the production of some kinds of out-law genres.

The kind of reworking of autobiography in bell hooks's writing is
expanded upon in the notion of "cultural autobiography" that Reagon
proposes in her essay, "My Black Mothers and Sisters or On Beginning
a Cultural Autobiography."[51] Here Reagon explores the conditions of
"home" and the precarious locations of coalition work without utilizing the conventions of identity celebrated in mainstream autobiography. Reworking a history of inspiration and affiliation, Reagon writes
about her mother, her grandmother, her great-grandmother, her teacher
(Ms. Daniels), and Miss Nana (a singer in her church). Reflecting on
the necessity for naming and remembering the people who have given
her the skills and inspiration to survive, Reagon theorizes a form of
autobiography that describes both a gendered community and a form
of nationhood: "Black women are nationalists in our efforts to form
a nation that will survive in this society, and we are also the major
cultural carriers and passers-on of the traditions of our people."[52]

Reagon's cultural autobiography expands the parameters and content of life writing. Reclaiming a history and constructing a community

of strength and diversity gives the cultural autobiographer a foundation for the difficult work of coalition. Expanding the borders of life writing to include coalition, the cooperative activities of people and groups with different points of view, challenges the terms of conventional autobiography. The process of distinguishing between friend and foe, self and others, between opposing parts of the self, while managing the connections and affiliations that constitute communities in the face of institutionalized racism, sexism, homophobia, and other forms of cultural violence, requires many strategies. Cultural autobiography as an out-law genre works to construct both the "safe" places and the border areas of coalition politics where diversity operates in crisis conditions to forge powerful temporary alliances. Bernice Reagon reminds us that coalition work is undertaken only by those who recognize no other solution to the systemic violence of racism, sexism, and other forms of modern oppression. "You don't go into coalition because you just *like* it," she writes. "The only reason you would consider trying to team up with somebody who could possibly kill you, is because that's the only way you can figure you can stay alive."[53]

Staying alive—cultural and personal survival—fuels the narrative engines of out-law genres. An oppositional relationship to writing and to genres such as autobiography requires the difficult embrace of unfamiliar narrative strategies as well as the validating insertion of your own familiar modes of expression and your own systems of signification. The histories of coalitions—their dynamism and their difficulties—can be charted as cultural autobiographies of communities in crisis and resistance. The struggle *in* writing remains to be read and recognized by literary criticism. First, it is necessary to read the narratives of coalition politics as cultural autobiographies. Second, personal histories that link the individual with particular communities at given historical junctures can be read as cultural autobiographies. The link between individual and community forged in the reading and writing of coalition politics deconstructs the individualism of autobiography's Western legacy and casts the writing and reading of out-law genres as a mode of cultural survival.

Regulative Psychobiographies: Postcolonial Subjects

Even as the interaction of coalition work and diverse identities presents opportunities for the expression of "subaltern" subject positions, Gayatri Spivak suggests that there is another subject who is so under-represented as to be absent even from "emerging" out-law genres. Drawing on the work of June Nash and Maria Patricia Fernandez-Kelly,

Spivak considers the difference between the colonial subject and a new international neocolonial subject who can be found in the proliferation of export-processing zones (otherwise known as EPZs).[54] EPZs, or "free-trade zones," have emerged as export-led industrialization has become the preferred mode of development since the mid-1960s. Protective trade barriers that worked in favor of individual nations such as the United States and Great Britain have been dismantled to construct the EPZs. The export-processing zones require a "free flow" of "capital and goods across national boundaries," thereby contributing to the creation of transnational culture.[55] Annette Fuentes and Barbara Ehrenreich report that the majority of the more than one million workers in EPZs are women, and that the preferred work force in the multinational-controlled plants and domestically owned subcontracting factories outside the EPZs is female.[56] This is the context for Spivak's analysis of the condition of women in transnational culture, "fractured by the international division of labor."[57]

Spivak describes a time when the traditional subject of colonialism was violently remolded by consumer capitalism. As territorial imperialism developed legal and social codes to legitimate the new colonial structure, the colonial subject entered the "struggle for individualism."[58] Drawing on Spivak's description of subaltern subject formation, I would argue that autobiographical expression, along with other cultural signposts of individualism, became part of the economy of colonialism, that is, part of the division of labor that produced subject positions and the artifacts of subjectivity. We can locate most resistance literatures and out-law genres on the borders between colonial and neocolonial systems, where subjectivity, cultural power, and survival are played out in the modern era.

Spivak argues that in neocolonialism, exemplified by the economy of the EPZs, the "elaborate constitution of the subject is not necessary":

> No legal structure need be laid down for the army of "permanent casuals," only the circumventing of rudimentary labor and safety regulations is on the agenda. No consistent training into consumerism is any longer needed. The industries can move on. The markets are elsewhere. . . . Thus these women and men are moving further and further away from us. Electronic capitalism is not making them enter post-modern culture. They are re-entering what Partha Chatterjee has called the "feudal mode of power."[59]

The division of labor in the free-trade zones bypasses both the modern and postmodern to catapult displaced populations into feudal

structures of domination. And, as women are favored by the multi-
nationals for their supposedly docile temperaments and nimble fingers,
long-established indigenous gender constructions become disrupted
and are renegotiated. Women are subject to what Spivak calls "the
double whammy":

> Unlike in the classical context . . . in this new feudalization the
> men are set against the women. The feudal mode of power
> cannot now be contested by invoking communal modes of
> power . . . from *below*, as in cases of pre-capitalist insurgency.
> In addition, accession to the bourgeois mode of power . . . is
> also made much more difficult for these women. Thus this
> new feudal mode of power cannot be easily resisted from
> *above* by these women and their representatives.[60]

Can the critical practice of out-law genres, as defined so far, address
this neocolonial subject? Are there out-law genres that interact with
the new feudal mode of production in operation in the EPZs? Out-
law genres challenge Western critical practices to expand their parameters and, consequently, shift the subject of autobiography from the
individual to a more unstable collective entity. If the individual subject
is not constituted in the social framework of the free-trade zones (in
any of its traditional areas: law, psychology, medicine, and so on),
what forms of cultural production work against domination and
exploitation?

Since poststructuralist psychoanalytic theories of subject formation
and object relations cannot adequately address the constitution of the
neocolonial subject and her oppressors, Spivak argues, feminist critics
must develop an alternative procedure, a more intensely collaborative
method. The "narrative" form that must be invented is "regulative
psychobiography": the expressions "that constitute the subject-effect
of these women, give these women a sense of their 'I.'"[61] The model
narratives that Spivak refers to as "regulative psychobiographies" are
less obvious to "us" at the present moment. Spivak asks: "What narratives produce the signifiers of the subject for other traditions? . . .
traces of this psychobiography can be found in the indigenous legal
tradition, in the scriptures, and of course, in myth."[62]

In her study of women in the free-trade zones of Malaysia, Aihwa
Ong found "four overlapping sets of discourses about factory women:
corporate, political, Islamic, and personal."[63] If we embrace Spivak's
project, the regulative psychobiographies produced in the Malaysian
context that Ong studied, for example, would require a densely layered
study, with input from people with various forms of expertise and

knowledge. Spivak urges Western feminists to develop the skills and methods necessary for this multilayered coalition project. Without this effort, she warns, we will leave transnational knowledge in the hands of the military-industrial complex.

Transnational Feminism and the Politics of Culture

A discussion of autobiographical out-law genres in the postcolonial and neocolonial era of transnational capital leads us to a conception of collaborative work that can best be described by Katie King's term "feminist writing technologies."[64] Taking Spivak's collaborative conception of "regulative psychobiography" into consideraiton, "feminist writing technologies" suggests a global project that employs the efforts of many people, rather than the act of a single hand lifting pen to paper or an individual pressing the keys on a keyboard. "Feminist writing technologies" can transform cultural production from individualized and aestheticized procedures to collaborative, historicized, transnational coalitions. Yet, because the electronic communications technologies we use are literally made by women in the free-trade zones and our "sisters" in the assembly plants in the West, Western feminists must be alert to our participation in the international division of labor. Transnational feminisms are enabled by the very conditions that have created the "Third World female subproletariat," the neocolonial subject. Therefore, to quote Saralee Hamilton, "If feminism is going to mean anything to women all over the world, it's going to have to find new ways to resist corporate power internationally."[65]

In this world-system of asymmetrical participation in cultural and industrial production, the activities of writing and reading cannot remain neutral. These power dynamics construct genres and counter-genres, including autobiography and criticism. Autobiography may not have enjoyed a central role in literary studies until recently, but its outsider status has not automatically aligned it with resistance. This essay has argued that resistance is a mode of historical necessity, that Western feminism must participate in this moment, and that the critical practice of out-law genres challenges the hierarchical structures of patriarchy, capitalism, and colonial discourse. Reading prison memoir, *testimonio,* ethnography, "biomythography," cultural autobiography, "regulative psychobiography," and other challenges to the conventions of autobiography in an oppositional mode moves Western feminist criticism into transnational coalition work. Feminist criticism as activism, in an expanded transnational sense, will produce theories and methods of culture and representation grounded in the material conditions of our similarities and differences. The deconstruction of autobiography in transnational feminist criticism marks the constitution of "writing technologies" that can work *for* and *with* women so that the law of genre will no longer dominate the representation and expression of women from different parts of the world.

Notes

I would like to thank Katie King, Inderpal Grewal, and Eric Smoodin for invaluable conversations and inspiration.

1. Chandra Talpade Mohanty, "Feminist Encounters: Locating the Politics of Experience," *Copyright* 1 (Fall 1987): 35.

2. Jacques Derrida, "The Law of Genre," trans. Avital Ronell, *Glyph* 7 (1980): 203–4.

3. Georges Gusdorf, "Conditions and Limits of Autobiography," trans. James Olney, in *Autobiography: Essays Theoretical and Critical,* ed. James Olney (Princeton, N.J.: Princeton University Press, 1980), 28.

4. James Olney, "Autobiography and the Cultural Moment: A Thematic, Historical, and Bibliographical Introduction," in *Autobiography: Essays Theoretical and Critical* (Princeton, N.J.: Princeton University Press, 1980), 5.

5. Gusdorf, "Conditions and Limits," 29.

6. Roy Pascal, *Design and Truth in Autobiography* (Cambridge, Mass.: Harvard University Press, 1960), 180.

7. Ibid., 22.

8. Georg Misch, *A History of Autobiography in Antiquity,* vol. 1 (Cambridge, Mass.: Harvard University Press, 1951), 272.

9. Leila Ahmed, "Between Two Worlds: The Formation of a Turn-of-the-Century Egyptian Feminist," in *Life/Lines: Theorizing Women's Autobiography,* ed. Bella Brodzki and Celeste Schenck (Ithaca, N.Y.: Cornell University Press, 1988), 154.

10. Domna C. Stanton, *The Female Autograph: Theory and Practice of Autobiography from the Tenth to the Twentieth Century* (New York: New York Library Forum, 1984), 6.

11. Useful discussions of the "politics of location" can be found in Adrienne Rich, "Notes toward a Politics of Location," in *Blood, Bread, and Poetry: Selected Prose 1979–1985* (New York: W. W. Norton, 1986), 210–31; Donna Haraway, "Situated Knowledges: The Science Question in Feminism and the Privilege of Partial Perspective," in *Simians, Cyborgs, and Women: The Reinvention of Nature* (New York: Routledge, 1991), 183–201; Mohanty, "Feminist Encounters"; and essays included in "Third Scenario: Theory and the Politics of Location," special issue, ed. John Akomfrah and Pervaiz Ichan, *Framework* 36 (1989): 4–96.

12. Barbara Harlow, *Resistance Literature* (New York: Methuen, 1987).

13. Barbara Harlow, "From the Women's Prison: Third World Women's Narratives of Prison," *Feminist Studies* 12 (Fall 1986): 502–3.

14. Ibid.

15. Ibid.

16. Harlow, *Resistance Literature,* 120.

17. Ibid.

18. Harlow, "From the Women's Prison," 508.

19. Harlow, *Resistance Literature,* 136.

20. Ibid., 142.

21. Ibid., 147–48.

22. John Beverley, "The Margin at the Center: On *Testimonio* (Testimonial Narrative)," *Modern Fiction Studies* 35 (Spring 1989): 16. This article is reprinted as Chapter 6 of this volume.

23. Robert Carr, "Re(-)presenting Testimonial: Notes on Crossing the First World/Third World Divides" (Unpublished manuscript, July 1990), 6.

24. Ibid., 21.

25. Ibid., 6.

26. Doris Sommer, "'Not Just a Personal Story': Women's *Testimonios* and the Plural Self," in *Life/Lines: Theorizing Women's Autobiography,* ed. Bella Brodzki and Celeste Schenck (Ithaca, N.Y.: Cornell University Press, 1988), 108.

27. Ibid., 111.

28. Ibid.

29. See George E. Marcus and Michael M. J. Fischer, eds., *Anthropology as Cultural Critique* (Chicago: University of Chicago Press, 1986); James Clifford and George E. Marcus, eds., *Writing Culture* (Berkeley: University of California Press, 1986); James Clifford, *The Predicament of Culture* (Cambridge, Mass.: Harvard University Press, 1988).

30. See James Clifford, "On Ethnographic Authority," in *The Predicament of Culture,* (Cambridge, Mass.: Harvard University Press), 21–54.

31. Deborah Gordon, "Writing Culture, Writing Feminism: The Poetics and Politics of Experimental Ethnography," *Inscriptions* 3/4 (1988): 21.

32. See Kamala Visweswaran, "Defining Feminist Ethnography," *Inscriptions* 3/4 (1988): 27–46.

33. Ibid., 33.

34. Ibid., 37.

35. Roger M. Keesing, "Kwaio Women Speak: The Micropolitics of Autobiography in a Solomon Island Society," *American Anthropologist* 87 (1985): 37.

36. Ibid., 27.

37. Biddy Martin, "Lesbian Identity and Autobiographical Difference(s)," in *Life/Lines: Theorizing Women's Autobiography,* ed. Bella Brodzki and Celeste Schenck (Ithaca, N.Y.: Cornell University Press, 1988), 77.

38. Ibid.

39. Ibid., 78.

40. Ibid., 82.

41. Ibid., 103.

42. Katie King, "Audre Lorde's Laquered Layerings: The Lesbian Bar as a Site of Literary Production," *Cultural Studies* 2 (1988): 331.

43. Ibid., 330.

44. Ibid., 331.

45. Ibid., 336.

46. Katie King, "Producing Sex, Theory and Culture: Gay/Straight ReMappings in Contemporary Feminism," in *Conflicts in Feminism,* ed. Marianne Hirsch and Evelyn Fox Keller (New York: Routledge, 1990), 82–101.

47. bell hooks, "Writing Autobiography," in *Talking Back: Thinking Feminist, Thinking Black* (Boston: South End, 1989), 158.

48. Ibid., 155.

49. Ibid., 159.

50. Bernice Johnson Reagon, "Coalition Politics: Turning the Century," in *Homegirls: A Black Feminist Anthology,* ed. Barbara Smith (New York: Kitchen Table: Women of Color Press, 1983).

51. Bernice Johnson Reagon, "My Black Mothers and Sisters or On Beginning a Cultural Autobiography," *Feminist Studies* 8 (Spring 1982): 81–96.

52. Ibid., 82.

53. Reagon, "Coalition Politics," 356–57.

54. June Nash and Maria Fernandez-Kelly, eds., *Women, Men and the International Division of Labor* (Albany: State University of New York Press, 1983). See also Annette Fuentes and Barbara Ehrenreich, *Women in the Global Factory* (Boston: South End, 1983).

55. Fuentes and Ehrenreich, *Women in the Global Factory,* 9.

56. Ibid., 11–12.

57. Gayatri Chakravorty Spivak, "The Political Economy of Women as Seen by a Literary Critic," in *Coming to Terms: Feminism, Theory, Politics,* ed. Elizabeth Weed (New York: Routledge, 1989), 219.

58. Ibid., 224.

59. Ibid. See also Partha Chatterjee, "Agrarian Relations and Communalism in Bengal, 1926–1935," in *Subaltern Studies,* vol. 1 (Delhi: Oxford University Press, 1982), 9–38; idem, "More on Modes of Power and the Peasantry," in *Selected Subaltern Studies,* ed. Ranajit Guha and Gayatri Chakravorty Spivak (New York: Oxford University Press, 1988), 351–90.

60. Spivak, "Political Economy of Women," 225.

61. Ibid., 227.

62. Ibid.

63. Aihwa Ong, "Colonialism and Modernity: Feminist Re-presentations of Women in Non-Western Societies," *Inscriptions* 3/4 (1988): 88.

64. See Katie King's works in progress, "Crafting a Field: Feminism and Writing Technologies" (Presentation at Princeton University, 12 April 1990); "Feminism and Writing Technologies" (Presentation at the annual meeting of the Modern Language Association, 28 December 1988).

65. Saralee Hamilton, coordinator of the AFSC Nationwide Women's Program, quoted in Fuentes and Ehrenreich, *Women in the Global Factory,* 59.

Chapter 8

Unspeakable Differences: The Politics of Gender in Lesbian and Heterosexual Women's Autobiographies

Julia Watson

The Unspeakable

In women's autobiographies, naming the unspeakable is a coming to voice that can create new subjects, precisely because women's marginality may be unnameable within the terms or parameters of the dominant culture.[1] Maxine Hong Kingston introduces the category of the unspeakable in *The Woman Warrior* to describe the lack of identity that surrounds the first-generation Chinese-American children who want to name and therefore erode the boundaries of ghostly silence that guard the old culture's hegemony:

> Those of us in the first American generations have had to figure out how the invisible world the emigrants built around our childhoods fit in solid America. . . . [The emigrants] must try to confuse their offspring as well, who, I suppose, threaten them in similar ways—always trying to get things straight, always trying to name the unspeakable.[2]

Refusing to name the unspeakable not only protects what is sacred in Chinese tradition by enshrouding it in silence, guarding it from the uninitiated; it also marks cultural boundaries within which what is operative does not need to be spoken. For the immigrant or multicultural daughter, naming the unspeakable is at once a transgressive act that knowingly seeks to expose and speak the boundaries on which the organization of cultural knowledge depends and a discursive strategy that, while unverifiable, allows a vital "making sense" of her own multiple differences.[3]

The unspeakable is a category that has also been used to designate sexual differences that remain unspoken, and therefore invisible. In a heterosexual order, the homosexual woman has been both unrepresented and unrepresentable within sanctioned cultural fictions. Since the early 1970s, Adrienne Rich's essays have underscored the unspeakability of lesbian women and their texts.

> Whatever is unnamed, undepicted in images, whatever is
> omitted from biography, censored in collections of letters,
> whatever is misnamed as something else, made difficult-to-
> come-by, whatever is buried in the memory by the collapse
> of meaning under an inadequate or lying language—this will
> become, not merely unspoken, but *unspeakable*.[4]

Indeed, many fictions of female development structure the incorporation of sexuality as the internalization of the only sexual identity to be spoken—that of female heterosexuality defined as the other of heterosexual masculinity. In autobiography, which as a genre has functioned as the keeper of the "law" of patriarchal identity, women's sexuality has usually been presumed as heterosexual except when spoken otherwise.[5] When it is spoken as lesbian in autobiography, it has been read as voicing a transgressive sexuality—as the naming of an unspeakable—whose difference is read as deviance.[6]

That is, in autobiography, only homosexuals have sexuality. Heterosexuality, because it does not have to be named, retains some of the disciplinary power that Adrienne Rich attributed to it in delineating its "compulsory" mechanisms.[7] But it should be possible to locate women's autobiographies with respect to sexual demarcations along an axis of sexualities, and to read their speaking of sexual identity as complex statements that may challenge or rethink contemporary ideologies of gender. I propose to begin from lesbian markings of sexuality, and to read these articulations of the "unspeakable" against autobiographies of women whose sexuality is assumed to be normatively heterosexual at the same time that it is repressed as superfluous, the object of another's desire. Reading sexual difference as, in Audre Lorde's phrase, "the house of difference" in lesbian autobiographies, we may trace a trajectory of naming the unspeakable. This voicing may in turn be read against autobiographies in which the presumption of heterosexuality makes trouble within and across cultures. Can the repressive unspeakables of heterosexuality be named or unknotted without a critique of sexuality such as lesbian manifestos and other feminist critiques of patriarchy enable? While the texts I will discuss are recent (from the 1950s to the present in the United States), much has changed during the four decades since the first of them was published. What was formerly unspeakable may now no longer be transgressive, as critiques of heterosexuality have begun to be named from several points within its "system." My project is, then, a double one: to read women's autobiographies as acts not just of coming to voice but as negotiations in naming the unspeakable, and to claim a critical location from which to read the sexual unspeakable from outside a polarized framework in which normative heterosexuality and oppositional homosexuality operate as authorized and mutually exclusive discourses.

I do this in part in the interest of my own autobiographical project, to locate myself with respect to the discourses of lesbian and feminist identity politics, which have been positioned as inimical at several points, and to consider my investment in each.[8] If in my own life these categories have seemed inadequate to describe the complexities of experience, if the formulas of sexual and identity politics and the fixities of gender have seemed insufficiently articulated for the particulars of relationships, perhaps the polarized discourse of gender itself needs to be renegotiated through the specifics of personal affiliation. Reading women's autobiographies of lesbian and heterosexual orientations, declared or not declared, against one another may help to frame a politics of reading that undoes their simple opposition. This speaking may be located at an Archimedean point, but it is one that frames the possibility of women's affiliation through, and not despite, sexual difference. To read outside a framework of either heterosexual or homosexual identity politics focuses our attention on the possibility of becoming, in a sense, the sexually "decolonized" readers that both alternative texts and nondominant theories of autobiography propose.

Framing the Unspeakable

Carolyn Heilbrun, in *Writing a Woman's Life,* has observed the difficulty of negotiating and describing women's friendships outside a patriarchal framework by calling eloquently for reading and writing affiliation with other women as a focus of women's autobiography.

Heilbrun states that affiliations have been conceived in women's writing as "this sense of identification with women alone, not as fellow sufferers but as fellow achievers and fighters in the public domain" and "the sole saving grace of female friendship."[9] In seeing Toni Morrison's *Sula* and Audre Lorde's *The Cancer Journal* as models of such friendship, Heilbrun both identifies and elides the differential politics of such affiliations: between remorseful heterosexuality that gestures toward a nonrepresentable elsewhere (*Sula*) and lesbianism that reads relationships to women through its multiple, exclusionary differences (Lorde). Though Heilbrun does not expand on this interplay between sexual ideologies and women's affiliations, her characterization of the dilemma extends into women's autobiography generally. She leaves open a space for asking what the possible practices and politics of women's affiliation are that could undo the rhetoric and claims to power of both heterosexual and lesbian hierarchies.

There are justifications for reading from outside the heterosexual framework within feminist theory as well as in the autobiographical practices of many women writers. Teresa de Lauretis, in analyzing how the technologies of gender collude in maintaining a repressive status quo, has called for disengaging gender from the binary terms of patriarchy and repositioning it in a necessarily unspecified elsewhere:

> To envision gender (men and women) *other*wise, and to (re)construct it in terms other than those dictated by the patriarchal contract, we must walk out of the male-centered frame of reference in which gender and sexuality are (re)produced by the discourse of male sexuality.[10]

De Lauretis cites Monique Wittig's claim that "the discourses of heterosexuality oppress in the sense that they prevent us from speaking unless we speak in their terms" as justification for her argument that women's desire is unspeakable within current gender arrangements. If women are to forge an identity politics that would not simply reproduce the terms of patriarchy, the multiplicity of women's differences must be spoken in terms other than the heterosexist concepts that designate "feminist" and "lesbian" as forms of difference from its norms.[11]

Arguments in support of de Lauretis's call for women to position themselves in an "elsewhere" outside the heterosexual framework are made from two positions, that of lesbian readings of women's texts and that of revisionist gender theory. In "Lesbian Identity and Autobiographical Difference(s)," Biddy Martin argues powerfully against what she sees as an emerging hegemonic discourse in women's autobiography that threatens to silence female difference in the name of "woman."[12] White heterosexual feminists, she argues, have replicated a politics of marginalization in which lesbian autobiography is rendered invisible by being presented as a unitary other. Martin points out that lesbian autobiography has been represented as different from all other life writing and as the same for all lesbians, its difference localized reductively in sexual practice (p. 98). The coming-out story is, she argues, not only a genre of writing, but a way of reading that reduces and institutionalizes lesbian difference. Its conventions, including the representation of a homogeneous, repressive past and the subject's discovery of her lesbian "essence" and desire, make for an oversimplified story. In suppressing their own and the larger group's active participation in creating a community through internal and external struggle, the authors of coming-out stories may help to sustain a unitary and polarized construct of lesbian identity.

In challenging this univocity in the representation of lesbian life writing, Martin argues against reading lesbianism as "a totalizing self-identification" (p. 82).[13] To relocate its differences, the concept of gender must be expanded and filtered through the multiple differences and intersecting sites of oppression that characterize women's life writings, particularly those of women of color. In turning to the politics of experience to indict the narrowness of theory, Martin focuses on the important antiacademic feminist text *This Bridge Called My Back: Writings by Radical Women of Color,* a collection of autobiographical poems, essays, stories, and sketches.[14] In *Bridge,* the many autobiographical writers point to their systematic exclusion from the dominant white—including white academic feminist—culture and invoke collective identification of women of color across multiple differences as a community in unspeakability. In *Bridge,* Martin argues, lesbianism is "less an identity than a desire that transgresses the boundaries imposed by structures of race, class, ethnicity, nationality . . . and figures as a provocation that . . . desires different kinds of connections" (p. 94). Martin's relocation of lesbian desire frees it from the polarized opposition to a dominant heterosexuality that has characterized much earlier theorizing.

Women such as the writers in *Bridge,* in voicing experiences of invisibility, necessarily write against the norms of autobiography, traditionally understood as an institutionalized discourse of patriarchal authority that has rendered their differences unspeakable. Martin argues that lesbian autobiography has to be rethought not as a genre of writing, but as a rhetorical figure of the negotiations around identity and difference in which many autobiographers are engaged. It is, then, exemplary of new-model autobiographies when it is least like the fixed genre of lesbian autobiography. Like other autobiographers of marginality, the woman writer has to break silence to question dominant structures of meaning. Martin's textual readings free lesbianism from its own generic orthodoxy, in the "law" of the coming-out story, and refigure it as a transgressive desire and a provocation to heretofore unspeakable connections and affiliations.

In ways that complement Martin's rethinking of lesbian difference and particularize and revise de Lauretis's analysis, Judith Butler critiques the system of gender by showing how established models of both heterosexuality and homosexuality are constructed around binary oppositions. Butler argues that "heterosexuality" is a falsely naturalized coherence that acts as a regulatory fiction to police and deny more complex constructions of cultural identity.[15] The implications of her argument for women's autobiography are considerable. Butler argues that Lacanian and feminist post-Lacanian critiques of the subject are rooted in a binary matrix in which variants of two heterosexual desires underlie all available notions of gender. She notes:

> Under Lacanian and anti-Lacanian story lines about gender acquisition gender meanings are circumscribed within a narrative frame which both unifies certain legitimate sexual subjects and excludes from intelligibility sexual identities and discontinuities which challenge the narrative beginnings and closures offered by these competing psychoanalytic explanations.
> (p. 329)

That is, representations of identity have been polarized within a binary matrix that prohibits what Butler terms "the subversive recombination of gender meanings" observable in historical subjects (p. 335). What Freud posited as a pre-Oedipal primary bisexuality turns out to be subsumed and refigured within a paternally organized culture. To achieve gender identity is to achieve coherent heterosexuality, according to both Lacanian and Freudian analyses. Gender has been a falsely stabilized category that acts to regulate and maintain heterosexuality as a fiction of great cultural power. That constituted coherence, Butler argues, conceals the gender discontinuities within any sexuality, whether its context be heterosexual, bisexual, gay, or lesbian. In none of these does gender necessarily follow from sex, nor desire from gender (p. 336). The need for a coherent fiction of sexual identity and for an oppositional model in which heterosexuality is the norm and all other sexualities are deviant, while claiming to describe sexuality, regulates it as a developmental law.

Equally important to Butler's argument is her claim that critics of "compulsory heterosexuality," notably Monique Wittig and Adrienne Rich, have categorically criticized being "straight" as a compulsory ideology and argued for the necessity of an oppositional politics and praxis. Butler both learns from and revises Wittig's attack on fixed gender identities rooted in heterosexual ideology and her use of gendered homosexuality as a critical instrument to examine the negotiations of women's bodies. In so doing, Butler "makes trouble" by opening up a space within the oppositional representation of hetero/homosexuality for undoing and complicating the definitional claims of both heterosexual and lesbian as categories of gender identity. Butler's challenge cuts both ways. On the one hand, she criticizes the power of heterosexuality as a norm that levels and marginalizes the diversity and fluidity of sexual possibilities. On the other hand, she criticizes the discourse of lesbian identity as replicating the oppositional structure of heterosexuality by imitating and inverting its binary oppositions, suggesting that radical feminist critics have not been able to undo its fundamental power. For Butler the notion of multiple, fragmentary, fluid postures around a set of dissonant sexual roles opens up an interplay between hetero- and homosexual categories that destabilizes both. Such a theory would have potential for a politics of reading identity differently—reading it, that is, as a negotiation among fixed possibilities that both resists and remakes the representation of human experience. In such a negotiation the unspeakable would be mapped as what becomes speakable when boundaries are traversed, articulated, confused, and undone.

The Unspeakable and "Colonization"

Both de Lauretis's insistence on reading gender outside the terms of the patriarchal contract and Martin's and Butler's loosening of "heterosexuality" and "lesbian" from their competing claims to delimit women's sexuality offer us a language for reading the sexual identities of women's autobiographies other-wise. Such reforms speak to a claim within lesbian theory and, for that matter, much feminist theory, namely, that women's autobiographical projects are "sexual self-decolonization," which seems to me problematic. *Sexual decolonization* refers to a recurrent debate among feminists about whether women are "colonized" by compulsory heterosexuality in ways that only decolonizing strategies and the practice of critical consciousness can undo. Such critiques of heterosexuality need not inevitably point outside it to a primary "lesbian continuum" or a lesbian refiguring of sexuality, as the consciousness-raising groups of the 1970s—which could be understood as collective acts aimed at liberation from sexist ideology—showed. But the rhetoric of sexual decolonization has been employed primarily by lesbian writers in the context of their "unspeakability" to argue that the situation of women in patriarchy is in some ways analogous to that of colonized peoples.

Adrienne Rich uses the "unspeakable" to name how women's love for and affiliation with one another, which she sees as primary, are silenced by the colonizing practices exerted literally upon the bodies of women in Western culture: "There is the heterosexist, patriarchal culture which has driven women into marriage and motherhood through every possible pressure—economic, religious, medical, and legal—and which has literally colonized the bodies of women."[16] To counter that "colonization," Rich calls upon women to resist gynephobia and affirm the radical complexity of women's bonds without reverting to a simpler "dyke separatism."[17] Affirming a primary affiliation as women and naming it "lesbian" is, Rich argues in several essays, necessary to undo both the unspeakables and the "colonizing" practices of heterosexism: "The word *lesbian* must be affirmed because to discard it is to collaborate with silence and lying about our very existence; with the closet-game, the creation of the *unspeakable.*"[18] Rich insists on the "primary intensity" of woman-to-woman relationships as a way of "desiring . . . and choosing oneself" and on naming that focus "lesbian" as a way of resisting collaboration with the "unspeakable" or forbidden status of women's relationships under patriarchy.[19]

Similarly, Mab Segrest, who describes her autobiographical project as "self-decolonization," intends to divest herself of the inherited cultural baggage of heterosexism, along with that of "good" English literature and southern conservative politics. Segrest observes: "If much of it is rooted in autobiography, much of this decade of lesbian-feminist writing has undertaken the work of decolonizing the self."[20] Within an American lesbian feminist context, then, "decolonization" has been used as a metaphor for self-investigation of sexual difference, by definition an autobiographical divestiture of the unspeakables that police sexuality. Before exploring how colonization, as a metaphor and a discursive strategy, is used in lesbian women's autobiographies and considering whether such a condition can be read back into autobiographies of heterosexual women, where it is often not marked, it is important to situate the American feminist use of "decolonization" within the framework of postcolonial critique. Is a concept of colonization even viable outside a network of political, externally imposed,

repressive practices that operate on entire peoples? Or is "sexual decolonization" an indication of the decadent and depoliticized discourse
of American feminism, which has often been criticized by its non-
European "Third World" sisters for being mired in personal and bourgeois issues rather than addressing the exploitation of entire classes
of women workers characteristic of late capitalism?

The Nigerian novelist Buchi Emecheta takes up these concerns in
denouncing Western feminism's preoccupation with issues of sexuality
as a kind of exoticism when projected onto non-Western women:

> I have not been relating well with Western feminists and have
> found myself at loggerheads with them from time to time.
> They are only concerned with issues that are related to them-
> selves and transplant these onto Africa. Their own preoccupa-
> tions—female sexuality, lesbianism, and female circumcision—
> are not priorities for women in Africa. . . . Many African
> women are involved in food production in the rural areas and
> are far removed from lesbianism. . . . Western feminists are
> often concerned with peripheral topics and do not focus their
> attention on major concerns like the exploitation of women
> by Western multi-national companies. They think that by
> focusing on exotic issues in the "third world" they have inter-
> nationalized their feminism.[21]

For Emecheta, colonization, and particularly the neocolonization of
African countries, creates macropolitical issues that are obscured or
distorted by a preoccupation with sexual politics at the micropolitical
level. While indifference to social responsibility might be entertained
by educated Western women, African women, situated in networks
of family responsibility, must resist it. Emecheta's critique strikes at
the heart of the feminist dictum "The personal is political," by reading
the phrase as a substitution of the personal for the political. For
Emecheta, as for other African women writers, a critique of sexual
politics is not a sufficient act of "self-decolonization," and practicing
heterosexuality does not necessarily signify the absence of a critique
of how sexual organization intersects macrosocial organization.

Similar cirtiques of sexual politics as exoticizing and trivializing
women's primary and proper concerns with economic and political
exploitation have been made with reference to women autobiographers
outside the Euro-American frame. Barbara Harlow notes that in many
women's autobiographies of resistance the personal tends to disappear
into the political, or to be renounced for it in specific historical situations.[22] Harlow recalls Gayatri Spivak's observation on the "inbuilt
colonialism of First World feminism toward the Third" and Hazel

Carby's criticism of the participation of Western feminists in "the self-proclaimed 'civilizing mission' of European and United States colonialism and imperialism" as indictments of Western feminist claims to a global sisterhood. Harlow also notes that Western readers of women's autobiography deemphasize that many resistance women writers have relocated their lives to the public sphere, where the historic struggles of their people are taking place (p. 187). The discussion of sexual colonization as an aspect of "de/colonizing the subject," therefore, needs to be bracketed as a problematic and potentially misleading concept within the privileged discourse of Western identity politics that autobiography has helped to create and sustain, while it has refused to read the real and devastating effects of economic and political colonization. As the critics mentioned above persuasively argue, *sexual colonization* is too historically specific a term to apply to the situation of all women or even to the heterosexism that oppresses lesbians when that is not complicated by racial or ethnic oppression of a class of people.

The case for sexual colonization, however, has been made persuasively at some sites by radical women of color writing in the United States. A situation of colonial domination was assuredly represented in Harriet Jacobs's *Incidents in the Life of a Slave Girl*.[23] Notably, in the autobiographies of Chicana feminists Cherríe Moraga (*Loving in the War Years*) and Gloria Anzaldúa (*Borderlands/La Frontera*) and in *This Bridge Called My Back,* the interpellation of marginalizations by gender, race/ethnicity, class, and sexual orientation may inform a postcolonial situation.[24] The writers in *Bridge* read the isolation and invisibility imposed on them by their self-proclaimed lesbianism not as analogous to their marginalization as women of color, but as another outcome of heterosexist domination in American life. By claiming Audre Lorde's proclamation, "The master's tools will never dismantle the master's house," in an essay of the same title published in *Bridge,* they look to a restructuring that is political and economic, as well as interpersonal.

Autobiography, then, has been in recent years a productive site for rewriting the arrangements of gender. In an influential essay, Barbara Smith points to the unspeakability of lesbian women of color in feminist theory and urges white women to "a sane accountability to all the women who write and live on this soil." Smith calls for "what has never been" in saying:

> I . . . want to express how much easier both my waking and my sleeping hours would be if there were one book in existence that would tell me something specific about my life.

One book based in Black feminist and Black lesbian
experience.[25]

Writing in the late 1970s, Smith asks that autobiography resituate black
women's experience outside cultural sanctions. Although canonical lesbian texts such as Gertrude Stein's *The Autobiography of Alice B. Toklas*
had long been in print, they remained texts of privileged white women
whose major identification was with male expatriate writers and the
cult of genius. (In fact, in the 1970s Stein's writings were not yet being
read as lesbian texts—not surprisingly, given Stein's own equivocation
about homophobia and her "ventriloquist" silencing of Alice in the
text.[26]) Barbara Smith points out a gap that oppresses by what it does
not permit to be spoken. The project of naming the unspeakable is
an effort to pose the problem of the relationship between personal
experience and political goals as an instrument for change.[27]

In this way, rereading women's autobiographies both *for* their voicing of oppressed identities and *against* a misapplied concept of decolonization may enable a reformulation of sexual identity in
autobiography. Reading lesbian autobiographies as, in Judith Butler's
term, "complex sites of dissonance around sexual identity" (p. 338)
implicitly dislodges heterosexual women's autobiographies from a
fixed concept of gender as stable heterosexuality. Displacing the rhetoric of binary and polarized sexual orientations in autobiography and
understanding that as a strategy that keeps attempting to, in Hong
Kingston's phrase, "name the unspeakable" may open up that dissonance.[28] While arguing that women in the United States are seldom
colonized only by sexuality anymore, I want to consider how they
negotiate the naming of the unspeakables of sexual identity. Adrienne
Rich and Audre Lorde are lesbian autobiographers who are, in different
ways, in search of an "elsewhere" for their marginalized subjectivities.
Conversely, some contemporary autobiographical writers resist the
oppositional politics of lesbian analysis while attempting to situate
themselves "outside" the heterosexual framework.

Adrienne Rich and Women's Otherness

Adrienne Rich's autobiographical project is diffused through several
of her books and essays and increasingly directed at reading herself
as a representative white woman whose life narration is a self-critique
of her "colonized" status. She writes as a "woman trying, as part of
her resistance, to clean up my act," as she states in her autobiographical
essay, "Split at the Root."[29] There Rich undertakes an inquiry into the

premises of her cultural identity and her inherited views of gender, race, and class in the United States. She locates herself through the silences, the unspeakables, that surround her family's ethnic and class status while she is growing up. The essay moves from discovering and voicing the silences that she participated in and enacted to formulating her identity as a collective and oppositional one—through participating in the civil rights movement, then through her growing solidarity with other women, in particular lesbian women, as a community united by its articulated, rather than inherited, goals. The essay's movement is from family as the locus of an identity that is configured negatively through its unspeakables to the possibility of a chosen, communal identification with explicit goals and a non-individualist concept of identity.

If compulsory heterosexuality is the great lie for Rich, the unspoken secret is the integration of love and power in personal and collective woman identificaion in the lesbian community. Her position has often been taken as a separatist manifesto, particularly in proclaiming the "lesbian continuum" of women that must remain unspeakable in heterosexist society. But in "Split at the Root," Rich traces a complex web of intersecting identifications that argues for a less dogmatic rethinking of identity politics through acts of self-inquiry. Rich represents her identity as a double consciousness incapable of integration, and locates it in an originary fissure or "split" that points up the fictive status of unitary concepts of identity. Rich sees her own history as fundamentally divided between what was spoken and what remained repressed in her family across gender, class, and ethnicity. She reads the denial of Jewish ethnicity in her middle-class family as constitutive of both her own racism and her lack of identity while growing up. Confessional and critique become inseparable autobiographical acts. Discovering how in childhood her identity was formed by her family's assimilative values, she finds herself scripted to live out an American dream of privilege without conscience. Rich recalls her father's insistence "I am a person, not simply a Jew" as a wish for assimilation that divests the family of its identity (p. 110). As the daughter of an eminent Jewish doctor who "passed" for WASP, she learned to collude in silence. By passing for a Christian southerner, her mother's heritage, she participated as well in the unspeakability of blackness—in skin color and social position—that in the 1950's perpetuated racism in the South. Not naming, Rich insists, reinforces the power of the unspeakable to sustain oppression; yet exposing the silences of racism by indicting her parents' caste and class would be a betrayal of the personal bonds of family. For example, when she first discovers the persecution of Jews in a newsreel of Allied liberation of Nazi concentration camps, Rich discovers both connection to and hatred for Jewish identity, as well as the potential to resist that identity by continuing to "pass": "I had never been taught about resistance, only about 'passing.' I had no language for anti-Semitism itself" (p. 107). Watching the film, she cannot say whether the dead in the film are "them" or "us." As Rich recalls her identity crisis, she constructs it as a choice between the personal myth of her family, grounded in individualism and false consciousness, and an affiliation with the collective and political history of her ancestors that that myth has rendered unspeakable.

Rich sees the notion that identity and assimilation are compatible, her family's message about outsiders becoming insiders, as a delusion to be uncovered. But if the family's identity is truncated, investigating it through acts of self-reclamation, while it can make the split visible, will not heal it. Self-reclamation means taking seriously the contradictory identity politics of her ethnicity, her class status, and her gender. Reading family relationships through a model of patriarchal domination creates both split consciousness and a double vision of Jewish identity as liberation and collusion. That reading finds an unspeakable web of interlocked oppressions.

Autobiographical narrative becomes a useful way of tracking her own movement through contradictory filiations and recognizing the difficulty of extricating herself from individualist concepts of identity. For example, though she claims affiliation with Jewish women at Radcliffe, she counterposes that to a moment in which she refuses identification as a Jew with an immigrant seamstress, a betrayal consonant with her upbringing (p. 109). Similarly, she marries a man of Eastern European Jewish origin in order to identify with her heritage against her family, but discovers that that heritage includes an oppressively patriarchal tradition in which she is figured as subordinate. For Rich, the crux of her realizations about identity politics comes in recognizing the anti-Semitism that she herself has objectified as "Jewish culture" and internalized as self-hatred, which the civil rights movement brings home to her. To complicate further her critique of the relationship of women to family and culture in Judaism by placing herself outside heterosexuality as a Jewish lesbian is, Rich argues, to chart "oppressions within oppression" (p. 121). To be inscribed in one tradition implies the unspeakability of the other. Finally, she characterizes this fundamental split only in negative terms: she was born "neither Gentile nor Jew, Yankee nor Rebel" (p. 101). And she is a "white, Jewish, anti-Semite, racist, anti-racist, once-married, lesbian, middle-class, feminist Southerner" who acknowledges her inability to speak with clarity or to speak for others, across multiple differences (p. 123). These strings of oppositions that configure American identity both display her multiple, interlocked splits and fix her within their binary logic. In speaking, she autobiographically recollects the unspeakables of private and collective history as a way to "clean up my act" (p. 123). Admitting her ongoing collaboration as a woman in her suppression as a lesbian shapes a split identity that is oppositional, without a means to heal its own fissures except in speaking its process of purgation and re-visioning.

Rich's self-investigation, applying the rhetoric of decolonization, argues for the necessity of rethinking identity in opposition to the framework of Western humanism. As an autobiographical writer employing identity politics to define autobiography as a process of "cleaning up my act," Rich makes one response to Emecheta's indict-ment of lesbian feminist critiques as decadent privatism. Rich bears witness to white Western women as living through a model of split subjectivity disciplined by its unspeakables. For her, articulating oppression and false consciousness is a necessary autobiographical prelude to larger political engagement.

Audre Lorde's House of Difference

Audre Lorde, though a contemporary of Adrienne Rich, formulates "sexual decolonization" in significantly different ways. Lorde's auto-biographical writings, in addition to much autobiographical poetry, include *Zami,* a coming-of-age narrative; *The Cancer Journals;* and several volumes of essays.[30] They have been little discussed by most contemporary critics of autobiography.[31] Lorde, a black lesbian fem-inist of Grenadan ancestry who grew up in the 1950s in New York, does not write autobiographical difference simply. In *Zami,* Lorde locates herself at the intersection of multiple differences, in *represen-tative* unspeakability as a lesbian woman of color. She notes of her first years as a black lesbian writer in the Village:

> Being women together was not enough. We were different.
> Being gay-girls together was not enough. We were different.
> Being Black together was not enough. We were different.
> Being Black women together was not enough. We were differ-
> ent. Being Black dykes together was not enough. We were dif-
> ferent. . . . It was a while before we came to realize that our
> place was the very house of difference rather than the security
> of any one particular difference.[32]

Voicing multiple specificities, Lorde names her unspeakability as that which is suppressed at any intersection of racism, sexism, and homophobia.[33] But naming through difference has to acknowledge its own unspeakability, its inevitable placement "elsewhere." The "house of difference," assuredly not the master's house, is a virtual space defined in negation, as always "different." So, I will argue, is the mythic space in which women can build a utopian community that Lorde's work proposes; it is not a "decolonized" territory but a vision of possibility that reorients the political and personal relationships of this world.

In *Zami,* Lorde self-consciously calls into question the norms of autobiographical representation as they have been inscribed in Western culture. She takes her own marginality—beginning as a legally blind, awkward, woman-identified black child at a time when any of those would have sufficed to make her an outsider—as a lens to interrogate normative concepts of women, whiteness, and sexuality. The oxymoron of her representative unspeakability is a central trope of Lorde's autobiography. To write is to exorcise her childhood of internalized oppression and the imposed ideological biases—sexism, racism, homophobia—that converged in her experiences of being invisible, other.

Lorde remakes both the genre of autobiography and the texture of its *bios.* In subtitling *Zami* as *A New Spelling of My Name,* she inverts the established order from A (Audre) to Z. *Zami* is a word used derogatorily in the West Indies for lesbians (*les amies*) that Lorde redefines as "a Carriacou name for women who work together as friends and lovers" (p. 255).[34] She embraces "zami" to spell her own name collectively and reworks her autobiography as explicitly a "biomythography" that defines that collectivity. Lorde proposes a semimythic place, Carriacou, an unlocatable island that her mother claims as home and that is famous for "how . . . women love each other," as the site of a community of women lovers that is both prior to and beyond patriarchal origins (p. 14).[35] Carriacou, as an origin and mythic goal of deindividuated identity in a nonoppressed lesbian community, redefines "house" as community in Lorde's metaphor of her autobiography as "my journey to this house of myself" (p. 43). In finally creating a satisfactory relationship with a lover, mythicized as the black lesbian goddess Afrekete, who can both move within and laugh at white patriarchy, Lorde uses autobiography to undermine its socially integrative purpose and to stage an alternative birthing of herself through writing her life as a movement toward an origin "elsewhere."

Lorde's myth of destiny as origin remade is less a nostalgic desire for originary unity than a self-conscious strategy for creating a context in which her painful consciousness of the price of her difference can be transformed into celebration. To rewrite her unspeakability through myth in the final chapters of *Zami* is to make an intervention in the political arrangements that have rendered her unspeakable and that provide an insistently historical counternarrative to the mythic time of Carriacou. In documenting, at several points in *Zami,* the ubiquitous racist practices of the 1950s—segregated housing, transportation, lunch counters—and its terrifying McCarthyism, Lorde emphasizes the inequitable power structures of Western society that cannot be mythically resolved. The counternarrative to the "biomythography" of *Zami,* then, is a personal story of struggle and pain in a stubborn present that is inflected by the difficulty of social change in a world driven by myths of white Western individuality. In her introductory interrogation of where her own power comes from, Lorde both acknowledges the force of encounters with battered, angry, and proud women and attests to how those experiences of women's cruelty to women helped to create herself: "I, coming out blackened and whole" (p. 5). Lorde's "I" works narratively to transform her experience of exclusion as a transgressive outsider into chosen, prized, collective difference. If the present remains uninhabitable because of its fractured political structure, Lorde's myth of nostalgic futurity, acknowledging its own fantasy, permits the unspeakables of her identity to be written.

Lorde's struggles are epitomized in the problematic inheritance of her Grenadan mother Linda, whose tough-mindedness bespeaks her strength in reformulating her native past into a modest American success story achieved through repressing her cultural origin. Lorde is raised to cooperate in the wall of restrictive injunctions her parents have internalized: social decorum, Catholic-school diligence, and racial assimilation. Lorde reads her mother's disciplining as an effort to make her own Grenadan identity as unspeakable as her mother's became in an alliance with heterosexual patriarchy that made her origin indecipherable. Yet her mother's unspeakables speak to her in an underlying contradiction that Lorde sees: her mother is "a very powerful woman" who was "different from the other women I knew, Black or white," a kind of "third designation" or sex beyond an ordinary woman or man (p. 15). Lorde sees her mother as a Carriacouan woman prior to her domestication to American heterosexuality, that is, as having a primal eroticism that Lorde names "lesbian." This vision of her mother's origin both legitimates her lesbian desire and explains the inevitablity of tension with a mother who represses her own "power." Lorde specifies her difference from her mother as much in her resistance to all assimilation—to heterosexuality, the middle class, compliant black femininity—as in her mythicizing of Carriacou as a locus of "root-truths" and "powers," healing and rituals from Africa (p. 13).

Lorde's reading of her childhood makes her transvaluation of all values clear. Childhood is for her a series of intensifying transgressions against the norms of heterosexual femininity that uncover and speak her female desire as transgressive because it is connected to the rhythms and practices of a forgotten, repressed origin. Several of her autobiographical stories are exemplary. As a child of four, for example, she first attempts an exploration of what is hidden in the clothing of another little girl, and retrospectively reads this encounter as her awakening to women's difference from the doll without sexual parts that she plays with and that stands for "woman." That she is both prevented from exploring and rebuked for her natural curiosity proves to her that becoming woman should be understood as an education in denial and repression.

Similarly, Lorde's adolescence is narrated as a series of transgressive liminal moments that defy her mother's way of negotiating the world by honoring its unspeakables. While her mother's world is full of secret shame about the signs, odors, and paraphernalia of female sexuality, Lorde figurally rewrites her mother's destiny in a homely, sensuous story of kitchen erotics. She recalls when, as an adolescent on the verge of menstruation, she helped to concoct a fragrant West Indian *souse,* a stew that has no American equivalent, like her Carricouan eroticism. As she is grinding ingredients with a mortar and pestle, she fantasizes a different connection to women's work in revising the pounding of the pestle to a sweeping circular movement. The adult Lorde makes of this "instinctual" pleasuring gesture an origin for her desire to remake the phallic order through a blood connection to the loamy tropical fruits and pungent smells of West Indian women that her mother has denied and policed. Lorde's kitchen erotics as a vision of affiliation can have no correlative in either the straight or the lesbian worlds of 1950s New York; its difference, with its mythic origin/goal in the "elsewhere" of Carriacou, organizes her world as the unspeakable inversion of all that she knows.

Yet Lorde, unlike Rich, explodes the oppositional logic of sexual difference. Finally the world is only women. She is as different from all those who name themselves different as she is from those who do not. She indicts the homophobia and racism of her white women lovers as signs of their own self-hatred. *Zami* invents a language of lesbian eroticism in a political climate in which it is as prohibited as is cross-dressing in the 1950s Village. She discovers that, even in the lesbian subculture, female relationships are coded within a hierarchy that is classist and racist. Her encounters with white women are infused with anxiety about her own excess—of blackness, of desire—that she is required to suppress in order to fit a norm in which her blackness can be only a devalued exoticism.

Recalling the aftermath of the Rosenberg executions, when McCarthyism raged, Lorde's vision of American life is one of repressive tolerance, subordinating women to abusive lovers, workers to life-destroying jobs in chemical industries, and blacks to a schizoid culture of official segregation and constant harassment. Finding the United States intolerable, Lorde sets out to explore an alternative world of brownness in Mexico that celebrates sensuality in eating and living. Yet there, too, in the lesbian community she seeks and encounters, the relationship politics of women are shaped by their own unspeakables—alcoholic rage, financial jealousy, and the mutilation, both psychological and physical, that American women have internalized as lesbian self-hatred. In this world of differences, Lorde must confront the alternative impulses of her "different" identity—for a mythic home and a permanent sense of exile. *Zami* provides both. In that sense her "biomythography," despite its gesture toward "elsewhere," is a historicized statement for political transformation, not transcendence, that remains embedded in the difficult political realities of racism and homophobia that define American life.[36]

In rewriting her life as "a bridge and field of women," Lorde makes naming evocative. The depersonalized, collective name of Afrekete, the mythic African goddess, "linguist, trickster, best-beloved, whom we must all become," is an identity that revises individuality into women's communality. She proposes a myth of noncolonizing harmony based paradoxically in a separate community of women who had been known only in a colonial context. Throughout the autobiography Lorde attempts to name "what has never been," an act that is rhetorically a metaphor but experientially a politics. She remakes the *bios* of autobiography into a collective, erotic possibility of connection that dreams of representing the unspeakable. No innocent naturalization of an originary past, Lorde's self-conscious mythmaking occurs on the site of its own impossibility in a counterdiscourse of the erotics of place that inverts and reformulates identity.

Unspeakability is conditioned by historical factors that shift rapidly. Certainly the 1980s made visible both the oppression of women of color and a multiplicity of voices that disclaimed white patriarchal identity politics and refused to read their lives through the ideologies of middle-classism, academic feminism, imperialism, or heterosexism. While it remains to be seen what positions women will adopt in the 1990s, the personal, intimate narratives that locate sexuality as not just a construct but a revising of identity, above all for women who look critically at heterosexism, whether from within or without heterosexuality, are likely to persist. I will discuss two life writings that attempt to undo the axis of oppositional sexual positioning. Both of these tests try to write beyond what Sidonie Smith has termed the "manifesto" quality of many lesbian autobiographies in the last two decades.

Does Mary Morris Have Nothing to Declare?

Mary Morris's *Nothing to Declare: Memoirs of a Woman Traveling Alone* is both "a travel book and a journey into the self," according to its jacket blurb.[37] The narrative claims to be a journey of *divesting* Western cultural assumptions about the woman who is unspeakable because she is, in every sense, "traveling alone." Morris presents her encounter with Mexican others of different language, ethnicities, and social practices as a means of divestiture that distinguishes her from the American expatriates of San Miguel de Allende, who cling to their own colony. But this autobiography also leads us to ask whether a mainstream American woman in a "Third World" culture can divest herself, relocate, and affiliate transnationally with other women if she has "nothing to declare."[38] Like Lorde, Morris stakes her identity on making a myth of an imagined elsewhere that both de- and recolonizes women; unlike Lorde, Morris does not reinvent social arrangements, but remains a traveler, passing through. Her insistence on a depoliticized world of intuitive connections and fluidity, however appealing, finally suggests that the book does declare something: namely, its own refusal to connect personal experience to the sociopolitical realities of women's lives. Morris's view of Mexican culture, as an otherness that remakes her identity as a traveler, spares her engagement, intervention, the possibility of concrete change.

Morris's travels from northern Mexico down through the Honduran jungles, to the Guatemalan highlands and back, describe the circular structure of a journey of recognition. She sees this journey ending not in the social reintegration of the heroine, but in her breaking away from the old—old friends, old myths, the necessity of situating and seeing herself in the old male-centered frame. Her travels point up several parallels between U.S. and Mexican women—brutalization by their male lovers, the difficulties of economic self-empowerment, and the desire for another Mexico than the facade of Spanish colonialism and Americanized sexist exploitation that confronts her. But despite her efforts at divestiture and nondeclaration, Morris's sense of women's analogous experience across cultures needs to be viewed critically, within a framework of the United States' historical exploitation of other American cultures. Despite her journey of divestiture Morris has difficulty in extricating herself both from her own white middle-class midwestern cultural heritage and from North American sentimentalization of Mexicans as dark-skinned Latino males and noble, self-sacrificing *madres*.

In crossing cultural boundaries, Morris presents herself as opening up interior frontiers of exploration across nationality, class, and sexuality. Stripping away the declaratives that have stood in for her identity, she interrogates her Chicago Jewish middle-class background, with its imperatives to do well and marry a good provider. Her private vision of self, recalled from childhood fantasy, comes to the fore: romantic images of a frontier world in which "the men were away and the women had to be brave . . . as an Indian hunter, riding bareback, or the boss of a ranch" (p. 77). Morris reflects on the role she served in her family, as a "demilitarized zone" for two incompatible parents, and her own role of enacting the daughter with cheerful patience until the day she could escape to live out her fantasy (p. 176). She recalls her mother as making a traveler of her by her own stasis. Staying in the suburbs at her husband's will, Morris's mother, for an event called the Suppressed Desires Ball, costumes herself elaborately as the globe. "Instead of seeing the world, my mother *became* it" (p. 21). In escaping her destiny as the inheritor of her mother's stasis, Morris tries to see while eluding self-definition. As a traveler, she disavows any stable identity. But she also claims the traveler's privilege, to refuse recognition of the indigenous culture's "otherness," preferring romantic myths of the hidden pre-Columbian Mexico to the harsh economic and social realities of its neocolonial present.

Morris discovers that her childhood desire to be an adventurer has to occur in an elsewhere that is truly "elsewhere." The cultural representations that name and contain women in Mexico frame her as "woman," American, and traveler. They hinder her access to the unofficial culture that she glimpses as an underlay of Mexico's Westernized public culture. Above all, her cultural status as *gringeta* marks her as vulnerable: "Initially I behaved like a hunted thing. It is not easy to move through the world alone, and it is never easy for a woman. . . . you should know how to strike a proud pose, curse like a sailor, kick like a mule, and scream out your brother's name, though he may be 3,000 miles away. And you mustn't be a fool" (p. 10). Rejecting the American expatriates who try to incorporate her, she attempts to cross literal and metaphorical borders to affiliation with other women—an illiterate peasant, Lupe, who advises Morris, "It is better not to depend on anyone," and a fellow traveler, Catherine, who deserts her for a boyfriend when she feels homesick (p. 39). Morris sees Lupe as a link to the indigenous culture, "mystical, magical, communal," that under-lies the conqueror's efficient reality (p. 64). But the reader is left with an uneasy sense of Morris's selective appropriation of Lupe's experi-ence and her denial of the confining realities of Lupe's life—spousal abuse, ineffective birth control and expensive abortions, lack of money for necessities for her children.

Finally, Morris opts for a vision of "Mexico" as the insubstantial, inaccessible world of the *bruja* or sorceress who appears mysteriously in the mountains several times, over Lupe's grim *barrio*. The possi-bility of an alternative matrilinear world supportive of affiliations among women remains for her a fantasy to be located outside a net-work of societal realities. When Morris finds a Mexican boyfriend, whom she prizes for his dark skin, he becomes a solution to the problems of either continuing to travel as a women alone or relying on other women who desert her. He offers her a means of entry into the urban culture of Mexico City, an exchange in which she both gains and loses social status; ultimately this is another relationship to be divested. Resisting fixities of location and declaration throughout this journey, Morris just keeps on walking.

In Morris's mysterious glimpses of the *bruja,* she finds a connection to the "other," precolonization Mexico. In disavowing explicit feminist politics and politically based affiliation with other women for the possibility of personal affiliations, Morris seems to hesitate between the old story of heterosexual ideology's power to fix women and an alternative possibility of free exchange. But her nondeclarative stance refuses to let her address the otherness of the other woman, in the figure of Lupe, who is not like her precisely because of the inequities of social status produced by Spanish and American colonization.

Morris sees travel as creating for her a provisional and temporary identity that escapes the declaratives of social ideology. As a moving point of perception she both makes momentary connections to other women and attempts to elude the strictures of definition as "woman" that would immobilize her. But can some of the essentialist baggage of "woman" be divested simply by repeatedly "walking out" to a new place? Morris creates a virtual space of textuality in which female identity would not be construed as the Other of a male universal, in which whiteness would not be normative, in which pre-Columbian myths would not be used to justify exploitative neocolonialist practices, but would contribute to imagining a different world. In such a world family would be reinterpreted communally, bonds with other women would occur across class and ethnicity, male violence would be suppressed, and women could wander freely, like powerful animals. But all this is transient, tentative, nondeclarative—finally a traveler's dream. In this evocation of an elsewhere in between cultural boundaries sexuality need not be negotiated and women's relationships are free and untroubled. But it is a mythic "elsewhere" of past futurity that cannot speak to the differences of "the other woman." In having "nothing to declare" Morris continues to hover between reliance on patriarchal authority that positions her as its "other" and the resistance of the unspeakable woman whose only alternative is to keep traveling alone.

Jo Spence—Decensoring the Unspeakable

Jo Spence is a British photographer whose work has ranged widely from commercial and portrait photography to social documentaries exhibited in collective galleries. In 1986 she published *Putting Myself in the Picture,* a book that combines images and text in an autobiography centered on the politics of sexuality—in the family, in relationships, in the history and imagery of photography itself.[39] Spence puts herself in the picture by retrospectively viewing her professional photographs of others against images of herself throughout her life, and making a chronological text of their interplay. To the photographs she appends essays that create a dialogue between her present "looking" and the texts of memory about the representational power of images to mold perception and behavior. This interplay of images and texts lets her study how the camera's "gaze" has fixed the poses and expressions of her "individuality" through stereotypes based in gender and class.

One of the aims of Spence's self-study is to "denaturalize" sexuality (p. 78). "Disrupting Sexual Stereotypes" is the title of a 1977 project for which she hired a male transvestite to play several women's roles before the camera's objectifying "gaze." Spence discusses the autobiographical significance of this project for her: "Denaturalizing sexuality meant facing the long held-at-bay limitations of the ways in which I lived out and negotiated my own sexuality" (p. 78). Those limitations, she explains, were the boundaries of both how she conceived herself as "feminine" and how she let herself see other women, including the women and girls she had photographed. She begins to read the limitations, indeed unspeakables, that constrained, naturalized, and defined her sense of being a subject as structured by determinants of class, nationality, and gender. Through the project she comes to see herself differently, recognizing that "woman" is constructed through both the spectator's gaze and the subject's participation in becoming "woman."

In several essays Spence focuses on how class and sexuality are determinants of identity that have "cross-fertilized" each other in what she thought was her individual history (p. 82). She turns to early family photographs to trace an autobiographical history of how she has been made a woman, a process that she sees as a way to deconstruct her own construction: "Deconstructing myself visually [was] an attempt to identify the process by which I had been 'put together'" (p. 83). Viewing successive photos of herself throughout her life, she sees how she has been caught trying to conform to role expectations at several stages when she believed she was asserting herself. Through this process Spence begins to depersonalize her autobiographical self and to speak in a collective "we" to other women about a feminist project of unmaking stereotypes of women. Such a process of dialogue and critique is, she implies, necessary for the formation of new subjects: "We must learn to see beyond ourselves and the stereotypes offered, to understand the invisible class and power relationships into which we are structured from birth" (p. 92). Though Spence plays autobiographically with versions of her photographed and remembered past, she argues that this personal restructuring is a means to a serious commitment to political change.

In particular, Spence employs the analytical frameworks of psychoanalysis and historical materialism to explore how interrogating gendered subjectivity provides possibilities for political change (p. 121). One extended project at this intersection is "photo-therapy," a "reframing technique" that she has developed from 1984 onward with Rosy Martin (p. 172). Martin is a lesbian; Spence characterizes herself as a (naturalized) heterosexual interested in undoing heterosexuality's naturalizing power. In photo-therapy Spence and Martin exchange roles between the subject/patient and the photographer/therapist. Spence sees this exchange as a means of mutual creation through a practice of dialogue in which they give each other permission to both re-view and let go of past constructed selves.

Spence and Martin play with restaging the absences and silences around childhood photos—being an infant, a schoolgirl, an adolescent in the shadow of her mother, a bride. When they look, the assumed heterosexuality of their subjectivity is exposed as falsely naturalized and repressive of the multidirectional impulses of childhood sexuality that become unspeakable in becoming "woman." Their dialogue opens up questions of how sexuality may be explored and expressed across the categories of "lesbian" and "heterosexual" (pp. 184-85). In their cowritten essay, each recalls and replays her childhood relationship with her mother to discover how her adolescent self was constructed as heterosexual. For Martin the process of sexual socialization is an "un-natural extra-ordinary distortion" to fit into a "natural" position (p. 175). For Spence it meant learning to become her mother, a role that she needs to enact and undo in order to claim her difference as a heterosexual woman. Spence and Martin claim that photo-therapy deconstructs the dominant fantasies, mystified processes, and image manipulations evident in what the photos do not show—the silences and gaps around the objectified roles they had learned to become. Photo-therapy is also a reconstructive process, one in search of other "truths" for potential healing and survival.[40] By finding and naming the powerful unspeakables that "made" both of them and fixed them in opposition to each other as the "natural" and the "unnatural" woman, Spence and Martin tell each other their autobiograhical stories as what their official "lives" screened from the record.

As a consequence of her own autobiographical "therapy," Spence urges women to reappropriate the camera. She views and reflects on the unspeakables of her life to gain control in a society that is structured as inaccessible to women. In so doing, she claims, women could enter into a larger autobiographical project of "keep[ing] the family archives" with a political consciousness (p. 209). In such a project the subject would focus on "areas of what you actually know and remember, as opposed to what you can allow yourself to speak about" (p. 216). That is, naming the unspeakables of personal and family history, hidden in the "occasions" of family photographs, can rewrite the silences that stucture family complicity in the making of "natural" men and women. Such naming is a step toward collective practices of discovering the history of one's assumed subjectivity in order to "re-imag(in)e who we are," both visually and verbally (p. 214). Women as phototherapists re-viewing their self-images and "inability to 'speak' about certain things" can restructure autobiography into a mode neither of nostalgic individuality nor simply of oppositional consciousness (p. 210). Rather, autobiography becomes a historicizing process that tries to "decensorize" unspeakables for women by making their operations and their normative power manifest (p. 214).

By framing the images and the implicit story of her life through a heterosexual imperative that she saw as repressing both multidirectional desire and the objective realities of being "woman," Spence takes up the critical challenges with which I began: De Lauretis's call to walk out of the heterosexual frame and Butler's call to both undo and complicate the binary oppostion of homosexual and heterosexual, falsely naturalized in the interest of policing gender identity. Spence's speculations on how to see/be as a subject in a society that tries to fix her as woman pose innovative directions for women's autobiographical writing. In critiquing women's investment in a history of images bound by their unspeakables, Spence redefines autobiography as process of re-vision. The Spence-Martin partnership in phototherapy, across sexualities fixed as "lesbian" and "heterosexual," begins to undo the power of images to control and restrict. Spence's double move, of partnered deconstruction and playful reconstruction, repositions autobiographical subjectivity within the objective class relations of gendered subjects. Her practice to some extent undoes the oppositional constructions of identity and the othering of non-Western women that the other autobiographers discussed here seem unable to escape. In an autobiographical project that is personal *through* its engagement in sexual and class politics, Spence reframes autobiography and negotiates a dialogue in which personal interrogation of her subjective history begins to create a new subject, one whose identity and sexuality aim at being critically chosen rather than assigned and unspeakable.

Conclusion

In the evocation of spaces outside a mapped and constricted social world, each of these autobiographers invokes the transformatory power of personal myths of alternative self-definition; yet each attempts to ground herself in a historically and politically specific present that displays the complexity of differences and the difficulty, especially for women of color, of maneuvering them. In confessing a personal history, each sketches a process of, and a will to, change that places these texts, framed as both transient and transpersonal, in gestures toward "naming the unspeakable." In progressing through these autobiographical texts around refigurings of sexual identity, I have attempted to respond to and reframe Buchi Emecheta's concern with a false analogy between the situations of postcolonial writers in non-Western countries and women in the West. Emecheta is surely correct that the colonization analogy is suspect because the conditions of colonial exploitation based solely in sexual identity do not exist here unqualifiedly. Reading First World heterosexual or lesbian women's autobiographies as processes of "sexual decolonization" misstates the conditions of colonialism, despite ongoing tensions and injustices rooted in homophobia and sexism. Emecheta also raises the question of whether Western women's focus on sexual politics is a frivolous process. I have argued that, in autobiography, reexamining one's sexual positioning is an aspect of reframing the history of one's subjectivity through a critical examination that intends to enable connectedness with other women as potential new subjects whose identity would have collective force.

But, depending on how the process of self-reflection and the construction of identity are conceived, how the system of gender is understood, and whether the multiple differences of women are acknowledged, it may not be possible to undo the binds created by autobiographical reflection on one's position as woman/women. Rich's delineation of her split consciousness as a product of her family's—and culture's—systematic refusal to speak its difference is autobiographically a process of "cleaning up my act." But, although her corpus of feminist writing is perhaps the single most important body of American work on the difficulty of naming, and the need to name, unspeakables, Rich's fixation on herself within the oppositional politics of lesbianism seems not to permit critical reflection on how it structures identity. For Lorde, the multiple differences of being a black Grenadan-American lesbian define her as outside all available systems of naming. If, for Lorde, her difference cannot be summed up as any single difference, and if the myth of a community of women loving women is inscribed in its own mythic wishfulness, speaking the unspeakables of her difference names it; but it cannot speak effectively to the situation of other nameless women whose lives mutely intersect her own. As Morris suggests, walking on nondeclaratively may be read as a refusal to participate in the fixed positions inscribed for women in the cultures she passes through as a traveler. In her engagements with other women across cultural boundaries, she can see, but not intervene in, brutalization and marginalization; women's autonomous assertion remains a magical glimpse. With Spence, however, an insistence that women move from reflecting on their own subjectivity to considering how they are all "framed" as images in the politics of representation resituates colonizing rhetoric while maintaining a focus on the ways in which, even for white women of privilege, identity is structured and policed by its unspeakables.

Notes

1. Rita Felski argues that feminist autobiographies, linking the personal and the political, have been an important moment for the self-definition of formerly voiceless groups in recent years by creating a "counter-public sphere" as a genre of autobiography that both interrogates and affirms gendered subjectivity. Such autobiographies of marginality thus create *new subjects*. *Beyond Feminist Aesthetics* (Cambridge, Mass.: Harvard University Press, 1989), 121.

2. Maxine Hong Kingston, *The Woman Warrior* (New York: Random House, 1975), 6. Kingston again refers to the unspeakable as the unnamed of traditional Chinese discourse: "If we had to depend on being told, we'd have no religion, no babies, no menstruation (sex, of course, unspeakable), no death. I thought talking and not talking made the difference between sanity and insanity. Insane people were the ones who couldn't explain themselves" (p. 216). Writing the book *names* the "secrets" on whose repression the perpetuation of traditional culture depends; figuring them out is both a transgression and, for the emigrants, a way of making sense of one's life. Compare this with the remark by Lena St. Clair in *The Joy Luck Club*: "I always thought it mattered, to know what is the worst possible thing that can happen to you, to know how you can avoid it, to not be drawn by the magic of the unspeakable." Amy Tan, *The Joy Luck Club* (New York: G.P. Putnam's Sons, 1989), 103.

3. Similarly, James Baldwin remarks, "Growing up in a certain kind of poverty is growing up in a certain kind of silence." The facts and injustices of everyday life cannot be named because "no one corroborates it. Reality becomes unreal because no one experiences it but you." Baldwin also attests to the power of another's witnessing to what seems unspeakable: "Life was made bearable by Richard Wright's testimony. When circumstances are made real by another's testimony, it becomes possible to envision change." Quoted by Margaret Spillane in a review, "The Culture of Narcissism," *The Nation,* 10 December 1990, 739.

4. Adrienne Rich, "It is the Lesbian in Us . . . ," in *On Lies, Secrets, and Silence: Selected Prose 1966–1978* (New York: W. W. Norton, 1979), 199.

5. See Caren Kaplan's essay, "Resisting Autobiography: Out–Law Genres and Transnational Feminist Subjects," in this volume.

6. Assuredly, as Sidonie Smith, Carolyn Heilbrun, and others have shown compellingly, women autobiographers are always writing against a history of their own cultural silencing, producing texts whose multiple, fragmentary discourses stand in no easy relationship to the empowered, coherent subjectivity that has been taken as a norm of autobiography. In the last ten years, a series of canons have emerged in women's autobiography, initially privileging texts by literary women autobiographers (Mary McCarthy, Lillian Hellman, Virginia Woolf, and Gertrude Stein, as well as earlier spiritual autobiographers), that has now shifted toward autobiographies of marginality (the work of Maxine Hong Kingston, Zora Neale Hurston, Maya Angelou, women's slave narratives). Significantly, Stein's texts have appeared in this canon as well, becoming a site of lesbian discourse/marginality. See Sidonie Smith, *A Poetics of Women's Autobiography* (Bloomington: Indiana University Press, 1987); Carolyn Heilbrun, *Writing a Woman's Life* (New York: W. W. Norton, 1988).

7. Adrienne Rich, "Compulsory Heterosexuality and Lesbian Existence," in *Blood, Bread, and Poetry: Selected Prose 1979–1985* (New York: W. W. Norton, 1986), 23–75. In her 1980 foreword to this essay (which first appeared in *Signs* in 1978), Rich notes, "I continue to think that heterosexual feminists will draw political strength for change from taking a critical stance toward the ideology which demands heterosexuality, and that lesbians cannot asume that we are untouched by that ideology and the institutions

founded upon it" (p. 26). Rich goes on to note that the intent of such a critique is not to make women into victims, but to voice the grounds for their resistance.

8. For their valuable suggestions and their help in hearing out and framing the perplexities of personal and textual issues raised in this essay, I am indebted, respectively, to Joy De Stefano and to Sidonie Smith.

9. Heilbrun, *Writing a Woman's Life,* 72, 75.

10. Teresa de Lauretis, *Technologies of Gender* (Bloomington: Indiana University Press, 1987), 17. Subsequent references to this book will include page numbers in parentheses in the text.

11. It is clear from de Lauretis's recent work that her own practice requires that she situate herself critically toward the claims of heterosexual feminism and speak from a lesbian position that she distinguishes from feminist ones and glosses autobiographically, as she did in papers presented at the 1989 meeting of the Philological Association of the Pacific Coast and at the 1990 Modern Language Association convention.

12. Biddy Martin, "Lesbian Identity and Autobiographical Differences," in *Life/Lines: Theorizing Women's Autobiography,* ed. Bella Brodzki and Celeste Schenck (Ithaca, N.Y.: Cornell University Press, 1988), 77-103. Page numbers for all subsequent citations to this work are included in the text in parentheses.

13. Similarly, in reviewing recent books on lesbian writing, Julie Abraham calls for reconsidering the contention of many lesbian critics that lesbian sexuality is central to lesbian representation and that the lesbian's marginality is the major factor informing her writing. Abraham asks, "How far do [these propositions] constitute an acceptance of the dominant culture's definitions?" Abraham calls for distinguishing "between representations of the lesbian and lesbian representations," and argues that "lesbian representation would be a theoretically infinite set of possibilities for lesbian cultural . . . expression." "Criticism Is Not a Luxury," *The Nation,* 3 December 1990, 711–12.

14. Cherríe Moraga and Gloria Anzaldúa, eds., *This Bridge Called My Back: Writings by Radical Women of Color* (New York: Kitchen Table, Women of Color Press, 1981).

15. Judith Butler, "Gender Trouble, Feminist Theory, and Psychoanalytic Discourse," in *Feminism/Postmodernism,* ed. Linda J. Nicholson (New York: Routledge, 1990), 338–39. Page numbers for all subsequent references to this essay appear in parentheses in the text. Butler's *Gender Trouble* (New York: Routledge, 1990) has also been informative for my analysis.

16. Adrienne Rich, "The Meaning of Our Love for Women Is What We Have Constantly to Expand," in *On Lies, Secrets, and Silence: Selected Prose, 1966–1978* (New York: W. W. Norton, 1979), 225. Similarly, Rich considers how women internalize the values of colonialism and participate in carrying out the colonization of self and sex in *Of Woman Born* (New York: W. W. Norton, 1976); see especially "The Kingdom of the Fathers."

17. Rich, "The Meaning of Our Love," 227.

18. Rich, "It Is the Lesbian in Us," 202.

19. Ibid., 201.

20. Mab Segrest, *My Mama's Dead Squirrel: Lesbian Essays on Southern Culture* (Ithaca, N.Y.: Firebrand, 1985), 126. Segrest reads lesbian coming-out stories as analogous to African American slave narratives because both are narratives of victimization, resistance, and transformation through the power to name oppressions. My attention was drawn to this essay by Biddy Martin's "Lesbian Identity and Autobiographical Difference(s)." While Segrest's analogy between lesbians and African American slaves as oppressed peoples seems to be untenable, her emphasis on the process of coming to speech is helpful.

21. Thelma Ravell-Pinto, "Buchi Emecheta at Spelman College" (interview), *SAGE* 2 (Spring 1985): 50–51. Emecheta states, "My novels are not feminist; they are part of the corpus of African literature" (p. 50). The editor points out that "[Emecheta's] perspective on women as portrayed in her novels is most definitely feminist" (p. 51).

22. Barbara Harlow, *Resistance Literature* (New York: Methuen, 1987). Page numbers for subsequent references to this book are in parentheses in the text.

23. Harriet Jacobs, *Incidents in the Life of a Slave Girl,* ed. Jean Fagan Yellin (Cambridge, Mass.: Harvard University Press, 1967; first published in 1861). See "The Changing Moral Discourse of Nineteenth-Century African American Women's Autobiography: Harriet Jacobs and Elizabeth Keckley," by William L. Andrews, in this volume.

24. Cherríe Moraga, *Loving in the War Years* (Boston: South End, 1983); Gloria Anzaldúa, *Borderlands/La Frontera* (San Francisco: Spinsters/Aunt Lute, 1987); Moraga and Anzaldúa, *This Bridge Called My Back.* For discussions of *Bridge*'s relevance as autobiography, see Martin, "Lesbian Identity," especially pp. 91–99. I am indebted to this essay and to discussion with Biddy Martin in July 1988 in formulating the concerns of my essay. My review of *This Bridge Called My Back* (*a/b: Auto/Biography Studies,* 4 [Fall 1988]: 77–79) also considers the collection as women's autobiographical writing.

25. Barbara Smith, "Toward a Black Feminist Criticism," in *The New Feminist Criticism,* ed. Elaine Showalter (New York: Pantheon, 1985), 183–84.

26. See Sidonie Smith: "The Impact of Critical Theory on the Study of Autobiography: Marginality, Gender, and Autobiographical Practice," *a/b: Auto/Biography Studies* 3 (Fall 1987). See also Catherine Stimpson's insightful essays on the complexities of Stein's position as a lesbian in drag in *The Autobiography of Alice B. Toklas,* notably the essay, "Gertrude Stein and the Lesbian Lie," in *Fea(s)ts of Memory,* ed. Margo Culley (Madison: University of Wisconsin Press, 1992).

27. Rita Felski discusses the force of women's confessional autobiography, in which women write self-consciously and explicitly as women, as a mode of shifting autobiography away from idiosyncratic individualism and toward a concept of representative communal identity of the sort Barbara Smith calls for. *Beyond Feminist Aesthetics;* see especially pp. 91–95.

28. Mary Jacobus calls for a similar rupturing of women's confinement in urging that women, while necessarily inscribed within "male" discourse, "work ceaselessly to deconstruct it: to write what cannot be written." Quoted in Heilbrun, *Writing a Woman's Life,* 41.

29. Adrienne Rich, "Split at the Root: An Essay on Jewish Identity," in *Blood, Bread, and Poetry: Selected Prose 1979–1985* (New York: W. W. Norton, 1986), 123. Subsequent references to this essay will include page numbers in parentheses in the text.

30. Lorde's autobiographical works have been published by small activist presses such as Persephone, Firebrand, and Crossing.

31. Claudine Raynaud has discussed the text as "a biography of the mythic self." Jeanne Perrault has discussed *The Cancer Journals* as a text that makes the body a site of subjectivity infused with "the ethics of a deeply and precisely historical, political, sexual, and racial consciousness." See Claudine Raynaud, "'A Nutmeg Nestled inside Its Covering of Mace': Audre Lorde's *Zami,*" in *Life/Lines: Theorizing Women's Autobiography,* ed. Bella Brodzki and Celeste Schenck (Ithaca, N.Y.: Cornell University Press, 1988), 221; Jeanne Perrault, "'That the Pain Not Be Wasted': Audre Lorde and the Written Self," *a/b: Auto/Biography Studies* 4 (Fall 1988): 1.

32. Audre Lorde, *Zami: A New Spelling of My Name (A Biomythography)* (Freedom, Calif.: Crossing, 1982; originally published by Persephone), 226. All subsequent page references appear in the text after quotations.

33. Amitai Avi-ram, in an essay on how Lorde creates a poetry of "eroticism, political consciousness, and social change," points out that Lorde celebrates "a strength in the community of difference rather than in its negation." "*Apo Koinou* in Audre Lorde and the Moderns: Defining the Differences," *Callaloo* 6, 3 (1983): 193, 201.

34. As Claudine Raynaud has pointed out, *zami* is patois for *les amies,* lesbians. Raynaud's reading places greater emphasis on the maternal nurturance of the mythic community postulated at the end of the book than does mine, which sees Lorde's unspeakability within American political life as pressing upon her at every point in the autobiography. "'A Nutmeg Nestled," 236, n. 32; Raynaud is citing Chinosole.

35. Lorde observes, "*Carriacou* . . . was not listed in the index of the *Goode's School Atlas* nor in the *Junior Americana World Gazette* nor appeared on any map that I could find, and so when I hunted for the magic place . . . I never found it, and came to believe my mother's geography was a fantasy . . . and in reality maybe she was talking about the place other people called Curaçao, a Dutch possession on the other side of the Antilles" (p. 14). In a footnote on that page, Lorde notes that at age twenty-six she finally found Carriacou on a map in the *Atlas of the Encyclopedia Britannica,* about where she had pictured it.

36. Lorde's historicizing is evident in her resistance to universals. She states, "What I insist upon in my work is that there is no such thing as universal love in literature. There is *this* love in *this* poem." Mary J. Carruthers, "The Re-Vision of the Muse: Adrienne Rich, Audre Lorde, Judy Grahn, Olga Broumas," *Hudson Review* (Summer 1983): 322.

37. Mary Morris, *Nothing to Declare: Memoirs of a Woman Traveling Alone* (New York: Penguin, 1988). Subsequent references to this book include page numbers in parentheses in the text.

38. Denise Riley explores the ambiguities of the category of "women" by considering how women have been fixed as historical subjects to one another and how the meanings of "women" have shifted with changes in social arrangements. Women become their gender, its fixities as well as its indeterminacies, and become other to one another. Riley urges a fluid concept of identity for naming oneself as a woman and for designating the other woman, but notes that the conditions under which this might be achieved do not exist at this time. Her analysis has informed my thinking about Morris's autobiography. *"Am I That Name?": Feminism and the Category of "Women" in History* (Minneapolis: University of Minnesota Press, 1988).

39. Jo Spence, *Putting Myself in the Picture: A Political, Personal, and Photographic Autobiography* (Seattle, Wash.: Real Comet, 1988; first published in 1986 in England by Camden). All subsequent references include page numbers of the U.S. edition in parentheses in the text. Spence's book includes twenty essays in chronological succession from 1949 to 1986, interspersed with more than one hundred photographs taken by—and many of—herself. It is, then, an autobiography, as the subtitle indicates, and not simply an allusion to the visual story that could be read from the history of Spence's photographs and self-images.

40. The epigraph to Spence's book is a citation from Adrienne Rich, part of which reads: "There is no 'the truth!' 'a truth'—truth is not one thing or even a system. It is an increasing complexity" (p. 9).

Chapter 9

"I Yam What I Yam": Cooking, Culture, and Colonialism

Anne Goldman

*I still think that one of the pleasantest of all emotions is to know that
I, I with my brain and my hands, have nourished my beloved few, that
I have concocted a stew or a story, a rarity or a plain dish, to sustain
them truly against the hungers of the world.*

—M. F. K. Fisher, *The Gastronomical Me*[1]

Cooking as a Metonym for Culture

Not, at first glance, a revolutionary statement. Yet, with respect to the
hierarchy of labor, the leveling tendencies of this passage are clear:
in this first of Fisher's two culinary autobiographies, writing literature
and cooking dinner are represented as equally significant and equally
satisfying forms of work. What is perhaps more important than the
equation made between the products of the writer's "brain" and
"hands," however, is the pride such labors engender in the speaker
herself. In addition to the domestic and literary labors foregrounded
in this personal narrative, another form of work is operating: that
process of self-reflection whose end product is the construction of
the subject.

The very title of this autobiographical foray insists that to write
about food is to write about the self as well. In the wartime reminiscences of the author, "the hungers of the world" provide a compelling
metaphor for writing about love and desire, her own wants, and those
of the numerous people she comes into contact with on her travels
between continents. Describing with equal relish her consumption of
caviar and cod, frijoles and boeuf bourguignon, Fisher's culinary

equations provide her with a means of asserting, through the rubric of her own "I" as representative human speaker, the existence of those less palpable hungers we all share. Erasing not only distinctions between writing and cooking, but differences of class and culture, Fisher implies that in producing a discrete "I" she is in fact representing, to a certain extent, "us" and "them" as well.

What appeared within the context of the Second World War as a humanistic effort to resist the divisive polemics of fascism and nazism becomes in the postmodern frame of reference a (cultural) imperialism of a different order; if the well-meaning Anglo-American appreciates the products of different people's culinary labor, she nevertheless consumes them, and in so doing, makes them a part of herself. If I have not persuaded you that the edible metaphor in fact may accord with the seriousness of the occasion, let me rephrase this formulation more conventionally. By writing about the food, and by implication the culture of people distinct from herself acquisitively—desirable to sample because "exotic"—Fisher represents such "foreign" traditions as commodities to be (literally) assimilated for her own use. Despite occasional acknowledgment of the material advantages that underwrite the independent self she is at pains to construct in this reminiscence, Fisher pays scant attention to the fact that her self-reliant feminine Anglo-American "I," who can savor a four-hour, five-course dinner alone, is in large part defined against, and thus contingent upon, the hurried digestions of others: the hasty, unrelished meals of the German Jews who are her shipmates on one trip home on the eve of the Second World War, for instance.

To take Fisher to task for collecting edible souvenirs of her travels abroad is, of course, to critique her culinary autobiography for its political agenda. We do not often perceive cookbooks as literature, let alone as the occasion, covert or explicit, for political commentary. But recently, critics of literature have begun to argue that we acknowledge the ways in which the exchange of recipes may communicate more than the culinary. In "Recipes for Reading: Summer Pasta, Lobster à la Riseholme, and Key Lime Pie," Susan Leonardi analyzes recipes "as highly embedded discourse akin to literary discourse,"[2] identifying this language practice as a gender-inflected one:

> In the earlier *Joy,* the establishment of a lively narrator with a circle of enthusiastic and helpful friends reproduces the social context of recipe sharing—a loose community of women that crosses the social barriers of class, race, and generation. Many women can attest to the usefulness and importance of this discourse: mothers and daughters—even those who don't get

along well otherwise—old friends who now have little in common, mistresses and their "help," lawyers and their secretaries—all can participate in this almost prototypical feminine activity. (pp. 342–43)

Before commenting on this compelling reappraisal of an apparently mundane practice, I would like to juxtapose against it two additional comments about recipe sharing:

While calling upon and taking one of my Spanish recipe cookbooks to one of my neighbors, our conversation for the moment centered around Spanish recipes. "Have you seen the article in *Holland Magazine* written by Mrs. D.?" she inquired. I had not seen it, so she gave me the magazine to take home to read it. It was a three-page article, nicely written and illustrated, but very deficient as to knowledge of our Spanish cooking. In giving the recipe for making tortillas it read, "Mix bread flour with water, add salt." How nice and light these must be without yeast or shortening! And still these smart Americans make money with their writing, and we who know the correct way sit back and listen.[3]

Diana Kennedy, the authoritative cultural missionary for the foods of Mexico, has been decorated with the Order of the Aztec Eagle, the highest honor of its kind bestowed on foreigners by the Mexican government. In addition to this now classic and definitive cookbook, she is the author of *The Tortilla Book, Mexican Regional Cooking,* and *Nothing Fancy* and she travels widely promoting authentic Mexican cuisine.[4]

So aptly does Diana Kennedy, the "ultimate authority, the high priestess of Mexican cooking,"[5] describe the "smart American" of Cleofas Jaramillo's cultural critique that, if three decades did not separate the promotional paean from the political complaint, it would be tempting to resolve the twin images of Ms. Kennedy and Mrs. D. into a single overzealous evangelical. That the author of *The Art of Mexican Cooking* and the now anonymous writer for *Holland Magazine* are in fact not one but two distinct missionaries for the intercultural faith does not, of course, date Jaramillo's criticism. Rather, the persistence of American forays into foreign ground—cultural rather than geographical here—merely makes such a critique more pointed.

Leonardi's thesis that a cookbook is a literary production deserving of critical comment is compelling. But, in light of passages like the two I have foregrounded here, her affirmation of recipe sharing as a practice uniting women across "social barriers" begs to be reconsidered. Precisely because art—in this case, the art of cooking—is produced, as Leonardi herself indicates, within a specific social context, it encodes a political problematic. I would like to refocus inquiry on the "barriers of class, race, and generation," which Leonardi invokes only to transcend, in order to suggest that we read the "embedded discourse" of the cookbook not as an archetypally feminine language but rather as a form of writing that, if coded feminine, is also a culturally contingent production. What kind of ideological impulses are operating in a cookbook such as *The Art of Mexican Cooking: Traditional Mexican Cooking for Aficionados,* the very title of which calls attention to the representation of a specific culture and the authority of "aficionados" to reproduce it in a text circulated for the benefit of English speakers? When does recipe sharing, that is, become recipe borrowing, with only a coerced "consent" from the domestic "help?"[6]

While *The Gastronomic Me* may strike some critics of autobiography and ethnography as a peculiar kind of self-reflexive text, the equations its author establishes between the presentation of recipes and the articulation of a self are clearly not idiosyncratic to M. F. K. Fisher. If writing of global food traditions may fashion the speaker-writer as culture plunderer, describing regional food traditions can enable self-reflexive writing to invoke, as Tey Diana Rebolledo has indicated of Cleofas Jaramillo, "a sense of place and belonging."[7] For those writers whose gender, race, or class may seem to preclude access to "high art" and its literary forms, the very domestic and commonplace quality of cooking makes it an attractive metonym for culture. For such autobiographers, presenting a family recipe and figuring its circulation within a community of readers provides a metaphor nonthreatening in its apparent avoidance of overt political discourse and yet culturally resonant in its evocation of the relation between the labor of the individual and her conscious efforts to reproduce familial and cultural traditions and values. That is, the reproduction of dishes such as okra gumbo and huevos rancheros works to maintain cultural specificity in the face of assimilative pressures attempting constantly to amalgamate cultures for the benefit of the "melting pot" or "national interests."

Yet reproducing a recipe, like retelling a story, may be at once cultural practice and autobiographical assertion. If it provides an apt metaphor for the reproduction of culture from generation to generation, the act of passing down recipes from mother to daughter works as well to figure a familial space within which self-articulation can begin to take place.[8] The connection between culture and identity toward which Ralph Ellison's "I yam what I yam" gestures in *Invisible Man* appears repeatedly in the culinary autobiographies of American women. Jessica Harris's recollections of her mother's cooking implicitly attest to the relationships among cooking, culture, and colonialism. "My mother, who trained as a dietician but was discouraged from work in the food presentation field in which she excelled because of her race, took her talents home," Harris writes. "Each night was a feast. No frozen dinners or cake mixes ever crossed our threshold. Made-from-scratch cakes, flaky pie crusts, and intricate finger sandwiches went along with the traditional African-inspired foods that my father loved."[9]

Maya Angelou more explicitly invokes food as the signifier of political well-being. Indicting what she sees as the Ghanian penchant for things European, a West African woman in *All God's Children Need Traveling Shoes* decries the absence of rice—a traditional African staple—at the university cafeteria in order to critique the inability of Ghanian culture-makers to use indigenous culture as the foundation for a healthy body politic:

> "No rye?" Again, "No rye? What country you peepo got? . . .
> You peepo, you got your Black Star Square. You got your university, but you got no rye! You peepo!" She began to laugh sarcastically, "You make me laugh. Pitiful peepo."[10]

The invocation of a specific food speaks on behalf of cultural nationalism here. The elaboration of cooking techniques may also provide a means of articulating an ethnic subject, however. In her 1945 autobiography, Jade Snow Wong devotes a considerable portion of one chapter to an extended description of a Chinese dinner she cooks for a group of (interracial) schoolmates. A narrative of assimilation gives way, for one reading moment, to an affirmation of cultural difference, as the author reproduces her recipes for "egg foo young" and "tomato-beef" in extended detail. Wong clearly designs this kind of cultural reproduction to be circulated for the benefit of a non-Chinese audience when she follows up her description of cooking techniques with this proverbial gesture: "[She] found that the girls were perpetually curious about her Chinese background and Chinese ideologies, and for the first time she began to formulate in her mind the constructive and delightful aspects of the Chinese culture to present to non-Chinese."[11] While this coda may be read as reaffirming on the gastronomic level the ideology of the melting pot her "perpetually curious" readers might expect to see reinstated, the very attention to a specific cultural practice as figured through a feminine discourse apparently bereft of political implications opens a space by which the author can affirm a tradition decisively Chinese-American. In effect, this passage declares

Jade Snow Wong's intentions to shape her friends'—and readers'—perceptions of Chinese-American culture.

More important, by constructing an empowering image of cultural tradition via her own cooking labor, the autobiographer writes herself into a prominent place in the narrative. Her apparently casual invitation to dinner, accepted with alacrity by friends Wen-Lien, Teruko, and Harriet, allows her to assert herself as deserving of attention at the same time it implies their cultural deficit: "Within half an hour, her comrades had raised Jade Snow high in their estimation. To be worthy of this new trust, Jade Snow racked her brains to decide what dishes she could cook without a Chinese larder" (p. 158). This apparently tentative appropriation of the limelight as effected through the agency of her friends is repeated several pages later, when the writer describes a dinner she cooks for a group of world-renowned musicians staying with her employer, the dean of Mills College. Again the text moves explicitly in the direction of erasing cultural difference while simultaneously encoding an affirmation of cultural specificity and autobiographical presence:

> That was a wonderful evening. . . . For the first time Jade
> Snow felt an important participant in the role of hostess.
> Because of everyone's interest in the kitchen preparations, she
> soon lost her shyness in the presence of celebrities and acted
> naturally. There was no talk about music, only about Chinese
> food. And Jade Snow ceased thinking of famous people as
> "those" in a world apart. She had a glimpse of the truth, that
> the great people of any race are unpretentious, genuinely hon-
> est, and nonpatronizing in their interest in other human
> beings. (pp. 172–73)

Ostensibly working to celebrate "universal" moral values through the lesson of the last sentence, the accolade nevertheless allows Jade Snow Wong to focus attention on herself; to construct a subject who, if located in the modest role of "hostess," is yet "important" as the recipient of the homage of "famous people." Significantly, it is the representation of racial difference that enables this kind of self-assertion. Like the talk of the musicians, the chapter itself speaks not so much about the accomplishments of the celebrities, or even about the virtues people share regardless of race, but instead about her own Chinese food.[12]

The Conflict Over Culture: Some Discursive Contexts

I would like to explore this symbiosis of autobiographical act and cultural affirmation in a reading of cookbooks by Cleofas Jaramillo and Fabiola Cabeza de Baca. The culinary histories the two women published mid-century provide for the beginnings of autobiographical assertion. They also demonstrate how political circumstance—in this case the struggle for control of Mexican culture that succeeds the struggle for proprietorship of Mexican land—helps to shape both the way people conceive of themselves and the manner in which they speak this sense of self-assertion. Self-reflection in both narratives is accordingly complicated by political and literary history, the demands of publishing and of the languages available to Hispana writers during the first half of the twentieth century.[13]

Working as a home demonstration agent on behalf of the state of New Mexico in the 1910s through the 1930s, Fabiola Cabeza de Baca published, in addition to her autobiography *We Fed Them Cactus* (1954) and a number of cookbooks celebrating nuevomexicano traditions, a series of pamphlets issued by the New Mexico State Agricultural Extension Service designed to instruct rural Hispano women in the new housekeeping and cooking methods being promoted by the U.S. government through its passage of the Smith-Lever Act in 1914. Her activities as an "agent" placed her in the position of cultural mediator between the Hispanos—whom the state clearly considered her a representative *of* as well as *for*—and the Anglo-American business interests promoted by the government's discourse of technological "advancement." To the extent that they recirculate this language of "the march of progress," Cabeza de Baca's pamphlets "Buletín de Conservar" (1931) and "Los Alimentos y Su Preparación" (1934) reflect the compromising—as well as compromised—role their author occupied by working on behalf of a government agency as eager to assume ignorance, incivility, and inability on the part of its Hispano residents as it was willing to trumpet the advantages of eastern farming and housekeeping methods over the nuevomexicano and Native American practices more appropriate to the arid environment Anglo "pioneers" were attempting to improve through industrialization.

In "Canning Comes to New Mexico: Women and the Agricultural Extension Service 1914–1919," Joan Jensen characterizes the response of Hispanas to the work of home demonstration agents including Cabeza de Baca as less than enthusiastic.[14] "Hispanic women, unlike Anglo women, did not feel at home in school houses or public buildings. They also preferred meeting without Anglo women," she suggests. "'Very retiring,'" according to one agent, even bilingual Hispanas would not come to meetings called for Anglo women as well (p. 213). It is not difficult to read in this recalcitrance a resistance to the pressures of assimilation exerted on women through a critique of their domestic work practices. Jensen herself acknowledges that the state's efforts to emphasize the virtues of "modernization" encoded a very conservative cultural agenda. Focusing here on the government's interruption of Navajo tradition by its edict forcing families to send at least one child away to boarding school, she comments that it was "part of the national program to replace traditional skills of the Indian woman with skills that would make them more dependent upon the Euro-American culture and occupy the place women were assigned in that culture" (p. 205).

But what of Cabeza de Baca's own efforts to further the march of progress through the state of New Mexico? In marked contrast to her later publications celebrating the nuevomexicano past as an Edenic era of abundance, prosperity, and self-sufficiency, "Los Alimentos y Su Preparación" reproduces the future-oriented discourse of progress employed by the state, often as justification for land fraud, illegal business practices, and the attempt at cultural obliteration. Paralleling changes in food preparation with changes in "civilization," Cabeza de Baca introduces this domestic instruction manual with an assertion that is half apologetic, half imperative: "Cada día hay una nueva invención y nuevos descubrimientos de la ciéncia y todos estamos listos para adoptarlos" (Every day there is a new invention and new scientific discoveries and we are all ready to adopt them).[15] Framing assimilation as the inexorable and inevitable outcome of history (the daily progression of new inventions and scientific discoveries), Cabeza de Baca reproduces the nation's teleology of industrial growth. "En esta época de progreso y descubrimientos científicos hay que seguir la marcha, no sólo en el modo de vivir, sino que también en el modo de comer" (In this era of progress and scientific discoveries it is necessary to follow the trend, not only in one's style of life, but also in one's style of eating) (p. 3). The politics of cooking here makes a virtue of necessity, as progress sweeps from the urban to the rural sector:

> Para progresar en el modo de vivir debíamos que estar listos para aprendar como alimentarnos para conservarnos saludables. ¿De qué sirve tener los mejores automóbiles, las mejoras carreteras, las mejores escuelas, y todo lo mejor del mundo si nos falta la salud? El pueblo que no se alimenta propriamente no puede producir y mantener una civilización próspera y fuerte. [In order to progress in our way of life we must be ready to learn how to eat in order to maintain our health. What use does having the best cars, the best highways, the best schools, and the best of everything in the world serve if we don't have our health? The town that doesn't nourish itself

properly can't produce and maintain a prosperous and strong civilization.] (p. 4)

Eating "properly" is to good bodily health what building the best cars, highways, and schools is to a strong body politic. Despite Cabeza de Baca's emphasis on the relationship between good nourishment and good health, learning how to eat "correctly" has a great deal more to do with accommodating to cultural change than it does with building strong bodies twelve ways.

The bright tone of this pronouncement notwithstanding, the appeal to assimilate carries with it a cost. Writing to women, the home demonstration worker defines cultural accommodation in the language of home management. Good table manners signify superior comportment, she asserts, and

> Una persona que tiene buenos modales en el modo de comer considerá superior a una que no los tiene. Es una de las pruebas de tener educación o buena crianza. Si la madre enseña a sus hijos seguir buenos modales de mesa cada día, no tendrá que avergonzar cuando tengan huéspedes. [A person who has good table manners is considered superior to one who doesn't have them. This is one of the proofs of having an education or being well brought up. If the mother teaches her children to follow good table manners every day, she will not have to be ashamed when she has guests.] (p. 44)

Superiority or shame: the subjugated must become convinced of their own desire for subjugation.[16] Here women, the reproducers of culture because of their work of child rearing, are urged to internalize those political dictates—framed as moral lessons—of the state discourse on home improvement. Cooking does not so much embody culture in this text, it turns out, as obliterate it. If "Los Alimentos y Su Preparación" explicitly appeals to its female readers' experience of maternal obligation, the pamphlet, complete with photos depicting the proper way to use knife, fork, and spoon and instructions detailing the "Reglas Para Poner y Como Servir La Mesa" (Rules for Setting and Serving at the Table) (p. 41) ultimately figures its audience not as parental educators but as children themselves, culturally speaking, requiring instruction in the new rules of the Anglo table.

Cooking and Colonialism: Speaking against Cultural Appropriation

A pamphlet on table manners may seem a rather slight subject with which to examine how cultural appropriation figures in works by

American women writers. Yet, like Jaramillo's complaint about the ingredients in tortillas, which associates the authenticity of a recipe with the integrity of a culture, Cabeza de Baca's juxtaposition of "el modo de vivir" with "el modo de comer" is a gesture made repeatedly by Hispana writers concerned with the maintenance of nuevomexicano cultural practices after 1848, in the wake of the U. S. conquest of northern Mexico. For women, this attention to the pressures of acculturation often takes the form not of explicit political statements but rather of a kind of composite genre: a combination of familial reminiscence and personal narrative, descriptions of custom, history, food, folklore. In the three decades between the 1930s and the 1950s, both Cabeza de Baca and Jaramillo, as Tey Diana Rebolledo notes, published cookbooks integrating recipes "with accounts of folk life, as if the female sense of rootedness and place is passed down through the distinctive foods nature offers" (p. 102). Evoking a specific place, I would suggest, allows the two writers to insist upon the cultural legacy of a long-settled Hispano community. Such attention to "rootedness" and "place," framed as it is in a feminine culinary discourse apparently far removed from the sphere of political contention, thus enables the two writers, whose sex and position within landed families would discourage the voicing of explicit discontent with Americano policy, to critique it.

Home economics, in other words, provides a suitably genteel forum for theorizing about the social and political economy. Descriptions of food and its preparation resonate with nostalgia for an Edenic past; as with Proust's concisely symbolic madeleines, evocations of flavors and cooking methods work efficiently to recall the manner of an entire way of life. "Try the recipes," Cabeza de Baca urges in *Historic Cookery:* "And when you do, think of New Mexico's golden days, of red chile drying in the sun, of clean-swept yards, outdoor ovens, and adobe houses on the landscape. Remember the green valleys where good things grow. And think too of families sitting happily at the tables."[17] "Chile drying" and "clean-swept yards" are indications of a well-ordered life; descriptions of a domestic economy where "good things grow" reflect the health of the Hispano community of the past, before it was besieged by Anglo land speculators, its culture "recovered" by white artists and writers.

Clearly Cabeza de Baca's description of familial and community harmony is modeled after nonnative accounts of Hispano culture, its nostalgic evocation complicit in a folkloric discourse that romanticizes both the land and its people as suspended in a kind of glorious sunset of fast-fading "traditional" rituals. Yet the author's figuring of cultural practice as a consciously reproduced strategy does provide her with a means to reassert cultural agency. Emphasizing the labor involved in the reproduction of cultural practices, however sentimentalized and classist such representations may be, does work (at least on the textual level) against the politics of assimiliation by insisting on a historically grounded sense of cultural specificity and by maintaining an ethnic difference that in turn provides the self with authority to speak. Thus the rose-colored tribute to "New Mexico's golden days," with its description of "historic" (read "unadulterated") Hispano cooking and pointed lack of reference to more contemporary cooking methods enables Cabeza de Baca to develop an unspoken comparison between the richness of traditional nuevomexicano life and the paucity of the presumably nonnative reader's "modern" cultural practices.

That the brief but tartly phrased admonishment of Cleofas Jaramillo's *Romance of a Little Village Girl,* with its proprietary emphasis on "our Spanish cooking" is, like Cabeza de Baca's romance of sun and adobe, aimed at Anglo appropriation of Hispano culture more generally becomes clear if we look more closely at the text by Jaramillo that precedes its publication. A response in part to the aplomb with which the Mrs. D.s of her day marketed recipes not of their own making, *The Genuine New Mexico Tasty Recipes,* is not simply a catalog of recipes correcting the absence of yeast and shortening.[18] Instead, it represents food and its preparation, within the context of personal narrative, as metonyms for the reaffirmation and maintenance of traditional Hispano cultural practices as a whole. Following a series of "Spanish" recipes—and note that this formulation is itself a colonial one, suppressing Native American contributions to New Mexican culture[19]—Jaramillo reprints a series of chapters from *Shadows of the Past*[20] describing, as Genaro Padilla notes, "familial and community occasions that contextualize the very preparation and consumption of food" (p. 55).

It is such a cultural context—and, more specifically, who is authorized to describe it—that is at issue in this text. The very title of the book, with its insistence on authenticity, foregrounds nuevomexicano tradition, under the rubric of the culinary, as subject to appropriation. To assert that the recipes in one's cookbook are the genuine articles, after all, is to imply that fabrications—nonauthentic recipes—exist. Emphasizing the antiquity of her collection (the subtitle is *Old and Quaint Formulas for the Preparation of Seventy-Five Delicious Spanish Dishes*), Jaramillo ensures that the bloodlines of her culinary products are pure, or nearly so. "In this collection of Spanish recipes," she announces, "only those used in New Mexico for centuries are given, excepting one or two Old Mexico recipes" (p. 1). While this attention to cultural commodification may be read as a critical move on Jaramillo's part, the very act of eulogizing Hispano tradition as "quaint"—an artifact, that is—suggests that this critique is itself intended to be circulated extraculturally. As Padilla argues:

> On the one hand, *Tasty Recipes* represents the popularization of ethnic cuisine, and, in that respect, represents a desire to cater to members of the dominant culture. On the other, Jaramillo contextualizes consumption in an explicitly cultural manner, and, therefore, suggests how intimately food is related to lived cultural experience. Hence, we discover a form of culinary resistance—Anglo-Americans can follow the recipe and still not eat nuevomexicano cooking (p. 55).

Yet, in *The Genuine New Mexico Tasty Recipes,* food is invested not only with a cultural register ultimately inaccessible to the non-native, but with a more overtly political signification as well. By historicizing his sister's evocation of food traditions in his introduction to the book, Reyes N. Martínez quite clearly directs readers to draw connections between good nutrition and good government:

> The early settlers introduced certain kinds of foods to this section of the country, which, although occasionally used now, are not appreciated for their nutritive and health value. No one questions the evidence of the superior physical ruggedness of the past generations of that era in comparison with that of their descendants of the present day, who, although enjoying the advantages of modern science and research along the lines of dietetics, do not generally attain the natural constitutional ruggedness of body that tradition tells us their ancestors possessed. (p. 28)

Taking up the dominant culture's discourse of progress, Martínez's appeal to science turns this language of the inevitable back upon itself.[21] Affirming "the advances of modern science" does not work here to celebrate the encroachment of Anglo business interests into a rural state of small landholders and self-sufficient homesteads, but rather to critique such a political situation as unhealthy. Martínez's historical distinction between "early settlers" and "their descendants of the present day," between "natural constitutional ruggedness" and "the advances of modern science . . . along the lines of dietetics" thus encodes a racial inflection as well. The loss of cultural integrity and authority is articulated through a parable about the devaluing of "traditional foods." Resonating with Jaramillo's insistence on the authenticity and antiquity of her collection, Martínez's generational focus here suggests that, like the Spanish colonists themselves, foods can have a lineage; the genuine landholders, whose land grants derive from the rulers of sixteenth-century Spain, eat *The Genuine New Mexico Tasty Recipes.* Just as those foods introduced by the conquistadores and enjoyed by their descendants resulted in good health, so abandoning them and replacing them with modern ("white") substitutes will produce a less constitutionally sound people. Clearly I am distorting the conscientiously neutral tone of Martínez's brief historical commentary by subjecting it to such extensive analysis and sardonic paraphrasing. Nevertheless, the implicit parallel between cooking and culture and the writer's refusal to glorify the advancements of science despite a discursive environment extolling its praises enable readers to draw from the passage a certain resistance to the rhetoric of assimilation.

If one takes even a cursory glance at the contemporary literature being produced by nonnatives, such a critique appears neither inordinately defensive nor unfairly acerbic. Like Jaramillo's preface to *The Genuine New Mexico Tasty Recipes,* Erna Fergusson's introductory remarks to her 1934 *Mexican Cookbook* stress the authenticity of her culinary catalog. "The recipes in this book," she affirms, "are limited to those which were in common use when the province of New Mexico was a part of the Republic of Mexico."[22] Like the folklorist author of *Shadows of the Past* and *Cuentos del Hogar,* Fergusson is concerned to demarcate a series of cultural traditions, using food as a signifier: "Nothing more surely reflects the life of a people," Fergusson asserts, "than what they ate and how they prepared it" (p. 4).

Yet, while Jaramillo's project is to recover nuevomexicano customs in a gesture of ethnic pride, however muted, Fergusson's interest is precisely in appropriating such practices on behalf of "national interests." Defining Mexican food in her foreword as "part of the Southwestern diet . . . since the 'American Occupation,'" the author traces the acceptance of "slowly-cooked and richly condimented dishes" by "people who could not even pronounce their names" in order to insist that such recipes "represent Mexican cookery that belongs to the U.S." Cultural appropriation is thus justified by a political event, the U.S. military takeover of Mexico. That Fergusson is not unaware that her coercive culinary history of the Southwest in some measure reiterates the forced invasion of the region she speaks of becomes clear later in the book, when she prefaces a series of recipes for tortillas with this derisive but nonetheless anxious comment about cultural authority: "The only way to be sure of making tortillas correctly is to have a line of Indian ancestry running back about 500 years" (p. 88). If her recipes for corn and wheat tortillas lack yeast, readers have been duly warned.

Yet it is cultural rather than culinary blunders that are most arresting here. Reading "Mexican Cooking Then and Now," Fergusson's history of cooking methods, one is struck by the degree to which narrative energy is invested in justifying the "'American Occupation'" by juxtaposing the "modern cook in a modern kitchen" with the "primitive conditions" of traditional domestic life (pp. 3, 5).

If Cabeza de Baca's "Los Alimentos" reluctantly espouses the new housekeeping and cooking methods as inevitable given the forward movement of "el progreso y civilización de la nación," Fergusson's text actively maligns Hispano cultural practices through a series of racist clichés. Consider, for instance, the caustic sarcasm of this passage:

> The menus are based on meals as served at a gentleman's table before the general adoption of American ways. Then eating was a serious matter, interfered with only by famine, war, or Lent. The day began with a preliminary breakfast in bed; coffee or chocolate and sweet rolls. About nine o'clock came the real breakfast which included eggs or meat and more bread and coffee. After that the Señora put in her heavy work of unlocking cupboards, storerooms, and chests; of dispensing food for the day; and of directing her servants. Naturally she felt fagged by 11 and ready for the *caldo colado* or clear soup, which came as a pick-me-up at that hour. (p. 6)

Small wonder, given this kind of representation of the nuevo-mexicano rancheros, that Jaramillo felt called upon to exact literary justice. The romantic picture of wealthy family life described for us in the pages of *The Genuine New Mexico Tasty Recipes,* a scene of "warm harvest sunlight" and "golden wheats and oats, stacked high on round" (p. 21) is thus in some measure a defensive portrait, its emphatically celebratory rhetoric a compensatory literary strategy. The impression of rural life here is one of busy industry and "self-sustaining" plenty, a harmony of blue corn and yellow wheat, a perpetual "Indian summer" where "servants and children" enjoy the harvest plenty in a bucolic landscape unmarked by time (p. 21). This "historical amnesia," which Padilla notes is characteristic of Jaramillo's work as a whole, clearly works as a palliative for the all-too-immediate economic losses and cultural conflict suffered by landed families like hers during the early years of the century (p. 48). So, too, the author's insistence on maintaining a feudalistic stability of rich and poor works as an implicit indictment of the contemporary, less happy relation between Hispanos and Anglos. In such a context of cultural contention, the sentimentalized picture of "*peones* [working] happily, taking great interest in doing their best for the *patrón,* whom they held in great esteem and respect" (p. 24) provides a critique of race relations precisely contingent upon a suturing over of class conflict. Likewise, given the collective loss of self-confidence after 1848, the representation of Jaramillo as authoritative subject is to a certain extent dependent upon the objectification of "Lupe" as "our Indian cook" (p. 23). The proprietary address subsumes both ethnic and class divisions, constructing a whole Hispano Subject greater than the sum of its cross-cultural parts.

This glowing picture of village life is not exclusive to Cleofas Jaramillo's *The Genuine New Mexico Tasty Recipes,* but in fact characterizes both Fabiola Cabeza de Baca's more recent *Historic Cookery* (1970) and her 1949 celebration of Hispano food and custom, *The Good Life: New Mexico Traditions and Food,* as well. I have previously argued that in her earlier bulletins, undertaken as home economist for the state, Cabeza de Baca neglects traditional domestic life in order to espouse the changes sanctioned by the government's agricultural "improvement" program. In *The Good Life,* by contrast, she does not look forward to some future technological utopia, but backward, recovering a history untranslatable in the dominant culture's lexicon of industrial progress.[23] Ethnographic description in *The Good Life,* as in Jaramillo's *Tasty Recipes* then, is nostalgic rather than analytic, with chapter headings such as "Winter's Plenty," "Christmas Festivities," and "The Wedding" celebrating that "happiness and abundant living" with which the author characterizes the Hispano past. The emphasis on cultural self-sufficiency invoked by the "full splendor" of an "Autumn Harvest" recalls Jaramillo's *Tasty Recipes,* as well as a series of mexicano personal narratives after 1848, in which the cataloging of farm and field provides an implicit contrast between a harmonious, richly lived past and a more difficult present (p. 5)[24].

While the language of *The Good Life* often shrouds historical struggles in a romantic fog, the reader response dynamic that the text establishes provides its author with a means for articulating a form of cultural critique. The cookbook is particularly well suited to engage this kind of critique because it exhorts readers to gloss its text not only as a series of declarative statements (if one were to peruse it without actually trying the recipes) but as a set of performative acts as well (provided one not only reads the recipes but reproduces them). As Leonardi notes: "Like a narrative, a recipe is reproducible, and, further, its hearers-readers-receivers are *encouraged* to reproduce it, and, in reproducing it, to revise it and make it their own" (p. 344). If she is able to equate "reproducing" with "sharing" only by ignoring the inequities of power across "the social barriers of class, race, and generation" (p. 342), Leonardi's emphasis on the performative aspect of cookbook reading is nevertheless a useful one for ethnographic inquiry. If the exhortation to reproduce a recipe may create a community, it may also call attention to the boundaries of such an affiliation, asking readers to question the conflations and distinctions between the community constructed within the text itself and the community of readers created outside it.

Encouraging readers to reproduce, revise, and make a recipe their own enables Cabeza de Baca to call attention to cultural commodification in *The Good Life*. If the text appears to encourage its audience to make "New Mexican traditions and food" their own, however, its author ultimately provides obstacles to such appropriation. "In order to have the dishes taste as one has eaten them in the New Mexican homes or genuine New Mexican restaurants, one must use New Mexican products," she counsels (p. 45). As with Jaramillo's text, "genuine" works here not merely as authorization of authenticity (with respect to the writer) but as barrier (vis-à-vis the reader) as well. Ostensibly allowing for the possibility of extracultural access, this admonishment to use "New Mexican products" works on another level to divide nonnative readers from the Hispano community the book itself so wholeheartedly celebrates, thus resisting cultural abstraction and insisting on rootedness and a sense of place. Appending the book with a glossary of Spanish terms allows Cabeza de Baca to remind her readership that reproducing the recipes of *The Good Life* does not necessarily lead to cultural ownership. "The words in this glossary may have other meanings," she asserts, "but the one given here explains the meaning as used in this composition" (p. 81). By calling attention to what is left over, the remainder that escapes translation, the author problematizes cultural access, depicting a web of associations and meanings ultimately ungraspable by the nonnative speaker.[25] Depictions of class conflict in *The Good Life* further complicate the text's representation of culture. As in Jaramillo's *Tasty Recipes,* cultural harmony is achieved largely at the expense of a sustained appraisal of class relations. This is not to say that relations between rancheros (landowning farmers) and peones (farmhands) are ignored, however. As in the later *We Fed Them Cactus,* anxiety about class conflict in *The Good Life* is relieved not by being overlooked but rather by being contained. Curiously, it is art that effects this defusing of class conflict in both of Cabeza de Baca's texts: consistently a laborer-artist figure simultaneously articulates the threat to the social order and resolves it. In *The Good Life,* the relation between art and politics is figured in Tilano, guitar-playing goatherd for Don Teodoro. His introduction early in the narrative indicates at once the affiliation of manual and mental labor and the marginal status such a worker occupies.

Describing the making of *ristras,* strings of dried red chiles, the author situates Tilano as follows: "Men, women, and children joined in the task. Each one, seated on the ground, deftly started tying the pods. Tilano, the goat herder and storyteller, stood at the door waiting for his chance to get in a word" (p. 6). Like Santiago, the grumbling ranch hand of *We Fed Them Cactus,* whose critique of class inequities is replaced by the harmonies of his own *corrido* (ballad) singing, Tilano is encouraged to forget his political complaints when the patron's wife, Doña Paula, urges him to exercise his musical skills instead:

> "The *Aleluyas* say that there is no future in being a Roman
> Catholic and they told me that if I joined them I would
> not have to herd goats for you for such low wages, Don
> Teodoro." . . . "Why don't you play the guitar for us Tilano,"
> said Doña Paula. . . . Tilano did not need coaxing. No sooner
> had Doña Paula spoken than Tilano was playing familiar
> strains. Some of the young folks joined in by singing which
> made Tilano so happy that he forgot the *Aleluyas.* (pp. 6–7)

In becoming the palliative to political ills, Cabeza de Baca's representation of art is a very conservative one. To the extent that it is defined by the laboring goatherd rather than the leisured gentleman, however, such a representation of the aesthetic carries with it quite radical implications. It is the cooks and *curanderas* (healers) in Fabiola Cabeza de Baca's books, after all, who in producing stories and recipes reproduce the cultural practices that constitute the folkloric reminiscences of both *We Fed Them Cactus* and *The Good Life.* Granted, the figure of the working musician in *The Good Life* ultimately underwrites the rule of the wealthy by creating an art that reveals class conflict only to contain it. Nevertheless, what we see in both *We Fed Them Cactus* and *The Good Life* are narratives sustained by the very people they explicitly work to keep down.

While the relation between the Turrieta family and their servants structures *The Good Life,* this insistently affirmative picture of social harmony is itself sustained through a gendered metaphor of class obligations. If the culinary reminiscences of this text figure ethnicity as actively reproduced, it is the working alliance between Señora

Martina and Doña Paula through which cultural labor is represented. Chapters titled "Autumn Harvest," "Christmas Festivities," and "Lent" celebrate nuevomexicano traditions across time, but the descriptions of the labor involved in preparing for such cultural events remain a constant throughout the text. In fact, the narrative emphasizes not so much descriptions of particular Hispano customs as the labor of preparing for such events. And if it is through the representation of work itself—always a community effort in this text—that Cabeza de Baca locates Hispano ethnicity, it is a characteristically feminine labor, cooking, that she calls attention to in order to signify both nourishment (material and moral) and the active labor involved in providing for such cultural sustenance.

While the book's nostalgic representation of cultural plenitude is contingent upon the joint labors of Señora Martina and Doña Paula, the vantage point from which readers observe this alliance does not accommodate both female subjects equally. We are initially introduced to "Señá Martina," as she is familiarly called by Doña Paula, not as a distinct individual but rather as the type of the ageless, timeless *curandera:*

> The medicine woman seemed so old to Doña Paula and she
> wondered how old she was. No one remembered when she
> was born. She had been a slave in the García family for two
> generations and that was all any one knew. She had not
> wanted her freedom, yet she had always been free. (p. 14)

Eulogizing her as "the medicine woman," such a perspective works to represent Señora Martina with respect to Doña Paula, wife of the ranchero, and to insist on a harmonious picture of relations between classes and cultures.

Succeeding references to "the Herb Woman," however, emphasize not only her willingness to work on behalf of Doña Paula ("After greeting Doña Paula she sat down beside her and without being asked, she took over the task of slicing small squashes into circles in preparation for drying"; p. 13), but her resistance to Anglo cultural authority as well. It is Señora Martina who voices opposition to acculturation, as this process is signified by changes in the practices of medicine. While Doña Paula, whose voice is closely linked with that of the narrator, may argue on behalf of accommodation ("Diphtheria is contagious Señá Martina. It is better to let the doctor treat that"; p. 15), the *curandera* responds: "Be as you say—but I cured all my children without assistance from the doctor which I could not have afforded anyway. . . . Today [Juanito, my youngest] is as well as any one can be, although deaf, he is a healthy man" (p. 15). If Señora Martina's stubbornness is treated a trifle sardonically here, the amount of narrative energy expended upon this figure alone suggests that her criticism of contemporary medical practices serves a significant function in the text. And comments such as the following more explicitly contrast the well-being of Hispano *antepasados* with the difficulties their modern counterparts face: "When I was young," Señora Martina recalls, "there were no doctors and we lived through many sicknesses" (p. 14). Comparing the competence of the *curandera* with the incapability of (presumably Anglo) doctors, I would argue, enables Cabeza de Baca to articulate a muted cultural critique. In addition, the meticulous detail with which the author lists herbs and their curative properties not only provides *The Good Life* with a model of cultural authenticity and antiquity but conveys practical information as well.[26]

Tey Diana Rebolledo has noted that "in Hispanic folklore the curandera has always had more freedom of movement than other women. Cabeza de Baca saw the herb woman as not only freer but clearly outside the confines of society" (p. 105). Yet her "freedom" seems to me questionable, since it is defined on behalf of the class that most benefits from her labor, and her marginal status does more to provide the author with the measure of a landed Hispano class than to elevate this working-class figure herself. I would suggest that it is precisely Señora Martina's distance from the voice of the narrator, her position as cultural Other vis-à-vis the Turrieta family, that enables Cabeza de Baca to maintain her own position as cultural mediator in a narrative location that provides her with authority over her non-Hispano readership and simultaneously allows a (muted) critique of Anglo imperialism. At once this eulogy to the herb woman provides Cabeza de Baca with a means to contain cultural difference (the relations between Hispanos and *indígenos* [Native Americans] remain harmonious, in implicit comparison with the current Hispano-Anglo conflict) and to articulate political difference (post–1848) without compromising the influence of her well-connected narrator. Señora Martina's censure of the medical establishment ("I hope to live another year, for when I am gone my remedies go with me and the doctors will get fat from your generosity"; p. 18) thus exploits the author's culinary trope for culture in order to provide her with a critique of it.

In this analysis of *The Good Life* I have suggested that a cookbook can reproduce the means to more than material nourishment: it may reproduce as well those cultural practices and values that provide a community with a means of self-definition and survival. I would argue

in addition that a text such as *The Good Life* may produce not only
a communal subject, but an individual authority as well. While the
subtitle insists that recipes speak a cultural history, the preface and
introduction establish an individual record of activities on behalf of
this collective. Two languages, then, appear to drive the narrative. If
at once the text grounds its authority in its capacity to provide readers
with an "example" of the good life as lived by Hispanos mid-century,
it simultaneously offers a representation of a particular life as lived by
Fabiola Cabeza de Baca, writer and home economist. This conflation
of ethnographic and autobiographic discourse, of the exemplary and
the idiosyncratic, is particularly marked in the book's preface, which
moves constantly between descriptions of "our Spanish forebears"
and references to the subject who in speaking of them associates
herself with nuevomexicano traditions. The first two sentences, for
example, negotiate between an ethnographic subject and an autobiographical speaker in order to define a life lived contextually:

> The recipes which are a part of *The Good Life* and the family
> traditions from which the recipes have developed have been a
> part of my life. They have been a part of the lives of Hispanic
> New Mexicans since the Spanish colonization of New Mexico.
> (p. v)

The equation of community traditions with personal development
established here is reinforced in the sentences that follow, where a
distinctly autobiographical recounting of birthplace and upbringing is
itself made representative of "the good life" (p. v).

Given that the play of discourses is often operating at the level of
the sentence, deciding whether or not to privilege the language of
ethnography or of autobiography as the ultimate narrative strategy
remains at issue. To a certain extent the recounting of the individual
life as a representative one is shaped by the demands of audience. Yet
if the author provides readers with two subjects, splitting the representative qualities of the autobiographic self from those set in opposition to it, she nevertheless avoids sacrificing a commitment to self-
assertion through syntactical arrangements that suggest the cultural
record is itself contingent upon personal narrative. The following
sentence, for instance, posits a singular "I" situated within a community of which the Turrieta family is the model: "This simple story
of the Turrieta family, the family in *The Good Life,* revolves around
the observance and traditions of what could have been any Hispanic
family in a New Mexican village during that period of my work as a
home economist" (pp. v-vi). If Cabeza de Baca's assertion of repre-

sentativeness ("What could have been any Hispanic family") establishes the text as an ethnographic record, she links the larger frame of reference within which the Turrieta family is located, curiously, to her own life. Time is measured not by the sweep of armies across the desert or the dictates of politicians, but by the discrete labor of the self: "that period of my work as a home economist."

A similar relationship between the personal and the collective is established in the closing sentences of the preface: "The fondest memories of my life are associated with the people among whom I have worked. The ways of life expressed in the book and the recipes which are a part of those lives have helped make for me *The Good Life*" (p. vi). Here the subject is interpolated through work—more specifically, the literary labor that mediates between two cultures. Yet the unexpected intrusion of the speaking subject—"for me"—where we might have expected to read without this formulation demands that we locate the text not only as a cultural record but as a self-reflexive narrative as well.

Books such as *The Good Life* confound the line traditionally drawn between autobiography proper, where the subject is presumed to constitute herself as unique, and ethnography, whose postcolonial origin has situated the subject as representative of a culture, typically a culture of "dying breeds." In so doing, they insist on the cultural practices that in part construct the self without privileging those qualities of the subject considered representative and without ignoring any articulations either ambivalent or set in opposition to the "I" as an ethnic "type." By making ethnicity concrete, representing it as it is experienced by the individual, rather than invoking Culture as an abstraction, such autoethnographic texts discourage cultural appropriation, be this within the domain of economics or of criticism. For those literary critics interested in ethnicity theory, the "hybrid" texts of writers such as Cleofas Jaramillo and Fabiola Cabeza de Baca—where the subject is situated in context, but is quite obviously a presence the reader cannot ignore—may discourage that form of critical imperialism (whether more explicit or spoken as nostalgia for a golden primitive past) encouraged by some "purer" forms of ethnographic criticism, in which the (cultural) subject under investigation is always romanticized as either an artifact or about to become one.

Cultural Practice as a Conscious Labor

Ethnicity is not something that is simply passed on from generation to generation, taught and learned. . . . Insofar as ethnicity is a deeply rooted emotional component of identity, it is often transmitted less through cognitive language or learning . . . than through a process analogous to the dreaming and transference of psychoanalytic encounters.[27]

One day when I was a happy six-year-old, I made the shocking discovery that I had Japanese blood. I was a Japanese. Mother announced this fact of life to us in a quiet, deliberate manner one Sunday afternoon as we gathered around for dinner in the small kitchen. . . . Now we watched as Mother lifted from a kettle of boiling water a straw basket of steaming slippery noodles. She directed her information at Henry and me, and I felt uneasy. Father paid strict attention to his noodles, dipping them into a bowl of fragrant pork broth and then sprinkling finely chopped raw green onion over them. "Japanese blood—how is it I have that, Mama?" I asked, surreptitiously pouring hot tea over my bowl of rice. Mother said it was bad manners to wash rice down with tea, but rice was delicious with obancha.[28]

So, you see, this book is the reflection of our pilgrimage "home," which revealed to us not only good food but the origins, early struggles, and life-styles of our family. . . . it is therefore a testimonial to those who lovingly fed us and at the same time gave us a better sense of ourselves by sharing themselves.[29]

Certainly the development of ethnic identity, as Michael M. J. Fischer suggests, is neither simple nor straightforward. The autoethnographic records discussed in this essay, despite their ideological, thematic, and formal differences, all demonstrate a complex series of linguistic maneuvers required to locate the self with respect to a sense of community and ethnic traditions. But what they share in addition is a sense of the conscious and careful work necessary to maintain and reproduce such cultural practices as a means of authorizing the subject. Despite Fischer's attention to the unconscious processes that in part construct ethnic identity—and clearly a sense of cultural awareness as it impinges on the self is developed simultaneously at the level of both conscious and unconscious faculties—the autobiographers of these culinary memoirs expend a great deal of narrative energy in order to affirm that the cultural work their feminine predecessors have undertaken is a difficult labor. In this sense, the disdained but serviceable "caldron and skillet" passed down from mother to daughter in Jessica Harris's *Iron Pots and Wooden Spoons* provides an appropriate metaphor for autoethnographic texts by women more generally.

If it is humble, it is nevertheless instrumental in providing (material) nourishment; just so, women autobiographers point to the mundane work of women, the common labors of their mothers, grandmothers, and daughters, as ultimately the most significant in providing the emotional and spiritual sustenance necessary for self-assertion. Merely because it is conscious, after all, does not assure that a labor is uncomplicated—if this were the case, the struggles for civil rights would have been resolved before now.[30]

This insistence on the conscious labor involved in the reproduction of cultural practice, I would suggest, provides a means of affirming the work of female predecessors often given little attention in texts by male autobiographers from Frederick Douglass to Herbert Gold to Richard Rodriguez. Hence the choice of gender-inflected metaphors of cultural practice and its maintenance: the culinary metaphor, distinctly feminine, the reproductive model of cultural development and identity, specifically maternal. Such a recuperation of a female legacy of course enables self-assertion at the same time it celebrates the lives of women family members as role models. The eulogy Norma Jean and Carole Darden provide for their grandmother, Dianah Scarborough Darden, in *Spoonbread and Strawberry Wine,* for example, implicitly stresses the self-assurance of the authors as it affirms their grandmother's strength of character: "She was not one to merely accept second-class citizenship, and instilled in each child what was then called 'race pride'; insisting that they hold their heads high and assert their equality before God and among men" (p. 28). Similarly, Cleofas Jaramillo's tribute to her mother in *Shadows of the Past* ("Mother would sometimes tell us lovely stories, of which I have written a Children's Story Book, translated into the English") at once acknowledges the literary debt she owes this maternal predecessor and fixes attention on her own publishing efforts (p. 36).

But there is a second, equally important, reason moving writers, including Jade Snow Wong and Fabiola Cabeza de Baca, to represent the relation between subjectivity and ethnicity as a conscious, practiced one. Over and over again, these authors emphasize the struggle involved in the process of self-assertion, an affirmation that is as much the task of family and community as of the subject herself. Figuring the development of an ethnic identity with the metaphor of domestic labor thus provides a means of associating struggle in the political domain with endeavors in the cultural sphere. Because it calls attention to the work involved in cultural reproduction, the culinary metaphor provides writers with a means of reexamining power. Eugene Genovese has described the relation between slaves and slaveholders in the plantation kitchen as one of "the culinary despotism of the quarters over the Big House."[31] Such a figure suggests that a kind of cultural authority may operate simultaneously with—and against— political sway. Such examinations of cultural work reconceptualize the fixed model of oppressor-oppressed power relations. Without sacrificing an acknowledgment of the physical and emotional burdens imposed by imperialism, these writers recuperate a sense of agency for people who, in traditional political and literary theory, have often been subjects in name only.

Notes

I thank Barbara Christian, Sandra Gunning, Genaro Padilla, and Susan Schweik for their comments on earlier drafts of this essay.

1. M. F. K. Fisher, *The Gastronomical Me,* rev. ed. (San Francisco: North Point, 1989; originally published in 1943), 18.

2. Susan Leonardi, "Recipes for Reading: Summer Pasta, Lobster à la Riseholme, and Key Lime Pie," *PMLA* 3 (May 1989): 342. Further references to this article will be cited within the text.

3. Cleofas M. Jaramillo, *Romance of a Little Village Girl* (San Antonio, Tex.: Naylor, 1955), 173. Further references to this book will be cited within the text.

4. Craig Claiborne, back cover notes for Diana Kennedy, *The Cuisines of Mexico,* rev. ed. (New York: Perennial Library/Harper & Row, 1986; originally published in 1972).

5. In full, Craig Claiborne's accolade to Diana Kennedy, reprinted on the back cover of *The Art of Mexican Cooking: Traditional Mexican Cooking for Aficionados* (New York: Bantam, 1989), reads as follows: "Diana Kennedy is the ultimate authority, the high priestess, of Mexican cooking in America. Her previous works have set the standard for any subsequent south-of-the-border cookbooks that might appeal to the English-speaking public. In this present work she has exceeded herself. If you want to cook with the most authentic Mexican taste, this volume should be your guide. I thought I knew Mexican food. This book has been an education!"

6. In the case of *The Cuisines of Mexico,* as Diana Kennedy acknowledges, the book's recipes are based on the meals the author's Mexican maids cooked for her during her various séjours in Mexico. Kennedy herself obliquely acknowledges her own anxiety about cultural appropriation in the acknowledgments to her most recent book, *The Art of Mexican Cooking,* which introduce the text as follows: "I should like to include . . . a quotation from Poppy Cannon (in her introduction to *Aromas and Flavours* by Alice B. Toklas): 'Little by little I began to understand that there can be value in giving a fine performance of another's compositions . . . that an exquisite interpretation can be in its own way just as creative, just as imaginative as an invention,'"(p. x).

7. Tey Diana Rebolledo, "Tradition and Mythology: Signatures of Landscape in Chicana Literature," in *The Desert Is No Lady: Southwestern Landscapes in Women's Writing and Art,* ed. Vera Norwood and Janice Monk (New Haven, Conn.: Yale University Press, 1987), 102. Further references to this work will appear in the text.

8. Clearly, power relations do not cease to operate at the front door of the family home. Nevertheless, I would argue that, despite being equally politically fraught, the intimacy of this space often makes it appear a less intimidating locus within which to work toward self-assertion.

9. Jessica B. Harris, *Iron Pots and Wooden Spoons: Africa's Gifts to New World Cooking* (New York: Atheneum, 1989), xxii. Further references to this book will appear in the text.

10. Maya Angelou, *All God's Children Need Traveling Shoes* (New York: Random House, 1986), 26.

11. Jade Snow Wong, *Fifth Chinese Daughter* (New York: Harper & Brothers, 1945), 161. Further references to this book will be cited within the text.

12. I am indebted to Genaro Padilla for his contributions to this discussion of *Fifth Chinese Daughter.*

13. As many scholars of Chicano literature have noted, native Mexican people of the United States use a variety of self-identifiers to signify their ethnic identity, Mexicano, Latino, and Hispano constituting only a partial list. Each of these terms, as Ramón Saldívar indicates, "has a different psychological, historical, and political connotation that sets it apart from the others." *Chicano Narrative: The Dialectics of Difference* (Madison: University of Wisconsin Press, 1990), 12. In this essay I use *Hispano* to refer to native Mexicans of the state of New Mexico, *nuevomexicano* as the adjectival form designating what is native Mexican New Mexican, and *Mexicano* to refer to Mexicans who are native to the United States.

14. Joan M. Jensen, "Canning Comes to New Mexico: Women and the Agricultural Extension Service 1914–1919," in *New Mexico Women: Intercultural Perspectives* (Albuquerque: University of New Mexico Press, 1986), 207. While I do not concur with Jensen's conclusions, I am indebted to her essay for its historical analysis of the work of the New Mexico home demonstration agents. Further references to the essay will be cited in the text.

15. Fabiola Cabeza de Baca, "Los Alimentos y Su Preparación," *Extension Circular* (New Mexico College of Agriculture and Mechanic Arts, Agricultural Extension Service) 129 (April 1934), 4. Further references to this pamphlet will appear in the text.

16. See Genaro Padilla, "Lies, Secrets and Silence in New Mexico: Cleofas Jaramillo and Fabiola Cabeza de Baca," in *Chicano Literary Criticism: New Essays in Cultural Studies and Ideology,* ed. Hectór Calderón and José David Saldívar (Durham, N.C.: Duke University Press, 1991). "The dominating culture . . . must make the subject forget the details of its domination and make it believe that it has not surrendered so much as availed itself of a more progressive sociocultural national experience. . . . The dispossessed elite, in addition to the modicum of political power they are granted, are also fitted with a socioideological discourse that not only accedes to their dispossession, but actually becomes the official cultural discourse through which the subject group makes sufferable its subordination" (pp. 43-44). Further references to this essay will appear in the text.

17. Fabiola Cabeza de Baca, *Historic Cookery* (Las Vegas, N.M.: La Galería de los Artesanos, 1970; orignally published in 1949), 2.

18. Cleofas M. Jaramillo, *The Genuine New Mexico Tasty Recipes,* rev. ed. (Santa Fe, N.M.: Seton Village, 1942; originally published in 1939). Further references to this book will appear in the text.

19. Clearly such nostalgia for a "Spanish" order, in that it attempts to define Hispanos as "pura Español" (of "pure" Spanish blood) invokes a colonial frame of reference. I will argue that Jaramillo and Cabeza de Baca both tend to signify Hispano/Native American cultural difference obliquely, class inflection, to an extent, simultaneously masking and speaking for this ethnic difference. (See the discussion below of "Señora Martina" in Cabeza de Baca's *The Good Life.*) Nevertheless, I would suggest that current power relations make it impossible to discuss Spanish imperialism over indigenous populations

separately from Anglo imperialism over both Mexicano and Native American people; just as gender relations within African American communities are to a degree informed by white-black race relations in the United States (not to mention race relations in this country more generally), so Anglo-Americans, Hispanos, and Native Americans exist in an unequal, sometimes triangulated, relation to one another. In the texts of both Jaramillo and Cabeza de Baca, colonial representations are to a degree contingent upon, and work as unattractive but nevertheless understandable responses to, that racism exerted over Mexicanos by the dominant Anglo-American order. Critiquing the dominant discourse that lumps all Mexican people together as other, Cabeza de Baca insists on a less monolithic picture of Hispano life, but she does so by invoking—obliquely—Hispano colonialism over Native Americans: "Many historians and writers have contended that there was no wealth in colonial New Mexico, but there was. It was strictly a feudal system and the wealth was in the hands of the few. The *ricos* of colonial days lived in splendor with many servants and slaves. Their haciendas were similar to the Southern plantations. To those coming from what was then the United States of America, the life of the New Mexican *ricos* was not understood because they kept their private lives secure from outsiders." *We Fed Them Cactus* (Albuquerque: University of New Mexico Press, 1954), x.

20. Cleofas M. Jaramillo, *Shadows of the Past* (Santa Fe, N.M.: Ancient City, n.d.). Further references to this book will appear in the text.

21. Compare this insistence on the better health of previous generations with the future-extolling text of Cabeza de Baca's "Los Alimentos": "Hay personas que afirman que nuestros antepasados guardaban mejor salud y vivían más años sin saber nada de la própria nutrición: estas eran las excepciones. Esto puede ser verdad hasta cierto punto. . . . El modo de vivir de nuestros antepasados era más favorable para la salud. Con el progreso y civilización de la nación, el modo de vivir ha cambiado y el resultado es que el modo de comer tiene que cambiar" (There are people who affirm that our ancestors enjoyed better health and lived longer without knowing anything about nutrition: these were the exceptions. This is true up to a certain point. . . . Our ancestors' way of life was more amenable to good health. With the progress and civilizing of the nation the way of life has changed and the result is that the way of eating must change) (p. 4).

22. Erna Fergusson, *Mexican Cookbook* (Albuquerque: University of New Mexico Press, 1934), foreword. Page numbers are provided in text for further quotes from this book. Quotes showing no page numbers are from the book's unpaginated foreword.

23. Fabiola Cabeza de Baca, *The Good Life: New Mexico Traditions and Food* (Santa Fe: Museum of New Mexico Press, 1982; originally published in 1949). This apparently unbridgeable rift in chronological, cultural and ideological perspective becomes easier to negotiate if one considers the different subject positions the author occupies in the two texts. I have previously suggested that "Los Alimentos" locates the author as a kind of cultural intermediary, a state "agent," if you will. Writing in Spanish, speaking to an Hispano readership, the author of the "Buletín" need not articulate her identity as nuevomexicano. Cultural difference is not at issue here; what is problematized instead is her position as worker for the state. *The Good Life,* on the other hand, assumes an extracultural audience and constructs its subject accordingly. Here it is her affiliation with an ethnic community that authorizes her to speak about "New Mexico traditions and food." The introduction to *The Good Life* concisely traces this shift in self-representation: "As a home economist I am happy to see modern kitchens and improved diets, but my artistic soul deplores the passing of beautiful customs which in spite of New Mexico's isolation in the past, gave us happiness and abundant living" (p. 4). Further references to this book will appear in the text.

24. For other representations of this "cultural plenitude," see the narrative of Leonardo Martínez, as transcribed by Patricia Preciado Martín in *Images and Conversations: Mexican Americans Recall a Southwestern Past* (Tucson: University of Arizona Press, 1983); see also that of Jesusita Aragón in Fran Leeper Buss, *La Partera: Story of a Midwife* (Ann Arbor: University of Michigan Press, 1980).

25. The same kind of attention to the limits of cultural translation is at work in the writer's *Historic Cookery*. See, for instance, her discussion of "guisar": "Your experiments in New Mexican cookery can be fascinating. Remember, though, that when you try any of these recipes, you should be prepared to spend plenty of time. *Guisar,* which has no exact English equivalent, is the most popular word in the native homemaker's vocabulary. Roughly translated, it means to dress up food, perhaps only by adding a little onion or a pinch of oregano; good food always deserves a finishing touch. Food must never taste flat, but it will—if it's not *guisado*" (p. 1).

26. In one sense, then, the author herself takes on the work of *curandera* by providing her readership with this description of alternative medical practices.

27. Michael M. J. Fischer, "Ethnicity and the Post-Modern Arts of Memory," in *Writing Culture: The Poetics and Politics of Ethnography,* ed. James Clifford and George E. Marcus (Berkeley: University of California Press, 1986), 195–96.

28. Monica Sone, *Nisei Daughter* (Seattle: University of Washington Press, 1987; originally published in 1953), 3–4.

29. Norma Jean and Carole Darden, *Spoonbread and Strawberry Wine: Recipes and Reminiscences of a Family* (New York: Fawcett Crest, 1978), 11. Further references to this book will appear in the text.

30. S. Frank Miyamoto's introduction to Monica Sone's *Nisei Daughter* provides an interesting example of how complex the reproduction of culture can be. Describing the kind of cultural work the Japanese Language School provided for Seattle Nisei before World War II, he comments: "The School . . . was minimally successful in teaching the language but highly effective in establishing lasting associations." "Introduction," in Monica Sone, *Nisei Daughter,* (Seattle: University of Washington Press, 1987), xi.

31. Eugene D. Genovese, *Roll Jordan Roll: The World the Slaves Made,* (New York: Pantheon, 1974); quoted in Harris, *Iron Pots and Wooden Spoons,* xvi.

Chapter 10

Subversive-Subaltern Identity
Indira Gandhi as the Speaking Subject

Gita Rajan

To speculate on the political agenda of a colonized woman's autobiography, one first locates a subject position from which the woman can speak, then traces the articulation of that speaking subject at the site of colonization. Finally, one decodes the language of that speaking subject in the theater of self-portrayal. Hence, to read a colonized woman's autobiography, one engages in a semiotic endeavor; that is, one reads woman-as-text. Even though this endeavor may sound like a three-step process, it does not proceed hierarchically or chronologically. It proceeds, instead, horizontally and simultaneously. To understand the complicated position of the subaltern woman who speaks in this way, one necessarily examines the social and political construction of the representative identity in question. Numerous factors contribute to creating and maintaining the subaltern woman's identity: the differential and differing relationships in the divided subject between the imaginary/symbolic modes (with attendant psychoanalytic implications), the complexity of gender identifications (with feminist and cultural implications), and the colonizer/colonized context (with historical and ideological implications).[1] The subaltern speaking subject stands therefore at the intersection of various sociocultural forces that must be accounted for in reconstructing her subjectivity.

By pointing to the different facets in the subaltern woman's identity, one can, adopting the oppositional stance taken by Gayatri
Chakravorty Spivak in "Can the Subaltern Speak?" posit that the female
is in the "double shadow" of the male and/or the colonizer and thus
can "never speak." One can also assume an integrative stance toward
the divided subject and argue that the simultaneity of her doubled
position refuses to cancel out these oppositions (of male and/or colonizer). Accordingly, if one extends Spivak's thesis to account for a
gendered identity instead of situating identity in the woman's body,
then one can argue that the gendered subaltern subject can indeed
speak. *Gendering,* in a broad sense, means extending the woman's
identity beyond her biological and sexual configurations to her cultural
and historical specificity. Further, gendering the female body achieves
two things: first, it allows for an expansion of Spivak's explanation of
the "subaltern woman"; second, and more important, it grants the
woman access, albeit a subversive access, to a speaking subject's
position.

Accordingly, this essay explores the notion of Indira Gandhi as the
gendered subaltern in order to reveal the calculated subversive trajectory of the speaking subject. Reading Indira Gandhi-as-text vis-à-
vis the cultural/political history of India, this essay focuses on the
oppositionality or polarization implicit in Spivak's argument by invoking Karl Marx's notion of the contradiction inherent in any subject
position between representation (political, as in speaking for) and representation (semiotic, as in signifying). I will suggest that Gandhi
subverted the gap in this contradiction by situating herself discursively
and gesturally between these two modes of representation, and thus
allowed herself to be read semiotically. In this frame, she successfully
voiced the desires of the dominant ideological parties of postcolonial
India, while simultaneously proclaiming her own agenda as widowed
mother of India. Thus, *she* became the site of overlapping discourses.
This deliberate double articulation allowed Gandhi to portray herself
on both sides of the ideological boundary—inside/outside, and before/
after subaltern subjugation.

Divided Subjectivity as Representative Politicocultural Identity

Indira Gandhi-as-text—that is, as a semiotic subject—cannot be read
as the normative example of an Indian woman's autobiography. Tex-
tualizing Indira Gandhi necessarily becomes a multivalent endeavor
because she must be explained as a woman, a historical event, a

political creature, and a site for viewing the spectacle of colonization. The issue of colonization is particularly fascinating because I have to situate her inside Indian history and culture while rendering these very tropes transparent to make her readable for a Western audience. Accordingly, I will discuss her accident of birth in this section and explore this factor in etching her *political* identity. Since India's history became intertwined with Indira's history, explanations of the influence of political events on her life and actions are crucial to understanding cultural and semiotic underpinnings of her subjectivity. Pointedly, one of the more popular election slogans (1972) claimed, "Indira Is India." Next, any theory postulated about colonial or subaltern identity must be read, in Indira Gandhi's case, against the grain of her privileged status. In other words, it is only when Indira Gandhi exploited her *cultural* lack of status as a widow that she gained access to power. In Indian culture, a widow has no exchange or use value, that is, no identity in society except through lack. From a feminist, poststructural viewpoint, then, she positioned herself as lack, or as the blind spot on which her colonizers and history wrote a master discourse. Ultimately, she exploited this very blind spot to subvert both.

Accident of Birth

The first facet of Indira Gandhi's representative identity was the legacy of her birth. She belonged to an elite family, class, and caste. As Motilal Nehru's granddaughter, Jawaharlal Nehru's daughter, Vijaya Lakshmi Pundit's niece, and Mahatma Gandhi's adoptive daughter, she belonged to a family of pioneers in the Indian freedom struggle. She was also the only child of one of the richest Kashmiri Brahmin families, one that lived within an Anglicized cultural environment. I make the distinction here between Brahmin and Anglicized cultures to show how she had access to Hindu tradition with the former and "schooled" cultural status with the latter.[2] Thus, at first glance, she does not fit the category of subaltern women. The very accident of her birth and her proximity to power render suspect her position as a subaltern woman. At the level of a privileged, well-schooled daughter, she participated in the decision-making political machinery of colonial, postcolonial, and independent India.

Growing up at the height of the freedom struggle forged a political consciousness and a sense of personal identity that was uniquely Indira Gandhi's. Nehru, in prison during most of her childhood and adolescence, maintained a tenuous father-child relationship with her through a steady stream of letters. Mahatma Gandhi, realizing the impact of Nehru's discourse, wrote in 1937:

> Your letters to Indu are excellent and should be pub-
> lished. . . . They have a value derived not from the truth of
> your conclusions, but from the manner of treatment [of India's
> freedom struggle] and from the fact that you have tried to
> reach Indu's heart and open the eyes of her understanding in
> the midst of your external activities.[3]

Nehru's catalog of his freedom struggle experiences and his evaluation of imperialistic politics through the letters undoubtedly played a large part in Indira's understanding of India. They gave her an indelible blueprint to use in conceptualizing and dealing with political crises, and created a sense of duty commingled with shades of martyrdom in the shaping of a destiny for free India. As Gandhi himself pointed out, it was not "the truth" of Nehru's "conclusions," but the "manner of treatment" of political crises from which Indira Gandhi learned her lessons. This is just one of many factors, albeit an elitist one, that contributed toward creating Indira Gandhi's political subjectivity.

Woman as Cultural Signifier

While one aspect of Indira Gandhi's divided subjectivity granted her access to elite political platforms, another allowed her to project herself as a daughter/widow serving her country. Her unwitting, perhaps unconscious, occupation of the two positions—daughter and mother—in the economy of Indian womanhood is remarkable from a poststructural, postrepresentational perspective. Even though she married Feroz Gandhi (no relation to Mahatma Gandhi), she chose to abort her relationship as his wife in the public arena so that she could become her father's political hostess. With unerring acumen, she chose to abnegate the place of *wife,* one of the easiest to appropriate and one that requires the unconditional surrender of agency in an Indian cultural context. In a letter dated 21 July 1959 to Dorothy Norman, her American friend, she says:

> A veritable sea of trouble is engulfing me. On the domestic
> front, Feroz has resented my very [political] existence, but
> since I have become President [of the Congress Party] he
> exudes such hostility that it seems to poison the air.[4]

That Indira Gandhi was conscious of her choice not to play "wife" was made graphically clear when she banned the film *Andhi (Tempest),* which was released during the period in which she had declared a state of national emergency (25 June 1975 to 20 March 1977). The film presents ironically the tension between filial and conjugal duties in an Indian woman who ultimately opts for the former, becomes her father's social/business affiliate, and abdicates her role as wife. After the Emergency period it was common for the media to mock Indira Gandhi for revealing her Achilles' heel.

Indira Gandhi chose self-consciously to reiterate her position, first as a daughter and then as a widowed mother, obeying and carrying out the dictates of elders in the Indian Congress party when she was first elected party president and later prime minister. In this configuration of "woman" she managed to create a cultural, representative identity for herself, both within the Indian cabinet and within the minds of the Indian electorate. And it was in this context that history, complicit with culture, created a double or divided subjectivity for Indira Gandhi—as privileged daughter and martyred mother. The Indian press constantly referred to her as *Mataji* (mother, where the suffix *ji* is the cultural signifier of respect) throughout her political career.[5]

Another self-conscious trick she used in creating an Indira Gandhi-as-cultural-icon was her staged appearance. A well-imprinted image of Indira Gandhi, both at home and abroad, was that of a stark, energetic figure in a white/beige *khaddar* sari (hand-spun and hand-woven fabric that immediately signaled Mahatma Gandhi's "buy Indian" slogan, calculated to work against British imperialism). A full-sleeved blouse, a cloth shoulder bag, and hands folded in a humble gesture of greeting—*Namaste*—lent an air of dignified maturity. She en-*gendered* power through the paradox of her simplicity and humility, such that all her biographers, and even her sincerest critics, acknowledge this mesmerizing semiotics of studied starkness. The energy, the *khaddar,* and the self-conscious *Namaste* evoked Mahatma Gandhi. She categorically established herself in the apostolic tradition,[6] as the Mahatma's follower, signifying that she was going to toil untiringly to carry on his tradition and fight valiantly for the Indian masses.

Indira Gandhi was conscious of her apostolic ploy, of projecting such a metaphoric substitution and creating a metonymic extension—of troping her very presence. This becomes even clearer when one examines her speeches. From the time she delivered one of her first national speeches she maintained a rhetorical strategy whereby she became linked to Nehru/Gandhi and pledged herself to the service of the country. In her keynote address as party president, titled "A Servant of the Nation" and delivered to the Congress Parliamentary party and broadcast to the nation by All India Radio on 19 January 1966, she said:

> My heart is full today, and I do not know how to thank you. As I stand before you, my thoughts go to the great leaders— Mahatma Gandhi, at whose feet I grew up; Panditji, my father; and Shri Lal Bahadur Shastri . . . who brought me into politics after Independence. . . . I have always considered myself a *desh sevika* [servant of the nation] even as my father regarded himself as the first servant of the nation. I consider myself a servant of the party, and especially of the great people of this country.[7]

This strategy, maintained in most subsequent speeches, became her signature as a politician. She systematically invoked the genealogy of the great leaders and reminded the people that she was their servant. Very subtly, she encoded the Indian cultural myth of *servitude.* Her duty to the Indian masses she performed willingly because she, as a widow, was now devoting herself to the country. She engulfed the country metaphorically in every public address by calling her audience "brothers and sisters," and maintained the illusion of the masses as her very family by referring to herself as "*Chacha* Nehru's *beti*" (Uncle Nehru's daughter), which became her winning campaign slogan in 1967 and in later elections. The rhetoric of "brothers and sisters" allowed Indira Gandhi to slide her discursive identity from the political register to the familial one. Embracing the nation as her family, she made the country responsible for her political success, her electoral victory (and, as I will discuss later, made the country an unconscious and sometimes unwilling partner in her crimes during the Emergency). It is crucial here to understand that Indira Gandhi did not ask for the country's fierce devotion; she asked instead to act as the "servant" through whom the country could channel its patriotism to the country/fathers.

Moreover, in moving from the political register to the familial one, Indira Gandhi split her representative identity between the elitist and the commoner. For the first time a member of the Nehru family embraced the masses; and she resembled the Mahatma more than she did her own father. Strategically, she healed the fissure between the two representations (political/Nehru/elitist and semiotic/Gandhi/commoner) through her encompassing role as "woman." She is perhaps one of the few women in the world who has showcased the signification of *woman* so eloquently. While one part of her subjectivity, as privileged daughter, disallowed her access to subaltern status, the second, as martyr/mother, guaranteed it. This simultaneity of roles allowed her to function under erasure as both a ruthless political strategist and a historicocultural "pathetic figurine."[8]

Indian Subjectivity/Western Theory

From a theoretical perspective the subaltern woman cannot speak, as Spivak so elegantly argues, because she is relegated to an always-already object position; she is either spoken for or spoken at. She lacks agency, according to Spivak, in the subaltern position. But Mrs. Gandhi adroitly turned the tables on her colonizers (the party elders) by assuming agency. By using her body as a "widow" and shielding her voice with that of the "fathers," Indira Gandhi made her presence felt. She appropriated what we have come to understand as the polemics of the political, semiotic, or cultural formula inherent in Karl Marx's notion of representation. It is at this point that I must unmask my own representation of Indira Gandhi: I am an Indian rereading an Indian critic (Spivak) in an attempt to situate an Indian subject-text (Indira Gandhi). My position is complicated because I both invoke and silence Indian culture, history, and politics to formulate a Western paradigm for understanding the agency behind the subaltern position and to show how Mrs. Gandhi turned it to her advantage. The West, at the risk of a generalization, has established lines along which subjectivity can be constructed. In *The Eighteenth Brumaire of Louis Bonaparte,* Marx discusses the subject positions available in representation with a play on *vertreten* and *darstellen. Vertreten,* according to Marx, involves political agency, as the subject becomes spokesperson for a class in society. *Darstellen* is the social construction of the subject that is both dependent on and independent of class.[9] Spivak underscores the point regarding class difference by citing Marx's own formulations about representation when she says:

> In so far as millions of families live under economic conditions that separate their mode of life . . . they form a class. In so far as the identity of their interest fails to produce a feeling of community . . . they do not form a class. The complicity of *vertreten* and *darstellen,* their identity-in-difference as the place of practice—since this complicity is what Marxists must expose, as Marx does in *The Eighteenth Brumaire*—can only be appreciated if they are not conflated by a sleight of word."[10]

It is this *"identity-in-difference"* that creates a unique lens for reading Mrs. Gandhi. That is, the status of Indira Gandhi as a "widow" (cultural class) is inseparable from her privileged class position (economic class) in an Indian cultural/political context. Unraveling her layered subjectivity would perhaps reveal a Foucauldian fallacy that Spivak warns against in her critical essay on the subaltern.[11] It is my attempt here to suggest a complicated subject position that could become a contingency in examining feminist/colonial agendas in *other* geopolitical contexts.

No doubt, Spivak's agenda is to posit a theory of cultural discourse centered on the oppressed class (the one who is represented) in order to show two things: one, that the oppressed person is indeed silenced, and two, that the situation reveals instances of colonial discourse in which mimicking the master discourse[12] has been misread as authentic colonial voice. Along the lines of such a hypothesis Spivak proves that the subaltern woman can be viewed only as a ventriloquist's dummy— never as a speaking subject.[13] However, in Indira Gandhi's case, the representation issue is more complicated. If we consider *vertreten,* or political agency, we see that Indira Gandhi had access to agency. But if we examine *darstellen,* or cultural identity, we see that she denounced any claims to agency. This paradox of her subaltern position must be considered. Because Indira Gandhi placed herself in such clear Indian political and cultural spaces, she challenges most readings framed by Western paradigms.

As Jawaharlal Nehru's daughter she belonged to the *sanctum sanctorum* of icons in the Indian freedom struggle. Her patriotism at the beginning of her career was unquestionable; her understanding of political issues during the early years of independence was certainly better than that of most other candidates. Hence, she was treated with (fatherly) affection by the senior cabinet ministers and with respect by the junior ministers. An example from her political life reveals her privileged access to legislative power in India and shows also how she manipulated it to suit her personal agenda. Late in 1958, Nehru made it possible for Lal Bahadur Shastri (India's second prime minister after Nehru's death in May 1964) and Kamaraj (Congress party elder, and acknowledged "king maker" who catapulted Indira to political fame) to nominate Indira Gandhi as Congress party president. R. K. Murthy, in *The Cult of the Individual,* notes that Indira was the "natural" choice but fails to recognize the metaphoric implications of "daughter" that are contingent upon "natural" and are implicit in the political move. He writes:

> Proximity to Nehru gave her the necessary training. . . . She
> absorbed the intricacies which eddied and undulated below
> the surface, shaping the course of history. Political leaders
> who wanted to influence Nehru saw in her an instrument to

achieve their objectives. She enjoyed, in unlimited measure, Nehru's complete confidence. She did not cower when Nehru lost his temper, stood up to him boldly, at times even defiantly. She had the steel with which to counter Nehru's rapier thrusts.[14]

This quotation reveals a certain dynamics of patriarchy that operated in the Indian political arena. The inner circle of political pundits wanted to appropriate or colonize the "daughter" Indira for their own needs. With this in mind, Shastri and Kamaraj went along with Nehru's unspoken command and elected her to power. They never wanted to see her function as the king, but merely as a pawn; all of Indian history from 1965 to 1977 testifies to that. Because Nehru's charisma had made him seem immortal and omnipotent, the cabinet felt secure about giving in to his covert request to give Indira a political position.

Dorothy Norman, perhaps because of her proximity to the Nehru family or her Western subjectivity, reiterates the well-rehearsed lie that Nehru was innocent of this gesture. She writes: "During my 1959 trip to India . . . she [Indira] had just been elected Congress Party President. Rumors spread that Nehru made this possible. He told me he had nothing to do with it; Indira confirmed this."[15] Norman's acceptance of Nehru's word as a *true* record of the incident is symptomatic of the portrayal of Indira Gandhi in Indian history. She hid behind the "word" of the fathers to achieve her own ends, and this in turn helped her to move alternately between subject and object positions in the discourse of Indian history. The presupposition behind Indira Gandhi's nomination was that she would toe the line inscribed by the party F/fathers, and, as daughter/object, would execute the political decisions or maneuvers. They never granted her or expected her to arrogate a subject position that assumed such a well-defined political agency.

Ironically, one of Gandhi's first steps as party president, her intervention in the communist situation in Kerala, reveals her subtle yet powerful arrogation of agency. In 1959, Kerala, one of India's southern states, became the first in the country to elect a communist majority to power. Assessing the political situation in a letter to Norman dated 21 July 1959, Gandhi writes:

The Kerala situation is worsening. The movement is not petering out as the Communists claim but gathering momentum. The women, whom I have been trying to organize for years, had always refused to come into politics. Now they are out in the field. Over 8000 have been arrested. I have heard that in Europe, perhaps even in America my father is being blamed for not taking action. He has given a very good lead from the beginning but he is incapable of dictatorship or roughshod-ding over the views of his senior colleagues. More and more I find that he is almost the only one who thinks in terms of ideology rather than personality. I cannot write much in a let-ter. . . . My father cannot go against the wishes of the Home Minister [Morarji Desai], for instance.[16]

The letter displays at least three levels of cognizance. First, Indira Gandhi never underestimated the power of the people, a power she could tap into through her own personality and rhetoric. Second, while Nehru could not ride "roughshod" over his colleagues, she herself had a different set of ethics. Both Thakur and Murthy record that Kamaraj, perhaps even more than Nehru, was disgruntled with the way she handled the Kerala situation.[17] Third, and most important, she recognized the almost magical way in which personality could spark "native" ideology. Accordingly, she single-handedly mobilized the people of Kerala to protest openly and overthrow the communist regime. Astutely, she consolidated "ideology" and "personality" to successful ends. Her strategy (ideology) was to mimic Mahatma Gandhi by hinting that she was working with the people against an alien, oppressive government. Her personality she projected through her resemblance to the Gandhi and the Nehru of the freedom struggle. The moment was also close enough (historically) to the independence effort for her to transform the alien, communist Kerala government into a metonymy of British imperialism. Inciting the people to rebel against the local government granted her a special place in their mem-ory; it invoked the independence struggle. Fortunately, history was complicit with her in this political strategy and recorded the Kerala incident as a "fight for democracy." In this brilliant move, even though she (seemingly) went against her father and other "senior colleagues," she endeared herself, her personality, and her values to India and to the Western world in general.[18] More important, she theatricalized her cultural lack of power as both a woman and a widow. By assuming political agency, yet rendering it void through identification with ide-ologues such as Gandhi/Nehru (through mirroring the Indian inde-pendence struggle), she slid from the object to the subject position without disturbing the surface of her discursive identity.

Pierre Macherey, discussing the role of ideology and its dissemi-nation into culture, makes an observation that can be used to explore some ramifications of Indira Gandhi's discursive identity:

What is important in a work is what it does not say. This is not the same as the careless notation "what it refuses to

say," . . . although that would in itself be interesting. . . . what
the work *cannot* say is important, because there the elaboration of the utterance is carried out in a sort of journey into
silence.[19]

In retrospect, what Mrs. Gandhi "did not" tell, "refused to say," and,
most important, *could* not say was that the struggling Keralites were
going against the very ethics of democracy. Her duplicity in over-
throwing a democratically elected government in Kerala never came
to light because she identified her *self* and her *actions* with Mahatma
Gandhi. In reality, she mobilized the march against Kerala and its
communist regime because she wanted to mandate the power of the
central government, that is, her father. Feroz Gandhi was the only
one who argued with Indira about her dubious political intentions.
She records the fact in a letter to Dorothy Norman: "He [Feroz] is
being so principled about Kerala."[20] Indira Gandhi's deliberate manipulation of the situation comes across in the very semantics ("principled") of her comment to Norman. In her complaint to Norman, she
reveals her (subversive) political agency and (machinated) subject consciousness, both of which Macherey emphasizes are *subtexts* to ideology and culture.

The Kerala incident reveals a contrived "silencing" by Gandhi, the
subject/agent, which is quite different from Spivak's argument of the
mandated "silencing" of the subaltern subject who is forced to perform
sati, that is, commit suicide. In this, Spivak's exemplary figure is
completely robbed of her subject position and placed in the "double
shadow" of male and/or colonizer. Thus, while both Spivak and I
focus upon examples of a "subaltern" subject, we differ in our ascrip-
tion of agency to that subject. Indira Gandhi exceeded signification
because she genderized representation. By occupying the subject position consciously from the first step (i.e., beginning with the apostolic
agenda) yet proclaiming her lack of subject status (i.e., signaling her
widowed status), Mrs. Gandhi merged ideology and personality, sub-
ject/object, and actor/mime with consummate skill.

To accent the position of a gendered subaltern subject and the
political agent that Indira Gandhi acted out, I will read her as a semiotic
subject through some discussions of representation raised by contemporary scholars of colonial discourse. One could argue that by not
stating her position at the point of "enunciation," Indira Gandhi created the aura of "ambivalence" or "indeterminacy" that Homi Bhabha
allows the colonized text.[21] Abdul R. JanMohamed, however, short-
circuits Bhabha's claim to a certain "ambivalence" by remarking that

to impute in this way, at this late date, and through the back door, an "innocent" or "naive" intention to colonialist discourse is itself a naive act at best. Wittingly, or otherwise, Bhabha's strategy serves the same ideological function as other older humanistic analyses: . . . he represses the political history of colonialism, which is inevitably sedimented in its discourse.[22]

In Indira Gandhi's case, the political history of the independence struggle that becomes "sedimented in the discourse" cannot be ignored. Because of this undertow, Indira Gandhi's every utterance, whether discursive or semiotic, needs to be examined in the light of the "other" (Indian/fathers/cultural) discourse that she deliberately invoked and erased.

If I were to argue that Indira Gandhi was *not* stating her position because she was caught unwittingly in the gap—in the "indeterminate" subject/agent position of a "colonized woman" that Bhabha grants to colonial discourse—I would need to trace the accidental nature of such a gap. However, examining the political agency she constructs through her acknowledged lack of cultural agency, one can argue instead that Indira Gandhi was always conscious of her subject position. By analyzing her discourse as deliberately articulated through the "colonial" register, the agency in the subject position becomes apparent.

I place Indira Gandhi in the colonial position because it is a well-documented historical fact that, from the beginning of her career (1958–60), the party elders, Kamaraj in particular, wished to map a history of India via Indira. All of them planned to use her name, her political acumen, and her personal charisma to control events from behind the scenes. They had banked upon the fact that the country, conditioned by centuries of monarchic rule, would make her ascent to power culturally automatic if not politically expedient. In fact, the Indian press, recognizing this master plan (also jokingly referred to as the "Kamaraj plan"), remarked during her overwhelming victory in the 1967 election to the post of prime minister that "Indira Gandhi is no *goongi-gudiya*" (dumb doll; the translation suggests connotations of puppetry).[23] It is in this frame that she should be congratulated for calculatedly colonizing her colonizers.

In conjoining the political and cultural axes of subjectivity, and in reading Indira Gandhi as text, one can see that she represented the agent who had *learned* the syntax of the dominant and dominating discourse and had the cultural good sense as a *woman* alternately to silence and amplify her own agenda. While rendering herself transparent to the polemics of sex due to her role as a widow (Indian culture demands a kind of sexlessness in a widow), she emphasized her presence through gender. By calling attention to her widowhood, Indira Gandhi emphasized her nurturing role as a woman who had sacrificed herself for the country. She positioned herself in a particular place in Indian culture that called attention to the attributes of her biological sexuality and deflected attention from her libidinal sexuality. In an interview for *Revista de Occidente* of Madrid, she declared, "My being Prime Minister had nothing to do with my being a woman. . . . would you ask that of a man. . . . indeed, Gandhiji's success was in no small measure due to the fact that he was able to mobilize women."[24] Like Gandhi, she was able in this way to project herself as an abstract, ahistorical entity.

It is at this juncture that Ketu Katrak's analysis of Mahatma Gandhi's (ab)use of women in the revolution reiterates my analysis of Indira Gandhi's colonization of her womanhood. Katrak records Mahatma Gandhi's well-publicized comment on the role of Indian women in the *satyagraha* (nonviolent revolution) formulated from 1921 onward: "The female sex is not the weaker sex; it is the nobler of the two; for it is even today the embodiment of sacrifice, silent suffering, humility, faith, and knowledge."[25] Indira Gandhi straddled two positions in a sophisticated manner. By identifying with the Mahatma at the point of enunciation, she became the subject of the discourse; she was the leader who could mobilize the swarming millions of women. But, by simultaneously merging with the image of the innumerable "noble" women thus mobilized, she became the object of discourse. By moving seamlessly between subject/leader and object/women positions, she became invincible. Mockingly, however, she took the Name of the Father, fully conscious of an intention to subvert it.[26] By portraying both the subject (Mahatma Gandhi) and the object (his willing troop of women), she systematically highlighted "F/father," erased her own womanhood, and rendered "womanhood" fictive.

Subverting a Subaltern Identity

The coalescence of two facets of representation (the political and semiotic) in Indira Gandhi-the-text enabled Gandhi to subvert her position as a "subaltern" by systematically occupying both the subject and object positions. It is necessary at this point, then, to consider the various meanings of the term *subaltern* in order to understand the ways in which Indira Gandhi both enacted and resisted subaltern status. In the British military frame the term denotes a rank just below that of captain. It connotes the responsibility of executing tasks *without* assuming the responsibility of making decisions. Indira Gandhi assumed this subaltern position purposefully, appearing to maintain a status below that of the captains of the cabinet and pretending to carry out their dictates. She used her subordinate status to achieve her own political agenda. In the cultural/historical frame, which is incidentally also the etymological frame, the term *subaltern* means "below the other."[27] Again we see that, in publicly proclaiming that she served "below" the party elders, and by implication the nation, she actively positioned herself as the subaltern.

There is a third frame through which to understand subaltern status. In his essay "Some Aspects of the Southern Question," Antonio Gramsci explains that the subaltern is constituted through the inferior/superior relationship established between socioeconomic classes. For Gramsci, subaltern identity may signal "class consciousness," which in turn leads to the construction of subjectivity (or a lack of it) depending upon the role of the subaltern in the writing of history itself.[28] Gramsci's theorizing comes closest to the issues at hand while examining Gandhi-as-text. He draws boundaries between subject/agency and object/lack along lines of bourgeois aspirations for power. In this frame, too, Gandhi cannot be read as having a typical subaltern identity because she deliberately breached the boundary between the Gramscian categories.

Ranajit Guha, an Indian theorist of subaltern studies, provides a fourth frame through which to understand subaltern identity in a colonial context. Guha suggests a four-part "dynamic stratification grid ascribing colonial social production at large."[29] Guha points out that the imperial subject was the only one allowed to speak because the native "people" or the "subaltern" got disseminated into categories of "dominant foreign group," or the "indigenous elite national" or the "indigenous local group," leaving no room for the "people" per se to speak. Reading Gandhi-as-text through Guha's grid, we see that she claimed a dual status that was "elite" on the one hand (based upon her political genealogy) and "part of the total Indian population" on the other (based upon her widowed mother claim). She thus becomes absorbed in almost all of Guha's registers so that it is difficult to see her occupying any one of his conceptual spaces fully. Consequently, one needs to consider all the above definitions of the term *subaltern*. In order to be able to categorize Indira Gandhi as "subaltern" we need to include her cultural position as "widow," her sexual position as "woman," her familial position as "mother," and her (carefully acknowledged) political position as "second in command," and note that *every* position denies her access to agency. But, as already seen, she systematically exploited this very lack and occupied the margin between presence/subject and absence/object—that is, she exercised agency because she appeared not to be exercising agency.

Due to this seeming inseparability of "representation" (both political and cultural) or subaltern/captain (both woman and widow) status in the "subject" Indira Gandhi, I must seek the precise place where she herself caused the scandal in her subjectivity. I must show how she became careless in observing the complicated rules that organize discourse and ideology. I must therefore focus upon the one incident wherein she moved from her *radical* straddling position (subject/ object) to a traditional one where she revealed her access to power (subject only). That opportunity came with her declaration of a state of national emergency.

The Emergency Rule

The pursuit of power makes us cunning, the possession of power makes us stupid.

Nietzsche

Indira Gandhi's strategy from 1958 onward was to traverse the gap between her cultural and political identities, and that slippage maintained her steadily in power. She always appeared before the nation not as prime minister, but as widowed mother working for the country. It was only with the declaration of the emergency rule that the synchronization between the two representative identities was broken. The nuances of her subaltern identity became traceable only when she betrayed the ideology of that position—during her reign of emergency (25 June 1975 to 20 March 1977). Then for the first time she emerged as a full political figure, acknowledged an agency for her political actions, and established a clear subjectivity behind her political decisions.

She became unidimensional—completely sacrificing her womanly/ cultural *darstellen* facet to assume a fully political *vertreten* one.[30] When she shed the cultural identity of widowed mother the nation was shocked to see her naked face. She had erased her gendered identity, exposed her desire for absolute power, and, hence, lost the people's unconditional admiration. The whole world was appalled by the dictatorial Indira Gandhi; Indian civilians were arrested, imprisoned, even killed without due process. She imposed new legislation that consolidated her claim to supreme authority, silenced the press, even amended the Constitution without the apparent gesture of obeisance to the fathers. The Indian newspapers used such phrases as "the rape of the judiciary" (*Times of India*), "gagging the media" (*Statesman*), and the "reign of terror" (*The Hindu*). Her American friend Dorothy Norman was so disillusioned that she first wrote letters to Indira Gandhi protesting the emergency rule and, when that failed, circulated a petition demanding a human rights inquiry (through Amnesty International) into the political state of chaos in the country.[31]

Rather than analyze the emergency itself, I will trace the semiosis behind the drastic action. One of the interesting points about reading Indira Gandhi as a semiotic text is to show how she used the economy of an Indian cultural/gendered discourse to break the rules in ideologically significant ways. By circumscribing herself as widowed mother, she inscribed herself across patriarchal discourse without violating the rules of the play. But when she chose to disobey these very rules, she destabilized her own subject position. In her new, yet-undefined role, she maintained an iron hold on the Indian judiciary and the press. Justifying the emergency to the country, she was often reported by the (controlled) press as saying: "We were confronted with counter revolutions against Indian policies." On the international front, she accused the Western press of indulging in "propaganda" about the "nuclear test in India in 1974" and/or claiming that the emergency was one obvious manifestation of a general *malaise* in the "Indian subcontinent."[32] By specifically calling attention to the arms race and the world market economy, she managed to move some of the criticism aimed at *herself* onto a geopolitical level. In a manner of speaking, she deflected the gaze of the West neatly away from her and back onto itself. She seemed to suggest (repeatedly) at international gatherings that the press's criticism was a reflection of Western, patriarchal hegemony. Raj Darbari records an incident with the British Broadcasting Corporation in which she made such a statement in London in the presence of Prime Minister Callaghan and Mrs. Thatcher and neither contradicted her. It is not as important to challenge the truth behind her allegations as it is to uncover her astute tactics in blatantly discrediting some of the Western press.

Mrs. Gandhi also joked to Dorothy Norman about the emergency in a letter dated 19 September 1975—"Dorothy dear . . . accept a [Christmas] gift from the 'Great Dictator'"—subtly forcing the "friend" who had turned "critic" to overlook the bad blood between them.[33] Astutely, Indira Gandhi realized the role Norman was playing in world politics, particularly in the wealthy, cultured Western world, and she wanted to rein Norman in. By this conciliatory gesture, she attempted to force Norman to compromise her ethics in favor of their friendship.

In short, she had a suave explanation for both her private and her public critics.

The note of admiration that runs through this segment of the essay is not to validate Indira Gandhi's political conduct, but to applaud her presence of mind. In the face of tremendous adversity, both domestic and foreign, she tried desperately to cope with her own fragmented identity. Sadly, she had to be punished for this very fracture: as a "woman" she had overstepped the boundaries of her cultural notation (in India); as a "person of color" she had overstepped the boundaries of her colonial notation (abroad). And having exposed her agency through the emergency, she was expelled from the public arena, by both the Indians and the foreigners. She bore the consequences of exposing that very subjectivity/agency and lost at the 1977 national polls. The Indians showed their wrath at her betrayal of her facade, and the West showed its hand in Third World politics by (covertly) aiding the opposition party.[34] Only at this moment did Indira Gandhi resemble the *sati* figure from Spivak's essay: she became a woman who had no use or exchange value in a traditional, patriarchal economy, and, consequently, was expendable. She was relegated to the position of the subaltern, was held in the "double shadow," stripped of speech and stature.

Resurrecting the Subaltern

After the 1977 election, Indira Gandhi realized that she had to resurrect the "daughter/widowed mother" image. There was only one place she could legitimately occupy that would grant her the agency and power she had become accustomed to having—that of the subaltern. Since in 1975 she had converted her personal emergency (major dissidence in the Indian Parliament) into a national emergency with unerring political acumen, she realized she could reverse the process. I will catalog only three examples out of innumerable others to show how she systematically retraced her steps back into the people's good graces. Indira Gandhi was equal to the task of launching a planned cultural/historical assault on the masses in India with calculated effect.

First on her agenda was to apologize publicly to the whole nation for the horrors of the emergency. Semiotically, begging for forgiveness allowed her to reinscribe herself in the feminine position of her cultural identity.[35] Her crime was the abuse of executive power during the state of emergency, which is perhaps the only corruption of power that is forgiven and forgotten in most political arenas. She had deftly colonized the position of "mother" without ever letting her power seep beyond the boundaries of her status as a widow. One obvious record of such a colonization was that she never allowed any hint of sexual scandal to blemish her status as a dedicated widow in the service of her people. Dressed in her pre-emergency-style *khaddar* sari, she stood with her head bowed, begging the nation's forgiveness. Such a planned representation exhausted the femininity of her cultural identity mentioned above; the people did not see the arrogant woman— they saw instead the contrite widow/mother. In short, she reappropriated her stature as widowed mother. The press was the first to be persuaded by her tactics; it labeled her the "pathetic figurine," and the people then picked up the cue.

Her next chance came when the opposition party arrested her for crimes committed during the emergency. It was a shock to the nation that Sanjay Gandhi, who was largely responsible for the abuse of power, was not even an elected official in the government.[36] Thus, the opposition was forced to arrest her to vent public spleen and appear *just* to the nation. At 5:00 p.m. on 3 October 1977, Mr. N. K. Singh from the Central Bureau of Investigations served Indira Gandhi with the arrest notice. She refused to be taken into custody without capitalizing on the situation. She waited for the press and wailed to the television cameras: "Where is my *hathkadi* [handcuff]?" By deliberately stepping into the shoes of the criminal, she was perceived as a martyr, and within hours she had projected herself as a "mother" who had paid for her son's indulgences. She also compared herself to the Indian freedom fighters who were handcuffed by the British. The country shifted its anger to a slow expression of sympathy for this contrite yet brave woman. She had played her abject femininity once more to the finish line. Between her Machiavellian strategies and the ineptness of the opposition party, she shifted from the position of the oppressor to that of the oppressed. With India as the enthralled audience, she choreographed an elaborate *pas de deux* in which her intricate planning stood out starkly against the inefficiency of the opposition; she had wrested political agency once again. Coupled with this strategy was the fact that the Shah Commission (set up to inquire into her nefarious plans during the emergency) could not indict her for any major crime. The people were divided, and the moment seemed right for a mood shift to her side again.

Her last step was to select weak spots in the opposition rule and exploit them, appearing always to serve the nation. One such graphic and opportune moment came with the Belchi incident. Belchi, a small town in northern India, had just burned three "untouchables" in a caste war.[37] The central government did not accord the racial/caste incident the correct political attention or suppress press coverage, and Indira Gandhi seized the opportunity. Even though she did not hold any political office at that time, she walked to the village in a torrential downpour, mobilizing all the towns and villages en route, just to express her sympathy. Immediately, the press compared her trek to Mahatma Gandhi's famous *Dandi*/salt march, paralleled her mission to his emancipation of the oppressed caste, and read a nobility in her deed that she herself had scripted. The villagers meanwhile had taken up the chant "Adhi roti khayenge, Indiraji loutayenge" (We will starve to get Indira reelected). Slowly, but deliberately, she had synchronized her image with that of the Mahatma again. Her theatrical caper caught the attention of the bored press, which highlighted her intention to make amends; the nation waited for her announcement that she was running for public office again.

I have chosen three examples that graphically display Indira Gandhi's deliberate attempt at reviving her image not only as daughter of the fathers but also as "widowed mother" of the nation. These examples are selected from innumerable others, all of which achieved the same end—she was elected for the fourth time as prime minister of India on 4 January 1980. She came back with a vengeance, flaunting the fact that she was "reelected" by popular vote. To Mark Frost, the BBC reporter, she remarked jubilantly: "We are the largest democracy in the world, and I am giving the people what they want."[38] What is even more staggering, in analyzing Indira Gandhi's life, is the fact that her charisma reached out from her grave. Gunned down by the Sikh faction in 1984, she died a martyr, a figure virtually the opposite of the dictator of the emergency days. More important, she ensured her son's political debut—Rajiv Gandhi became the prime minister after her death. Here was the Nehru dynasty ruling India again.

Conclusion

Indira Gandhi situated herself simultaneously on the cusp of two modes of discourse—narrative and descriptive—to enunciate her life. To gather the *meaning* of her words, one must necessarily glance at her *posture* as she spoke. From the examples cited above we see that Indira Gandhi's posture was deliberately wrought to give the intended impact to her words. Indira Gandhi-as-text forces the critic to speculate on the possibility of a speaking subject on the spectrum of the sub-altern arc who exceeds signification within the traditional Western categories of speech/silence, subordinated/subordinating. Indira Gandhi—the woman, the speech maker, the mother, the politician, the historical figure—becomes unified under the rubric of "sign" and thus must be read as such. Germaine Brée addresses the question of women's autobiography in general with a similar kind of latitude that I use in reading Indira Gandhi-as-text. She suggests that to uncover a feminist agenda in women's writing, one must

> explore the many "lines" women have devised to speak of themselves for themselves and their readers, going beyond the constraints of traditional boundaries. It [such an interrogation] eschews the temptation to elude questions of specificity of the self, of its "presence" in the writing, in its informing strategies. These are inseparable from our further understanding of the genre and its creative potential.[39]

In this sense, Indira Gandhi functions as a semiotic text in which one can read the desire for power intersecting the domain of gender to reveal positions not usually available to women in the world, colonized or otherwise.

Notes

I wish to thank Gurudev, Robert Con Davis, and Radhika Mohanram for challenging my presuppositions constantly while I wrote this article, and for reading the drafts patiently.

1. The definitions and elaborations of the "subject" in theoretical postulations come from a variety of fields. For the purposes of this chapter, the main points from the following texts have been summarized and synthesized, and certain nuances of the original arguments may have been erased. Sigmund Freud, *Beyond the Pleasure Principle*, in *The Standard Edition of the Complete Psychological Works of Sigmund Freud*, ed. James Strachey (London: Hogarth, 1953–66); Norman Holland, "Human Identity," *Critical Inquiry* 4 (Spring 1978): 451–70; Jacques Lacan, *Ecrits: A Selection*, trans. Alan Sheridan (New York: W. W. Norton, 1977), especially "The Mirror Stage as the Formation of the Function of the I" (pp. 8–29), "The Agency of the Letter in the Unconscious or Reason since Freud" (pp. 146–78), and "The Subversion of the Subject and the Dialectic of Desire in the Freudian Unconscious" (pp. 292–325); Anthony Wilden, *The Language of the Self* (Baltimore: Johns Hopkins University Press, 1968), especially "Lacan and the Discourse of the Other" (pp. 159–310); Roman Jakobson, "Two Aspects of Language and Two Types of Aphasic Disturbances," in *The Fundamentals of Language* (The Hague: Mouton, 1965), 55–82; Jacques Derrida, "Structure, Sign and Play, and the Discourses of the Human Sciences," in *The Structuralist Controversy*, ed. Richard A. Macksey and Eugenio Donato (Baltimore: Johns Hopkins University Press, 1972), 247–72. See Frederic Jameson's Marxist version in *The Political Unconscious: Narrative as Socially Symbolic Act* (Ithaca, N.Y.: Cornell University Press, 1981) and, particularly, *Marxism and the Interpretation of Culture*, ed. Cary Nelson and Lawrence Grossberg (Urbana: University of Illinois Press, 1988); Gayatri Chakravorty Spivak's essay "Can the Subaltern Speak? Speculations on Widow Sacrifice" is also printed in this edition (pp. 271–313). See also Julia Kristeva, *Desire in Language*, trans. Léon S. Roudiez (New York: Columbia University Press, 1980); Toril Moi, *Sexual/Textual Politics: Feminist Literary Theory* (London: Methuen, 1985), particularly the section on the French

feminists. By pointing to the various facets of subjectivity, I will discuss the historical construction of Indira Gandhi as Nehru's biological daughter, Gandhi's cultural daughter, and Sanjay and Rajiv's mother, exploring the nuances of imaginary/pre-oedipal daughter, and symbolic/post-oedipal m(other). It is also important to mention that Indira Gandhi was not related to Mohandas Karamchand Gandhi (hereafter referred to as Mahatma Gandhi).

2. I quote just one instance here from Dorothy Norman, *Indira Gandhi: Letters to an American Friend—1950–1984* (San Diego, Calif.: Harcourt Brace, 1985), 41–42, to make my point about Mrs. Gandhi's appreciation of Western culture: "During her [Indira's] 1958 visit to the U.S. with Nehru . . . she had dinner at the White House [Roosevelt's era], . . . saw *My Fair Lady,* by Lerner and Lowe, . . . during that afternoon we saw Marguerite Duras' *Hiroshima, Mon Amour.* The film by Alain Renoir struck us both as magnificent. We then went directly to Mrs. Franklin D. Roosevelt's for tea. . . . Indira and I visited the Museum of Modern Art and also the Metropolitan Museum, so she might see, among other work, Richard Lippold's sculpture *Sun.* . . . Blanchette and John D. Rockefeller III were deeply interested in Indira [and] graciously invited [her] to their home in Tarrytown. . . . At a dinner I gave for Indira . . . the other distinguished guests were the French diplomat and Nobel Prize-winner poet Alexis Léger (St. John Perse). . . . We attended Samuel Beckett's *Krapp's Last Tape* and Edward Albee's *Zoo Story.*" As indicated, this is merely a two-day itinerary, and Mrs. Gandhi usually absorbed this much in every foreign tour. Another incident (in 1961) shows the difference in familiarity with Western culture between Nehru and Indira: "We saw Lawrence Olivier and Anthony Quinn in Jean Anouilh's *Becket* . . . [and] Nehru asked me . . . whether it was by Tennyson. . . . I took Indira to Henry Denker's *A Far Country.* Because it was about Freud's approach to psychoanalysis, I thought it might interest her; it made a vivid impression" (p. 56). From a Lacanian viewpoint, it is interesting to note how she charmed the Western world by creating the semblance of sameness (i.e., participating on a par with Westerners) while emphasizing her *otherness* (i.e., maintaining her image as the Indian visitor). From a semiotic point of view, she graciously (adroitly) accepted a "foreign" culture and made it her own while slowly rendering it transparent. See also note 18, below.

3. R. K. Murthy, *The Cult of the Individual: The Study of Indira Gandhi* (New Delhi: Sterling, 1977), 4. See this volume generally for more information on the impact of Gandhi and Nehru on India.

4. Norman, *Indira Gandhi,* 57. The Norman book represents a collection of Gandhi's letters that is carefully edited for publication. I want to add here that part of Indira Gandhi was torn by the choice she had made, because she admits to being "distraught . . . feeling empty" when her husband died of a heart attack in 1960; ibid., 61. It is tempting to read guilt into her grief because she abandoned her husband to set up house with her father. While only a few biographers record the exact nature of the relationship between Indira and Feroz, fewer speculate on the degree of "love" in this love-match. However, it is common knowledge that Indira married Feroz against her father's wishes, in an alliance formed by the two young lovers when they were in Europe. However, a Western biographer, Mary C. Carras, records otherwise, in what can best be termed as conjecture at this point. Carras notes (with no textual or historical evidence) that "Indira Gandhi married Feroz because while he loved her, she probably would not have married at all if she had not wanted children." *Indira Gandhi in the Crucible of Leadership* (Boston: Beacon, 1979), 59. In an ironic way, Indira Gandhi was never perceived as anybody's wife, even though she was constantly referred to as Mrs. Gandhi.

5. However, the *Mataji* had at least three distinct tonal variations. During her first term as prime minister, from 1967 to 1972, the word held respect, then from 1972 to 1974 it became sarcastic because she was becoming dictatorial (it was also the period preceding her declaration of national emergency). During the emergency (1975–77) it was whispered by the underground press with terror, coupled with the horrors of matriarchy.

6. Most biographers valorize Indira Gandhi, reading a "true Gandhian" spirit in her posture. Some of the more readable biographies are as follows: N. Currimbhoy, *Indira Gandhi: An Imprint Biography* (New York: F. W. Watts, 1985); Franchia Butler, *Why a Biography: Indira Gandhi* (New York: Chelsea House, 1985); Nayantara Sehgal, *Indira Gandhi: Her Road to Power* (New York: Unger, 1982); and Tarik Ali, *An Indian Dynasty: The Story of the Nehru/Gandhi Family* (New York: Putnam, 1986). Also worth noting are the *Time* and *Newsweek* issues that covered her assassination in October 1984.

7. Publicity Division of the Information and Broadcasting Ministry, comp., *Selected Speeches of Indira Gandhi* (New Delhi: Government of India Publications, 1971), 4.

8. Janardan Thakur draws attention to Indira's "womanly ways" in a chapter titled "The Lady in Tears" to point to various instances when she had to get out of a difficult political situation. The exact phrase, "the pathetic figurine" was a reporter's description of her when she made her final public appearance after losing the 1978 national elections. Even though Thakur reveals his clear admiration for Gandhi, he analyzes her political life with a remarkable degree of unbiased accuracy. Janardan Thakur, *Indira Gandhi and Her Power Game* (Uttar Pradesh: Vikas, 1979), 16. The context of this comment decodes some of Indira Gandhi's practiced charisma. After her loss in the national elections of March 1977, she made a speech as the outgoing party president. On the dais was a small photograph of Mahatma Gandhi. Suddenly, one party official, Mouriya, shouted, "Where is Panditji's [Nehru's] portrait. . . . where is Mataji's [Indira Gandhi's] portrait? All this is the doing of *chamchas* [sycophants]" (p. 15). Within minutes, photos of Mrs. Gandhi and Nehru were produced. Of course, Mrs. Gandhi's photo was the largest, signaling her larger-than-life image, and reiterating her carefully planned agenda of apostolic succession. Mrs. Gandhi arrived late, on the crest of a surging crowd chanting her name, thanked those assembled in a hushed, defeated voice for their "unstinted support, in good times and bad," and dissolved in tears (p. 16).

9. For the purposes of this essay, the basic explanation of the difference in representation will suffice, whereas Spivak goes into rhetorical understanding of the terms. For more on this matter, see Karl Marx, *The Eighteenth Brumaire of Louis Bonaparte*, in *The Marx-Engels Reader*, ed. Robert Tucker (New York: W. W. Norton, 1978; originally published as *Papers in Exile* in 1852).

10. Spivak, "Can the Subaltern Speak?" 277. See Spivak's essay for the full context of this argument.

11. Spivak asks an excellent question of Western cultural critics in their attempts to posit a theory for the "speaking subject" in non-Western cultures. She argues that most critics, Foucault in particular, short-circuit the Third World subject by turning the central query into a formula "West as subject." For more on this, see Spivak, "Can the Subaltern Speak?" introduction.

12. Homi K. Bhabha presents a somewhat similar idea of the notion of "identity in difference" without granting an agency to the colonized text. His exploration of "ambivalence," however, can be applied to Indira Gandhi's portrayal of her subjectivity only where she herself consciously blurs the differences. "Of Mimicry and Man: The Ambivalence of Colonial Discourse," *October* 28 (1984): 125–33; see also another Bhabha essay that approaches the same issues, "Sly Civility," *October* 35 (1985): 71–80.

13. See Jenny Sharp, "Figures of Colonial Discourse," *Modern Fiction Studies* 35 (Spring 1989): 137–55, for a clear summary of Spivak's position on the issue. See also Benita Parry, "Problems in Current Theories of Colonial Discourse," *Oxford Literary Review* 9 (1987): 27–58.

14. Murthy, *Cult of the Individual*, 7.

15. Norman, *Indira Gandhi*, 58.

16. Ibid., 57.

17. Murthy notes that Kamaraj was openly vitriolic about Indira Gandhi's decision because she failed to consult him as party elder. Nehru, on the other hand, gave in to her demand, even to the extent of invoking the constitution in one instance. Murthy notes that Nehru "agreed to exploit the provision of Article 356 of the [Indian] Constitution, and on August 1, 1959, the Communist Government in Kerala was dismissed." *Cult of the Individual*, 14. This proves that Indira was fully conscious of both her place as daughter and her authority as Congress president. In another incident she divided Maharashtra and Gujarat over the bilingual issue in Bombay. Murthy writes: "Nehru buckled under her pressure and the bi-lingual issue was mandated on Dec. 4, 1959." Ibid., 16. Having proved her mettle, and her political agency, Indira retired as Congress party president in 1960.

18. Norman, *Indira Gandhi*, repeatedly mentions that even though Indira Gandhi was not a head of state, European leaders and American presidents such as Truman, Kennedy, and Eisenhower competed to entertain her. Gandhi had also discovered a very elite circle of rich, powerful, and cultured friends in the United States, such as the Rockefellers, who treated her with warmth and respect. The record reveals Indira Gandhi's privileged place in Western society. All this attention, of course, was lavished upon her before her declaration of national emergency.

19. Pierre Macherey, *A Theory of Literary Production*, trans. Geoffrey Wall (London: Routledge, 1978), 87. I take Macherey's comment from the frame of a larger argument about silences in texts, but I choose to highlight it because Spivak conceptualizes it also, and denies the Indian woman, forced to perform the *sati*, any agency. Spivak writes: "When we come into the concomitant question of the consciousness of the subaltern, the notion of what the work *cannot* say becomes important. In the semiosis of the social text, elaborations of insurgence stand in the place of 'the utterance.' . . . 'The subject' implied in the texts of insurgency can only serve as a counter-possibility of the narrative sanctions granted to the colonial subject in the dominant groups." "Can the Subaltern Speak?" 287.

20. Norman, *Indira Gandhi*, 59.

21. For more on these factors, see Homi Bhabha, "The Other Question—Stereotype and Colonial Discourse," *Screen* 24 (November–December 1988): 19–25.

22. Abdul R. JanMohamed, "The Economy of Manichean Allegory: The Function of Racial Difference in Colonialist Literature," in *Race, Writing, and Difference,* ed. Henry Louis Gates, Jr. (Chicago: University of Chicago Press, 1986), 79. JanMohamed discusses various instances of intersections of literature and politics in analyzing colonial discourse. I have taken the liberty of substituting "class" for JanMohamed's "race" in Indira Gandhi's case, however, playing on the range of connotations that this term evokes in her particular case.

23. The caption was first printed in the *Hindustan Times* after her victory at the polls in 1967; then the whole nation picked it up as a way of showing their support of this valiant figure who had outwitted the masters. Of course, history once again helped because Kamaraj of the "Congress Syndicate/party elders" was trounced during the same elections. Whether or not it is a valid comment to read *racism* in Kamaraj's

attitude toward Indira Gandhi, it is tempting, nonetheless. She was so clearly "Angli-cized" in his eyes that he felt confident about subordinating her because he (and the elders) had defeated the English just two decades before. For a clearer understanding of this last statement, see note 2, above.

24. For other instances in which Indira Gandhi used such a strategy to situate herself into the sign of a "woman," see Publicity Division of the Information and Broadcasting Ministry, *Selected Speeches*. There does not seem to be any conscious denial of her womanhood, but she substitutes the cultural signification for the biological one. She always projects herself as "widow/mother" serving her country. Similarly, it is through gender—that is, cultural definitions of other—that she places herself in the "lack" place in the global nuclear arms race. In her keynote address at the Commemorative Session of the Twentieth Anniversary of the First Summit Conference of Non-aligned Countries in New Delhi in February 1981, she plied the assembled delegates from Third World countries with her signatory sophistic rhetoric: "Peace is not that which teeters on the brink . . . that is absence of war, yet it threatens war. . . . True peace is not the peace of negation, not the peace of surrender, not the peace of the coward, not the peace of the dying, not the peace of the dead, but the peace, militant, dynamic, creative, of the human spirit which exalts." K. Ramamurthy and Govinda Narain Srivastava, eds. and comps., *Indira Gandhi on Non-Alignment: A Collection of Speeches* (New Delhi: Indian Institute of Non-Aligned Studies, 1983), vi.

25. Ketu H. Katrak, "Decolonizing Culture: Toward a Theory of Post Colonial Wom-en's Texts," *Modern Fiction Studies* 35 (Spring 1989): 167. Katrak's incisive reading critiques Gandhi's incomplete "liberation" of women. She argues that Gandhi's purpose was to signal graphically the role of women as repositories of cultural tradition and their sense of higher duty in following the elders, who could lead them, and the country, to liberation. My point here is to reveal the method by which Indira Gandhi situates herself as "woman," signaling her relationship to Mahatma Gandhi. My interest in bringing Katrak into the discussion is to show the planned politics behind using women's bodies by both Mahatma Gandhi and Mrs. Gandhi. Also of interest on this subject are Partha Chatterjee's critique of the Indian independence struggle in *National Thought and the Colonial World* (London: Zed, 1986); and Kumari Jayawrdena's insightful reading of some of the women of the Indian freedom struggle, in *Feminism and Nationalism in the Third World* (London: Zed, 1986). See also Chandra Talpade Mohanty, "Under Western Eyes: Feminist Scholarship and Colonial Discourse," *Boundary* 2, 12 (1984): 333–58.

26. Spivak discusses the psychoanalytical and colonizing implications of using the "Name of the Father" in Marx as a way of invoking the transparent, absolute power structure. She elaborates on the incapability of the Indian woman to call upon the name to save her from either the *sati* or the British colonists. In Indira Gandhi's case, the name would include not only the direct political giants on the Indian scene who brought her to power, but Nehru and Mahatma Gandhi (to name only two) as well, the original fathers in the freedom struggle. And Spivak's position on the other aspect of represen-tation, the semiotic one, focuses on repression or object status, because the subjugated female in Spivak's example (*sati*) is unable to perform independently, and is recirculated in the colonizer's economy as one more signification of British imperialism. In Gandhi's case, she carefully maintained her subject status veiled behind an apparently object facade. Yet, in fairness to Indira Gandhi, simultaneous with her desire for power was her genuine love for India when she embarked on her political career. Not only was Indira Gandhi connected to the influential people mentioned in this essay, but as Vijaya Lakshmi Pundit's niece she was emulating another example of how the Nehru woman

could take the lead from the "fathers" for the good of the country. Gandhi's affiliation to Nehru as "father" is somewhat similar to that of Violeta Barrios de Chamorro to the United States. But, while such an affiliation brought the Nicaraguan candidate dubious popularity, Gandhi's connections guaranteed her access to power. I do not want to muddy the issue by making direct comparisons; instead, I want to suggest the potency of the politicocultural implications.

27. From the Latin *subalternus* = *sub (below)* + *alternus* (alternate) > alter. *American Heritage Dictionary,* 2nd ed. (Boston: Houghton Mifflin, 1982).

28. See Antonio Gramsci's "Some Aspects of the Southern Question," in *Selections from Political Writings 1921–1926,* trans. Quintin Hoare (New York: International Publications, 1986). Gramsci's argument is based upon reading Italy's class struggle and the recording of the struggle as history (truth). Gramsci elaborates upon the *vertreten/darstellen* principles that Marx discusses in *The Eighteenth Brumaire.*

29. Quoted in Spivak, "Can the Subaltern Speak?" 284. Ranajit Guha examines the subaltern thesis from a different angle, stressing that the imperialists were the only ones allowed to narrate history, and other accounts of history must be read as transcriptions or translations of imperialist power through willing, subjugated subalterns. He proposes a place for the "people" based upon a four-part division as follows: "a) dominant foreign groups, b) dominant indigenous groups on the all-India level, c) dominant indigenous groups at the regional/local level, and d) the 'people' or 'subaltern' (used synonymously throughout this note), wherein the social groups and elements included in this category represent the demographic differences between the total Indian population and all those whom we have described as elite" (p. 284). For more details on Guha's work, see Ranajit Guha, ed., *Subaltern Studies III: Writings on South Asian History and Society* (London: Oxford University Press, 1984).

30. It is common knowledge, though never documented, that Sanjay Gandhi (Indira's second son) was the brain behind the scenes, but she, as prime minister, mandated his wishes. Ironically, she amplified her political decision because she wanted to silence her biological position as Sanjay's mother. Because he was *Mataji's* son he could tyrannize the country. A fact that came to light after the emergency was that the Congress party could not fire Sanjay because he had no actual political office in the Indian government. He committed the atrocities because he was "Mrs. Gandhi's son," and the level of sycophancy built into Third World governmental politics sanctioned such behavior.

31. Norman writes: "We issued a statement that expressed our concern. Sidney Hertzberg, former U.S. correspondent of the *Hindustan Times* of New Delhi, Indian born author Ved Mehta, and I drafted a joint appeal. . . . We released it to the press, radio, and television, and tried to publicize it in . . . India. I also held several meetings for Indian dissidents. . . . I sent a further note to Indira. . . . I received three short notes from her." *Indira Gandhi,* 148–49.

32. Mrs. Gandhi was in London during the period 12–19 November 1978. Despite the speculations of the press, and a general note of censure by Western politicians, Mrs. Gandhi was received with official courtesy by British Prime Minister James Callaghan; the Opposition leader, Margaret Thatcher; former conservative Prime Minister Michael Foot; and others. At Heathrow, one reporter mocked, "Mrs. Gandhi, are you trying to make a comeback?" to which she quipped, "But where had I gone?" This degree of self-confidence was a facade, no doubt, but also part of the identity that she had created for herself. Later, at a press conference, she neatly turned the tables on the reporters by cataloging the reasons for the bad press and "exaggerations" about the Indian national emergency. She said: "It could hardly have been accidental that India's

upheaval came about the same time as major transformations took place in other parts of the Indian subcontinent [in Bangladesh, Mujibur Rehman was assassinated; in Pakistan, General Zia-ul-Haq, in a military coup, wrenched power from Bhutto, whom he then jailed; in Srilanka, Mrs. Bandaranaike lost bitterly to Mr. Jayawardhane]. . . . In Bangladesh and Pakistan assassinations and arrests of government leaders swiftly followed the counter-revolutions against my own policies." She went on to list two "developments" that "inconvenienced" the Western powers. The first was "India's test blast . . . a peaceful nuclear device in 1974 which thrust the world's first developing country into the atomic league. The second was that India, through its industrialization programme, was beginning for the first time to compete against Western markets." Raj Darbari and Janis Darbari, *Indira Gandhi: 1028 Days* (New Delhi: Hindustan Press, 1983), 78. See this work generally for another view of the emergency. For the purposes of my essay, I want to emphasize how Indira Gandhi drew attention to the arms race and economic discrimination to wash away some of the harshness of the criticism of the Western press.

33. Norman, *Indira Gandhi*, 149. Norman writes that she did not correspond with Indira Gandhi during the emergency period, even though she mobilized an Amnesty International inquiry into the whole situation. Norman also gracefully bows out of any controversy about this point in her book, claiming "facts about it [emergency] and about the activities of her younger son, Sanjay Gandhi, lie outside the scope of this volume" (p. 151).

34. It was well known to the Indian electorate that the West had backed Morarji Desai and, further, that it was a covert operation not publicly acknowledged. Murthy notes that "it was not known whether the president-elect of America, Jimmy Carter, before assuming office on January 20, sent a personal message to Mrs. Gandhi, asking her to indicate some semblance of return to democratic process so that he need not, during his inaugural address, be forced to indict India." *Cult of the Individual*, 131. Within the Indian scene, when she was questioned by the Shah Commission, the Indian political or judiciary system could level no serious charges against her. Her astute maneuvers saved her from total political annihilation. There was tremendous world attention focused on Indira Gandhi at that time. A commentary by the *Detroit Free Press* summed up the situation best when it reported on 10 October 1977 that the case against her was not about the "forfeiture of fundamental freedoms," but about the "misuse of some government jeeps," that she was ultimately charged only with "picayune crimes."

35. Feminist critics, too numerous to name here, have pointed out that the gesture of "begging" for forgiveness grants women a degree of power that does not overtly threaten patriarchal hegemonic structures.

36. Mr. Barooha, the president of the Congress party during this period, was satirized by the press for granting Sanjay such unlimited power. He was mocked ruthlessly for exhibiting such dangerous levels of sycophancy in attempting to please Mrs. Gandhi. When the rest of the Congress party asked for Sanjay's resignation after Mrs. Gandhi's arrest, they discovered his nonstatus within the political system. See also note 30, above, for more on this.

37. *Harijans*, or untouchables, are the lowest rank in the caste system in India. Even though Mahatma Gandhi tried to abolish the caste system, there is, even today, discrimination within the caste levels. In 1978, the burning of *harijans* had risen to alarming proportions in northern India.

38. Thakur, *Indira Gandhi and Her Power Game*, 85.

39. Germaine Brée, "Foreword," in *Life/Lines: Theorizing Women's Autobiography,* ed. Bella Brodzki and Celeste Schenck (Ithaca, N.Y.: Cornell University Press, 1988). See this volume generally for discussion of various theoretical positions used to analyze women's autobiography.

PART III

Negotiating Class and Race

Chapter 11

The Changing Moral Discourse of Nineteenth-Century African American Women's Autobiography: Harriet Jacobs and Elizabeth Keckley

William L. Andrews

Nineteenth-century African American women's autobiographies can teach their readers much about the effects of intellectual colonization on oppressed people in the United States and about the role of auto-biography in the efforts of oppressed people to decolonize their thinking and writing. If one considers Christianity one means of subjecting the nonwhite peoples of America to the role of benighted children of Jehovah, the transcendent White Father of the Western spiritual tradition, then the abiding commitment to Christianity among the American slaves and freedmen and -women who produced autobiographies in the nineteenth century poses real questions about what constitutes colonization and what does not. In no tradition of nineteenth-century African American autobiography was there a more pronounced concern with or use of the ideals of Christian morality as a standard by which to judge individuals or institutions than in the first-person narratives of black women. When Nancy Prince concluded her mid-century autobiography with the assertion, "Fearful indeed is this world's pilgrimage," she applied a spiritual metaphor to her experience that spoke to many black women narrators' sense of life as a perilous journey in which only "the power of God" and "the spirit of Christ" could be counted on ultimately to shield the "dependent children" of the Almighty.[1] Knowing that they could not depend on the secular law for justice, black women narrators of the antebellum era looked to the laws of God and the maxims of Christ for spiritual solace and a moral bulwark against a threatening and corrupt world.

African American women's spiritual narratives of the nineteenth century record their authors' sense of unique empowerment as a consequence of conversion to Christ and sanctification by the indwelling Holy Spirit. Prompted by a renewed and spiritually purified selfhood, such autobiographers as Jarena Lee, Zilpha Elaw, and Julia A. J. Foote confronted the mutifarious sins of American society with a unified, all-embracing message of repentance and acceptance of the gospel of Christ.[2] Similarly, the earliest feminist in black America, Maria W. Stewart, was unequivocal in her analysis of the source of her people's troubles in freedom as well as slavery. In her first tract she wrote:

> Why is it, my friends, that our minds have been blinded by ignorance, to the present moment? 'Tis on account of sin. Why is it that our church is involved in so much difficulty? It is on account of sin. Why is it that God has cut down, upon our right hand and upon our left, the most learned and intelligent of our men? O, shall I say, it is on account of sin! Why is it that thick darkness is mantled upon every brow, and we, as it were, look sadly upon one another? It is on account of sin.[3]

Her remedies for her people's travail included unity of effort and self-help on a broad social front, but she held out no hope for the success of any antislavery or civil rights program unless blacks first "cultivate among ourselves the pure principles of piety, morality and virtue."[4] This belief in the primacy of moral improvement as the key to racial advancement was echoed by Frances Ellen Watkins Harper, one of the best-known and most widely read black women of letters in the nineteenth century. In an 1859 essay titled "Our Greatest Want," she called for "a higher cultivation of all our spiritual faculties. We need more unselfishness, earnestness and integrity. Our greatest need is not gold or silver, talent or genius, but true men and true women."[5]

The idea that a "true woman" should be a repository and conservator of the highest Christian virtues was as much an article of social faith in the nineteenth-century black American community as in that of whites. Although racist myths disqualified black women from the pedestal to which white celebrators of "true womanhood" elevated their domestic angels, many black autobiographers, male as well as female, disregarded what Hazel Carby has called "the polarity between ideologies of black and white womanhood"[6] in the nineteenth century by extolling enslaved women of surpassing good character in their personal histories.[7] In general, nineteenth-century black autobiographers singled out their mothers, sisters, and grandmothers for special praise. In the "true, steadfast heart and noble soul" of the slave mother, female slave narrators epitomized their highest ideals of Christian womanhood, celebrating the indomitable heroism of the slave mother in particular for her moral activism, her resolute will, and her steadfast devotion to her duty to family and loved ones.[8]

As every student of African American women's autobiography knows, the most famous of the female slave narratives, Harriet A. Jacobs's *Incidents in the Life of a Slave Girl* (1861), inaugurated the tradition of black women's autobiography in a profound interrogation of the relationship of power, sex, and morality within the slave system.[9] Yet a reading of female-authored slave narratives of the postbellum era reveals a studied refusal to explore the kinds of moral problems attendant to the slave woman's sexuality that surface often in the discourse of the antebellum antislavery movement. Why did Jacobs's successors not follow her? Did she answer the questions and resolve the problems raised by antislavery's moral discourse on the slave woman's sexuality? Or did *Incidents* reveal problematic aspects of the discourse itself, which later female autobiographers in the postbellum era simply refused to admit into the discourse they used to judge their own? Though it will be impossible to answer these questions definitively in this essay, a look at the key transitional text, Elizabeth Keckley's *Behind the Scenes; Or, Thirty Years a Slave, and Four Years in the White House* (1868), can be helpful in exploring reasons for the apparent disparities separating Jacobs from her postbellum sisters in autobiography.[10]

Because the main focus of Keckley's autobiography is Lincoln family life as seen from her privileged position as Mary Todd Lincoln's modiste, *Behind the Scenes* might well be regarded as more a book of gossip about whites than a key contribution to black women's first-person writing. Yet in some respects *Behind the Scenes* represents a stronger reaction to the issues raised in *Incidents* than is evident in any other black woman's autobiography of the nineteenth or early twentieth century. Labeling *Behind the Scenes* a transitional text is not meant to imply that it was a kind of midway station in the evolution of the black women's tradition from one extreme position to another. The discursive alternatives that Keckley posed to the problems raised in Jacobs's narration would not be adopted by Lucy Ann Delaney, Kate Drumgoold, or their counterparts in the revival of the woman's slave narrative that began at the end of the nineteenth century.[11] The sense of tacit agreement among the late nineteenth- and early twentieth-century female ex-slave narrators, particularly in deemphasizing questions of sexual morality, may be attributable in some degree to their awareness of the unresolved dialectic formed by the antithetical moral positions taken in *Incidents* and *Behind the Scenes*. Thus it is possible to read both of these texts of the 1860s as staking out extreme positions that enabled a post-Civil War black women's autobiographical tradition to get under way, if only by showing where the inheritors of that tradition would not want to go.

The narratives of Jacobs and Keckley were published only seven years apart by women who lived and worked in the Washington, D.C., area from 1862 to 1865, both of them active participants in relief efforts for the "contrabands" from the South. The chances of their meeting each other or knowing about each other were more than slight. But even if the two women never met, it seems unlikely that Keckley would never have heard or taken notice of *Incidents,* given the publicity it received in the early 1860s, the public presence of its activist author in Keckley's hometown for three years, and, perhaps most important, the striking parallels between what Jacobs revealed about her slave past and what Keckley knew to be true about her own. Though Keckley telescopes her life in slavery in *Behind the Scenes* so that she can get on to her account of her relationship to the Lincolns, the details that Keckley does record about her youth inevitably recall that of Harriet Jacobs. For instance, the two women, born only about five years apart, grew up among the comparatively privileged of the slave population. They were raised under similar circumstances—that is, as house servants, not field workers. No effort was made to keep them from learning how to read and write. They were both light complexioned and considered good-looking by blacks and whites alike. They had strong family ties, particularly with a mother or grandmother. Though both wanted to escape slavery as teenagers, neither secured her freedom until she was a mature woman, Jacobs at almost thirty years of age and Keckley some seven years older. Perhaps the most remarkable of all the links between these two women, however, was the fact that both bore children by white men while each was a slave in her early twenties.[12]

In the well-known tenth chapter of *Incidents,* titled "A Perilous Passage in a Slave Girl's Life," Jacobs confesses her desperate decision, at the age of fifteen, to "plunge into the abyss" of an illicit affair with a white lover rather than become the concubine of her master. Asking that her reader "not judge the poor desolate slave girl too severely,"

Jacobs pleads, "I wanted to keep myself pure; and, under the most adverse circumstances, I tried hard to preserve my self-respect; but I was struggling alone in the powerful grasp of the demon Slavery; and the monster proved too strong for me" (p. 54). This characterization of slavery as a superhuman, demonic force, implacably committed to the obliteration of the slave's self-respect as a moral being, together with the strong suggestion that the individual slave is overmatched in her struggle to resist such a force, points up the grounding of *Incidents* in what we might call the rhetoric of antislavery moral absolutism.[13] The idea of abolitionism as a holy crusade against slavery, "the sum of all villainies," in John Wesley's often-quoted phrase, encouraged numerous antebellum slave narrators to subscribe to the abolitionist association of slavery with hell and slave owners with the satanic legions of darkness.[14] Following this precedent, Jacobs denounces the South and its institutions without reservation or compromise: the land of the narrator's birth is represented as a "pit of abominations" (p. 2) where "the shadows are too dense for light to penetrate" (p. 37); slaveholders become "fiends who bear the shape of men" (p. 27); whites and blacks alike are subjected to "the all-pervading corruption produced by slavery" (p. 51), from which there is no escape. Living in this atmosphere of unmitigated evil, it is no wonder the female slave "is not allowed to have any pride of character" (p. 31). It is no wonder that she, "one of God's most powerless creatures" (p. 19), becomes "the helpless victim" (p. 27) of the white man's lust.

For Harriet Jacobs, "the painful task of confessing" her deliberate decision to transgress the fundamental norm of antebellum true womanhood—chastity before marriage[15]—was compounded by her extensive use of antislavery's rhetoric of moral absolutism in the first nine chapters of her narrative. Having allied herself with a popular moral position that "condemned slavery because it excluded slave women from patriarchal definitions of true womanhood,"[16] Jacobs faced a dilemma when she tried to plead the mitigating circumstances of her own individual case. If she did not place moral blame somewhere for her transgressions, she would risk offending those among her readers whom she had cultivated with her own absolutist rhetoric. On the other hand, if she simply uttered *mea culpa* to the charge of sexual impurity, she would absolve slavery of its agency in the "wrong" that she did as a slave. Given this difficult choice, Jacobs's ambivalent summation of her confession in chapter 10 is not surprising: "I know I did wrong. No one can feel it more sensibly than I do. The painful and humiliating memory will haunt me to my dying day. Still, in looking back, calmly, on the events of my life, I feel that the slave woman ought not to be judged by the same standard as others" (pp. 55-56). Clearly, in speaking of her specific case Jacobs was reaching for an alternative to the moral categories that buttress her characterizations of the slave woman's condition in general. But the extent to which she was able to escape the ambivalence and contradictoriness of her own moral position to articulate an alternative standard of morality for black women in slavery remains a matter of debate.[17]

The tenth chapter of *Incidents* comes to an end without a statement of resolution of this dilemma. Jacobs penitently accepts the moral onus for her sexual transgressions while at the same time pleading her special entitlement to her reader's "pity" in view of "the most adverse circumstances" she faced as a beautiful slave girl. She acknowledges moral responsibility for her sexual liaison with the man she calls Mr. Sands, yet she argues that because she was "entirely unprotected by law or custom" and was "entirely subject to the will of another" (p. 55), her actions were not exactly condemnable or even wholly unjustifiable. Her ambivalent problematizing of her own moral responsibility indicates that Jacobs wanted somehow to reconcile an absolute moral standard for womanly virtue prescribed by white culture with the actual circumstances of a slave woman's complex lived experience. Even as a teenager, "I had resolved that I would be virtuous, though I was a slave" (p. 56). Yet the opening chapters of her autobiography plainly show that while a female slave may value herself according to an essential principle, namely, that she was a morally responsible being, the law identified her according to a relative standard, namely, that of property, whose value is subject always to the whims of those who control the market. That Jacobs insists on "confessing" her sexual transgressions in chapter 10 to her "virtuous reader," of whom she asks "pardon" as well as pity, indicates that she felt obliged to pay at least lip service to the idea that the loss of her sexual virtue created a moral deficit in her character for which she had to atone. Unable to resolve her contradictory feelings about the morality of her actions vis-à-vis Sands, Jacobs devotes the remainder of her narrative to the amassing of evidence that will recoup her honor in the eyes of her reader.

As her story progresses, the author of *Incidents* describes how she gradually recovered her "woman's pride" by exercising "a mother's love for my children." Dedicating herself to her family and aided by a sub rosa women's community in her hometown, Jacobs pits her "determined will" (p. 85) against her master's patriarchal power. In the end her will wins out. She achieves freedom for herself and her

children. Ironically, however, the route to freedom demands the sacrifice of her essential principles in an accommodation with slavery.
Her master's family insists on her buying her freedom, but Jacobs
insists, "I could not possibly regard myself as a piece of property"
(p. 187). That "seemed too much like slavery" (p. 199). Nevertheless,
Mrs. Bruce, Jacobs's northern protector and sponsor, purchases the
fugitive woman without her knowledge or consent, leaving Jacobs at
the end of *Incidents* in a marginal status curiously analogous to her
free yet unfree situation when she was ensconced for seven years in
the garret of her grandmother's house in North Carolina. Mrs. Bruce's
gift, like grandmother Martha's garret, inevitably circumscribes the
freedom that it bestows; to obtain one sort of freedom, Jacobs must
submit to another form of powerlessness.

At the end of her narrative Jacobs acknowledges her contradictory
situation in her ambivalent tribute to Mrs. Bruce herself. "God so
orders circumstances as to keep me with my friend Mrs. Bruce. Love,
duty, gratitude, also bind me to her side. It is a privilege to serve her"
(p. 201). Thus the final irony of Jacobs's fealty to absolute principle—
by refusing to submit her sense of absolute selfhood to a property
standard, she finds herself in a classic "bind"—obligated and indebted,
by virtue of her principles, namely, "love, duty, gratitude," to "serve"
Mrs. Bruce. This "freedom," as Jacobs maintains, may be an "inesti-
mable boon," but it is not enough. "I still long for a hearthstone of
my own" (p. 201). Behind this admission lies the former slave's implicit
recognition of the relative powerlessness of her supposed absolute
freedom. Jacobs seems to be saying that power, the ability to act on
and *realize* freedom, stems, in the North as well as the South, not
from principle but from property, from that which can be claimed
like a home or a hearthstone as "my own."

Turning to Keckley's *Behind the Scenes,* we find explicitly articulated the materialist discourse that Jacobs was reaching for at the end
of her narrative. From early childhood, Keckley states, "I had been
raised in a hardy school—had been taught to rely upon myself, and
to prepare myself to render assistance to others. . . . Notwithstanding
all the wrongs that slavery heaped upon me, I can bless it for one
thing—youth's important lesson of self-reliance" (pp.19–20). This idea
of slavery as a schooling in self-reliance, which anticipates Washington's famous use of this metaphor, diverges almost diametrically from
Jacobs's portrayal of slavery as an initiation into perversion. To the
extent that Jacobs thought of "that cage of obscene birds" as a place
of learning, she could say only that "the influences of slavery . . .
made me prematurely knowing, concerning the evil ways of the

world" (p. 54). Instead of gaining "self-reliance" from slavery's school of hard knocks, Jacobs emphasizes what she lost—her "self-respect," which in part her narrative itself is designed to help her reclaim. Nowhere in *Behind the Scenes,* however, is slavery imaged as demonic or superhuman, even though Keckley suffered physical abuse from white men that could readily have been represented in these terms. Nowhere in *Behind the Scenes* does Keckley portray herself as helplessly struggling against forces "too strong for me," even when she narrates the circumstances under which she became a mother.

Keckley's comments on her sexual liaison with an unnamed white man during her time in slavery are confined to a mere five sentences:

> I was regarded as fair-looking for one of my race, and for four years a white man—I spare the world his name—had base designs upon me. I do not care to dwell upon this subject, for it is one that is fraught with pain. Suffice it to say, that he persecuted me for four years, and I—I—became a mother. The child of which he was the father was the only child that I ever brought into the world. If my poor boy ever suffered any humiliating pangs on account of birth, he could not blame his mother, for God knows that she did not wish to give him life; he must blame the edicts of that society which deemed it no crime to undermine the virtue of girls in my then position. (p. 39)

There is no reason to think that the memory of this experience was any less "fraught with pain" for Keckley than for Jacobs, yet while Jacobs struggles to declare herself, Keckley refuses to articulate her pain and "deep mortification" to her reader. The whole vexed question of moral responsibility, which Jacobs wrestles with in a plea for empathy from her reader, is simply shunted aside in Keckley's bold pronouncement, "He could not blame his mother." Clearly, Keckley faults southern white society, but she has no interest in pursuing the matter of moral responsibility. "The virtue of girls in *my then position*"— note the emphasis on the difference between her past and current positions in society—is basically irrelevant to the image Keckley intends to create for herself in the postbellum social order. That was then, this is now, Keckley implies. But no such easy differentiation of past and present self is possible for Jacobs.

While Keckley refuses to accept the blame for her transgression of middle-class sexual morality, she expends much of her narrative in claiming credit for herself as an upholder of bourgeois economic standards. Unlike Harriet Jacobs, Keckley offers no principled objection to buying herself and her son out of slavery, a process to which she proudly devotes a twenty-page chapter. In fact, Keckley insists on paying full value for herself and her child, in conformity to the laws of the slaveocracy, even when her master offers to pay the passage for her and her son on a ferry across the Mississippi to Illinois. Before going to New York to raise money for her purchase, Keckley must find six St. Louis men who will reimburse her mistress the price of Keckley and her son should the slave woman fail to return South. Keckley's conversation with a Mr. Farrows, the last of the six signatories to her bond, centers on a question of business ethics. Will she return from the North with the money for her purchase price once she achieves her freedom? Readers of Jacobs's narrative will be surprised to discover Keckley refusing to accept Farrows's signature as long as "he had no faith in my pledges" (p. 52). "No," Keckley writes, "slavery, eternal slavery rather than be regarded with distrust by those whose respect I esteemed" (p. 53). This woman whose "stubborn pride" could not be broken by a series of brutal beatings from white men narrated earlier in *Behind the Scenes* describes herself leaving Farrows's house empty-handed, "with humbled pride."

Whether Keckley actually felt so solicitous of the confidence of southern gentlemen cannot be determined, of course. My concern here is with her motives in reconstructing this incident as she did in *Behind the Scenes*. If Keckley's pride was humbled it was certainly not because she had lost what Jacobs would have called her "self-respect." What Keckley is disturbed about is losing the respect of *other* people, namely, those moneyed whites "whose respect I esteemed." No one, least of all Keckley herself, is concerned about this slave woman's sexual respectability; at issue is something much more important—her financial reputation. Whether or not having a spotless business reputation in the antebellum South mattered all that much to Keckley, we may be sure that she wanted her *postbellum* audience to know of her unswerving fealty to the ethics of the marketplace. A self-supporting businesswoman like Keckley could hardly afford to do otherwise. Thus she links her sense of pride and respectability to an external standard—that of the marketplace—rather than an internal principle—what Jacobs would have called her "virtue." Immediately thereafter, almost as though effect follows cause, Keckley is delivered from slavery by a white female benefactor named—what else?—Mrs. Le Bourgois, who confirms the white community's respect for Keckley by raising the $1,200 needed to set her and her son free. In return Keckley postpones her plans to go North for five years so that she can pay back "every cent that was so kindly advanced by my lady patrons of St. Louis" (p. 63).

Behind the Scenes is an unabashed and often plainly self-congratulatory success story. After leaving the South, Keckley portrays herself inexorably climbing the social and economic ladder to intimacy with the First Family of the United States based on her work as a modiste for Mary Todd Lincoln. Jacobs, by contrast, had to live as a hunted fugitive for ten years after her flight from the South. Unlike Keckley, whose teenaged son virtually disappears from her narrative once she arrives in the North, Jacobs had the welfare of two children, not just herself, to think of when she got to New York. Thus employment was for her primarily a way of amassing the money necessary to buy her children and make a home for them, not for advancing herself. This does not mean that Jacobs does not use her narrative of her years as a fugitive in the North to enhance her respectability in her reader's eyes. But, consistent with the discourse of the first half of her story, Jacobs's means of enhancing her image in the North remains dependent on the rhetoric of moral absolutism, in particular that associated with the cult of true womanhood.

Consider what Jacobs writes of her first encounter with respectable people in the North, a black minister and his wife, whom Jacobs meets upon her arrival in Philadelphia. To these evidently sympathetic people Jacobs divulges her background and her identity as a mother with no husband. The minister warns her that such openness, while doing her credit, might leave her vulnerable to the "contempt" of "heartless people." Jacobs replies, "God alone knows how I have suffered; and He, I trust, will forgive me. If I am permitted to have my children, I intend to be a good mother, and to live in such a manner that people cannot treat me with contempt" (p. 161).

Proving herself a "good mother," devoted, vigilant, and formidable, becomes the burden of the latter chapters of *Incidents in the Life of a Slave Girl*. Undeniably, Jacobs succeeds in proving herself thus. But there is also no denying that Jacobs's determination to prove herself a "good mother" puts her once again on the moral, and thus the rhetorical, defensive. She may question the applicability of true womanhood's negative stereotype—the fallen woman—to her case in the South, but in the North she affirms her allegiance to true womanhood's feminine ideal—the self-sacrificial mother. Only in the penultimate paragraph of *Incidents,* when Jacobs speaks longingly of a "home of my own," repeating three times her desire for something of "my own," do we begin to sense that she is moving away from the idealist rhetoric that she has both adopted and reacted against in her attempts to image herself as a slave girl and a free woman. Being "a good mother" has its obvious compensations, but having a home of one's own, a tangible sphere of personal power, is clearly the unrealized goal at the end of *Incidents in the Life of a Slave Girl*.

It is interesting, in light of Jacobs's desire for a home, that nowhere in *Behind the Scenes* does Keckley take the time to discuss the home she made for herself in the North. She makes a great deal of her southern home, to which she returns in a joyful reunion with her former mistress, in a chapter titled, significantly, "Old Friends."[18] Keckley also observes, in a comment on the freedmen and -women who came to Washington, D.C., in the last few months of the war, "The colored people are fond of domestic life, and with them domestication means happy children, a fat pig, a dozen or more chickens, and a garden" (pp. 142–43). "They make a home, and are so fond of it that they prefer it, squalid though it be, to the comparative ease and luxury of a shifting, roaming life" (pp. 139–40). It is not hard to hear in these two remarks Keckley's ambivalence toward home as she understood it in African American life. "Domestic life," marked by a happy family enjoying rural self-sufficiency, is appealing, but, compared with "a shifting, roaming life," the settled sphere of home leaves something to be desired. Certainly Keckley did not want the "shifting, roaming life" forced on many emancipated ex-slaves at the end of the war, but, on the other hand, she did not want "domestic life" either. When she left the South for good in 1860, she went alone. She left behind her mother and her feckless husband and apparently sent her son to be educated at Wilberforce College in Ohio. Emotionally baggageless in the North, she devoted herself entirely to her career.

What Jacobs epitomizes in her idea of a "home of my own"—that is, freedom *realized* and thus empowered in the socioeconomic realm—Keckley accrues to herself via the idea of employment. It is not just employment, however, but career, that emerges from *Behind the Scenes* as Keckley's chief goal in life. She does not just want to work as a self-supporting seamstress; she wants to work for the most highly placed women in Washington, D.C. Moreover, Keckley is not content to be one woman's dressmaker; she hires a contingent of twenty assistants so that she can garner the trade—and the confidence—of the wives of Lincoln's cabinet, not just Mrs. Lincoln herself. To read *Behind the Scenes* is to realize that Keckley shared with Jacobs a strong desire to prove herself—though by strikingly different means—through the publication of her autobiography.

Early in her story, Keckley recalls that her first owners, in an effort to break what they called her "stubborn pride," told her endlessly "that I would never be worth my salt" (p. 21). While still a slave in

St. Louis, Keckley discovered in work both emotional and economic compensation:

> With my needle I kept bread in the mouths of seventeen persons for two years and five months. While I was working so hard that others might live in comparative comfort, and move in those circles of society to which their birth gave them entrance, the thought often occurred to me whether I was really worth my salt or not; and then perhaps the lips curled with a bitter sneer. (pp. 45–46)

Speaking in this way about her past, Keckley makes it clear that even as she realized her exploitation as a southern black female wage slave, she also found the role of the superworker to be rewarding and, in a certain sense, empowering. It is not surprising, therefore, that she made a career of this kind of work in the North and that she proudly identified herself with it in her autobiography.

Keckley's emphasis on what she had accomplished as a black worker, not on what had been done to her as a slave, freed her from some of the binds that restricted Jacobs when she tried to define herself in terms other than those of victimization in her narrative. Yet Keckley's readers should not be blind to the enforced agenda that she also felt obliged to follow in her story. Rejecting idealism and moral absolutism in favor of a materialist and pragmatic measure of self-valuation empowered Keckley to redefine the terms in which a black woman in a postbellum slave narrative might explain "whether [she] was really worth [her] salt or not." But imaging the black woman as superworker, instead of supermother, as Jacobs does, did not provide a solution to the common problem of self-valuation that underlies both women's narratives. Just as Jacobs's idealist discourse both enhanced and detracted from her efforts to represent herself respectably in *Incidents,* so Keckley's materialist discourse was at best a double-edged weapon in her similar effort to claim respect from the white readers of *Behind the Scenes.*

In my work on the antebellum slave narrative in the United States, I have argued that until the mid-nineteenth century, the large majority of slave narrators were strongly motivated by a sense of obligation, born of their situation in a racist society, to *prove* themselves deserving of freedom and the rights of freemen and women. *Incidents in the Life of a Slave Girl,* like Frederick Douglass's *My Bondage and My Freedom* (1855) and a handful of other slave narratives from the 1850s and 1860s, evidences growing resistance to this traditional strategy of self-valuation expected of African American autobiographers.[19] Nevertheless, as I have tried to suggest here, Jacobs's attitude toward the moral categories of antislavery perfectionism and the cult of true womanhood, however questioning, is expressed and thus conditioned by the discourse of moral idealism. While her espousal of that discourse is designed to enhance her moral standing in the eyes of her reader—"I wanted to keep myself pure. . . . I tried hard to preserve my self-respect"—applying this discourse to her circumstances inevitably brands her as alien and deviant and forces her to combat her oppression in the discourse of the oppressor.

Elizabeth Keckley seems to have recognized the handicaps that this discourse placed on her sister slave narrator and sought in a materialist and pragmatic mode of self-valuation an alternative to the idealism and essentialism of Jacobs's moral standard. However, while delivering her from the moral problematic that Jacobs wrestles with, Keckley's revaluation of herself according to her social and economic status in the white world did not release her from the slave narrator's traditional problem of fashioning a mode of self-valuation that was not dependent on the standards of the hegemonic socioeconomic order. Indeed, Keckley's resorting to a materialist discourse as though it is somehow in diametric opposition to an essentialist discourse is itself indicative of the hegemonic culture's divide-and-conquer strategy on the intellectual and linguistic level, where assumed and enforced binary oppositions enable a class as well as caste structure to be treated as natural, not arbitrary. Thus, while Keckley's discourse seems to have offered her a way out of the dilemmas imposed on Jacobs by her choice of discourse, Keckley can also be seen to have invited her readers, particularly those who were black and female, to buy into an economy of selfhood consistent with the interests of the newly emerging capitalist order in the postwar North.

It is beyond the scope of this essay to analyze the ways in which later black women autobiographers of the nineteenth century negotiated the discursive dilemmas posed by the alternative moralities in *Incidents* and *Behind the Scenes*. The famous turn-of-the-century conflict between Booker T. Washington's pragmatism and W. E. B. Du Bois's idealism recapitulated in some important ways the problem of choosing between a materialist and an essentialist orientation for moral action illustrated in the divergent discourses of Jacobs and Keckley. Yet, even as we can see these prominent male-authored first-person narratives addressing a problem posed by earlier women's discourses, we should not assume that the polarities between the Washington and Du Bois camps continued to delineate black women's thought and writing at the turn of the century. Nor should we assume that by that time black women writers had neither sought nor found ways out of the Bookerite and anti-Bookerite factionalism that would come to define so much early twentieth-century African American writing. At this point in the reconstruction of African American literary history, we do not know to what extent black women writers, as a group, were prepared to interrogate the terms in which Jacobs and Keckley and, later, Du Bois and Washington posed the problems of self-valuation and social ethics that the latter two (male) writers have become so famous for having explored.

What we do know at least is that Anna Julia Cooper in *A Voice from the South* (1892) acceded to the notion that "the world" judged individuals and races according to the pragmatic question, "What are you worth?"[20] A reading of black women autobiographers of the late nineteenth century will reveal that many did not hesitate to affirm their worth in worldly terms by noting their economic independence, leadership in social organizations, and educational achievements. Yet students of late nineteenth-century black women's autobiography should not see in the genre's increasing attention to socioeconomic success a growing disenchantment with traditional Christian idealism, particularly as applied to and upheld by women. When Lucy Ann Delaney concluded her autobiography by claiming to have "made the best use of my time" in answering affirmatively the question, "Can the negro race succeed, proportionately, as well as the whites?" she rested her case in the assertion that her work had been done for the glory of God and the benefit of those "for whom I live." "What better can we do than to live for others?" she asked her reader rhetorically.[21] Nevertheless, before readers of today find in Delaney's conclusion yet another evocation of the self-sacrificial ideal of nineteenth-century true womanhood, we should bear in mind that she does not explain what "living for others" might really mean for an African American woman, especially one who had experienced in slavery all too many self-destructive facets of "living for others." Nor does Delaney make clear who the "others" are for whom she has lived. If we take *A Voice from the South* as a gloss on Delaney's text, however, we can find ample suggestion that living for others, which Cooper also endorses as an ideal to which African American women should aspire, does not include indiscriminate self-abnegation to any and all "others"—indeed, in her insistence on the higher education of black women, Cooper *precludes* black women's thoughtless living for white others through the traditional domestic roles and black women's automatic subjection to black male others through the traditional submissive wifely role.[22] Cooper's readers today may find her tantalizingly vague about how black women could set about "developing a self respecting freedom" that would not alienate and threaten whites in general and black men in particular.[23] And we may also wonder whether she thought she was being pragmatic or idealistic—or both—when she argued that African Americans should concentrate on "supplying the great demands of the world's market"—namely, "better, nobler, truer men and women"—whose "intrinsic worth" could be safely left to the judgment of "the cool, calm, unimpassioned, unprejudiced second thought of the American people."[24] Only through further study of Cooper's contemporaries in black women's autobiography will we be able to understand fully whether she spoke for the many or the few among black women at the end of the nineteenth century when she tried to reconcile the idealist and pragmatic discourses pioneered in *Incidents* and *Behind the Scenes* to yield her ultimate solution to the problem of racial and sexual injustice in America.

Notes

1. Nancy Prince, *A Narrative of the Life and Travels of Mrs. Nancy Prince,* in *Collected Black Women's Narratives,* introd. Anthony B. Barthelemy (New York: Oxford University Press, 1988), 87.

2. See the autobiographies of Lee, Elaw, and Foote in William L. Andrews, ed., *Sisters of the Spirit: Three Black Women's Autobiographies of the Nineteenth Century* (Bloomington: Indiana University Press, 1986).

3. Marilyn Richardson, ed., *Maria W. Stewart, America's First Black Woman Political Writer: Essays and Speeches* (Bloomington: Indiana University Press, 1987), 35.

4. Ibid., 30.

5. Frances Ellen Watkins Harper, "Our Greatest Want," *Anglo-African Magazine* 1 (May 1859): 160.

6. Hazel V. Carby, *Reconstructing Womanhood: The Emergence of the Afro-American Woman Novelist* (New York: Oxford University Press, 1987), 32.

7. For examples of slave narrators' tributes to morally upright black women, see William Wells Brown's description of his mother in his *Narrative of William W. Brown, a Fugitive Slave,* ed. Larry Gara (Reading, Mass.: Addison-Wesley, 1969); the idealized Antoinette in William Craft's *Running a Thousand Miles for Freedom,* in *Great Slave Narratives,* ed. Arna Bontemps (Boston: Beacon, 1968), 282; John Thompson's admiring portrait of his sister Delia in *The Life of John Thompson, a Fugitive Slave* (Worcester, Mass.: Author, 1856); Lewis and Milton Clarke's similarly respectful account of their sister in their *Narratives of the Sufferings of Lewis and Milton Clarke,* ed. Joseph C. Lovejoy (Boston: B. Marsh, 1846); Francis Frederick's tribute to his grandmother in his *Autobiography of Rev. Francis Frederick* (Baltimore: Author, 1870), 7; and Allen Parker's eulogy of his mother in his *Recollections of Slavery Times* (Worcester, Mass.: Author, 1895), 80.

8. For a representative portrayal of the slave mother, see Lucy Ann Berry Delaney's tribute to Polly Berry in *From the Darkness Cometh the Light or Struggles for Freedom,* in *Six Women's Slave Narratives,* introd. William L. Andrews (New York: Oxford University Press, 1988). For other tributes to the slave mother in black women's

autobiographies of the nineteenth century, see Andrews's introduction to *Six Women's Slave Narratives,* xxx–xxxi.

9. Harriet A. Jacobs, *Incidents in the Life of a Slave Girl,* ed. Jean Fagan Yellin (Cambridge, Mass.: Harvard University Press, 1987; originally published in 1861). Further references to *Incidents* will include page numbers to the 1987 edition in text.

10. Elizabeth Keckley, *Behind the Scenes: Or, Thirty Years a Slave, and Four Years in the White House* (New York: Oxford University Press, 1988; originally published in 1868). Further references to this book will include page numbers to the 1988 edition in text.

11. Delaney's *From the Darkness Cometh the Light* and Drumgoold's *A Slave Girl's Story* are reprinted in *Six Women's Slave Narratives.*

12. See the chronology of Jacobs's life in *Incidents,* 223–25, and excerpts from her letters in Dorothy Sterling, *We Are Your Sisters* (New York: W. W. Norton, 1984), 256–58. For a list of reviews and notices of *Incidents* in the United States and Great Britain, see *Incidents,* 248–49. For biographical information on Keckley, see the sketch of her life in Rayford Logan and Michael R. Winston, eds., *Dictionary of American Negro Biography* (New York: W. W. Norton, 1982), 375–76; and in John E. Washington, *They Knew Lincoln* (New York: E. P. Dutton, 1942), 205–41.

13. For further discussion of the antislavery movement's ideology of moral perfectionism and its associated rhetorical style, see John L. Thomas, "Romantic Reform in America, 1815–1865," *American Quarterly* 17 (Winter 1965): 656–81; and George M. Fredrickson, *The Black Image in the White Mind* (New York: Harper & Row, 1971), 28–31.

14. See Jean Fagan Yellin's discussion of the apocalyptic imagery on the masthead of William Lloyd Garrison's *The Liberator* in *Women and Sisters: The Antislavery Feminists in American Culture* (New Haven, Conn.: Yale University Press, 1989), 22. In the *Narrative of the Life of Frederick Douglass, an American Slave,* ed. Houston A. Baker (New York: Viking/Penguin, 1982), 129, Douglass describes the white men who capture him after an abortive escape attempt as "fiends from perdition."

15. Barbara Welter, *Dimity Convictions: The American Woman in the Nineteenth Century* (Athens: Ohio University Press, 1976), 23.

16. Yellin, *Women and Sisters,* 25.

17. Yellin states of *Incidents:* "The book is double, linking Linda Brent's confessions as what the patriarchy called a 'fallen woman' with her heroic account of her successful struggle as a slave mother." *Women and Sisters,* 92. Carby argues that *Incidents* is much more internally consistent in its critique of "conventional standards of female behavior" and its challenge to "their relevance and applicability to the experience of black women." *Reconstructing Womanhood,* 47. See also Foster's discussion of Jacobs's resistance to the antebellum slave narrative's "monolithic characterization of slave women as utter victims" in Frances Foster, "'In Respect to Females . . .': Differences in the Portrayals of Women by Male and Female Narrators," *Black American Literature Forum* 15 (Summer 1981): 67.

18. For further analysis of scenes of reunion between former slaves and former slaveholders in post-Civil War black autobiography, see William L. Andrews, "Reunion in the Postbellum Slave Narrative: Frederick Douglass and Elizabeth Keckley," *Black American Literature Forum* 23 (Spring 1989): 5–16.

19. See William L. Andrews, *To Tell a Free Story: The First Century of Afro-American Autobiography, 1760–1865* (Urbana: University of Illinois Press, 1986), 167–79.

20. See Cooper's essay "What Are We Worth?" in *A Voice from the South* (New York: Oxford University Press, 1988; originally published in 1892), 228–85.

21. Delaney, *From the Darkness Cometh the Light,* 63.

22. See Cooper's essay, "The Higher Education of Woman," in *A Voice from the South,* 48–79.

23. Ibid., 283.

24. Ibid., 283, 284.

Chapter 12

Rosario Castellanos: "Ashes without a Face"

Debra A. Castillo

Mas já que se há de escrever, que ao menos não se esmaguem com palavras as entrelinhas.

Since it is necessary to write, at least do not smudge the space between the lines with words.

Clarice Lispector[1]

—¿Quienes son los nueve guardianes?
—Niña, no seas curiosa. Los mayores lo saben y por eso dan a esta región el nombre de Balún-Canán. La llaman así cuando conversan entre ellos. Pero nosotros, la gente menuda, más vale que nos callemos.

"Who are the nine guardians?"
"Don't be curious, child. The old ones know, and for that reason give this area the name Balún-Canán. They call it that when they converse among themselves. But for us, the little people, it is better to be quiet."

Rosario Castellanos, Balún-Canán[2]

In a recent *New Yorker* article, John Updike noted "the curious but widespread autobiographical impulse in men still enjoying middle age," and theorized that this Eurocentric, male, mid-life need to testify to the progress of life in the midst of living it "possibly stems from a desire to set the record straight before senility muddles it, and a hope of lightening the ballast for the homeward leg of life's voyage."[3] Almost every word of Updike's tongue-in-cheek comment would sound hopelessly foreign to a Latin American woman.

Let me begin with what is only a slightly hyperbolic statement: Latin American women do not write autobiography. The occasional exception—Western-trained and European-oriented women such as Victoria Ocampo or, on the contemporary Mexican scene more pertinent to this study, women such as Margo Glantz, Barbara Jacobs, and Elena Poniatowska (whose non-Hispanic-sounding last names are almost too suggestive)—neatly demonstrates the point, and even these women refuse to subscribe to the synthetic, neatly patterned style typical of the traditional male autobiography. Their works, like their lives, are fragmented, other-directed, marginally fictionalized. Yet these women are the privileged minority. Latin American women, unless they have the great good luck of the access to the advantages implicit in names like Glantz or Poniatowska, the advantages of birth, education, and affluence, do not write at all. Black, mestizo, and Indian women tend to be poor and illiterate.[4] The extraordinary campesina may, in extraordinary circumstances, dictate her testimonial to a more privileged, politically compromised poet, anthropologist, or novelist: examples include *Si me permiten hablar . . . Testimonio de Domitila, una mujer de las minas de Bolivia,* dictated to Moema Viezzer (Bolivia); *Me llamo Rigoberta Menchú y así me nació la conciencia,* dictated to Elizabeth Burgos (Guatemala); Alegría's *No me agarran viva: La mujer salvadoreña en la lucha* (El Salvador); Verdugo and Orego's *Detenidos-desaparecidos: Una herida abierta* (Chile); and Poniatowska's nonfiction novel, *Hasta no verte Jesús mío,* recreating the life of Mexico City laundrywoman and ex-*soldadera* Jesusa Palancares in (more or less) her own words. All of these works—and I do not exclude those of the Ocampos and Glantzes of Latin America— are significant ones; all represent important contributions to the still nascent emergence of women's voices into the public forum, with all of the revisionary resonances implicit in the unstifling of radically different perspectives.[5] However, the general, if trite, conclusion to be drawn from such works as appear in adequate press runs, from mainstream Latin American presses, and that make it to English translation is that, in Poniatowska's words, "La literatura de mujeres es parte de la literatura de los oprimidos" (Women's literature is part of the literature of the oppressed).[6] It is an observation that has been made many times, in slightly different terms, by writers of the First World as well as the Third. Poniatowska's statement is, nonetheless, true on a variety of levels, and has specific implications for Latin America that are more than trite ones.

Literature by Latin American women can clearly afford neither the luxurious impulses nor the strange urges besetting (in Updike's mixed metaphor) middle-aged Eurocentric men. The record that needs to be set straight is always a more than personal one; the threat, in countries where intellectuals regularly "disappear," is not encroaching senility but government security forces. In the words of well-known Mexican novelist Carlos Fuentes, "To write on Latin America, from Latin America, for Latin America, to be a witness of Latin America in action or in language is now, will be more and more, a revolutionary fact. Our societies don't want witnesses."[7] Implicit in this statement is the peculiarly Latin American artistic compromise with practical politics as filtered through creative works of great technical difficulty and limited distribution. Radical artistic compromise, in a society ruled by censorship, often flirts with radical estrangement, at times coming together only in an art that conceals or subverts, as it illuminates, truth. It is an art continually, intentionally, disrupted by a surreptitious, meticulously engineered dispersal through the agency of what Fuentes calls, in the original Spanish title of the essay cited above, "la palabra enemiga" (ambiguously, the word "enemy," the word-enemy, the enemy word), with all the gravity of that phrase's implicit linguistic, cultural, and political density.[8] Women's "autobiography," in such a context, necessarily wears a non-Eurocentric face, as the subjective realm must continually, and on all levels, renegotiate its implicit contract with the social and ideological imperatives.

The problem of situating Latin American women in relation to the question of self-writing is much too large for this essay; the twenty-three countries of Indo-Ibero-America are much too diverse for facile generalization. Instead, I will look at one country, Mexico, and one writer, Rosario Castellanos (1925–74) in order to explore one case of self-writing that both stretches the limits of autobiography as traditionally defined and asks us to think about the cultural assumptions behind apparently "universal" generic categories.

Historically, the tradition of women's autobiography in Mexico is extremely thin. Women have been discouraged from participation in the public arena for centuries, their role in the literary and political debates surrounding their male counterparts obscured or denied. Their voices are only now finding entry into the national discourse. Thus, when Rosario Castellanos, in her various articles on autobiography, looks for Mexican foremothers, she can identify only two: Sor Juana Inés de la Cruz, the brilliant seventeenth-century nun whose impassioned "Respuesta a Sor Filotea" includes a two- or three-page autobiographical sketch, and the Marquesa Fanny Calderón de la Barca, the English wife of a Spanish ambassador to Mexico, whose memories of her two years in that country (1839–41) serve as one of the most cherished historical documents of the nineteenth century. The lack of access to the written word was such that when one of the heroines of the fight for independence, Doña Josefa Ortiz de Domínguez, "quiere avisar al cura Hidalgo que han sido descubiertos, no puede manuscribir su recado porque no sabe" (wants to inform Father Hidalgo that they have been discovered, she can't write the message because she doesn't know how to write).[9] In 1946 Mexican women were officially given citizenship, including the right to primary (now junior high) education; economic factors still affect actual literacy rates.

Rosario Castellanos spent the first sixteen years of her life in the town of Comitán in the state of Chiapas, a community that was completely isolated from the central government until the Pan-American

Highway reached it in 1951. The Revolution of 1910 passed it by; the 1934 Agrarian Reforms of president Lázaro Cárdenas took years to arrive, and when they did, in 1941, the neofeudalistic life-style of Castellanos's family was swept away almost entirely. Her father lost his ranches and the economic and social power that went with them, and emigrated with the family to Mexico City. Rosario Castellanos eventually returned to Chiapas for several years as an employee of the Instituto Nacional Indigenista; by all accounts, these later experiences confirmed her early sympathy for the Tzeltal-speaking Indians of the area and inspired almost all her prose works. Says Aurora M. Ocampo, "Rosario Castellanos supo escuchar las voces de los desposeídos porque ella también fue una desposeída, las voces de los oprimidos porque ella también fue una oprimida y las de los verdugos porque también tuvo ocasión de serlo" (Rosario Castellanos knew how to listen to the voices of the dispossessed because she too was dispossessed, the voices of the oppressed because she too was oppressed, and the voices of the executioners because she also was one of them).[10] Castellanos never forgets that, by writing her story and the story of the Tzeltal-speaking Indians in Spanish, she is making herself complicitous in one of the most tortuous ambiguities of the "palabra enemiga"—giving voice to herself and to them in the language of the oppressors, in a form and a style inaccessible to the people she represents.[11]

Rosario Castellanos was essentially a poet, whose best-known and most highly appreciated works are her volumes of poetry, and she was an artist who could not permit herself the facile distinctions other writers and thinkers maintain between art and life. For her personally, literature was, in a quite literal sense, her life; her work kept her alive by saving her from the abyss of impotent anxiety. For her politically, literature carried the power of changing reality through the act of naming. Unsurprisingly, *Balún-Canán,* although "esencialmente un libro autobiográfico" (essentially an autobiographical book),[12] violates almost all the normative requirements of the autobiographical genre as traditionally conceived. Castellanos elaborates: "Es la *narración* de mi infancia; es, además un *testimonio* de los hechos que presencié en un momento en que se pretendió hacer un cambio económico y político en los lugares donde yo vivía entonces. . . . pero claro, están contados a manera de *literatura,* no a manera de crónica, ni a manera como podría contarse en el 'cauch' de un psicoanalista." (It [*Balún-Canán*] is the narration of my infancy; it is also a testimonial to the events I witnessed at a time in which efforts were made to effect a political and economic change in the places I lived at that time. . . . but obviously, these events are told as literature, not as a chronicle, nor in the way one would talk from a psychoanalyst's couch.)[13] In another interview, Castellanos adds, "En forma estricta, esta obra no puede considerarse *prosa*" (Strictly speaking, this work cannot be considered prose).[14]

Briefly, then, to recapitulate the disjunctions with traditional expectations for an autobiography: it is a narration, but not, "strictly speaking," a prose one. It is a testimonial, but not a chronicle of events. It is a literary autobiography, but not psychoanalytical. If it can be said to conform to any established form, *Balún-Canán* seems to fit in best with that protean variety of feminine autobiography described by Françoise Lionnet:

> It should not be surprising for an autobiographical narrative to proclaim itself as fiction: for the narrator's process of reflection, narration, and self-integration within language is bound to unveil patterns of self-definition (and self-dissimulation) with which we are not always consciously familiar. . . . the female narrator . . . exists in the text under circumstances of alienated communication because the text is the locus of her dialogue with a tradition she tacitly aims to subvert.[15]

The tradition she wishes to subvert is triply her own: hers by right of class, race, and access to education. All three terms are problematized in this poetic novel, as it is precisely in respect to this privileged position that Castellanos grounds her critique, confusing the distinction between autobiography and fiction intentionally so as to call attention away from the failed ideal of a meaningful, complete, and self-directed life toward the (for her) more essential questions of the contribution of an ideological critique of a society that actively prevents self-direction in a significant majority of its citizens.

Rosario Castellanos's tale begins and ends with the social upheavals among both her own landholding class and Indians following the tardy arrival of Cárdenas's land reforms during her seventh year. The closure of this abbreviated life is marked by the girl-child-narrator's access to the written word, as it is by means of the very fact of writing that the child inserts herself unwittingly into the rejected conventions of devalued tradition and, moreover, confirms her identity as property of the male, confirming in a minor key the historical circumstances of the systematic, and systematically congruent, domination of non-whites and creole women by creole men. This oral tale, finally and inevitably lost in the appropriations of writing, is paralleled by a second tale, that of the Tzeltal-speaking Indians, also oral, also a story of loss and expropriation of the word that spoke identity and so gave it being. For the Indians, the idea of an individual autobiography is, however, incomprehensibly alien, as their mode of telling the self is not personal but communal, the story of an interrelated identity forged by the voice of the storyteller, the Elder Brother, the Tribal Memory. This tale, too, was once put into Spanish, and into writing, at the request of the landowners; frighteningly, the resulting document was preserved by the male heirs of the landowning family as a written acknowledgment of their legal claim to traditional Indian territories. The girl's story incorporates and recuperates this tale alongside and tangential to her own, but the older and wiser Rosario Castellanos is clearly aware of the potential for co-optation of her dual text as well— hence the elusive poetic style that seems to operate in flight from all such potential betrayals, including those of generic conventions. Alongside these two tales of oppression, both cast in a lyrical prose, Castellanos also offers two tales of domination. First, the girl sees her own story as subordinate to the more important story of the only child who really counts in the family: her brother Mario. Second, *Balún-Canán* is actually divided into three parts, only the first and third of which are narrated from the point of view of the seven-year-old child. In the central, far more pedestrian, section, the story of a bloody uprising against the landholders is narrated mostly from an omniscient third-person point of view. The work as a whole, then, develops as a series of confrontations between oppressor and oppressed sparked by the new government requirements: César Argüello, the landowner father, versus Felipe, the Indian leader; César versus his wife, Zoraida; Zoraida versus the girl child; the brother, Mario, versus the girl; the girl, finally, versus the Indian nana. For all these caveats, I would argue, nevertheless, that Castellanos's poetic novel provides a true plumb line, given the only partially Westernized cultural context, into the autobiographical impulse as adapted to a Mexican provincial climate.

"Underreading" describes the most common critical reaction to *Balún-Canán*. When the work first came out in 1957, it was safely classified as an *indigenista* novel and read as an elaboration on the traditional political commitment and social consciousness of that particular, politically charged variation on the more general exoticist recuperations of *costumbrismo*. Such readings are plausible, if narrow, but in order to function they must repress the most arresting and original features of the narrative as imperfections in achievement of the *indigenista* form. Recent reevaluations of the work often attempt to recuperate it for a content-based protofeminism by focusing on the figure of the woman in the text; curiously, most of these readings ignore

the most central female—the seven-year-old girl—and all of them
ignore the Indian nana, who disappears critically into the invisibility
that, ironically, she bitterly predicted as her tribe's communal fate.[16]
Balún-Canán opens *in medias res* with the voice of the nana as she
dresses the child, and I will at this point permit myself the luxury of
a long, essential quote:

> —. . . y entonces, coléricos, nos desposeyeron, nos arrebata-
> ron lo que habíamos atesorado: la palabra, que es el arca de la
> memoria. Desde aquellos días arden y se consumen con el
> leño en la hoguera. Sube el humo en el viento y se deshace.
> Queda la ceniza sin rostro. Para que puedas venir tú y el que
> es menor que tú y les basta un soplo, solamente un soplo . . .
> —No me cuentes ese cuento, nana.
> —¿Acaso hablaba contigo? ¿Acaso se habla con los granos
> de anís?
> No soy un grano de anís. Soy una niña y tengo siete años.
> Los cinco dedos de la mano derecha y dos de la izquierda. Y
> cuando me yergo puedo mirar de frente las rodillas de mi
> padre. Más arriba no. Me imagino que sigue creciendo como
> un gran árbol y que en su rama más alta está agazapado un
> tigre diminuto. Mi madre es diferente. Sobre su pelo—tan
> negro, tan espeso, tan crespo—pasan los pájaros y les gusta y
> se quedan. Me lo imagino nada más. Nunca lo he visto. Miro
> lo que está a mi nivel. [. . .] Y a mi hermano lo miro de
> arriba abajo. Porque nació después de mí y, cuando nació, yo
> ya sabía muchas cosas que ahora le explico minuciosamente.
> Por ejemplo ésta:
> Colón descubrió la América.
> [. . .]
> —No te muevas tanto, niña. No puedo terminar de peinarte.
> ¿Sabe me nana que la odio cuando me peina? No lo sabe.
> No sabe nada. Es india, está descalza y no usa ninguna ropa
> debajo de la tela azul del tzec. No le da vergüenza. Dice que
> la tierra no tiene ojos.
> —Ya estás lista. Ahora el desayuno.
> Pero si comer es horrible. Ante mí el plato mirándome fija-
> mente sin parpadear. Luego la gran extensión de la mesa. Y
> después . . . no sé. Me da miedo que del otro lado haya un
> espejo.[. . .]
> —Quiero tomar café. Como tú. Como todos.
> —Te vas a volver india.
> Su amenaza me sobrecoge. Desde mañana la leche no se
> derramará. (pp. 9–10)

"... and then, angrily, they dispossessed us, they tore away
what we had treasured: the word, which is the ark of memory.

And since that time they have burned and been consumed
with the wood in the fire. The smoke rises on the wind and
dissolves. All that remains is ashes without a face. So that you
can come, and the one that is younger than you, and with a
breath, with only a breath . . ."

"Don't tell me that story, nana."

"What makes you think I was talking to you? Do people
talk to anise seeds?"

I am not an anise seed. I am a girl and I am seven years
old. Five fingers on the right hand and two on the left. And
when I stretch up I can look straight at my father's knees. No
higher. I imagine that he grows upward like a tree and that in
his highest branch crouches a diminutive tiger. My mother is
different. Above her hair —so black, so thick, so curly—pass
the birds, and they like it there so they stay. I'm only imagining. I have never seen it. I look at things on my level. I can
look at my brother from top to bottom. Because he was born
after me and, when he was born I already knew lots of things
that I now explain carefully to him. For example, this:

Columbus discovered America.

"Don't move so much, child. I can't finish combing your
hair."

Does my nana know I hate her when she combs my hair?
She doesn't know. She doesn't know anything. She's an
Indian, she's barefoot, she doesn't wear anything under the
blue cloth of her tzec. She doesn't care. She says the earth has
no eyes.

"You're ready. Now breakfast."

But eating is horrible. In front of me the plate stares up
without blinking. Then the long stretch of table. And then . . .
I don't know. I'm afraid there might be a mirror on the other
side.

"I want coffee. Like you. Like everybody."

"You're going to turn into an Indian."

Her threat chills me. From now on the milk will not spill.
(pp. 13–14)

The nana's frightening tale of an ongoing conquest is twice interrupted: once in the white space before the beginning of *Balún-Canán*,
once by the child's imperious demand that the nana not tell that
particular story. The nana's incomplete story is further displaced by
the child's "knowledge," her counterhistory, complete in one simple
sentence, that erases the Indian from the tale: "Colón descubrió la
América." The love/hate relationship of mutual dependence and shifting lines of power between the white child and her Indian nurse is

exquisitely captured in the war between storytelling styles: the metaphorical, lyrical mode of the woman, cut off by the child and obliterated by the matter-of-fact European version of Spanish arrival in the
Americas; the child's petty assumption of the nana's ignorance, the
nana's revenge in suggestively setting the metaphor of an eyed earth
into the child's mind so that plate and table become leering faces or
horrific mirrors; the childish demand for coffee, the nurse's menacing
response couched in terms of the simple declarative sentence of the
whites, foregrounding the child's secret fear: "Te vas a volver india."
The work opens, then, with two competing author figures battling
uneasily for control over the text—the girl child, the least valued
individual of the dominant class, and the nana, the most marginalized
member of the communal culture—a battle, from one point of view,
for the lowest possible stakes.

This is not a traditional autobiography that begins with some version
of the sentence, "I was born . . ."; the opening gesture invalidates
such trite phrasings. Instead of the emergence of the individual self
as a function of the acquisition of language, we are thrown into contact
with a primary and soon-eradicated "we" that defines itself through
the historicomythic account of an originary loss of language that has
come to endow reality with its present form. Without ever leaving
their homeland, the natives of Chiapas have been disenfranchised,
morally exiled, dehumanized, marginalized, silenced, and then re-
admitted once again, as barely tolerated semislaves, on the fringes of
a geographical and historical space that was once their own. Furthermore, the nana's tale, pointedly *not* one of those other stories she
tells to amuse the child, functions most importantly as a kind of
narrative revenge. "¿Acaso hablaba contigo?" erases the child as much
as possible and in the same manner as her people have been erased:
by denying her access to or participation in the storytelling cycle, the
history of the nation. See me, she seems to be whispering to her
charge, see *us* if only in the ashes left by your burnings, see us in
the traces that slaveholding leaves in the faces of slave holders. And
at the same time, shouting, these faces, these remnants of words are
not for you. I am contemplating my private word-self and you have
no right to intervene. And yet again, insinuatingly, I am watching you
listen/refuse to listen to me as I tell myself (but implicitly you) this
story, and you are angry because you want me to hear you. But in
seeing me you see the unwanted, unspoken, rejected side of yourself
and refuse that story, that mirror. The child is caught up in this seductive, tangled plot. "For listening," says Gerald Bruns, "is not the spec-

tator's mode; listening means involvement and entanglement, participation or belonging for short."[17] As we read this novel (eye work) we are forced to recall the entirely different work of the ear, which, helpless, cannot turn away from the story—but cuts it off. "No me cuentes," says the child, though the expropriation of the ear has no recourse. However, the child has become the woman, has rejected the ear for the power of the written word, the "Columbus discovered America" that silences the nana's speech.

From another vantage, however, the essential issue in such an exercise is to point to the operative questions that guide a sensitive reader of the text. Of what significance are traditional distinctions between "fact" and "fiction"? How valid are the kinds of conventional demands we are likely to make of an (autobiographical) work of this sort, such as, Is it authentic? Is it correct? Is it complete? What does it tell us about the author? And, for Third World texts, is it politically useful? The double lines of the initial act of storytelling—two individuals, two cultures, two traditions, and implicitly, two languages—imply an ambiguous textual space, and an uncomfortable textual reality, in which such problems and questions become, at best, undecidable; at worst, irrelevant. Basic tenets of knowledge that anchor reality— Columbus discovered America—are revealed, in context, as purely fictional, laying open the flayed knower to other fictional perversions: eyes in plates, metamorphosis into an Indian.

The nana's metaphorical/spiritual "word" has been ripped away from the Indians in what looks to Western eyes like a translated version of the biblical rape of the Ark of the Covenant. This "word," transmuted, reappears later in *Balún-Canán* in concrete form as the document composed by the embodied memory of the tribe and preserved by César Argüello as proof of his right to the lands of Chactajal. "Los que tenían que venir, vinieron" (Those who were destined to come, came), says the Elder Brother of the tribe. "Nos preservaron para la humillación, para las tareas serviles. Nos apartaron como la cizaña del grano. Buenos para arder, buenos para ser pisoteados, así fuimos hechos, hermanitos míos. He aquí que el cashlán difundió por todas partes el resplandor que brota de su tez. Helo aquí, hábil para exigir tributo, poderoso para castigar, amurallado en su idioma como nosotros en el silencio, reinando" (pp.57–58). (They preserved us to humiliate us, to make use of us in servile tasks. They separated us like the chaff from the grain. Good for burning, good for trampling, that's the way we were made, my brothers. See how the cashlán diffused everywhere the splendor born of his skin. See him here, able in demanding tribute, powerful in punishment, walled up in his language as we in our silence, ruling [pp. 56–57].)

The Elder Brother's tale forces us to reevaluate the nana's story, which has the same metaphorical base in its focus on issues of memory and silence, on the coming of the Castilian whirlwind, the burning, and the dispersed face of the tribe, forces us to read the nana's second "they" ("arden y se consumen") more ambiguously than we first imagined: they (the "cashlánes") burn in a metaphorical hell for their blasphemy; they (the Indians, "buenos para arder") burn with humiliation and oppression; they (the words) burn away, leaving only silence, dispersed chaff, ashes without a face. The Elder Brother's words suggest as well the degree to which the nana's charge, the seven-year-old girl, has absorbed the conquest stories she rejects; her lyrical imagining of her parents' inaccessible faces has the same tone as the Elder Brother's reference to the shining splendor of the Castilian skin, a tone quite different from the matter-of-fact voice used for official knowledge.

It is the persistence of this "knowledge," moreover, rather than the child's rather petulant "No me cuentes ese cuento" that poses the essential narrative dilemma in foregrounding the existence of a force so strong that it leaves no place for the nana's voice, no room to trace her tribal silencing back to its inexpressible origin, no space in which the erased face of the Indian can meet the blinding features of the Castilian. It is this dilemma of the impossible confrontation that drives the narration, that requires the intervention of the reader in order to project and reinscribe it elsewhere, here, in the political act of bringing it into existence by naming it.

Furthermore, the concrete "arca de la memoria" of the tribe comes to be reinscribed into the the text of *Balún-Canán* through the girl's secret robbery of the word, in the reappropriation of the Indian's writing as the genealogy of the Argüello family, the history of abuses that is the family's story in the eyes of the oppressed, which is, in this book, the only full account taking of the girl's ancestors. Significantly, it is the mother who interrupts the girl's reading, barring her way to the dangerous pages of this potentially subversive, unofficial history: "No juegues con estas cosas," she warns her daughter after giving the pages her own surreptitious skimming. "Son la herencia de Mario. Del varón" (p. 60). (Don't play with these things. . . . They are the inheritance of Mario. Of the boy [p.59].)

The central issue in relation to *Balún-Canán*, then, is not one of historical correctness or congruence with verifiable personal experiences; it is not even a question of philosophical or intellectual adequacy. Rosario Castellanos turns aside from such traditional expressions of value, as such requirements tend to short-circuit discussion. "La lucidez," she writes in an essay on Simone de Beauvoir, "aparentement, es una calidad (¿o desgracia?) que se acuerda a las mujeres con suma parsimonia y escasísima frecuencia" (Lucidity, apparently, is a quality [or disgrace?] that is awarded to women with great parsimony and very scarce frequency). Instead, she continues, "se les concede . . . el relámpago fugaz de las intuiciones que alumbra un fenómeno . . . sin que requiera ninguna disciplina previa, ningún esfuerzo de la inteligencia ni de la atención, ninguna constancia de la voluntad" (they are conceded the flickering lightning of intuition that lights up a phenomenon without necessity for any effort of intelligence or attention, without any willed concern).[18] Castellanos is unconvinced by either the traditional male value of lucidity (in its standard definition) or the traditional female value of intuition (as a second-rate substitute). Simone de Beauvoir's distinctive quality, for Rosario Castellanos, is a poetic one: "Va descubriendo, poco a poco, los aspectos más escondidos de las cosas" (She uncovers, little by little, the most hidden aspects of things).[19] It is this quality, rather than a strictly defined veracity or even verisimilitude, that is most outstanding in her own text as well, counteracting the impacted, overdetermined murmurings of official history. To uncover the hidden aspects of things and name them represents, for her, the primary use value of the double-voiced text as a recontextualization of specific reading and writing practices as political strategies. The story of the self is defined partly by the historical abuses and the continuing imposition of one culture on another, and partly by the incongruous and unexpected infiltration of Indian discourse into the very founding gesture of the dominant class, while at the same time the two languages and two cultures retain their mutual incomprehensibility. The juxtaposition of the two creates not a harmonious whole, but a strategic positioning of an entire set of resistances to repression. To bracket the child and the nana, as critics of this text traditionally have, is to ignore its most radical contribution; it is, in Lionnet's analogy, "acting like the surgeon who blithely 'cures' feminine hysteria by doing hysterectomies."[20] In what follows, I would like to explore some of the various responses to oppression (and to repression) in this text, and to examine its implicit criteria for value in naming the undiscovered.

One reaction to the pressures of the dominant social force is silence. Initially, however, silence is not a response but a condition imposed from outside: silencing, rather than silence freely chosen. The Indians, says the Elder Brother, are walled up in their silence at the time of the conquest; the contemporary landowners continue to enforce this historically established linguistic tradition: "Ningún ladino que se respete," says César, "condescenderá a hablar en español con un indio" (p. 188). (No self-respecting white man will condescend to speak in Spanish with an Indian [p. 177].) The females of the dominant social class, likewise, are condemned to silence and invisibility. The child's mother, Zoraida, accepts the traditional role allotted her in exchange for the material comforts accruing from her husband's name: "'Zoraida de Argüello.' El nombre me gusta, me queda bien" (p. 90). ("Zoraida de Argüello." I like the name, it fits me [p. 89].) She maintains her minimal hold on her marriage rights through abject self-humiliation, even though she knows she was sold into marriage like a hen and is about as highly appreciated as one, even though her husband now ignores her since she cannot produce more children, even though she knows of his Indian mistresses and unrecognized children, even though the rest of the family and society at large follow his lead, walling her up in an official silence as profound as, if of a different sort from, that imposed on the Indians. A deromanticized distancing of the feminine and repressive silencing of her needs are still at the heart of the control mechanism.

The revolutionary response to silencing is resemanticization: to use silence as a weapon (resorting to silence) or to break silence with hypocrisy. One scenario for a response of the repressed to the oppressor may take form in the strong woman whose mode of resistance consists of playing with the cherished myths of dominant society and secretly reversing their charge—for instance, this hoary tale, much repeated: "[La mujer] pasivamente acepta convertirse en musa para lo que es preciso permanecer a distancia y guardar silencio" (Women passively accept conversion into muses, for which it is necessary to stay at a distance and remain silent).[21] A woman who is neither passive nor accepting may yet preserve the advantages of distance and silence for her own reasons, using distance to her advantage, using the mask of silence to slip away. Another scenario makes use of misleading speech to mask an essential silence. Says Castellanos, "Se ha acusado a las mujeres de hipócritas y la acusación no es infundada. Pero la hipocresía es la respuesta que a sus opresores da el oprimido, que a los fuertes contestan los débiles, que los subordinados devuelvan al amo." (Women have been accused of being hypocrites, and the accusation is not unfounded. But hypocrisy is the response the oppressed give their oppressors, the response of the weak to the strong, of the subordinates to the master.)[22] That is, give the oppressors the response they want to hear, but maintain the mental reservations that permit a minimal independence of thought.

In the first striking use of the properties of silence in this work, neither the child nor the nana is named; the silencing of their "proper" names leaves them free to act as markers or position holders while escaping implication through the definition of their functions. This silence as to name marks a transferral of value; silence accrues a positive value as the power of concealment, the necessary and elided missing element (nana, child, Elder Brother) carving out the path for narrative. "Daughter," for example, means child of no value, a perceived mistake, a familial burden to be passed on to the future husband who will (finally) give her a name, his name. The son, Mario, however, encodes the hope of the family for persistence of the name and the heritage. The girl, then, as a thing of no account, has a freedom not allowed the boy; as long as she maintains her passive exterior she can engage in the subtle hypocrisies of invention and storytelling, creating a space for the quietly subversive counterknowledge that is this book, the expanded counterpart to the nested tale of the Elder Brother, the gloss on the doubly interrupted story of the nana. Too much knowledge may, in fact, infringe upon the possibilities encoded in this productive silence. Toward the end of the novel, the old Indian known as tío David (Uncle David) offers to take the girl up to the mountain to the "mero corázon de Balún-Canán, al lugar donde viven los nueve guardianes. Los mirarías a todos, tal y como son, con su veradera cara, te dirían su verdadero nombre" (p. 274) (right to the heart of Balún-Canán, to the place where the nine guardians live. You could look at them all, as they really are, with their real face, they would tell you their real name [p. 256]). The girl refuses such intimate knowledge, turning away the invitation with a lie. She has learned that names told her by others are less significant than the names she tells, in her own way, with her words or with her silence, with her own truth that is the product of her imagination.

As a political strategy, however, to embrace silence is clearly of limited value. Silence alone cannot provide an adequate basis for either a theory of literature or concrete political action. The girl child must, eventually, break silence and write, negotiating the tricky domains of the said and the unsaid, the words written down, as Lispector would have it, smudging the page, and the words left, for whatever reason, between the lines. I am reminded of Eugen Gomringer's concrete poem,[23] which raises the question of silence as a wall of silence and at the same time enacts the speaking/writing of the word *silence* in a disembodied command, a fact without a speaker, bricks in the wall:

> silencio silencio silencio
> silencio silencio silencio
> silencio   silencio
> silencio silencio silencio
> silencio silencio silencio

Only in breaking silence—the chink in the wall—can the writer hope to establish any form of critique, any potentially revolutionary opposition to the oppressive system.

The second response to repression is negation, the questioning of dominant meaning structures through positing the inverse. Negation, in its various permutations, has become identified as one of the most significant oppositional strategies of feminist critics, who, by standing outside the system as willfully "different," propose an alternative epistemology derived from rejection of conventional truth claims, now revealed as problematic social constructions. Ludmer's seminal discussion of Sor Juana Inés de la Cruz's letter to the Bishop of Puebla focuses on just such a strategy in terms that, unsurprisingly, given Sor Juana's crucial influence on Mexican women of letters, are highly relevant to this discussion of Rosario Castellanos:

> La escritura de Sor Juana es una vasta máquina transformadora que trabaja con pocos elementos; en esta carta ["Respuesta a Sor Filotea"] la matriz tiene sólo tres, dos verbos y la negación: *saber, decir, no.* . . . Saber y decir, demuestra Juana, constituyen campos enfrentados para una mujer. . . . Decir que no se sabe, no saber decir, saber sobre el no decir: esta serie liga los sectores aparentemente diversos del texto (autobiografía, polémica, citas) y sirve de base a dos movimientos fundamentales que sostienen las tretas que examinaremos: en primer lugar, separación del saber del campo del decir; en segundo lugar, reorganización del campo del saber en función del no decir (callar).[24]

> Sor Juana's writing is a vast transformatory machine that works with very few elements; in this letter ["Response to Sor Filotea"] the matrix has only three: two verbs and the negative: *to know, to say, no.* . . . To know and to say, Juana shows, constitute opposing fields for a woman. . . . To say that she does not know, not to know how to say, not to say what she knows, to know about not saying: this series links the apparently diverse sectors of the text (autobiography, polemic, quotes) and serves as basis for two fundamental movements that sustain the tactics we will examine: in the first place, sep-

aration of the field of knowledge from the field of speech, in the second place, reorganization of the field of knowledge in the function of not saying (silence).

Ludmer, then, traces in Sor Juana's letter what we might call a symbolic logic of minimalist transformation: A not-A, B not-B, in which the negative functions as the performative metaphor of difference, setting the pace for the transformation. The negation represents the signal mark of internal division of the field, creating the signifying gap but also motivating potential reconstruction on other terms. To know and to say, mediated by the "no," displays the concealment of both knowledge and speech as the presence of the irrecuperable other. The tactic of silence and distance, examined earlier, is only one step of the process defined by Ludmer, of which the next step is the displacement and deferral organized through the agency of negation itself.

In *Balún-Canán,* the doubled storyteller at the opening of the work suggests a doubled field of operations; the elements involved, however, are exactly those defined by Ludmer: "to know," "to say," and "no," with the permutations defined through the unstable relations of the nana and the child and their mutual ability to limit knowledge and speech in the other. The first and last speeches of the opening chapter are given to the nana; in the first case, the speaking is interrupted by the child's "no"; in the second, the nana's implicit "no" silences the child and ensures obedience. Between these two instances, the narrator weaves the shifting, and destabilizing, patterns of knowledge and speech as relative positionalities rather than absolute concepts.

The nana's opening tale is a story of negation, of memory as the memory of loss; accordingly, her language figures the violent institutionalization of racial difference as a primary division between saying and not saying. What the nana tells, therefore, is nothing less than the tale of forcible silencing: "nos desposeyeron, nos arrebataron . . . la palabra" (they dispossessed us, they tore away . . . the word), and later, "queda la ceniza sin rostro" (all that remains is ashes without a face). No face, no word. For the nana, no name, no genealogy, no story but the interrupted story of the loss of name, genealogy, story, speech, a recognition confirmed, chillingly, from the other side of the vexed relationship by the girl-child at the end of the novel when, thinking to recognize her nana in the crowd, she realizes, "Nunca, aunque yo la encuentre, podré reconocer a mi nana. . . . Además, todos los indios tienen la misma cara" (p. 291) (Even if I find her, I will never be able to recognize my nana. . . . Besides, all Indians have the same face [p. 271]). The worst of racist clichés, that all Indians look alike, represents, in the context of this work, the nearest approximation a white girl can make to the most profound reality of Indian life—the loss of face that is their irremediable historical tragedy, the loss of face that makes a mockery of the narcissistic impulses of conventional autobiography. In this book, accordingly, the collective "no" of the Indians profoundly complicates any other individual's speech.

What is lacking is the essential, unequivocal knowledge of the Indian's nature, established by the framing of the *Balún-Canán* with reference to the nana, and by markedly denying the nana identity and speech. Such a lack, and such knowledge, is clearly defined as something that urgently requires interpretation, but for which interpretation is impossible because of an act of willful disfiguration and effacement: the silencing of the other. Castellanos's work, uncomfortably, opens with a tale of silencing and closes with a strictly parallel act of silencing: the negation turned against itself.

The nana's uncomfortably effaced knowledge is repeatedly rejected in favor of the child's own set of things she knows. First, however, the child uses her own negation—"No me cuentes ese cuento" (Don't tell me that story)—as a way of interrupting the telling and discrediting the teller—"No lo sabe. No sabe nada" (She doesn't know. She doesn't know anything)—before inserting the list of her own, highly controversial, bits of counterknowledge: "Colón descubrió la América" (Columbus discovered America), "suiza quiere decir gorda" (p. 10) ("Swiss" means "fat" [p.14]), and later, "todos los indios tienen la misma cara." The first and the third "facts" in the child's list represent cultural clichés so deeply engrained that they represent the essential cornerstones of knowledge at the basis of the construction of the national identity. The defamiliarization operative in placing such truisms in relation to the nana's deeply disturbing tale reveals their deeply flawed nature, and makes a political statement of considerable force. By also placing these bits of knowledge in a series with the statement "'Swiss means fat'" as facts of similar incontrovertibility, the narrator also implies their absurdity.

The same pattern is repeated when the child steals into the father's library and gets access to the forbidden tale of the Elder Brother. Again, knowledge of loss is the basis of the Indian's tale; again, the telling (reading) is interrupted by the authoritative "no"—"No juegues con estas cosas" (Don't play with these things), says the mother—again, the negation is followed by the controverted knowledge of the dominant society implicitly rejected in this context: "Son la herencia de Mario. Del varón" (Such things are the heritage of Mario, the male). In such a context, the idea of knowledge about a person as revealed through a background of concrete, individualized, and objectively verifiable historical fact that is at the heart of traditional autobiography demonstrates itself to be either insufficient or distinctly distorting. The negation operates across the board.

Although her discussion of Sor Juana does not develop the implications of the insight, Ludmer also points to another possibility for resistance that goes beyond both silence and negation as tactics of the weak and marginalized. This tactic, she suggests, "consiste en que, desde el lugar asignado y aceptado, se cambia no sólo del sentido de ese lugar sino el sentido mismo de lo que se instaura en él" (consists in that, from the assigned and accepted place, she change not only the meaning of that place but meaning itself of what is installed in it),[25] and, I would add, the meaning of meaning as well. In such a practice, negation does not serve only as an oppressor's means of establishing difference, recuperated for other reasons by the oppressed. It also implies a methodology for retaining a fertile spatial and temporal distance that allows the action of thought to occur, while at the same time suggesting the potential for a creative reappropriation of the negated elements, a transvaluation of values that permits bridging the gap of difference *on her own terms*. The logic of such reappropriation is neither symbolic nor political, but poetic, and based on the affirmative and constitutive power of the metaphor. One concrete result is that already theorized by Ludmer: "Los espacios regionales que la cultura dominante ha extraído de lo cotidiano y personal y ha constituido como reinos separados (política, ciencia, filosofía) se constituyen en la mujer a partir precisamente de lo considerado personal y son indisociables de él. Y si lo personal, privado y cotidiano se incluyen como punto de partida y perspectiva de los otros discursos y prácticas, desaparecen como personal, privado y cotidiano." (The regional spaces that dominant culture has extracted from the quotidian and personal and has constituted as separate realms [politics, science, philosophy] are constituted in the woman as derived precisely from what is considered personal, private, and quotidian. And if the personal, private, and quotidian are included as the point of departure for these other discourses and practices, they disappear as personal, private, and quotidian.)[26] Accordingly, we would be justified in concluding that the oft-repeated critical distinction between marginal and dominant cultures is itself a seductive fiction reflecting the hypostatization of that which is different into a conveniently distanced, merely antagonistic "Other," at which point intervention stops. Negation in the first, simple, sense neglects the possibilities for individual or communal agency in effecting reciprocal adjustments. The double negation—refusal of subsumption in the dominant, refusal of alienation in the marginal—creates a disturbance in the fields of discourse, reminding us of the mutual dependence and reciprocal relations bridging the metaphorical gap between antagonistic ideologies. Or, in Derrida's words, "There are always two *pas*'s, the one in the other, but without any possible inclusion, the one immediately affecting the other, but overstepping it by distancing itself from it. Always two *pas*'s, overstepping even their negation, according to the eternal return of the passive transgression and the repeated affirmation. . . . *Pas* is forgetting, *pas* of forgetting, doubly affirmed (yes, yes)."[27]

The crucial element that Rosario Castellanos would add to this two-step reversal is that of the essential fictiveness of experience, her realization that a system of signs, recognized as arbitrary, remotivates itself, inducing the entire history of being. In relation to the working woman, for example, Castellanos points to the "manera de asumir el trabajo" (the way of taking a job) that prevents her from acquiring with the salary "un cierto grado de independencia, que aunque es real se experimenta como ficticio" (a certain degree of independence, which, although real, is lived as a fiction).[28] To "overstep" this "*pas* of forgetting" Castellanos counterposes her work, "*pas* is forgetting," a story of what is long lost, long forgotten, long relegated to the realm of old wives' tales, kitchen fictions, freeing her in the heady independence that, although fictitious, is lived as real and thus negates negation itself. The prose/poetry, autobiography/fiction of *Balún-Canán* is a natural product of this impulse. Consider the dynamics of this exchange, part of which was quoted earlier, out of context:

> INTERVIEWER: ¿Hasta qué punto la poesía ha influído en tu prosa?
> CASTELLANOS: Este influjo se nota fácilmente in *Balún-Canán,* sobre todo en la primera parte. En forma estricta, esta obra no puede considerarse prosa . . . .
> INTERVIEWER: ¿Cómo llegaste a la prosa?
> CASTELLANOS: . . . Escribí dos cuentos: uno de ellos, "primera revelación," que es un germen de *Balún-Canán.*
> Deseaba contar sucesos que no fueron esenciales como los de la poesía: sucesos adjectivos. . . . Así, casi sin darme cuenta, di principio a *Balún-Canán:* sin una idea general del conjunto, dejándome llevar por el fluir de los recuerdos.[29]

> INTERVIEWER: Up to what point has poetry influenced your prose?
> CASTELLANOS: This influence is easily noticed in *Balún-Canán,* especially in the first part. Strictly speaking, this work cannot be considered prose. . . .

INTERVIEWER: How did you come to prose?

CASTELLANOS: . . . I wrote two stories; one, "First Revelation," is the germ of *Balún-Canán*. I wanted to tell of events
that, unlike poetry, were not essential: adjectival events. . . . In
this way, almost without realizing it, I began *Balún-Canán,*
without any controlling idea, allowing myself to be carried
along by the flow of memory.

Prose, let us say, is typically conceived of as a concatenation of
nouns and verbs; Castellanos's intuition of the basically adjectival
nature of her work surely deserves note as a revolutionary transvaluation of prose, rejecting agency and action (the essential and the
essentialist, both typically male preserves) in favor of what is often
downgraded as mere ornamentation: superficial, attractive surely, but
of lesser significance. In Castellanos, "la palabra enemiga" is transformed, polished, held close to the body and to the reader, and that
reader, Castellanos's ideal reader, knows the precise mechanism of its
formal construction, the particular resources and uses of its form. I
do not want to imply that the interviewer, in this case Emmanuel
Carballo, is insensitive to these issues because he is a man; I do want
to pose the hypothesis that his program, his apparent unwillingness
to depart from his prepared script for idiosyncracies of the writer, is
typical of a certain common misunderstanding that is in itself culturally
determined by a series of concerns that involve what is proper, what
is property, and how property relations are negotiated linguistically.
In Castellanos's metaphorical history of language as an instrument for
domination, she writes, "La propiedad quizá se entendió, en un principio como corrección lingüística. . . . Hablar era una ocasión para
exhibir los tesoros de los que se era propietario. . . . Pero se hablaba
¿a quién? ¿O con quién?" (Perhaps property/propriety [the word *propiedad* means both] was originally understood as a linguistic correction. . . . Speaking was an opportunity to exhibit the treasures of which
one was proprietor. . . . But to whom or with whom did one speak?)[30]
     In her seminal article, "On the Superficiality of Women," Susan
Noakes points out, through her readings of Rousseau, Sterne, Flaubert,
and Dante, among others, that "it is Christianity that stresses that
superficial reading (for 'adventure,' plot, to find out 'what happens')
is not, as one might suppose today, merely stupid but, more importantly, morally wrong. . . . Readings that remain *on* the surface . . .
engage the reader's desires rather than the reader's ideas."[31] Through
the agency of desire, bad reading and carnal desires come to be associated; from there, says Noakes, it is only a small step to the effective
conflation of terms: "Woman as seducer behaves like woman as reader;

thus, woman reads in the same way she seduces."[32] Reading for enjoyment is reading as a woman, is reading in a morally deficient manner, is reading woman, woman reading: reading or seducing, she is the tempting, destructive figure of Eve. The horror of that notoriously damning eroticism is evident in Cortázar's text as well as Flaubert's; reading as a woman reads (that is, badly, superficially) is associated with moral depravity or mental derangement:[33] on the one hand, Morelli's pedantic reminder that the new, antinovel "debe ser de un pudor ejemplar" (must have an exemplary sense of decorum),[34] on the other, Horacio Oliviera's fall, at the end of the novel, from the madhouse window.

One response is to deny the superficiality. Thus, while Marta Traba acknowledges a system of judgment based on "nivel de autonomía, de su capacidad para crear un campo simbólico mediante una nueva estructura lingüística y de su alcance universal" (its degree of autonomy, on her capacity to create a symbolic field by way of a new linguistic structure, and on its universal reach),[35] the traditional criteria for evaluating literary quality, she suggests that women's writing attends to a second, equally profound and valuable, set of criteria. First, women's literature can serve a mediating function: "Si el texto femenino queda situado en el espacio próximo a los . . . marginados culturales . . . podría perfectamente intermediar como lo hacen todas las contraculturas, entre el productor solitario y el receptor desconfiado." (If the feminine text can be situated in the space next to . . . the culturally marginalized . . . it, like all countercultures, can serve as a perfect intermediary between the solidarity producer and the suspicious receiver.)[36] Second, says Traba, and following upon the recognition of the woman writer's role as a representative marginal and intermediary with the center, the woman writer can learn to speak for herself (ironically, Traba, herself a woman writer, expresses this thought through Pierre Bourdieu): "Hablar, en cambio de *ser hablado*, podría ser una de las tareas de la contracultura." (To speak, instead of *to be spoken*, should be one of the tasks of the counterculture.)[37] Women reading/women writing provide, then, a viable, profound, and morally defensible alternative to the dominant cultural mode. Their work is different, surely, but not superficial; rather, it is complementary to the established norms of universality.

Castellanos's "lector hembra" (female reader—I use Julio Cortázar's derisive term from *Hopscotch* in a willed reversal) has another value. Implicitly recognizing and taking into account once again a tradition that marks women readers as superficial and morally deficient, she realigns the terms to right the misappropriation of the reading woman as immoral, while reversing the negative charge on the accusation of superficiality. Openly marked as a celebration of the unexplored potential of the female reader and of the female novelist, her essay on María Luisa Bombal provides a counterpoint to Cortázar's meditations on moral and intellectual deficiency and Traba's call for a strategic appropriation of marginality, and offers other possibilities for appropriation of texts, for establishment of rights of property and propriety. Hers is another program, another face, another place, another force, another interlocutor:

> Cuando la mujer latinoamericana toma entre sus manos la literatura lo hace con el mismo gesto y con la misma intención con la que toma un espejo: Para contemplar su imagén. [. . .] El cuerpo se viste de sedas y de terciopelos, que se adorna de metales y de piedras preciosas, que cambia sus apariencias como una víbora cambia su piel para expresar . . . ¿qué?
>
> Las novelistas latinoamericanas parecen haber descubierto mucho antes que Robbe-Grillet y los teóricos del *nouveau román* que el universo es superficie. Y si es superficie pulámosla para que no oponga ninguna aspereza al tacto, ningún sobresalto a la mirada. Para que brille, para que resplandezca, para que nos haga olvidar ese deseo, esa necesidad, esa manía de buscar lo que está más allá, del otro lado del velo, detrás del telón.
>
> Quedémonos, pues, con lo que se nos da: no el desarrollo de una estructura íntima, sino el desenvolvimiento de una sucesión de transformaciones.[38]

When a Latin American woman picks up a piece of literature she does it with the same gesture and with the same intention as that with which she picks up a mirror: to contemplate her image. . . . Her body is dressed in silks and velvets, adorned with metals and precious stones that change her appearance like a serpent changes its skin to express . . . what?

Latin American women novelists seem to have discovered long before Robbe-Grillet and the theoreticians of the *nouveau roman* that the universe is surface. And if it is superficial, let us polish the surface so that it leaves no roughness to the touch, no shock to the look. So that it shines, so that it glows, so that it makes us forget that desire, that necessity, that mania for seeking out that which is beyond, on the other side of the veil, behind the curtain.

Let us keep, then, what is given us: not the development of an intimate structure, but the unenveloping of a series of transformations.

Castellanos here confronts directly the rhetorical tradition that defines good prose as clear, straightforward, and masculine, and bad taste in prose as a fondness for the excessively ornamented, and therefore effeminate. In her challenge to this ingrained metaphor, she intuits the startling possibilities of a feminine aesthetics as a model for feminist politics, in her evocation of the unmistakable image of the bored upper-class woman, filing her nails (sharpening her claws?), slipping, menacingly, out of her Eve-snake skin, creating herself affirmatively in the appropriation of the polished, superficial, adjectival existence allotted her, making the fiction yet more impenetrably fictive until it glows as the revolutionary recognition of a forgotten truth.[39] The mirror is her talisman; it is, like those flashing mirrors worn by the famous Knight of the Mirrors in *Don Quixote,* a weapon for dispelling, as it creates, illusion: aesthetics and politics brought home, as it were, from their travels, made homey, personal, private, quotidian, made adjectival rather than absolute.

Balún-Canán does not provide a model to imitate or a mimetic reflection to contemplate, but a polished surface to triangulate desire (nana, niña, and a third term, the female reader), a free space for self-invention. Castellanos writes elsewhere: "No basta imitar los modelos que se nos proponen y que son las respuestas a otras circunstancias diferentes de las nuestras. No basta siquiera descubrir lo que somos. Hay que inventarnos" (It is not enough to imitate the models that are proposed to us and that are the answers to circumstances different from ours. It is not even enough to discover what we are. We have to invent ourselves).[40] Implicitly, we have to invent ourselves in a continual process of reelaboration.

Back in Comitán, in the provincial schoolroom, a tired schoolmistress displays before the bored little girls under her tutelage the catalog of her meager knowledge, permitting "que cada una escoga los [conocimientos] que mejor le convengan. Yo escogí, desde el principio," says the narrator, "la palabra *meteoro.* Y desde entonces la tengo sobre la frente, triste de haber caído del cielo" (p. 13) (each of us to choose the knowledge that best fits us. From the beginning I chose the word *meteor.* And from that time on I have worn it on my forehead, sad from having fallen from the sky [p. 16]). The sun emanating from the Castilian skin of the conquerers shines, blinding the Indian; the child's light is a nighttime light, a fugitive, "fallen" track across the sky. Her identity is never meant for monumentalization in a bulky autobiography. Instead, we note her passage briefly and she is gone, aged eight, almost before we have time to register her existence, restored and effaced/defaced in a single gesture. "Me da miedo,"

says the child in the opening pages of the book, "que del otro lado
[de la mesa] haya un espejo" (I'm afraid that on the other side of the
table there might be a mirror)—a mirror that might reveal, for example,
that not only do all Indians have the same face, but the single face
of the Indian is one she too shares; that all oppressed people, not
only Indians, share the same mirror-face. And so she invents herself
in the metaphorical slicing of a fugitive word across her sky—
"meteoro"—in the beginning of her schooling. It is a word treasured
in memory for the evanescent bright path it traces in her life, her
badge of accomplishment and her mark of Cain. She should never
have been the bright child, the child of words; that destiny was
reserved for the only child who mattered in the family, the dead son.
Thus, for her, the word *meteoro,* like the unpronounceable word of
the nana's lost heritage, passes forceably into the hands of another.
Deformed to "Mario" in the last untold story, *meteoro* initiates the
story of her brother's short life and premature death, the beginning
of writing. And yet, in the interstices of this adjectival prose, the
"lectora hembra" can catch glimpses of this falling star, still falling,
still burning in the hands of the "lector enemigo" who has appropriated it as his property.

Rousseau ends his *Confessions* with the act of reading his *Confessions.* It was, as H. Porter Abbott says, "a shrewd idea" that initially
resolves the thorny problem of the slippage between property and
propriety, positing a specific audience to or with whom this prize
possession is to be shared. Abbott continues: "Rousseau selected for
this event an audience of the highest breeding and most exquisite
sensitivity. Yet the observable effect of this reading (silence, disturbed
only by the enigmatic trembling of Madame d'Egmont) . . . only heightened the pathos of his effort to control response through the control
of form."[41] I am disturbed by the silence and "enigmatic trembling"
of exquisitely sensitive Madame d'Egmont; however, since my topic
is not Rousseau but Castellanos I merely point out the careful negotiation of the issues of self-writing and the reception of that writing
as acts of self-possession and repossession. Castellanos's work ends,
as the nana began it, with empty hands. The narrator is dispossessed,
deprived of voice, and in the enforced muteness finds the strength to
take up her pencil and begin to write: "Con mi letra inhábil, torpe,
fui escribiendo el nombre de Mario. Mario en los ladrillos del jardín.
Mario en las paredes del corredor. Mario en las páginas de mis cuadernos. Porque Mario está lejos. Y yo quisiera pedirle perdón" (p. 291).
(With my awkward, unsteady handwriting I began writing the name
"Mario." Mario on the bricks of the garden. Mario on the walls in the

hall. Mario in the pages of my notebooks. Because Mario is far away. And I want to ask his forgiveness [p. 271].) The story is, ironically, as her mother predicted, the posthumous inheritance of someone else, if not of the son, Mario—for he has, in death, gone far indeed—then of some other heir, equally beloved, equally hated, equally foreign. Although very different from Rousseau's concluding gesture, Castellanos's final words also offer an implicit commentary on the communal/self-portrait she is in the process of drawing/erasing: that the conflictual rescue of buried memories is as much a decomposition as a recuperation, that it is all but impossible for the forgotten trace to speak of more than the process of its repression, that it is as much her torment as her salvation that the reader, male or female, mirror or reflection, must complete the shifting development of appearances, that what we do with this property, this *Balún-Canán,* is, by her license, a matter for our own sense of decorum.

Notes

1. Clarice Lispector, *A legião estrangeira* (Rio de Janeiro: Editôa do antor, 1964), 137.

2. Rosario Castellanos, *Balún-Canán* (Mexico City: Fondo de cultura económica, 1957), 26. This book has been published in English as *The Nine Guardians,* trans. Irene Nicholson (London: Faber & Faber, 1959), but that edition is now out of print. Translations appearing in this chapter are my own. Further references to this book include page numbers from both Spanish and English editions for ease of consultation by non-Spanish speakers.

3. John Updike, "Michel Tournier," *New Yorker,* 10 July 1989, 94.

4. Examples of a general anesthesia to class and race issues could be multiplied almost indefinitely. Castellanos herself was well aware of her own blindness in this regard. She has written feelingly about both her nana, whose real name was Rufina, and about her *cargadora,* María Escandón, the woman and the child whom her parents handed over to her as if they were playthings. Her behavior, if not extraordinarily exploitative, was not exemplary either: "Yo no creo haber sido excepcionalmente caprichosa, arbitraria y cruel. Pero ninguno me había enseñado a respectar más que a mis iguales y desde luego mucho más a mis mayores. . . . El día en que, de manera fulminante, se me reveló que esa cosa de la que yo hacía uso era una persona tomé una decisión instantánea: pedir perdón a quien había yo ofendido. Y otra para el resto de la vida: no aprovechar mi posición de privilegio para humillar a otro." (I do not believe I was exceptionally capricious, arbitrary, and cruel. But no one ever taught me to respect anyone other than my equals and those older than me. . . . The day that it was suddenly revealed to me that the thing I had been using was a human being, I took an instantaneous decision: to beg forgiveness of the person I had offended. And I made another vow, that for the rest of my life I would never take advantage of my privileged position to humiliate another person.) Elena Poniatowska, *¡Ay vida, no me mereces!* (Mexico City: Joaquín Martiz, 1985), 6. This realization of the essential humanity of a plaything is both wrenching and horrifying, and Castellanos did dedicate much of her life to the cause of indigenous Mexicans. Her dedication, nevertheless, had a curious and inexplicable omission, a blind spot or, harshly, a hypocritical element. After María Escandón

had passed thirty-one years at her side, Castellanos, at the time of her marriage, released her old companion to the service of another woman. By Castellanos's own account, that new mistress, Gertrudis Duby, was amazed that during those thirty-one years, Castellanos never found the time to teach her servant to read or write. As Castellanos herself notes, "Mientras yo andaba de redentora . . . junto a mí, alguien se consumía de ignorancia" (While I was running around playing redeemer, . . . someone was consumed by ignorance at my side) (p. 121). The commitment was an inconsistent and unreliable one at best; the risk, if such a word can be used in the context, no risk at all.

5. I refer the reader interested in pursuing the question of the testimonial to Doris Sommer's magnificent study, "'Not Just a Personal Story': Women's *Testimonios* and the Plural Self," in *Life/Lines: Theorizing Women's Autobiography,* ed. Bella Brodzki and Celeste Schenck (Ithaca, N.Y.: Cornell University Press, 1988), 107-30. Jean Franco provides a solid historical and critical background to the broad scope of Mexican literary history in *Plotting Women: Gender and Representation in Mexico* (New York: Columbia University Press, 1989). Among the best works produced in the nascent field of Hispanic feminist criticism are Franco's article "Apuntes sobre la crítica feminista y la literatura hispanoamericana," *Hispámerica* 15, 45 (1986): 31-43; and her chapter "Beyond Ethnocentrism: Gender, Power, and the Third World Intelligentsia," in *Marxism and the Interpretation of Culture,* ed. Cary Nelson and Lawrence Grossberg (Urbana: University of Illinois Press, 1988), 503-15.

6. Elena Poniatowska, "La literatura de las mujeres es parte de la literatura de los oprimidos," *Fem* 6, 21 (1982): 23.

7. Carlos Fuentes, "La palabra enemiga," in *La nueva novela latinoamericana* (Mexico City: Joaquín Mortiz, 1972), 120. An English translation of this work by Suzanne Jill Levine has appeared as "The Enemy: Words," *Triquarterly* 23, 4 (1972): 111-22.

8. Pragmatism is also involved. One of Mexico's typical modes of censorship is to withdraw funding for state-sponsored projects *when those works are already far advanced.* The policy is breathtakingly Machiavellian, and inspires considerable baroque subterfuge on the part of artists and writers.

9. Rosario Castellanos, *Mujer que sabe latín . . .* (Mexico City: Fondo de cultura económica, 1984), 27.

10. Aurora M. Ocampo, "Debe haber otro modo de ser humano y libre: Rosario Castellanos," *Cuadernos americanos* 250, 5 (1983): 201.

11. Besides land redistribution, the other highly disputed element of Cárdenas's agrarian reforms was to require landowners to teach Spanish to the Indians. This measure was considered almost blasphemous, as one of the major means of control over the Indian population was to discourage them from learning any more Spanish than absolutely required to follow commands. Since their own language, of course, had no official recognition, the Tzeltal speakers were thus effectively disenfranchised.

12. María Luisa Cresta de Leguizamón, "En recuerdo de Rosario Castellanos," *La palabra y el hombre* 19 (1976): 10.

13. Ibid., 3; emphases mine.

14. Beth Miller and Alfonso González, *26 autoras del México actual* (Mexico City: B. Costa-Amic, 1978), 125.

15. Françoise Lionnet, *Autobiographical Voices: Race, Gender, Self-Portraiture* (Ithaca, N.Y.: Cornell University Press, 1989), 92–93.

16. Examples of the first, *indigenista,* reading, include the following: Mario Benedetti, "Rosario Castellanos y la incomunicación racial," in *Letras del continente mestizo* (Montevideo: Arca, 1969), 165–70; Jean Franco, *An Introduction to Spanish American Literature* (Cambridge: Cambridge University Press, 1969); Joseph Sommers, *After the*

Storm (Albuquerque: University of New Mexico Press, 1968). Typical of the protofeminists are María Rosa Fiscal, "La mujer en la narrativa de Rosario Castellanos," *Texto crítico* 5 (1979): 133–53; Donald H. Frischmann, "El sistema patriarcal y las relaciones heterosexuales en *Balún-Canán* de Rosario Castellanos," *Revista iberoamericana* 51 (1985): 665–78; Regina Harrison MacDonald, "Rosario Castellanos: On Language," in *Homenaje a Rosario Castellanos,* ed. Maureen Ahern and Mary Seale Vásquez (Valencia: Albatros, 1980), 41–64, especially "La mujer," pp. 54–64. See also Sandra Messinger Cypess, "*Balún-Canán:* A Model Demonstration of Discourse as Power," *Revista de estudios hispánicos* 19 (1985): 1–15. Cypess's fine discourse analysis does take into account the importance of the girl child as narrative figure.

17. Gerald Bruns, "Disappeared: Heidegger and the Emancipation of Language," in *The Play of Negativity in Literature and Literary Theory,* ed. Sanford Budick and Wolfgang Iser (New York: Columbia University Press, 1989), 127.

18. Rosario Castellanos, *Juicios sumarios* (Mexico City: Fondo de cultura económica, 1984), 19.

19. Ibid., 22.

20. Lionnet, *Autobiographical Voices,* 205.

21. Castellanos, *Mujer que sabe latín,* 23.

22. Ibid., 25.

23. Eugen Gomringer, "Schweigen," in *Worte sind schatten die Konstellationen 1951–1968,* ed. Helmut Heissenbüttel (Hamburg: Rowohlt, 1969), 27.

24. Josefina Ludmer, "Tretas del débil," in La sartén por el mango, ed. Patricia Elena González and Eliana Ortega (Río Piedras, P.R.: Huracán, 1985), 48.

25. Ibid., 53.

26. Ibid., 54.

27. Cited and translated in Joel Fineman, "'The Pas de Calais': Freud, the Transference and the Sense of Woman's Humor," *Yale Journal of Criticism* (1988): 140.

28. Castellanos, *Mujer que sabe latín,* 29.

29. Miller, *26 autoras,* 125–26.

30. Castellanos, *Mujer que sabe latín,* 177.

31. Susan Noakes, "On the Superficiality of Women," in *The Comparative Perspective on Literature: Approaches to Theory and Practice,* ed. Clayton Koelb and Susan Noakes (Ithaca, N.Y.: Cornell University Press, 1988), 347.

32. Ibid., 344.

33. I am referring here to Julio Cortázar's novel, *Rayuela* (Buenos Aires: Sudamericana, 1963), translated in 1966 by Gregory Rabassa as *Hopscotch* (New York: Random House), and particularly to the furious intercontinental debate that erupted around the use by one of his characters of the term *el lector hembra* (the female reader) to describe a lazy, superficial, hedonistic reading style.

34. Cortázar, *Rayuela,* 454 (*Hopscotch,* 408).

35. Marta Traba, "Hipótesis sobre una escritura diferente," in *La sartén por el mango,* ed. Patricia Elena González and Eliana Ortega (Río Piedras, P.R.: Huracán, 1985), 23.

36. Ibid., 25.

37. Ibid., 26.

38. Castellanos, *Mujer que sabe latín,* 145.

39. Puerto Rican writer Mayra Santos-Febres adduces another variant of the uses of superficiality. In her country, there is a movement among certain young women to dress, for their own pleasure and to make a political statement, in clothes traditionally seen as sexually provocative, while retaining specific subtle markers of untouchability. In more extreme circumstances, another counterpart for the sophisticated woman in

the mirror is the "disappeared" poet, of whatever race or social class (I am thinking here, in part, of Mahasveta Devi's wonderful story, "Draupadi," and of Gayatri Spivak's carefully considered "foreword"; see Mahasveta Devi, "Draupadi," trans. and fwd. Gayatri Chakravorty Spivak, *Critical Inquiry* 8 [1981]: 381–402). I am indebted to the Argentine poet and former political prisoner Alicia Partnoy for reminding me that, furthermore, in the context of the prisons, the writer must direct her work to a sympathetic reader outside the walls, while at the same time remembering that the only guaranteed audience for her work is a "lector enemigo" (an enemy reader): the official prison censorship. Each of these manifestations would require its own carefully nuanced study.

40. Rosario Castellanos, *El eterno femenino: farsa* (Mexico City: Fondo de cultura económica, 1975), 194.

41. H. Porter Abbott, "Autobiography, Autography, Fiction: Groundwork for a Taxonomy of Textual Categories," *New Literary History* 19 (1988): 610.

Chapter 13

Expressing Feminism and Nationalism in Autobiography
The Memoirs of an Egyptian Educator

Margot Badran

There are different reasons for writing autobiography and different ways of reading autobiography. As a reader who is a historian of modern Egypt specializing in women's history and feminist history, I am interested in the feminist content of women's autobiography. Many years ago, while I was doing research on the feminist movement led by Huda Sha'rawi from the 1920s through the 1940s, a relative introduced me to her unpublished memoirs of her childhood and life up to the time she began to lead a feminist movement. Sha'rawi's memoirs helped me answer questions I had about origins of feminist consciousness and nascent forms of feminist activism.[1] Over the years, as I read writings of women in Egypt, I came to see other expressions of feminist consciousness and activism as part of daily life.[2] Through my historical study and activism in Egypt I have been continuing to speculate about what *may* have existed there beyond the realm of formal feminist movements or explicitly articulated feminist ideology.[3]

In 1989, while doing research at Dar al-Kutub, the National Library in Cairo, I came across the autobiography of Nabawiyya Musa published serially from 5 May 1938 to 2 August 1942 in her periodical, *Majallat al-Fatah* (The Magazine of the Young Woman, which was published from 20 October 1937 to 5 June 1943), under the title

270

Dhikriyyati (My Memoirs). This was a major discovery for me as a feminist historian. It was the highly detailed life of a woman who was a pioneering educator and who had made a lifelong commitment to nationalist and feminist issues. Musa, of modest middle-class origins, was a self-made woman whose everyday language was Arabic, as it was for the majority of Egyptians. Huda Sha'rawi and other upper-class feminists who spoke French appropriated the ready-made feminist terminology of that language, which generated the term *feminism* in the late nineteenth century.[4] In Musa's time there was no word for *feminist* or *feminism* in Arabic; to this day there are no unequivocal words for these concepts. However, there are forms of consciousness and behaviors that can be understood as feminist even in the absence of the label.[5] Knowing about the past experiences of particular women and how they viewed those experiences helps us in this. The revelations of an autobiographical text such as Musa's are critical for a fuller understanding of the history of Egyptian feminism.

Nabawiyya Musa's *Dhikriyyati* is a treasure trove. It describes concrete ways in which Egyptian women were oppressed in the early twentieth century and how one woman overcame these structural and behavioral modes of oppression. Musa's autobiography enables us to demonstrate that Egyptian women's feminist consciousness and activism exceeded what most people have been able to see or willing to concede. *Dhikriyyati*, a major document in the history of Egyptian feminism, also contributes to expanding and refining feminist theory in general.

Musa achieved her highest form of self-expression in her autobiographical writing, which she began at the age of fifty-two, long after she had established herself as a formidable educator. Much earlier in her career, at the age of thirty-four, she had published a short treatise called *al-Mar'a wa al-'Amal,* (The Woman and Work), supporting education and work for women.[6] Her feminist exposition in these two kinds of writing is strikingly different, with far freer expression exhibited in her autobiography. *Dhikriyyati* is thus critical to an understanding of the possibilities of the autobiographical mode for feminist expression in Egypt.

Musa's life and the reconstruction of her life operated as counter-discourses cutting through indigenous and colonialist patriarchal overlays. Through autobiography, Musa produced a feminist and nationalist manifesto bolder, more sweeping, and far more radical than the feminism and nationalism she articulated in *The Woman and Work*. This early publication, which announced the author's feminist and nationalist agenda, was a brave work published at the height of the national revolution in Egypt. *Dhikriyyati,* begun nearly two decades later and serving at once as a historical record and a feminist model, was, I would argue, however, her supreme political work.

Biographical Contexts

Nabawiyya Musa (1886–1951), pioneering educator in modern Egypt, was born thirteen years after the first state school for girls was established and four years after the start of British colonial occupation. She was thirty-nine years old when the first state secondary school for girls opened and thirty-six when British occupation ended—except for a military presence in the Suez Canal Zone, which was not expelled until 1956. In that year the state granted Egyptian women the vote, declaring them equal citizens in the official ideology; also that year, the state suppressed women's right to organize independently as feminists as part of a larger drive to curtail free political expression.

Musa was from the modest middle class in a highly stratified society. She was a female in a patriarchal society. She was a citizen (for her first thirty-six years) in a colonized country. She was born fatherless in a culture where the patriarchal family was paramount.[7] Within the heavy constraints imposed by indigenous patriarchal society and colonial domination, as well as by family circumstances, Nabawiyya Musa managed to build a life for herself.[8] As a teacher, headmistress, and founder of girls' schools, she engaged in a lifelong struggle to advance the cause of Egyptian women. Musa studied in the Girls Section of the 'Abbas Primary School, passing the primary school examination in 1903, two years after girls first were allowed to take this state-administered test.[9] She then entered the Saniyya School (established in 1889), where she took a teacher training certificate in 1906. Triumphing over the objections of the colonial educational authorities, in 1907 she became the first Egyptian girl to be allowed to sit for the state baccalaureate examination and the last until after independence.

Musa was one of the first Egyptian women to become a teacher in the state school system when she began to teach in the Girls Section of the 'Abbas Primary School in 1906. She was the very first Egyptian Muslim woman to become a headmistress, taking direction of the Girls School in Fayyum in 1909. She went on to become headmistress of the Girls School in Mansura from 1910 to 1914. Meanwhile, Musa spoke in the women's lectures series in Cairo for women-only audiences organized by Huda Sha'rawi and other upper-class women in 1909. Musa also gave lectures in the Women's Section of the Egyptian University (established in 1908), which lasted for three academic years, from 1909 to 1912.[10] (When Musa had sought unsuccessfully to enroll in the new Egyptian University the year before, after it first opened, she was not even allowed to enter the building without permission from the director.)

From 1914 to 1916, Musa was assistant headmistress (the headmistress was an Englishwoman) at the Bulaq Women Teachers Training School in Cairo (part of the state school system and more prestigious than the provincial schools where she had been headmistress), and from 1915 to 1924 she was headmistress of Wardiyyan Women Teachers Training School in Alexandria. In 1924 she was appointed chief inspector of female education in the Ministry of Education, the year the decision was made to create the first state secondary school offering girls the same curriculum offered to boys.[11] In 1926 she was dismissed from the Ministry of Education. Thereafter, she devoted herself to running the two schools for girls she had struggled successfully to found: al-Tarqiyya al-Fatah Primary School for Girls in Alexandria and Banat al-Ashraf Secondary School for Girls in Cairo.[12]

In 1923, the year after independence was declared, when the first public, organized feminist movement started, Nabawiyya Musa became a member of the newly founded al-Ittihad al-Nisa'i al-Misri, the Egyptian Feminist Union (EFU). Along with EFU President Huda Sha'rawi, she attended the conference of the International Alliance for Women Suffrage in Rome, where she spoke on women's educational needs in Egypt. This was Musa's first and last formal role in the EFU-led feminist movement, which agitated for a range of social, economic, and political rights for women for the next quarter century under the leadership of Huda Sha'rawi.[13]

Although she appeared only for a brief moment on the scene as an EFU activist, Musa, who was gifted in Arabic, used her pen throughout her life to advance her causes. As a young schoolteacher she wrote articles on education for the press under the pseudonym Damir Hai fi Jism Raqiq (A Living Conscience in a Delicate Body) because employees of the Ministry of Education were forbidden to write for the newspapers. She published the already-mentioned *al-Mar'a wa al-'Amal* in 1920 and *al-Ayat al-Bayyinat fi Tarbiyat al-Banat* (The Clear Model in the Education of Girls) at an uncertain date. In 1938 she published *Diwan al-Fatah* (The Young Woman Collection of Poems) and, during the same decade, *Riwayya Nabhutub* (Nabhutub, a Novel). In 1937 Musa started her own periodical, *Majallat al-Fatah,* as a "weekly political and general magazine" aimed at a wide audience of women and men; it sold for one piaster. In her weekly editorial, "Kalima al-Muharrira," she criticized government policy, especially concerning education.[14]

Musa's career came to an abrupt end when the Egyptian government imprisoned her for speaking out against the government's compromising position after British tanks menaced Abdin Palace in 1942. Her magazine ceased publication in 1943, and she died in retirement eight years later, at the age of sixty-four.[15]

Early this century, Musa not only sought new opportunity for herself but advocated the entry of other domestically confined middle- and upper-class women into the life of society. Although she objected to the enforced seclusion of women in the home, she supported the separation of the sexes in public. Musa's strict application of the practice of gender segregation secured for her, and for other women, space in the public arena of education and work where direct male interventions in women's lives could be held at bay. Musa operated within the framework of Egyptian sexual and moral ideologies, and they became for her weapons to keep men in their place.

Although Nabawiyya Musa was active in Egypt for nearly half a century and was a prominent figure in education, she has been neglected in general accounts of modern Egypt, a fate shared with other women. Even Amir Boktor, in his more specialized history of education in Egypt, overlooked her. When attention later turned to women's history, Musa began to receive some notice, but she still remains little known.[16]

Autobiography as an Indigenous Form

Recording one's life story is a centuries-old practice in Egypt and elsewhere in the Arab and Islamic worlds. The earliest self-narratives are from the medieval period. As far as we know, however, only in this century have Arab women written accounts of their lives; of course, it is possible that future research may unearth earlier texts that are currently unknown.[17]

In Egypt the rise of the modern autobiographical tradition occurred following independence in 1922. It was developed by middle- and upper-class women and men who had played important roles in the political, intellectual, and sociocultural life of the country. The modern genre of autobiography is called in Arabic *tarjama hayat* (literally, interpretation of life) or *sira dhatiyya* (literally, self-created life story).[18] Egyptians often inscribed their life stories under the rubric of memoirs (in Arabic, *mudhakkirat* or *dhikriyyat*), suggesting the process of recall. The first modern autobiography was writer Taha Husain's *al-*

Ayyam (The Days), which appeared serially in *Majallat al-Hilal* from 1926 to 1927 and in a separate volume in 1929.[19] By the 1930s both women and men were publishing autobiographies, a practice that accelerated from the 1940s onward.

Nabawiyya Musa is one of the first two women, according to our current knowledge, to have published her life story, which she began in installments in May 1938. Umm Kulthum, the legendary Egyptian singer, serialized her memoirs several months earlier in the journal *Akhir Sa'a,* from November 1937 to January 1938. Hers, unlike Musa's, were written with the help of, or "with the pen of" Muhammad Hammad.[20] Other early autobiographical writings of women include the *Mudhakkirat* (Memoirs) of feminist leader Huda Sha'rawi, recorded around the middle 1940s but not published until the 1980s, and journalist and feminist Munira Thabit's *Thaura fi al-Burj al-'Aji: Mudhakkirat fi 'Ashrin 'Aman* (Revolution in the Ivory Tower: Memoirs of Twenty Years) published in 1945. Women's autobiographies continued into the 1950s. Actress and journalist Ruz al-Yusif's *Dhikriyyat Ruz al-Yusif* was published in 1953 and again in 1959, after her death.[21] Professor of Islamic thought and writer Bint al-Shati' (pseudonym for 'Aisha 'Abd al-Rahman) published *Sirr al-Shati'* (Life of al-Shati') in 1951 and a second autobiography in 1967 called *'Ala Jisr: Usturat al-Zaman* (On a Bridge: A Myth of Time).[22] 'Asma Fahmi, a teacher, published *Dhikriyyat 'an Madrasa al-Hilmiyya al-Thanawiyya lil-Banat* (Memories of the Hilmiyya Secondary School for Girls) in 1955. Singer 'Asmahan, of Lebanese origin, told about her life and singing career in Egypt from the late 1920s to the middle 1940s under the title *'Asmahan Tirwi Qissatuha* ('Asmahan Tells Her Story), "with the pen of" Muhammad al-Taba'i in 1965.[23] Another well-known performer of the same period, also of Lebanese origin, Bad'ia Masabni, published *Mudhakirrat Bad'ia Masabni* (The Memoirs of Bad'ia Masabni) "with the pen of" Nazik Basila.[24] The Egyptian actress Fatma Rushdi, born in 1910, recounted her story in the first half of the century in *Kifahi fi Masrah wa Sinima* (My Struggle in Theater and Cinema), published in 1971.[25] Feminist Duriyya Shafiq, active in the 1940s and early 1950s, began to write her memoirs after her house arrest in 1957 and continued period of self-imposed withdrawal from society. Her memoirs, in family hands, have not been published.[26] Feminist and social welfare activist Hawa Idris wrote about her mission from the 1930s onward in *Ana wa al-Sharq* (I and the East); she completed the work in the early 1970s, and it has been made available in limited numbers of privately bound copies. Feminist and artist Inji Aflatun, first active in the student movement of the middle 1940s, began her memoirs, but she died in 1990, before she could complete them.[27] Women's auto-biographical writing has covered later periods and continues to the present time.

Not all women were, or are, prepared to write autobiography. Some have appropriated distancing devices to mask the autobiographical. Women in Egypt have sometimes used biography to speak *auto*-biographically. Writer and critic Safinaz Kazim explained to me that her series of biographies in the paper *al-Watan* in the 1980s, which included a portrait of Nabawiyya Musa, carried autobiographical over-tones.[28] Marilyn Booth, a historian and literary specialist, detected a similar impulse in Lebanese writer May Ziyada's biographies of three women writers published early this century.[29] The writer Nawal al-Saadawi employed still another strategy in creating a fictional auto-biography, *Mudhakirrat al-Tabiba* (The Memoirs of a Woman Doctor), published in 1960.

Although both participated in the creation of the modern genre of autobiography, presentation of one's life had different connotations for Egyptian women and men. Writing about the self was a radical act for women, but not for men. Women's voices were considered *awra,* something shameful to be covered. *Awra,* which means puden-dum, carries specifically sexual connotations. Moreover, not simply women's voices but their entire beings were construed in sexual terms as *awra.* The prevailing ideology held that women as essentially sexual beings posed dangers to men, family, and society.[30] Men secluded women in order to control them—that is, women of the middle and upper classes, Muslims, Christians, and Jews alike, whose labor outside the home was not needed. Their lives were to be private and unseen. In the early decades of this century, as a result of continuing socio-economic and technological change in the urban world, middle- and upper-class women gradually emerged from domestic confinement to become an increasing presence in society.[31] They began to remove the facial veils that had rendered them invisible and deprived them of individual identity in society. Non-Muslim women were the first to do this.[32] Around 1909, when Musa began to run a school for girls in the Fayyum oasis, where veiling was generally not practiced, she quietly uncovered her face. Huda Sha'rawi removed her veil as an overt and confrontational political act in the train station in Cairo after returning from the feminist conference in Rome in 1923. Their two different ways of unveiling symbolized Musa's and Sha'rawi's divergent approaches to the process of women's liberation.

For all the controversy and antagonism connected with the issue of uncovering the face, the public disclosure of a woman's own life was far more challenging. Much of women's early practice of auto-biography can be seen as a feminist act of assertion, helping to shatter the complicity with patriarchal domination that had been effected through women's invisibility and silence.[33] Women's autobiography was exposure—it was entry into public discourse in a particular way and it was a shaping of it. It was a shedding of the patriarchal surrogate voice. Many of the pioneering autobiographers mentioned above, as we can see, were feminists. Most of the early female autobiographers who were not feminists were entertainers whose lives already, atyp-ically, *were* public, and as such had challenged or flaunted convention; by recounting what may not have been known, however, and shaping their larger life stories, these women, too, assumed special agency.

The Text

When Nabawiyya Musa set down her life for public consumption, she embarked on a radical enterprise. She chose her own periodical, *The Young Woman Magazine,* as the forum in which to publish her *Dhikriyyati* in weekly installments. As mentioned earlier, despite its title, the magazine aimed at a general readership.[34]

The mature Musa was a still feisty woman in the thick of battle when she began to resurrect her earlier defiant and victorious selves.[35] She opened the narrative of her life with the episode, "How I Started My Work Life and When My Troubles Began," establishing what would be a trope of trials and triumphs and a focus on her educational mission. She produced 91 installments, with little heed for historical sequence. She then started a new series, beginning chronologically by filling in the void of her early years, but soon abandoned this approach. The old and new series together contain a total of 152 episodes, many repetitive.

Musa presented her life as a struggle, a pattern of skirmishes and successes with her patriarchal enemies, whom she scathingly exposed in their perpetual attacks. She narrated how a young woman con-structed her own life, came of age as a teacher and headmistress, and played a role in shaping modern education in Egypt. If, as we have said, Musa's autobiography is the life of a pioneering educator in mod-ern Egypt, it is equally a testament to the evolution of her feminist and nationalist consciousness and activism. *Dhikriyyati* affords the reader an unprecedented opportunity to see a mode of feminism and a mode of nationalism that were not expressed in the context of a formal political organization or movement. It shows how an acute gender consciousness, coupled with a strong personal drive further heightened by nationalist awareness, incited her to manipulate her environment in order to transcend the limitations that might have stifled her. Her feminism did not announce itself as did the movement feminism of Huda Sha'rawi, with its highly visible discourse of protest and demands and its use of explicit feminist terminology and dramatic symbolic gestures. Although Musa had evolved a feminist consciousness and had honed feminist tools, she did not articulate her life in the language of feminism as did Sha'rawi.

Since Musa was from the modest middle class and Sha'rawi from the wealthy landowning class, they were positioned very differently and accordingly observed and operated from diverse vantage points. Musa's position was self-achieved, and one she had to struggle to maintain. She was in a relationship of dependence on the Ministry of Education for much of her career. Sha'rawi, on the other hand, was born into her circumstances and operated from a position of private wealth and elite social status that gave her considerable independence. Her status and condition were ascriptive. Musa's use of Arabic, the language of the majority, made her more widely accessible to her compatriots. If she had employed an explicit feminist vocabulary— which she would have had to coin—she would have risked antagonizing large segments of the population, including superiors in the Ministry of Education who held power over her.[36] On the other hand, because Sha'rawi spoke and wrote in French, the language of the elites, her outreach was restricted. These realities, combined with different personal choices and proclivities, set these two women from different classes on diverse paths in the service of their gender and nation.

Musa's autobiographical account affords us access to her less explicit, more pragmatic, and idiosyncratic brand of feminism. Musa was not part of a movement, and her memoirs do not indicate that she consciously considered herself a feminist. Musa never mentions her passing connection with the Egyptian Feminist Union. Musa clearly belongs to the history of feminism in Egypt, albeit among those historical actors whose feminism was less explicitly expressed. I, therefore, use a vocabulary for her feminism that is mine, not hers.

Self-Construction

This brief outline of Nabawiyya Musa's life confirms that she overcame barriers to self-expression in the kind of society and circumstances in which she found herself. In his memoirs, Egyptian writer and journalist Salama Musa (no relation), a contemporary of Nabawiyya Musa who came from the same town, gives a sense of the world into which she as a female was born: "Once I was struck by my sister because I had called her name in the street. It was considered just as improper for a girl's name to be heard in public as for her face to be seen."[37] How did Musa overcome the barriers in front of her? Clearly eager for her Egyptian readership to know, Musa tells the story of her self-construction in *Dhikriyyati.*

Musa relates that she was raised in a female-headed household on the pension of her army colonel father, who died before her birth. Her secondary status was impressed on her by her mother, who took Nabawiyya and her brother, ten years her senior, from Zagazig, the small town in the eastern Delta where she was born, to Cairo to advance *his* schooling.[38]

Musa, however, advanced *her own* education through self-creation, a leitmotif in her writing. Extracting help from her brother, she acquired the rudiments of Arabic through memorization. When she had taught herself the elements of writing, progressing from the mnemonic to the creative, she triumphantly composed her first verse. She narrates a painful scene in which her brother denigrated her first effort to write, but dispels the pain by saying that her uncle told her, "Don't pay attention to what he said. When you become educated none of us will be able to touch your writing."[39] Mastery of the word and mastery of the self converge, as domination by language becomes another trope in Musa's narrative of self-creation.

While memorizing served Musa in the first stages of learning and in acquisition of basic skills, she soon insisted on using her own mind and creative abilities, even in sacrosanct matters of religion. When the young Nabawiyya proceeded from the more passive and imitative task of memorizing the Koran to the active and individualist enterprise of interpretation, she again incurred censure and established victory. She recounts that a male relative studying at al-Azhar, the center of Islamic learning, chastised her for trying to interpret the Koran on her own without a religious guide, something even he, as a (male) student of religion, would not attempt, as it was tantamount to heresy. Ignoring this, she challenged him to explain a Koranic *aya* (verse). When he blundered through a blatant misreading of the Arabic, she pointed out his error and scorned him in verse. In a culture permeated by religion, Musa established her own ability to understand Islam and rejected passive acquiescence to the not infallible interpretation of male authority.[40]

In this episode Musa and her male relative represent two approaches to religion (and authority): acquiescence to the authority of religious figures (which the male relative could one day become, but Nabawiyya, as a woman, could not) and the reliance upon oneself to interpret religion. Individual interpretation, or *ijtihad,* was an Islamic method for understanding religion resurrected by the late nineteenth-century reformer Shaikh Muhammad 'Abduh as part of his doctrine of Islamic modernism, encouraging Muslims to reject non-Islamic practices and to apply religion to new circumstances. Within this context of Islamic modernism, pioneering feminists in Egypt, including Musa and Sha'rawi, articulated their approach to women's liberation.[41]

Finding her way to school (possible then only for middle-class girls, as tuition of elites was still strictly confined to the home) opened up a whole new life for Musa. She narrates how her brother played an initially helpful role in informing her about entry requirements for the Saniyya School.[42] Again, there was a pattern of obstacles and resistance. When, at her request for a mathematics tutor, her mother sought the help of her uncle, he responded with a famous proverb, saying, "Teach them to say words of love, not to write [learn]," advocating a sexual destiny (of marriage and motherhood) and implying the irrelevance, or impropriety, of literacy for females. Musa adds flippantly that her mother taught her neither, whereupon she solved the problem on her own by getting a mathematics book and teaching herself.[43]

In recounting her determination to attend school, a domain outside the domestic, family-centered world, Musa's narrative displays a break with maternal authority. When Musa announced her intention to go to school, her mother told her it "was a violation of decorum and modesty, and an affront to [her] good upbringing and to religion" and threatened to disown her.[44] The text then ironically discloses the unwitting collusion of the mother with the daughter's project as Nabawiyya marched off to register at the school, armed with the signet ring of her illiterate mother. When Nabawiyya learned she had passed the entrance examination, she gave her mother an ultimatum. If her mother stood in her way she would leave home and enter school as a boarder, paying her tuition out of her portion of her late father's pension. Her mother acquiesced—reluctant to forfeit the money, remarks Musa. At this point her brother enters the narrative reconstruction, warning his sister, "If you go to the Saniyya School I shall cease to know you." She snapped, "Then I shall have one less (male) relative and that's fine with me."[45] Musa paid her fees as a day student with the money she received from selling the jewelry her mother had given her, the conventional gift of feminine adornment from mother to daughter; she remarks that she found jewelry inappropriate to her newfound status as a student. The redeployment of elements of her social and cultural inheritance to rewrite her gendered destiny and serve her new self-chosen objectives is yet another trope in Musa's life narrative.

In her text Musa challenges the commonplace belief that an educated girl is a frivolous girl, exploding the stereotype with her portrayal of the young Nabawiyya. Earlier, in *The Woman and Work,* she had argued that education for women would make them more serious and better able to protect themselves.[46]

In Musa's youth, as we have seen, schooling was not the norm for a girl, but it was possible. Notions that female education constituted a violation of religion had been dispelled in state-encouraged tracts published in the nineteenth century that also explained that Islam favored the quest for knowledge by male and female believers alike.[47] Marriage, however, was a norm backed by religious injunction. Musa's rejection of marriage was her most obvious act of defiance, but gaining an education was also integral to this rebellion, as she shows in her autobiography when she links her pursuit of education to her escape from marriage:

> It [marriage] repelled me and perhaps my leaving home at the age of thirteen to go to school was because of my hatred for marriage. If I had stayed without work I could not have remained unmarried. I did not have the resources adequate to my needs.[48]

Musa relates how a series of suitors, who learned of her existence through articles she published in the newspapers, presented themselves for marriage. At some length she describes how she turned each down; she was earning good money that they could not match. When one suitor suggested that she continue to work after marriage, she rejected it as an absurd notion in words that showed she had no interest in what later would be called the "double burden." (Society also frowned on what might have been termed "split loyalties," for not until the 1930s were married women allowed to teach in the state schools.)[49] The burden, Musa implies, was not simply a pragmatic one, but included the general weight of male domination that came with marriage. In the context of discussing her escape from marriage she declares: "I preferred to live as the master of men, not their servant."[50] Musa also surely rejected the specter of reconfinement in the domestic sphere from which she had adroitly escaped by going to school and then to work.

Publication of such astonishingly blunt views on marriage as Musa's is unusual in the context of Egyptian society and culture, both in her day and now, at the end of the century. She makes her deep aversion to marriage evident:

> I hated marriage and considered it dirt and had decided not to soil myself with this dirt. Since childhood, I had believed that marriage was animalistic and degrading to women and I could not bear [the thought of] it.[51]

When we contrast the approaches Musa takes to marriage in her treatise and in her autobiography, we see that she is careful to uphold the ideal of marriage and motherhood as women's first and paramount roles in *The Woman and Work,* while in *Dhikriyyati* she gives firm reasons for her rejection, even denigration, of marriage. In her treatise, Musa's main aim was to promote schooling and work for women early this century, when they were still barely possibilities even for middle-class women; accordingly, she took care to dispel fears she knew people would have that education and work might divert women from what were deemed their "natural" roles. But by the late 1930s, major battles for women in education and work had been won. Musa herself was at the pinnacle of her own career and no longer an employee of the Ministry of Education but an independent educator, heading her own private schools. She could also more "safely" make her position known by presenting it as her experience and commenting upon it.

A different sort of contentious matter Musa takes up in her auto-biography is the controversy over *sufur* (unveiling) and *hijab* (veiling). On this subject, her position is the same in both *The Woman and Work* and *Dhikriyyati.* In *Dhikriyyati* she borrows from her intro-duction to *The Woman and Work,* where she had written:

> I have dealt with all the subjects relating to Egyptian women, but I have not dealt with what they now call *sufur* and *hijab* because I believe these are academic terms the meanings of which we are quite ignorant. I cannot call the peasant woman unveiled because she does not wear the transparent veil that is known to us city women. The peasant woman goes about her way modestly. . . . I cannot call some of the city women veiled when they go out immodestly covered with ornaments and jewelry attracting the eyes of the passerby while on their face they wear a veil that conceals nothing but timidity.[52]

Musa wanted to shift the debate away from *sufur* versus *hijab* to an emphasis on *hishma,* or modesty, which also transcends categories such as "traditional" and "modern" (veiling being seen as traditional and unveiling as modern). In *Dhikriyyati,* Musa illustrates her point when she narrates an encounter she had with a woman on a tram who asked her if she was Christian because her face was uncovered (as already noted, Christians in Egypt began to unveil earlier than Muslims). Musa replied to the woman that she was behaving more correctly than she, herself, was, telling her that not only did her transparent veil not hide her face, but, she said, "I see what I should not see of your bosom and I see your arms [which Muslim women are enjoined to cover] from beginning to end but you cannot see anything of me but my face [which Islam does not enjoin women to cover]."[53] She also reconstructs an exchange she had with a male writer in the offices of the Cairo daily, *al-Ahram,* who insisted on the face veil for women. After reminding him that his female relatives in the village did not cover their faces (it was not customary among peasant women) she said: "Sir, you claim that men are wiser and more rational than women. If women are not seduced by your faces, and some of you are indeed handsome, how could you men who are more rational be seduced by women's faces? You should be veiled and women unveiled."[54]

At the end of the 1930s and the beginning of the 1940s, she observes in *Dhikriyyati,* "What I foresaw came true. Now the women of Egypt are unveiled and men have started to attack the mentality of the veiled woman. Yes, what I envisioned came true but not in the way I had wanted. Unveiling was accompanied by *tabarraj,* flashiness, which I did not expect the respectable Egyptian woman to fall prey to, especially the educated women. But who knows, maybe it is a passing thing. Perhaps later we shall return to modest unveiling."[55] Musa's prescient speculation about the future has been echoed with the renewed concern for modesty and the reveiling of the head and body (and sometimes the face) that surfaced in the 1970s, two decades after Musa's death.

By early adulthood, Musa had achieved considerable self-definition and had secured her personal independence. She had acquired status and her own means of support, and in so doing was able to thwart society's project of making marriage her destiny. Yet, she was still a female in a patriarchal society and subject to controls imposed, in part, by the (patriarchal) culture's code of morality. Musa, unveiled and single, hence vulnerable, upheld this code to protect herself in her everyday life and made it serve her wider ends.

Lines of Battle: Colonialism

Musa's autobiography sets up a model in which a daughter's girlhood is distinguished from adult, outer-directed womanhood and autonomy.

Until the age of twenty Musa narrates her efforts as directed toward the "feminist project" of constructing her own life. When she enters the work force she represents her "feminism" as taking on a more collective and public dimension. Defying the conventional life script, and those who sought to impose it, Musa enters into a new stage of combat lasting the rest of her life. For nearly the first two decades of her work life, as during her school days, Musa had to contend with the omnipresence of British colonial rule. Colonialism oppressed Egyptians in gender- and class-specific ways, often doubly oppressing women. At the same time, it sometimes promoted new roles for women and in so doing gave rise to tensions across (indigenous) gender lines, an unexplored form of colonial divide and rule.[56] In the struggle against colonialism, Egyptians played roles determined in certain ways by class and gender. Musa's nationalism, like her feminism, was articulated in the context of her professional life. Unlike Sha'rawi, whose nationalist activism during the independence struggle was conducted (like her postindependence feminism) within the framework of a political organization and was militantly expressed in slogans, demands, and demonstrations,[57] Musa's nationalist activism (like her lifelong feminist activism) was embedded in her regular life and articulated more subtly. Musa's *Dhikriyyati* illuminates intersections between her feminism and nationalism and sheds light on forms of indigenous and colonial patriarchal oppressions she experienced.

Musa used her autobiography to elucidate her mode of nationalist activism. Her nationalism—a nationalism with a feminist dimension— has to be understood in the context of her position as a middle-class teacher in a government school. Unlike Sha'rawi, whose life was secured by her upper-class status and wealth, Musa could not politically agitate without professional and economic risk. It was not, however, simply pragmatic considerations that moved Musa, but the conviction that building an educated citizenry, especially educated female citizens, was integral to achieving real independence and preserving national identity. In *The Woman and Work* (which, as mentioned previously, was published during the national revolution) she stresses women's central role in strengthening Egyptian identity and expanding the national work force:

> The best service that can be done for the country that we are ready to die for is to direct the attention of women toward education and work. . . . This conviction has inspired me to publish this book in the hope that it will have some effect.[58]

Recounting her position and actions during the revolution of 1919-22, when she was headmistress of the Wardiyyan Women Teachers

Training School in Alexandria, Musa discloses how class and gender operated in the nationalist struggle. During that period when (male) students and teachers were frequently out on strike, Musa did not allow herself, her teachers, or her students, to participate in demonstrations. That could have led to the closure of her school and the end of her career, neither of which she believed would have benefited Egypt.[59] Demonstrating, she says, would also have played into the hands of her (Egyptian male) enemies within the educational system who would have been relieved to have her out of the way. She writes:

> I loved, and still love, education which fully preoccupied me and kept me from involvement in politics because I believed that a person serves their country through the work in which they excel and through that alone. . . . In my view striking in schools does not help the country.[60]

> We can help in our own ways such as advocating the spread of girls' education which our country greatly needs. It is a non-threatening endeavor with which no one can interfere and something noble that will greatly benefit the country and have a long-term impact.[61]

The moral dimension was salient as well. Musa objected to women under her charge going out on demonstrations with men because it would endanger the women's reputations and pose a moral threat to them:

> I was unhappy that nationalist activity might be a reason for women teachers to violate codes of modesty and decorum and be an occasion for frivolity.[62]

Later, she states, "I explained to them that taking part in street demonstrations was not fitting to our dignity as oriental women."[63]

Musa discloses to her readers how the men who were her adversaries in the Ministry of Education called into question her nationalist credentials as a way to goad her into striking in order to bring about her downfall as an anti-British agitator. She reveals how gender strife perpetrated by certain Egyptian men in the Ministry of Education overrode nationalist solidarity even during the independence struggle.

Representing Victory

As an illustration of Musa's imbrication of issues of gender and nationalism, I want to consider an episode representative of her confrontation with authority. Musa had been active in state education for two

decades, a period full of battles with both colonial and Egyptian superiors and colleagues in the Ministry of Education. Her text is replete
with tales of traps set on all fronts to bring her down and of her
skillful maneuvers to maintain her position. She claims the British
authorities in the Ministry of Education preferred to keep her inside
the system and under their control rather than allowing her to slip
into private education, where she might become a threat to the colonial
presence. In the first two decades of the century, the schools were
sites of nationalist agitation and resistance, and teachers and students
alike were closely watched. Musa relates incident after incident in
which her Egyptian foes inside the Ministry of Education tried to create
her downfall by reporting to the colonial authorities that she was a
threat to their rule.

However, it was not during colonial occupation but four years after
independence that Musa's downfall came, in March 1926, when she
was fired by the Ministry of Education. One report says she was
dismissed because she opposed new appointments of foreign headmistresses in government schools, motivated Egyptian headmistresses
and women inspectors against the Ministry of Education, and accused
senior officials in the Ministry of Education of making sexual advances
toward women teachers. While these may have been among the reasons, complete understanding of the truth of the matter requires more
research.[64] She tells her readers that accusations leveled against her
could not be substantiated by her employment record at the Ministry
of Education; consequently, she claims a new file was fabricated, "one
hundred and forty-eight pages filled with nonsense and imaginings."[65]
Musa further relates how the two lawyers she had retained, one after
the other, allowed themselves to be manipulated by the judges in court
into agreeing that the testimony on Musa's behalf be read *in camera*
rather than aloud in the courtroom. She claims that this caused her
to lose her case against the government and tells her readers how she
appealed the case and decided to take up her own defense. This was
the ultimate act of agency in quest of self-vindication by the woman
who had created and protected herself:

> I appealed the decision the same day. I wrote in the news-
> papers that I had dismissed my lawyers and that I would take
> up my own defense in court. The announcement created an
> uproar in various circles. People awaited the day the court
> would convene to examine my case in order to see the
> woman defend herself in an important case against the gov-
> ernment. That was what I wanted. I had seen that a defense
> conducted between four walls would not shame the court but

if it were done before the general public it would be an important force pushing the court towards justice.[66]

Musa elaborates on how, rallying the people to her side, she defended herself:

> I wanted to speak on the matter of the claim but the court wanted to prevent me. However, I insisted upon my right to speak. The people in the courtroom went into an uproar. Some of them shouted, "Let her speak. Let her speak. Where is justice?" I spoke and gave a full explanation of my case without the court being able to stop me. Whenever the court wanted to stop me from introducing some facts, I adamantly insisted on my right to speak and the public increased their uproar and show of disgust. When the session ended those present were convinced that I had been treated unfairly and that what I had demanded was just and that my explanations were sound. The representative of the government stood up to give the government defense in the case but was unable to say anything significant. His arguments were weak and the public was against him. Whenever he started to speak the people went into an uproar. . . . When the court adjourned newspaper photographers were waiting for me and took pictures.[67]

Musa won her case for compensation. She adds that Fikri Abaza (a prominent journalist) wrote: "In doing what she did Nabawiyya blocked the way for lawyers to earn a living."[68] Musa says that winning her defense and passing her baccalaureate examination, which also gained her public acclaim, were achievements that gave her the two happiest days of her life.

Possibilities of Autobiography

The Moroccan feminist scholar Fatima Mernissi writes, "Memory and recollection are the dawn of pleasure; they speak the language of freedom and self-development."[69] This assessment applies to Nabawiyya Musa's *Dhikriyyati*. At the peak of her life, when she began to record it with a zest and fierceness, she was having, as it were, her day in court. Declarative and defiant, Musa speaks the language of freedom in *Dhikriyyati*.

During the militant phase of the national revolution, eighteen years before she began her autobiography, Musa enunciated her agenda in *The Woman and Work,* supporting education and work for women while upholding moral/cultural values, for the betterment of women and the good of the nation. Hers was a program for female relief from patriarchal oppression and for the rescue of the nation from colonial oppression. In her treatise Musa refuses binary oppositions: the prevailing social construction of gender that essentialized male and female as "two separate species"[70] and the contest between veiling and unveiling, with implications of modest or immodest, (morally) right or (morally) wrong, "traditional" or "modern."

I have deliberately given space for Musa's autobiographical voice to resonate. Hers is an unfamiliar voice, long silenced through neglect, one that displays the range of fine-tuning and concretizing she found possible in the self-narrative but not the treatise. *Dhikriyyati* illustrates how a feminist and nationalist project can be embedded in autobiography and elucidates Musa's process in a highly particularized and historicized way that allows space for intersections and contradictions. Autobiography enabled Musa to expound and reveal the feminism and nationalism that inflected her educational mission. Through autobiography she could delineate the contours and details of patriarchal oppressions and expose levels of hypocrisy.

At one level Musa was simply a historical scribe, yet she was also the shaper of the tale and the interpreter of the past. Not only had she entered the public arena of active struggle and achieved personhood in an asymmetrically gendered world, but she entered the public arena of written discourse. Her life was best re-presented as a struggle with the trope of trials and triumphs. As a woman Musa was kept out of the new Egyptian University, was unable to fulfill her wish to become a lawyer, was professionally buffeted by colonial authorities, and was fired outright by the Ministry of Education after independence. But she managed to construct a meaningful life for herself against all odds and opposition.

Musa showed how it was a struggle to be both the same and equal in a society where difference was minutely gendered and the male was highly privileged and empowered. The male Egyptians pioneering in writing modern autobiography narrated lives lived at the center and the top of the new "democratic" order; they lived and wrote their lives as full citizens in the newly independent Egypt. In writing the history of the female Egyptian, Musa "celebrated" struggle, using the narrative re-creation of it as both mirror and prism. Her autobiography recorded the experience and furnished a model of an Egyptian Muslim woman who had forged and sustained a life for herself. For Musa autobiography was finally "the dawn of pleasure," if pleasure is satisfaction that a life has been lived and retold with purpose.

Notes

1. See Huda Sha'rawi, *Harem Years: The Memoirs of an Egyptian Feminist,* trans. and ed. Margot Badran (New York: Feminist Press, 1987). I first saw the memoirs in 1967. The copy of the memoirs in the possession of 'Abd al-Hamid Fahmi Mursi was published in 1981 under the title *Mudhakirrat Ra'ida al-'Arabiyya al-Haditha Huda Sha'rawi* (Memoirs of the Modern Arab Pioneer Huda Sha'rawi) (Cairo: Dar al-Hilal).

2. For some of these writings, see Margot Badran and Miriam Cooke, *Opening the Gates: A Century of Arab Feminist Writing* (Bloomington: Indiana University Press, 1990).

3. Two of my works that explore feminist ideologies and activisms in Egypt from the late nineteenth century to the present are "Idependent Women: More than a Century of Feminism in Egypt," in *Arab Women: Old Boundaries, New Frontiers,* ed. Judith Tucker (Bloomington: Indiana University Press, with the Institute for Contemporary Arab Studies, Georgetown University, forthcoming); "Competing Agenda: Feminists, Islam, and the State in Nineteenth and Twentieth Century Egypt," in *Women, Islam, and the State,* ed. Deniz Kandiyoti (Philadelphia: Temple University Press, 1991). Also see Akram Khater and Cynthia Nelson, "Al-Harakah al-Nissa'iyah: The Women's Movement and Political Participation in Modern Egypt," *Women's Studies International Forum* 2 (1988): 465–83. Concerning the meanings of feminism, see my article, "Ma hiyya Ma'na al-Nisa'iyya?" (What Is the Meaning of Feminism?), *Nisf al-Dunya* (Cairo), 21 September 1990. As a member of the Arab Women's Solidarity Association (AWSA), I participated in an AWSA conference in Cairo in 1988 where feminism was debated and presented a paper titled "Feminism as a Force in the Arab World," which was later published in *Contemporary Thought and Women* (Cairo: AWSA Press, 1989 [Arabic]; 1990 [English]).

4. On the origin of the term *feminism,* see Karen Offen, "Defining Feminism: A Comparative Historical Approach," *Signs* 14 (Autumn 1988): 119–47.

5. See Margot Badran, "Gender Activism: Feminists and Islamists in Egypt" (Paper presented at the Roundtable on Identity Politics and Women, United Nations University World Institute for Development Economics Research, Helsinki, October 1990).

6. Nabawiyya Musa, *al-Mar'a wa al-'Amal* (Alexandria: National Press, 1920).

7. Her father, Musa Muhammad, was an army colonel who died before she was born, while on a mission to the Sudan.

8. Recalling the same period, Amir Boktor wrote: "Women from the poorest homes were attracted to the teaching profession. . . . Only in the last ten years [mid 1920s to mid 1930s] have more Egyptian girls come into the profession." *School and Society in the Valley of the Nile* (Cairo: Elias Modern Press, 1936), 185. "Work for a girl of a middle class family, or even of a lower class status, is an act of indecency." Ibid., 75.

9. Musa was 78th out of a total 2,783 male and female students. She did better in the Arabic examination that the future writer Muhammad 'Abbas al-'Aqqad, who came out 166th overall, and the future prime minister, Muhammad al-Nuqrashi, who was 64th overall. See Ahmad 'Atiya 'Abd Allah, "al-Taliba alati Tafqwwaqat 'ala al-Nuqrashi and al-'Aqaad" (The Female Student who Topped al-Nuqrashi and al-'Aqqad), clipping dated 11 May 1951, in Nabawiyya Musa file 3 2357, Dar al-Hilal (the source of the clipping was not appended). The author was then director of the Education Museum.

10. On the beginnings of the Egyptian University and the Women's Section, see Donald Reid, *Cairo University and the Making of Modern Egypt* (New York: Cambridge University Press, 1990), 51–56; on Musa's lecturing experience, see Nabawiyya Musa, "al-Muhadarat al-Nisa'iyya fi al-Jam'ia al-misriyya" (Women's Lectures in the Egyptian

University), *al-Ahram,* 16 April 1912 (reprinted in *al-Ahram, Shuhud al-'Asr 1876–1986* [Cairo, 1986], 38–42; cited in Reid, *Cairo University,* 244); Margot Badran, "The Origins of Feminism in Egypt," in *Current Issues in Women's History,* ed. Arina Angerman, Geerte Binnema, Annemieke Keunen, Vefie Poels, and Jacqueline Zirkzee (London: Routledge, 1989); idem, "From Consciousness to Activism: Feminist Politics in Early Twentieth Century Egypt," in *Problems of the Middle East in Historical Perspective,* ed. John Spangolo (London: Ithaca, 1991).

11. A secondary school for girls with the same curriculum as that for boys had been one of the first two demands the Egyptian Feminist Union made in 1923.

12. The information on Musa's life is obtained mainly from her *Dhikriyyati* (henceforth referred to as NM). Brief biographical profiles include Khair al-Din al-Zirkali, *al-'Alam Qamus Tarajam li Ashar al-Rijal wa al-Nisa' min al-'Arab wa Must'aribin wa Mustashriqin* (Biographical Dictionary of the Most Famous Arab, Arabist, and Orientalist Men and Women), 2nd ed., vol. 8 (Cairo, n.d.), 321–22; Ahmad Zaki 'Abd al-Halim, *Nisa' fawq al-Qima* (Extraordinary Women) (Cairo: Dar al-Faisal, n.d.), 18–24.

13. It is interesting that Musa speaks only once of Huda Sha'rawi in her memoirs, in "Musa'adat al-Sayyida al-Jalila Huda Hanim Sha'rawi" (The Help of Huda Sha'rawi), First Series, no. 14. (The autobiographical installments of *Dhikriyyati* that appeared in *Majallat al-Fatah* are cited throughout according to series and number.) She tells how, in response to Musa's request, Sha'rawi made emergency funds available to Musa to secure new premises for her school. Huda Sha'rawi's feminist movement was the subject of my D. Phil. thesis, "Huda Sha'rawi and the Liberation of the Egyptian Woman" (Oxford University, 1977).

14. The first issue of *Majallat al-Fatah* appeared on 20 October 1937. It is worth noting that the EFU's Arabic language journal, *al-Misriyya (The Egyptian Woman,* counterpart to EFU's *L'Egyptienne,* established in 1925) was first issued seven months earlier, on 15 February 1937.

15. The government put her in prison alongside prostitutes. Safinaz Kazim has spoken of this indignity in "al-Ra'ida Nabawiyya Musa wa In'ash Dhakirrat al-'Umma" (The Pioneer Nabawiyya Musa and the Reviving of the Nation's Memory), *Majallat al-Hilal,* January 1984.

16. For example, she is mentioned briefly in Ijalal Khalifa, *al-Haraka al-Nisa'iyya al-Haditha* (The Modern Feminist Movement) (Cairo, 1974). Musa has received more attention over the years in short articles in the Egyptian press than in books.

17. Early autobiographies in the Islamic Middle East include, for example, al-Ghazzali (d. 1111), *al-Munqidh min al-Dalal;* and Idn Khaldun (d. 1406), *al-Ta'rif.* On early or "traditional" autobiography, see Franz Rosenthal, "Die Arabische Autobiographie," *Analecta Orientalia* 14, *Studie Arabica* (1937); Gustave E. von Grunebaum, "Self-Expression: Literature and History," and "The Human Ideal," in *Medieval Islam,* 2nd ed. (Chicago, 1953), 221–93; Fadwa Malti-Douglas, *Blindness and Autobiography* (Princeton, N.J.: Princeton University Press, 1988), 9–10. On Arab women's autobiographies, see Badran and Cooke, *Opening the Gates,* xxxv. For an example from South Asia, see Stephen Frederic Dale, "Steppe Humanism: The Autobiographical Writings of Zahir al-Din Muhammad Babur, 1483–1530," *International Journal of Middle East Studies* 22 (February 1990): 37–58.

18. I cannot date the start of the use of the terms *tarjama hayat* or *sira dhatiyya,* although the term *sira,* or biography, is ancient, *al-Sira* being the biography of the Islamic prophet, Muhammad. It is interesting to note that the English word *autobiography* first appeared in print only in 1809. On autobiography, see Shawqi Dayf, *al-Tarjama al-Shakhsiyya* (Cairo: Dar al-Ma'arif, 1979); Ihsan 'Abbas, *Fann al-Sira* (Beirut: Dar al-Thaqafa, 1956).

19. See Malti-Douglas, *Blindness and Autobiography.*

20. "With the pen of" is a direct translation from the Arabic; it can indicate merely scribal help or possibly further assistance in shaping the narrative. Awad says that "Umm Kulthum wrote it [her memoirs] out for me." However, ascertaining the extent of assistance that "with the pen of" represents for the other autobiographies mentioned below in the text would require further research. Umm Kulthum's memoirs published in *Akhir Sa'a* were republished in *Umm Kulthum alati la Ya'rifuha Ahad* (The Umm Kulthum Nobody Knows) (Cairo: Mu'assat Akhbar al-Yaum, 1971) by Mahmud Awad, who added more material; an English translation of the memoirs, "Excerpts from *The Umm Kulthum Nobody Knows,*" is found in Elizabeth Fernea and Basima Qattan Bezirgan, eds., *Middle Eastern Muslim Women Speak* (Austin: University of Texas, 1977), 135–67.

21. Her autobiography was written by the then young journalist Ahmad Baha al-Din. See Sonia Dabbous, "Studying an Egyptian Journalist: Rose al-Youssef, a Woman and a Journal," *Islamic and Mediterranean Women's History Network Newsletter* 1 (Spring/Fall 1988): 11–12.

22. See C. Kooij, "Bint Al-Shati': A Suitable Case for Biography?" in *The Challenge of the Middle East: Middle East Studies at the University of Amsterdam,* ed. Ibrahim A. El-Sheikh, C. Aart van de Koppel, and Rudolf Peters (Amsterdam: Institute for Modern Near Eastern Studies, University of Amsterdam, 1982).

23. 'Asmahan, *'Asmahan Tirwi Qissatuha* (Asmahan Tells Her Story), with the pen of Muhammad al-Taba'i (Cairo: Mu'assat Ruz al-Yusif, 1965).

24. Bad'ia Masabni, *Mudhakirrat Bad'ia Masabni* (The Memoirs of Bad'ia Masabni), with the pen of Nazik Basila (Beirut: Dar Maktabat al-Hiyat, n.d.).

25. Fatma Rushdi, *Kifahi fi Masrah wa Sinima* (My Struggle in Theater and Cinema) (Cairo: Dar al-Ma'aris).

26. See Cynthia Nelson, "The Voices of Doria Shafiq: Feminist Consciousness in Egypt, 1940–60," *Feminist Issues* (Fall 1986): 15–31.

27. A leftist and feminist in the student movement after World War II, she was jailed under Nasser from 1959 to 1963 and afterward kept a low profile, working exclusively as an artist. In an interview in 1988 Aflatun told me she was working on her memoirs. She published *Thamanun Maliyun Imraa Ma'na* (Eighty Million Women with Us) in 1948 and *Nahnu al-Nisa al-Misriyyat* (We Egyptian Women) in 1949. Michelle Raccagni has written an unpublished paper titled "Inji Efflatoun, Author, Artist, and Militant: A Brief Analysis of Her Life and Works."

28. Personal communication, Cairo, March 1989.

29. Marilyn Booth, "Biography and Feminist Rhetoric in Early Twentieth-Century Egypt: Mayy Ziyada's Studies of Three Women's Lives," *Journal of Women's History* 3 (Spring 1991): 38–64.

30. See Fatna A. Sabah, *Women in the Muslim Unconscious,* trans. Mary Jo Lakeland (New York: Pergamon, 1984).

31. On the life of an upper-class woman, see Sha'rawi, *Mudhakirrat Ra'ida al-'Arabiyya al-Haditha Huda Sha'rawi* and *Harem Years.*

32. See Beth Baron, "Unveiling in Early Twentieth Century Egypt: Practical and Symbolic Considerations," *Middle Eastern Studies* 25 (July 1989): 370–86.

33. About Huda Sha'rawi's memoirs I have said, "Writing about her life during the harem years was a final unveiling. It can be seen as Huda Shaarawi's final feminist act." Sha'rawi, *Harem Years,* 1.

34. Musa had also called her poetry collection *Diwan al-Fatah,* or *The Young Woman Collection of Poems. Al-Fatah* means "young woman," but it could also signify an unmarried woman. Using *al-Fatah* could be an assertion of her independent status—

which she fought to preserve in a society expecting every woman to marry. *Diwan al-Fatah* celebrated the status of the independent woman. *The Young Woman Magazine* was a woman speaking to women and men, and not in the tradition of the women's journals aimed at female audiences. And as an Arabic periodical, its largest audience was middle class. On the early Arabic women's press, see Beth Ann Baron, "The Rise of a New Literary Culture: The Women's Press of Egypt, 1892–1919" (Ph.D. diss., University of California, Los Angeles, 1988).

35. By the time she began to publish her memoirs, Musa had long since been the butt of ridicule in the press and the subject of numerous cartoons portraying her covered from tip to toe in the traditional *abaya* (the long black wrap that by then was worn mainly by more conservative women and those of the lower class), bespectacled and "ugly," usually in a haranguing posture. She actually appropriated this kind of caricature in her own magazine, turning to her own ends. The woman who broke convention in writing about her own life had already gained a notoriety that gave her a certain freedom.

36. For an analysis of the sociocultural significance of language for the transmission of feminist thought, see Irene Fenoglio-Abd El Aal, *Defense et Illustration de l'Egyptienne: aux Debuts d'une expression feminine* (Cairo: Centre d'Etudes et Documentation Economique, Juridique, et Sociale, 1988).

37. Boktor, *School and Society,* 7.

38. NM, "Tufulati" (My Childhood), First Series, no. 70, and Second Series, no. 1.

39. NM, "Tufulati," Second Series, no. 1.

40. Ibid.

41. On Islamic modernism, see Albert Hourani, *Arabic Thought in the Liberal Age* (Cambridge: Cambridge University Press, 1983), 130–63.

42. The Saniyya School was created in 1889, incorporating the Siufiyya School founded by Tcheshme Hanim, a wife of the Kehdive Tawfiq, in 1873 (the first state-connected school for girls) and the Qirabiyya School, founded the following year. At the beginning of the twentieth century the Saniyya School became the training ground for middle-class women in Egypt to become teachers. For reminiscences on the early classes, see NM, "Nahda Ta'lim al-Banat fi Misr" (The Renaissance of Girls' Education in Egypt), Second Series, no. 3.

43. NM, "Kaifa Dakhaltu Madrasat al-Saniyya" (How I Entered the Saniyya School), Second Series, no. 3.

44. Ibid.

45. Ibid.

46. "Ta'thir al-Kutub wa Riwayyat fi al-Akhlaq" (The Effects of Books and Novels on Morals), in Musa, *The Woman and Work,* 89–96.

47. See Shaikh Ahmad Rifa'i al-Tahtawi, *Tariq al-Hija wa al-Tamrin 'ala Qawaid al-Lugha al-'Arabiyya* (The Intelligent Way and Exercise in Employing the Rules of the Arabic Language) (Cairo: 1869) and 'Ali Pasha Mubarak, *al-Murshid al-Amin lil-Banat wa al-Banin* (The Faithful Guide for Girls and Boys) (Cairo: 1875).

48. NM, "Athar Husuli 'ala al-Bakkaluriyya wa Madhhabi fi al-Zawwaj" (The Result of My Success in the Baccalaureate Examination and My View of Marriage), Second Series, no. 18.

49. NM, "Madhhabi fi al-Zawwaj" (My View of Marriage), First Series, no. 22.

50. Ibid.

51. Ibid.

52. Musa, "al-Muqaddima" (Introduction), in *The Woman and Work;* NM, "Sufuri" (My Unveiling), Second Series, no. 15.

53. NM, "Sufuri," Second Series, no. 15.

54. Ibid.

55. Ibid.

56. On women's new roles, see Judith Tucker, *Women in Nineteenth Century Egypt* (Cambridge: Cambridge University Press, 1985).

57. See Margot Badran, "Dual Liberation: Feminism and Nationalism in Egypt, 1870s–1925," *Feminist Issues* (Spring 1988): 15–34.

58. Musa, "al-Muqqadima," 3–5.

59. A woman who had been a teacher in one of Musa's schools in a latter period recalled how Musa instilled a nationalist spirit in her students and that she invited outside speakers to talk on current events. See "Mudhakkirat Mudarissa" (Memoirs of a Teacher), *al-Jumhuriyya,* 16 November 1970. The teacher's name is not given.

60. NM, "Wathifa Wakila" (The Job of Deputy Headmistress), Second Series, no. 61.

61. NM, "Insha' Madrasat Tarqiyya al-Fatah" (The Establishment of the Tarqiyya al-Fatah School), Second Series, no. 75.

62. NM, "Kaifa Kuntu U'aqab 'ala al-Qiyam bi-Wajab Siyanat al-Akhlaq" (How I Was Punished for Performing the Duty of Maintaining Morals), First Series, no. 9.

63. NM, "Insha' Madrasat Tarqiyya al-Fatah."

64. Muhammad Abu al-Hadid, "Misriyya Tathada al-Rijal" (An Egyptian Woman Who Challenged Men), *al-Jumhuriyya,* 21 August 1975.

65. NM, "Qissa al-Dhi'ab wa al-Hamal" (The Story of the Wolf and the Lamb), First Series, no. 37.

66. NM, "Yaum al-Mahkama" (The Day in Court), First Series, no. 38.

67. Ibid.

68. Ibid.

69. Fatima Mernissi, *Women and Islam: An Historical and Theological Enquiry,* trans. Mary Jo Lakeland (Oxford: Basil Blackwell, 1991), 10.

70. Musa, "al-Farq bain al-Rajil wa al-Mar'a" (The Differences between Men and Women), in *The Woman and Work,* 21–36.

PART IV

The Counterhegemonic "I"

Chapter 14

The Subject of Memoirs: *The Woman Warrior's* Technology of Ideographic Selfhood

Lee Quinby

In his 1982 essay "The Subject and Power," Michel Foucault argues that the modern era places individuals in a "kind of political 'double-bind,' which is the simultaneous individualization and totalization of modern power structures." He further suggests that "maybe the target nowadays is not to discover what we are but to refuse what we are," adding that, since this is the case, "we have to promote new forms of subjectivity through the refusal of this kind of individuality which has been imposed on us for several centuries."[1] I do not know whether Foucault was familiar with Maxine Hong Kingston's *The Woman Warrior*, published six years earlier. But Kingston, it seems, in the words she uses to describe her childhood dream of becoming a warrior woman, had anticipated that "the call would come."[2] In *The Woman Warrior* she promotes "new forms of subjectivity" by refusing the totalizing individuality of the modern era.

Kingston's refusal rejects the fields of representation that have promoted that subjectivity. The subtitle of *The Woman Warrior* specifies its genre: *Memoirs of a Girlhood among Ghosts*. Kingston has emphasized the importance of this subtitle in an essay called "Cultural Misreadings by American Reviewers," in which she reemphasizes her work's genre by stating that she is "not writing history or sociology but a 'memoir' like Proust." She writes approvingly of two reviewers who recognize this point, stating that she is, "as Diane Johnson says, 'slyly writing a memoir, a form which . . . can neither [be] dismiss[ed] as fiction nor quarrel[ed] with as fact,'" and confirming Christine Cook's comment that "the structure is a grouping of memoirs. . . . It is by definition a series of stories or anecdotes to illuminate the times rather than be autobiographical."[3]

Despite these efforts at clarification, critics have continued to ignore or resist the implications of Kingston's work as memoirs. The insightful and eloquent discussions of Paul John Eakin and Sidonie Smith acknowledge that Kingston's work challenges distinctions between fact and fiction, but they still treat the work as an autobiography rather than as memoirs. Although their respective discussions convert the *autos* or self of autobiography into a "self" understood as self-invention (Eakin) or self-representation (Smith), their readings of the work *as an autobiography*—even a postmodern one—delimit its full-scale assault on modern power structures.[4] My contention is that autobiography is a field of self-representation that has historically promoted the normalizing and disciplinary form of subjectivity that, as Foucault points out, we should "target." In what follows, I examine the ways in which the five memoirs that constitute *The Woman Warrior* subject modern power formations to the scrutiny of one who has been subjected by them.[5] I want to illuminate the ways in which *The Woman Warrior* constructs a new form of subjectivity, what I call an *ideographic selfhood*. This new subjectivity refuses the particular forms of selfhood, knowledge, and artistry that the systems of power of the modern era (including the discourses of autobiography) have made dominant.

Reading *The Woman Warrior* as memoirs rather than as autobiography has more at stake than redressing aesthetic assumptions regarding genre. It serves to direct attention to the particular formation of subjectivity constructed by these different discourses and the technologies of power within which they operate as self-constituting practices. Modern memoirs as a genre emerged more than two centuries prior to modern autobiography; the *Oxford English Dictionary* (*OED*) lists the date of the first appearance of the singular *memoir* as 1567 and of the plural *memoirs* as 1659. *Autobiography* makes its first appearance in 1809. But as James M. Cox has argued, the term *autobiography* is now "so dominant that it is used retroactively to include as well as to entitle books from the present all the way back into the ancient world."[6] This expansion of autobiography is a form of discursive colonization that, both as an authorial choice of genre and as a critical designation, produces and is produced by the normalizing subjectivity that has come to dominate the post-Enlightenment West.

The ways of constituting an "I" within these respective discursive formations demonstrate some of the key differences between them, differences that have been instrumental in establishing autobiography as a privileged aesthetic and ethical discourse of the modern era and in maintaining a marginalized status for memoirs. Whereas autobiography promotes an "I" that shares with confessional discourse an assumed interiority and an ethical mandate to examine that interiority, memoirs promote an "I" that is explicitly constituted in the reports of the utterances and proceedings of others. The "I" or subjectivity produced in memoirs is externalized and, in the Bakhtinian sense, overtly dialogical.[7] Unlike the subjectivity of autobiography, which is presumed to be unitary and continuous over time, memoirs (particularly in their collective form) construct a subjectivity that is multiple and discontinuous. The ways that an "I" is inscribed in the discourse of memoirs therefore operate in resistance to the modern era's dominant construction of individualized selfhood, which follows the dictum to, above all else, know thy interior self. In relation to autobiography, then, memoirs function as countermemory.

In situating autobiography historically as a self-normalizing practice of the modern era, it is important to recognize the ways in which autobiographies by marginalized people have often challenged the conventions and power relations of traditional autobiography, as recent feminist scholarship such as Sidonie Smith's work and the essays in such collections as *The Private Self* and *Life/Lines* demonstrate.[8] If I risk making too harsh a case against autobiography, it is certainly not to dismiss those challenges. But it is to insist that we scrutinize the extent to which such writings promote, despite their challenges, the subjectivity—the totalized individuality—of the modern era.[9] It is also to point out that applying the label "autobiographical" to all types of life writings—even when their titles announce them as memoirs, testimonials, confessions, or the like—tends to reduce and narrow our reading of the text.[10] On the other side of the issue, my argument risks overvalorizing memoirs. Memoirs as a discourse could, of course, be used to promote reprehensible political programs, but my point is that—in the modern era, at any rate—it would provide a less effective means of doing so, given its marginalized status in relation to autobiography or other more dominant genres and given its dialogical format, which destabilizes unified selfhood. What I wish to show are the ways in which Kingston's use of memoirs negotiates a confrontation with disciplinary power relations, a confrontation that can be suggestive for feminist theorizing as well as for literary criticism.

As an ensemble of several discourses, the genre of memoirs rejects the discursive unity that constructs subjectivity as simultaneously individualized and totalized, for, as the *OED* indicates, *memoirs* names a type of writing that is a composite of several generic discourses. The *OED* defines *memoir* as a "note, memorandum; record" and the collective plural *memoirs* as "a record of events, not purporting to be a complete history, but treating of such matters as come within the personal knowledge of the writer, or are obtained from certain particular sources of information"; and "a person's written account of records in his [sic] own life, of the persons whom he has known, and the transactions or movements in which he has been concerned; an autobiographical record"; also, "a biography, or biographical notice"; "an essay or dissertation on a learned subject on which the writer has made particular observations. Hence *pl.* the record of the proceedings or transactions of a learned society"; and, finally, "a memento, memorial." *The Woman Warrior* is precisely such a composite.

The etymology of *memoirs* is also particularly resonant for characterizing *The Woman Warrior*. Again from the *OED*: "F. *memoire* masc., a specialized use, with alteration of gender, of *memoire,* fem., MEMORY. The change of gender is commonly accounted for by the supposition that the use of the word in this sense is elliptical for *écrit pour mémoire;* Sp. Pg. and It. have *memoira* fem. in all senses." English usage retains a quasi-French pronunciation but has anglicized the spelling, making the word, according to the *OED,* "somewhat anomalous." Thus the word itself may be understood as a metonymy of Kingston's particular discursive position. As a Chinese-American, her linguistic heritage is informed by two different language systems. As a woman, she is a "somewhat anomalous" memoirist, using a grammatically feminine term that has been colonized by a masculine form. The word *memoirs* in Kingston's subtitle is in this sense a signifier of subjugated femininity subversively erupting against linguistic and literary exclusion.

Even as Kingston draws on the term *memoirs* as a generic description, the word *ghosts* in her subtitle indicates that memoirs are not an exclusively empirical record of events and individuals. This use of ghosts places her in lineage with Virginia Woolf, who, as Shari Benstock points out, also associates memoir writing with the inclusion of material on "invisible presences." In *Moments of Being,* which includes five pieces Benstock calls "fragments of a memoir," Woolf describes the importance of these "invisible presences": "This influence, by which I mean the consciousness of other groups impinging upon ourselves; public opinion; what other people say and think; all those magnets which attract us this way to be like that, or repel us the other and make us different from that; has never been analyzed in any of those Lives which I so much enjoy reading, or very superficially." Benstock explains that Woolf's mother is one of these "invisible presences," not because she is absent from the memoir, but rather because she is so much present, "too central, too close, to be observed." Woolf argues, "If we cannot analyze these invisible presences, we know very little of *the subject of the memoir.*" [11]

In *The Woman Warrior* ghosts have their own specificity as "invisible presences." Kingston represents her girlhood as triply displaced because of America's deeply embedded Sinophobia, her parents' ambivalence about America and the poverty they face, and the misogynistic attitudes she finds in both her American and Chinese heritages. The idea of ghosts thus suggests the profound confusion she felt as a child amid the concealed but felt hatreds of both China and America. She is haunted by the stories of China that her mother told her, stories of women's oppression and female infanticide. She discloses that she also lived in fear of those who performed the regular but often unseen services of quotidian life in America, which was, she says, "full of machines and ghosts—Taxi Ghosts, Bus Ghosts, Police Ghosts, Fire Ghosts, Meter Reader Ghosts, Tree Trimming Ghosts, Five-and-Dime Ghosts" (pp. 96–97)—members of American society who came regularly but without friendship, who filled the world with frightening noises and kept her family under surveillance. Both kinds of ghosts haunt her even into adulthood. But in adulthood the writing of her memoirs serves as a ritual of exorcism that "drives the fear away" (p. 205). As Woolf points out, memoirs confront what other forms of life writing too often ignore—the pervasive "invisible presences" that are the most profound determinants of subjectivity.

The form of subjectivity explored in *The Woman Warrior* may be located at the nexus of two patriarchal technologies of power, the deployment of alliance and the deployment of sexuality, which operate in interlocking ways in the American nuclear family. Foucault argues that the deployment of alliance—the "mechanisms of constraint" that operate through "a system of marriage, of fixation and development of kinship ties, of transmission of names and possessions"—predominated in the West prior to the eighteenth century.[12] With the decline of monarchical rule and the emergence of modern nation-states, a second technology of power—the deployment of sexuality—came to be superimposed on this system. Rather than operating through constraint and the law, this technology functions by "proliferating, innovating, annexing, creating, and penetrating bodies in an increasingly detailed way, and in controlling populations in an increasingly comprehensive way."[13] In *The Woman Warrior* the deployment of alliance is associated with Kingston's Chinese heritage and the deployment of sexuality with hegemonic American culture.

Although, as Foucault demonstrates, the deployment of sexuality took shape from the practices of alliance, particularly the confession and penance, it now operates through and within the domains of medicine, education, police surveillance, and psychiatry. In regard to women in particular, one of the primary axes of the deployment of sexuality is the process of "hysterization of women, which involved a thorough medicalization of their bodies and their sex . . . carried out in the name of the responsibility they owed to the health of their children, the solidity of the family institution, and the safeguarding of society." The bourgeois family is the "interchange of sexuality and alliance."[14]

Kingston situates the events of *The Woman Warrior* within her family's interchange of these two systems of power.[15] Through her depiction of her relationship to her mother, she portrays the dramatic intensity given to mother-daughter relations within these interlocking power structures, for within the family the mother is a site of intersection between the systems of alliance and sexuality, and so too the daughter is constituted as a future mother. In keeping with the dynamics of alliance, the mother's body perpetuates the father's lineage, oversees the exchange of daughters in marriage, and maintains kinship ties. In keeping with the dynamics of sexuality, the mother's body is the site of integration (for herself and her children) into the medical sphere, and her fecundity is integral to the social body through the reproduction and moral education of children.[16]

Within the nuclear family, then, it is the mother's obligation to turn her daughter into a mother. To the extent that she succeeds, she aligns her daughter with herself at the point of intersection between the deployment of alliance and the deployment of sexuality. *The Woman Warrior* is a discourse of resistance to the subjectification of the daughter within this family dynamic. Such resistance is fraught with difficulties. Paramount among them is that, in trying to push away from the constraints of alliance's patriarchal law, daughters are pulled toward the enticements of sexuality's medicalizations. And in regard to mother-daughter bonds, a daughter's resistance carries with it a danger of completely severing her ties with her mother.

This dilemma is a paradigm of female subjectivity as it has been constituted in the modern era in the West. It is also a dilemma that plagues feminist theorizing. On the one hand, insofar as feminist discourse rejects patriarchal constraint by valorizing what Foucault has called "a hermeneutics of desire," it enters the domain of the deployment of sexuality; such a hermeneutics constructs subjects for whom the "truth of their being" is to be found in desire (including but not limited to sexual acts).[17] On the other hand, insofar as feminist discourse rejects the proliferating mechanisms within the deployment of sexuality by valorizing womanhood, matriarchal kinship, and feminine essence, it reverts to the system of alliance. *The Woman Warrior* is a particularly important work in this regard, for it combats both deployments of power by saying no to the repressions of patriarchal constraint without saying yes to the enticements of the sexualized body. At the same time, it forges mother-daughter bonds in which the daughter is not required to become yet another "dutiful daughter" in preparation for patriarchally circumscribed motherhood.[18]

Throughout *The Woman Warrior,* language, both oral and written, is one of the "invisible presences" that constitute the subject of memoirs.[19] The memoirs recount extensively Kingston's own difficulties with language, focusing on them as a feature of the conflict of cultural impulses within Chinese-American culture generally and her Chinese-American family specifically. As Sidonie Smith has pointed out, Kingston suggests that her difficulty with language "originates in the memory of her mother's literally cutting the voice out of her" when her mother cut her daughter's frenum.[20] In Kingston's words: "She pushed my tongue up and sliced the frenum. Or maybe she snipped it with a pair of nail scissors. I don't remember her doing it, only her telling me about it, but all during childhood I felt sorry for the baby whose mother waited with scissors or knife in hand for it to cry—and then, when its mouth was wide open like a baby bird's, cut" (pp. 163–64). The cut frenum serves as a figure for the dilemma of the conflicting subjectivities produced by the systems of alliance and sexuality, for the frenum is a membrane that both restrains and supports the tongue. "The Chinese," Kingston reports, "say 'a ready tongue is an evil'" (p. 164). Yet her mother tells her that she cut her frenum in order to *give* her a ready tongue, telling her that her "tongue would be able to move in any language," that she would be "able to speak languages that are completely different from one another" (p. 164). By the end of the text, this capacity is shown to be necessary in an interdependent world.

Whatever her mother's motives, the predicament that Kingston discloses as the result of the cutting is that of being caught between alliance's imposition of muteness on women and sexuality's pathology of hysterical babbling. Finding herself suspended in the spaces between her family's use of Chinese and her birth society's use of English, Kingston recounts that she fell into semi-muteness and experienced physical pain when required to speak aloud. After an episode of cruelty to another young girl, in many ways her double but one who had been less resistant to the imposed passivity of Chinese-American femininity, she herself experienced an eighteen-month-long "mysterious illness" in which she, like "the Victorian recluses," remained indoors, a virtual invalid. Upon returning to school, she had "to figure out again how to talk" (p. 182). But to talk is to risk becoming garrulously incoherent. Kingston cites examples of several women who are called insane, including her mother's sister, and fears that she too might lapse into mental illness. "Insane people," she observes, seemed to be "the ones who couldn't explain themselves" (p. 186). Her own self-explanations are so often blurred by the mix of two incommensurate languages that as a child she feels unable not only to explain herself but even to understand the explanations of others. She finds consolation in talking to the "adventurous people inside [her] head" but fears that such a practice is yet another sign of abnormality.[21]

From the perspective of adulthood, the point of view from which the memoirs are composed, Kingston indicates that these problems derived not so much from within her as from the refusal of others to listen to the experiences of those they deem Other and their readiness to designate that otherness as abnormal. "A Song for a Barbarian Reed Pipe," the last of the five intertwining accounts that make up *The Woman Warrior*, relates a humiliating incident that crystallizes the sense of confused self she had as a child. Asked by her first-grade teacher to read a lesson aloud to the rest of the class, she falters over the word "I." "I could not understand 'I,'" she recalls. The teacher, enmeshed in the disciplinary pedagogical regime of the modern era, exiles her to a site of public shame—"the low corner under the stairs . . . where the noisy boys usually sat" (pp. 166–67).

The irony, of course, is that the child has stumbled onto a profundity about which the teacher is unaware: the first person pronoun "I" is not at all simple; nor is it as unified as the "I" of autobiography implies. To clarify this point, Kingston invites readers to see through her eyes as a Chinese-American child for whom writing had hitherto been ideographic. "The Chinese 'I' has seven strokes, intricacies. How could the American 'I,' assuredly wearing a hat like the Chinese, have only three strokes, the middle so straight?" (p. 166). The child's question challenges the sense of self associated in Kingston's memoirs with nonideographic writing, a self that promises autonomy, certainty, and unequivocal moral righteousness. The memoirs record that the phallic American "I" systematically denies its multiplicity and interconnectedness, masquerading as self-contained, independent subjectivity and imposing its will on others, often in the name of justice. The self/other dichotomy concealed within the American "I" stationed immigrant families in slums, then paved over the slums with parking lots; relegated immigrants to menial, low-paying labor; sneered at Chinese voices; used logic, science, and mathematics against "superstitious" modes of knowing; and branded children unable to read English with a "zero IQ" (pp. 48, 183).[22] Such an "I," she warns, is not merely a harmful illusion, it is a form of imperialism.

Yet the alternative Chinese "I" is not without its own traps, for Kingston also points out that there is a "Chinese word for the female I—which is 'slave,'" adding with a note of bitterness that the Chinese "break the women with their own tongues!" (p. 47). Thus the ideographic conjunction of slave and female "I" makes visible the added problem for selfhood confronting Kingston—her gender redoubles the second-class status imposed on Chinese-Americans. So pronounced is the legacy of female inferiority that it unsettles the love her family gives her. Even after she has left home as an adult, conflicting experiences of familial love and female disdain haunt her. "From afar I can believe my family loves me fundamentally," she writes. "They only say, 'When fishing for treasures in the flood, be careful not to pull in girls,' because that is what one says about daughters." But such rationalization fails to satisfy in the face of nagging memories: "I had watched such words come out of my mother's and father's mouths; I looked at their ink drawing of poor people snagging their neighbors' flotage with long flood hooks and pushing the girl babies on down the river. And I had to get out of hating range" (p. 52).

Kingston's "I" does not remain caught between the American "I"'s facade of autonomy (belied, in any case, for women by the demands of what Kingston calls "American-feminine" behavior) and the Chinese "I"'s designation of women as inferior. Rather, even at the level of writing as graphic inscription, *The Woman Warrior* challenges the operations of power that have historically and culturally been invested in the Chinese ideograph and the American alphabet.[23] Kingston's resistance to these graphic signifiers of power/knowledge rejects the notion that one can discover (invent or find) a language that "transcends" existing power formations. Instead, *The Woman Warrior* problematizes inherited intertwinings of writing, meaning, artistry, and experience and constructs a technology of the self that resists the subjectivities promoted by patriarchal ideographic and alphabetic language.[24] In other words, Kingston uses each tradition to intervene against the other. From this intervention, she constructs a subjectivity through a form of writing that forces the American script of her text to reveal its intricacies in the way Chinese ideographs do.

The ideographic "I" of Kingston's memoirs valorizes individual freedom while at the same time defining selfhood as an ensemble subjectivity. In terms of narrative time, the ideographic "I" of *The Woman Warrior* intersects the distanced time of a retrospective point of view with a displayed time of processive narration.[25] This use of time past and time present thus disrupts Western conventions of historical and sociological discourse that promote the notion of objective reporting of events. Instead, Kingston's memoirs display the intersection of knowing subject and known object. The subjectivity that emerges from this conjunction is interdependent and interrelational, a self that acknowledges separation and difference from others even while cultivating intimacy and interconnection. It is a subjectivity that recognizes the selfhood of the other and acknowledges its own alterity.[26] In short, Kingston's interventions in her inherited subjectivity constitute a new technology of ideographic selfhood.

As Foucault has argued and as Kingston's critique of the Chinese and American "I"s demonstrates, writing is a significant exercise of selfhood. Kingston's memoirs challenge the ways that the deployment of alliance and the deployment of sexuality function to, in Foucault's words, turn "real lives into writing." *The Woman Warrior* rejects alliance's "procedure of heroization" that has traditionally chronicled the lives of powerful men, those who have power over others, by relating instead stories about women who have been subordinated by such men. The memoirs also refuse the deployment of sexuality's "procedure of objectification and subjection" that disciplines and normalizes individuals in modern society.[27] Those practices of writing construct a subjectivity that either monumentalizes individuals in the system of alliance or normalizes them in the system of sexuality. Although different from one another, both of these forms of subjectivity deny or conceal the incoherencies, confusions, contradictions, and gaps constituting any selfhood. In opposition to claims for a unified and coherent subjectivity, Kingston's memoirs accentuate the conflicts and confusions of identity that constitute her discursive "I."

The evocation of an ideographic selfhood acknowledges a complex, discontinuous, multilayered subjectivity.

Kingston's technology of ideographic selfhood and its corresponding aesthetics and ethics entail putting into written discourse stories from the Chinese oral tradition, many of them told to her by her mother. Each story adds a stroke to her ideographic selfhood, and each stroke is a form of resistance to the deployments of power that would either constrain women's sexuality or hystericize it. Structurally, the five titled accounts that make up *The Woman Warrior* clarify the operations of these power formations and Kingston's oppositions to each. The first two enact, in the telling of the stories of No Name Woman and Fa Mu Lan, respectively, limited attempts to counter the deployments of alliance and of sexuality. The third and fourth reveal, through representing the lives of Kingston's mother and aunt, respectively, the detrimental effects of alliance and sexuality. And the final piece combines stories about the poetess Ts'ai Yen and Kingston's grandmother, who "loved the theater," to represent a subjectivity that emerges in resistance to both systems of power.

The first chapter of the memoirs, "No Name Woman," retells a story told to Kingston by her mother on the occasion of the daughter's onset of menses. It rehearses the plight of her father's sister, whose pregnancy by a man not her husband brands her a transgressor of village morality. No Name Woman refuses to identify the father of her child, thus giving her designation a double meaning—she has no name because she refuses to reveal his name. "She kept the man's name to herself throughout her labor and dying," Kingston writes. "She did not accuse him that he be punished with her. To save her inseminator's name she gave silent birth" (p. 11). The villagers live by the deployment of alliance's code of patriarchal justice, which entitles them to slaughter the family's animals, smear blood on the walls and doors, and yell curses at the pregnant woman. Facing a life of such ostracism for herself and her family, the aunt kills herself and her newborn baby by plunging into a well. This is a "spite suicide," Kingston notes, for it ruined the family's water supply; but drowning the baby with her is an act of love: "Mothers who love their children take them along" (p. 15).

Over the years her aunt's drowned, "weeping" body with "wet hair hanging and skin bloated," seemed always to wait "silently by the water to pull down a substitute" (p. 16). In keeping with alliance's system of power, her mother had told her this story of family shame as a warning against women's transgressive sexuality, with a strict injunction never to tell of No Name Woman's existence, adultery, and suicide. Kingston not only tells her readers about her aunt, she embellishes her version of the story with an empathy and her aunt with a sexuality that her mother would not tolerate, perpetuating as she does the villagers' sense of justice and the aunt's immorality. Twenty years after hearing about No Name Woman, Kingston refuses to continue her silent complicity in the code of moral vengeance and strictures on women that had exacted her aunt's death. In her public disclosure she too transgresses the code of alliance and thus allies herself with her aunt. As Sidonie Smith has argued, Kingston's "story thus functions as a sign, like her aunt's enlarging belly, publicizing the potentially disruptive force of female textuality and the matrilineal descent of the texts."[28]

Kingston's revelation of the story of No Name Woman serves as her memoirs' first act of self-empowerment through writing and a rejection of village morality. As such, it demarcates the nexus of alliance and sexuality within the family, a place where transgression within the system of alliance readily converts into the confessional mode of the system of sexuality.[29] *The Woman Warrior* allows us to see the ways in which feminist efforts to liberate women from the repressions of the patriarchal juridical code run the risk of entrenching women more deeply within the deployment of sexuality's proliferating dynamics of power. More important, Kingston's work manages to resist this pull by employing what Foucault has called a "movement of de-sexualization," which displaces the apparatuses of morality, normality, and artistry operating within the deployment of sexuality; such de-sexualization looks for "new forms of community, co-existence, pleasure."[30] "White Tigers," the second piece in the memoirs, may be understood as a point of departure for diffusing the power dynamics that would otherwise pull her sexual/textual transgression into the confessional dynamic inherent to the deployment of sexuality with which autobiography is complicit.

It should be stressed that "White Tigers" is a beginning point of resistance, for the blending of self-sacrifice and justice enacted at this stage is a child's fantasy of heroics, a fantasy that powerfully but *playfully* brings together the legend of Fa Mu Lan—derived from a chant her mother had taught her about a woman warrior who had avenged her village—and heroes from American movies.[31] As a child, Kingston had become infatuated with this woman warrior, a woman who, in contrast to the American and Chinese women she knew, received honor for her deeds both in battle, from which women are traditionally excluded, and in patriarchal motherhood, through which women have been subordinated. Imagination thus provides an outlet against the double devaluation she has experienced as a Chinese-American girl, and in her theater of the mind she herself becomes this woman warrior who undergoes strenuous years of discipline and training so that she may take her place as both soldier and mother. Ultimately, however, like No Name Woman, whose sexual transgression is limited in its challenge to the system of alliance, Kingston's fantasies of being a female avenger deflect, without fully challenging, the process of sexualization to which an adolescent female is subjected in the United States.

Ideographs inaugurate the fantasy world of "White Tigers" and mark points of development of an ideographic selfhood. Initially, nature's ideographs summon the child to the challenge of greater humanity. "The call would come," she writes, "from a bird that flew over our roof. In the brush drawings it looks like the ideograph for 'human,' two black wings" (p. 20). When the call comes, the girl of seven leaves home to join an old man and old woman who train her to become a warrior, a training that includes exercises resembling body writing. "I learned to move my fingers, hands, feet, head, and entire body in circles. I walked putting heel down first, toes pointing outward thirty to forty degrees, making the ideograph 'eight,' making the ideograph 'human.' . . . I could copy owls and bats, the words for 'bat' and 'blessing' homonyms" (p. 23). After years of preparation, she returns home to bid her parents farewell before leaving for battle. Again, the theme of inscription is repeated as her parents mark her body with their love and desire for revenge. By carving into her back their "oaths and names," they transform her body into a testament of family honor. "My father first brushed the words in ink," she records. "Then he began cutting; . . . My mother caught the blood and wiped the cuts with a cold towel soaked in wine. It hurt terribly—the cuts sharp; the air burning; the alcohol cold, then hot—pain so various. . . . If an enemy should flay me, the light would shine through my skin like lace" (pp.34–35). In battle, the woman warrior avenges her family and village, regaining their lands; she marries her childhood friend, bears a child, and upon victory returns to her village to live out her days in honor.

The fantasy portion of "White Tigers," with its heroic deeds and "happily ever after" ending, is juxtaposed in it concluding section against feelings of frustration, impotence, and confusion in bringing about gender, racial, and class equality. Marching and studying at Berkeley in the 1960s does not turn Kingston into the boy her parents would have preferred. Confronting an employer with his racism, she is dismissed from her job. In describing the death of an uncle in China who was killed by the Communists for stealing food for his family rather than giving it to the "commune kitchen to be shared," she admits that it is "confusing that my family was not the poor to be championed" (p. 51). And she laments her inability to avenge her family: "I'd have to storm across China to take back our farm from the Communists; I'd have to rage across the United States to take back the laundry in New York and the one in California. Nobody in history has conquered and united both North America and Asia" (p. 51).

Although the heroics of Fa Mu Lan are naive in terms of political practice, the story of the female avenger constitutes a bold stroke in Kingston's ideographic selfhood. The avenger's feats of courage are an inverse expression of the powerlessness imposed on Kingston as a Chinese-American female, but an expression that ultimately empowers her as an author and allows her to become a different kind of warrior, one who makes public the wrongs done against her people. Comparing herself to the woman warrior of her fantasy, as the title of the memoirs also does, she observes that what "we have in common are the words at our backs. The ideographs for *revenge* are 'report a crime' and 'report to five families.' The reporting is the vengeance— not the beheading, the gutting, but the words. And I have so many words—'chink' words and 'gook' words too—that they do not fit on my skin" (p. 53). As a writer-warrior, then, Kingston's image of words *in excess* of her body suggests that writing itself must veer away from monumentalizing and normalizing regimes of power and serve instead to corporealize a subjectivity that can take revenge on forces of domination. This excess of words disrupts racist and sexist categories of containment through which the dominant and dominating regimes of power are constructed.

Much of the drama of *The Woman Warrior* derives from Kingston's representation of her mother as a force of domination.[32] Rather than denying or suppressing the deeply embedded ambivalence her mother arouses in her, Kingston unrelentingly evokes the powerful presence of her mother, arduously and often painfully exploring her difficulties in identifying with and yet separating from her. Her record of differentiation from her mother involves confrontation with the two systems of power that intersect within the family. This ethical-political process of separation is a precarious one, for it threatens repudiation of the mother or abandonment by her, the two opposing responses that Kingston depicts as terrifying to her as a child. Yet emulating her mother would perpetuate two modes of oppression: the subordination of women under the Law of the Father within the deployment of alliance, and the proliferating hysterization of women within the deployment of sexuality. Writing the memoirs provides a means for altering this dynamic by separating herself from her mother without severing their ties.

Kingston does this by weaving together two intertwined discursive threads integral to her technology of ideographic selfhood: healing and artistry. In order to create a new pattern, she must first unravel the preexisting designs of alliance's shamanism and maternal orality as well as that of the medicalization of sexuality and paternal literacy. Throughout *The Woman Warrior,* particularly in "Shaman," the third chapter, devoted to her mother, Brave Orchid, Kingston describes her mother's practices of midwifery and healing. Brave Orchid's shamanistic practices seem to the child a form of magic in comparison to the science and logic learned by the American-educated daughter as "American-normal." Although Kingston admires her mother and the other women of the To Keung School of Midwifery as "outside women," and "new women, scientists who changed the rituals," she deems her mother's practices to be superstitious and frightful. Such is the case, for example, with the "big brown hand with pointed claws stewing in alcohol and herbs" stored in a jar from which Brave Orchid would draw "tobacco, leeks, and grasses" to apply to her children's wounds (p. 91). Such is also the case with the power over life and death that her midwife mother possessed in China. Furthermore, her mother's diploma is disparaged by American health agencies, and as a result Brave Orchid must labor long hours as a laundry worker and tomato picker instead of in the profession for which she was trained. "This is terrible ghost-country," she reports her mother as saying, "where a human being works her life away" (p. 104).

Although Kingston sympathizes with her mother's professional exclusion in America, she nonetheless indicates that she holds many of the American attitudes that devalue her mother's methods of shamanistic healing. These conflicting feelings are intensified when her mother's treatments prove ineffectual and possibly harmful to the mental health of her sister Moon Orchid, whose story of deterioration is the subject of the fourth account, "At the Western Palace." Brave Orchid's ministrations might well have worked in the sisters' Chinese village decades before, where alliance's system of knowledge and morality prevailed. But in America they lead Moon Orchid to be declared insane by Western medical authorities, and she is placed in a California state mental asylum. Acceptance of her mother's beliefs, Kingston implies, might impose this judgment on her as well. She determines to differentiate herself from her mother through adherence to Western science and logic.

Yet this determination has another side, revealed in the description of Moon Orchid's response to the mental asylum. There she finds happiness in the company of other women, all of whom "speak the same language" (p. 160). The combined dread of and longing for insanity that Kingston expresses throughout *The Woman Warrior* results from the deployment of sexuality's process of hysterization of women. For to be a "proper" (procreative) woman within this technology of power means to be medicalized, means becoming either the "American-normal" Good Mother or the abnormal hysterical woman. In describing her own eighteen-month illness, when she lived "like the Victorian recluses," she reveals the thrill of invalidation that is so central to the invalidism of hystericized womanhood: "It was the best year and a half of my life. Nothing happened" (p. 182). Such yearning for nothingness is a consequence of overidentification with patriarchally inscribed motherhood: a paradoxical desire to return to prelinguistic infancy and remain forever a dependent daughter in order to evade the subjectivity that becoming a mother entails in the nexus of alliance and sexuality. This yearning may be understood as a form of resistance to women's subordination in a misogynistic society, but it is a resistance that turns back on itself, destroying not misogyny but the woman who suffers it.

Instead of entering this sphere of hysterization, Kingston creates a self-healing aesthetics. This requires differentiation from her mother's artistry, for, as with Brave Orchid's medicine, her form of art functions primarily within the system of alliance. Throughout her childhood, her mother's talk-stories had filled her imagination with "pictures to dream," some of them reveries of hope, as with the legend of Fa Mu Lan, and others leaving nightmarish images, as with the story of No Name Woman and the monkey story, in which eaters feast on the brain of a still-living monkey. Even though Brave Orchid is an artist, then, she is one who remains exclusively within the oral tradition and whose stories are often accompanied by the admonition not to tell anyone else. Kingston's written memoirs are a sign of separation from her mother's oral tradition and women's enforced silences, but they are also a sign of tribute to her mother: to the vividness of her stories and to her readiness to confront some of life's most terrifying moments.

Enthralled by her mother's courage and yet aware of her vulnerability in both China and America, and caught within her mother's complicated and often hostile attitude toward females, Kingston situates her childhood in the interstices of her two cultures, a place where she is in danger of plunging into either "feminine" muteness or hysteria. Acquiring a new voice is a feature of her new subjectivity. When she first gains a voice, however, she finds it through an over-zealous repudiation of her mother. One day as they work together in the family laundry, she blurts out angrily, "I won't let you turn me into a slave or wife. . . . They say I'm smart now. Things follow in lines at school. They take stories and teach us to turn them into essays. . . . And I don't want to listen to any more of your stories; they have no logic. They scramble me up. You lie with stories" (pp. 201–2). Although the memoirs suggest that such vehemence was crucial for Kingston's construction of a new subjectivity, she follows this passage with a note of regret: "Be careful what you say. It comes true. It comes true. I had to leave home in order to see the world logically, logic the new way of seeing. I learned to think that mysteries are for explanation" (p. 204). Acquisition of the deployment of sexuality's empirical knowledge displaces the system of alliance's shamanistic knowledge.

But the acquisition of Western logic as constitutive of Kingston's new subjectivity does not entirely supplant Brave Orchid's way of knowing, and the memoirs are neither talk-stories nor logical essays but something of each and a challenge to both. In *The Woman Warrior* Kingston brings together her mother's talk-stories and conventions of Western logic in order to tell (her) truth without reducing its complexities. She divulges about No Name Woman what Brave Orchid has declared must never be revealed beyond the family. And she gives tribute to her mother as artist and healer even as she separates herself from her mother. In these ways, the memoirs show how through writing one can symbolically revisit one's mother, not as a child but as an adult who gives birth to herself as artist with the aid of her mother's midwifery.

Despite the troubled relationship between Kingston and her mother, and the difficulties that arise between them because of their clashing views of morality, healing, and artistry, that relationship nonetheless ultimately provides the momentum for Kingston's new—but never complete, never closed—subjectivity. Kingston's memoirs refuse alignment with phallic conceptualizations of art that ignore the mother's role as a teacher of language, define the mother tongue as crude in relation to the fatherly text, or see artistry as a symbolic playing out of the oedipal conflict between father and son. *The Woman Warrior* gives tribute to Brave Orchid's talk-stories and shamanism even as it marks Kingston's turn toward a written art that reveals and heals the wounds of patriarchal motherhood and daughterhood.[33]

The story of Ts'ai Yen, which concludes the memoirs with a tribute to the power of a woman who transformed sounds of captivity into piercingly beautiful music, enacts this turn. Kingston writes that this is a "story my mother told me, not when I was young, but recently, when I told her I also am a story-talker. The beginning is hers, the ending, mine" (p. 206). Her mother's story is about her own mother, Kingston's grandmother, who so loved the theater that she moved the entire family, as well as some of the household furnishings, to the theater when the actors came to her village. Although this is done in order to ensure the household's safety from bandits while the family is away enjoying the performance, as the story goes, the bandits attack the theater. They scatter the family and very nearly kidnap Lovely Orchid, Kingston's youngest aunt. By the end of the ordeal, however, "the entire family was home safe, proof to my grandmother that our family was immune to harm as long as they went to plays." She adds, "They went to many plays after that" (p. 207).

The family's frequent attendance at the theater is both a logical non sequitur and a meaning-producing narrative thread between her mother's story and Kingston's. "I like to think that at some of those performances, they heard the songs of Ts'ai Yen," writes Kingston (p. 207). This telling phrase, "I like to think," encapsulates the poetics and politics of Kingston's memoirs. As Trinh Minh-ha has observed, Kingston's writing, which is "neither fiction nor non-fiction, constantly invites the reader either to drift naturally from the realm of imagination to that of actuality or to live them both without ever being able to draw a clear line between them yet never losing sight of their differentiation."[34] Just as the village theater serves in her mother's story as the space of both fear and fortune, of cause and effect, so too the phrase "I like to think" serves in her memoirs as the field of the represented and the unrepresented, the recalled and the constructed. And the ending of the tale demonstrates that what is representable— and what is not—is subject to change.

The tale of Ts'ai Yen, a poet born in A.D. 175, is that of a young woman captured at the age of twenty by a barbarian tribe. By day over the twelve years of her captivity, she could hear only the "death sounds" of war; but night after night, the desert air would be filled with the sharp, high notes of her captors' reed flutes. Fascinated by their disturbing music, she finally taught herself to sing "a song so high and clear, it matched the flutes," a song in her own language, in words her captors could not understand, but filled with a "sadness and anger" that they could not fail to comprehend. When she was later ransomed and returned home, she brought her songs with her.

One of these songs is "Eighteen Stanzas for a Barbarian Reed Pipe," a song the Chinese now "sing to their own instruments" (pp.206-9).

Perhaps, like Ts'ai Yen's song, Kingston's memoirs sustained her in a hostile land. But unlike Ts'ai Yen, who eventually returned home, the hostile land from which Kingston writes *is* her homeland. The endemic ethnic, gender, and class hatreds that the memoirs document give rise to a sense of displacement and corresponding yearning for place akin to the ambivalence evoked by her mother. As with her relationship to her mother, Kingston poses a rethinking of women's place in regard not only to the family but also to territoriality.[35] This issue arises during a visit to her parents' home when she is an adult. Upon witnessing her mother's distress over having had to relinquish the last of their land in China, she responds: "We belong to the planet now, Mama. Does it make sense to you that if we're no longer attached to one piece of land, we belong to the planet? Wherever we happen to be standing, why, that spot belongs to us as much as any other spot" (p. 107). This is a remark that consoles, even as it refuses a mythologized evocation of an originary homeland.

Kingston's proposal of belonging to the planet also contrasts with the ways Edward Said, Tzvetan Todorov, and Julia Kristeva have proposed the metaphor of perpetual exile as an ethical guide. Both Said and Todorov have quoted Erich Auerbach (who was quoting Hugh of St. Victor, from the twelfth century): "The man who finds his country sweet is only a raw beginner; the man for whom each country is as his own is already strong; but the man for whom the whole world is as a foreign country is perfect."[36] And Kristeva has argued that exile "is an irreligious act that cuts all ties," a severing necessary for "*thought.*"[37] *The Woman Warrior* suggests that even such a stance is too much a denial of the ties between individuals and their planet. To hold that one belongs to the planet, and to claim as one's own the spot wherever one stands, presents a signifying space that resists nation-state mythologies without mythologizing exile.

"Chinese-Americans, when you try to understand what things in you are Chinese, how do you separate what is peculiar to childhood, to poverty, insanities, one family, your mother who marked your growing with stories, from what is Chinese? What is Chinese tradition and what is the movies?" asked Kingston in the opening pages of *The Woman Warrior* (pp. 5-6). Over the course of her memoirs she indicates that she cannot, in fact, separate what is peculiar to her own life and family from what is Chinese, or even from the American version of what is Chinese. Indeed, the memoirs insist that experience is neither separable nor unmediated, but is instead always a knot of significations. One can, however, perhaps especially through the genre of memoirs, give new meanings to the twists and ties of knotted experiences, new meanings that challenge those prescribed by and inscribed in hegemonic technologies of power and selfhood.

A metaphor of knotmaking opens the final memoir of *The Woman Warrior*. Kingston contrasts her form of storytelling with her brother's, which is notable for its barrenness: it is not "twisted into designs" like hers. She points to the dangers of such knotmaking but insists on its importance. "Long ago in China," she writes, "knotmakers tied strings into buttons and frogs, and rope into bell pulls. There was one knot so complicated that it blinded the knotmaker. Finally an emperor outlawed this cruel knot, and the nobles could not order it anymore." "If I had lived in China," she adds, "I would have been an outlaw knotmaker" (p. 163). In this vignette, as in her discussion of the American and Chinese "I"'s, Kingston uses a practice from the Chinese tradition to intervene in American traditions. Storytelling as knotmaking alludes to the ancient Chinese practice called *chien sheng,* or knotted cord, which was used as a method for keeping records and communicating information.[38] By knotting together her life experiences, even when it means tying a "cruel knot" of blinding truth, Kingston becomes an "outlaw knotmaker," a not-maker or negator of patriarchal law and normalizing power.[39]

Just as the ideograph's several intersecting strokes display its polysemy, so too the knot as discursive form suggests the possibility of untying old meanings and retying new ones. Through such untying and retying, Kingston seeks to "figure out how the invisible world the emigrants built around our childhoods fit in solid America" (p. 5). In this figuring out—which is a figuring of—what is peculiar to her, Kingston thinks the limits of her subjectivity. As Foucault has observed, "The critique of what we are is at one and the same time the historical analysis of the limits that are imposed on us and an experiment with the possibility of going beyond them."[40] As *The Woman Warrior* demonstrates, ideographic self-stylization is a practice of going beyond imposed limits.

Notes

I would like to thank Tom Hayes, Sidonie Smith, and Julia Watson for their suggestions in revising this essay.

1. Michel Foucault, "The Subject and Power," in *Art After Modernism: Rethinking Representation,* ed. Brian Wallis (New York: New Museum of Contemporary Art, 1984), 424.

2. Maxine Hong Kingston, *The Woman Warrior: Memoirs of a Girlhood among Ghosts* (New York: Alfred A. Knopf, 1977), 20. All further citations of this book will include page numbers in parentheses in the text.

3. Maxine Hong Kingston, "Cultural Mis-readings by American Reviewers," in *Asian and Western Writers in Dialogue*, ed. Guy Amirthanayagam (London: Macmillan, 1982), 64.

4. Despite my disagreement with Eakin and Smith regarding the genre of *The Woman Warrior*, I find their readings of the work compelling and am in agreement with them in their treatment of a number of textual details. See John Paul Eakin, *Fiction in Autobiography: Studies in the Art of Self-Invention* (Princeton, N.J.: Princeton University Press, 1985); Sidonie Smith, *A Poetics of Women's Autobiography: Marginality and the Fictions of Self-Representation* (Bloomington: Indiana University Press, 1987). Also see Patricia Lin Blinde, "The Icicle in the Desert: Perspective and Form in the Works of Two Chinese-American Women Writers," *MELUS* 6 (1979): 51-71; Suzanne Juhasz, "Towards a Theory of Form in Feminist Autobiography: Kate Millett's *Fear of Flying* and *Sita;* Maxine Hong Kingston's *The Woman Warrior*," *International Journal of Women's Studies* 2 (1979): 62-75; Jan Zlotnik Schmidt, "The Other: A Study of Persona in Several Contemporary Women's Autobiographies," *CEA Critic* 43 (1981): 24-31, for discussions of the search for self and autobiographical form.

5. Elizabeth Bruss discusses the disappearance of autobiography in our time as a result of changes in our cultural formation. Such changes, which include a shift from writing to film and video, constitute changes in "our notions of authorship, the difference between narrating (on the one hand) and perceiving or 'focalizing' (on the other), the conventions of representational realism." "Eye for I: Making and Unmaking of Autobiography in Film," in *Autobiography: Essays Theoretical and Critical,* ed. James Olney (Princeton, N.J.: Princeton University Press, 1980), 299.

6. James M. Cox, "Recovering Literature's Lost Ground through Autobiography," in *Autobiography: Essays Theoretical and Critical,* ed. James Olney (Princeton, N.J.: Princeton University Press, 1980), 124. Cox makes this point in regard to Thomas Jefferson's memoir, which he reads as part of Jefferson's efforts as an American revolutionary "to destabilize everything fixed before him" (p. 145).

7. It would be in keeping with Bakhtin's arguments to see memoirs as novelistic in their accentuation of dialogue. This is not to say that a memoir is a novel, but, rather, that novelization is a process by which genres move toward "liberation from all that serves as a brake on their unique development, from all that would change them along with the novel into some sort of stylization of forms that have outlived themselves." M. M. Bakhtin, "Epic and Novel," in *The Dialogic Imagination,* ed. Michael Holquist, trans. Caryl Emerson and Michael Holquist (Austin: University of Texas Press, 1981), 39.

8. In an analysis of Simone de Beauvoir's memoirs, Kathleen Woodward comments on Estelle Jelinek's characterization of female "life stories" as "more often discontinuous and fragmentary, written in a straightforward, objective manner, yet nonetheless emphasizing the personal rather than the public" by saying that she (Woodward) would "reserve Jelinek's characterization of the female life story for the *memoir.*" See Kathleen Woodward, "Simone de Beauvoir: Aging and Its Discontents," in *The Private Self: Theory and Practice of Women's Autobiographical Writings,* ed. Shari Benstock (Chapel Hill: University of North Carolina Press, 1988), 99. I generally concur with this point, but would place less stress on the memoir's emphasis of the personal over the public. Kingston's memoirs blur traditional distinctions between the personal and the public.

9. For an example of such analysis, see Biddy Martin's exploration of the complexities of lesbian autobiography in light of a variety of questions involving generic

normalization versus the challenge of lesbian politics. "Lesbian Identity and Autobiographical Difference(s)," in *Life/Lines: Theorizing Women's Autobiography*, ed. Bella Brodzki and Celeste Schenck (Ithaca, N.Y.: Cornell University Press, 1988), 77–103.

10. Doris Sommer underscores this point in her analysis of testimonials by Latin American women, pointing out that accepting these works as autobiographical tends to divert attention away from the significance of the testimonials' collective self. "'Not Just a Personal Story': Women's *Testimonios* and the Plural Self," in *Life/Lines: Theorizing Women's Autobiography*, ed. Bella Brodzki and Celeste Schenck (Ithaca, N.Y.: Cornell University Press, 1988), 107–30.

11. Woolf, quoted in Shari Benstock, "Authorizing the Autobiographical," in *The Private Self: Theory and Practice of Women's Autobiographical Writings*, ed. Shari Benstock (Chapel Hill: University of North Carolina Press, 1988), 26–27; emphasis mine.

12. Michel Foucault, *The History of Sexuality*, vol. 1, trans. Robert Hurley (New York: Vintage, 1980), 106. For a feminist corrective to Foucault's lack of focus on the patriarchal dimensions of the deployment of sexuality, see the essays in Irene Diamond and Lee Quinby, eds., *Feminism and Foucault: Reflections on Resistance* (Boston: Northeastern University Press, 1988).

13. Foucault, *History of Sexuality*, 107.

14. Ibid., 146–47, 108.

15. Kingston's *China Men* also relates family difficulties in America but focuses in that work on the men of her family. Regarding the changing family power dynamics between Chinese men and women upon coming to America, see Linda Ching Sledge's argument that because of the "deleterious effects of male emigration," the "mother from China is forced by the father's increasing passivity to take on 'masculine' traits of aggressiveness and authority." "Maxine Kingston's *China Men:* The Family Historian as Epic Poet," *MELUS* 7 (1980), 10–11.

16. Foucault, *History of Sexuality*, 104–6.

17. Michel Foucault, *The Use of Pleasure*, trans. Robert Hurley (New York: Pantheon, 1985), 5.

18. Kingston's use of the word *memoirs* in her subtitle also places her work alongside Simone de Beauvoir's account of resistance to bourgeois daughterhood in *Memoirs of a Dutiful Daughter*, trans. James Kirkup (Cleveland: World, 1959).

19. For an insightful comparative discussion of the issue of language and silence, see King-Kok Cheung, "'Don't Tell': Imposed Silences in *The Color Purple* and *The Woman Warrior*," *PMLA* 103 (1988): 162–74.

20. Smith, *Poetics of Women's Autobiography*, 168.

21. As Foucault argues, the deployment of sexuality operates through oppositional categories of normality versus abnormality. The desire to attain "normality" is thus a generative function of power in contrast to alliance's juridical and prohibitive mode. *History of Sexuality*, 42–43.

22. Kingston reports a variation on this particular form of pedagogical domination by citing a *Teachers Newsletter* review that "gave the book a seventh grade reading level by using a mathematical formula of counting syllables and sentences per one hundred-word passage." "Cultural Mis-readings," 62.

23. Woon-Ping Chin Holaday has compared Ezra Pound and Kingston in regard to their respective involvement with China and the use of the ideograph to represent that relationship. Holaday notes that in Pound's writings China tends to be "an ideal abstraction" drawn from written sources, whereas Kingston's "Chinese-American world is a tangible, changeable reality drawn from a living culture" and oral sources. "From Ezra Pound to Maxine Hong Kingston: Expressions of Chinese Thought in American Literature," *MELUS* 5 (1978): 15–24.

24. "Technology of the self" is Foucault's term for the specific techniques that "permit individuals to effect by their own means or with the help of others a certain number of operations on their own bodies and souls, thoughts, conduct, and way of being, so as to transform themselves in order to attain a certain state of happiness, purity, wisdom, perfection, or immortality." "Technologies of the Self," in *Technologies of the Self: A Seminar with Michel Foucault,* ed. Luther H. Martin, Huck Gutman, and Patrick H. Hutton (Amherst: University of Massachusetts Press, 1988), 18. My analysis seeks to show that the technology of ideographic selfhood put forward in *The Woman Warrior* operates in opposition to the technologies of self produced through the formations of power that are hegemonic in the modern era.

25. Norman Bryson argues for this distinction in painting by associating the distanced time technique with the tradition of Western painting and the displayed, processive time technique with the visible brush strokes of Chinese painting. See *Vision and Painting: The Logic of the Gaze* (New Haven, Conn.: Yale University Press, 1983), 89–92.

26. Carol Gilligan's analysis of gender differences in conceptualizations of selfhood and morality helps illuminate Kingston's depiction of an interrelational self insofar as it resembles the model of interdependence that Gilligan associates with women at a mature stage of moral development. Gilligan's theories, however, do not attend to cultural and ethnic differences in moral development. *The Woman Warrior* problematizes that blind spot in Gilligan's model. See *In a Different Voice* (Cambridge, Mass.: Harvard University Press, 1982).

27. Michel Foucault, *Discipline and Punish,* trans. Alan Sheridan (New York: Vintage, 1979), 192.

28. Smith, *Poetics of Women's Autobiography,* 156.

29. Foucault observes, "For us, it is in the confession that truth and sex are joined, through the obligatory and exhaustive expression of an individual secret." And also: "The obligation to confess is now relayed through so many different points, is so deeply ingrained in us, that we no longer perceive it as the effect of a power that constrains us; on the contrary, it seems to us that truth, lodged in our most secret nature, 'demands' only to surface; that if it fails to do so, this is because a constraint holds it in place, the violence of a power weighs it down, and it can finally be articulated only at the price of a kind of liberation." *History of Sexuality,* 60–61.

30. Michel Foucault, "The Confession of the Flesh," in *Power/Knowledge,* ed. Colin Gordon, trans. Colin Gordon et al. (New York: Pantheon, 1980), 219–20.

31. Kingston calls the "White Tigers" fantasy a "sort of kung fu movie parody" in her critical review of American reviews of her work. "Cultural Mis-readings," 57. I had a similar Saturday serial fantasy in my own girlhood, styled on a wild-west Zorro-like character. Clad boldly in black, and riding a black horse, I would valiantly fight off desperadoes (always men) who preyed upon defenseless men, women, and children.

32. Although they have been both astutely critiqued and further developed, the pioneering discussions about mother-daughter ambivalence by Chodorow, Dinnerstein, and Flax have been helpful here. See Nancy Chodorow, *The Reproduction of Mothering* (Los Angeles: University of California Press, 1978); Dorothy Dinnerstein, *The Mermaid and the Minotaur* (New York: Harper & Row, 1976); Jane Flax, "The Conflict between Nurturance and Autonomy in Mother-Daughter Relationships and within Feminism," *Feminist Studies* 4 (1978): 171–89.

33. Also see Leslie Rabine's important reading of "Kingston's work as a unique kind of feminine writing that in its own way fractures the logic of opposition into a play of

difference . . . [which] clarifies relations between social and symbolic gender." "No Lost Paradise: Social Gender and Symbolic Gender in the Writings of Maxine Hong Kingston," *Signs* 12 (1987): 474. And see Celeste Schenck's discussion of the story of Ts'ai Yen as representing a "return to the exiled mother as the source of poetry and the difference between mother and daughter which allows this female subject to find her own writing voice." "All of a Piece: Women's Poetry and Autobiography," in *Life/Lines: Theorizing Women's Autobiography,* ed. Bella Brodzki and Celeste Schenck (Ithaca, N.Y.: Cornell University Press, 1988), 303.

34. Trinh T. Minh-ha, *Woman, Native, Other: Writing Postcoloniality and Femininity* (Bloomington: Indiana University Press, 1989), 135.

35. Kingston thus broaches from a different register many of the questions raised by Julia Kristeva. Kristeva sees a new generation of women whose "attitude" toward issues raised by feminism "could be summarized as an *interiorization of the founding separation of the socio-symbolic contract,* as an introduction of its cutting edge into the very interior of every identity whether subjective, sexual, ideological, or so forth." "Women's Time," in *The Kristeva Reader,* ed. Toril Moi (New York: Columbia University Press, 1986), 210.

36. Tzvetan Todorov, *The Conquest of America,* trans. Richard Howard (New York: Harper Colophon, 1984), 250.

37. Julia Kristeva, "A New Type of Intellectual: The Dissident," in *The Kristeva Reader,* ed. Toril Moi (New York: Columbia University Press), 298–99.

38. Paul Carus, *Chinese Astrology* (La Salle: Open Court Press, 1974), 2–3. This edition is an abridgment of the 1907 text.

39. Also see Nancy K. Miller's discussion of "quipos," a system of knotting used in the Inca empire, which she interprets as a "signature" of feminist writing. *Subject to Change: Reading Feminist Writing* (New York: Columbia University Press, 1988), 137–42.

40. Foucault, "What Is Enlightenment?" in *The Foucault Reader,* ed. Paul Rabinow (New York: Pantheon, 1984), 50.

Chapter 15

Of Mangoes and Maroons
Language, History, and the Multicultural Subject of Michelle Cliff's *Abeng*

Françoise Lionnet

In a well-known essay, "Conditions and Limits of Autobiography," Georges Gusdorf states that "the prerogative of autobiography consists in this: . . . that it reveals . . . the effort of a creator *to give the meaning of his own mythic tale. . . .* Artistic creation is a struggle with the angel, in which *the creator . . . wrestles with his shadow.*"[1] The invention of a personal (i.e., private and individual) mythology is the project of many canonical authors whose writings constitute the basis of much Western, male theorizing about the nature of self-consciousness. This individualistic approach to the genre contrasts sharply with the one used by most postcolonial writers, male and female.[2] For them, the individual necessarily defines him- or herself with regard to a community, or an ethnic group, and their autobiographical mythologies of empowerment are usually mediated by a determined effort to revise and rewrite official, recorded history. Gusdorf's belief that "autobiography . . . expresses a concern peculiar to Western man" is based on a view of autobiography that is rather reductive and narrow, since it does not take into account the culturally diverse forms of self-consciousness, or the necessarily devious and circuitous modes of self-expression that colonized peoples have always had to adopt in order to come to terms with their own subject

321

positions.[3] The (formerly) colonized are marked, as Gusdorf rightly points out, by "a sort of intellectual colonizing to a mentality that was not their own,"[4] but *also,* it should be added, by ancient, often occluded traditions that need to be articulated through new discourses and new images. Postcolonial writers have had to invent mythologies of their own, stories and allegories of "self" and "other" that can translate this complex heritage, and perhaps make a difference in helping transform the mentality of the oppressed as well as their self-perception.

Postcolonial autobiography, in all its myriad forms, is best defined by this transformative and visionary dimension: by the convictions that writing matters and that narrative has the power to transform the reader. Writers from a variety of colonial backgrounds are often moved by a sense of urgency, by what Roland Barthes and Nadine Gordimer have called the writer's "essential gesture as a social being," that is, the writer's sense of responsibility and his or her ability to take risks that might help change the form of the genre as well as relations of power in society.[5] For a writer to "wrestle with his shadow," he must be certain of casting one: women of color have yet to define the shape of the shadow that they are beginning to cast, and autobiography is helping them in the task of achieving self-definition in a multicultural context. Their acts of self-portraiture increasingly bear testimony to the diversity and richness of the traditions that subtend their innovative narrative projects.

Among recently published autobiographies, Audre Lorde's "bio-mythography," *Zami,* is a prominent example of the kind of revisionist mythmaking that a writer engages in when she does not feel legitimated and validated by a long tradition of self-conscious self-exploration.[6] Because she breaks new ground, Lorde can "give meaning to [her] own mythic tale" and have it serve as testimony for others who have not yet had the opportunity to experience a life story whose shape could in some way compel, attract, or interest them. That is why I would argue that *Zami* constitutes the condition of possibility of Michelle Cliff's *Abeng,* the novel that I shall deal with in this essay.[7] By inventing a new way of narrating her experiences as a lesbian poet, Audre Lorde has made it possible for others like herself and Cliff, both immigrants from the Caribbean, to continue to shape and enrich their common cultural heritage.

Published in 1984 in the United States by a small feminist press, and written by a Jamaican-born author who focuses her narrative on the history, culture, and processes of gender and racial identity formation in the Caribbean, *Abeng* is at once fiction and autobiography in the third person. Written in English, it incorporates dialogue in Jamaican Creole. It appears, however, to be meant for a non-Caribbean audience, since it gives the reader the benefit of numerous cultural explanations and translations. The literal meaning of the word *abeng,* for example, is clarified on the title page: "*Abeng* is an African word meaning conch shell." Michelle Cliff goes on to add that in the West Indies, the *abeng* was used as an instrument of communication, the blowing of the conch serving either to call the slaves to work for the master in the canefields or to send messages that could be passed to maroon armies.[8] The *abeng* is thus a culturally polysemic object, having both positive and negative connotations in the context of Caribbean slave societies. Because its main function is to facilitate communication, the *abeng* stands in an obvious parallel relationship to the novel we are reading: both are objects by means of which different messages can be passed on (sometimes simultaneously) to different receivers; both are "double-voiced," duplicitous, and susceptible to ambiguous reception and interpretation.

That is why I would like to examine the way in which the multi-lingual context of Caribbean societies demarcates a specific set of cultural parameters that must be taken into consideration when discussing subjectivity and self-conscious agency in relation to a postcolonial form of historical consciousness distinguished by the absence of "master narratives."[9] Not surprisingly, autobiographical practice reflects this lack, and Michelle Cliff achieves a particularly successful rendering of the cultural discontinuities that form the basis of her protagonist's inquiry and motivation.

The Polyglot's Subjectivity

To remain speechless, or else to live in the third person.

And the past, which can still split the first person into the second and the third—has its hegemony been broken?
Christa Wolf, *Patterns of Childhood*[10]

Michelle Cliff chooses the *abeng* as an emblem for her book because, like the conch, the book is an instrument of communication whose performative function seems to be valorized. The story she tells is meant to inform and educate Jamaicans and non-Jamaicans alike, and she goes to great lengths to demystify the past in order to imagine, invent, and rewrite a different collective and personal history for the protagonist. The narrative weaves the personal and the political together, allowing the protagonist Clare Savage, who is but a thinly disguised alter ego of the author, to negotiate the conflicting elements of her cultural and familial background. She thus succeeds in reclaiming the multifaceted identity her family and society had "taught [her] to despise," namely, her mixed racial heritage, her femininity, and her homosexuality.[11]

The narrative sets up an uneasy and duplicitous relationship with its audience. It begins with the standard disclaimer, "This work is a work of fiction, and any resemblance to persons alive or dead is entirely coincidental," despite its clearly autobiographical themes, which echo and repeat similar themes treated from a first-person perspective in Cliff's poetry and essays.[12] But *Abeng* discloses far more about the author than does the poetry, while engaging the reader in a dialogue that confronts the fictions of self-representation. It would seem that, for Cliff, the third person is a self-protective device that creates sufficient distance, and thus helps her deal with the burden of history. Acts of disclosure are always painful, and since Cliff admits that she has labored "under the ancient taboos of the assimilated" (*LLB*, 16), the "hegemony of the past" cannot easily be broken by a straightforward act of self-portraiture. Like German writer Christa Wolf and Chinese-American writer Maxine Hong Kingston, Cliff uses postmodern fictional techniques that, in the words of Sidonie Smith, "challenge the ideology of individualism and with it the ideology of gender."[13]

The use of Creole accentuates some of these structural ambiguities. Numerous instances of patois fragment the linguistic unity of the book, and limit the range of textual understanding for the non-Jamaican reader. Cliff, however, includes a glossary of Creole terms as a posttext, without giving any prior indication of that fact; this is tantamount to a gesture of inclusion/exclusion that forces the reader to situate him- or herself with regard to his or her particular understanding of Jamaican Creole. Thus American readers who approach this book for the first time may well remain unaware of the glossary, and feel "excluded" unless they flip through to the last page of the book while reading.[14] This move from Standard English to Creole speech is meant to underscore class and race differences among protagonists, but it also makes manifest the double consciousness of the postcolonial, bilingual, and bicultural writer who lives and writes across the margins of different traditions and cultural universes.[15] For Cliff, to attempt to define her own place is also to undermine all homogeneous and monolithic perspectives—especially those constructed by the official colonial historiography—and to situate her text within the prismatic field of contemporary feminist discourse.[16]

For these very reasons, Cliff's reception in Jamaica is quite problematic. It is in fact symptomatic of the alienated status of the feminist postcolonial writer: relatively unknown outside of intellectual feminist circles, Cliff is seen, like many other West Indian female intellectuals, as an expatriate, and is accused of exhibiting a feminism colored by Euro-American ideology. Lloyd Brown, for example, in his introduction to a volume of selected conference papers (1981–83) titled *Critical Issues in West Indian Literature,* states that "one needs to be very sceptical about claims on behalf of 'radical' feminism and 'revolutionary' women's movement in the Caribbean." Although ostensibly sympathetic to the feminist perspective, Brown sees the whole issue as still largely foreign to the culture of the region:

> The need to address Caribbean literature and society through feminist and pro-feminist perspectives has been long-standing and embarrassingly neglected, but attributing some sort of mass "radicalism" to a pervasively conservative, often reactionary, society is quite another thing. There is the possibility that the exercise can be little more than the smuggling in of so much foreign (North American) baggage rather than a demonstrated reality of West Indian life.[17]

While this tendency to discount feminism is bemoaned in the recent and ground-breaking work of Carol Boyce Davies and Elaine Savory Fido, who have produced the first comprehensive anthology of feminist criticism of Caribbean literature, the impulse to regard Cliff's ideology as suspect remains strong among Caribbean critics.[18] Cliff has been influenced by the American women's movement and the work of lesbian poets such as Audre Lorde and Adrienne Rich, whom she acknowledges at the beginning of *Abeng.* Like Audre Lorde, Cliff does not position herself as a "representative" of West Indian life, nor does she mean to be. Certainly, her lesbianism is bound to be controversial in the Caribbean cultural context (where homosexuality, like feminism, is generally viewed as a "foreign import"). Unlike Lorde, however, whose *Afro*-Caribbeanness is never in question, Cliff's self-representation is more problematic. And it is her position as a racially mixed Jamaican, who can "pass" for white but prefers to recover the African heritage of her matrilineal ancestry, that draws the interest of critics such as Pamela Mordecai and Betty Wilson:

> The only one of the recently published Caribbean writers who does not affirm at least aspects of being in the Caribbean place is Michelle Cliff, who along with [Jean] Rhys could be regarded as being more in the *alienated tradition* of a

"francophone" than an anglophone consciousness. Personal history perhaps provides important clues: like Rhys, who felt isolated, Cliff is "white"—or as light skinned as makes, to the larger world, little difference. Also like Rhys, she went to the kind of school—quite comprehensively described in *No Telephone to Heaven*—which promoted the values of the metropole. Like Rhys, she left her island early and never really came home. One of the prices she has paid is a *compromised authenticity* in some aspects of her rendering of the creole.[19]

As an exile who has lived and studied in England and the United States, where she now lives, Cliff is clearly marginal to the Jamaican cultural mainstream. But what writer ever was truly part of a "mainstream"? Indeed, exile and marginality are perhaps the necessary preconditions for what Myra Jehlen terms "the extraordinary possibility of our seeing the old world from a genuinely new perspective."[20] To blame Cliff for belonging to an "alienated tradition" of Caribbean writers is to misunderstand the point of Cliff's representational strategies, which aim at reclaiming a lost heritage, at affirming what had been devalued while simultaneously re-presenting and narrativizing the processes and experiences that had obscured and obfuscated those traditions in the first place. Indoctrination into the culture of the metropole was an integral part of the "elite" private school system, and Cliff painstakingly shows *how* middle-class Jamaicans were assimilated by that system. It is true that her project is comparable to those of Francophone authors Maryse Condé (*Heremakhonon*) or Myriam Warner-Vieyra (*As The Sorcerer Said . . . Juletane*), whose heroines are ambiguously passive.[21] But the theme of alienation has been central to women's literature in the Caribbean and in the United States, whether it is alienation because of what Mary Helen Washington has called the "intimidation of color"—the values used to breed conformity to white culture's expectations and standards of behavior and beauty—or the self-hatred generated by "passing" and self-denial.[22] The right pigmentation and "good" hair were always overvalued in the colonial context. Having both light skin and straight hair, Clare Savage embodies the physical ideal of the assimilated—a situation that estranges her from her darker sister and mother, and thus isolates her from that part of her own heritage. Alienation is therefore a given that must be dealt with before the narrator can begin to make sense of the past. As Cliff's prose poem puts it, to face the past becomes a matter of personal survival:

In the family I was called "fair"—a hard term. My sister was darker, younger. We were split: along lines of color and order of birth.

That family surface: treacherous—always the threat the heritage would out: that blackness would rise like slick oil and coat the white feathers of seabirds. Lies were devised. Truth was reserved for dreams. . . .
This kind of splitting breeds insanity. (*CI*, 11)

It is this split subjectivity of the narrator that is mirrored accurately in the self-conscious move from English to Creole, since the appropriation of the vernacular sets off the discontinuous and fragmented nature of the postcolonial subject. Indeed, as Daryl Dance has observed, "there are many language forms available" to the Caribbean writer, so that the question of *"which* word" to use becomes inseparable from the way subjectivity is defined. Because "language and identity are inseparable," poets have always known that in order to liberate the world one must start by liberating the word.[23] Aimé Césaire and Derek Walcott have made extensive use of neologisms that attempt to capture the uniquely hybrid, *métis,* and heteroglot world of the Caribbean.[24] Since it is in the nature of oral languages not to have a fixed and codified system of orthography, it is not entirely fair to state, as Mordecai and Wilson do, that Cliff's rendering of Creole is "compromised" by a lack of "authenticity." For Cliff, the use of written Creole becomes essential to the project of

> retracing the African part of ourselves, reclaiming as our own, and as our subject, *a history sunk under the sea, or scattered as potash in the canefields,* or gone to bush, or trapped in a class system notable for its rigidity and absolute dependence on color stratification. On a past bleached from our minds. It means finding the artforms of these of our ancestors and speaking the *patois* forbidden us. (*LLB*, 14; emphasis mine)

That is why, Evelyn O'Callaghan can write of Cliff that

> this deliberate counterbalancing is crucial for "a writer coming from the culture of colonialism" [*LLB,* 14] and has politically influenced the direction her writing has taken. . . . In consolidating *the literary potential of the Jamaican Creole continuum,* . . . writers are challenging the hegemony not only of the 'Queen's English,' but of any outward-looking value system.[25]

The cultural nationalism at work in the Caribbean has encouraged writers to develop a new hybrid language, based on the oral traditions of the area and capable of capturing the elusive—and often subversive—subtext of those ancient and "noncanonical" traditions.[26] Linguists increasingly agree that the language situation no longer fits the binary model of "bilingualism" or "diglossia" that used to be applied to the region. There is in fact a linguistic "continuum" that allows speakers to vary their speech along the spectrum from Standard English at one pole to what is known as "Broad Creole" at the other, despite the fact that, as Pauline Christie points out, it is still true that

> for most people in the community, the roles of Creole and English seem to be clearly demarcated, as are the individuals and groups they associate with each. The fact is, that the roles are not always easily definable and what is usually considered English more often than not includes a number of features which characterize it as distinctly Jamaican or West Indian, while the so-called Creole reveals the continued influence of English. . . .
>
> On the one hand, increasing social and cultural interaction within the society has led to *greater acceptance of Creole forms in formal usage.* . . . On the other hand, the physical and psychological distancing from expatriate models . . . has given rise to innovations in formal speech and writing which can be seen as *developments from English structure.*[27]

Indeed, Caribbean languages are shaped by an all-encompassing syncretism that generates new forms of social and national identities for speakers and writers. Hence, any attempt at establishing rigid demarcations between users of one or the other form of speech reveals itself to be an artificial gesture favoring a view of identity and subjectivity that perpetuates a false ideal of purity—an ideal that is, however, the aim of all assimilationist ideologies.

As Cliff discusses it in her essay "A Journey into Speech," the West Indian writer's relationship to language has been extremely problematic, because of what O'Callaghan terms "the outward looking value system" and Christie calls the "expatriate models." These have strongly influenced the educational system, creating an Anglocentric cultural mold that some contemporary writers have been unable to resist, mimicking in their work the canonical models of British literature:

> One of the effects of assimilation, indoctrination, passing into the anglocentrism of British West Indian culture is that you believe absolutely in the hegemony of the King's English and in the form in which it is meant to be expressed. Or else your writing is not literature; it is folklore, and folklore can never be art. Read some poetry by West Indian writers—some, not all—and you will see what I mean. You have to dissect stanza after extraordinarily anglican stanza for Afro-Caribbean truth; you may never find the latter. But this has been our educa-

tion. The anglican ideal—Milton, Wordsworth, Keats—was held before us with an assurance that we were unable, and would never be enabled, to compose a work of similar correctness. No reggae spoken here. (*LLB,* 13)

Elsewhere in the Caribbean, Francophone writer Maryse Condé has acknowledged that "lullabies that rocked [her] to sleep were sung in metropolitan French . . . while [her] neck was strait-jacketed by French verbal conjugations." But in the same essay, she also adds, "Today, we can summon to memory the languages of our ancestors. . . . French and English together with Creole and indigenous Caribbean languages, Bambara and other African tongues form a matrix for the breaking of new linguistic ground and unexplored derivatives."[28] Cliff's project is to explore this hybrid dimension of vernacular speech, and to dig beneath the linguistic surface so as to comprehend the power of individual words to recall and connote a forgotten cultural matrix. She is involved in an "archaeological" enterprise, not unlike that of Michel Foucault in his *The Archaeology of Knowledge.* Digging underneath the colonial process of subject formation, Cliff examines the various cultural strands that make up Creole culture: the European and the African influences, braided together, the experience of dispossession that is characteristic of slave societies, and the concomitant need to question the tenets of Western humanism.

When history is recognized to be full of gaps, it is impossible to subscribe to a traditional notion of the subject as theorized by Western humanism. As Foucault explains:

> Continuous history is the indispensable correlative of the founding function of the subject: the guarantee that everything that has eluded him may be restored to him; the certainty that time will disperse nothing without restoring it in a reconstituted unity. . . . Making historical analysis the discourse of the continuous and making human consciousness the original subject of all historical development and all action are two sides of the same system of thought.[29]

That system of thought has created the illusion that memory and history can define the self and give meaning and authority to each utterance. By contrast, Cliff's strategy is to let the narrative show how authority is a construction of language, and how the multicultural subject is always the site of contradictions.[30]

Similarly, Martinican critic Roger Toumson has also cautioned that we must approach the issue of identity with a full understanding of the role that Western philosophy has played in the rationalization of inequality, in the subjugation of an "other" defined and coded negatively vis-à-vis a master who is the only "proper" person and full subject of history. Thus, Toumson adds, "humanism was able to legitimize a praxis of barbariousness [sic]."[31] A system of thought that represents the "other" as a variation of the "same" cannot do justice to the multicultural environment of the Caribbean, and, for Toumson, the questions that must now be asked are the following:

> What philosophy of the subject, what concept of difference
> can bear witness to the Caribbean cultural particularity with-
> out the experienced difference being neither put as difference
> in relationship to the European or African model nor brought
> back to a repetition of one or the other of these models? How
> else can we conceive ourselves *otherwise?*[32]

Echoing Frantz Fanon's formulation in *Toward the African Revolution,* Toumson goes on to say:

> The Caribbean logic of experience no longer authorizes the
> transfer of the biological to the anthropological. . . . [We must]
> try to put an end to the binary theory of identity as soon as
> possible by preventing the morbid resurgence of the discourse
> of absolute otherness. When, for example, the White illusion
> is followed by the Black illusion there is passage only from
> the same to the same.[33]

"To conceive ourselves otherwise" means to scrutinize the assumptions that buttress our systems of ideology, including the ones that would tend to essentialize language as an entity that is not permeable to its "other" or that can be judged inauthentic, depending on the subject position adopted or evinced by the speaker. Because linguistic innovations tend to undermine the separation between standard language and vernacular speech, this highly creative process of cultural Creolization also forms the basis for a praxis of self-invention through and in language that is the virtual project of many writers (from Marie-Thérèse Humbert to Abdelkebir Khatibi, from Zora Neale Hurston to Jean Rhys, from Toni Morrison to Salman Rushdie) who are the products of colonial encounters and whose works experiment with the emancipatory potential of language.

The 'Noises' of History

> *The real world—that is the world outside country—could be just as*
> *dreamlike as the world of make-believe—on this island which did not*
> *know its own history.*
>
> Michelle Cliff, *Abeng* (p. 96)

How can we theorize this possibility of thinking "otherwise"? In order to scrutinize the role played by the vernacular in the constitution of a postcolonial subjectivity that truly reflects the discontinuities of Caribbean history, I want to turn to a brief discussion of communication theory. It will help me show how Creole can function as "noise" in the alienated discourse of the assimilated subject. As stated above, Cliff's book, like the *abeng,* is a polysemic means of communication that addresses different audiences simultaneously. What is "message" for a Creolophone audience may be construed simply as "noise" by an Anglophone reader. What does this self-conscious articulation of "noise" and "message" tell us about the discourse of the postcolonial writer?

It has become a truism—at least since Claude Shannon and Warren Weaver published their path-breaking research on the mathematical theory of communication in the 1940s—that there is no message without noise, that any channel of communication contains some form of interference that impedes, to a greater or lesser degree, the reception of a message.[34] It has also been a tenet of poststructuralist theory to argue against the binary sterility and linearity of subject-object and sender-receiver models of analysis, precisely because this linear formal approach evacuates the noise, that is, the contextual and connotative dimensions of the message being communicated. By contextual dimensions, I mean the heterogeneities and pluralities that subtend any act of language, any act of representation, and that we have to take as *givens* in any culture.

Thus, also, French mathematician and philosopher Michel Serres, in his book *Le Parasite,* relates noise in the communicative context to biological parasitism: in French, the word *parasite* means "interference" or "static," as on the sound waves of telecommunication systems, as well as referring to parasitism in general, to the organisms that thrive on a host's body while keeping it healthy. Michel Serres's point about noise is that what may be perceived as interference is perhaps simply another message trying to get through, trying to be heard against the background of existing discourses. Serres gives in particular the example of the ringing telephone that interrupts a dinner conversation: on one level it is random, unwelcome noise, but by answering the phone one receives a message in its own right, a message with which the dinner-table conversation interferes because *it* will now function as noise.[35]

Viewed from this perspective, any message can become the noise or static that disrupts the orderly proceedings of another communicative act; the more obvious the disturbance, the easier the task of containing, ignoring, or neutralizing the disruptive factors. The point I want to get to, however, is this: if the discourse of an author is outside of the acceptable norms of common linguistic practice, and if he or she wants to use it to disrupt or resist those dominant norms, one way to proceed is to undermine from within, in order to avoid being too easily neutralized. Of course, the author might also run the risk of having his or her message mistaken for meaningless noise, if he or she communicates it in a language that is not a part of the general frame of reference of that dominant discourse.

The predicament I have just outlined is that of all so-called marginal writers who belong to several hierarchized cultural universes, and who generally express themselves in a "dominant" language. Such is the case with African American writers, who have the choice between Standard English and vernacular traditions, and with postcolonial writers, whose mother tongue may be patois, Creole, Joual, Wolof, Bambara, Berber, or Arabic, but who write in French or in English. This vernacular mother tongue will produce interferences in the text, interferences that only a reader trained to recognize the—sometimes duplicitous, sometimes obvious—use of the vernacular, and receptive to its message, will not dismiss as noise.

In his essay "Bilinguisme et Littérature," Abdelkebir Khatibi discusses this "translation" problem as it relates to North African literature:

> Tant que la théorie de la traduction, de la bi-langue et de la pluri-langue n'aura pas avancé, certains textes . . . resteront imprenables selon une approche formelle et fonctionnelle. La langue "maternelle" est à l'oeuvre dans la langue étrangère. De l'une à l'autre se déroulent une traduction permanente et un entretien en abyme, extrêmement difficile à mettre au jour. . . . Où se dessine la violence du texte, sinon dans ce chiasme, cette intersection, à vrai dire, irréconciliable? Encore faut-il en prendre acte, dans le texte même: assumer la langue française, oui *pour y nommer cette faille et cette jouissance de l'étranger* qui doit continuellement travailler à la marge.[36]

> [As long as a theory of translation, of this double- and multi-language has not progressed, some texts . . . will remain beyond appropriation by a formalist or functionalist approach. The "mother" tongue is at work within the other tongue. There is a permanent movement of translation from one to the other, a dialogue as with a mirror, extremely hard to elucidate. . . . The violence of the text takes shape precisely in this chiasmus, this intersection, this irreconcilable difference. We must however take note of it within the text itself: we need to

assume the French language, but in order *to name this divide, this fault, and this joyful use of what is foreign,* with its process of undoing the margin continually.]

It is important to note that the term *jouissance* is not used here simply in the sense made familiar by psychoanalysis (Lacan, Kristeva, Barthes, and so on). What is also implied in Khatibi's text is the *legal* aspect of the term, as in the legal phrase *jouissance d'un bien,* which means to have the use and possession of a piece of property (the usufruct). This meaning is related here to the use and possession of a language, to the process of "making a language one's own" as Bakhtin also understands it: that is, the way an individual appropriates a language, a cultural code, transforms it, and makes it his or her own, despite the fact that the code may continue, on a certain level, to resist appropriation.[37]

But, what is most important for Khatibi is that the fact of recognizing and naming the proliferation of textual gaps between different levels of discourse effaces territorial boundaries and continually undoes the margin: this, for him, is the function of the vernacular in the text when it operates as message in its own right and not as noise—it undoes and undermines the binary relation between center and periphery, message and noise, history and fiction, language and "dialect." In other words, the vernacular offers a continual play of resistance. Although it may clearly be marked as "other"—thus leaving itself open to the possibility of cooptation—it can also create tensions and contradictions within the dominant discourse, setting in motion the dynamics of dissent, intervention, and change that can ultimately allow a "minority" position to resist integration and assimilation, and even to become its own exclusionary system (that might eventually exist in a symbiotic relationship with the dominant ideology, just as the parasite does in the host's body). When viewed from this perspective, the vernacular can help us understand particular configurations of power at a given historical moment.

When Michelle Cliff strives to reinvent the past, she is guided by its traces as they exist and show up in the everyday world. More often than not, these traces are present in language in the form of words whose etymology is "foreign" and often unknown to the majority of the people using them. In such cases, the vernacular is "parasitic," its existence depending upon the relative unrecognizability of its origins. That is why Cliff takes on the role of cultural translator, stating: "The people . . . did not know that their name for papaya—*pawpaw*—was the name of one of the languages of Dahomey. Or that the *cotta,* the circle of cloth women wound tightly to make a cushion to balance baskets on their heads, was an African device, an African word" (p. 20). Interestingly, words such as *pawpaw* and *cotta* function as noise in *both* Standard English and Jamaican Creole. Although commonly used in everyday speech, and assimilated into the language, they retain a radical difference that can point to their submerged origins on the palimpsest of history. Now, in Anglocentric "literary language," *pawpaw* and *cotta* could of course be recuperated as "folkloric" cultural detail, but for Cliff they become polyvalent signifiers, lifelines to a different past, the means by which a different art form, closer to an oral tradition of storytelling and self-representation, can begin to take shape.

This linguistic practice confirms Trinh T. Minh-ha's recent views on the matter. She suggests that "vernacular speech . . . is not acquired through institutions—schools, churches, professions, etc.—and therefore not repressed by either grammatical rules, technical terms, or key words."[38] Its intent and purpose, she goes on to explain, are outside of the realm of persuasion. Vernacular speech does not aim at clarity, for "clarity as a purely rhetorical attribute serves the purpose of a classical feature in language, namely, its instrumentality."[39] Echoing Khatibi, Trinh adds: "Clarity is a means of subjection, a quality both of official, taught language and of correct writing, two old mates of power: together they flow, together they flower, vertically, to impose an order."[40] The presence of Creole creates for the non-Jamaican reader an opacity that places Cliff's text beyond appropriation, demarcating it as radically "other" for an English speaker, preventing any simplistic understanding based on its purely referential value. Hence, that opacity has a doubly subversive function: it does not aim simply to suggest (*pace* Mordecai and Wilson) a specific link to a more or less "authentic" cultural past, *and* it prevents the ideological adoption of a static form of humanism, because it stresses the distance between narrator and reader, between insiders and outsiders, Creole speakers and their others, while undermining the reader's belief in the value of "clarity."

Not unlike Zora Neale Hurston, who has been a major influence on her work and her thinking, Cliff is what I have called an *auto-ethnographer*, because her narratives belong in a new genre of contemporary autobiographical texts by writers whose interest and focus are not so much the retrieval of a repressed dimension of the *private* self, but the rewriting of their ethnic history, the re-creation of a *collective* identity through the performance of language.[41] Thanks to the appropriation of the oral tradition, the written text becomes a patchwork of discontinuous influences, and Cliff points out that her experience as a writer, her "struggle to get wholeness from fragmentation while working within fragmentation, producing work which may find its strength in its depiction of fragmentation, through form as well as content," is similar to the experience of many other writers coming from colonial backgrounds (*LLB* 14–15).

That is why the reconstruction of her fictive ancestors' past is translated through what Glissant has called an "économie parcellaire."[42] She has recourse to a textual economy of "small plots" that seems to correspond to the economy of "small plot farming" that maroon slaves used to engage in. Because she wants to claim the cultural heritage of the maroons who survived in large numbers in Jamaica, Cliff uses a narrative fragmentation that is but the mimesis of another form of cultural and economic dispersion and segmentation. In order to survive in the high mountain regions of the island, the maroons would cultivate small plots of land that were alternatively cleared out and left fallow because they were always on the move so as to avoid being captured by their former masters. Whereas the totalizing discourse of colonial historiography would appear to correspond to the economy of large, self-sustaining plantations, the small "portions" of texts, episodes, and plots in Cliff's narrative would rather seem to reapportion and reassign authority and agency to a different set of elusive actors, always on the move, and present on both the public and the private stages of history. The narrative discontinuities and the polyphonic tone of *Abeng,* as well as the shifts among different linguistic registers, all suggest a form of subjectivity bound to the fluid configurations of memory, language, and landscape, and representable only in nonlinear forms.

Cliff's search for a means of cultural representation that can do justice to the heterogeneities of the present and to the absent categories of the past is echoed throughout the Caribbean in the work of male and female, Francophone and Anglophone, writers (C. L. R. James, Brathwaite, Césaire, Maximin, Schwarz-Bart, Condé, to name just a few). This is how Edouard Glissant formulates it:

> The past, to which we were subjected, which has not yet
> emerged as history for us, is, however, obsessively present.
> The duty of the writer is to explore this obsession, to show
> its relevance in a continuous fashion to the immediate present.
> This exploration is therefore related neither to a schematic
> chronology nor to a nostalgic lament. It leads to the identifica-
> tion of a painful notion of time and its full projection forward
> into the future, without the help of those plateaus in time
> from which the West has benefited, without the help of that
> collective density that is the primary value of an ancestral

cultural heartland. That is what I call *a prophetic vision of the past.*[43]

Contemporary Caribbean writers address and reject the Hegelian view of history as a single hierarchical and linear process that would run its unique—European—course, bypassing the Caribbean as it did Africa.[44] But this intolerable absence in the realm of self-conscious representations can in fact allow the postcolonial writer to invent and re-create a sense of continuity and community rooted in this absent temporal landscape. It is by becoming an agent in this shared process of cultural mutation that writers such as Cliff or Condé free themselves from the straitjacket of a Eurocentered vocabulary.

Unlike the previous generation of Caribbean writers, from Césaire to Lamming, whose discourse on *exile* established the parameters within which much of negritude was to become understood, Cliff's effort rejoins the patient reconstructions of history and physical landscape already attempted by Glissant:

> Landscape is more powerful in our literature than the physical size of countries would lead us to believe. The fact is that it is not saturated with a single history but effervescent with intermingled histories, spread around, rushing to fuse without destroying or reducing each other. . . .
>
> We are finished with the fight against exile. Our task today is reintegration. Not the generalized power of the scream, but the painstaking survey of the land. . . . [We have] the difficult duty of considering the function of language and the texture of self-expression. In particular, [we must be careful] not to use Creole in a mindless fashion, but to ask in all possible ways, *our* question: How do we adapt to the techniques of writing an oral language that rejects the written? How do we put together, in the dimension of self-expression, the use of several languages that must be "mastered"?[45]

By situating herself on the postmodern side of the ideological fence separating different generations of Caribbean writers, Cliff sets the stage for the kind of "historiographic metafiction" that locates postcolonial subjectivity within the interstices of heteroglossia and in the "lived rhythms" of orality.[46] But she also belongs in the tradition that begins with Césaire's "Notebook," a work James Clifford has described as "a tropological landscape in which syntactic, semantic, and ideological transformations occur."[47] Like Césaire, Cliff undermines the colonial language and transforms reality by her use of tropes.[48] These tropes function as subversive or "deviant" historical categories that allow her to redefine the private and public genealogies of the Savage family.[49]

Wild Mangoes and Windward Maroons

The present always invents a past for itself out of its own desire.
           Daniel Maximin, interview with Clarisse Zimra[50]

In the forest of your dreams you seek the key to your fruits.

Because you must know which one is your dream fruit, your fruit of pleasure. Litchi? Mango? Apple?

           Daniel Maximin, *Lone Sun*[51]

Two of the tropes that Cliff uses quite consistently in *Abeng* are "mangoes" and "maroons." Both mangoes and maroons connote the "wild," the uncultivated, the free, and both imply radical resistance to any form of hegemonic control: "Some of the mystery and wonder of mangotime may have been in the fact that this was a wild fruit. Jamaicans did not cultivate it for export to America or England—like citrus, cane, bananas. . . . For them the mango was to be kept an island secret" (p. 4); "The Windward Maroons . . . held out against the forces of the white men longer than any rebel troops. . . . Nanny was the magician of this revolution—she used her skill to unite her people and to consecrate their battles" (p. 14).

In Cliff's mythmaking, the mango becomes a heterogeneous signifier that can readily be opposed, on the symbolic level, to the rigid classificatory practices of the colonial system. The following example of schoolyard gossip amply demonstrates the systematic stratification of social classes according to the color line, and the divisive impact of this rigid classification on children:

> The shadows of color permeated the relationships of the students, one to one. When the girls found out that Victoria Carter, whom everyone thought was the most beautiful girl in school, was the daughter of a Black man who worked as a gardener and an Englishwoman who had settled in Jamaica, her position in their eyes was transformed, and girls who had been quite intimidated by her, now spoke about her behind her back. (p. 100)

In order to create her own counterdiscourse to this disabling situation, Cliff establishes, on the first page of the text, the mango as emblem of the hybrid, mixed-race people of the island:

It was a Sunday morning at the height of the mango season. . . . There was a splendid profusion of fruit. The slender
cylinders of St. Juliennes hung from a grafted branch of a
common mango tree in a backyard in town. Round and pink
Bombays seemed to be everywhere. . . . Small and orange
number elevens filled the market baskets at Crossroads. . . .
Green and spotted Black mangoes dotted the ground at bus
stops, schoolyards, country stores—these were only to be
gathered not sold. The fruit was all over and each variety was
unto itself—with its own taste, its own distinction of shade
and highlight, its own occasion and use. In the yards around
town and on the hills in the country, spots of yellow, pink,
red, orange, black, and green appeared between the almost-
blue elongated leaves of the fat and laden trees. (p. 3)

The use of food imagery as a marker of cultural identity is common
to several African-American women writers: Maya Angelou, for example, also refers to the variety of skin colors among blacks by using
similar tropes and metaphors.[52] By consciously using the mango, Cliff
alludes to the nineteenth-century discourse of scientific racism: her
poem "Passing" echoes and repeats these pages of *Abeng,* but there
the emphasis is on the ideological constructions of racial ambiguity
in terms of *animal* referents:

In Jamaica we are as common as ticks.
We graft the Bombay onto the common mango. The Valencia
    onto the Seville. We
mix tangerines and oranges. We create *mules.*
    (*CI,* 6; emphasis mine)

I will not dwell on the question of institutionalized scientific racism.
As Nancy Stepan has argued, the discourse of "races and proper
places" was grounded in the monogenists' and polygenists' belief in
the necessity to keep races "pure" and "apart," for their fear was that
interracial breeding would create subhumans akin to the mule, that
is, infertile mulattoes who would cause the white race's degeneracy
and its eventual extinction.[53] What interests me here is the fact that
this discourse is turned on its head: images of abundance and fertility
are generated by the height of the mango season, and are linked to
the idea of variety and diversity. That this diversity is a source of
strength is constantly stressed by Cliff. Furthermore, she makes an
explicit rapprochement between Clare's mother's light skin color and
the fruit—"She was in fact quite light-skinned, the shade of her

younger daughter, like the inside of a Bombay mango when the outside covering is cut away" (p. 127). The mango represents femininity and fertility, and is as central to the islanders' experience as the sea ("The smell of the sea and the smell of mangoes mixed with each other"; p. 20) or the cool tropical nights (in which "the scent of ripe mangoes was present and heavy"; p. 22), which are also ambiguous maternal symbols.

As pointed out above, *Abeng* underlines the matrilineal filiation, which, under the laws governing slave societies, would have been the only permissible filiation, the only acknowledged genealogy, and hence the only possible means of retracing memory and charting the contours of a historical past that, in the Caribbean, is both submarine and subterranean, "sunk under the sea, or scattered as potash in the canefields" (*LLB,* 14). This representation of the mother serves the double purpose of establishing both filiation and affiliation. Described as a strong and passionate woman who suffers from the absence of the kind of historical legitimacy that the narrative simultaneously creates for her daughter, Kitty is a virtual descendant of the famous maroons. But, locked in a negative image of the past (see, for example, the narrator's comments on p. 128), she clings to the condition of "victim" of her people, ignoring the existence of strong female maroon figures, such as Nanny, and initially passing on to her daughter the belief that "speaking well" and reading English books would be her passport to freedom, and to integration into the white world. Although Kitty is "more comfortable speaking patois and walking through the bush" (p. 99), she remains the "phallic mother," the one who helps buttress the patriarchal foundations of language, and who deprives her daughter of that Creole dimension of her own subjectivity because it is a dimension trapped in silence.[54] Wishing to grant Clare an "easier" life than her own, she tries to prevent the development of a double vision and a double consciousness in the child. As Clarisse Zimra argues, the patriarchy hides "the silent presence of a Mother not yet fully understood."[55]

But Cliff can use the broken threads of the colonial diaspora to weave a different narrative of belonging, inclusion, and kinship. *Abeng* becomes the performative rewriting of the web of multicultural influences that her mother could not—and would not—pass on to her. It is in the reconstructions of Kitty's—fictive—childhood memories that the narrative most explicitly reveals the narrator's desire for a past that can transform her view of the present, and be the antidote for the Anglocentric obsessions of the father. In naming their daughter Clare, Kitty allows her husband to believe that this choice signals her acceptance of a patriarchal legacy of learning, since Clare is the name of the college his grandfather attended at Cambridge University. But this naming is a stunning act of "signifying," a gesture of dissimulation on the part of the mother who thus also honors and recalls a devoted young black woman, Clary, who had played the role of surrogate mother to Kitty when she was seven.[56] By creating such a mythical link between her own name and her mother's past, Cliff's protagonist situates Kitty within a long tradition of female resistance and invents a new identity for herself, in accordance with her desire for a different personal history. This history begins with the life of the legendary slave and maroon woman whose presence in the text allows for the development of a counternarrative that challenges established historical practices and compels reinterpretation of the past through a different, Afrocentric, lens.

The conventions of the dominant historical and anthropological discourses are used to express Cliff's own subversive perspective, just as slaves used the *abeng* to "signify." Combining descriptions of geography and religion, of social and familial arrangements, Cliff does linguistic archaeology (e.g., the comments on the word *pawpaw*) while giving "folk" details (e.g., "They did not know . . . that Brer Anancy, the spider who inspired tricks and tales, was a West African invention"; p. 20). She directly relates Jamaican popular culture to African *practices,* establishing the links in the necessary process of cultural resistance to the theoretical and mythic adherence to European models of culture. This retrieval of the collective, and of the collectively repressed dimension of the cultural self, is mediated by the recognition that writing is an act of language that refigures the real. Cliff's apparently disconnected narrative moves generate interruptions and suspensions that allow her to take possession of all the threads in her multicultural background and to articulate a form of multivalent subjectivity capable of resisting shifting networks of power. By appropriating the repressed otherness of patois, she writes across the margins while questioning the very notion of marginality, since her position demonstrates that marks of difference and otherness are ambiguous and shifting. Much like the fading wallpaper in the mansion that used to belong to the slave owners, her father's ancestors (see p. 25), the English language is shown to be but a thin veneer barely hiding a Creolized, *métis* culture where the woman as native and the native as other merge with, and emerge from, the blind spots of official historiography.

It is by means of linguistic *practices* embedded within the apparently hegemonic function of the colonizer's language that *Abeng* enacts this transformation of culture. It clearly illustrates what Foucault has pointed out, namely, that "a change in the order of discourse does not presuppose 'new ideas,' a little invention and creativity, a different mentality, *but* transformations in a practice, perhaps also in neighboring practices, and in their common articulation."[57] This suggests that one of the ways in which one might account for the transformation of discursive apparatuses within a postcolonial context would be to identify and highlight those categories (such as "dialect" or "noise" in language, and "maroons" in historical narrative) that, in Foucault's terminology, would be labled "deviant," and to focus on the way they function in the larger culture. To the extent that new practices can provide means of resistance, they enable us to understand the conditions of possibility for a true paradigm shift in postcolonial culture.

Abeng accomplishes just such a modification in autobiographical discursive practice, bearing testimony to the pluralities of postcolonial existence, and thus challenging us, its readers, to become multicultural subjects as well, capable of recognizing the different shapes that a postcolonial artist's shadow might cast on the conventions of genre, as outlined by Gusdorf, and on the ideology of authenticity, as romanticized by some critics. Only then will we be able to understand fully the "conditions and limits" of autobiographical practice outside of a narrowly defined idea of self-writing, or of community.

Notes

1. Georges Gusdorf, "Conditions and Limits of Autobiography," in *Autobiography: Essays Theoretical and Critical,* ed. James Olney (Princeton, N.J.: Princeton University Press, 1980), 48; emphasis mine.

2. And, I should add, it contrasts with the approach used by many women and/ or non-Western writers since colonial times, as numerous critics have indeed noted. See, for example, William L. Andrews, *To Tell a Free Story: The First Century of Afro-American Autobiography, 1760-1865* (Urbana: University of Illinois Press, 1986), and the special issue on Afro-American autobiography Andrews edited for *Black American Literature Forum* 24 (Summer 1990); Bella Brodzki and Celeste Schenck, eds., *Life/ Lines: Theorizing Women's Autobiography* (Ithaca, N.Y.: Cornell University Press, 1989); Sidonie Smith, *A Poetics of Women's Autobiography: Marginality and the Fictions of Self-Representation* (Bloomington: Indiana University Press, 1987); Joanne M. Braxton, *Black Women Writing Autobiography: A Tradition within a Tradition* (Philadelphia: Temple University Press, 1989); Susan Stanford Friedman, "Women's Autobiographical Selves: Theory and Practice," in *The Private Self: Theory and Practice of Women's Autobiographical Writings,* ed. Shari Benstock (Chapel Hill: University of North Carolina Press, 1988).

3. Gusdorf, "Conditions and Limits," 29.

4. Ibid.

5. See Roland Barthes, *Writing Degree Zero* (New York: Hill & Wang, 1968), and Nadine Gordimer's reference to this text in *The Essential Gesture* (New York: Alfred A. Knopf, 1988), 286-87.

6. Audre Lorde, *Zami: A New Spelling of My Name (A Biomythography)* (Freedom, Calif.: Crossing, 1982).

7. Michelle Cliff, *Abeng* (Trumansburg, N.Y.: Crossing, 1984). Futher references to this book will include page numbers in parentheses in text. All quotations by permission of Michelle Cliff. For an interesting reading of *Zami* as revisionist mythmaking, see Claudine Raynaud, "'A Nutmeg Nestled inside Its Covering of Mace': Audre Lorde's *Zami,*" in *Life/Lines: Theorizing Women's Autobiography,* ed. Bella Brodzki and Celeste Schenck (Ithaca, N.Y.: Cornell University Press, 1988).

8. *Maroons* is a term applied to runaway slaves in many parts of the New World. In Jamaica, they were able to hide in the mountainous central regions of the island to evade capture and started a "remarkable tradition of revolt . . . [that] as slave societies go, [was] an unusual, perhaps unique record." Orlando Patterson, "Slavery and Slave Revolts: A Sociohistorical Analysis of the First Maroon War, 1665-1740," in *Maroon Societies: Rebel Slave Communities in the Americas,* ed. Richard Price (Garden City, N.Y.: Anchor, 1973), 275. In 1739 a treaty was signed between the British and the maroon leaders, acknowledging the existence of a free and independent maroon community with its own settlement. See Barbara K. Kopytoff, "The Maroons of Jamaica: An Ethnohistorical Study of Incomplete Polities, 1655-1905" (Ph.D. diss., University of Pennsylvania, 1973) (Ann Arbor, Mich.: University Microfilm 73-24, 169).

9. I use this phrase in the sense made familiar by Jean-François Lyotard, *The Postmodern Condition: A Report on Knowledge,* trans. Geoff Bennington and Brian Massumi (Minneapolis: University of Minnesota Press, 1984).

10. Christa Wolf, *Patterns of Childhood,* trans. Ursule Molinaro and Hedwig Rappolt (New York: Farrar, Straus, & Giroux, 1985), 3 and 406.

11. See Michelle Cliff's volume of poetry titled *Claiming an Identity They Taught Me to Despise* (Watertown, Mass.: Persephone, 1980). This book is hereafter cited as *CI,* with page numbers in parentheses.

12. See in particular Michelle Cliff, *The Land of Look Behind* (Ithaca, N.Y.: Firebrand, 1985). This book is hereafter cited in text as *LLB,* with page numbers in parentheses.

13. Smith, *A Poetics of Women's Autobiography,* 150. See Wolf, *Patterns of Childhood;* Maxine Hong Kingston, *The Woman Warrior: Memoirs of a Girlhood among Ghosts* (New York: Random House, 1977). In the final chapter of her *Poetics,* Sidonie Smith discusses Kingston's work and the question of postmodern self-representation in an illuminating way.

14. This was indeed the experience of some undergraduate students in my course on Caribbean women writers at Northwestern University: the nonlinear narrative and the unfamiliarity of Creole initially prevented them from appreciating this book as much as they did, say, Jamaica Kincaid's *Annie John* or Myriam Warner-Vieyra's *Juletane,* which do not require as much sustained attention and involvement from the reader.

15. This double consciousness was first described by W. E. B. Dubois in *The Souls of Black Folks: Essays and Sketches,* in 1903. The volume has been reprinted, with an introduction by Saunders Redding (New York: Fawcett, 1961), 16, 17.

16. For a recent discussion of the question of feminist discourse in the context of the Caribbean, see Carole B. Davies and Elaine S. Fido, "Preface: Talkin' It Over: Women, Writing and Feminism," in *Out of the Kumbla: Caribbean Women and Literature* (Trenton, N.J.: Africa World, 1980), ix-xx. Also in that volume, an article by Lemuel Johnson, "A-beng: (Re)Calling the Body (In)to Question," makes use of many different strands of contemporary feminist theory (pp. 111-42).

17. Lloyd Brown, "Introduction," in *Critical Issues in West Indian Literature,* ed. Erika Sollish Smilowitz and Roberta Quarles Knowles (Parkersburg, Iowa: Caribbean, 1984), 3.

18. Carle B. Davies and Elaine S. Fido, eds., *Out of the Kumbla: Caribbean Women and Literature* (Trenton, N.J.: Africa World, 1980). See also note 16, above. I want to thank Belinda Edmondson for contributing to my understanding of the problematic reception of Cliff in Jamaica. Her unpublished paper "Race, Audience and the Use of Feminism in Two Contemporary West Indian Works" was especially useful because of her comparison of Cliff's *Abeng* to the Sistren Collective's *Lionheart Gal* (London: Women's Press, 1986).

19. Pamela Mordecai and Betty Wilson, eds. *Her True-True Name: An Anthology of Women's Writing from the Caribbean* (Portsmouth, N.H.: Heinemann, 1989), xvii; emphasis mine.

20. Myra Jehlen, "Archimedes and the Paradox of Feminist Criticism," in *The Signs Reader: Women, Gender and Scholarship,* ed. Elizabeth Abel and Emily K. Abel (Chicago: University of Chicago Press, 1983), 94.

21. For a discussion of Maryse Condé, *Heremakhonon,* trans. Richard Philcox (Washington, D.C.: Three Continents, 1982), see Françoise Lionnet, *Autobiographical Voices: Race, Gender, Self-Portraiture* (Ithaca, N.Y.: Cornell University Press, 1989), chap. 5. For a brief discussion of Myriam Warner-Vieyra, *As the Sorcerer Said . . . ,* trans. Dorothy S. Blair (Burnt Mill, Harlow: Longman, 1982), and *Juletane,* trans. Betty Wilson (London: Heinemann, 1987), see also Françoise Lionnet, "Myriam Warner-Vieyra," in *Fifty African and Caribbean Women Writers,* ed. Anne Adams (Westport, Conn.: Greenwood, forthcoming). Also useful in that context are Audre Lorde, "The Transformation of Silence into Action," in *Sister Outsider* (Trumansburg, N.Y.: Crossing, 1984), 40-44; Adrienne Rich, "Resisting Amnesia: History and Personal Life," in *Blood, Bread and Poetry: Selected Prose 1979-1985* (New York: W. W. Norton, 1986), 136-55.

22. See Mary Helen Washington, "Teaching Black-Eyed Susans: An Approach to the Study of Black Women Writers," in *All the Women Are White, All the Blacks Are Men, but Some of Us Are Brave: Black Women's Studies,* ed. Gloria T. Hull, Patricia Bell Scott, and Barbara Smith (Old Westbury, N.Y.: Feminist Press, 1982), 210.

23. Daryl Cumber Dance, "Introduction," *Fifty Caribbean Writers: A Bio-Bibliographical Critical Source Book* (Westport, Conn.: Greenwood, 1986), 4-5.

24. See Aimé Césaire, "Notebook of a Return to the Native Land," in *The Collected Poetry,* trans. Clayton Eshleman and Annette Smith (Berkeley: University of California Press, 1983); Derek Walcott, *The Castaway* (London: Cape, 1965).

25. Evelyn O'Callaghan, "Feminist Consciousness: European/American Theory, Jamaican Stories," *Journal of Caribbean Studies* 6 (Spring 1988): 157, 158; emphasis mine.

26. See also Maryse Condé's latest novel, *Traversée de la Mangrove* (Paris: Mercure de France, 1990), in which she uses images, turns of phrase, and sounds that give the text a particular flavor, unlike any other she has written before: the use of everyday "Antillean" language and speech patterns gives this novel a singular beauty.

27. Pauline Christie, "Language and Social Change in Jamaica," *Journal of Caribbean Studies* 3 (Winter 1983): 207, 226; emphasis mine. As Christie points out, the linguistic situation is by no means simple: "The continuum designation, however, not only obscures the fact that a range is not equally or at all observable in all parts of the 'system,' it also fails to take into account local stereotypes. In the mind of most members of the speech community, the situation involves English on the one hand and Creole on the other. In other words, they tend to ignore the marked variation in what they actually include under each label and the practical impossibility of drawing a dividing line between the two codes" (p. 206).

28. Maryse Condé, "Beyond Languages and Colors," *Discourse* 11 (Spring–Summer 1989): 110, 111–12.

29. Michel Foucault, *The Archaeology of Knowledge and the Discourse on Language,* trans. Alan M. Sheridan Smith (New York: Pantheon, 1972), 12.

30. Cliff's protagonist is adept at manipulating codes, switching from "patois" to "backra" whenever she needs to reassert her class superiority. *Backra,* or *buckra,* is a Creole term meaning "white person" and, by extension, "white" language. See *Abeng,* pp. 100-101, 122-23, and 133-34, for particularly interesting episodes in which Clare reveals her problematic relationship to Zoe and her ability to manipulate the social dissymmetry between them in order to maintain power and control.

31. Roger Toumson, "The Question of Identity in Caribbean Literature," *Journal of Caribbean Studies* 5 (Fall 1986): 134.

32. Ibid., 139.

33. Ibid., 141. See Frantz Fanon, "West Indians and Africans," in *Toward the African Revolution,* trans. Haakon Chevalier (New York: Grove, 1969). Fanon states: "Then, with his eyes on Africa, the West Indian was to hail it. He discovered himself to be the transplanted son of slaves; he felt the vibration of Africa in the very depth of his body and aspired only to one thing: to plunge into the great 'black hole.'

"It thus seems that the West Indian, after the great white error, is now living the great black mirage" (p. 27).

34. See Claude Shannon and Warren Weaver, *The Mathematical Theory of Communication* (Urbana: University of Illinois Press, 1949).

35. Michel Serres, *Le Parasite* (Paris: Grasset, 1980), 93.

36. See Abdelkebir Khatibi, "Bilinguisme et Littérature," *Maghreb pluriel* (Paris: Denoël, 1983), 179; translation and emphasis mine.

37. Jacques Lacan, *Le Séminaire,* Livre XX "Encore" (Paris: Seuil, 1975); Julia Kristeva, *Desire in Language: A Semiotic Approach to Literature and Art,* trans. Tom Gora, Alice Jardine, and Léon Roudiez (New York: Columbia University Press, 1980); Roland Barthes, *Le Plaisir du texte* (Paris: Seuil, 1973); Mikhail Bakhtin, "Discourse in the Novel," in *The Dialogic Imagination* (Austin: University of Texas Press, 1981), 258-422.

38. Trinh T. Minh-ha, *Woman, Native, Other: Writing, Postcoloniality and Feminism* (Bloomington: Indiana University Press, 1989), 16.

39. Ibid.

40. Ibid., 16-17.

41. See Lionnet, *Autobiographical Voices,* chap. 3.

42. Edouard Glissant, *Le Discours antillais* (Paris: Seuil, 1984), 69. This volume appears in English as *Caribbean Discourse: Selected Essays,* trans. J. Michael Dash (Charlottesville: University Press of Virginia, 1989).

43. Glissant, *Caribbean Discourse,* 63-64.

44. "Jenes eigentliche Afrika ist, soweit die Geschichte zurückgeht, für den Zusammenhang mit der übrigen Welt verschlossen geblieben; es ist das in sich gedrungene Goldland, das Kinderland, das jenseits des Tages der selbsbewußten Geschichte in die schwarze Farbe der Nacht gehüllt ist." See G. W. F. Hegel, *Vorlesungen über die Philosophie der Geschichte, Werke 12* (Frankfurt: Suhrkamp Verlag, 1970), 120. (As far back as history goes, the true Africa has remained cut off from all contact with the rest of the world; it is the golden land pressed in upon itself, and the land of childhood removed from the daylight of self-conscious history, wrapped in the dark mantle of night. My translation.)

45. Glissant, *Caribbean Discourse,* 154.

46. I borrow the phrase "historiographic metafiction" from Linda Hutcheon, *Narcissistic Narrative: The Metafictional Paradox* (New York: Methuen, 1984), xiv: "Historiographic metafiction . . . works to situate itself in history and in discourse, as well

as to insist on its autonomous fictional and linguistic nature." In *The Politics of Postmodernism* (London: Routledge, 1989), Hutcheon adds: "Subjectivity is represented as something in process, never as fixed and never as autonomous, outside history. It is always a gendered subjectivity" (p. 39); and "Postmodern texts consistently use and abuse actual historical documents in such a way as to stress both the discursive nature of those representations of the past and the narrativized form in which we read them" (p. 87). "Lived rhythms" is from Glissant, *Caribbean Discourse,* 154. The term "heteroglossia" is a Bakhtinian one. See "Discourse in the Novel."

47. James Clifford, *The Predicament of Culture: Twentieth Century Ethnography, Literature, and Art* (Cambridge, Mass.: Harvard University Press, 1988), 175.

48. This clearly suggests that the oversimplification of traditions in terms of periodization and/or colonial languages (i.e., Francophone versus Anglophone) becomes inappropriate in the Caribbean. The lines of literary filiation and affiliation are as complex as the bloodlines of slave cultures.

49. I use the word *deviant* here in the sense made familiar by Michel Foucault in *Discipline and Punish* (New York: Vintage, 1979); I will return to it in my conclusion. His concept of "heterotopia" can also clarify my point. See Michel Foucault, "Of Other Spaces," *Diacritics* 16 (Spring 1986): 22-27. The tropes used by Cliff contribute to the delineation of new spaces within the old landscapes.

50. Interview appears in Clarisse Zimra's introduction to Daniel Maximin, *Lone Sun,* trans. Clarisse Zimra (Charlottesville: University Press of Virginia, 1989), xvi.

51. Maximin, *Lone Sun,* 5.

52. See, for example, Maya Angelou, *Gather Together in My Name* (New York: Random House, 1974), 14; see also the discussion in Lionnet, *Autobiographical Voices,* 156.

53. See Nancy Stepan, "Biological Degeneration: Races and Proper Places," in *Degeneration: The Dark Side of Progress,* ed. J. Edward Chamberlin and Sander Gilman (New York: Columbia University Press, 1985); see also the discussion in Lionnet, *Autobiographical Voices,* 9.

54. For a discussion of the term "phallic mother" as used here, see Julia Kristeva, *Desire in Language,* especially pp. 190-208.

55. Clarisse Zimra, "Righting the Calabash: Writing History in the Female Francophone Narrative," in Davies and Fido, *Out of the Kumbla,* 157.

56. For a detailed discussion of the term *signifying* and its role in the cultures of the African diaspora, see Henry Louis Gates, Jr., *The Signifying Monkey: A Theory of Afro-American Literary Criticism* (New York: Oxford University Press, 1988).

57. Foucault, *Archaeology of Knowledge,* 209.

Chapter 16

Terms of Empowerment in Kamala Das's *My Story*
Shirley Geok-lin Lim

A popular approach to Western women's writings is to categorize the best of them as the achievements of exceptional women, women who were able to move beyond the sociocultural confines that kept other women "domesticated" and invisible. Such exceptional women forced a reordering and re-visioning of seemingly stable social relations and roles for women; their works, therefore, have been privileged in the canon of Euro-American women's literature.[1] In Sappho, Aphra Behn, Jane Austen, the Brontë sisters, Emily Dickinson, and Sylvia Plath, Western women persistently find models of exceptional women to study and emulate.

Recently, the privileging of exceptional Anglo-American women has become open to interrogation in critical exchanges about the intersections of race, class, and gender and the sociopolitical implications of "sisterhood." Bonnie Thornton Dill, succinctly outlining the racist and classist biases that have historically accompanied white American middle-class women's liberation movements, tells us that "contemporary scholarship on women of color suggests that the barriers to an all-inclusive sisterhood are deeply rooted in the histories of oppression and exploitation that Blacks and other groups encountered upon incorporation into the American political economy."[2] Dill calls, therefore, "for the abandonment of the concept of sisterhood as a global construct based on unexamined assumptions about our similarities" and urges us to "substitute a more pluralistic approach that recognizes and accepts the objective differences between women."[3]

American readers, however, are generally ignorant of non-Western women writers whose literary production has set them apart in their traditional societies. In the Asian world, the works of such women writers as Ding Ling and Kamala Das possess a power to enable their readers to reread social relations and to participate in a revolution of consciousness.[4] Such a revolution, Julia Kristeva rightly insists in *Revolution in Poetic Language,* must precede changes in the materialist/political horizon.[5] The transforming power in Ding Ling's and Das's work and its impact upon readers precede and/or parallel the effects of works by Anglo-American and ethnic women writers and critics such as Adrienne Rich, Alice Walker, and Barbara Smith. Ding Ling's and Das's writings contain the themes of women's revolt and the interrogations of the processes of women's subjectivity as it is situated in frankly portrayed male-female power relations that many Western readers associate chiefly with Anglo-American feminist literature.

Kamala Das is a prolific bilingual Indian woman poet, fiction writer, and essayist. She is the author of numerous novels in Malayalam, collections of English-language fiction and poetry, and an autobiography, *My Story*, published in 1976.[6] She is not entirely unknown to American readers; Sandra Gilbert and Susan Gubar have included her as the only representative from Asia in their *Norton Anthology of Literature by Women.*[7] As none of her Malayalam novels has been translated into English, I will address only her English-language writing.

For the purposes of this essay, I am interested in Das's autobiography as a document expressing the writer's own ambiguity—what Bakhtin characterizes as "the internal dialogism of double-voiced prose"[8]—as a woman asserting subjective power in a traditional patriarchal society. Her materialist critiques propose precisely those themes that give her writing its vividness and compelling power to arouse and disturb. Her female subjects destabilize our notions of what is female or feminine and dislocate given Indian cultural and social relations; in short, they give her writing a transformatory dimension that accounts for both the repulsion and the fascination it has provoked.[9]

Das's autobiography is a strongly public work, exhibiting a deliberate consciousness of audience. The audience is both the reader of the autobiography and the readers of her poetry prior to the writing of the autobiography; that is, the poet's audience appears in her life

story as an active catalyst and agent. Before turning to the autobiography, however, I would like to summarize her critical reception to
date, as that reception helps explain the "double-voicedness" of her
narrative.[10]

Das has had two audiences. Her own native Indian audience is
mostly English-educated and middle-class. Its class mobility and its
choice of the English language for expression are generally associated
with a modern, Westernized mentality (that is, with an unstable indigenous cultural identity related to an assimilation of sociopolitical values
influenced by Anglo-American norms and cultures).[11] Her other, more
vocal and welcoming, audience is an international group of readers,
chiefly from Australia. These non-Indian critics are interested in non-
Western writing in English. They represent the old Commonwealth
literature school of thought reincarnated as postcolonial, post-
Orientalist sensitivities to new or national or world literatures in English.[12] While the emphases are different, both audiences share common assumptions and make similar conclusions in approaching Das's
writing.

Das is acknowledged by both Indian and Anglo critics as working
within a "strong tradition of female writing . . . with a venerable ancestry."[13] The consensus from both interpretive communities is that her
achievement is limited to themes of female sexual and physical experience. Hostile readers, both Indian and international, debunk her
subjects, describing them variously as "a poetry of thighs and sighs,"
"salacious" fantasies of sexual neuroticism, and "flamboyant," "weak,"
"self-indulgent" obsessiveness.[14] Friendly critics valorize her as "a poet
of feminine longings."[15] She is praised (chiefly by male critics) for that
"feminine sensibility [that is] manifested in her attitude to love, in the
ecstasy she experiences in receiving love and the agony she feels when
jilted in it."[16] According to her most fervent defenders, both Indian
and Western, her feminine sensibility is expressed in her total involvement with the sexual male Other.

The recent publication of a selected collection of her work by the
Centre for Research in the New Literatures in English in Adelaide,
Australia, accompanied by critical essays, all by white Australian critics,
would seem to confirm a hardening of these interpretive lines.[17] Many
of the essays in the volume argue that the theme of Das's heterosexuality receives its highest apotheosis, its Indian rationale, in Das's
identity as a devotee of Krishna. As Dorothy Jones informs us, Krishna,
eighth avatar of Vishnu, is traditionally represented in Indian culture
as "an important focus in Hinduism of Bhakti, the experience of
intense religious adoration in which the soul [the female representa-

tion] abandons itself in ecstasy to the divine [the male representation]."[18] Jones is only repeating a paradigm, first articulated by Das herself, whereby the "vulgar" (and arguably Westernized "confessional") topos of brutal or illicit sexuality becomes transformed into the "high" topos of licit Brahminic mysticism.

In approaching Das's evident concentration on sexual themes, however, the non-Indian reader would do well to keep in mind that erotic sexuality is strongly inscribed in Indian, specifically Hindu, culture. In using these materials, Das is able to appeal to both the Western tradition that emphasizes confessional writing and the Hindu tradition that places a high and visible valuation on male-female eroticism. By a shift in authorial (and critical) perception, the sensual complexities of a "sensational"—because exceptional—life are reduced to an abstract allegory of religious quest and devotion. (No American reader, however, would find Das's so-called confessions of extramarital affairs memorable if set among the Hollywood memoirs appearing today!)

Many critics have participated in this sanitization of the female subject Das constitutes in her autobiography and her poetry, and have acquiesced, even contributed, to obfuscating the notable "revolt" against male-dominant terms of sexuality in her themes. They have interpreted the persona in her poems and autobiography to be a "smoothly" acceptable, because traditional, worshiper of that most adulterous, most privileged male Indian god, Krishna. Mohan Lal Sharma, for example, argues that Das's career exhibits a "pilgrim's progress" toward Krishna-worship; thus, he congratulates her for her faults in poetic style, since, for him, they demonstrate her religious achievement. "'He shining everything else shines' is the ultimate Upanishadic dictum," Sharma advises us, unself-consciously reflecting his patriarchal reconstruction of Das's work in his choice of dictums.[19] Sharma's male-centered critical orientation, moreover, is itself a reflection of the patriarchal structure of communities dominated by Krishna-worship. Adopting a similar critical approach, non-Indian critics such as Syd Harrex, Vincent O'Sullivan, and Dorothy Jones similarly turn Das's very specifically located materialist critiques of class and gender into a phantasm of Krishna-worship.[20]

I argue that Das's writing and life display the anger, rage, and rebellion of a woman struggling in a society of male prerogatives. Her best work cannot be read either as a celebration of love or as an allegorical abstraction of Radha, the Gopi cowmaid, worshiping Krishna in his many manifestations. I find that the informing energy in the autobiography springs, like the pulsating rhythm of a popular 1960s rock 'n' roll song, from its central poetics, "I Can't Get No Satisfaction."

Teresa de Lauretis, among other feminist commentators, has pointed out that "to feminism, the personal is epistemologically the political, and its epistemology is its politics."[21] "Satisfaction," therefore, while it encompasses the notion of sexual desire, emerges in the autobiography, as it does in Das's novel, *Alphabet for Lust,* as epistemologically the domain of female struggle in a patriarchal society.[22] The inequalities and social oppressions suffered by Indian women are many and profound. As Marilyn French reports in a 1985 United Nations-sponsored publication, "Most Indian women are married young by their families to men they have not met before. . . . They then move to their husbands' parents' home, where they are, essentially, servants."[23] French documents a series of social horrors: the dowry system, bride-burning, male abuse, the ban against divorce, women's isolation, job discrimination, female infanticide, poorly paid or unpaid female labor, high female illiteracy. Das's autobiography specifies the connections between personal/sexual and social/political struggles for a female protagonist in this traditional male-dominated society.

In her preface, Das locates the origin of her autobiography in the confessional impulse attending the deathbed. She indicates that the autobiography was written during her "first serious bout with heart disease," and that she "wanted to empty myself of all the secrets so that I could depart when the time came with a scrubbed-out conscience." This intention indicates a particular understanding of the autobiographical genre, one attuned to the confessional tradition of Christianity exemplified in Augustine's *Confessions.* The expressed wish for a "scrubbed-out conscience" itself prepares the reader for representations of "sinful" or immoral subjects, secrets that defile a conscience, and for some kind of remorse undertaken within a religious or spiritual frame of reference. Yet Das candidly reveals that she wrote her autobiography as a commercial publication, a series of articles for a popular magazine, because she needed money to pay off her medical bills. The spiritual impulse and the commercial intention are both evident in the dialogic, ambiguous, and contradictory features of the text.

The autobiography, republished in book form in 1976, possesses the characteristics that mark it as a book written hurriedly and structured to the formulaic requirements of serial publication. It has fifty chapters, each from two and a half to about four and a half pages in length. The organization of materials into so many short chapters is clearly governed by the necessity of chopping the life into as many marketable pieces as possible, thus revealing more about the magazine format and the attention span of its popular audience than about the

writer's craft. Moreover, the serial form dictates the anecdotal, superficial essayistic structure, allowing little room for analysis of difficult
issues or exploration of psychological experience.

The contradictions between the commercially dictated features of
the text and the narrator's stated "spiritual" intention have led many
critics to view Das as unreliable. "After reading such a confession,"
Vimala Rao says astringently, "it is difficult to determine where the
poseur ends and the artist begins."[24] Dwivedi describes the work as
"more baffling and dazing [sic] than her poetry," and Jones admits
that "it is hard to know how to respond to this book which, while
adopting an openly confessional tone, conceals quite as much or more
than it reveals."[25] Because they cannot read her autobiography as a
faithful account of her life, critics have generally preferred to treat it
as an appendix to her poetry. Sharma claims that Das's autobiography
"is the single best 'Reader's Guide' to the design and meaning of her
work."[26] Jones more cannily allows that "if considered as a literary
rather than a factual recreation of the writer's life, it often serves as
an illuminating comment on her poetry and fiction, exploring many
of the same dilemmas and situations."[27]

In fact, the obvious unreliability of the author's intention foregrounds the postmodernist qualities of Das's "autobiography." Thus,
instead of approaching it as a text containing an authentic account of
a life unmediated by literary conventions, I argue that our understanding of the constituted "autobiographical" female subject should be
informed by features of the text. These features include ones that
conform to a mass-market strategy (the simple anecdotal structure,
unrelenting focus on sensational and popular themes, attention to
domestic and marital relations as appealing to a female readership) and
ones that derive from the self-reflexive nature of the prose. In "deconstructing" Das's autobiography, then, I want to elaborate how it
achieves its impact less from its separate parts than from their sum.
While each chapter offers a distinct picture or theme, together the
chapters resonate in their emphasis on the domestic details of food,
familial relations, marriage, childbirth, sexual liaisons, and the internal
and external struggles of one woman in a sociopolitically repressive
world.

The opening chapters, for example, depict a colonized childhood,
resonant with the later theme of oppressed womanhood. The father,
a Rolls Royce and Bentley salesman, stood as a middleman between
the British corporation and the Indian upper class. Das similarly
showed the characteristic alienation of being suspended between
indigenous and colonized cultures. Unhappy as one of the few brown

children in a white school, the young girl "wondered why I was born to Indian parents instead of to a white couple, who may have been proud of my verses" (p. 8). Significantly, the child's very mastery of the colonial language, English, provoked the psychic break between herself and her (native) parents. This separation between English-language child-poet and Indian parents, a consequence of colonialism, prefigures the later rupture between the English-language woman writer, engaged in the Westernized project of claiming her own subjective autonomy, and traditional patriarchal Indian society. Das's autobiography, therefore, in its very "doubleness" of commercial and spiritual intentions and of suspension between colonized or Westernized and indigenous cultures, provides a valuable recording of the hybridized, "impure" cultural conditions in which postcolonial English-language writers from non-Western societies often find themselves writing.[28]

Setting the opening scene on the internal division in the colonized subject, Das prepares the reader for the move to the theme of an older division, the division between genders. By implication, the colonized child brings to her womanhood those perceptions of division arrived at when she learns to value her talent and simultaneously learns to reject her Indian parents, who do not value it. The longing for "white parents" is a powerful psychic aberration, expressing and demonstrating the embedded racism in the colonizing (and colonized) experience that the child has internalized. As the opening psychological drama, it contains those contradictions and ambivalences, between the privileging of "verse" and "self," at times recognized as a specifically "white" or Western-based value, and the respect to be accorded to one's "parent" society. In her representations of gender divisions, Das similarly oscillates between two contradictory positions: one the exceptional woman in conflict with her traditional society, struggling for a subject status specifically endowed through her writing, and the other, that most unexceptional of Indian women, the Krishna devotee. Das's subsequent examinations of her woman's experiences are informed by these postcolonial ambivalences—the contradictions between Westernized and indigenous sociopolitical values—as well as by gender and feminist concerns.

In the autobiography's dialogic representations, therefore, the interest does not lie in the frank revelations of illicit sexual encounters. In fact, the autobiography has so little of the pornographic in it as to make credible a critic's description of Das as "Matthew Arnold in a sari."[29] Instead, it compels our reading because it offers, among other things, a critique of the victimization of women in a patriarchal society.

The autobiography is itself a gesture enunciating the empowerment of the female when she speaks in protest, in rejection, in an infinitely recessive "desire" within a powerfully restrictive psychosocial matrix.

The dominant figure in her autobiography, also present in her fiction and poems, is the female as "desiring" subject. Female "desire" is figured in the psychological longing of a neglected daughter for a remote father, the physical drive of a virgin for sexual experience, the marital yearning of a young wife for emotional union with her husband, the ecstatic enjoyment of a mature woman with her lover, the depraved lust of a disillusioned older woman with a host of unloving and unlovely paramours, and finally as the ecstasy of the older devotee in the ancient worship of Krishna, a female soul seeking her divine bliss. "Desire," as embodied in the autobiography, is multiply manifest, attending a range of female roles. The narrator presents herself in turn as a girl-child with a crush on a teacher, the naive object of lesbian exploration, an innocent child bride, the victimized wife, loyal and loving wife, adoring mother, sexual tease, easy lay, and spiritual goddess seeking union with the divine. The narrator lives out these stereotypic roles.

The central attribute of this "desiring" female is that, in order to maintain her subject condition and the economy of energy that constitutes her being, she cannot be satisfied. As "self" is constituted in desire, and desire is given shape by the energy of an absence of satisfaction (whether in innocent longing, brutalized sex, cynical promiscuity, the range of female sexual experiences), the story of "self" is constructed on a continual series of arousals and deferments of satisfaction. The life in the autobiography is continuously plotted as a drama of desire, and the female protagonist becomes the representation of female desire.

Significantly, the narrative first provides the reader with a series of empowered female subjects. Chapter 4 is a rewriting of Das's matriarchal past. The narrative is yet another version of the legends surrounding her grandmother's home, Nalapat House, which had been mythologized in earlier poems.[30] The poem, "My Grandmother's House," for example, identifies the place with an idealized time in the poet's life, "where once / I received love" (*KD,* 14). In Das's automythology, the maternal home is also the trope for the condition of proud and loving freedom, a condition that the poem raises as absent in the degraded adult woman's life:

> . . . you cannot believe, darling,
>
> Can you, that I lived in such a house and

Was proud, and loved . . . I who have lost
My way and beg now at strangers' doors to
Receive love, at least in small change?

In the autobiography, Nalapat House becomes a symbol of the way in which the contradictions in traditional Indian women's roles can be resolved. Das traces her lineage to her ancestress, Kunji, a wealthy aristocrat who, at age fifteen, fleeing from the war between the English and Dutch, "was made to change her route by an amorous chieftain who brought her over to his village and married her" (p. 11). The delicate phrasing masks the more sensational possibilities of abduction, rape, and forced marriage; it suggests instead a romantically blurred portrayal of a male figure motivated by "amour," a male figure moreover who "was well-versed in Astrology and Architecture" and who set his bride up in the magnificent Nalapat House. The maternal home was dominated by "the old ladies"—"my grandmother, my aunt Ammini, my great grand-mother, her two sisters" (p. 12). Only two males intrude in this woman-universe, the remote and idealized political saint, Mahatmaji Ghandi, whom the uncomprehending girl saw as a brigand whose "diabolic aim was to strip the ladies of all their finery so that they became plain and dull"; and her grand uncle, the famous poet-philosopher Narayana Menon, who is seen as lonely and indigent. The girl-child falls under the influence of these women, especially her aunt Ammini, "an attractive woman who kept turning down all the marriage proposals that came her way." Ironically, it was from this virginal literary woman that Das "sensed for the first time that love was a beautiful anguish and a *thapasya*" (p. 12). Deepening the theme, the following chapter is devoted to an even earlier ancestress, "my great grandmother's younger sister," Ammalu, "a poetess." Like Ammini, Ammalu "was a spinster who chose to remain unmarried although pretty and eligible" (pp. 14–15).

What kind of female models do these two relatives offer the girl-child? Both women were ascetics. Ammini "chose to lead the life of an ascetic" (p. 12), while Ammalu "was deeply devout and spent the grey hours of dusk in prayer" (p. 15). Both loved poetry. The former recited it and the latter "read profusely and scribbled in the afternoon while the others had their siesta" (p. 15). Das locates the existence of an ancient female ambition for writing, expressed, and perhaps only capable of being expressed, in the strict and narrow social structures of the time and place, as religious longing. This writing ambition, while associated with female spinsterhood or chastity, is made more complex by its juxtaposition with intimate symbols of female sensuality. As a middle-aged woman, Das returns to her maternal home and discovers books containing Ammalu's poems. Together with "the leaves of her books, yellowed like autumn-leaves," Das finds "in the secret drawer of [Ammalu's] writing box, a brown bottle shaped like a pumpkin that smells faintly of Ambergris" (p. 16). The archetypal resonances in the symbols of "bottle" (container, receptacle, vagina, womb, female desire), pumpkin (roundness, swelling, female, fecundity), and ambergris (perfume, sensuality, arousal, sexuality) are meaningful cross-culturally, and the significance of their placement in "the secret drawer of her writing box" is deliberate and emphatic. If these ancestresses are literary spinsters, they also are familiar with female desire, with the knowledge "that love was a beautiful anguish." For Das, their biographies offered a knowledge of the complex intersections of asceticism and sexuality that form major thematics in her autobiography.

What separates this knowledge, the surface thematics of Das's autobiography and much of her poetry, from the usual sentimental drift of popular women's romances is that it is inseparably, intricately woven and innately situated in the thematics of woman as writer and as speaking subject. The identity of her ancestresses, while associated with love or yearning, remains woman- or subject-centered; and this subject condition is integral to and invested in the literary enterprise. In these maternal figures, therefore, the protagonist is able to find an indigenous tradition that her English-educated childhood had denied her. Only in Nalapat House, in a matriarchal society, do the identities of Indian, woman, and writer coalesce. Only here, as the poem suggests, are love and pride coeval, in contrast to the patriarchal society, where love becomes coeval with degradation.

Nalapat House and the women in it, while representing ideologically one pole of female empowerment, are also perceived as limited in what they can offer the active child. In the poem "Blood," for example, Das shows in painful detail the decline and fall of this matriarchal tradition. Its "chastity" and isolation from "the always poor" and "the new-rich men," its venerable ancestry ("Now three hundred years old, / It's falling to bits / Before our very eyes"; *OP*, 17) result in its destruction. The adult Das, while finding her source of identity in it, cannot resurrect this matriarchy:

> O mother's mother's mother
>
> I have plucked your soul
>
> Like a pip from a fruit
>
> And have flung it into your pyre. (*OP*, 19)

Yet, even as the autobiography narrates the sordid "reality" of a bad marriage and unsuccessful affairs, the matriarch as native spinster and writer remains a powerful representation that resonates in the background.

Similarly, foregrounding the native sources of the narrator's feminism, the early chapters narrate an active engagement with those Indian cultural elements that valorize unchallenged female power. The strongest symbol of female empowerment in the protagonist's early ancestral memories is Kali. Kali is the most feared deity in the Indian pantheon, the goddess to whom powers of death and destruction are attributed. Significantly, the narrator devotes her longest description to her worship. Describing the annual ceremonies, she writes, "When Kali danced, we felt in the region of the heart an unease and a leap of recognition. Deep inside, we held the knowledge that Kali was older than the world and that having killed for others, she was now lonelier than all. All our primal instinct rose to sing in our blood the magical incantations" (p. 26).

What is constituted in this "recognition"? The shift from "I" to the communal "we" emphasizes Das's explicit recognition here of a collective female "primal instinct" associated with the repressed aspects of womanhood, the un-nurturing, destructive forces of female passion. Paradoxically, Kali represents a collective identity of powerful isolation. Thus she is called the "lonely goddess." Her affection, we are told, is specially reserved for the aboriginal pariahs, people who are normally "regarded as outcasts and held at a distance" (p. 25). Only in the month of Makaram, between January and February, a time set aside for the worship of Kali, do the pariahs become important members of Indian society. Kali-worship, as a form of carnival, permits the reversal of social hierarchy and encourages the transgression of social rule. Kali's power in Indian society is such that it also permits a crossing of gender identity; in the Kali rituals, the oracle who takes on the role of Kali is a male: "He ran up and down through the crowd of people brandishing his scimitar before a trance thickened. . . . His voice changed into the guttural voice of the angry goddess" (p. 26). During the month of Makaram, young women perform a processional ritual in which they enter into a trance-like condition: "The drums throbbed against their ears, mesmerizing them so that their walk began to resemble the glide of a somnambulist and their eyes began to glow, nesting in their pupils the red flame of their lamps" (p. 26). The passage describes an ecstatic state at the level of sensuous experience that Kali-worship permits these young women, and stands in contrast to the later devotional passages on Krishna-worship, in which the god is described in abstract terms of nonphysicality, as "the bodyless one."

The Kali figure returns in a later chapter, to represent again those forces of fearful female isolation that can protect the outsider, the pariah, against "feudal enemies" (p. 178). In response to the villagers' persecution, Das decided she "too should try some magic to scare my foes away. I hung a picture of Kali on the wall of my balcony and adorned it daily with long strings of red flowers, resembling the intestines of a disemboweled human being" (p. 178). The Kali figure therefore represents the usually repressed energies of the female psyche whose release transgresses and crosses social hierarchy and gender. This mythic female power is capable of both destruction and protection, and it therefore has to be pacified through intercession.

In the early chapters Das sets up female figures, each of which, like the iconic representation of Kali, provided her as a girl-child with a "leap of recognition." In Ammina and Ammalu we recognize the woman writer influenced equally by sensual and ascetic passions, a woman recognizable in Amherst's Emily as well as in Nalapat House's Ammalu. In her grand-uncle's wife, we recognize yet another face of the empowered female. The wife is woman as voluptuary and seducer. She is "never seen even at night without her heavy jewellery, all gem-encrusted and radiant, and the traditional cosmetics of the Nair woman" (p. 19). And the object of her life is to "*enslave*" the man "with her voluptuous body" (p. 20; emphasis mine).

These early portrayals of female types make apparent, contrary to general critical consensus, that Das's focus is less on the male (or male-female relations) than it is on the female. The female types that fascinate the young girl range from those in the women-centered community in Nalapat House to the self-authored woman as subject (Ammalu) and the fearfully empowered Kali figure. Together they form an original patterning of proud and powerful womanhood against which the narrative of patriarchal marriage and abuse develops.

Despite the rhetoric of scandal Das employs to describe them, the male-female relations depicted in the autobiography, therefore, are significant more for their sociopolitical themes than for any scandal in them. For instance, in the narrative of her arranged marriage we see a critique of that institution beneath the apparently confessional surface. The fifteen-year-old Das, having experienced only schoolgirl crushes, the attentions of lesbians, and clumsy seduction attempts, is married to an older man because "I was a burden and a responsibility neither my parents nor my grandmother could put up with for long" (p. 73). Her marriage begins in sexual brutality. She calls the wedding-night encounter an unsuccessful rape (p. 79). She suffers through her husband's selfishness and neglect of her emotional and physical needs. The cook prepares only breakfast and dinner, and the young pregnant bride falls ill. After an early separation, she and her husband attempt a reconciliation when they move to Bombay, but she has a nervous breakdown at twenty, after the birth of her second son. Das's critique of Indian marriage as patriarchal oppression is more damning when the reader keeps in mind that middle-class and professional Indian women, a very small minority of Indian society, generally receive greater legal and social protection than the vast numbers of poor and peasant Indian women.

Exactly in the middle of the autobiography, in chapter 25, the narrator locates an instance of insight, an epiphany that permits the protagonist to move beyond the passivity of her female bondage to a more integrated existence. Faced with the failure of her marriage and the impossibility of leaving it, her son's illness, and her husband's rejection of her in favor of a homosexual attachment, the protagonist finds herself poised on a balcony in a moment of suicidal temptation: "I felt a revulsion for my womanliness. The weight of my breasts seemed to be crushing me. My private parts was only a wound, the soul's wound showing through" (p. 94). In this moment of recognition, the young wife acknowledges the imposed powerlessness of the female body, that understanding that woman's fate as suffering victim is tied to her physical body. The narrator expresses for us the knowledge that, for the victimized woman in a patriarchal society, sexuality not only makes her vulnerable physically, a prey to rapacious men; it is inherently bound up with her emotional and spiritual vulnerability. This moment of insight reinterprets the Freudian maxim that anatomy is destiny. It is a powerful, because profoundly ironic, reconceptualizing of woman's fate as victim; her victimization, we cannot be reminded too often, goes beyond the plane of material pain to encompass mental and spiritual conditions in which her very identity as woman and her own body become the instruments of her torment.

But the woman does not throw herself off the balcony. Instead, she "lit the reading lamp . . . and began to write about a new life, an unstained future" (p. 94). Again, as in the early chapters, the autobiography shows a female subject coming to her own ministry, becoming herself a mistress/ancestress of "an unstained future." Centrally located in the text, the passage repeats the central theme, of woman writing her self, not only as one act of identity among other acts, but as the primary act. She saves her life by telling her life. It is perhaps an example of cross-cultural concerns that this passage foreshadows a later passage by French feminist Hélène Cixous, who asserts that a woman must write her self to mark "her shattering entry into history which has always been based on her suppression. . . . To become at will the taker and initiator, for her own right, in every symbolic system, in every political system."[31] The protagonist chooses writing against suicide, self-inscription against self-destruction, and so takes the first steps of revolt against a symbolic/political system that has oppressed her.

The passage therefore also marks the convergence of the thematics of female psychic emergence with a continued critique of female sexuality in a patriarchal society. It is in the light of this thematic of emergence that we should read the rest of the book, which is heavily interlaced with accounts of extramarital affairs, sexual flings, cynical portrayals of deceit and betrayal, and yearnings for spiritual consolation. After her breakdown and her grandmother's death, the protagonist who emerges is a different sexual person. No longer a naif or passive "object" of her husband's actions and victim of the rapes of various strangers, she is now able to take her pleasure, to reappropriate her sexual self, "with my pride intact and blazing" (p. 100). Her sexual adventures, however, have less to do with actual male others than with her own internal identity needs. As Das aptly points out, "Like alms looking for a begging bowl was my love which sought for it a receptacle" (p. 105). Here the conventional association of woman with receptacle, of woman as passive receiver of male desire and sperm, is inverted. In this passage, woman's desire is dominant, aggressively seeking "a [male] begging bowl." In the bold reversal, the male is passive, the female active and full, signifying plenitude and wealth.

But *My Story* does not conclude with this seeming female victory. Although it continues with the narrative of extramarital affairs (Das apparently had an open marriage; according to her poems and the autobiography, her husband accepted her love affairs rather than encourage the prospect of a divorce), it becomes clear that sexual empowerment in no way satisfies the protagonist's internal identity needs. Thus, even as the narrative dwells on lovers and husband, it incorporates a poem that resists an equation of "liberated" sexuality with satisfaction of female desire:

We lay
On bed, glassy-eyed, fatigued, just
The toys dead children leave behind,
And we asked each other, what is

The use, what is the bloody use? That was the only kind of love,

This hacking at each other's parts

Like convicts hacking, breaking clods

At noon. (115)

The poet rejects the sexual act as a brutal and futile action committed by "toys dead children leave behind," or by "convicts." Rather than representing or enacting desire, male-female sexual interactions are anomic, penitential, dead.

Curiously, then, what we can read in Das's autobiography is a re-visioning of female desire. Contrary to the Lacanian thesis of female desire as "lack," a wanting, which is itself an extension of the Freudian view of female as that which is deficient in or missing the potency of the penis, the protagonist of the autobiography emerges from passive victim to active agent possessing fullness and plentitude, needing only a proper recipient. But this female desire, assertive, aggressive, and confident, must still await satisfaction in a sociopolitical context that denies it any expression except in the area of sexuality. The area of sexuality that the adult Das explores, however, is defined in a patriarchal society to the advantage of men, and the narrative's tales of extramarital affairs are also tales of male abuse. Thus, in the narrative of her most intense affair, she interrogates the sadomasochistic nature of her relationship: "Years after all of it had ended, I asked myself why I took him on as my lover, fully aware of his incapacity to love. . . . I needed security. . . . Perhaps it was necessary for my body to defile itself in many ways, so that the soul turned humble for a change" (p. 163). Here is yet another recognition of the mental and spiritual damage women suffer on account of their sex; the masochistic rationalization of drives, while more conventionally expressed as religious growth, is itself a chilling example of psychic damage in the female protagonist.

The struggle for sexual and other forms of autonomy in the female protagonist in Das's autobiography is "exceptional" in the tradition of Indian writing in English, whether by men or women. In the Indian context, female desire, because it breaks social conventions of marital and sexual property and propriety, is inherently illegitimate and therefore doubly exceptional. As French reports it:

[Indian women's] primary duty, a duty so emphatic as to override their children's well-being and certainly their own, is to "make the marriage work." This means that a woman must adjust to her husband. Whatever he is or does—if he is cold or cruel, if he is never home, or does not give her money, if he drinks or gambles or has other women, if he beats her—is her lot. She is expected to submit, serve, and produce a son.[32]

The myth of her origin in the woman-centered matriarchy of Nalapat House enables the protagonist to stand outside and to interrogate the abusive patriarchal world in which she (or her sexuality) functions only as an economic object with market value. When her husband complains that she has not read "the prestigious report of the Rural Credit Survey Committee"—that is, not given him due respect—she answers, "But I let you make love to me every night . . . isn't that good enough?" (p. 114). The protagonist has learned to balance what is "due" to her husband in terms of her sexual availability, and understands that the exchange of her sexual self in the economy of the marriage is a kind of market exchange, "a good" sufficient for the shelter and material security he provides. In this passage, Das makes explicit what is more often concealed or silenced in both Indian and Western literature, that the relationship between male and female is often baldly an economic exchange. This relocation of male-female relationship in an economic world makes it evident that the protagonist's claim to female subject autonomy in matters of sexual relations outside of marriage is even more illegal, for it breaks both the cultural and economic codes.

Das goes beyond the economic/sexual bond to examine the place of class in her society. Observing the lives of the working-class and poor who surround the protagonist and commenting specifically on the protagonist's fascination with the poor, the narrator offers these lives in moral contrast to the protagonist's own middle-class ennui. In one striking passage, the poet is in her "drawing room" while "cultured voices discussed poetry" (p. 190). She hears the song that the poor who live in the builders' colony behind the "large new structures" are singing. "Finally," she writes, "unable to control myself any longer, I dragged my husband to the colony one evening" (p. 190). In the squatters' welcome for her, she is able to revise her subjective perspective:

I was pining for yet another settee for the drawing-room
while these grand men and women were working from morning till dusk carrying cement and climbing the scaffoldings.
And yet they had more vitality than I had of optimism. . . .
My gloom lay in its littlest corner like a black dog. I had had
the idiocy to think of myself as Kamala, a being separate from
all the rest and with a destiny entirely different from those of
others. (p. 191)

This incident, isolated as it is from any larger examination of the issues of class and caste in Indian society, may be read as a shallow idealization of the working class. To my mind, however, its inclusion in a subjectivist genre such as autobiography indicates the writer's unease with her own subjective project, the project of constituting "Kamala, a being separate from all the rest and with a destiny all her own." The passage contains less a materialist critique of class inequalities than an interrogation of the Westernized, middle-class privileging of the individual, which forms the autobiography's subtext. In its valuation and equation of vitality and "singing," a communal activity, with the working class (in contrast to "poetry," a private affair, equated with middle-class ennui), the passage offers another example of narrative "double-voicedness." The incident represents another instance of the protagonist attempting to break the psychic isolation of a middle-class marriage; but the attempt on this occasion, dragging "my husband with me," is licit and legal and serves to underline her identification with, rather than separation from, the larger Indian society.

In the autobiography, Das comes to a point in her life when she questions her own sense of being exceptional. The same kind of necessity to open consciousness to the dialogic presence of others, whether of a different race (as in the case of the young girl yearning for white parents), class, or gender, also admits into the autobiography the other aspect of self, of tradition. Yet it is this aspect of woman as patriarchal mate, that most unexceptional of women in Indian society, that the autobiographical discourse has been most energetically displacing.

As befitting the story of a woman mediating among and mediated by multiple and contradictory cultures, *My Story* in its Krishna-consciousness shows the ideological interpenetrations of the Hindu worldview with a feminist, although not necessarily wholly Westernized, text. For example, in locating the woman as autonomous sexual subject in her familiar world, the narrator moves from the image of plenty looking for a begging bowl to that of devotee: "I was perhaps seeking a familiar face that blossomed like a blue lotus in the water of my dreams. It was to get closer to that bodyless [sic] one that I approached other forms and lost my way. I may have gone astray, but not once did I forget my destination" (p. 105). The immediate contradictions between this passage and the bulk of the book are so large as to suggest the complicated indeterminacy of identity that forms the site of conflict for Westernized Asian women in strongly regulated, traditionally patriarchal societies. Marginalized by their gender, their colonial English education and language, their rejection of patriarchy and its given social and familial norms, and their bourgeois interests in a chiefly peasant society, women writers such as Das negotiate their identity needs among contradictory dominant discourses, each of which offers more grounds for tension than for resolution. As a work by a major English-language Indian woman writer, Das's "story" is less a seamless product of hybridity than it first appears, although the cultural differences between Indian and Western values and ideas are obviously present and affect her work. Her autobiography, in fact, shuttles between the gaps, articulating the space between cultures, displaying rather than resolving these differences in the narrative. The conclusion of the autobiography moves out of the discourse of feminism that occupies the foreground of the first two-thirds of the text to the more conventional discourse of the confessional autobiography.

Arguably, therefore, it is possible to read the major locus of meaning in Das's autobiography in the slippage between the two tropes, that of alms looking for a begging bowl (that is, female subject desiring/enacting its terms of empowerment/identity) and that of devotee worshipping the blue Krishna (female desire as passively situated in the hierarchical construction of patriarchal stasis or tradition). For in the shift of tropes, Das places a Hindu screen before her feminist project, which is up to this point to treat the domain of the sexual as also the field of political struggle. In shifting from the psychosexual and sociopolitical to the Hindu view of woman as Krishna-worshiper, Das attempts to move from the position of the exceptional (and illegitimate) woman to that of the legal, central, and iconic Indian female figure.

The presence of Krishna-consciousness (that is, of acceptance of female submission to male godhood) in Das's autobiography, I would argue, is evidence of the process of creative play that Bakhtin describes in *The Dialogic Imagination,* the "struggle and dialogic interrelationship of [the categories of authoritative discourse and an internally persuasive discourse that] usually determine the history of an individual ideological consciousness."[33] Krishna-consciousness in Das's work makes evident the presence of the "authoritative word" of patriarchal Indian culture. The "authoritative word," as Bakhtin defines it, is the word of the fathers, a prior discourse, located in a distanced zone, with a hieratic language akin to taboo.[34] Das's slippages between straightforward feminist discourse, the subjective writing of the body—her internally persuasive discourse—and this "authoritative word" of Krishna-consciousness, testify to the gaps that result from the simultaneous existence of plural, dominant, yet contradictory discourses in the same consciousness. The "intense struggle within . . .

for hegemony among various available verbal and ideological points of view, approaches, directions and values"[35] defines her inscribed ideological development.

In this regard, Das's inscriptions of the struggles for autonomy of the female are themselves placed in jeopardy, under interrogation. Aspects of female identity are polarized. The autonomous subject actively creating her destiny in an unstained new world stands in contrast to the iconic figure of the female as passive, culturally fixed in an object relationship in which she is always the inferior in search of the Divine Krishna. The weight of these polarities indicates the enormous contradictions that beset a woman living in a strongly male-dominant society. As an Indian woman, she participates in and endures simultaneously those constructed systems of Hindu rationalization that have existed in India for centuries.

To privilege one polarity over the other, however, is to reduce falsely the dialogic complexities of Das's themes and the totality of her achievement. It is to silence the libido that speaks in and through relations with others. Her autobiography reshapes both our consciousness and our unconscious, by means of its raw, experimental edges. The internally persuasive dialogue of her autobiography shares characteristics with the kind of writing described as "écriture féminine" in Western literature. The enabling myth of matriarchal origin; the genealogical constructions of chaste spinster-writers; the sociopolitical critiques of arranged marriages, child brides, and loveless middle-class marriages; the portrayals of male abuse of women as sexual objects and prey; the narrative of emergence of woman as subject and writer—all these form a counterdiscourse to the later confessional closure. This counterdiscourse, contradicting and attacking patriarchal constructions of male superiority and female passivity, appears forcefully in the early reconstructions of empowered female figures. The Kali figure, for example, sets up a clear female antithesis to Krishna-consciousness that forms part of the authoritative word of the father in the second half of the autobiography; this "savage" goddess reminds us especially of "the forceful return of a libido, which is not so easily controlled, and by the singular, by the noncultural, by a language which is savage and which can certainly be heard."[36]

Despite the later development of the Krishna theme, Das's autobiography springs from the same impulses of revolt as the rest of her oeuvre. Indigenous cultural elements, such as the Kali figure and the matriarchal structure of Nalapat House, provide sources for her critiques of patriarchally constructed heterosexuality. These critiques form major themes in her autobiography and poetry, contributing to a self-reflexivity that provides an intertextual web in which whole plots, incidents, acts, characters, concerns, even sentences and phrases from her other works appear. For example, about halfway through the autobiography, at the point where the protagonist arrives at full, although emotionally unsatisfying, sexuality (in a chapter titled "For the First Time in My Life I Learned to Surrender Totally"), the chapters are prefaced by her poems (e.g., pp. 99, 107, 115, 124, 127). Many of these poems had been published previously and were already notorious.[37] Their appearance in the autobiography suggests that coming to adult sexuality for the protagonist is also a coming to speaking subjectivity for the poet.

Das's critique of patriarchally constructed heterosexuality and her struggle to construct her own terms of sexual empowerment, while sharing similar concerns with Western feminists such as de Beauvoir, Kate Millett, and Hélène Cixous, remain one exceptional Indian woman's life story. The concluding chapters suggest not so much a retreat as a reconfiguration of her feminist project. A bad heart condition and her aging body lead the protagonist to turn away from male-female sexual relations as the site of conflict: "I had shed carnal desire as a snake sheds its skin" (p. 170). Her sexual desires are imaged, ironically, in the stereotypical figure of the spiritual lotus, as "now totally dead, rotted and dissolved, and for them there was no more to be a re-sprouting" (p. 186). She returns to Nalapat House "like a lost woman" (p. 175), in a gesture of retreat into female chastity: "I should never have taken to wearing the coloured clothes of the city. I should have dressed only in white. . . . I belonged to the serenity of Nalapat House" (p. 176). But the retreat is not a defeat; instead, the protagonist's libido becomes invested in the writing project, which is described in suggestively erotic terms: "I learnt for the first time to be miserly with my energy, spending it only on my writing which I enjoyed more than anything else in the world. I typed sitting propped against pillows on my wide bed" (p. 183).

Yet this emergence of the woman as empowered writer, recalling the return of the ancestral figures of Ammini and Ammalu, is still patriarchally restricted. The narrator represents her readers as lovers: "I had realized by then that the writer had none to love her but the readers" (p. 183). The desire to write, therefore, signifies the desire for a collective libidinous intercourse, a female exposure fantasy: "I have often wished to take myself apart and stick all the bits, the heart, the intestines, the liver, the reproductive organs, the skin, the hair and all the rest on a large canvas to form a collage which could then be donated to my readers" (p. 183). Although a different subject from the woman as sexual being, the woman as writer is again presented as consciousness constructed under the gaze of a patriarchal other, in this case a voyeuristic male deity: "Each time I walked into my lover's houses dressed like a bride, my readers have walked with me. . . . Like the eyes of an all-seeing God they follow me through the years" (p. 183). It is in her intercourse with her readers that the narrative finally arrives at anything like a recognition of satisfaction: "But how happily I meddled to satisfy that particular brand of readers who liked me. . . . And it certainly brought me happiness" (p. 184). This satisfaction, however, while it is a sign of empowerment (privileging) of the woman writer, continues to be expressed in the terms of patriarchal (inter)discourse, demonstrating the continued submission of Das's feminist project to patriarchy.

The social restrictions on women writers against expressing the kind of sexual and professional autonomy that we find in *My Story* are as strongly embedded in many Asian cultures today as they were in 1976, when Das's book appeared, and will probably prevent any imitators soon. The negative responses of Indian women critics such as Monika Varna, Vimala Rao, and Eunice de Souza to Das's work and to the work of other candid Indian women writers such as Gauri Deshpande and Mamta Kalia demonstrate that perceived transgressions of social decorum and traditional behavior still affect literary evaluation.[38] Moreover, Asian women generally might not find Das's exploration of female subjectivity as chiefly desire-centered or her portrayal of sexual relations as politically engaged congenial or helpful. After all, Das's writing can be said to have little material transformatory effect in Indian society. Some 80 percent of India's 700 million people live in the countryside. The status of Indian women, moreover, is woefully precarious, reflecting profound gender inequality and urgent material deprivations. The age for sacramental marriage, for example, is fourteen years for girls; the 1987 birthrate was 32 percent per one thousand population. More than 75 percent of Indian women are illiterate.[39] Moreover, Das's English-language Indian audience is extremely limited; India has fifteen languages included in its Constitution, and it has been reported that only about 3 percent of the Indian population, a Westernized and class-differentiated elite, uses English with any regularity. Her engaged and disruptive work, however, serves to remind Western readers to avoid any stereotyping of women from postcolonial developing nations. Even in the oppressive sociocultural conditions the autobiography delineates—conditions too often elided and stereotyped as Third World backwardness—Das's *My*

Story, proving the exception in her revolt against patriarchal oppression, helps to write the terms of empowerment for Indian women.

Notes

I wish to thank Nancy Miller, Graduate Center of the City University of New York, and Larry Lipking, Northwestern University, for their support; Wimal Dassanayake and the East-West Center, Hawaii, for the time and resources that led to this paper; Julia Watson, who gave me the occasion for the paper; Sidonie Smith, whose critical eye sharpened my argument; and the many critics, both East and West, who have provided me with their readings.

1. Adrienne Rich notes that for centuries Western women have been "mothered" by the "unchilded"—that is, exceptional—woman: "Throughout recorded history the 'childless' woman has been regarded . . . as a failed woman. . . . seen as embodiments of the great threat to male hegemony; the woman who is not tied to the family, who is disloyal to the law of heterosexual pairing and bearing. . . . Without the unacclaimed research and scholarship of 'childless' women, without Charlotte Bronte (who died in her first pregnancy), Margaret Fuller (whose major work was done before her child was born), without George Eliot, Emily Bronte, Emily Dickinson, Christina Rossetti, Virginia Woolf, Simone de Beauvoir—we would all today be suffering from spiritual malnutrition as women." *Of Woman Born: Motherhood as Experience and Institution* (New York: W. W. Norton, 1976), 251–52.

2. That we can and should find parallels between Asian and Western women's texts does not imply that we must accept "the concept of sisterhood as a global construct." See Bonnie Thornton Dill, "Race, Class, and Gender: Prospects for an All-Inclusive Sisterhood," *Feminist Studies* 9 (Spring 1983): 145.

3. Ibid, 146.

4. See Ding Ling, *Miss Sophie's Diary,* trans. W. J. F. Jenner (Beijing: Panda, 1985); idem, *I Myself Am a Woman: Selected Writings of Ding Ling,* ed. Tani E. Barlow with Gary J. Bjorge (Boston: Beacon, 1989).

5. See Julia Kristeva, *Revolution in Poetic Language,* trans. Margaret Waller (New York: Columbia University Press, 1984), 17.

6. Kamala Das, *Alphabet of Lust* (New Delhi: Orient Paperbacks, 1972); *A Doll for the Child Prostitute* (New Delhi: India Paperbacks, 1977); *Summer in Calcutta* (Calcutta: Rajinder Paul & Everest, 1965); *The Descendants* (Calcutta: Writers Workshop, 1967); *The Old Playhouse and Other Poems* (*OP* in the essay) (New Delhi: Orient Longman, 1973); *Tonight, This Savage Rite: The Love Poems of Kamala Das and Pritish Nandy* (New Delhi: Arnold-Heinemann, 1979); *Collected Poems,* vol. 1 (Kerala State: Trivandrum, 1984); *My Story* (New Delhi: Sterling Paperbacks, 1976) (all page references to this text will be given in the body of the essay); Syd C. Harrex and Vincent O'Sullivan, eds., *Kamala Das: A Selection with Essays on her Work* (*KD* in the essay) (Adelaide: Centre for Research in the New Literatures in English, 1986). Page references to poems in *KD* will be given in the essay.

7. Sandra M. Gilbert and Susan Gubar, eds., *The Norton Anthology of Literature by Women: The Tradition in English* (New York: W. W. Norton), 1985, 2247–49. Das, the only Asian writer in the anthology, is represented by one poem, "An Introduction," which encapsulates some of the material worked in her autobiography.

8. M. M. Bakhtin, *The Dialogic Imagination,* ed. Michael Holquist, trans. Caryl Emerson and Michael Holquist (Austin: University of Texas Press, 1981), 326–34. Bakhtin's notion of "the internal dialogism of double-voiced prose" that "draws its energy,

its dialogized ambiguity, not from individual dissonances, misunderstandings or contradictions . . . but sinks its roots deep into a fundamental, socio-linguistic speech diversity and multi-languagedness [heteroglossia]" (325–26) applies to Das's multilanguage background and specifically to what Harrex has termed "cultural dissonances" in the postcolonial Indian world.

9. Das has attracted an enormous critical response, resisting and laudatory, in her relatively brief writing career. There are more bibliographical items on her work than on any other Indian writer in English, living or dead. It is curious that the majority of Indian women critics persist in reading Das's subjects as strongly physical, a "profanity" of love, in contrast to the male and Anglo tendency to sacralize her subjects, to read them counter to the body as manifesting transcendent and Hindu mentality.

10. Bakhtin, *Dialogic Imagination,* 324.

11. The phenomenon of erosion or changes within native cultures in response to aggressive colonial education and colonial language imposition has been the focus of numerous studies. See, for example, Chinweizu, Onwuchekwa Jemie, and Ihechukwu Madubuike's classical polemical study of this phenomenon in African states, *Toward the Decolonization of African Literature* (Washington, D.C.: Howard University Press, 1983).

12. See Bruce King's introduction in *Literatures of the World in English* (London: Routledge & Kegan, 1974), 1–21, for a discussion of the evolution of these literatures from their colonial sources to their complex contemporary national identities.

13. Harrex and O'Sullivan, "Introduction," in *KD,* 2.

14. See Vimala Rao, "Kamala Das: The Limits of Over-exposure," in *Studies in Contemporary Indo-English Verse,* vol. 1, *A Collection of Critical Essays on Female Poets,* ed. A. N. Dwivedi (Bareilly: Prakash Book Depot, 1984), for one of the sharpest attacks on the sexual themes and craft of Das's work. See also Eunice de Souza, "Kamala Das, Gauri Deshpande, Mamta Kalia," in *Contemporary Indian Poetry,* ed. Saleem Peerandina (Bombay: Macmillan India, 1972), 85.

15. A. N. Dwivedi, *Kamala Das and Her Poetry* (Delhi: Doaba House, 1983), 20–21.

16. Anisur Rahmin, *Expressive Form in the Poetry of Kamala Das* (New Delhi: Abhinav, 1981), 7.

17. Harrex and O'Sullivan, *Kamala Das.* The essays in the volume are by S. C. Harrex, Vincent O'Sullivan, Dorothy Jones, and Curtis Wallace-Crabbe.

18. Dorothy Jones, "'Freedom Became My Dancing Shoes': Liberty and the Pursuit of Happiness in the Work of Kamala Das," in *KD,* 203.

19. Mohan Lal Sharma, "The Road to Brindavan: The Theme of Love in Kamala Das's Poetry," in *Studies in Contemporary Indo-English Verse,* 100.

20. See Harrex and O'Sullivan, "Introduction," 1–3; and Vincent O'Sullivan, "Whose Voice Is Where? On Listening to Kamala Das," in *KD,* 179–94. O'Sullivan asserts that, with Das, "We are reading religious poems of a kind that it would be impossible to find in any other woman now writing in English" (190).

21. Teresa de Lauretis, *Alice Doesn't: Feminism, Semiotics, Cinema* (Bloomington: Indiana University Press, 1984), 235.

22. For a discussion of Das's novel, *Alphabet of Lust,* see Shirley Geok-lin Lim, "Semiotics, Experience, and the Material Self: An Inquiry into the Subject of the Contemporary Woman Writer," *Women's Studies,* 18 (Summer 1990): 153–75.

23. Marilyn French, "Women and Work: India," in *Women, a World Report* (New York: Oxford University Press, 1985), 174–201.

24. Rao, "The Limits of Over-exposure," 88.

25. Dwivedi, *Kamala Das and Her Poetry,* 42; Jones, "'Freedom Became My Dancing Shoes,'" 192.

26. Sharma, "The Road to Brindavan," 108.

27. Jones, "'Freedom Became My Dancing Shoes,'" 197.

28. See Homi Bhabha, "Signs Taken for Wonders: Questions of Ambivalence and Authority under a Tree outside Delhi, May 1817," in *Europe and Its Others,* ed. F. Barker et al. (Colchester: University of Essex, 1985), 89–105, for an insightful discussion of the dynamics of hybridity in colonialist and postcolonialist cultures. In Das's case, her texts are further complicated by the intersections of gender conflict with postcolonial cultural ambiguity, multiplicity, and indeterminacy.

29. Syd C. Harrex, "The Strange Case of Matthew Arnold in a Sari: An Introduction to Kamala Das," in *KD,* 155–75.

30. See, for example, "My Grandmother's House," in *KD,* 14; and "Blood," in *OP,* 16–19.

31. Hélène Cixous, "The Laugh of the Medusa," trans. Keith Cohen and Paula Cohen, *Signs: Journal of Women in Culture and Society* 1 (Summer 1976): 880.

32. French, "Women and Work," 179.

33. Bakhtin, *Dialogic Imagination,* 342.

34. Ibid.

35. Ibid., 346.

36. Cixous, "The Laugh of the Medusa," 880.

37. For example, untitled poems beginning chapters 37 (p. 137) and 41 (p. 154) are "The Freaks" and "The Sunshine Cat," both published in her 1965 collection, *Summer in Calcutta.*

38. See Monika Varna, "Gauri Deshpande," in *Studies in Contemporary Indo-English Verse,* vol. 1, *A Collection of Critical Essays on Female Poets,* ed. A. N. Dwivedi Bareilly: Prakash Book Depot, 1984), 65–75; Eunice de Souza, "Kamala Das, Gauri Deshpande, Mamta Kalia," in *Contemporary Indian Poetry,* ed. Saleem Peeradina (Bombay: Macmillan India, 1972), 84–87; Gauri Deshpande, *Between Births* (Calcutta: Writers Workshop, 1968); idem, *Lost Love* (Calcutta: Writers Workshop, 1970); Mamta Kalia, *Tribute to Papa and Other Poems* (Calcutta: Writers Workshop, 1970).

39. These statistics are taken from *Women: A World Report* (New York: Oxford University Press, 1985).

Chapter 17

Autobiographical Storytelling by Australian Aboriginal Women

Kateryna Olijnyk Longley

It is only very recently that the written autobiographies of Aboriginal people have begun to be published in Australia.[1] So extreme has been the degradation and virtual erasure of Aboriginal culture that it is impossible for white readers to imagine the scale of obstacles that have to be negotiated and compromises that have to be made in order for Aboriginal people to offer their personal stories to a white reading public, and to do so in genres and modes that are not only foreign to Aboriginal culture but have been brutally efficient agents of its destruction for two hundred years.[2] Much Aboriginal history is difficult to relate because it is literally unspeakable. For white readers there are also difficulties that go well beyond the challenges of cross-cultural comprehension. Even the most sympathetic white observers and promoters of Aboriginal culture face the now familiar risk of consolidating the old patterns of domination each time they attempt to act as interpreters of Aboriginal production. It can be argued, however, that there is a much more serious risk of perpetuating the negation of Aboriginal culture by ignoring the new work and remaining silent, and it is from this position that this essay is written.[3] Further, Aboriginal autobiography offers much more than a window for viewing authentic "firsthand" presentations of black experience; it also contributes to a more general understanding of the genres by which cultures tell their personal and communal stories and so define themselves. In other words, the window enables vision and reflection both ways, upon fundamentally different worlds and their representations.

Australian Aboriginal women have been doubly disadvantaged: as well as suffering racial subjugation, they have lost their traditional tribal power base as women and so have become victims of alien patterns of sexual discrimination within the new urban class and family structures imposed upon them by a notoriously masculinist white Australia.[4] Now, in a climate of cultural curiosity and growing respect for Aboriginal culture, fostered in part by Aboriginal outspokenness during the recent bicentenary, Aboriginal women are claiming new power by speaking from a variety of positions, drawing upon both cultures in ways that are expedient but not necessarily obedient to the conventions of either. By publishing their stories of double disempowerment, they are reconstructing the past in their own ways, challenging the entrenched history-book accounts. They are also redefining themselves in the present as crucial agents of Australia's dawning postcolonial understanding. Autobiography provides an ideal medium for this process because it has the authority of a primary historical record while enjoying the freedom of an unashamedly personal vision.

European autobiography traditionally depends upon a strong sense of self. However, it has been pointed out by feminist theorists that this is because it has evolved primarily as a white male genre. Autobiographies of white women are more likely to question and decenter the autobiographical subject.[5] For Aboriginal women the genre provides an ideal platform from which to reveal the fragmentation of the subject and of the culture that has occurred as a result of these women's displaced cultural situation. The lack of unity shows up all the more strikingly because it is displayed within the framework of a genre that, in its classical form, is dependent on the coherence of the subject. Further, as well as having solidly masculine assumptions, classical autobiography also depends upon specific Western cultural value systems in ways that become visible only when other cultures use the genre to write life narratives based on very different traditions of living and storytelling. Rules of authorship, ownership, and authority, for example, are so differently understood by Aboriginal people that the term *autobiography* is immediately problematized when it is used in an Aboriginal context. In many cultures "autobiography" did not exist at all in the past and exists now only as a cultural transplant. As Georges Gusdorf has pointed out, autobiography does not develop in cultures where "the individual does not oppose himself to all others; [where] he does not feel himself to exist outside of others, and still less against others, but very much with others in an interdependent existence that asserts its rhythms everywhere in the community . . . [where] lives are . . . thoroughly entangled."[6] In other words, according to this model, autobiography is dependent upon a sense of the "isolated being" or the "individual." If we were to accept Gusdorf's highly conservative view, we would have to exclude from the genre all life narratives by people who have been denied the privileged illusion of individuality or those who do not seek or value that illusion.[7] While contemporary autobiography and theory have advanced far beyond such restrictive conceptions of the genre, Gusdorf's views are nevertheless useful because they sum up a familiar traditional approach to autobiographical writing.[8]

How does contemporary Australian Aboriginal autobiography look in the light of this "individualistic" tradition? Because it is so varied, there is no clear answer. Some of it is written by Westernized, white-educated women who have had little contact with tribal organization. Some has been transcribed and translated in a tribal context. However, two recurring features set this writing apart from more conventional forms of autobiography. One is the sense of communal life that is evoked through the individual story, and the other is the intimate relationship with tribal land. It is in the context of these two defining drives—to consolidate or reestablish links with Aboriginal communities, and to restore crucial links with traditional tribal lands—that contemporary life narratives are being written, even when those drives emerge indirectly from the texts as absences, as lost or forgotten frameworks that the works have to do without. This is not to say that the narratives are necessarily nostalgic. Most are deeply concerned with the present and the future. As a result, they look backwards not just to "preserve" their recent history but with the more urgent need to justify their demand for a revision of all Australian history to incorporate crucial Aboriginal histories into ways of reading the contemporary world. As with other Fourth World writing, Aboriginal autobiography is passionately polemical in its impulses. The focus of this chapter is the ways in which this new body of work draws upon traditional Aboriginal strategies for recording history while at the same time utilizing white genres to gain power in an intercultural contemporary political arena.

An important study that has contributed greatly to white Australian understanding of Aboriginal women's tribal life is Diane Bell's *Daughters of the Dreaming*. In it she describes in detail the degree to which women have autonomy, power, and control over their lives and the specific ways in which their rituals preserve these in everyday life. Central to these rituals are the women's secret ceremonies and meetings, forbidden to men, even unreportable to them. In fact, men can be punished by women for violation of their domains by being inflicted with illness or death.[9] Among women's primary responsibilities is protection of the *kukurrpa* or "dreaming," from which, Bell explains, "flowed rights and responsibilities in land, a power base as independent economic producers and a high degree of control over their own lives in marriage, residence, economic production, reproduction and sexuality" (pp. 50–51). Obviously, much of the content of these ceremonies is unavailable to a general reading public, but the structures are being revealed because of Aboriginal women's desire to publicize the strengths of their cultures to as wide an audience as possible.

Diane Bell's book is remarkable in that it is written from the outside (she is a white anthropologist) and from the inside (she won the trust of the women among whom she lived and worked sufficiently to be included in their secret ceremonies and permitted to record and publish her knowledge). Essential to her understanding are the autobiographical fragments that she scatters throughout her work. Through these accounts it becomes clear that within Aboriginal cultures telling one's own story is a very complicated process that is heavily controlled by taboos and other traditional constraints. For example, a senior Napanangka, when asked about her first sighting of a white man, had to ask a younger woman to speak because she was too closely related to a man killed in the encounter and was therefore under a speech taboo. An older woman, also closely related to the deceased, could only confirm the account of her younger sister in sign language since she too was forbidden to speak. While this silence appears to withdraw the story from firsthand reporting as it is known in the West, it actually gives it greater authenticity for an Aboriginal audience than an isolated first-person narrative precisely because it is delivered and confirmed communally. As Bell explains:

> Story-telling is a group activity: the presence and assistance of an audience ensures that there will always be a number of persons to bear witness to the content of the story and to quell any accusations that the story-teller may have erred or touched upon matters which were improper. (p. 44)

For the story itself, the younger sister uses the first-person plural, highlighting the fact that it presents a shared experience to which she has no special claim. She begins:

> We [Napanangka and Napurrula] were only young girls, about
> that big [eleven or twelve]. It was the killing time [late 1920s].
> We were in Miyikampi country, playing in the water with
> Nampijinpa's mother [a Nungarrayi now deceased]. We saw a
> white man coming. "What is this?", we asked ourselves.
> "Looks like a ghost." We were frightened. He was leading a
> camel. We didn't know that camel. My grandfather [Jungarrayi,
> Napurrula's mother's father], old Pampa [blind one] was hand-
> cuffed and tied to the tail of that camel. He was "showing"
> the white man the country. They were going to "muster up"
> all the Yapa [Aboriginal people]. We ran away. We dragged
> leaves behind us to cover our tracks. We hid in a rabbit hole.
> (p. 44; bracketed explanations are Bell's)

In different circumstances the women would sing their stories, many
of which celebrated rather than lamented aspects of their world. During their food-gathering expeditions, for example, they would sing of
the travels of ancestors in order to explain and preserve the stories
by which the land gained meaning and shape. Accompanying the
storytelling would be rituals of food preparation and other ceremonies
by which the sustaining world of the Dreaming was constantly integrated into daily life. Through these expeditions the women gained
knowledge of and power over the land, its stories, and its produce.
It was this secure power base that they lost when they were driven
into Western forms of organization. With that loss the stories changed
radically, because they were no longer connected to the land from
which all stories arose or to the very different understanding of time
that governed the narrative. While it is impossible for outsiders to
grasp the enormity of that change, Bell's account gives some insights
into it when she explains that "the way in which Aborigines have
made sense of the past century is not in terms of an event-person
oriented chronology. They have asserted continuity and found it in
the dogma of the immutability and the omnipresence of the Dreamtime
Law. . . . The past has been encapsulated in the present, the present
permeates the past" (p. 46).

The autobiographical stories of the women Bell listened to repeatedly display this quality of temporal integration, an integration linked
with the communal aspects of narration: times interweave, memories
flow into each other, all contributing to an understanding that no time
is distinct and separate and no person is isolated from the tribal group
and its complex, deeply interlocking traditions. The result is a mesh
of ever-present stories, rituals, and history-laden landmarks that make
up the Dreaming. Because personal stories constantly replenish and

reinforce this essential common pool from which all law and self-understanding derive, it is impossible to think of autobiography as an individual activity in traditional Aboriginal society. Women dream about the country in which they are living and hunting or over which they wish to claim rights, and they do this either in the context of ritual or simply as part of their day-to-day contact with the area. The distinction between dreaming and daily life or between personal story and communal knowledge is not well defined. Both, if significant enough to be repeated and passed down, become part of the Dreaming of the particular tract of land (p. 92).

The example given by Diane Bell of a song from an Alyawarra woman's repertoire illustrates this process. The woman sings of a boy of a Japangardi subsection who is *kirda* (related through the father) for the same country for which she is also *kirda*. As Bell explains:

> I had heard the song many times but on one occasion when I was translating songs with the woman, she explained that the Japangardi was her younger brother's son who had fallen from a windmill and died while still a child. She told of his place in the family and how old his siblings were when he died. From this I was able to fix a date to the song. To her this was interesting but unimportant. She related how she dreamt of him on the day he died. When she returned to the camp she knew of the death before she was told. This song is considered to be her song and when she dies it will be put aside as will all her property, name, swag, camp site and so on. (p. 93)

Yet the song is not exclusively "her" song in the sense that even after many years it may be refound and performed. By then any "correction" of the song by older women who may have heard it in the past is accepted and so it may change repeatedly in the retelling. It gradually grows to be a part of the recurring activity of the area and eventually becomes ancestral knowledge that nourishes the Law and the Dreaming. And so, while each song bears "the stamp" of its creator, it is "reinvented" so many times that its connection with the place and the community of people in that place becomes much more important than the specific personal and temporal details of the original event. For the story to be renewed and refashioned in this way, access to its country is essential, since, in its evolution into an ancestral Dreaming song, the story retains its many references to other local stories and their locations long after the precise human origins have been forgotten or become irrelevant. In other words, the story, which might originally have corresponded roughly to a reverse autobiographical Western model, becomes more significant in terms of communal validation as it loses the characteristics of historical accuracy and personal authenticity upon which the Western genre depends.

Before approaching contemporary published forms of Aboriginal autobiography in the context of this oral tradition, it is important to make one final point about the depth of the relationships among stories, community, and people in the tribal tradition. When Aboriginal people say, "This is my place," they are likely to be referring to a site; but when they speak of "my country," they refer to a kinship network as much as to a piece of land. Country is for them constituted inter-semiotically by storytelling and communal activity, as against geography, geology, and real estate legislation. Referring to *country*, they list the relatives through whom they can claim it: "This is my country from my father, grandfather, mother, aunty, uncle." When speaking of two countries, they may even say that these countries are their "brothers, grannies, mother." Ancestors, relatives, dreaming tracks and Dreaming itself are all so active in the landscape and so essential to its practical and spiritual significance that in many cases people take the name of the land as their own name, in accordance with kinship rules. Thus in Kaytej country, for example, *altyerre* (the word for dreaming) becomes the name of the persons who call the country mother, while those who call the country father affix the word *arenye* (associated with). In this way, from names such as Akwerlpartyerre, one can know the country that a person is from (in this case, Akwerlpe) as well as the kinship relation with the land. Evident in this naming practice is the closeness of bonding with the land. Diane Bell describes it as a "mode of mapping people directly onto country" (p. 138).[10] In maintaining these bonds women play an essential role, because they hold special knowledge that is encoded everywhere around them in rituals and ceremonies, in traditional designs, in objects and features of the landscape, but most of all in the songs and stories they tell each other and their children.[11]

The most commercially successful Australian Aboriginal autobiography produced to date is Sally Morgan's *My Place,* published in 1987 and now a best-seller, reprinted in the United States and England, translated into German and soon to be translated into Indonesian.[12] Various factors have contributed to its success, but one of these is undoubtedly the fact that it is not obviously Aboriginal in its presentation, with the exception of the transcribed autobiographies of Morgan's grandmother, mother, and uncle at the end of her own story. By using a conventional linear mode of narration the writer has reached a huge audience and raised public awareness enormously. There is no doubt that her work has acted as a catalyst for other

Aboriginal writers and for publishers. Appearing just before the Australian bicentenary, the book foreshadowed and exploited the rising interest in Aboriginal work in a culture that has traditionally given it neither recognition nor access to white means of production.

While Morgan's book is open to criticism for its lack of activism and its uncritical adoption of a white mode of storytelling, it is important to consider that the writer was brought up in a white middle-class family and "protected" from the knowledge of her Aboriginality almost until she reached adulthood.[13] She therefore had no choice but to use the forms she knew. Her autobiography is not simply an account of the transition from a white to a black perception of herself, though that in itself would be a complex enough subject; it is the record of a conscious process of reentry into a culture whose traces had repeatedly erupted in inexplicable ways into her comfortable suburban life without ever adding up to anything coherent until she found out about her Aboriginal origins. It therefore provides a crucial positive model for other projects that seek reinstatement and redefinition for subjugated cultures from positions and moments in history when almost all appears to have been lost. From within the framework of conventional Western autobiography, Morgan makes many discoveries about the loss of her "place" in Aboriginal life. While these are often personal discoveries that help her to redefine herself, they also weave a web of communal connections with families, kinship groups, traditions, lands, and stories that have little to do with her as an "individual."

Some of the most moving moments of the book are those that reveal some element of the old culture breaking into the conventionally autobiographical narrative. This happens when her elderly uncle asks her, just before his death, to "look after" his story (p. 166), and again when Morgan's mother tells of her realization that the scar across her chest was an initiation mark, given to her by her mother for protection (p. 252). Most of all, it happens in the stories of her older relatives as they tell of their experience of the horrors of white treatment of them and their families and their desperate efforts to fight back with rituals that were powerful in their own world but useless in the other. A victim of the routine legalized abduction of Aboriginal children for "assimilation" and labor, her uncle describes the moment he was taken away:

> They told my mother and the others we'd be back soon. We
> wouldn't be gone for long, they said. People were callin',
> "Bring us back a shirt, bring us this, bring us that". . . . When
> they came to get me, I clung to my mother and tried to sing*
> them. I wanted them to die. I was too young. I didn't know

how to sing them properly. I cried and cried, calling to my
mother, "I don't want to go, I don't want to go!" She was my
favourite. I loved her. I called, "I want to stop with you, I
want to stop with you!" I never saw her again.
[*sing—to sing an incantation that is believed to have the
power to kill the person against whom it is directed] (p. 182).

Other stories leave gaps and silences at crucial moments. Morgan,
eager to find out all that she can to allow her story to reach out as
far as possible into the world from which she was excluded, comes
up against moments of resistance when the older people refuse to
speak further. At those times it becomes clear that some things are
unspeakable for them in such a public arena. Much of the unspeakable
is related to landowners' violation of white and Aboriginal laws, including those relating to incest, in their sexual abuse of Aboriginal women.
These blank moments remind both the reader and the writer of the
crudeness and invasiveness of the genre of transcribed autobiography
when compared with the oral tradition of shared stories told on tribal
lands, a central communal activity that these people can still
remember.

Another autobiography that uses straightforwardly linear modes of
narration within an explicitly Christian moral framework is Glenyse
Ward's *Wandering Girl,* the first autobiography to be published by
the Aboriginal press, Magabala Books.[14] This, too, is the story of an
uprooted childhood spent in a totally alien culture. As disturbing as
the story itself, of Ward's being taken away from her family as a baby
to an orphanage and then eventually to domestic "employment" on
a white settler's farm, is the weirdly "empty" quality of the narrative.
In spite of the extraordinary sequence of events, there is something
missing, certainly if we take the expectations of Western autobiography
as the baseline. This is because *Wandering Girl* repeatedly expresses
its position as a text produced between cultures. Unlike Morgan, Ward
does not have a high level of Western education, and she has lost
access to Aboriginal traditions of living and storytelling. She adopts
a Western mode to tell the story of that loss, even though she now
lives and works in an Aboriginal community, simply because it will
reach more people; but neither mode is comfortably her own. More
moving than the account of the details of her difficult and disconnected life is the constant sense, underlying the entire narrative, of
the narrator's loss of a cultural base from which to speak. While the
work is not explicitly activist, it provides important material for the
Aboriginal cause in its revelation of that dispossession and its devastating effects. It has the power to shock readers by the very fact of

its understatement of those effects, which are felt everywhere in the narrative. At the beginning of her story, Glenyse Ward writes:

> You see in the early days of survival and struggle, there was a
> lot of hardship and agony amongst the Aboriginal people.
> Through the misguided minds of earnest white people we
> were taken away from our natural parents. This affected all of
> us. We lost our identity through being put into missions,
> forced to abide by the European way. I was a baby when I
> was put into an orphanage called Saint Joseph's in Rivervale,
> run by the Order of St John of God. When I became the age
> of three I was put into another home, called Wandering Mis-
> sion. It was here that I spent the next thirteen years of my
> life. (pp. 1–2)

The mission's name is loaded with irony. With its connotations of both freedom and homelessness, and its obvious reference to the much misconstrued notion of walkabout, it points to the widespread white misconception that Aboriginal nomadic traditions leave Aboriginal people free to go anywhere without being tied to a particular place. The title of Morgan's *My Place,* in a more positive way, but still ironically, points to the centrality of place—land and cultural space— in Aboriginal cultural reempowerment.

A completely different kind of autobiography, *An Aboriginal Mother Tells of the Old and the New,* was written in 1972 (published in 1984) by a Mornington Island woman, Elsie Roughway Labumore, who had experienced mission life in her childhood in the 1930s but was able to return to her family and tribal life when the missionaries left during the war.[15] Although her story is framed by the work of white editors, it nevertheless retains a strong feeling of the writer's speech and writing patterns (the book was written by Labumore, not transcribed) and provides amazing insights for white readers into tribal laws, customs, and beliefs. Written with passionate conviction primarily for a white audience, this work sets out to describe and celebrate traditional Aboriginal life and so to try to make Europeans understand something of the depth and wealth of the culture their "civilization" has all but wiped out. Fundamental to this work is a commitment to family, community, place, and tradition that makes this much more than an autobiography in the usual Western sense. Also driving the narrative is anger at all that has been lost. As Labumore explains:

> The Europeans have not the slightest idea of all that the tribes
> have, or what they have lived with. Though you hear some
> legends, customs, laws and rules, but you just cannot under-
> stand how on earth have these people found to raise them-

selves as these people. I suppose the black race has something
that no one today can look downwards on. Of my people, of
asking more questions about all this, only I can say they were
men and women of rich wisdoms and knowledge.

Then you would ask how they've forgotten about all their
ways of living, as one of these early days people, if the laws,
customs, rules, Government of their own people . . . had them,
and now they gone from them. The big reasons . . . the white
man's law came in and made the people of the past to wipe it
off and look and take the laws of the white man.

. . . Why should they [white people] do these things of selfishness . . . or whether these wrongdoers have no parents or bigger
sisters and brothers, uncles and aunties or grandparents from
both sides of the families, to help and talk to them not to do
these sort of a thing. If they had, these people too should be
responsible of them. There would not be too much sorrowful,
worried, unhappy people in the world today. (pp. 95–96)

Labumore also presents more specific descriptions of methods of
healing, of traditions associated with giving birth, naming, courtship,
food gathering and other major events in everyday life, the ceremony
of the corroboree, the powers of mythical creatures, daily courtesies,
rituals and taboos, all interwoven with her wider vision of people
living in a supportive community. The book is a wonderful source of
information, "a veritable encyclopaedia of Aboriginal beliefs and practices," as the Aboriginal writer Mudrooroo Narogin calls it,[16] as well
as a powerful story of a woman's life, one that actively demonstrates
the claim that Aboriginal women had much greater power in relation
to men when they lived in traditional tribal situations. (Much of Bell's
book provides specific evidence of this in various tribes.) More than
any other published Aboriginal text, Labumore's works against white
ignorance and misconception about tribal life without bowing to white
conventions of genre and representation. There is no doubt that this
work gains strength from its double cultural perspective, as a firsthand
record of Aboriginal tribal traditions and as a written text published
by a major international publishing house. This is not to say that every
Aboriginal work needs to emulate these strengths. *An Aboriginal
Mother* was written from an unrepeatable moment and unique situation
in history. It provides not so much a model as a demonstration of the
need for writers to work from various positions, exploiting and adapting whatever genres are available in order to represent the multiple
and changing nature of Aboriginal experience, especially in increasingly urbanized circumstances.

An important recent autobiography that deals specifically with urban Aboriginal life is Ruby Langford's *Don't Take Your Love to Town*.[17] In a preface called "Names," the list of her own names foreshadows the writer's concern with multiple identities and worlds. After listing the names of her nine children (two now dead) and their fathers, she writes of herself:

> You can think of me as Ruby Wagtail Big Noise Anderson Rangi Ando Heifer Andy Langford. How I got to be Ruby Langford. Originally from the Bundjalung people. (p. 2)

The list highlights the power of naming in oral narrative and its peculiar effacement into the signature in individualistic autobiography. Langford's story of pub brawls, domestic violence, failed relationships, repeated imprisonment, and desperate urban poverty is a far cry from Labumore's celebration of traditional life, but it can be seen as the silent underside of that story in that it confronts and explains the realities of contemporary city life for Aboriginal people who have been irrevocably cut off from their lands and traditions in the way that Labumore feared. Where traces of the old world remain they rise out of the narrative as shadowy or parodic reminders of lost communal codes and lands:

> White people had given us all kinds of technological comfort, but the tribal ways still need to be strong. I thought of the difference between white people saying "I own this land" and blacks saying "We belong to this land." I looked out at the street and the tall weeds in the railway yard opposite. The phone-lines, the traffic. And I wondered who had been the custodian of Henderson Road, Alexandria. The Eora tribe.
> Eora country was at La Perouse but it reached this far into the city, to Redfern. (p. 262)

While Ruby Langford repeatedly laments the passing of tribal culture she is too caught up with surviving and providing for her children to be able to seek it out actively or sustain it. She spends her time battling against police, government bureaucracies, hostile suburban neighborhoods, unreliable partners, and even friends. But, far worse than these battles, the most harrowing aspect of her story is the absence of a sustaining community and base. Always on the move, reeling from repeated blows, Ruby Langford is never going anywhere; she is only escaping from one untenable situation to another. This is how she describes her way of life:

> I felt like I was living tribal but with no tribe around me, no close-knit family. The food-gathering, the laws and songs were

broken up, and my generation at this time wandered around
as if we were tribal but in fact living worse than the poorest
of poor whites, and in the case of women living hard because
it seemed like the men loved you for a while and then more
kids came along and the men drank and gambled and disappeared. One day they'd had enough and they just didn't come
back. It happened with Gordon and later it happened with
Peter, and my women friends all have similar stories. Neddy
and I have talked about it often as we get older, and how it's
not always different for our daughters and their kids, but
those stories are for later. (p. 96)

In Ruby Langford's narration we see how her adoption of an individualistic mode of autobiographical reporting, one that in no way
reflects traditional Aboriginal experience, actually highlights the isolated and dislocated way in which she is forced to live. The narrator
rebels but cannot escape that mode. Even her body seems to rebel
by growing so obese that major surgery is necessary to remove vast
amounts of fat to make walking possible again. This disorder becomes
a strong metaphor for the book's powerful expression of life out of
harmony and out of control.

What do the very different autobiographical works discussed in this
essay collectively contribute? Apart from providing specific insights
into Aboriginal women's lives in the past and in the present in Australia,
they, with other contemporary autobiographical works, particularly
those of immigrants, are presenting a major challenge to official Australian histories. Autobiography, by the very fact of its first-person
narrative position, claims the authority of firsthand knowledge as it
speaks against the grain of the dominant historical discourses, which
depend on precisely the opposite kind of perspective, that of the
authoritative but detached observer. The new autobiographical coun-
terhistories not only challenge the content of official narratives, they
also question the forms of narration by using other forms or by using
familiar forms strangely. The essential communal spirit of traditional
storytelling cannot survive if the narrative is carried by an individualistic subject, nor can the conception of time that allows past and
present, mythological and contemporary life to flow into each other
function properly within a plot-driven sequential narrative. By violating the rules of history and biography as they have developed in
the West, the Aboriginal life stories allow us to stand outside those
genres and so learn to read European as well as Aboriginal culture
differently. Not surprisingly, it is those autobiographical narratives that
conform least to conventional European forms that most effectively

extend the possibilities of the genre and reveal many of its conventional rules to be culturally coercive and imperialistic. Further, the autobiographical narratives remind us of the oral tradition from which they have only recently been drawn and the centrality of song, ritual, and storytelling in that tradition. But perhaps the most useful lesson provided by Aboriginal women's autobiography is that flexibility, specifically literary flexibility, is needed so that all genres can continue to be loosened to accommodate differences of personal and cultural vision at any time and in any place.

Notes

1. Many stories were collected by anthropologists during the nineteenth century and well into the twentieth, but they were constructed as mythology rather than as life stories. This can be explained partly by the bias of anthropology itself toward common features of cultural groups rather than the details of individual lives, and partly by the absence in Aboriginal culture of anything resembling the genre of individualistic autobiographical narrative. More powerful than either of these is the racist explanation: that Aborigines were regarded, until very recently, as objects of study rather than as subjects of their own discourses. The Aboriginal writer Mudrooroo Nyoongah, formerly Colin Johnson, identifies Robert Bropho's *Fringedweller* (Sydney: Alternative Publishing Cooperative, 1980) as the first "true autobiography" with "an authentic Aboriginal voice perhaps speaking for the first time without the intrusion of an editor." For a brief discussion of the history of Aboriginal "autobiography," see Colin Johnson, "White Forms, Aboriginal Content," in *Aboriginal Writing Today,* ed. Jack Davis and Bob Hodge (Canberra: Australian Institute for Aboriginal Studies, 1985). For further background information, particularly as it relates to Aboriginal women, see Peggy Brock, ed., *Women, Rites and Sites: Aboriginal Women's Cultural Knowledge* (Sydney: Allen & Unwin, 1989).

2. Some of these obstacles are considered in this paper, but for more detailed discussion, see Johnson, "White Forms, Aboriginal Content"; and Kateryna Arthur, "Fiction and the Rewriting of History: A Reading of Colin Johnson," *Westerly* 1 (March 1985): 55–60.

3. As an immigrant Ukrainian and therefore a member of another colonized and marginalized group, I write from the position of an outsider who is critical of Anglo-Irish Australian attitudes, but, as a white middle-class academic, I am aware that I cannot escape being implicated in white Australia's racist history. I venture, nevertheless, into the world of Aboriginal women's stories as a woman, encouraged by Aboriginal women who want to promote and publicize their readings of their own lives and culture to a white readership in ways that avoid at least some aspects of white patriarchal traditions of interpretation.

4. For a discussion of changes in Aboriginal women's roles since European settlement, see Fay Gale, ed., *We Are Bosses Ourselves* (Canberra: Australian Institute for Aboriginal Studies, 1983).

5. Shari Benstock, ed., *The Private Self: Theory and Practice of Women's Autobiographical Writings* (London: Routledge, 1988), 19–20.

6. Quoted by Susan Stanford Friedman, "Women's Autobiographical Selves: Theory and Practice," in *The Private Self: Theory and Practice of Women's Autobiographical Writings,* ed. Shari Benstock (London: Routledge, 1988), 35.

7. Ibid., 39.

8. See Friedman, "Women's Autobiographical Selves," for a critique of Gusdorf's theories, particularly in relation to women's autobiographical writing. The limitations of traditional definitions of autobiography are further discussed by Rita Felski, who redefines the genre in order to accommodate contemporary forms; see *Beyond Feminist Aesthetics: Feminist Literature and Social Change* (London: Hutchinson Radius, 1989), 89–91.

9. Diane Bell, *Daughters of the Dreaming* (Sydney: Allen & Unwin, 1983), 37. Further references to this book will include page numbers in parentheses in the text.

10. Although this is not a universal tradition, a high degree of bonding with the land is a universal feature of aboriginal culture, and this example shows it being expressed in a very visible way.

11. For a detailed account of the nature of women's land-maintaining activities, see Bell, *Daughters of the Dreaming*, chap. 3.

12. Sally Morgan, *My Place* (Fremantle, W. Australia: Fremantle Arts Centre Press, 1987). Further references to this book will include page numbers in parentheses in the text.

13. Mudrooroo Narogin makes this kind of criticism in "Disguising the Fringe," in *Writing from the Fringe: A Study of Modern Aboriginal Literature* (Victoria: Hyland House, 1990), 148–49.

14. Glenyse Ward, *Wandering Girl* (Broome, W. Australia: Magabala, 1987). Further references to this book will include page numbers in parentheses in the text.

15. Elsie Roughway Labumore, *An Aboriginal Mother Tells of the Old and the New* (Victoria: McPhee Gribble, 1984). Further references to this book will include page numbers in parentheses in the text.

16. Narogin, *Writing from the Fringe,* 161.

17. Ruby Langford, *Don't Take Your Love to Town* (Victoria: Penguin, 1988). Further references to this book will include page numbers in parentheses in the text.

PART V

The Body and the Colonizer

Chapter 18

Disembodied Subjects: English Women's Autobiography under the Raj

Nancy L. Paxton

In *Growing,* the second volume of his autobiography, which describes his life as a civil servant in Ceylon from 1904 to 1911, Leonard Woolf describes the world created by British imperialism as a hall of mirrors:

> The white people were also in many astonishing ways like the characters in a Kipling story. I could never make up my mind whether Kipling had moulded his characters accurately in the image of Anglo-Indian society or whether we were moulding our characters accurately in the image of a Kipling story.[1]

In this text, Woolf presents himself as the colonizer performing before a captive audience and describes himself as someone "always, subconsciously or consciously, playing a part, acting upon a stage. The stage, the scenery, the backcloth before which I began to gesticulate . . . was imperialism" (p. 24). While Leonard Woolf thus acknowledges the crisis in legitimation of the "imperial I" that accompanied modernism and psychoanalytic thought, he did not publish his confession until fourteen years after the British surrendered control of their Indian empire in 1947. His remarks invite us to see the world created by British colonialism in India as a stage where the "imperial I" was consolidated and protected against the subversive threats he admits.

Autobiographies written by British men and women during the Raj in India provide useful ground, then, for the study of the imperial I because they literalize and foreground its construction, demonstrate how gender acts as a variable in it, and reveal how the colonizers' confrontations with colonized people shaped their understanding of their own position and agency as speaking subjects.

By analyzing the autobiographies by English men and women writing about their life under colonialism, we can begin to demystify the imperial I by identifying the ways that many nineteenth-century "technologies of gender" operated to define and "implant" it.[2] The following comparison of representative autobiographies written by British men and women in India suggests that gender opened a gap in colonial discourse that imperialistic ideologies of class, race, and religion could not close.

The classic autobiographies of William Henry Sleeman (1788–1856) and Rudyard Kipling (1865–1936) epitomize the essence of the "imperial I" in the compelling, serene, rationalistic voice that speaks in these works. Autobiographies written by English women, by contrast, often express more ambivalence about the colonial project, ambivalence that was more systematically silenced in texts by men who were their contemporaries. The autobiographies by Emily Eden (1797–1869), Harriet Tytler (1828–1907), and Flora Annie Steel (1841–1929), who lived and worked in India during comparable periods, reveal, for example, considerably more ambiguity in their efforts to construct and claim the power and agency of the imperial I. Likewise, these texts are doubly marked by the authors' sense of their sexual difference and by mysterious "disruptions" caused by their confrontations with the colonized Other. Englishwomen's experience of breaking out of their own place as a silent Other thus inscribes itself on the representation of Indian men and women who appear in their narratives.

One particularly troubled site of "disruption" and displacement in both men's and women's autobiographies in this sample can be located by tracing how the physical body, as subject and object, writes itself into these texts. The autobiographer's representation of his or her own body reveals how deeply gender and sexuality engraved themselves into colonial discourse about India. Francis Barker has argued that the imperial I began to appear in English discourse in the seventeenth century, when it became "necessary to narrate the outer world from an inner place, by means of a clarified and transparent instrumental language."[3] This instrumental view of language made representation possible by creating oppositions not only between self and Other but also between self and body, so that the body was "confined, ignored, exscribed from discourse, and yet remains at the edge of visibility, troubling the space from which it has been banished" (p. 63).

Barker focuses our attention on that moment in English literature when, as Raymond Schwab has argued, the Orient was rediscovered.[4] While the autobiographies in this sample written by colonizing men were composed more than two centuries later, they show that the "tremulous private body" remained banished from the text. The autobiographies of colonizing women reveal, by contrast, how the private body not only "troubles" the text but overwrites the imperial I, limiting its position and agency as speaking subject.

William Sleeman's *Rambles and Recollections of an Indian Official* was written before the Raj was officially consolidated by the Government of India Act in 1858.[5] It demonstrates how the male prerogative of speaking for British and Indian women helped to consolidate the imperial I, and thus it reveals how technologies of gender helped transform seventeenth- and eighteenth-century travel accounts into manuals of colonial domination. Throughout his autobiography, Sleeman presents himself as a liberal, curious, cool, rational, and objective male observer.

In 1835, Sleeman suffered a serious illness for which a journey through North India was the prescribed cure, yet he "excises" nearly all traces of the private body from this curiously disembodied text. He remains similarly silent about the objects of his desire. Though his wife and young son accompanied him on his travels, he rarely mentions either of them.[6] In fact, the only words his wife speaks in this 650-page narrative demonstrate how profoundly she functions "as the silent groundwork of male subjectivity."[7] Sleeman reports that she was awestruck by the beauty of the Taj Mahal and declared, "I know not how to criticize such a building, but I can tell you what I feel. I would die to-morrow to have such another over me" (p. 317). Assigned only this fragment of the language of feeling, she is otherwise silent in this text; the rest of the universe of discourse is claimed by her husband.

The body that most "troubles" this autobiographical text, however, is the body of an Indian woman made Other by age and religion as well as race and gender. Sleeman interrupts his travel narrative to describe an occasion in 1829 when he saw a Hindu woman perform *sati,* the Indian ritual of widow immolation.[8] He begins by alluding to her physical body by noting that this older woman sat upon the riverbank "with only a thin sheet thrown over her shoulders" (p. 20) and that she had "broken her bracelets in pieces, by which she became dead in law, and for ever excluded from caste" (p. 20). Focusing on the most spectacular moment in this ritual, Sleeman recounts how the widow "walked up deliberately and steadily to the brink, stepped into the centre of the flame, sat down, and leaning back in the midst as if reposing upon a couch, was consumed without uttering a shriek or betraying one sign of agony" (p. 23). Sleeman watches this spectacle with a moral detachment only a little troubled by fears that he could be "charged with wanton abuse of authority" (p. 19), since he tried to outlaw sati in his district before the governor-general, Lord William Bentinck, officially prohibited it throughout British India later that year (p. 19). Because he knew several Indian languages, Sleeman was able to speak directly to this woman, but his efforts to dissuade her failed. Once he realized that "it would be unavailing" to attempt to save her life (p. 22), he permitted the performance of sati on the condition that the survivors in her family sign written agreements that "no other member of their family should ever do the same" (p. 22). Thus, Sleeman enacts the prerogatives of the male colonizer as lawgiver and historian, by describing how his word, his desire, is written over the heads of his subjects. The relationship between body and word in his text thus helps reveal the central place of gender in the emerging reformist political ideology Sleeman articulates, the ideology that justified the first official British interventions in Indian culture in order to eradicate certain "dreadful" practices such as sati.[9]

Rudyard Kipling's *Something of Myself,* written almost a century later, demonstrates how Victorian science was also later appropriated in service to the Raj.[10] Kipling's autobiography shows how social Darwinism acted as a technology of gender to shore up the imperial I in the decades after what the British call the Indian Mutiny, that "seminal event in the history of British India."[11] Unlike Sleeman, Kipling includes a narrative about his childhood that suggests how colonialism restructured the colonial English family in order to install more efficiently the gender- and race-inflected view of self that made the body central to the definition of the imperial I during the most intense phase of British imperialism in India.

Throughout his autobiography, Kipling allows much more expression of the needs and desires of the "tremulous private body" than does Sleeman. He begins with a sensuous description of his "first impressions," of "daylight, light and colour and golden and purple fruits" (p. 3). Kipling's narrative also indicates that he felt less inhibited by the discipline of race when he was a child. He relates how his Indian *ayah* entertained him with stories, and his bearer took him to the local Hindu temples,where "being below the age of caste, I held his hand and looked at the dimly seen, friendly Gods" (p. 4). Kipling's autobiography shows that racially segregated colonial society would collapse if, as adults, colonizers and colonized were permitted such intimacy.

Kipling's account of his separation from his parents when he was six years old, and his "exile" in the "house of Desolation" during his stay in England, dramatizes how the discipline of the body becomes one of the most important functions of the colonizer's education. Christian evangelicalism lent itself to this process in Kipling's case, for he describes how he was "regularly beaten" by his "aunt" who exercised the "full vigor of the Evangelical as revealed to the Woman" (p. 8) in the household where he was boarded. Likewise, his narrative about his formal education demonstrates how the male body was indeed disciplined by the compulsory games and by the repression of all homosexual "perversion" (p. 27) at schools like Westward Ho. As a consequence of these lessons, Kipling learned to cultivate an "invincible detachment . . . towards all the world" (pp. 30–31) and to regard "words . . . as weapons" (p. 36).

In describing his life after he returned to India at sixteen, Kipling includes a detailed representation of his own "bodyscape" that indicates how social Darwinist ideologies about race operated to widen the prescribed distance between colonizer and colonized.[12] Freed from the military discipline that may have constrained Sleeman, Kipling details the physical discomforts he experienced working in a newspaper office in Lahore, writing, for example, "I never worked less than ten hours and seldom more than fifteen per diem. . . . I had fever too, regular and persistent, to which I added for a while chronic dysentery. Yet I discovered that a man can work with a temperature of 104, even though the next day he has to ask the office who wrote the article" (p. 47).

Kipling's description of the circle of his intimacies as a young adult reveals how social Darwinist ideas about "race" operated to reinforce the imperial I, for he represents his social world as bounded by whiteness. The Indians he describes are nearly all anonymous and figure primarily as domestic servants, club members at that home away from home (p. 58), or his subordinates in the workplace. While his domestic servants mitigated some of his physical suffering by offering, among other things, the luxury of being shaved while he slept, the rest of the world of India—life in "the liquor shops and opium dens, the puppet shows and the native dances" that he describes—comes to be regarded as spectacle, observed for the "sheer sake of looking" (p. 59). Indian men are thus relegated to the middle distance, and Indian women disappear entirely.

Kipling's representation of his own "bodyscape" also suggests how the "technology" of race was deployed to redefine acceptable expressions of male sexuality for British men under the Raj. While Kipling mentions his marriage to Caroline Ballestier, he, like Sleeman, says almost nothing about his wife in his autobiography, referring to her only occasionally as a member of the curiously anonymous "Committee of Ways and Means" (p. 118) that helped to organize his professional, financial, and domestic life. Twenty years later, Lord Kitchener identified one typical source of this reticence when he explained how sexual repression was used to enforce prevailing notions of white superiority under the Raj; he insisted that "no soldier who is unable to exercise due restraint" in expressing his sexual desires could "be expected to be entrusted with command over his comrades. . . . Every man can, by self-control, restrain the indulgence of these imprudent and reckless impulses that so often lead men astray."[13] This definition of proper sexual behavior for Englishmen not only widened the gap between the races but also was used to discriminate class divisions among the British colonizers.

Yet the body subtly "troubles" Kipling's text, nonetheless, for the radical severing of self from sexual desire is anticipated by a macabre episode included in his narrative about his childhood, in which a dead child's hand is dropped into the Kiplings' garden by carrion birds feeding over the Towers of Silence. The shadow of this separation of the body from its sexual desires reappears in Kipling's account of his life in Lahore, for the Indian bodies that most haunt his text appear as corpses. He writes, "The dead of all times were about us—in the vast forgotten Moslem cemeteries round the Station, where one's horse's hoof of a morning might break through to the corpse below; skulls and bones tumbled out of our mud garden walls, and were turned up among the flowers by the Rains" (p. 48).

Colonizing British women could not so easily divorce themselves from the body and its desires, in part because they lived in a colonial economy that assigned white women the labor of reproduction but prohibited them from serving the Raj more directly by working in the military or in the civil service. Consequently, British women in India were confined by a culture that prevented them from experiencing the power of the spoken or written word in the public realm. It is hardly surprising, then, that the autobiographies of Emily Eden, Harriet Tytler, and Flora Annie Steel display a much less certain claim on the imperial I.

Eden's, Tytler's, and Steel's autobiographical narratives all indicate that they performed the roles assigned to the "incorporated wife," serving as hostess, wife, and mother.[14] Yet, all three escaped some of the constraints of this conventional gender role, in part, by claiming the right to narrate their own life stories rather than allow their men to write the stories for them.

From the beginning, *Up the Country* shows that Emily Eden experienced a certain immunity from these conventions because she went to India not as a wife but as the sister and confidant of her brother, Lord Auckland, who succeeded William Bentinck as governor-general of India in 1836.[15] She and her sister lived in India with Auckland until he was recalled in 1842, after five thousand British soldiers died in the retreat from Kabul.[16] While Eden confesses that her brother had "always been a sort of idol" to her, her narrative shows that their affection was mutual. She writes that after coming to India he was "fonder of me than ever, and more dependent on me, as I am his only confidant. I feel I am of use to him, and that I am in my right place when I am by his side" (2:177). Moreover, she enhanced his diplomatic capabilities because she was able to pay formal visits to the secluded wives of Indian rulers, a courtesy males could not perform.[17]

Emily Eden was thirty-eight years old and unmarried when she left for India. Her wealth as well as her age allowed her to exempt herself from participation in the Calcutta marriage market,[18] though she presided at countless formal dinners, dances, and receptions that were held to honor Lord Auckland. Nonetheless, Eden recognized that her gender prescribed her place in colonial society, as is evident in her representation of her own body in this text. While the body was virtually erased in Sleeman's autobiography, which narrated events during these same years, Eden's "tremulous private body" appears as the focal point of her account. One essential ritual in many of the formal meetings between Auckland and various Indian princes involved the exchange of gifts. Over and over, Eden describes how her body was loaded with jewels and other displays of "Arabian Nightish" luxury (1:87). When Auckland and his entourage visited the Rajah of Scindia, for example, Eden writes: "The Rajah had ordered that [the Ranee] should put all the jewellery on us with her own little hands. I had a diamond necklace and a collar, some native pearl earrings that hung nearly down to the waist, and a beautiful pair of diamond bracelets and the great article of all was an immense diamond tiara. . . . They were valued altogether at £2,400" (2:231). These exchanges were almost entirely ritualistic since the Edens, like all representatives of the East India Company at the time, were forbidden to accept gifts, but they served to dramatize the central importance of the female body as the symbolic common ground uniting British and Indian men of the ruling class.

Like Sleeman, Eden does not mention her childhood, but her letters describing her preparations for travel to India outline another discipline that British colonialism imposed on the female body and suggest how class operated in concert with gender to shape the body and its relation to the imperial subject. In one of her letters, Eden discloses how English ladies maintained the fashions that were a sign of their class and race, despite the discomforts of the Indian climate: "Poor Goliath himself would have been obliged to lie down and rest if he had tried on 6 pairs of stays consecutively . . . . It is so irritating to want so many things and such cold articles. A cargo of large fans; a silver busk, because all steel busks become rusty and spoil the stay; nightdresses with short sleeves, and net night-caps, because muslin is so hot."[19]

Like Kipling, Eden could call on a large retinue of domestic servants to help ease the physical discomforts of her life in India; she was even assigned two bearers whose job it was to wait beside a sedan chair to carry her up the marble stairs at Government House in Calcutta should the heat overcome her.[20] Thus, while the colonial ideology defining Eden's class position set rigid standards of fashion for upper-class memsahibs, it allowed them to surrender periodically to the presumed weaknesses of the female body.

Eden's autobiography recounts her travels with Lord Auckland on his diplomatic mission in 1838–39 to the court of Ranjit Singh, the most powerful ruler in the Punjab. Her experience of "camp life" prompted her to interrogate, however playfully, the definitions of self and body, English and Indian, right and wrong that provide the underlying structure of this colonial discourse. Eden ruefully describes the enormous entourage that accompanied them up the Ganges, overland to Delhi and Simla, and on to the Punjab. By the end of their journey, the numbers of their party swelled to include more than 260 personal servants and bearers, 500 camels, 800 horses, and 20 elephants, which seemed to Eden to be a ludicrously pompous display of English power and wealth.[21]

Though Eden often frets about the rigors of her journey, her account shows how camp life taught her to appreciate more fully her body's physical strength and agency. When an accident forced her to "march" some distance under the hot afternoon sun, she discovered, to her amazement, that she was strong enough to survive such an ordeal: "I had no idea that I could have walked a mile and a half without dropping down dead. That is something learnt" (2:118).

Likewise, while racial stereotypes often distorted her perceptions of the Indian men whom she regarded as her social inferiors, her gender allowed her, on occasion, to see through some of the barriers dividing colonizer from colonized. Eden was scandalized by the naked male mendicants at a Sikh temple, calling them "the most horrid-looking monsters it is possible to see. They never wear any clothes, but powder themselves all over with white or yellow powder, and put red streaks over their faces" (1:161). Yet, when she met the Rajah of Nahun, near Simla, she noted that he was "one of the best-looking people I have seen, and is a Rajpoot chief, and rides, and hunts, and shoots, and is active" (1:170). Facetiously imagining a marriage to the rajah, which would allow her to escape permanently from the heat of Calcutta, Eden writes, "Nothing can be prettier than the scenery, and altogether Nahun is the nicest residence I have seen in India; and if the rajah fancied an English ranee, I know somebody who would be very happy to listen to his proposals" (1:170). This episode thus suggests the power of the female body and its (usually repressed) desires to subvert the oppositions of self and Other most central to colonial discourse.

Eden's perspective on Indian women suggests that her fleeting sense of gender solidarity is perhaps even more subversive of colonial discourse than the heterosexual eroticism inspired by Indian men. In one episode, the spectacle of the exotic is interrupted when Eden's attention is drawn by the Indian women in a crowd along the Ganges at Benares: "They are more clothed here than in Bengal, and the women wear bright crimson veils, or yellow with crimson borders, and sometimes purple dresses with crimson borders and have generally a little brown baby, with a scarlet cap on, perched on their hips" (1:16). Unable to maintain the distance Sleeman assumes, Eden comments, in an aside to her correspondent, "I wish you would have one little brown baby for a change; they are so much prettier than white children" (1:16). After this extraordinary expression of racial disloyalty, Eden surrenders to convention and resumes her class-bound position as distant sightseer, describing the "boats of rich natives in front with gilded sterns and painted peacocks at the prow." "In short," she concludes, "just what people say of India; you know it all, but it is pretty to see" (1:16).

Moreover, though Eden is rarely sentimental about anything, including motherhood, her sympathetic response to the "horrible" sights of starving women and children in one district ravaged by famine prompted her to try to save at least one Indian child and its mother. In describing her efforts, Eden admits: "I am sure there is no sort of

violent atrocity I should not commit for food, with a starving baby.
I should not stop to think about the rights or wrongs of the case"
(1:93–94). Eden's narrative thus suggests the subversive power of gender solidarity not only to overcome racial barriers but even to transform moral definitions of "right and wrong."

Finally, Emily Eden is critical of the "merchandising" sensibility
she sees as characterizing British colonialism in India. Viewing some
of the grandest monuments of Moghul rule in Delhi and noting the
beautiful half-caste women who attended a ball given in her honor,
Eden writes:

> Delhi is a very suggestive and moralizing place—such stupen-
> dous remains of power and wealth passed and passing away—
> and somehow I feel that we horrid English have "gone and
> done it," merchandised it, revenued it, and spoiled it all. I am
> not very fond of Englishmen out of their own country. And
> Englishwomen did not look pretty at the ball in the evening,
> and it did not tell well for the beauty of Delhi that the
> painted ladies of one regiment, who are generally called "the
> little corpses" (and very hard it is too upon most corpses),
> were much the prettiest people there, and were besieged with
> partners. (1:130)

In contrast to Kipling who excises all upper- and middle-class Indian
women from his text and imagines dead bodies in place of the "painted
ladies" and veiled women he, no doubt, saw on the streets of Lahore,
Eden recognizes the beauty and vitality of these "little corpses." For
her, the female body thus forms some basis for shared sympathy with
multiply colonized Indian women.

Harriet Earle Tytler highlights her role as the"incorporated wife"
of Robert Tytler and the mother of his children. As the daughter of
a British officer stationed in India and later as the wife of a captain
of the 38th Native Infantry, she in some ways conformed most thoroughly to the role of the "incorporated wife." Tytler authorizes her
text and claims her readers' attention by describing herself as the
"only lady at the siege" of Delhi,[22] one of the most important battles
during the Indian Uprising of 1857. Her autobiography centers on her
eyewitness account of the British retreat from Delhi on 11 May 1857,
and the campaign to regain control of the city, which came to a
successful conclusion on 20 September 1857.[23] Tytler mutes the bodily
cause of her presence at the siege, though she indicates indirectly that
because her pregnancy was so far advanced she could not tolerate
travel by elephant, the only means available to transport wives and
children from the scenes of battle. Tytler gave birth to her third child

on 21 June 1857, virtually on the battlefield. Finally, like the proper "incorporated wife," Tytler maintains a decorous wifely silence; she did not write her account until she was over seventy years old, she did not describe her private life after the Indian Uprising, and she did not try to publish her narrative in her lifetime.

Harriet Tytler's autobiography reveals other "technologies" as well that operated in concert with class to construct the gender-inflected imperial I. Like Kipling, Tytler begins with lyrical descriptions that display the child's wonder over many small details of Indian life, but Tytler's account also dramatizes her family's far more precarious hold on those middle-class comforts that Kipling enjoyed.[24] Tytler describes playing with broken bits of china and the decorative end of a scabbard, the only toys her parents could afford to give her, until she received a precious and expensive doll as a gift from a friend.

The child-self that Tytler presents also lacks the naive egocentricity that Kipling reveals in his narrative about his childhood, and her autobiography thus suggests how evangelical Christianity contributed to the construction of the gender-inflected imperial I. Tytler's evangelicalism profoundly determined her subjectivity, chastening her self-regard and opening her eyes more frequently to the suffering and privation of the Indians she observed as a child and later as an adult. Early in her autobiography, for example, Tytler recalls that her father offered food to members of a Brahmin family who were literally starving to death and had come to the shores of the Ganges to die:

> I was at this time standing on the prow of the boat, looking
> on with childlike curiosity, when I observed a little infant
> crawl up to its dead mother and try in vain to obtain some
> nourishment from her. I recollect perfectly well the whole
> scene, little child as I was, for I could scarcely have been six
> years old, and I said to myself, "When I grow up to be a
> woman I will save all the little starving children and bring
> them up as Christians." (p. 10)

Though she echoes Eden's desire to save starving Indian children, Tytler lacks the same financial means and so can envision only the spiritual salvation she would offer to them instead.

Likewise, though Tytler, like Kipling, also describes the pain of exile often experienced by Anglo-Indian children when they were sent to England to school, her account is prefaced by descriptions of her fear that she would be denied the "good English educations" her male siblings received (p. 21), since she was not sent to school until she was eleven years old. Moreover, Tytler's text suggests that the cross-cultural dislocation, alienation, and loss experienced by Anglo-Indian girls operated to separate them not only from the maternal body but from their own bodies as well, restricting their sense of its power and agency in profound and gender-determined ways. Tytler's account of her five years in England shows how deeply her gender prescribed her education, for her training amounted to little more than the direct disciplining of her body and her sexuality.

The physical privations and psychological isolation Tytler felt during her five years in England were not designed to teach her to claim the power of the word as a compensation for the body's subordination. Tytler's narrative, in contrast to Kipling's autobiography, omits any details about her formal schooling and focuses, instead, on the rigorous regimen she was subject to in her aunt's household, a program similar to those Elaine Showalter outlines as directed toward the disciplining of adolescent Victorian girls' emergent sexuality.[25] Each morning Tytler reports that she breakfasted on bread and water, which her aunt required that she eat while running fifty times around the garden, making, she calculates, "four and a half miles of running daily" (p. 39). Similarly, because she was only permitted to wear a "low necked, short-sleeved print dress all year around" and "only allowed to wear a small plaid shawl" in winter (p. 39), Tytler suffered excessively during the cold English winters. She provides a particularly vivid image of how the female body was sacrificed as part of her preparation for Victorian ladyhood when she describes how, during her two hours of piano practice every morning in the pre-dawn cold, the "chilblains at the root" of her fingers would "burst and bleed" (p. 39), leaving blood upon the piano keys.

Unlike Sleeman and Kipling, Tytler recognized the misogyny at work in the Anglo-Indian family, and she is uncharacteristically severe in her criticism of the women who enforced the patriarchal bias of family life both in England and in colonial India. Tytler labels her aunt as "horribly strict" and "really cruel" (p. 39), and describes her mother as "inexorable" in imposing duty on her daughters but not on her sons. Tytler reports that when she returned to India at sixteen and learned of her father's recent unexpected death, her mother greeted her with the chilling news that she must remain in India alone in order to collect her father's pension while her mother returned to England to oversee the schooling of her youngest sister and brother. Protesting the misogyny of colonial society that thus reproduced itself in subsequent generations, Tytler writes: "I do think as a rule mothers are hard on their girls where a darling son is concerned, engendering selfishness in men in after-life, especially toward their daughters and wives" (p. 8). Raised in a family organized by these principles, Tytler came to see herself at sixteen as an "orphan" in "the truest sense" (p. 56).

Effectively separated from her mother's body and from her own, Tytler later plays the part often assumed by native servants in other British travel writing,[26] when she recounts the chaotic British retreat from Delhi and shows how she carried not only her own "emotional baggage" but that of her husband and children. In relating the harrowing circumstances of her family's escape from Delhi, Tytler vividly catalogs the precious possessions they left behind and describes the physical suffering they experienced, traveling in a crowded carriage in the "burning sun" and drinking the "greeny mire" in roadside ditches to slake their thirst (p. 117). When their carriage broke down, Tytler reports that she and her young children were forced to walk several miles, all the while fearing for their lives.

Tytler's account of the battle to retake Delhi also suggests how this colonial emergency reshaped the colonial family by further restricting the Englishwoman's apprehension of her body, its agency, and its capacity for pleasure. Tytler's experience of motherhood during the Indian Uprising taught her to regard motherhood as requiring the heroic sacrifice of her body and its pleasures, a sacrifice analogous to those of British soldiers.

In her description of the first battle she witnessed, Tytler, like many incorporated wives, foregrounds the suffering of her husband and children rather than herself. In the heat of battle, she grew so anxious for her husband's safety that she "did not realize any danger" for herself though "bullets whizzed and pinged in the air" and buried themselves in the wall behind which she sheltered (p. 154). Likewise, though Tytler lived through the last month of her pregnancy under the blazing sun of May and delivered her son during the monsoon rains of June, her description of her son's birth focuses on his body rather than her own. She describes her son's "advent into this troublesome world" by noting, with her wonderful gift for understatement, that the circumstances of his birth were "not very promising": "There he lay near the opening in the cart with only a small square piece of flannel thrown over him, with the setting moon shining brightly on him, with nothing but the sound of the alarm call and shot and shell for music to his ears for the rest of the siege" (p. 147).

The moment when the body creates the most extraordinary disruption in this text occurs, however, when Tytler describes her efforts to confine and amuse her two-year-old daughter, Edith, who was seriously ill. Bedridden herself and still weak from childbirth, Tytler describes her efforts to control her daughter: "To keep her in the cart was so difficult that I was at my wit's end what to do. At last a bright idea entered into my head. It was rather a unique one, which was to scratch holes in my feet and tell her she must be my doctor and stop their bleeding. This process went on daily and for hours. No sooner did my wounds heal, than she used to make them bleed again for the simple pleasure of stopping the blood with my handkerchief" (p. 149). Lacking the agency that Sleeman and Kipling could claim to turn words into laws or weapons, Tytler, like the Woman Warrior in Maxine Hong Kingston's autobiography,[27] feels compelled to offer her body as the blank page upon which the text of her daughter's survival could be written. Pain becomes the body's most eloquent language as the daughter writes, unknowingly, upon the maternal body.

Tytler's autobiography suggests that her experience in a female body, her experience of subordination, self-division, and self-sacrifice and the surrender of her body to childbearing nonetheless allowed her, on occasion, to see beyond the racial boundaries reinforced by this war. Looking at the bodies of the mutineers who were killed in battle, Tytler recognizes several sepoys who once served in her husband's company and dares to describe their naked bodies as they lay unburied in the sun: "I saw some of our fine, tall, handsome men lying somewhat swollen by the heat of those four hours and stark naked, for every camp follower robbed them of their gold and silver jewels and the last comers of the clothes on their bodies, leaving the poor fellows just as God had made them. Such handsome, splendid specimens of high casted Hindus" (p. 145).

In closing this passage, Tytler reveals her own divided loyalties as a colonizer, torn between Christian forgiveness and British chauvinism, and as a woman, caught between pity and vengeance. "At any other time my heart would have been full of pity and sorrow at such awful sights, but after all we had suffered, at the hands of our treacherous sepoys, pity had vanished and thirst for revenge alone remained" (p. 145). Remembering the British casualties of war, remembering the Englishwomen whose ravished bodies interposed themselves spectacularly in subsequent British histories of the Indian Mutiny—remembering the "beautiful young girl, the wife" of an English officer who was found dead and "perfectly nude with her unborn babe lying on her chest" (p. 113)—Tytler resists Christian forgiveness.[28] "Such are the effects of warfare upon the hearts of gentle, tender-hearted women," she explains (p. 145). She concludes by praying that the world will someday be delivered from war: "May God's millennium soon come and all strife and war be at an end, which until then I fear will never be" (p. 145).

Thus, Tytler's autobiography suggests how profoundly gender operated to modify a colonizing woman's sense of her class position, her response to Christian evangelicalism, and her sense of her body's power and agency, especially in her view of motherhood. Moreover, her life story provides eloquent testimony about how British nationalism at mid-century redefined the duties owed to the Mother Country, reorienting, as a consequence, the military's claims on the bodies not only of men but of women as well.

When she is compared with Emily Eden and Harriet Tytler, Flora Annie Steel appears to be the most successful in escaping the prescribed gender roles of the "incorporated wife" in British India. Married when she was twenty-one years old, Steel came to India as the "baby bride"[29] of a civil engineer who worked in the Indian Civil Service in North India from 1868 to 1881. Steel saw herself as sharing the duties of colonial rule with her husband rather than subordinating herself to serve his needs, and she worked outside as well as inside the home. Her autobiography, *The Garden of Fidelity,* demonstrates the powerful effects of the Indian Uprising of 1857 in reorganizing colonial life and discourse.[30] Though Steel's text shows how late nineteenth-century British feminism authorized her claims to greater autonomy and power in colonial society, it reveals, as well, her endorsement of social Darwinist analyses of racial and sexual difference, and her internalization of the more repressive sexual ideology characterizing Anglo-Indian society after 1857.[31] As such, it provides a cautionary tale about how the multifarious ideologies of gender have operated to subvert the most radical potential of feminist thought.

In her autobiography, Steel identifies herself as a "suffragette" and outlines her participation in the British campaign for women's vote in the first two decades of the twentieth century. Steel's account of her earlier life in India demonstrates how her egalitarian feminism provided a justification for her efforts to escape some of the restrictions that gender usually imposed on British women in colonial society. Steel's narrative about her life in India shows, first of all, that feminism opened a gap in colonial society by teaching Englishwomen like herself to find pleasure in the greater physical freedom it sometimes offered. Unlike Emily Eden, Steel particularly enjoyed "camp life," and found great satisfaction riding with her husband, for example, through fields of wildflowers in Kashmir. Likewise, camp life gave Steel an excuse to cut her hair "short," to wear "knickerbockers," to write and paint, and to forgo the formalities that otherwise structured colonial life (p. 146).

Steel's feminism, however, did not operate independently of other technologies of gender at work in colonial society. Rejecting arguments that her gender justified her own subordination in colonial society, Steel nonetheless assumed a conservative political ideology, like Kipling's, that justified her own claims to rule by appealing to specious social Darwinist arguments about the class and race superiority of the British elite. Hoping to seize the same power and authority she saw conferred on her husband because of his superior position in the colonial hierarchy, Steel rejected arguments to democratize colonial life: "I saw clearly that everything—order, method, punctuality, efficiency—depended upon one's individuality only. So I gripped the fact, to which I have held ever since, that the best form of Government is beneficent Autocracy. Democracy went by the board as a thing of mediocrity, the Apotheosis of Bureaucracy" (p. 46). Without apparently investigating the sources of her husband's—or her own—authority, Steel insisted on the "absolute necessity for high-handed dignity in dealing with those who for thousands of years have been accustomed to it. They love it. It appeals to them" (p. 133). She concludes illogically that because colonial subjects submit to British authority, "it is legitimate" (p. 133).

Steel's brief account of her childhood in Scotland reveals some of the roots of her racism and suggests how British nationalism implanted this sense of racial superiority in young British boys and girls. Describing the impact of the anti-Indian propaganda that swept England after the Indian Uprising, Steel writes, "The waves of horror that had spread through Great Britain as one after another of the Great Mutiny tragedies came through, reached even the nurseries and school rooms. Nana Sahib was hung, drawn, and quartered by children hundreds of times" (p. 15). Later in India, Steel resorts to these same brutal techniques in asserting mastery by physical domination, lessons that Kipling also describes as part of his experience at Westward Ho.

Nonetheless, as an adult living in colonial India, Steel occasionally recognized a gap between her gendered self and her impersonation of the imperial I that prompted her to adopt such tactics of mastery. In *The Garden of Fidelity*, for example, she unabashedly describes horsewhipping an Indian servant who mistreated her mule, but she acknowledges that her gender makes this expression of mastery through physical domination seem unseemly (and indeed, to us, obscene). She writes, "I confess that I never do get angry without an intense desire to hit, but I know it is unladylike, and condemn myself, as a rule, to inaction" (p. 155).[32] This episode, like many others in her autobiography, suggests how Steel's adoption of a conservative politics helped bridge this gap between masterful colonizer and "lady."

Steel's representation of the place and condition of the female body under the Raj reveals even more ambiguity. Like Harriet Tytler, Steel experienced motherhood as a "wounding experience." She identifies her grief over the loss of her first daughter, who died in childbirth, as one of only two regrets she felt about her life in India. Likewise, she characterizes her separation from her surviving daughter, Mabel, at sixteen months, as a "wound" that "never heals" (p. 105). Assuming that this pain of separation was necessary to the colonial enterprise, Steel observes matter-of-factly that many Anglo-Indian mothers felt that "though their children have been good, considerate, friendly, it seemed as though something were lacking" in the bond between mother and child (p. 105), but Steel could not envision any alternative. This view of motherhood indicates how colonial technologies of gender undermined the grounds of female solidarity that were usually fostered within the family. Thus, we can see how Steel's individualist understanding of feminism encouraged her to recommend that Englishwomen in India adopt the same masochistic stoicism valorized by upper-class British men.

Moreover, Steel unsexes herself and identifies female sexuality as the force that has the power to destroy civilization in order to enhance the moral superiority that she feels justifies her own claims as colonial ruler. Steel moved one step beyond the repression of heterosexual eroticism that Lord Kitchener recommended, for she expressed her natural immunity to the movement of sexual desire not only outside marriage but inside it as well. In her autobiography she represents herself as having achieved a subjectivity untroubled by the body's desire. On the opening page of *The Garden of Fidelity*, Steel baldly states that she did not love her husband and proudly asserts her "inborn dislike of the sensual side of life" (p. 1). Regarding her self-proclaimed lack of heterosexual desire as a sign of her moral superiority, Steel criticizes other British memsahibs whose passion allows them to become the "victims of sex" (p. 292).[33]

Steel's autobiography also shows perhaps more clearly than Kipling's how a social Darwinist technology of race cooperated with the technologies defining the colonial woman's sexuality in order to erect more impermeable racial barriers. "Women's jealousy," Steel writes, "was the primal cause of that disharmony of the racial instincts which is the root of so many of our social evils" (p. 292). Not recognizing how her analysis of gender and sexuality was shaped by the exigencies of imperial rule, Steel observed the greater sexual freedom of a younger generation of Englishwomen at home and concluded that they were "oversexed" and overly possessive, and recommended that "woman find her lost reserve and man his lost sense of fatherhood" (p. 291).

Still, Steel's autobiography, like Eden's and Tytler's, reveals the subversiveness of her gendered vision, for this same narrative demonstrates how her conflicted sense of gender solidarity occasionally allowed her to glimpse life beyond the narrow and confining vision of the male colonial I/eye. Her autobiography reveals more sympathy for Indian women than for Indian men, and details her efforts to improve the material conditions of their lives. Steel worked as an inspector of Indian girls' schools and worked on marketing schemes to sell handicrafts made by Indian women (p. 167). Moreover, she nominally supported suffrage for Indian women, though her conservatism prompted her, like many other English suffragettes, to insist on property qualifications as the basis for enfranchisement.[34] She argued, for example, that though "many" Indian women "doubtless are as intelligent and as well educated as the males," their "dependent position precludes them at present from outside interests," so that "few women in India" can properly qualify for suffrage because they do not meet the "property qualifications" (pp. 252–53).

The site in Steel's text where the body most troubles the narrative occurs in several episodes where she represents the sexuality of Indian women, for it is here that her own gynephobia and fear of female sexuality act most obviously to prevent her from seeing what she had herself lost in learning to unsex herself. In 1894, Steel traveled alone to India in order to gather material for a novel. During this trip she lived for a few weeks on a rooftop near Kasur with some Moslem women she knew and consequently gained entrance to a female world usually off limits to British colonizing men. Yet the colonizing I/eye obscures her vision, nonetheless, for she concludes that "the Mohomedan women in towns and therefore in the purdah were inevitably over-obsessed with sex. It was not their fault; they were strangely unaffected by the fact; but they had nothing else about which to think" (p. 121). In speculating about how Indian women were "to be released from this stagnation," Steel proposed that purdah should be made "less endurable" to Indian women. Later in her autobiography Steel asserts that "pain is Nature's strongest fulcrum," and explains that she always opposed "zenana missions or zenana doctors" because she "firmly" believed that "but for our efforts to make seclusion more bearable, India would now be half free of the curse of purdah" (p. 245). In this grotesque application of laissez-faire social Darwinism, we can see how Steel's experience as a British woman in colonial India prompted her to adopt a very punitive analysis not only of her own but also of Indian women's sexuality. Steel's partially repressed violence and aversion to "the sensual side of life" suggest how her feminism lent itself to British ideologies of control and so undermined the basis for a shared sympathy with her secluded sisters.

The effects of Steel's complicity with the patriarchal Raj and her resolute denial of the pain of her wounds and self-division may also be seen in her representation of herself as writer. In contrast to Tytler, Steel not only resisted her place as incorporated wife under the Raj; she later refused to assume the wife's silent and self-effacing role when she returned to England. Instead, at age forty-two, she began an active career, writing more than a dozen best-selling novels, numerous collections of short stories, and *The Complete Indian Housekeeper and Cook*. Her description of her career shows, nonetheless, how her habit of impersonating the imperial I undermined her authority as writer. While this skill initially helped advance her career—she successfully concealed her sex from her editor for three years and deceived several reviewers into thinking that her novels were written by Kipling—she confesses in her autobiography to feeling like a fraud. Throughout her life, despite her success, Steel admits that she felt ill educated, and in assessing her writing, she concludes that her novels "therefore must in some ways be poor" (p. 197).

Steel's most famous novel, *On the Face of the Waters,* presents a fictionalized account of the siege of Delhi and focuses on the same battles that Tytler witnessed during the Indian Uprising.[35] Unlike Tytler, however, Steel expresses skepticism about the power of Christianity to promote genuine "forgiveness," and asserts her faith in the power of her own words to heal the remaining wounds that prevent the English from "forgiving" the Indians for their part in the Mutiny (p. 15). Though she is fairly successful in excising overt Christian ideology from *On the Face of the Waters,* Steel's conservative politics writes itself instead into this novel, for she casts John Nicholson as the hero of the text and eroticizes the brutal tactics he employed in this decisive battle.

Moreover, after so many years of enjoying borrowed authority, Steel could not take full responsibility for her creative power with words.[36] Steel felt that some of her work was not written by her, but rather was dictated to her. In her fantasy about her creative processes, we can see how the Indian man, who is completely effaced in her autobiography, speaks nonetheless. She explains how an Indian man "in the white uniform of an Indian railway guard" appeared to her in a dream-vision and told her "word-for-word the story called *The Permanent Way*" (p. 197). Unable to adopt Kipling's attitude that words were "weapons," Steel knew, at least unconsciously, that the colonizer's language spoke her.

In conclusion, the autobiographies of Eden, Tytler, and Steel represent the experience of three successive generations of British women in Indian colonial society. Their narratives show that their lives were perhaps more constrained than those of British women in England because gender roles were more directly subordinated to the imperializing policies of the Raj. All three women include episodes that reveal they found some pleasure in exercising power over Indian men and women, suggesting how difficult it was for them to imagine ways to escape from the hierarchies that British imperialism imposed. On the other hand, their experiences of colonial life permitted them to recognize analogies between themselves and colonized Indian women that exposed larger social, economic, and political forces that subordinated them both. Certainly, the most insidious force at work shaping the subject in all three autobiographies was one that was most difficult for them to recognize and name: the technologies that defined their own sexual identity and experience of maternity. Eden, Tytler, and Steel demonstrate less expansiveness and certainty in claiming the prerogatives of the imperial I than do their male counterparts. Ultimately, their accounts demonstrate vividly why colonizing women had trouble imagining their bodies as entirely their own.

Like several other critics whose work is included in this volume, I have been troubled by the way that an attention to the subjectivity of the colonizer can erase the subjection of the colonized. In fact, what the autobiographies discussed here suggest, finally, is that there is no single duality that encompasses colonial oppression. Subjectivity can perhaps be better understood as constructed by a series of technologies that operate with greater or lesser effectiveness in particular times and places. The speaking subjects in all of these autobiographies show how women's experience of power and agency was limited by a colonial world that presented itself as a hall of mirrors that magnified gender, class, and racial differences in concert with other ideologies defining market economies, political power, and national identity. To understand more fully the various ways that the gender-inflected imperial I was constructed and later called into question, we must examine the other side of Kipling's mirror by rereading the literature not only of colonizing women but also of Indian writers of both sexes.

While the preceding analysis of how Englishmen and -women have been colonized by gender and sex may bring us closer to understanding how the imperial I was—and is—formulated, a fuller understanding of this problem can be achieved only if we look beyond the limits of studies of complicity such as this one. A more complete analysis of texts written by those colonized by race as well as by gender will shed necessary light on the colonial stage on which the uncertainties of the self are revealed.[37] By listening to the voices of those who have been multiply colonized, we can begin to reconstruct that unwritten history of different modes of subjection and expose the complicity that limited and deformed the lives of colonizing men and women who wrote, though not always self-consciously, in service to the Raj.

Notes

The research for this essay was supported by the Andrew W. Mellon Faculty Fellowship Program at Harvard University and by the Mary Ingraham Bunting Institute at Radcliffe College. I wish to thank Johanna Drucker, Julia Watson, Sidonie Smith, and Beverly Grier for many helpful suggestions for the revision of this article. This essay was inspired by Alice Jardine's call for a "new theory and practice of the speaking subject" in *Gynesis: Configurations of Woman and Modernity* (Ithaca, N.Y.: Cornell University Press, 1985), 44. I see my essay as part of a larger effort to analyze colonial discourse in relation to that of the colonized.

1. Leonard Woolf, *Growing: An Autobiography of the Years 1904–1911* (New York: Harcourt, 1961), 46. Further citations will include page numbers in parentheses in the text.

2. For a more complete discussion of these terms, see Teresa de Lauretis, *Technologies of Gender: Essays on Theory, Film, and Fiction* (Bloomington: Indiana University Press, 1987), 1–30.

3. Francis Barker, *The Tremulous Private Body: Essays on Subjection* (London: Methuen, 1984), 53. Further citations of this volume will include page numbers in parentheses in the text.

4. Raymond Schwab establishes a larger context for colonial discourse about India in his magisterial *The Oriental Renaissance: Europe's Rediscovery of India and the East, 1680–1880* (New York: Columbia University Press, 1984); see especially pp. 190–92. For a survey of autobiographies written by the colonizing British, see K. K. Dyson, *A Various Universe: A Study of the Journals and Memoirs of British Men and Women in the Indian Subcontinent* (Delhi: Oxford University Press, 1978).

5. William Henry Sleeman, *Rambles and Recollections of an Indian Official,* ed. Vincent A. Smith (Karachi: Oxford University Press, 1973). Further citations of this volume will include page numbers in parentheses in the text.

6. For Sleeman's rare comments about his wife, see *Rambles and Recollections,* 148, 210, 212, 317, 560.

7. Rosi Braidotti, "Envy: Or with Your Brains and My Looks," in *Men in Feminism,* ed. Alice A. Jardine and Paul Smith (New York: Methuen, 1987), 233–41.

8. For relevant discussions of the role of sati in British colonial discourse, see Gayatri Chakravorty Spivak, "Can the Subaltern Speak?" in *Marxism and the Interpretation of Culture,* ed. Cary Nelson and Lawrence Grossberg (Urbana: University of Illinois Press, 1988), 271–313; Anand A. Yang, "Whose Sati? Widow Burning in Early 19th Century India," *Journal of Women's History* 1 (1989): 8–33; Lata Mani, "Contentious Traditions: The Debate on Sati in Colonial India," in *Recasting Women: Essays in Colonial History,* ed. Kumkum Sangari and Sudesh Vaid (New Brunswick, N.J.: Rutgers University Press, 1990), 88–126; Ashis Nandy, "Sati: A Nineteenth-Century Tale of

Women, Violence, and Protest," in *At the Edge of Psychology: Essays in Politics and Culture,* ed. Ashis Nandy (New Delhi: Oxford University Press, 1980), 1–31. On the role of British liberalism, see, for example, Misra Udayon, *The Raj in Fiction: A Study of Nineteenth-Century British Attitudes towards India* (New Delhi: B. R. Publishing, 1987), 1–11.

9. Sleeman later served as the commissioner for the suppression of thuggee and dacoity, another example of the "dreadful practices" the English discovered in Indian culture at this time.

10. Rudyard Kipling, *Something of Myself: For My Friends Known and Unknown* (Garden City, N.Y.: Doubleday, Doran, 1937). Further citations of this book will include page numbers in parentheses in the text.

11. Louis Wurgaft, *The Imperial Imagination: Magic and Myth in Kipling's India* (Middletown, Conn.: Wesleyan University Press, 1983), 6.

12. Anthony Appiah demonstrates persuasively that "race" is an artificial construct in "The Uncompleted Argument: Du Bois and the Illusion of Race," *"Race," Writing, and Difference,* ed. Henry Louis Gates, Jr. (Chicago: University of Chicago Press, 1986), 21–37.

13. Wurgaft cites this remark by Kitchener in *The Imperial Imagination,* 10–11. For another view of Kipling's psychology, see John McClure, *Kipling and Conrad: The Colonial Fiction* (Cambridge, Mass.: Harvard University Press, 1981).

14. For a fuller discussion of the concept of the "incorporated wife," see the introduction to Hillary Callan and Shirley Ardener, eds., *The Incorporated Wife* (London: Croom Helm, 1984), 1-16.

15. Emily Eden, *Up the Country,* 2 vols. (London: Bentley, 1866). Further citations of these volumes will include volume and page numbers in parentheses in the text.

16. Janet Dunbar, *Golden Interlude: The Edens in India, 1836–1842* (Gloucester: Sutton, 1985), 216.

17. See Eden's account of her visit with Baiza Bae (*sic*), in *Up the Country,* 1:57

18. Margaret MacMillan, *Women of the Raj* (London: Thames & Hudson, 1988), 75.

19. Marian Fowler, *Below the Peacock Fan: First Ladies of the Raj* (New York: Penguin, 1987), 21.

20. Ibid., 39.

21. Dunbar, *Golden Interlude,* 63.

22. Harriet Tytler, *An Englishwoman in India: The Memoirs of Harriet Tytler, 1828–1858,* ed. Anthony Sattin (New York: Oxford University Press, 1986), 109. Further citations of this book will include page numbers in parentheses in the text.

23. S. B. Chaudhuri analyzes English writing on the Indian Mutiny and provides a useful chronology in *English Historical Writings on the Indian Mutiny* (Calcutta: World Press, 1979), 365–68.

24. Tytler's detailed description of her childhood seems to be shaped by the evolutionary model that Sidonie Smith describes as characterizing Victorian autobiography in *A Poetics of Women's Autobiography: Marginality and the Fictions of Self-Representation* (Bloomington: Indiana University Press, 1987), 126–27. Tytler's life story also suggests how evangelicalism acted on occasion to counter the more categorical racism seen, for example, in Kipling's autobiography. Often, however, Christian evangelicalism lent itself to British imperialism, as Homi K. Bhabha, in "Signs Taken for Wonders: Questions of Ambivalence and Authority under a Tree outside Delhi, May 1817," in *"Race," Writing, and Difference,* ed. Henry Louis Gates, Jr. (Chicago: University of Chicago Press, 1986), 163–84, and others have convincingly argued.

25. Elaine Showalter, *The Female Malady: Women, Madness, and English Culture, 1830–1980* (New York: Pantheon, 1985), 56–57.

26. Mary Louise Pratt, "Scratches on the Face of the Country: Or, What Mr. Barrow Saw in the Land of the Bushmen," in *"Race," Writing, and Difference,* ed. Henry Louis Gates, Jr. (Chicago: University of Chicago Press, 1986), 138–62.

27. Maxine Hong Kingston, *The Woman Warrior: Memoirs of a Girlhood among Ghosts* (New York: Vintage, 1975).

28. I discuss the role of rape in British colonial discourse about the Mutiny in "Rape under the Raj" (paper presented at the Sexualities and Nationalism Conference, 24 June 1989, Harvard University). I am currently revising this essay for publication.

29. Flora Annie Steel, *The Garden of Fidelity: Being the Autobiography of Flora Annie Steel, 1847–1929* (London: Macmillan, 1930), 31. Further citations of this book will include page numbers in parentheses in the text.

30. Wurgaft, *The Imperial Imagination,* 6.

31. For more details about the conflicts between feminism and conservatism in Steel's writing, see Nancy L. Paxton, "Feminism under the Raj: Complicity and Resistance in the Writings of Flora Annie Steel and Annie Besant," *Women's Studies International Forum* 13 (Spring 1990): 333–46. I outline the troublesome relationship I see between nineteenth-century feminism and Spencerian evolutionism in more general terms in *George Eliot and Herbert Spencer: Feminism, Evolutionism, and the Reconstruction of Gender* (Princeton, N.J.: Princeton University Press, 1991).

32. Steel's remarks about such acts of mastery suggest provocative parallels with comments about hunting in the autobiographies of other colonizing women, such as Isak Dinesen.

33. Sidonie Smith has identified a similar attitude toward female sexuality in Harriet Martineau's autobiography; see *Poetics of Women's Autobiography,* 123–49.

34. For more on the conservative wing of the British suffrage movement, see Olive Banks, *Becoming a Feminist: The Social Origins of First Wave Feminism* (Athens: University of Georgia Press, 1986).

35. Flora Annie Steel, *On the Face of the Waters* (London: Heinemann, 1896).

36. Mary Mason has observed that many women writing spiritual autobiographies establish their authority by describing their writing as an act of dictation, whereby they simply record the voice of the Divine. See "The Other Voice: Autobiographies of Women Writers," in *Life/Lines: Theorizing Women's Autobiography,* ed. Bella Brodzki and Celeste Schenck (Ithaca, N.Y.: Cornell University Press, 1988), 19–44. Steel's *Garden of Fidelity* represents a more secularized variation on this traditional theme.

37. See, for example, Malavika Karlekar, "Constructions of Femininity in Nineteenth-Century Bengal: Readings from *Janaika Grihabadhur* Diary," *Samya Shakti* 4–5 (1989–90): 11–29; Janaki Nair, "Uncovering the Zenana: Visions of Indian Womanhood in Englishwomen's Writings, 1813–1940," *Journal of Women's History* 2, 1 (1990): 8–33; and all the essays in Kumkum Sangari and Sudesh Vaid, eds., *Recasting Women: Essays in Colonial History* (New Brunswick, N.J.: Rutgers University Press, 1990).

Chapter 19

The Other Woman and the Racial Politics of Gender: Isak Dinesen and Beryl Markham in Kenya

Sidonie Smith

Africa meant a variety of things to the Europeans who settled there in the early decades of the twentieth century. For representatives of the British Empire, the land was an outpost of national expansion, a source of natural resources and inexpensive labor necessary for the defense and expansion of the empire. For the average citizen, the land represented the possibility of wealth and privilege unavailable in the home country. For the wealthy who had squandered their inheritance at home, Africa represented a place of new beginnings. For the truly wealthy, Africa represented a new kind of playground, "a winter home for aristocrats," as one Uganda Railroad poster advertised.[1] In its unknown and unmapped expanses, "man" could test himself against the elements, the animals, and time. "Untamed" and "undomesticated," it seemed a frontier of relaxed mores and unimaginable adventures not yet contaminated by bourgeois conventionality and emasculating comforts. The Africans, decentered and disempowered in their own space, watched as they continued to lose ownership of their land, labor, and culture.

Coming to this land, European settlers brought with them the "discursive territory" of Africa. And so, before turning to the autobiographical texts of Isak Dinesen and Beryl Markham, I want to follow one strand of the ideology of blackness that emerged in the nineteenth century as prelude to the great colonializing moment of the early twentieth century. Until it was abolished in the early nineteenth century, the slave trade reflected and effected certain justificatory discursive practices pertaining to black sexuality. Categorized as less civilized, located closer to nature, black Africans were identified with reproductive capacities that serviced the slave economy. Significantly, after the slave trade was abolished and imperialist expansion into the continent gained momentum, Europeans shifted their locus of identification, linking black Africans increasingly to "uncivilized" practices. "When the taint of slavery fused with sensational reports about cannibalism, witchcraft, and apparently shameless sexual customs," suggests Patrick Brantlinger, "Africa emerged draped in that pall of darkness that the Victorians themselves accepted as reality."[2] In identifying the physical characteristics of black sexuality as markers also of prostitutes (the most sexualized of white women) and in describing the sexual practices of primitive tribes as forms of prostitution, medical anthropologists during the century linked black sexuality and prostitution as two sources of social corruption and disease (syphilis in particular).[3]

European scientists and scholars thus projected onto the native African abnormal sexual appetite, that "dark" force lurking inside "civilized man," threatening the very basis of Western culture. Yet this "Africa" beckoned to Europeans, inviting the adventurer and the missionary into its vast spaces with its promise of illicit pleasure and imperial power. Journey into the jungle in search of treasure became journey into "the heart of darkness," as treasure and pleasure, economic and erotic desires, tangled. The image of Africa constructed by Europeans both invited and justified colonization, on one hand the project of "civilizing" the native Africans, on the other the aggressive expression of the will to power, the desire to dominate, appropriate, and transform. Thus Africa itself became, as did the Orient, a space effectively "feminized" by an imperial Europe.[4]

There are resonances here between colonial ideologies of race and patriarchal ideologies of gender, as well as radical differences. Western discursive practices assigned to woman the potential for a contaminating and disruptive sexuality that it ascribed also to the very body and the body social of the African. Thus both (black) African and (white) woman threatened to lure Western man into some forbidden, unholy, sexually clandestine place. Tellingly, Freud invoked the Victorian phrase describing Africa as "the dark continent" in his twentieth-century metaphor for the inscrutability of female sexuality. Coupling sexuality and Africa in this way, argues Sander Gilman, "Freud ties the image of female sexuality to the image of the colonial black and to the perceived relationship between the female's ascribed sexuality and the Other's exoticism and pathology."[5] This discursive conjunction of the erotic, exotic, and pathologic points to the specular bases upon which the (white, male) subject of Western humanism identifies himself as disembodied. "Masculine disembodiment," argues Judith Butler, "is only possible on the condition that women occupy their bodies as their essential and enslaving identities. . . . From th[e] belief that the body is Other, it is not a far leap to the conclusion that others *are* their bodies, while the masculine 'I' is a noncorporeal soul."[6] The patriarchal assignment of embodiedness to woman, mapped by Butler, parallels the colonial assignment of primitive sexuality to the African. As a result of in/corporation, woman and African remain other-than-fully human, on the one hand childlike and on the other monstrous.[7] And always, they require some kind of "parental" oversight.

Yet despite or, rather, because of this essentializing gaze, both woman and African remain the potential site of disruption—subjects waiting to speak. As Hélène Cixous warns: *"The Dark Continent is neither dark nor unexplorable.*—It is still unexplored only because we've been made to believe that it was too dark to be explorable. And because they want to make us believe that what interests us is the white continent."[8] What interests me here is "the white continent" of autobiography and the way in which two white women living on the frontier of colonial Kenya traversed the discursive borderlands of gender, race, and autobiographical practice. Since canonical Western autobiography functions as one of those discourses that inscribe white male subjectivity, Isak Dinesen and Beryl Markham of necessity engaged the colonial discourses of African otherness as they engaged the androcentricity of Western autobiography.

Isak Dinesen and Beryl Markham knew each other, if casually. They loved the same man at the same time. As white women in colonial Kenya, however, they shared more than a lover. On the one hand, they shared their privileged status vis-à-vis the native Africans, a privileged status manifest throughout their texts in the offhanded assumptions and conventional rhetoric of colonialism. (Of this, I will say more later.) On the other, they shared a marginal positionality in relation to white men, caught as they were in their embodiment; and this embodiment they shared with the Africans, who vis-à-vis Europeans were cast in the essentialism of race as surely as the women were cast in an essentialism of gender. (I do not mean to imply here that they experienced the same degree of marginalization as the Africans. They did not.) Chafing at the confinements of female embodiment, they discovered that residency on the colonial "frontier" provided them an arena of resistance. At the margins of the empire, far from the European center's hold, they could as white women break through the borderland of female embodiment and achieve a mobility of auto-biographical script unavailable to them in the "home" country.[9] Thus both Markham and Dinesen claim to be born "out of Africa" to use the phrase as horse trainers such as Markham use it. Attesting to the mystery that for them is "Africa," both represent the space of this mysterious otherness as a territory in which to escape the kind of identity that would have been theirs had they remained in Denmark or England. And yet, while both wrote haunting autobiographical accounts of their African experience, they offer the reader radically divergent readings of subjectivity in and through Africa. I want to read *West with the Night* and *Out of Africa* against one another, and to read them in ways attentive to the textual figure of the indigenous African woman, in order to explore the complications of colonized place, gender, and race in the politics of self-representation.

The Modern-Day Athena and Jebbta's Identity Politics

At the beginning of chapter 7, "Praise God for the Blood of the Bull," Markham re-creates the story of her participation in the initiation rite through which all Nandi boys mark their passage to manhood. In the midst of the narrative, she inserts an exchange with Jebbta, a young Nandi girl who confronts her before she sets out with the Nandi warriors on the hunt for wild boar:

> "The heart of a Murani is like unto stone," she whispered, "and his limbs have the speed of an antelope. Where do you find the strength and the daring to hunt with them, my sister?"
>
> We were as young as each other, Jebbta and I, but she was a Nandi, and if the men of the Nandi were like unto stone, their women were like unto leaves of grass. They were shy and they were feminine and they did the things that women are meant to do, and they never hunted.
>
> I looked down at the ankle-length skins Jebbta wore, which rustled like taffeta when she moved, and she looked at my khaki shorts and lanky, naked legs.
>
> "Your body is like mine," she said; "it is the same and it is no stronger." She turned, avoiding the men with her eyes, because that too was law, and went quickly away tittering like a small bird.[10]

In this scene Markham positions Jebbta as the other woman who attempts to identify (with) her: "Your body is like mine." Jebbta's undifferentiated sisterhood, posited as it is on a version of identity politics, would essentialize Markham as woman, reduce her autobiographical possibilities to the script of the sexed body. Yet Markham's very narration of the exchange resists Jebbta's insistence on the similarity between white and black girls. Positioning herself as a "boy," she emphasizes the contrast between her own hardy and naked strength and Jebbta's weak, fragile, and demurring "femininity." Gazing into the mirror of the other, Markham establishes her difference. In doing so she assigns the colonized woman to full embodiment and thereby denies her an autobiographical pretext, a future in genre.

In another passage toward the close of her narrative, Markham once again introduces the other woman. Describing her final flight from Kenya to England, she recalls the layover in Benghazi, where she and Blor Blixen spend the night in a brothel. Of the brothel keeper she writes:

> Her own face held the lineage of several races, none of which had given it distinction. It was just a husk with eyes. She spoke, but we understood nothing. Hers was a language neither of us had ever heard. . . . She was dressed in purple rags and they hung upon her in the unmistakable manner of the livery of her trade. And yet, I thought that a transformation would have been easy. Put her in an apron and soak the mask of paint from her face and she could be used as a fit subject for any artist wanting to depict the misery and the despair and the loneliness of all women driven to drudgery. (pp. 267–68)

Blixen discovers that the woman, a colonized victim of the white slave trade, can now neither recall her country of origin nor speak her native language. Here represented as grotesque, the other woman once again functions to secure the distance of Markham's difference. With contorted and debilitated body, cavernous face, vacuous grin, without origin or comprehensible speech, the brothel keeper is the figure of the subaltern woman whose only identifying mark is her body. Moreover, in the gaze of the exceptional woman, she becomes a representational artifact, a "portrait" of the drudgery of woman's colonized existence. Markham's autobiographical gesture is to comment unsentimentally, and stoically pass this other woman by: "Well, it's very sad, but you can't do anything about it," she reports saying to Blixen.

As anyone familiar with Markham's rather remarkable life knows, her own adventures as horse trainer and aviatrix testified to her mobile, dramatic, empowering existence on the frontier of colonial Kenya.

Not surprisingly then, Markham's autobiographical project functions to enact in the textual arena a resistance to Jebbta's identification of and with a limiting fate. As it celebrates the exceptional woman's escape from the script of female embodiment, her narrative intervenes in the conventional autobiographical script of a homogenized sisterhood. Situating essentialized gender differentiation in racialized and class-based frameworks, Markham foregrounds her own "liberation" from the structures of engendered identity.

The photograph on the cover of the recent paperback edition of *West with the Night* suggests certain dynamics of Markham's resistance to female essentialism and her identification with Western man's autobiographical narratives. Posing for a head shot, Markham looks away from the camera rather than directly into the eyes of the spectator. She effectively distances herself, remains elegantly aloof and self-contained. Moreover, the facial configuration and profile seem truly classical: the long, thin nose, the high cheekbones, the sculpted lips and eyes, the serious set of the mouth. In addition, the hair is held in erasure by the aviator's helmet. The figuration of Markham as an almost "flawless beauty" introduces the reader to a certain cultural "register of being" and of classic beauty.[11] Only the goggles interrupt the classical elegance of Markham's image. But despite the apparent dissonance between large goggles and refined visage, both visage and goggles signal Markham's appropriation of the Western gaze, her entrance into the scopophilic domain and its masculine positionality.

Allegiance to her patrimony is signaled in the triple inscription at the beginning of the autobiography: Markham dedicates the book to "my Father," expresses "gratitude to Raoul Schumacher for this book," and cites Shakespeare's *Henry IV:* "I speak of Africa and golden joys" (Act V, Scene iii). She proceeds to maintain narrative allegiance to male scripts by means of two powerful fabulations of male heroism that underwrite her text. Looking to the popular mythos of Hollywood films in the late 1930s, she inscribes the autobiographical equivalent of a swashbuckling adventure story with a female Errol Flynn as hero.[12] Looking back to the heroic world of ancient Greece for authoritative myths with which to ground a modern tale, she entangles her twentieth-century story with Homeric structures of adventure, travel, and contest. As she does so, Markham figures herself an avatar of Athena, the powerful, fleet goddess who emerges full blown from the head of her father, Zeus. A modern-day Athena, Markham structures her teleological narrative around her successful completion of three (patriarchal) tests: her early initiation into the hunting rites of Murani warriors, her conquest of the horse-racing world of Kenya, and her acceptance into the circle of male aviators crisscrossing Kenya during the 1920s and 1930s. Through mythic plotting, Markham re-creates a world in which men, and Markham with them, test their courage, intelligence, instinct, and skill against "the elemental forces and purposes of life" (p. 7).

Through each stage of her adventures, Markham entwines her story and identifies her achievement with that of a male mentor, from her father to Arab Maina to Denys Finch-Hatton to Tom Black to Blor Blixen, each of whom she ennobles in turn. She allies herself as well with the world of animals, and animals of a particular kind—the horse, the lion, the wild boar, the elephant, with its mammoth tusks. These are willful, proud, powerful, fleet, awesome animals, and she presents herself sometimes as hunter, sometimes as tamer of them. As modern hero she also identifies herself with the world of adventurous aviation and with the new instrument of colonial expansion in the 1920s and 1930s. Both animals of flesh and the animation of technology give her access to movement, aid her life as a "wanderer." They also provide her with powerful antagonists against which to test her heroic mettle. Describing the male honor code of this life early in her narrative, Markham captures both ethos and mythos of her adventurous life: "For all professional pilots there exists a kind of guild, without charter and without by-laws. It demands no requirements for inclusion save an understanding of the wind, the compass, the rudder, and fair fellowship. It is a camaraderie *sans* sentiment of the kind that men who once sailed uncharted seas in wooden ships must have known and lived by" (pp. 11–12). In the language of this code, Markham, as a modern Athena, links contemporary and ancient heroism and places herself securely inside the circle of both, thereby centering her unconventional narrative within traditional (Western male) autobiographical boundaries.

Such phallic heroism promotes certain narrative orientations toward the world, experience, and subjectivity. First among them is the celebration of her own unique destiny. Manifesting throughout her text what Georges Gusdorf describes as the "conscious awareness of the singularity of each individual life,"[13] Markham privileges her own individuality and consequently makes little effort to decenter her own experience, to incorporate experience from the margins of her story. Even in that strangest of all passages, where she drops the narrative voice of Beryl Markham to assume the narrative view of the horse Camiscan (pp. 109–16), she maintains the young Markham as the center of the horse's "consciousness."

As she foregrounds an idealized individualism, Markham presents herself as an unencumbered subject, an isolated, singular self, purposeful and solitary. Describing her experiences as an aviator, she figures the plane as a mechanical instrument to be manipulated and controlled, but also a machine that takes her to the limits of a precarious and lonely existence. "Night envelops me entirely," she writes, "leaving me out of touch with the earth, leaving me within this small moving world of my own, living in space with the stars" (p. 15). She says of the plane that it is "your planet and you are its sole inhabitant" (p. 10). Isolated in the cockpit, she becomes the figure of self-sufficiency, a self-sufficiency permeating the narrative voice.

Emphasizing throughout the narrative her ability to "read" the signs on the ground of life, Markham implies that such self-sufficiency derives from an education in hermeneutics. The narrative begins *in medias res* as she struggles to interpret signs of the earth—animal tracks, smoke, the silver wings of an airplane—in an effort to rescue the downed flyer Woody in that "vast unmarked desert" of the Serengeti. Circling back to her childhood, she continues by chronicling the childhood education in sign reading she received from the Murani hunters. The narrative of her early experiences as horse trainer focuses on her ability to "read" the potential in the horse and the rider. The transition between the early education and the later achievements that enable her to leave her mark (on the horse-racing scene, on aviation) follows seamlessly. The airplane she pilots and about which she writes becomes a machine to map what by Western standards are "unmapped" spaces.

In this way, the airplane becomes a topographic machine, extending the borders of empire, including the empire of the Western subject. Thus secure in the actual cockpit of the plane and the discursive cockpit of the autobiographical text, Markham celebrates the appropriative activity of the imperial subject, a pleasurable experience she recalls Tom Black elucidating:

> "When you fly," the young man said, "you get a feeling of possession that you couldn't have if you owned all of Africa. You feel that everything you see belongs to you—all the pieces are put together, and the whole is yours; not that you want it, but because, when you're alone in a plane, there's no one to share it. It's there and it's yours. It makes you feel bigger than you are—closer to being something you've sensed you might be capable of, but never had the courage to seriously imagine." (pp. 152–53)

So, too, Markham's text enacts the self-enhancement explicit in Black's romantic reverie. And that project requires a concomitant diminution of both the other woman and the "feminine" as a way of registering the distance Markham has placed between her aerial self flying high above any domesticated settlements and the embodied drudgery of a woman's life lived on the ground.

Thus in pursuing this scopophilic textuality, Markham constitutes "woman" and her script in particular ways. She resists sisterhood by positioning herself outside the narrative of maternal origins and domesticity, erasing the traces of motherhood and mothering, the script embodying traditional "woman." Her mother is elided, her name unspoken, her relationship unacknowledged. Presenting herself as an unmothered daughter, Markham, echoing the Athena of the *Oresteia*, implies that she is not of woman born. She also erases her own mothering, never mentioning her first or second husbands or her son, never positioning herself inside relationships and their consequent social roles. Resisting embeddedness in the world of domesticity, she divests herself of the textual encumbrances of a selfhood fettered to the female body, to Jebbta's undifferentiated sisterhood.

But Markham goes beyond erasing the traces of that autobiographical script that would enclose woman in stillborn postures. She goes so far as to position herself discursively as a male speaker. As befits the phallic hero, she adopts the rhetoric of stoic toughness, a stance through which she resists any kind of untidy textual emotion, any maudlin sentimentality, a toughness through which, to use an aerial metaphor, she remains above it all. Thus the topographic distance in flight functions analogously to her rhetorical distance in narrative voice. Moreover, she locates the feminine in particular textual spaces. Talking about another aviator's plane, Markham writes: "The silence that belonged to the slender little craft, was . . . a silence holding the spirit of wanton mischief, like the quiet smile of a vain woman exultant over a petty and vicious triumph" (p. 49). She describes the Klemm as "frivolous and inconstant," "the sad and discredited figure of an aerial Jezebel" (p. 53), powered by "an hysterical engine" (p. 47). She recalls Woody calling the Klemm "a bitch" (p. 54). In such passages, Markham participates in patriarchal assignments of gendered characteristics. Elsewhere she mimes the cultural use of the female body as a sign of emasculated manhood. To Makula, who refuses to enter her plane, she quotes the proverb: "A wise man is not more than a woman—unless he is also brave" (p. 233). Positioning herself as the male adventurer, Markham "ventrilocates male ideologies of gender," to use Felicity A. Nussbaum's phrase,[14] particularly the ideology of the "fallen," "contaminating," "potentially disruptive" woman, as much a threat to man as the plane gone wrong is a threat to the aviator.

Finally, Markham effectively "feminizes" her discursive "Africa." A place where she lives "free from the curse of boredom" (p. 10), constantly finds "a release from routine, a passport to adventure" (p. 198), Markham's rhetorical "Africa" is a space of mystery, wisdom, wildness, fluidity, virginity, silence, timelessness, an unknowable space rendered exotic and erotic by a subject who positions herself as a mythical figure. It is virgin land to be entered, conquered, the place where desire saturates landscape, the field on which the male hero can mark his imperial manhood. A conventionally mythic text, Markham's autobiography participates in what Teresa de Lauretis describes as the androcentricity inherent in the semiology of plotting. "As [the mythic hero] crosses the boundary and 'penetrates' the other space," suggests de Lauretis, "the mythical subject is constructed as human being and as male; he is the active principle of culture, the establisher of distinction, the creator of differences." In this same mythic space, the "untransformable" is marked as "female . . . an element of plot-space, a topos, a resistance, matrix and matter."[15]

West with the Night mimes, with haunting elegance and incontestable narrative power, the androcentric lineaments of traditional Western autobiography. Surrounding herself in the text with the accoutrements of the heroic figures of Greek mythology, figuring herself textually (and photographically) as "the radiant centre of a transcendent individualism,"[16] Markham aestheticizes her identity as bourgeois (male) individual. In this enactment of identity, then, the gender of performer (narrator), performed (narratee), and performance, to draw upon Judith Butler's analytical phraseology, is distinct from the anatomical sex of the woman whose name appears on the cover.[17] Markham's narrative of male experience, narrative, and voice undermines the stability of any "true" or essential origin of masculine or feminine identity. "Reveal[ing] that the original identity after which gender fashions itself is itself an imitation without an origin," the narrative promises to "deprive hegemonic culture and its critics of the claim to essentialist accounts of gender identity."[18] In this sense her autobiographical practice threatens to subvert ideologies of gender.

Moreover, her practice hints at the possible disruption of racial ideologies. Her resistance to Jebbta's identity politics, her embracing of masculine adventure narratives, leads Markham to ally herself with certain male Africans. She obviously learns from and admires the prowess of the male Africans with whom she hunted as a child (Arab Maina, Arab Ruta, the young Kibii) and later as an adult (the tracker

Makula). Her celebration of the aristocratic camaraderie of adventurers who test themselves against the elements leads her to contest conventional racial hierarchies in favor of cross-racial identifications: "Racial purity, true aristocracy, devolve not from edict, nor from rote, but from the preservation of kinship with the elemental forces and purposes of life whose understanding is not farther beyond the mind of a Native shepherd than beyond the cultured fumblings of a mortarboard intelligence" (pp. 7–8). It also leads her to offer slight but stinging critiques of the "modernization" and bureaucratization of colonial Kenya because it positions her with "heroic" natives against the "domesticated" Westerners who threaten to empty life of adventure itself.

But Markham's commitment to male scripts, her resistance to female figuration and fate, is only compromisingly promissory. As the text operates to resist the essentializing identification of Jebbta's universal sisterhood, it effectively reproduces that cultural script of essentialist difference, now displaced onto the body of the other woman. And thus what of Markham's naming of the other woman whose naming of her she forswears? For the other woman is the native African too. Even as she uncouples her identity from female embodiment, she maintains her allegiance both to what Hélène Cixous calls "the white continent" of subjectivity and to the literal white continent by supporting the colonization of the other woman and thus of the African generally, reminding us that transgressions of the assignment of gender do not inevitably lead to radical interventions in imperial assignments of racial characteristics.

We see the traces of an imperial subjectivity in other ways Markham positions native Africans in her text. She evinces very little of the ethnographer's fascination with the indigenous community and its cultural specificity. Thus the lives of Africans are marginalized through summary passages, except for those who serve her purposes, that is, the male natives who, with their courage, prowess, intuition, and camaradarie, participate in the "male" rites so central to her childhood. Moreover, the Murani warriors are given a major role as educators only in her presentation of her childhood. Once she moves to the narration of her adult experiences she accepts a different social and textual contract with the black Africans as they become her servants. Acknowledging this change with some irony, she nonetheless accepts its inevitability: "What a child does not know and does not want to know of race and colour and class, he learns soon enough as he grows to see each man flipped inexorably into some predestined groove like a penny or a sovereign in a banker's rack" (p. 149). While her ironic commentary here suggests that she glimpsed the economic dimension of a predestinarian social order, such politically charged commentary is rare in the narrative. And it is compromised by her own narrative practice of inserting the African male in Western narrative tropes of the great white hunter and "his" native guide/servant. Markham leaves the cultural and narrative economies of colonialism unchallenged. The native Africans are thus doubly servants: in literally serving whites they also serve the ideological economy of a "masculinity" central to the maintenance of European colonialism.

The relationship between Markham's transgressive autobiographical positioning as "man" and her conservative autobiographical positioning as "white" is therefore fascinating, if vexing. Ironically, of course, she could appropriate phallic selfhood in Africa because, as a white child growing up among black Africans, she had the cultural prerogatives and power to gain access to native male experiences inaccessible to the native girl; and because, on a culture's "frontiers," formalized arrangements of gender often surrender to practicalities. Life in colonial Kenya offered her the freedom to cross-dress as a young boy and consequently to assume the identity of the boy-child. As a result she could take from native Africans, all men, the education they could provide; and she used the power of that education to claim the spoils of male adventure and the pleasures of male bonding at the exclusion of identification with both white and native women. But she failed to contemplate the source of her access to male rites of passage or the consequences of her participation in the very Western practices that both spawned and necessitated the colonization of Africa, symbolized in the ivory of the elephant, that commodity that beckoned white hunters to the land and its treasures. Precisely on the "exotic frontier" of Africa, in that "orientalized" space distant from England, what might have been playful, destabilizing parody in the "home" country becomes complicit miming in the "wilderness."

In the geographical and discursive territories of colonialism, oppositionalities—male and female, black and white, colonized and colonizer, wild and tame—simultaneously confuse and compound one another. Instead of leveraging her destabilizing gender identification into a broader cultural critique, Markham leaves the boundaries of racialized territories relatively unbreached. Autobiographical transvestism here tends to reaffirm a colonizing poetics, that romanticized troping of the mythic adventure story that promotes generic stability, a stability dependent upon the literal and discursive marginalization of the African other, particularly the other woman. To acknowledge the other (woman, African) would be to contaminate "the white continent" of Western subjectivity and its autobiographical practices. The body of the other woman may trouble the edges of this narrative, but Markham keeps the other woman there, at the edges, since to incorporate her into the text would be to invite her own identification as "woman" across the borderland of race and class rather than as "man." It would be to emasculate and deracinate the white man and to contaminate "the white continent" of Western adventure narratives.

The Somali Smile and the Subversive's Pleasure

In contrast to Markham, who presses Jebbta's story into the margins of her narrative, Isak Dinesen incorporates the story of the other woman at the very center of *Out of Africa*. "In my life at the farm," she writes, "I saw few women, and I got into the habit of sitting, at the end of the day, for a quiet hour with the old woman and the girls in Farah's house."[19] Dinesen figures the Somali women as mothers, wives, and sisters sequestered within patriarchal institutions and systems of meaning, what she elsewhere called "ancient citadels of males."[20] Furthermore, the women are physically enclosed within yards of elaborate clothes, signs of male ownership of and in/vestment in them. Embodied testaments to male privilege, they are "luxuries," commodified in systems of exchange. Yet Dinesen insinuates into this locale of enclosure a politics of agency by foregrounding the other woman's sources of power: her intelligence, her cunning, her sophisticated manipulation of male investments. Most important, she identifies the other woman, as she identifies herself, with Scheherazade, the colonized woman who escapes literal and symbolic death by fabricating bold and imaginative tales. "Sometimes, to entertain me," she writes, "they would relate fairy tales in the style of the Arabian Nights, mostly in the comical genre, which treated love with much frankness" (pp. 179–80). Only apparently passive, the Somali women stake out a locale of female desire, empowerment, subversive laughter: "It was a trait common to all these tales that the heroine, chaste or not, would get the better of the male characters and come out of the tale triumphant" (p. 180).

Dinesen identifies the old Somali mother with a former dispensation characterized by matriarchal rule. A "Sibylline" figure "with a little smile on her face" (p. 180), she is the wise witch, the living trace of an earlier dispensation. "Within this enclosed women's world," she writes,

> I felt the presence of a great ideal, without which the garrison would not have carried on so gallantly; the idea of a Millen-

nium when women were to reign supreme in the world. The old mother at such times would take on a new shape, and sit enthroned as a massive dark symbol of that mighty female deity who had existed in old ages, before the time of the Prophet's God. (p. 180)

The old mother becomes the great mother, to use Erich Neumann's phrase,[21] a matriarchal witch-goddess predating the great prophet Mohammed. And her subversive smile signals the residual matrilineal linkage backward in time through this maternal heritage. It also points forward to a fictive Millennium, an already and always deferred possibility, yet an always potential site of laughter's disruption.

While Dinesen elsewhere presents herself as entertainer and her guests as entertained, in this scene the white woman reverses the pattern, presenting herself as the listener who sits at the feet of the other woman. The reversal signals not the subordination of white woman to black woman, but rather membership in a sisterhood of female storytellers, in a community of women who "remember" the time past when the great goddess reigned supreme. For Dinesen too has lost "the forest matriarchy" she figures in her representation of Africa. In 1931, after seventeen years in colonial Kenya, the Danish woman was forced by bankruptcy to return to her family home in Rungstedlund, Denmark, where she would remain the rest of her life. Describing the circumstances in which the *Ngoma* about to be danced in honor of her leaving is canceled, Dinesen writes toward the end of her narrative: "Perhaps they realized at once how completely the Ngoma was off, for the reason that there was no longer anybody to dance to, *since I no longer existed*" (pp. 382–83; emphasis mine). Abjection, the dispersal of "identity," attended expulsion from the paradisiacal Africa.[22] And so, "out of Africa," Karen Blixen experienced the loss of autobiographical story that comes from returning to the same old story of bourgeois embodiment. Enclosed in her mother's house, she could only dream of the past and in dreaming create the myth of an "African" identity. Like the Somali women, then, she is forced to tell stories to save her very "life," to abandon herself to writing in an elegant dance of loss.[23]

"The discovery of the dark races was to me a magnificent enlargement of all my world" (p. 17), Dinesen writes early in the text. In this expanded universe she claims to have discovered a truer "home" than the one she left in Denmark: "In the highlands you woke up in the morning and thought: Here I am, where I ought to be" (p. 4). Figured as a place of sensual pleasure, a garden of delight profoundly different and distant from the repressive, cold environment of Denmark, this "Africa" invites Dinesen to luxuriate in a rich, thick sensuality—a sensuality whose traces are then deployed throughout the text from the very first pages when she immerses the reader in descriptive passages ranging across the landscape and through the smells, colors, sounds, sights, the very feel of Africa. Sensuality resonates through the music of Africa and the music of the text's voice: "When you have caught the rhythm of Africa, you find that it is the same in all her music" (p. 16). Africa's very air is a sensual medium. Walking in the morning, she writes, "you are not on earth but in dark deep waters, going ahead along the bottom of the sea" (p. 228). Living becomes "swimming" as life takes place inside a global amniotic fluid always washing across the body.

Learning from the Africans how to live "in accordance with [the landscape]" this white woman represents herself as being at one with Africa in a powerful commingling of subjectivity and place: "The grass was me, and the air, the distant invisible mountains were me, the tired oxen were me. I breathed with the slight night-wind in the thorn-trees" (p. 272). Geographically her farm blurs seamlessly into the wild space of Africa. She writes of the adopted Lulu that she "came in from the wild world to show that we were on good terms with it, and she made my house one with the African landscape, so that nobody could tell where the one stopped and the other began" (pp. 76–77). Boundaries between human and animal are likewise blurred. Animals take on attributes of human beings; human beings are identified through animals. And metaphysically good and evil blend into one another. She writes of the Africans that their "assurance, [their] art of swimming, they had, I thought, because they had preserved a knowledge that was lost to us by our first parents; Africa, amongst the continents, will teach it to you: that God and the Devil are one, the majesty coeternal, not two uncreated but one uncreated, and the Natives neither confounded the persons nor divided the substance" (pp. 19–20). In Dinesen's "Africa," human beings, animals, space, metaphysical forces commingle with one another in revelries and reveries of interdependence and nondifferentiation.

"Africa distilled" thus signifies for Dinesen a space outside the menacing borders of a European "enlightenment" that brutally disjoins "self" and "other," a space uncontaminated by patriarchal arrangements and representational repertoires with their self-splitting repressions, an "Eden" uncalibrated by "man's" time and its gendered autobiographical scripts.[24] Identified with animism, sensuality, transport, pleasure, mystery, music, laughter, power,[25] "she" is the great goddess, nourishing "matrix space," locale of union and of jouissance, all that Julia Kristeva ascribes to the semiotic and Dinesen herself to female sexuality.[26]

In this space Dinesen positions herself as the great goddess's daughter, recovering from patriarchal representations of female subjectivity through reclamation of the repressed body and enactment of an empowered autobiographical script. "To ride, to shoot arrows, to tell the truth" reads the inscription that opens the text—a manifesto of a mythical Diana, the active, effectual, independent woman, not the enclosed woman of bourgeois domestic scenes.[27] Throughout the narrative "the lioness Blixen" assumes by turns the roles of empress, creatrix, healer, priest, protector, judge, genie (or *jinn,* in Islamic mythology). Figuring herself as honorable, resourceful, courageous, dependable, hardworking, and socially responsible, she identifies herself as a hybrid of "manliness" and "womanliness."[28]

The desire to posit an independent subjectivity suggests why Dinesen says little about her relationship with Denys Finch-Hatton. In fact, the little she presents of the relationship is purposefully cast in an idealized mold as she makes of that relationship one of coequals, based on the classical Greek model of homosexual liaisons.[29] Their hunting experiences, for instance, become metaphors of idealized lovemaking. In the first lion-killing adventure Finch-Hatton lends her his rifle so she can participate actively in the action rather than remain a passive observer. Dinesen describes his gesture as "a declaration of love" and asks: "Should the rifle not then be of the biggest caliber?" (p. 230). The experience of shooting takes on the quality of orgasm: "I stood, panting, in the grass, aglow with the plenipotence that a shot gives you" (p. 230). In the second scene the man and woman meet the male and female lions alone in the moonlight. There, in a gesture of reckless courage ("risk[ing] our lives unnecessarily"; p. 233), they enter "the centre of the dance," where two human beings face two animals, male and female together. Life, death, silence, darkness, pleasure, coalesce in a scene of unity: "We did not speak one word. In our hunt we had been a unity and we had nothing to say to one another" (p. 237).[30] Precisely in this imaginative Africa, Dinesen finds the opportunity to contest the Old World arrangements between men and women, to refigure herself against the conventional cultural assignments of gender, and to celebrate a unification that collapses the binary opposition of male and female into silence and elides consciousness and animality.

Like Markham, Dinesen contests conventional gender assignments. Unlike Markham, however, Dinesen situates her empowerment in the recovery of female sensuality. In this text the female body is not the source of evil and contamination; female labor is not alienated but a source of pleasure; woman's body is not what Christine Froula calls "the symbol of patriarchal authority." "No longer divided and no longer inscribed with the designs of an external mastery,"[31] body and spirit commingle.

But, of course, this "life" is but a dream, for Dinesen's tale is ultimately the tale of loss. Once again domesticated in Denmark, Dinesen can only revisit in fierce nostalgia and lyrical imagination that "preexilic state of union"[32] and that former dispensation, the reign of the goddess's daughter. Now, this invocation of nostalgia leads me to ask of Dinesen as we asked of Markham: Does her intervention in traditionally engendered autobiographical scripts imply an intervention in Western ideologies of race and the old arrangements between black and white?

On the one hand, Dinesen, as Susan Hardy Aiken argues, quarrels with the very ideologies of race that stabilized colonial regimes in early twentieth-century Kenya and does so through her narrative practices.[33] For instance, she contests the old autobiographical arrangements sexualized in the androcentric ideology of the autonomous individual by deploying her speaking voice fluidly through the "I," the "you," and the "we," especially in the first pages of the text. Opening this way, she signals an alternative autobiographical practice, one that testifies to the ways in which her subjectivity emerges "out of Africa" and the Africans. She describes how the Africans name her "Lioness" Blixen, assigning to her the power identified with the "king" of the beasts. Making of her "a brass serpent," symbol to them of one who bears burdens, *they* elevate her above other Europeans (pp. 106–7). With this belief in her, she writes home, the natives effectively cast a "spell" on her, constituting her identity as Lucifer, light-giver, rebellious angel.[34] They also create her as storyteller by laying their stories before her.[35] Moreover, the African environment intensifies existence, alchemically changing the mundane into the poetic, the mythic.[36] Only here, she seems to suggest, can she bring to light the "dark continent" of her sexuality and the full resources of her hybridized subjectivity.

Recognizing the mutuality of identifications between herself and the native Africans, Dinesen in turn re-creates the mystery of Africa as mythic space, in turn elevates the Africans above the mundane by turning their stories and their land into poetry through a thick web of allusion and compelling prose. And she does so without making a spectacle out of them, without serving a voyeuristic reader. In fact, as Aiken elaborates, she undercuts any voyeurism on the part of narrator and reader by rendering "Africa" narratively unmasterable: "As with Africans, so with the book-as-Africa: no more than the colonists can we finally 'know its real nature' or subject it to hermeneutic mastery."[37] It can never be contained in a Western gaze.

Other narrative practices in *Out of Africa* destabilize colonial gestures of power. Dinesen often directs the focus of her text away from herself to those people inhabiting what Lord Delamare and his fellow colonists would label the "margins" of the "civilized" world—to Kamante Gatura and Kinanjui. Surrounding them with majesty, mystery, and power, she ennobles rather than denigrates Africa and Africans for failing to meet the measures of Western practice, experience, and identity. Honoring the orality of African culture, she "speaks" in the sonorous storytelling voice that resonates with the elegant rhythms and tonal richness of Africa. As her letters indicate, she adopts from Farah Aden, her Somali house servant, the metaphor of life lived underwater. She takes her worldview from the Africans, discovering in their philosophical conjunction of good and evil a compatible orientation to the world and experience. Unwilling to make her narrative the totalizing whole of a unitary self, she joins together bits and pieces of African life, allowing Africa and herself to exist in fragmented, multiple forms, refusing the clear boundedness and certainty of the Western "I."[38] She also multiplies the specificity of native Africans by differentiating the tribes and incorporating the diversity of peoples into her text. Implicitly rejecting European rationalism, she contests the denigrating embodiment of native and of woman by turning the ideology of sexual contamination on its head, ennobling the body— of the African, of woman. Celebrating African culture, she resists the colonizing tendency to stabilize, explain, judge, and hierarchize the other's differences, as if to recognize that to do other/wise would be to suppress the story of the great mother, to oppress the racial other, and ultimately to repress her own subjectivity.

Dinesen's keen consciousness of her own marginality as a woman who sought to "achieve something *as myself*"[39] and of the larger cultural politics of gender, and her consequent positioning of herself as an "outsider" in the British colony, encouraged her to embrace native African culture in more sympathetic ways than the British colonials who assumed their privileges and their cultural superiority unquestioningly. Unlike other European settlers, whose racism was reflected in such pronouncements as that of Lord Delamere that "the British race . . . was superior to heterogeneous African races only now emerging from centuries of relative barbarism,"[40] Dinesen expressed what other colonists at the time termed "pronative" sentiments, implemented "pronative" practices. And yet, Dinesen was herself one of the colonizers, a woman who participated in the appropriation of native land, who hoped to profit from native labor, who enjoyed native service and idolization. Thus other of her narrative practices collude in the exploitative agenda of colonialism. The recurrent possessive ("my farm," "my boys"), the generalizations about native tribes, position her as a "European" speaker and reinscribe colonial relationships. By embedding native Africans rhetorically in an intricate web of literary allusions, she textually contains Africans and Africa in Western discursive nets of meaning and reference. Beyond these rhetorical gestures, however, lies a more complex and ambiguous colonial practice. Dinesen's nostalgia works to constitute "Africa" as a romanticized territory, inhabited by romanticized "natives" and "animals." "Africa" functions therefore as a kind of "Afro-disiac."[41] The distanced setting ("I had a farm . . ."), the achronological rather than linear time, the elegance and distance of the narrative voice, the "artifice" of a text that constantly insists, through its dazzling display of metaphor, on its imaginative status, all aid and abet Dinesen's romanticism. Certainly it is a different kind of romanticism from Markham's cavalier and stoic brand, but it is a brand nonetheless. And so, without dismissing the very real practices of subversion in the text, I want to pursue certain problematic implications of Dinesen's autobiographical practices.

Since the native Africans name her with the natural aristocratic title of "Lioness Blixen" as replacement for the derived nobility of "Baroness Blixen," Dinesen in turn must maintain their nobility as essential to her own by resisting the conventional racial stereotypes of the white settlers. Thus she privileges a certain alignment of African "difference." Dinesen assigns imagination, bondedness with nature, elegance of style, and sensuality to the native Africans as she pursues her conspiracy of nobility in the face of bourgeois philistinism. She thereby distances native Africans and herself from the repressive, prosaic, paternalistic culture of the white settlers and situates herself as romantic outsider whose bravado and rebellious excess are evident in her identificatory gesture, "I am a Hottentot" (p. 296), a gesture she directs defiantly at white passengers on a ship returning to Africa, not at black Africans. Dinesen invokes the politics of race to engage in her own class resistance because it is within bourgeois institutions that she experiences imaginative, economic, and sexual oppression. But as class disidentification encourages her to align difference along a certain axis, it also leads her to participate in a mystifying essentialism.

Dinesen's positioning of the body in the text reveals the potentially conservative effects of mystification in the midst of colonialism. Pressing the patriarchal myth of Christianity in the crucible of her African experience, Dinesen locates the source of female oppression in male mastery of the female body and promotes the recovery of that body as the beginning of a liberated female subjectivity. Doing so, she celebrates the body and its pleasures, the romanticized identification of woman with nature and the maternal body. Thus when Dinesen identifies herself as a "Hottentot," she invokes a body politics that "extolls" the "shadowy, nocturnal, oneiric domain" of the great goddess as "the interior locus of mystery and creativity."[42] This return to the body through maternal metaphorization becomes what Domna C. Stanton calls "a heuristic tool for reworking images and meanings."[43] A strategy of subversion, it works to "countervalorize the traditional antithesis that identifies man with culture and confines woman to instinctual nature,"[44] to the primitive and childlike. But the problem is that, in pursuing this "enabling mythology" as "a negation/subversion of paternal hierarchies,"[45] Dinesen takes the Africans with her into the textual forest. The African is once again allied with the natural world, a nativistic alliance already deployed in the justificatory discourses of racism and colonialism. Thus, in the historically specific context of early twentieth-century colonialism, the assignment of animal names to native Africans as part of her mythography operates racially, not just mythically. It is one thing for a white woman to be positioned metaphorically in the "black continent" of her sexuality and for her to identify herself and other white settlers with animals. It is quite another for the black Africans, no matter how regal and untamed the animals with which they are identified, to be positioned metaphorically where they are already positioned literally and discursively.[46] The material realities of racial politics disrupt the largess of metaphorical politics.

Furthermore, any utopian myth of unification, even if an admittedly failed one, is problematic. In Denmark the exiled Dinesen crafts her imaginative return to Africa as a return to an empowering origin, "the maternal continent,"[47] and the effect of that return is the mythification of the mother, the figure Luce Irigaray has called "the dark continent of the dark continent."[48] But mythification of a paradigm of maternal origins, warns Bella Brodzki, even as it contests hegemonic myths, potentially betrays the same "inherent dangers of privileging principles" as patriarchal mythification.[49] There are many motherhoods, not just one reified "motherhood." Mythification, however, wears everything to a patined homogeneity; it universalizes. Dinesen's dream of imaginary at-oneness requires the erasure of multiple and calibrated differences among and between people, races, and classes, between women, between mothers. Thus the textual identification of the narrator and the Somali women, while acknowledging certain realities of female oppression, glosses such complex material realities as their doubled colonization.

She also takes the native Africans into an oneiric realm that, however effectively it disperses coherent and totalizing interpretive possibilities,[50] distances the Africans from history itself. Such "nativism," as Edward Said cautions, "reinforces the distinction [between colonizer and colonized] by revaluating the weaker or subservient partner. And it has often led to compelling but often demagogic assertions about a native past, history, or actuality that seems to stand free not only of the colonizer but of worldly time itself."[51] There was such a past, certainly, but that past was past long before Dinesen journeyed to Africa. While Said cautions specifically against the excesses of nativist nationalism, his admonition captures my own concern about Dinesen's passionate countervalorization of native culture, which seems to abandon specific histories in favor of oneiric and aestheticized myth.

Moreover, her powerful evocation of the sense of loss and dispossession that supports her ethics of self-dispersal seems to suggest that only by losing does one gain, an ethics of love as letting go elaborated by Aiken.[52] Yet this reverence for loss and dispersal leads the narrator to position the native Africans in an irrecoverable past, to identify them with an inevitable loss, to ennoble them certainly but also to contain them. Distilling native Africans through specific axes of identification, she locates them in an exoticized and timeless place, in a nostalgically crystallized past, even as she acknowledges the historical changes being wrought on the land and on native culture through the historical march of colonialism. Positioned in such spaces, they function as passive subjects of history's corrupt and corrupting march into the future. Thus they are positioned as victims of history, not as active agents within vibrant, ongoing, complex histories.

Dinesen's fictive "Africa" becomes an imaginative map on which we see projected a white woman's desire for an irrecoverable past of empowered subjectivity. Mapping can be disruptive; it can be complicit. It is not innocent, as Dinesen herself understood. The romanticized cartography of "Africa distilled" is an expression of an "artistic primitivism" that in its reification of the other reveals certain totalizing investments in an imperialist autobiographical practice.[53] Against what might have been her own best intentions, and certainly in tension with very real and sophisticated contestatory practices, Dinesen's "I" participates in the "imaginative opportunism" that characterizes all manner of imperial projects.

In an essay titled "Changing the Subject," Nancy K. Miller elaborates a central strand of current feminist practice: "The formula 'the personal is the political' requires a redefinition of the personal to include most immediately an interrogation of ethnocentrism; a poetics of identity that engages with the 'other woman.'"[54] Gayatri Spivak, in "French Feminism in an International Frame," argues too for "a simultaneous other focus: not merely who am I? but who is the other woman? How am I naming her? How does she name me?"[55]

The concern for the "other woman" that now weaves throughout feminist theory in the West derives from a profound rethinking of a hypostasized sexual difference, a homogenized "woman." It is a rethinking that problematizes with postmodernism generally the Western notion of a sovereign "self," but also a rethinking that insists that historical specificities are the "grounds" outside the text that position us complexly and relationally in consciousness, behavioral practices, and politics.[56] The shift derives also from a rethinking that rejects any simplistic or romanticized notion of "marginality," recognizing instead that positions of marginalities and centralities are nomadic, that each of us, multiply positioned in discursive fields, inhabits margins and centers. Thus the call for reading the other woman requires that we consider the multiplicity of differences between one woman and another, the multiplicity of differences within each of us. It is an acknowledgment that the other woman troubles Western theories. It is a recognition that the other woman also troubles generic rules that function to govern and discipline identifications, and that she forces us to remap the ideology of identity and the horizons of subjectivity within autobiographical texts.

I have tried here to read *West with the Night* and *Out of Africa* through one another in search of the other woman and the meaning she makes of the autobiographical subject and her complex negotiation of subjectivity under colonialism. And I have learned that the autobiographical gesture of resisting sisterhood with the other woman (Markham) or embracing sisterhood (Dinesen) cannot be read simply or dichotomously, because for white women sojourn in the colonial territory both stimulates and confounds identification, crystallizes and obscures differences, subverts and conserves prevailing ideologies.

Notes

1. The Uganda Railroad advertised through travel posters aimed at aristocrats, sportsmen, and "students" of natural history. See G. F. V. Kleen, ed. and trans., *Blor Blixen: The Africa Letters* (New York: St. Martin's, 1988), 70ff.

2. Patrick Brantlinger, "Victorians and Africans: The Genealogy of the Myth of the Dark Continent," in *"Race," Writing, and Difference,* ed. Henry Louis Gates, Jr. (Chicago: University of Chicago Press, 1986), 217.

3. The "shameless sexual customs" of the Hottentots, evidencing as they did unrepressed sexual appetite, were, according to Sander Gilman, identified specifically in medical and anthropological discourse with the female Hottentot. From the less authoritative discourse of the chain of being to the more scientifically respectable discourse of medical pathology, black female sexuality became synonymous with abnormal sexual appetite. In fact, the assignment of "'primitive' genitalia" to the female Hottentot encouraged Europeans to read the signs of a regressive species evolution on the body of the Hottentot. See "Black Bodies, White Bodies: Toward an Iconography of Female Sexuality in Late Nineteenth-Century Art, Medicine, and Literature," in *"Race," Writing, and Difference,* ed. Henry Louis Gates, Jr. (Chicago: University of Chicago Press, 1986), 240–57.

4. See Ali Behdad, "Images of the Harem and Colonialism in Eighteenth-Century European Narratives" (paper presented at the annual meeting of the Modern Language Association, December 1988).

5. Gilman, "Black Bodies," 257.

6. Judith Butler, "Gender Trouble, Feminist Theory, and Psychoanalytic Discourse," in *Feminism/Postmodernism,* ed. Linda J. Nicholson (New York: Routledge, 1990), 133.

7. Always, as Albert Memmi argues, "the distance which colonialization places between [the colonialist] and the colonized must be accounted for and, to justify himself, [the colonialist] increases this distance still further by placing the two figures irretrievably in opposition; his glorious position and the despicable one of the colonized." *The Colonizer and the Colonized* (New York: Orion, 1965), 54–55. Critically, this "opposition" is essentialized: "Once the behavioral feature, or historical or geographical factor which characterizes the colonialist and contrasts him with the colonized, has been isolated, this gap must be kept from being filled. The colonialist removes the factor from history, time, and therefore possible evolution. What is actually a sociological point becomes labeled as being biological or, preferably, metaphysical. It is attached to the colonized's basic nature. Immediately the colonial relationship between colonized and colonizer, founded on the essential outlook of the two protagonists, becomes a definitive category. It is what it is because they are what they are, and neither one nor the other will ever change" (pp. 71–72). For a discussion of the "mythical portrait of the colonized," see pp. 79–89.

8. Hélène Cixous, "The Laugh of the Medusa," in *New French Feminisms: An Anthology,* ed. Elaine Marks and Isabelle de Courtivron (New York: Schocken, 1981), 255.

9. In invoking the language of margins and centers I realize I seem to hypostasize those spaces. Certainly the Europeans who lived in Kenya inhabited an imperializing center. Thus there were centers and margins in the colonial space, even centers and margins on the farms of Isak Dinesen and of Beryl Markham's father. Centers and margins shift against various horizons of power.

10. Beryl Markham, *West with the Night* (San Francisco: North Point, 1983), 77–78. All further citations of this book will include page numbers in parentheses in the text.

11. See Peter Stallybrass and Allon White, *The Politics and Poetics of Transgression* (Ithaca, N.Y.: Cornell University Press, 1986), 21.

12. And, in fact, Markham wrote her autobiography at the same time she became involved in Hollywood filmmaking, serving as consultant on a film about Africa, hoping for a successful screen test. See Mary S. Lovell, *Straight on Till Morning: The Biography of Beryl Markham* (New York: St. Martin's, 1987), chaps. 11, 12.

13. Georges Gusdorf, "Conditions and Limits of Autobiography," in *Autobiography: Essays Theoretical and Critical,* ed. James Olney (Princeton, N.J.: Princeton University Press, 1980), 29. Susan Stanford Friedman refers to this passage at the beginning of her essay, "Women's Autobiographical Selves: Theory and Practice," in *The Private Self: Theory and Practice of Women's Autobiographical Writings,* ed. Shari Benstock (Chapel Hill: University of North Carolina Press, 1988), 34.

14. Felicity A. Nussbaum, "Eighteenth-Century Women's Autobiographical Commonplaces," in *The Private Self: Theory and Practice of Women's Autobiographical Writings,* ed. Shari Benstock (Chapel Hill: University of North Carolina Press), 149. Nussbaum uses the phrase in discussing women's autobiography written in the eighteenth century.

15. Teresa de Lauretis, *Technologies of Gender: Essays on Theory, Film, and Fiction* (Bloomington: Indiana University Press, 1987), 43–44.

16. Stallybrass and White, *Politics and Poetics,* 21.

17. Butler, "Gender Trouble," 338.

18. Ibid. Or, as Denise Riley argues, "a category" such as masculinity or femininity "may be at least conceptually shaken if it is challenged and refurbished, instead of only being perversely strengthened by repetition." *"Am I That Name?": Feminism and the Category of "Women" in History* (Minneapolis: University of Minnesota Press, 1988), 113.

19. Isak Dinesen, *Out of Africa* (New York: Random House, 1965), 179. All further citations of this book will include page numbers in parentheses in the text. This passage comes at the midpoint of the narrative.

20. For reference to a lecture in which Dinesen uses this phrase, see Susan Hardy Aiken, "The Uses of Duplicity: Isak Dinesen and Questions of Feminist Criticism," *Scandinavian Studies* 57 (Autumn 1985): 401.

21. See Erich Neumann, *The Great Mother: An Analysis of an Archetype* (Princeton, N.J.: Princeton University Press, 1963).

22. See Julia Kristeva, *Powers of Horror: An Essay in Abjection* (New York: Columbia University Press, 1982), especially chaps. 1, 2. Judith Lee makes this connection in "Isak Dinesen in and out of the Place with No Name" (Paper presented at the annual meeting of the Modern Language Association, San Francisco, December 1987). Interviewed in 1934, after the publication of *Seven Gothic Tales* and before the publication of *Out of Africa,* Dinesen commented, in response to a question about why she published a book of short stories before publishing her recollection of Africa, that to write such a book so soon after leaving Africa would be like writing "about a child the day one buried it. One must have things at a distance. In my tales I have put a whole century between me and the events." Quoted in Judith Thurman, *Isak Dinesen: The Life of a Storyteller* (New York: St. Martin's, 1982), 281. The distance of a century in the tales becomes in *Out of Africa* the distance of recollection after several years and seven gothic tales.

23. For an analysis of the decomposition of narrative and identity in *Out of Africa,* see Susan Hardy Aiken, *Isak Dinesen and the Engendering of Narrative* (Chicago: University of Chicago Press, 1990), 209–46. Aiken explores how "this story of desire, dislocation, and loss is told repeatedly, not only in the trajectory of the book as a whole but also in the many parables that serve as its microcosmic reenactments" (p. 222). Aiken's analysis is rich and elegantly written. I hope in my own engagement with Dinesen's text to suggest the importance of reading her text against Markham's, and to emphasize more than Aiken does Dinesen's complicit participation in colonialist practices, even though I too acknowledge her very significant contestatory practices.

24. Dinesen's narrative erasure of linear time, the medium of the father and his law, in favor of cyclical time compounds the spaciousness of Africa and the mythic quality of the text.

25. All the accoutrements of the great goddess surround her: the animals, the aquatic air, the cowrie shells, the joyful artwork.

26. In her essay, "Women's Time," Julia Kristeva talks about the relationship of women to "the problematic of space, which innumerable religions of matriarchal (re)appearance attribute to 'woman,' and which Plato . . . designated by the aporia of the *chora,* matrix space, nourishing, unnnameable, anterior to the One, to God and consequently, defying metaphysics." "Women's Time," in *Feminist Theory: A Critique of Ideology,* ed. Nannerl O. Keohane, Michelle Z. Rosaldo, and Barbara C. Gelpi (Chicago: University of Chicago Press, 1982), 34. See also Aiken, "Uses of Duplicity," 410, n. 11.

27. Writing to her brother Thomas in 1926, Dinesen laments her early upbringing, claiming that the kind of childhood she had precluded "any possibility for me to live and act, achieve something *as myself." Letters from Africa,* ed. Frans Lasson, tran. Anne Born (Chicago: University of Chicago Press, 1981), 245. Writing to her Aunt Bess, Dinesen describes the different desires of contemporary women and women in the past and then elaborates on the relationship of aspiring women to men: "In my opinion 'manliness' is a human concept; 'womanliness' as a rule signifies those qualities in a woman or that aspect of her personality that is pleasing to men, or that they have need of. Men had no particular need for or pleasure from, and therefore no reason to encourage, women painters, sculptors, composers,—but they did have for dancers, actresses, singers, and it was the sensible and natural thing for artistically gifted women to adopt such careers. A man might well be attracted to and admire a woman who took a passionate interest in the stars, or who cultivated flowers with which to beautify his home; but she would be sinning against the idea of womanliness if she sought to establish a direct relationship with nature in these branches by taking up astronomy or botany,—for how could such ambitions have anything to do with him and his happiness?" (p. 261).

28. On hybridity, see Judith Lee, "The Mask of Form in *Out of Africa," Prose Studies* 8 (September 1985): 51. See also Aiken, *Isak Dinesen,* 234–38.

29. Dinesen elaborated this notion of the "human ideal" of "'homosexuality,'— sincere friendship, understanding, delight shared by two equal, 'parallel moving' beings" in a letter to her Aunt Bess in *Letters,* 264. See also Lee, "The Mask of Form," 53–55.

30. Judith Lee notes the differences between Dinesen's descriptions of the shooting events in the letters and in *Out of Africa.* "The Mask of Form," 54.

31. Christine Froula, "When Eve Reads Milton: Undoing the Canonical Economy," *Critical Inquiry* 10 (December 1983): 342.

32. The phrase is Bella Brodzki's. "Mothers, Displacement, and Language in the Autobiographies of Nathalie Sarraute and Christa Wolf," in *Life/Lines: Theorizing Women's Autobiography,* ed. Bella Brodzki and Celeste Schenck (Ithaca, N.Y.: Cornell University Press, 1988), 246.

33. Aiken, *Isak Dinesen,* 209–46.

34. Dinesen, *Letters,* 160.

35. As Aiken suggests in reading the passage where Dinesen re-creates Jogona Kanyagga as autobiographical speaker, "In laboring to give birth to his story, for which the narrator is only a kind of midwife, he also provides her with a story to tell, thus bringing about *her* birth as an author and permitting the making of *her* name. . . . the creation of his autobiographical narrative prefigures and enables, even as it inhabits, her own." *Isak Dinesen,* 241.

36. Dinesen, *Letters,* 42. "Through experiences of this kind," suggests Anders Westenholz, "Karen Blixen became conscious of the Power within her. By seeing her as magnified into myth, the natives showed her how to control the Power: through recognition of one's mythos, every detail in life achieves enormous significance and acquires importance far beyond its everyday triviality. It becomes, in other words, worthy of the Power." *The Power of Aries: Myth and Reality in Karen Blixen's Life* (Baton Rouge: Louisiana State University Press, 1982), 5.

37. Aiken, *Isak Dinesen,* 232.

38. Ibid., 220, 228–34.

39. Dinesen, *Letters,* 245.

40. Quoted in Elspeth Huxley, *White Man's Country: Lord Delamere and the Making of Kenya,* 2 vols. (New York: Praeger, 1968), 282. See also Thurman, *Isak Dinesen,* 169–83.

41. I am indebted to Thomas Connelly, who suggested this phrase at a conference titled "Autobiography Visual and Verbal," State University of New York—Binghamton, September 1989.

42. Domna C. Stanton, "Difference on Trial: A Critique of the Maternal Metaphor in Cixous, Irigaray, and Kristeva," in *The Thinking Muse: Feminism and Modern French Philosophy,* ed. Jeffner Allen and Iris Marion Young (Bloomington: Indiana University Press, 1989), 167.

43. Ibid.

44. Ibid.

45. Ibid.

46. For counterarguments to mine here, see Aiken, *Isak Dinesen,* 212–16; and Abdul K. JanMohamed, *Manichean Aesthetics: The Politics of Literature in Colonial Africa* (Amherst: University of Massachusetts Press, 1983).

47. "To be exiled from the maternal continent," suggests Bella Brodzki, "is to be forever subjected to the rules of a foreign economy for which one also serves as the medium of exchange." "Mothers, Displacement, and Language," 246.

48. Luce Irigaray, *Corps à corps avec la mère* (Paris: Editions de la Pleine Lune, 1981), quoted in Brodzki, "Mothers, Displacement, and Language," 247.

49. Brodzki, "Mothers, Displacement, and Language," 247.

50. See Aiken, *Isak Dinesen,* 231.

51. Edward W. Said, "Yeats and Decolonization," in *Nationalism, Colonialism, and Literature* (Minneapolis: University of Minnesota Press, 1990), 82.

52. Aiken, *Isak Dinesen,* 242.

53. On the textual politics of artistic primitivism, see Helen Carr, "In Other Words: Native American Women's Autobiography," in *Life/Lines: Theorizing Women's Autobiography,* ed. Bella Brodzki and Celeste Schenck (Ithaca, N.Y.: Cornell University Press, 1988), 146.

54. Nancy K. Miller, "Changing the Subject: Authorship, Writing, and the Reader," in *Feminist Studies/Critical Studies,* ed. Teresa de Lauretis (Bloomington: Indiana University Press, 1986), 110.

55. Gayatri Chakravorty Spivak, "French Feminism in an International Frame," in *In Other Words: Essays in Cultural Politics* (New York: Methuen, 1987), 150.

56. See, for instance, Teresa de Lauretis, *Alice Doesn't: Feminism, Semiotics, Cinema* (Bloomington: Indiana University Press, 1982), 178; Miller, "Changing the Subject"; Tania Modleski, "Feminism and the Power of Interpretation: Some Critical Readings," in *Feminist Studies/Critical Studies,* ed. Teresa de Lauretis (Bloomington: Indiana University Press, 1986), 135.

Chapter 20

Writing the Subject: Exoticism/Eroticism in Marguerite Duras's *The Lover* and *The Sea Wall*

Suzanne Chester

Until now, the main body of critical work on Duras has explored the relationship between her writing and the category of the feminine—defined variously in cultural, linguistic, and psychoanalytic terms.[1] However, the colonial aspect of Duras's work has been largely ignored and is, I argue, crucial to a reading of sexual difference and the construction of a gendered writing subject. Therefore, my essay will focus on Duras's representation of the particular power relations emerging from the confrontation of the female Other with the "exotic" Other in a French colonial situation. In my reading of *Un barrage contre le pacifique* (*The Sea Wall*) and *L'Amant* (*The Lover*), I will examine the relationship between structures of dominance and strategies of representation, especially as the latter pertain to questions of autobiography.[2]

Since my analysis of Duras lays special emphasis on the notion of a gendered writing subject, my reading of colonial discourse is to be distinguished from Abdul R. JanMohamed's theory of "colonialist literature."[3] Basing his analysis on Frantz Fanon's account of the Manichean structure of the colonizer/colonized relationship, JanMohamed identifies "colonialist literature"—writing produced by the European colonizer—as a monolithic discourse constructed around the central trope he calls "Manichean allegory."[4] He defines this trope as "a field of diverse yet interchangeable oppositions between white and black, good and evil, superiority and inferiority, civilization and savagery, intelligence and emotion, rationality and sensuality, self and Other, subject and object."[5]

While JanMohamed's approach is important in that it emphasizes the historical, social, and political context of colonial discourse, his argument is ultimately reductive insofar as it suggests that colonial power is possessed entirely by the colonizer. As a result, it cannot account for the conflicting textual strategies occasioned by a split in the colonial writing subject, a split that may occur when this subject is a woman and, as such, already defined as the Other of patriarchal society. Because JanMohamed's analysis relies on an absolute opposition between colonizer and colonized, it cannot engage with what I consider the specificity of writing produced by certain women in a colonial society. I maintain that the factors of gender and class produce a split in the colonial writing subject that challenges the fixed opposition between subject and object and the stable process of othering central to JanMohamed's conception of Manichean allegory.

Another pitfall in JanMohamed's approach to colonialist literature lies in its tendency, as Tzvetan Todorov has observed, "to elicit a similarly Manichean interpretation, with good and evil simply having switched places; on your right the disgusting white colonialists; on your left the innocent black victims."[6] My analysis of two texts written by, and dealing with, the female Other in the patriarchal society of French colonial Indochina examines how the intersection of gender and colonialism in Duras's writing avoids the trope of Manichean allegory, thereby generating readings that escape the moralistic tendencies of Manichean interpretation. In *The Sea Wall* and *The Lover,* the factors of gender and class problematize the relationship of the colonizer to the colonized, and consequently disrupt the economy of colonial discourse as defined by JanMohamed.

Published in 1950, *The Sea Wall* is Duras's third novel. As she has made clear in interviews with Michèle Porte and Xavière Gauthier, this novel contains many autobiographical elements dealing with her childhood and adolescence in colonial Indochina.[7] In 1914, Duras was born into the family of two French schoolteachers attracted to French Indochina by colonial propaganda, tales of exotica, and the promise of making their fortune. When Duras was four years old, her father died, leaving her mother with three young children. After teaching in a French colonial school by day and playing the piano in a cinema by night for twenty years, the mother put all her savings into the purchase of a concession from the colonial administration. Realizing that the administration had deliberately allotted her an unworkable piece of land that was periodically flooded by the salt water of the Pacific, she employed a group of local peasants to help build a series of dams to prevent the sea from invading. After the collapse of the dams, the mother's anger and bitterness at her exploitation by the colonial administration plunged her into depression and near insanity. Duras spent her first seventeen years in French Indochina, now southern Vietnam, and received her education in the *Lycée de Saigon*. In 1931, the family moved to Paris, where Duras obtained degrees in law and in political science before embarking on her career as a writer.

As a *roman à thèse, The Sea Wall* is an ironic indictment of the French colonial administration, from its corrupt policy of allocating infertile concessions and its collusion with the colonial banks, speculators, and property holders to its callous refusal to alleviate the abject poverty of the indigenous population. The novel also contains an implicit critique of the status of women in patriarchal, colonial society, structured as it is around the endeavors of Suzanne's mother and brother to secure her marriage to a series of white colonial suitors: Mr. Jo, son of a wealthy planter; John Barner, sales representative for a cotton factory in Calcutta; and Jean Agosti, local pineapple farmer and opium smuggler.

The Lover, published in 1984 and an international best-seller, explores the issues raised in *The Sea Wall* through an autobiographical account of Duras's childhood in Indochina and her relationship with her family. Centered on the affair Duras had with a Chinese man, *The Lover* rewrites the cultural and sexual politics of *The Sea Wall*. This rewriting is exemplified by a shift from the representation of the protagonist as a object of prostitution and of male desire in *The Sea Wall* to the construction of a female subject with an active relationship to desire in *The Lover.* Related to this transformation of the status of the female protagonist is the move from the overt anticolonialism of *The Sea Wall* to the feminization and subordination of the exotic Other in *The Lover.* An analysis of the representation of the female protagonist in *The Sea Wall* as an object of prostitution and of male desire provides the backdrop for an understanding of the subversive strategies at work in *The Lover. The Sea Wall* is a narrative in which the protagonist has no active relationship to desire. As a commodity in a colonial, patriarchal society, Suzanne shares the characteristics of both virgin and prostitute, neither of whom has the right to her own pleasure.[8] Suzanne's status as a young girl with neither money nor looks emerges from the following exchange concerning plans for a visit to Ram, the capital city of the colony.

> "So it's not tonight that we're going to Ram," said Suzanne.
> "We'll go tomorrow," said Joseph, "and it's not in Ram you'll find what you're looking for. They're all married, except Agosti."
> "I'd never give her to Agosti," said the mother, "not even if he came and begged for her."
> "He'll not ask you for anything," said Suzanne, "and it's not here I'll find what I'm looking for."
> "He wouldn't ask better," said the mother. "I know what I'm saying. But he can go on chasing her."
> "He never even thinks about her," said Joseph. "It's going to be hard. Some girls manage to marry without money, but they have to be awful pretty and even then it's a rare thing."(27)[9]

Occurring early in the novel, this exchange among Suzanne, her brother Joseph, and their mother establishes class as one of the determining factors in the quest to find a husband for Suzanne. It also points to important hierarchies within the dominant group of white colonialists. Since the family's poverty severely limits their choice, the chances of finding Suzanne a suitable husband are slim. What emerges from this conversation is that the mother and Joseph will ultimately decide whom Suzanne will marry. Therefore, although the father is absent from the novel, his traditional function within patriarchal society, as the one who controls the daughter's sexuality, is assumed by the mother and the older brother.

Once Mr. Jo falls in love with Suzanne, her status is radically transformed from that of a liability to that of a highly lucrative asset. As the only son of rich colonial speculator, Mr. Jo represents a potential source of enormous wealth for the family. Consequently, the mother does everything in her power to expedite his marriage to her daughter. Referring to Mr. Jo's daily visits to the house to see Suzanne, the narrator observes: "These visits delighted the mother. The longer they lasted the higher her hopes rose. And if she insisted they leave the bungalow door open, it was in order to give Mr. Jo no alternative but marriage to satisfy his strong desire to sleep with her daughter" (p. 53; translation modified).[10]

The mother recognizes the role Mr. Jo's desire plays in the family's quest for a suitable husband. Such desire is the basis upon which a daughter's value is established, as Luce Irigaray argues in her elaboration of the commodified status of women in patriarchal society. Since a woman's value in society lies in her capacity to be exchanged, her value is not intrinsic to her but is a reflection of a man's desire/need for her: "The exchange value of two signs, two commodities, two women, is a representation of the needs/desires of consumer-exchanger subjects: in no way is it the "property" of the signs/articles/women themselves."[11] This dynamic is clearly at work in the bathroom scene in *The Sea Wall*. As Suzanne prepares to take a shower in the bathroom, the frustrated and pathetic Mr. Jo begs her to open the door and show him her naked body. While her first reaction to Mr. Jo's entreaty is a decisive refusal, Suzanne gradually begins to wonder if her body is not, after all, intended to gratify the male gaze.

> He had a great desire to see her. After all, it was the natural desire of a man. And there she was, worth seeing. There was only that door to open. And no man in the world had yet seen this body of hers that was hidden by that door. It was not made to be hidden but, on the contrary, to be seen and to make its way in the world, that world to which belonged, after all, this Mr. Jo. (57)[12]

Suzanne is on the point of opening the door when Mr. Jo promises to give her a new record player. Realizing that he is trying to prostitute her, she opens the door only to spit in his face.

Although the young girl rebels against this overt prostitution of her body, she does not recognize that the marriage being arranged for her is an institutionalized form of prostitution orchestrated by her mother and Joseph. Thus, despite her initial rebellion, Suzanne comes to appreciate the value of her body when Mr. Jo, his humiliation notwithstanding, presents her with the promised record player. While a glimpse of her body was enough to secure the record player, the sexual favors demanded and the rewards offered begin to increase in direct proportion. Next, Mr. Jo promises her a diamond in exchange for a three-day visit to the city with him. Suzanne's perception of her body as a valuable entity temporarily blinds her to the alienation inherent in her newly commodified status: "And it was thanks to her, Suzanne, that it was now there on the table. She had opened the bathroom door just long enough for Mr. Jo's loathsome and unwholesome gaze to penetrate her body and now the record player lay there, on the table" (p. 59; translation modified).[13]

Similarly, in *The Lover*, the narrator repeatedly acknowledges the ways in which the white colonial woman becomes the object of the gaze and desire of both the indigenous and the colonial male: "I'm used to people looking at me," the narrator remarks, and then explains:

"People do look at white women in the colonies; at twelve-year-old girls too. For the past three years white men, too, have been looking at me in the streets, and my mother's men friends have been kindly asking me to have tea with them while their wives are out playing tennis at the Sporting Club" (p. 17).[14] Her awareness of the objectification of the white woman by the male gaze of both colonizer and colonized indicates that sexual difference functions in a particular way in a colonial situation.

While the narrator of *The Lover* alludes to the male gaze that constructs the young girl as an object of desire, *The Sea Wall* vividly stages the negativity of her self-alienation and indicates that, far from being in the dominant position of the subject, as JanMohamed's argument implies, the lower-class white colonial woman is objectified and prostituted by the male gaze. This self-alienation emerges clearly when Suzanne goes to the colonial capital to sell Mr. Jo's diamond. Carmen, the resident prostitute in the Hotel Central, suggests that, since her marriage prospects are limited by the family's poverty, Suzanne earn her living through prostitution, thereby forcing on the young girl a certain image of her precarious status. Unaware of the class divisions within the colonial capital, Suzanne wanders alone through the fashionable district, attracting the attention of the wealthy white residents and unwittingly making a spectacle of herself: "People looked at her. They turned to look, they smiled. No young white girl of her age ever walked alone in the streets of the fashionable district" (p. 149).[15] Furthermore, as Suzanne walks through the white, upper-class district, her consciousness of herself as an object of another's gaze causes her to see herself as she believes others see her: "The more they looked at her the more she was convinced that she was something scandalous, an object of complete ugliness and stupidity" (p. 150).[16]

Finally, the price of being the object of the male gaze results in the fracturing of any residual sense of identity as Suzanne's perception of her body now centers on its fragmentation, each part an object of shame, revulsion, and ridicule:[17] "She herself, from head to foot, was contemptible. Her eyes—where to look? These leaden, obscene arms, this heart, fluttering like an indecent caged beast, these legs that were too weak to bear her along" (p. 151; translation modified).[18]

Subjectivity is further denied to the protagonist of *The Sea Wall* as a result of the omniscient narrator, who, like the proverbial fly on the wall, effaces its own subject position within the text while aligning the reader with its disembodied point of view. Although there is an implicit critique of the objectification of the young girl, the ominiscient narrator also contributes to her objectified status by remaining a hidden observer of this process. Duras's use of a realistic, novelistic convention that depends on an unproblematized narratorial gaze makes both narrator and reader of *The Sea Wall* complicitous in the voyeurism that objectifies the female protagonist.

JanMohamed's Manichean allegory is further problematized by the class divisions within white colonial society—divisions that reveal the structures of dominance existing within that society. In *The Sea Wall,* Suzanne's body becomes the site of the class conflict between her family and the colonial powers. When Suzanne's brother Joseph refuses to allow Mr. Jo to have sex with her before marriage, he is not interested in the morality of the issue but in the measure of power such an interdiction affords the family. Helpless in the face of the colonial powers that have thwarted them, namely, the administration and the banks, their only remaining power lies in the control of Suzanne's body. By forbidding her to sleep with this wealthy planter's son, Suzanne's mother, situated at the bottom of the colonial hierarchy, finds a way to avenge herself psychologically on the whole colonial system. Joseph brazenly tells Mr. Jo where they stand on the issue of his sister's sexuality: "She can sleep with whoever she likes. We don't stop her. But in your case, if you want to sleep with her, you've got to marry her. That's our way of saying to hell with you" (p. 75).[19]

This censorship of Suzanne's relationship to her body reaches a climax when her mother physically beats her, refusing to believe she has not slept with Mr. Jo in exchange for the diamond he has given her. In fact, it is this diamond that really arouses the mother's wrath, since for her it symbolizes an object that has no use value, only exchange value: "There's nothing more disgusting than a diamond. It has no use, no use at all" (p. 108; translation modified).[20] The mother's revulsion at the diamond is related to her ambivalent feelings about her own part in the prostitution of her daughter, feelings that alternate between shame at handing her daughter over to Mr. Jo, who epitomizes the worst aspects of the dominant white colonials, and pride in the economic rewards that result from the relationship. The mother's ambivalence is symptomatic of her own alienated position within this colonial society, since it is the family's impoverishment—a direct result of colonial corruption—that predisposes her to use Suzanne's body as bait to lure Mr. Jo into a marriage with her daughter.[21]

As an object of pure exchange value, the diamond symbolizes the commodification of the daughter by a society in which a woman's value is realized in exchange. The final sale of the diamond at the end of the novel coincides with Suzanne's first experience of sexual pleasure with Agosti, the local pineapple farmer, an experience that is above all a "useful" one in bringing to an end the circuit of exchange, violence, and prostitution in which the young girl has been involved.

> The mother knew about it. No doubt she thought it was *useful* for Suzanne. She was not mistaken, for it was during that week, from the time of the first excursion to the pineapple field to the time of her mother's death, that Suzanne at last unlearned her senseless waiting for the hunters' cars and abandoned her empty dreams. (p. 281; translation modified; emphasis mine)[22]

However, Suzanne's sexual pleasure with Agosti is itself a direct result of the mother's authority in relation to her daughter's sexuality: "Still, they had made love together every afternoon for a week until yesterday and the mother knew, she had left them together, she had given him to her so that she might make love with him" (p. 284; translation modified).[23] While *The Sea Wall* ends with the sexual awakening of the protagonist, her life remains circumscribed by the desires and authority of her mother, lover, and brother. After the death of her mother, Suzanne must choose between remaining with Agosti or leaving with Joseph.

> "It's not important whether she stays with me or someone else, for the time being," said Agosti suddenly.
> "No, it's not very important," said Joseph. "It's up to her to decide."
> Agosti had begun to smoke and had turned a little pale.
> "I'm leaving," Suzanne said to him. "I can't do anything else." (p. 288)[24]

Although the protagonist of *The Sea Wall* achieves some small degree of autonomy, and a real, if circumscribed, relationship to sexual pleasure, the overriding emphasis of the novel, both formally and thematically, is on the young girl's body as the site of domination by both colonizer and colonized, and on the marginalized position of the lower-class, white colonial woman.

More than thirty years later, Duras rewrote the autobiographical material of *The Sea Wall,* this time availing herself of the possibilities offered by the autobiographical "I" in order to establish her own subjectivity and an active relationship to desire. In 1984, *The Lover* appeared—an "exotic, erotic autobiographical confession" that, I maintain, radically transforms the subordinate status of the female protagonist of *The Sea Wall*.[25] Given that some critics regard the genre of *The Lover* as ambiguous, vacillating as it does between a confessional mode in the first person and novelistic narration in the third person,

I will first suggest a reading of the text that resolves what Sharon Willis calls "the text's doubleness" and its refusal "to be pinned to the conventional confessional or fictional modes."[26]

The narrator of this text both adheres to and transgresses the conventions of confessional autobiography. On the one hand, in typical modernist fashion, she points to the impossibility of transposing her life into a story with a consistent identity at its center, saying: "The story of my life doesn't exist. Does not exist. There's never any center to it. No path, no line. There are great spaces where you pretend there used to be someone, but it's not true, there was no-one" (p. 8).[27] The use of the novelistic third person is also evidence of Duras's departure from a traditional autobiographical mode, a point I shall return to later.

On the other hand, the text is presented as a traditional autobiography in that its goal is the seemingly unproblematic reconstruction of personal identity. Alluding to *The Sea Wall* in her reference to the autobiographical content of her previous work, Duras indicates her intention to fill in the blanks and restore the omissions necessitated by the conditions of her life as a writer at that time.

> The story of one small part of my youth I've already written, more or less—I mean, enough to give a glimpse of it. Of this part, I mean, the part about the crossing of the river. What I'm doing now is both different and the same. Before, I spoke of clear periods, those on which the light fell. Now I'm talking about the hidden stretches of that same youth, of certain facts, feelings, events that I buried. I started to write in a milieu that drove me to modesty. (p. 8; translation modified)[28]

Despite the narrator's claims of merely elucidating what had previously been concealed, Duras's rewriting of this "one small part" of her youth radically transforms her own subject position within the economy of sexual desire.

By designating herself as the subject of *The Lover*, Duras avails herself of the autobiographical "I" in order to realize her own subjectivity. As Emile Benveniste has observed, language provides the possibility of subjectivity because it is language that enables the speaker to posit herself as "I," the subject of discourse.[29] Instead of being subjected to the voyeuristic gaze of the ominiscient narrator/reader, Duras claims control over the representation of her body, transforming it into an active display of her life as spectacle. Referring to the image of herself as a young girl, Duras writes: "It could have existed, a photograph could have been taken, just like any other, somewhere else, in other circumstances. But it wasn't. . . . And it's to this, this failure to have been created, that the image owes its virtue: the virtue of representing, of being the author of, an absolute". (p. 10; translation modified).[30]

Duras's image of herself is thus likened to a nonexistent photograph. It is this nonexistent photograph that allows Duras to create her own image of herself, an image in which "I" and "me" coincide and subjectivity is realized:[31] "It's the only image of myself I like, the only one in which I recognize myself, in which I delight" (pp. 3–4).[32] Whereas the reader of *The Sea Wall* is aligned with the disembodied point of view of the omniscient narrator, the reader of *The Lover,* by contrast, is a spectator whose presence and gaze are actively solicited. "Look at me" (p. 16), commands the narrator, as she constructs a new image that replaces the negative self-alienation of the young girl in *The Sea Wall.*[33]

The narrative vacillation between "I" and "she" that occurs at different points in the text has provided some critics with evidence of the failure of the narrator's search for identity. Sarah Capitanio, for example, argues as follows:

> Quant à la focalisée toutefois, sa designation comme 'elle' à ce moment marque une séparation définitive entre elle et la narratrice et, par la, la non-résolution de cette recherche si fondamentale.[34]

I read the question of narrative identity differently: the autobiographical "I" allows Duras to posit an identity between the narrator of *The Lover,* the young girl in the nonexistent photo, and the protagonist of *The Sea Wall,* thereby enabling her to reconstitute an identity fragmented by her experience as a white woman in the colonies. By designating herself alternately by the pronouns "I" and "she," Duras in fact undermines the objectification to which she was subjected. She appropriates the masculine position of the observer and, as we shall see, she rewrites the traditionally femininized position of the observed. In the following description, for instance, the actions of the Chinese man, later to become her lover, take place as though before the eye of a moving camera. Through this discursive strategy, the narrator ultimately appropriates the position of the mastering gaze as she watches the man from Cholon watching the young girl: "The elegant man has got out of the limousine and is smoking an English cigarette. He looks at the girl in the man's fedora and the gold shoes. He slowly approaches her" (p. 32).[35]

In the narrative shift to the third person, the young girl is also designated by the way white colonial society perceives her—that is, as "the little white slut" (passim). However, through the device of reported speech, Duras subverts the tone and meaning of the original utterance by permeating the reported speech with her own ironic intonation.[36]

> Fifteen and a half. The news spreads fast in Sadec. The clothes are enough to show. The mother has no idea, and none about how to bring up a daughter. Poor child. Don't tell me that hat's innocent, it means something, it's to attract attention, money. The brothers are layabouts. They say it's a Chinese, the son of the millionaire, the villa in Mekong with the blue tiles. And even he, instead of thinking himself honored, doesn't want her for his son. A family of white layabouts. . . . It goes on in the disreputable quarter of Cholon, every evening. Every morning the little slut goes to have her body caressed by a filthy Chinese millionaire. (pp. 88–89)[37]

By drawing attention to the clichéd speech, dogmatic worldview, and racist doxa of colonial society, Duras undercuts its tone of scandalized self-righteousness.

The representation of her lover as the exotic Other constitutes the second discursive strategy that enables Duras to appropriate the position of the subject. This construction of subjectivity is inextricably linked to her position of domination and power as she constructs it in relation to the Chinese man. In *The Lover*, the narrative strategies that effect the subordination of the cultural Other belong to what Edward Said terms the discourse of "Orientalism."[38] The most significant of these strategies are the eroticization of the exotic, the feminization of the figure of the Other, and the representation of the Orient as an ontological and unchanging essence. The Orient of *The Lover* figures as a set of topoi that Duras deploys for aesthetic and personal/political reasons. Thus, her exploitation of Orientalist discourse is instrumental in the textual transformation of the subordinate status of the poor white woman in French colonial patriarchal society and the construction of a female subjectivity. Although *The Lover* exemplifies many aspects of "Orientalism," the text is not structured by the Manichean allegory that JanMohamed sees at the heart of colonialist literature. Rather, Duras's inscription of many of the themes of Orientalist discourse is in service to the constitution of a subject position for the female protagonist of *The Sea Wall*, who, although she belongs to the group of French colonizers, is already defined as object/Other.

The eroticization of the exotic—figured by Indochina and the lover's Chinese heritage—is a key element of Duras's text. Said has identified the association of sex with the Orient as a persistent motif in Orientalist discourse.[39] The formal structure of the text reflects the binary opposition of intellect and sensuality that informs the representation of Europe and the Orient. While the erotic theme dominates in Indochina, intellectual and political affairs take place in France.

While Mr. Jo in *The Sea Wall* and the man from Cholon in *The Lover* represent two different versions of "the rich man in the black limousine," the transformation of the European Mr. Jo into an Asian is particularly important. By making the lover a Chinese man, Duras takes advantage of the erotic topoi associated with the Orient. Indeed, the exotic and the erotic are so inextricably merged in the text that even Duras's French school friend, Hélène Lagonelle, is imbued with Eastern eroticism. As object of the young girl's homoerotic desire, Hélène is "orientalized" through association with the Chinese lover: "I see her as being of one flesh with the man from Cholon. . . . Hélène Lagonelle is the mate of the bondsmen who gives me such abstract, such harsh pleasure, the obscure man from Cholon, from China. Hélène Lagonelle is from China" (p. 74).[40] Here, the geographical referent, China, disappears and is appropriated as a trope for the private sexual fantasy of the narrator. Nor is it insignificant that this orientalized body provokes fantasies of sadistic power: "[Hélène Lagonelle] makes you want to kill her, she conjures up a marvellous dream of putting her to death with your own hands" (p. 73).[41] Similarly, the conflation of the erotic with the exotic and the related dynamic of sexual domination are implicit in the narrator's incestuous desire for her younger brother, whose body she compares to that of an Indian servant: "Even the body of my younger brother, like that of a little coolie, is as nothing beside this splendour" (p. 72).[42]

A similar configuration of power and desire is suggested by the feminization of the Chinese lover. This feminization results from the description of his body and his role during sex. In the former, the emphasis is on traditional markers of femininity: smooth skin, fragile physique, and hairless body. The only sign of virility, the penis, is undermined by the lover's inability to carry through the initial seduction: "The skin is sumptuously soft. The body. The body is thin, lacking in strength, in muscle, he may have been ill, may be convalescent, he's hairless, nothing masculine about him but his sex, he's weak, probably helpless prey to insult, vulnerable" (p. 38).[43] Far from being a passive object of this man's desire, the young girl orchestrates and controls her initiation into sex and pleasure: "She was attracted to him. It depended on her alone. . . . She tells him she doesn't want him to talk, what she wants is for him to do as he usually does with the women he brings to his flat" (pp. 37–38). And then again, "She tells him to keep still. Let me do it. And she does. Undresses him" (p. 38). The act of penetration, traditionally associated with activity and virility, is reduced to an elliptic "And weeping, he does it" (p. 38), with the emphasis more on his feminine tears than on the act of penetration itself.[44]

The lover's feminization also results from his position in relation to the discourse of love. As Roland Barthes has noted, this discourse has historically been elaborated by woman in the absence of her beloved.[45] As a result, something feminine is revealed in the man who speaks in the voice of love. In Duras's text, these roles are exchanged: the female protagonist speaks from the place of desire, and the Chinese lover elaborates that of love and passion (passion as suffering): "He's started to suffer here in this room, for the first time, he's no longer lying about it. He says he knows already she'll never love him . . . . He says he's lonely, horribly lonely because of this love he feels for her"(p. 37).[46]

Similarly, the fickleness of the traditional male lover is transposed onto the narrator as a young girl as the Chinese man anticipates her future unfaithfulness: "Talks to me, says he knew right away, when we were crossing the river, that I'd be like this after my first lover, that I'd love love, he says he knows now that I'll deceive him and deceive all the men I'm ever with" (p. 42).[47]

Sailing away on the boat to France and leaving behind her lover, the narrator also usurps the position of the man whose seduced and abandoned women grieve in his absence. Years after their affair, the lover telephones the narrator to tell her he is still in love. This reversal of the gendered economy of the discourse of love is echoed in the shift in roles related to the traditional departure.

> Departures. They were always the same. Always the first
> departures over the sea. Men always left the land in the same
> sorrow and despair, but that never stopped them from going,
> Jews, philosophers, and pure travellers for the journey's own
> sake. Nor did it ever stop women from letting them go, the
> women who never went themselves, who stayed behind to
> look after the birthplace, the race, the property, the reason for
> the return. (p. 109)[48]

The father's authority over his son and his refusal to allow him to marry "the little white slut" place the Chinese man in the feminine position of the woman, entrusted with the care of the domestic hearth and the perpetuation of the race. Reinforcing the young girl's position of dominance as she constructs it in relation to her lover is her explicit identification with the authority of his father: "Then I said I agreed with his father. That I refused to stay with him (p. 83).[49] Later, the narrator confirms the finality of the young girl's decision: "The man from Cholon knows his father's decision and the girl's are the same, and both are irrevocable" (p. 97).[50] In this manner, Duras's text constructs a subordinate position for the Chinese lover through a variety of textual strategies that contribute to his feminization. By making him occupy the traditionally subordinate feminine position, Duras appropriates a position of dominance for herself.

This configuration of power is also related to the racial politics of the text. The transformation of the European Mr. Jo of *The Sea Wall* into "the man from Cholon" in *The Lover* is significant in that race is integral to the balance of power in the relationship. Although the young girl prostitutes herself to the Chinese man, and thereby places herself in what is typically a subordinate position, the fact that he does not belong to white colonial society relegates him to the subordinate position in the eyes of her family, who maintain their sense of superiority by believing the girl is sleeping with the "Chinese scum" only for his money. The young girl's failure to disabuse her family of this assumption allows her to continue to enjoy the intense sexual pleasure she experiences in her relations with him.[51]

> My brothers never will say a word to him, it's as if he were invisible to them, as if for them he weren't solid enough to be perceived, seen or heard. This is because he adores me, but it's taken for granted I don't love him, that I'm with him for the money, that I can't love him, it's impossible that he could take any sort of treatment from me and still go on loving me. This because he's a Chinese, because he's not a white man.
> (p. 51)[52]

Although the narrator exposes and denounces her complicity as a young girl in her brothers' exploitation of the Chinese man, Duras reinscribes this exploitation through the discursive strategies she deploys in her own representation of her Asian lover. Belonging to the discourse of "Orientalism," these strategies reinforce the subordinate racial status of the "man from Cholon."

Moreover, the lover's superior economic status—which enables him to "colonize" the young white girl through prostitution—is specifically connected to his Chinese origins. The wealth of "the man from Cholon" is tarnished through his association with the colonial history of the Chinese in Indochina and their continuing financial exploitation of the French colony. By drawing attention to the colonialist activities of the father and his son's complicitous attitude, the narrator transforms the superior economic power of her lover into a position of moral inferiority.

> I ask him to tell me about his father's money, how he got rich. He says it bores him to talk about money, but if I insist he'll tell me what he knows about his father's wealth. It all began in Cholon, with the housing estates for natives. He built three hundred of these "compartments," cheap, semi-detached dwellings let out for rent. Owns several streets. . . . The people here like living close together, especially the poor, who come from the country and like living out-of-doors too, on the street. And you must try not to destroy the habits of the poor. (pp. 47-48)[53]

In *The Lover,* the significance of the gaze further reinforces the Chinese man's subordinate position, as constructed by the narrator. Duras rewrites the semiotics of the gaze by transforming the negative associations of the gaze, which subordinates and reifies its object in *The Sea Wall,* into an action that signifies the recognition of the value of the other in *The Lover.* Referring to the hostile relations within her family, the narrator observes:

> It's a family of stone, petrified so deeply it's impenetrable. Every day we try to kill one another, to kill. Not only do we not talk to one another, we don't even look at one another. When you're being looked at, you can't look. To look is to feel curious, to be interested, to lower yourself. No one you look at is worth it. Looking is always demeaning. (p. 54)[54]

To be looked at, then, is to enjoy the privilege of exciting interest and curiosity. The Chinese lover, however, is denied the recognition of this gaze because his liaison with "la petite blanche" transgresses the racial arrangements of French colonial society. "My brothers never will say a word to him, it's as if he were invisible to them, as if for them he weren't solid enough to be perceived, seen or heard" (p.51). By contrast, the narrator flaunts the heroine's transgressive behavior in the face of the reader/spectator by actively soliciting the latter's attention with her imperious "regardez-moi," thereby demanding the recognition implicit in this gaze.

Duras's naturalization of the young girl's French identity further contributes to her position of authority over her lover. The narrator both relates the young girl's mockery of the Chinese man's French pretensions—"I tell him his visit to France was fatal. He agrees. Says he bought everything in Paris, his women, his acquaintances, his ideas"

(p. 49)—and undercuts these pretensions through the use of irony—
"He talked. Said he missed Paris, the marvellous girls there, the riotous
living, the binges, ooh là là, the Coupole, the Rotonde, personally I
prefer the Rotonde, the nightclubs, the 'wonderful' life he'd led for
two years" (p. 34).[55] This ironizing of the lover's predilection for things
French stems from the split between the narrated "I" and the narrating
"I." While the former—the subject of the narration—refers to the white
fifteen-year-old born and raised in colonial Indochina, who has never
been to France, the latter—the narrating subject—is the narrator whom
the text explicitly associates with the authorial identity of Marguerite
Duras—the embodiment of a certain Frenchness. It is this split that
both authorizes the mockery of the young girl and enables the narrator
to undercut the Chinese man's pretensions by infiltrating his reported
speech with ironic authorial intonation.

Another textual strategy that effects the subordination of the cultural
Other is the representation of the Orient as an unchanging essence
of which the lover clearly partakes. That he remains nameless is the
first sign of his lack of individuality, a characteristic that is reinforced
by the generic nature of the epithets used to designate him—"the
lover," "the man from Cholon," and "the Chinese man" (passim).
Although an individual, the lover functions as a representative type
who embodies the atmosphere of the Orient. Years later, when he
calls the narrator in France, his fear and his trembling voice are represented as belonging to the very essence of the Orient: "He was
nervous, afraid, as before. His voice suddenly trembled. And with the
trembling, suddenly, she heard again the voice of China (p. 116).[56]

The idea of the Orient as timeless and unchanging is conveyed by
the absence of a history to which the lover can lay claim since his
affair with the young girl. In contrast to the narrator's development
as a writer, his life is defined by his love for her, which dissolves the
future into an inescapable, eternal present: "He knew she'd begun
writing books, he'd heard about it through her mother whom he'd
met again in Saigon. . . . Then he didn't know what to say. And then
he told her. Told her that it was as before, that he still loved her, he
could never stop loving her, that he'd love her until death" (p. 117).[57]

In this display of her life as spectacle, Duras is also the ultimate
spectator. By exploiting the possibilities of autobiographical discourse,
Duras appropriates the privileged masculine position of observer and
rewrites the feminine position of the observed. By constructing a
position of dominance in relation to the "man from Cholon," the
author of *The Lover* radically transforms her relationship to both desire
and prostitution in order to establish a female writing subject.

Because JanMohamed's trope of Manichean allegory posits a stable process of othering in which the colonizer occupies the position of subject and the colonized that of object/Other, it fails to account for the ways in which gender and class affect the economy of colonial discourse. As a lower-class woman in the patriarchal society of French colonial Indochina, Duras was *already* in the position of Other. Her subordinate status as object of both prostitution and the male gaze is clearly represented in *The Sea Wall*. In *The Lover*, Duras establishes a female subjectivity through the appropriation of the masculine position of the observer, through the construction of an active relationship to desire, and by recourse to a variety of Orientalist topoi—the eroticization of the exotic, the feminization of the Asian lover, and the representation of an unchanging Oriental essence. Despite Duras's overt anticolonialism in *The Sea Wall* and her occasional contestation of the discourse of colonialism in *The Lover*, in which the narrator both satirizes and explicitly denounces the racist doxa espoused by her family and by French colonial society, she nonetheless also *reinscribes* a variety of Orientalist/colonialist themes in order to transform her own marginalized position as Other and to achieve a position of power and dominance in relation to her Chinese lover. Through her participation in colonialist politics in service to a "white" female subjectivity, Duras engages in textual strategies that have disturbing implications for the politics of women's autobiography.[58] This gendered subject position is also constructed through Duras's use of the rhetorical strategies made possible by autobiographical discourse. Just as the nonexistent photograph provides Duras with the means to authorize her favorite image of herself as a young girl, so autobiography affords the possibility to *create* a self/subject liberated from the oppressive realities of poverty, prostitution, and the patriarchal order of French colonial society.

Notes

1. For a psychoanalytic reading of the feminine in Duras's *oeuvre,* see Sharon Willis, *Marguerite Duras: Writing on the Body* (Urbana: Illinois University Press, 1987). Willis uses hysteria as a metaphor for Duras's narrative discourse and analyzes how her texts explore "the limits of narrative representation"—a discursive space coded as feminine within a particular historical moment. See also Michèle Montrelay, "Sur le Ravissement de Lol V. Stein," *L'Ombre et le nom* (Paris: Minuit, 1977). Situated within a psychoanalytic framework, Montrelay's article offers a reading of Duras's *Le Ravissement de Lol V. Stein* as an example of a text that gives a place to femininity defined as non-sense, silence, and nonspeech. In *Territories du féminin avec Marguerite Duras* (Paris: Minuit, 1977), Marcelle Marini reads Duras's disruptive writing style and her creation of silences and gaps as a feminine space that attempts to circumvent women's oppression within patriarchy. Trista Selous, in *The Other Woman: Feminism and Femininity in the Work of*

Marguerite Duras (New Haven, Conn.: Yale University Press, 1988), offers a cultural critique of the representations of women in Duras, challenging the claims that Duras's work is truly feminist.

2. All citations will include page numbers in parentheses in the text from the following editions, except where otherwise noted. Marguerite Duras, *The Sea Wall,* trans. Herma Briffault (New York: Harper & Row, 1986); *The Lover,* trans. Barbara Bray (New York: Pantheon, 1985). I have altered the English translations in places in order to stress nuances of the French text that are important to my analyses. I shall indicate "translation modified" wherever such changes occur. French quotations are provided in the notes and are from the following editions: Marguerite Duras, *L'Amant* (Paris: Minuit, 1984); *Un Barrage contre le pacifique* (Paris: Gallimard, 1950).

3. Abdul R. JanMohamed, "The Economy of Manichean Allegory: The Function of Racial Difference in Colonialist Literature," *Critical Inquiry* 12 (Autumn 1985): 59–87.

4. Frantz Fanon notes that "the colonial world is a Manichean world." *The Wretched of the Earth,* trans. Constance Farrington (New York: Grove, 1968), 41. He demonstrates the mechanism of this Manichean world in *Black Skin, White Masks,* trans. Charles Lam Markmann (New York: Grove, 1967).

5. JanMohamed, "Economy of Manichean Allegory," 63.

6. Tzvetan Todorov, "Critical Response III: 'Race', Writing Culture," trans. Loulou Mack, *Critical Inquiry* 12 (Autumn 1985): 178.

7. Marguerite Duras and Michèle Porte, *Les Lieux de Marguerite Duras* (Paris: Minuit, 1977); Marguerite Duras and Xavière Gauthier, *Les Parleuses* (Paris: Minuit, 1974).

8. For a more extensive discussion of this issue, see Luce Irigaray, *This Sex Which Is Not One,* trans. Catherine Porter (Ithaca, N.Y.: Cornell University Press, 1977). Irigaray describes women's censored relationship to desire as follows: "Mother, virgin, prostitute: these are the social roles imposed on women. The characteristic of (so-called) feminine sexuality derive from them: the valorization of reproduction and nursing; faithfulness; modesty; ignorance of and even lack of interest in sexual pleasure; a passive acceptance of men's activity; seductiveness, in order to arouse the consumers' desire while offering herself as its material support without getting pleasure herself. . . . Neither as mother nor as virgin nor as prostitute has woman any right to her own pleasure" (pp. 186–87).

9. "'Ce n'est pas ce soir qu'on ira à Ram,' dit Suzanne.

'On ira demain,' dit Joseph, 'et c'est pas à Ram que tu trouveras, ils sont tous mariés, il y a qu'Agosti.'

'Jamais je ne la donnerai à Agosti,' dit la mère, 'quand même il me suppliérait.'

'Il ne demande pas mieux,' dit la mère, 'je sais ce que je dis, mais il peut toujours courir.'

'Il ne pense même pas à elle,' dit Joseph. 'Ce sera difficile. Il y en a qui se marient sans argent, mais il faut qu'elles soient très jolies, et encore c'est rare'" (p. 35).

10. "Ces tête-à-tête enchantaient la mère. Plus ils duraient et plus elle espérait. Et si elle exigeait qu'ils laissent la porte du bungalow ouverte, c'était pour ne laisser à M. Jo aucune issue que le mariage à l'envie très forte qu'il avait de coucher avec sa fille" (p. 68).

11. Irigaray, *This Sex,* 180.

12. "Il avait très envie de la voir. Quand même c'était l'envie d'un homme. Elle, elle était là aussi, bonne à être vue, il n'y avait que la porte à ouvrir. Et aucun homme au monde n'avait encore vu celle qui se tenait là derrière cette porte. Ce n'était pas fait pour être caché mais au contraire pour être vu et faire son chemin de par le monde, le monde auquel appartenait quand même celui-là, ce M. Jo" (p. 73).

13. "C'était grâce à elle qu'il était maintenant là, sur la table. Elle avait ouvert la porte de la cabine de bains, le temps de laisser le regard malsain et laid de M. Jo pénétrer jusqu'à elle et maintenant le phonograph reposait là, sur la table" (p. 76).

14. "J'ai déjà l'habitude qu'on me regarde. On regarde les blanches aux colonies, et les petites filles de douze ans aussi. Depuis trois ans, les blancs aussi me regardent dans le rues et les amis de ma mère me demandent gentiment de venir goûter chez eux à l'heure ou leurs femmes jouent au tennis au Club Sportif" (p. 26).

15. "On la regardait. On se retournait, on souriait. Aucune jeune fille de son âge ne marchait seule dans les rues de haut quartier" (p. 185).

16. "Plus on la remarquait, plus elle se persuadait qu'elle était scandaleuse, un objet de laideur et de bêtise intégrale" (p. 185).

17. For a more extensive discussion of women's relation to their bodies in patriarchal society, see John Berger, *Ways of Seeing* (London: Penguin, 1972). According to his analysis, a woman is constantly accompanied by her own image of herself because she is the object of the male gaze. Consequently, a woman's sense of self is split into two and "she comes to consider the surveyor and the surveyed within her as two constituent yet always distinct elements of her identity as a woman" (p. 46).

18. "C'était elle, elle qui était méprisable des pieds à la tete. A cause de ses yeux, ou les jeter? A cause de ses bras de plomb, ces ordures, à cause de ce coeur, une bête indécente, de ces jambes incapables" (p. 187).

19. "C'est pas qu'on l'empêche de coucher avec qui elle veut, mais vous, si vous voulez coucher avec elle, faut que vous l'épousiez. C'est notre façon à nous de vous dire merde" (p. 96).

20. "Il n'y a rien de plus dégoutant qu'un bijou. Ca sert à rien, à rien. Et ceux qui les portent n'en ont pas besoin, moins besoin que n'importe qui" (p. 135).

21. See Marianne Hirsch, "Feminist Family Romances," in *The Mother/Daughter Plot: Narrative, Psychoanalysis, Feminism* (Bloomington: Indiana University Press, 1989), for an illuminating reading of the mother-daughter relationship in *The Lover*. Hirsch argues that Julia Kristeva's psychoanalytic reading of Duras in "The Pain of Sorrow in the Modern World: The Work of Marguerite Duras," *PMLA* 102 (March 1987): 138–52, ends up "eclipsing the mother's own voice, her own story, allowing her only the status of object, or of 'Other'" (p. 152). I concur with Hirsch that the figure of the mother in *The Sea Wall* and *The Lover* needs to be read in the political and economic context of colonialism in order to avoid "conflating [the political dimensions of women's lives] with the psychological" (p. 152).

22. "La mère le savait. Sans doute pensait-elle que c'était utile à Suzanne. Elle n'avait pas tort. Ce fut pendant ces huit jours-là, entre la promenade au champs d'ananas et la mort de la mère que Suzanne désapprit enfin l'attente imbécile des autos des chasseurs, les rêves vides" (p. 357).

23. "Pourtant ils avaient fait l'amour ensemble tous les après-midi depuis huit jours jusqu'à hier encore. Et la mère le savait, elle les avait laissés, le lui avait donné pour qu'elle fasse l'amour avec lui" (p. 360).

24. "'Ca n'a pas d'importance qu'elle soit avec moi ou un autre, pour le moment,' dit brusquement Agosti.

'Je crois que ça n'a pas tellement d'importance,' dit Joseph, 'elle n'a qu'à décider.' Agosti s'était mis à fumer, il avait un peu pâli.

'Je pars,' lui dit Suzanne, 'je ne peux pas faire autrement'" (p. 365).

25. The 9 June 1985 issue of the *New York Times Book Review* carried an advertisement for *The Lover* that included a *Saturday Review* comment that "this exotic, erotic autobiographical confession will deservedly become one of the summer's hottest books."

26. Willis, *Marguerite Duras,* 5.

27. "L'histoire de ma vie n'existe pas. Ca n'existe pas. Il n'y a jamais de centre. Pas de chemin, pas de ligne. Il y a de vastes endroits où l'on fait croire qu'il y avait quelqu'un, ce n'est pas vrai, il n'y avait personne" (p. 14).

28. "L'histoire d'une toute petite partie de ma jeunesse, je l'ai plus ou moins écrite déjà, enfin je veux dire, de quoi l'apercevoir, je parle de celle-ci justement, de celle de la traversée du fleuve. Ce que je fais ici est différent, et pareil. Avant j'ai parlé des périodes claires, de celles qui étaient éclairées. Ici je parle des périodes cachées de cette même jeunesse, de certains enfouissements que j'aurais opérés sur certains faits, sur certains sentiments, sur certains événements. J'ai commencé à ecrire dans un milieu qui me portait très fort à la pudeur" (p. 14).

29. See Emile Benveniste, *Problèmes de linguistique générale* (Paris: Gallimard, 1966), 258–65.

30. "Elle aurait pu exister, une photographie aurait pu être prise, comme une autre, ailleurs, dans d'autres circonstances. Mais elle ne l'a pas été. . . . C'est à ce manque d'avoir été faite qu'elle doit sa vertu, celle de représenter un absolu, d'en être justement l'auteur" (p. 17).

31. Susan Cohen notes that "the story [of *The Lover*] is essentially one of creativity, in particular the self-making of a woman and of a writer whom we watch in the process of creating out of that very initial non-presence." "Fiction and the Photographic Image in Duras' *The Lover,*" *L'Esprit Créateur* 30 (Spring 1990): 59. Cohen's article explores the relationship of absence to seeing and creativity.

32. "C'est entre toutes celle qui me plaît de moi-même, celle où je me reconnais, où je m'enchante" (p. 9).

33. Although I consider *The Lover* a feminist autobiography, it needs to be distinguished from the definition of "feminist confession" offered by Rita Felski in *Beyond Feminist Aesthetics* (Cambridge, Mass.: Harvard University Press, 1989). Whereas Felski's examples of feminist confession belong to the realist convention and continually refer to the question of truth as their ultimate legitimation, Duras is clearly less concerned with producing an image of herself faithful to a preexisting reality and more interested in the rhetorical and creative possibilities offered by the autobiographical genre. Felski makes the interesting observation that feminist confession is a rare phenomenon within the Catholic and rhetorically conscious French tradition on account of the strong Protestant element in the feminist preoccupation with subjectivity as the discovery of an authentic self (p. 114).

Clearly, Duras's writing of the "subject" differs from the pervasive quest for truth and self-understanding that Felski finds in the Protestant tradition of feminist confession. As Sharon Willis remarks, "Part of the appeal of *The Lover* lies in its duplicity, its pretense to confession coupled with its refusal to swear to truthfulness," *Marguerite Duras,* 5. In *The Lover,* the autobiographical "I" uses a variety of formal and rhetorical strategies in order to create a subject position for the female Other within a specific sexual and cultural economy. Rather than seeking validation through an appeal to authenticity, Duras's construction of a female subject relics on the colonialist politics of *The Lover* and a specific use of the autobiographical mode, both of which rework the sexual and cultural economy of *The Sea Wall.*

34. Sarah J. Capitanio, "Perspectives sur l'écriture durassienne: *L'Amant,*" *Symposium* 41 (Spring 1987): 18. The English translation of the cited passage is as follows: "The designation of the focalized as 'she' at this point, however, indicates a permanent split between her and the female narrator and, consequently, the nonresolution of this fundamental search [for personal identity]."

35. "L'homme élégant est descendu de la limousine, il fume une cigarette anglaise. Il regarde la jeune fille au feutre d'homme et aux chaussures d'or. Il vient vers elle lentement" (p. 42).

36. See V. N. Volosinov, *Marxism and the Philosophy of Language* (Cambridge, Mass.: Harvard University Press, 1973), 115–23, for an analysis of the infiltration of reported speech with authorial intonation.

37. "Quinze ans et demi. La chose se sait très vite dans le poste de Sadec. Rien que cette tenue dirait le déshonneur. La mère n'a aucun sens de rien, ni celui de la façon d'élever une petite fille. La pauvre enfant. Ne croyez pas, ce chapeau n'est pas innocent, ça veut dire, c'est pour attirer les regards, l'argent. Les frères, des voyous. On dit que c'est un Chinois, le fils du milliardaire, la ville du Mékong, en céramiques bleues. Même lui, au lieu d'en être honoré, il n'en veut pas pour son fils. Famille de voyous blancs. . . . Cela se passe dans le quartier mal famé de Cholen. Chaque soir cette petite vicieuse va se faire caresser le corps par un sale Chinois millionaire" (pp. 108–10).

38. As Edward Said demonstrates, the Orient represents "one of Europe's deepest and most recurring images of the Other." *Orientalism* (New York: Random House, 1979), 1. For political and economic reasons, the relationship between the West and the Orient has been one of power and domination. Said defines "Orientalism" as the discourse produced by the West about the Orient, a discourse in which the Orient is less a place than "an idea that has a history and a tradition of thought, imagery and vocabulary, that have given it presence and reality for the West" (p. 5).

39. Ibid., 188.

40. "Je la vois comme étant de la même chair que cet homme de Cholen. . . . Hélène Lagonelle, elle est la femme de cet homme de peine qui me fait la jouissance si abstraite, si dure, cet homme obscur de Cholen, de la Chine. Hélène Lagonelle est de la Chine" (p. 92).

41. "Hélène Lagonelle donne envie de la tuer, elle fait se lever le songe merveilleux de la mettre à mort de ses propres mains" (p. 91).

42. "Même le petit corps de petit coolie de mon petit frère disparaît face à cette splendeur" (p. 89).

43. "La peau est d'une somptueuse douceur. Le corps. Le corps est maigre, sans force, sans muscles. Il pourrait avoir été malade, être en convalescence, il est imberbe, sans virilité autre que celle du sexe, il est très faible, il paraît être à la merci d'une insulte, souffrant" (p. 49).

44. "Il lui plaît, la chose ne dépendait que d'elle seule" (p. 48); "Elle lui dit qu'elle ne veut pas qu'il lui parle, que ce qu'elle veut c'est qu'il fasse comme d'habitude il fait avec les femmes qu'il emmène dans sa garconnière" (p. 49); "Elle lui demande de ne pas bouger. Laisse-moi. Elle dit qu'elle veut le faire elle. Elle le fait. Elle le déshabille" (p. 49); "Et pleurant il le fait" (p. 50).

45. Roland Barthes, *A Lover's Discourse,* trans. Richard Howard (New York: Hill & Wang, 1978).

46. "Il a commencé à souffrir là, dans la chambre, pour la première fois, il ne ment plus sur ce point. Il lui dit que déjà il sait qu'elle ne l'aimera jamais. . . . Il dit qu'il est seul, atrocement seul avec cet amour qu'il a pour elle" (p. 48).

47. "Il dit qu'il a su tout de suite, dès la traversée du fleuve, que je serai ainsi, après mon premier amant, que j'aimerais l'amour, il dit qu'il sait déjà que lui je le tromperai et aussi que je tromperai tous les hommes avec qui je serai" (p. 54).

48. "Les départs. C'était toujours les mêmes départs. C'était toujours les premiers départs sur les mers. La séparation d'avec la terre s'était toujours faite dans la douleur et le même désespoir, mais ça n'avait jamais empêché les hommes de partir, les juifs,

les hommes de la pensée et les purs voyageurs du seul voyage sur la mer, et ça n'avait jamais empêché non plus les femmes de les laisser aller, elles qui ne partaient jamais, qui restaient garder le lieu natal, la race, les biens, la raison d'être du retour" (p. 132).

49. "Alors je lui ai dit que j'étais de l'avis de son père. Que je refusais de rester avec lui" (p. 103).

50. "L'homme de Cholen sait que la décision de son père et celle de l'enfant sont les mêmes et qu'elles sont sans appel" (p. 119).

51. Although the relationship between the young girl and her lover is a form of prostitution in that it involves monetary exchange, it needs to be distinguished from Suzanne's prostitution in *The Sea Wall* and the notion of prostitution elaborated by Irigaray in *This Sex,* 187–88. In *The Lover,* it is the exchange of money that makes the young girl's relationship with the Chinese man tolerable in the eyes of her family. Consequently, it serves as a screen for the sexual pleasure the young girl derives from the affair, and thereby enables her to continue the relationship.

52. "Mes frères ne lui adresseront jamais la parole. C'est comme s'il n'était pas visible pour eux, comme s'il n'était pas assez dense pour être perçu, vu, entendu par eux. Cela parce qu'il est à mes pieds, qu'il est posé en principe que je ne l'aime pas, que je suis avec lui pour l'argent, que je ne peux pas l'aimer, que c'est impossible, qu'il pourrait tout supporter de moi sans être jamais au bout de cet amour. Cela, parce que c'est un Chinois, que ce n'est pas un blanc" (p. 65).

53. "Je lui demande de me dire comment son père est riche, de quelle façon. Il dit que parler d'argent l'ennuie, mais que si j'y tiens il veut bien me dire ce qu'il sait de la fortune de son père. Tout a commencé à Cholen, avec les compartiments pour indigènes. Il en a fait construire trois cents. Plusieurs rues lui appartiennent. . . . La population ici aime bien être ensemble, surtout cette population pauvre, elle vient de la campagne et elle aime bien vivre aussi dehors, dans la rue. Et il ne faut pas détruire les habitudes des pauvres" (pp. 60–61).

54. "C'est une famille en pierre, pétrifiée dans une épaisseur sans accès aucun. Chaque jour nous essayons de nous tuer, de tuer. Non seulement on ne se parle pas mais on ne se regarde pas. Du moment qu'on est vu, on ne peut pas regarder. Regarder c'est avoir un mouvement de curiosité vers, envers, c'est déchoir. Aucune personne regardée ne vaut le regard sur elle. Il est toujours déshonorant" (p. 69).

55. "Je lui dis que son séjour en France lui a été fatal. Il en convient. Il dit qu'il a tout acheté à Paris, ses femmes, ses connaissances, ses idées" (p. 62). "Il parlait. Il disait qu'il s'ennuyait de Paris, des adorables Parisiennes, des noces, des bombes, ah là là, de la Coupole, de la Rotonde je préfère, des boîtes de nuit, de cette existence 'épatante' qu'il avait menée pendant deux ans" (p. 45).

56. "Il etait intimidé, il avait peur comme avant. Sa voix tremblait tout à coup. Et avec le tremblement, tout à coup, elle avait retrouvé l'accent de la Chine" (p. 142).

57. "Il savait qu'elle avait commencé à écrire des livres, il l'avait su par la mère qu'il avait revue à Saigon. . . . Et puis il n'avait plus su quoi lui dire. Et puis il le lui avait dit. Il lui avait dit que c'était comme avant, qu'il l'aimait encore, qu'il ne pourrait jamais cesser de l'aimer, qu'il l'aimerait jusqu'à sa mort" (p. 142).

58. Gayatri Spivak argues that a certain body of liberal feminist criticism "reproduces the axioms of imperialism" through "a basically isolationist admiration for the literature of the female subject." "Three Women's Texts and a Critique of Imperialism," *Critical Inquiry* 12 (Autumn 1985): 243. I concur with this argument and have emphasized the colonialist politics involved in Duras's constitution of a female subject position.

CONTRIBUTORS

William L. Andrews is Joyce and Elizabeth Hall Professor of American Literature at the University of Kansas. He is the author of *To Tell a Free Story: The First Century of Afro-American Autobiography, 1760–1865* (1986) and editor of a number of books on American autobiography, including *Sisters of the Spirit: Three Black Women's Autobiographies of the Nineteenth Century* (1986) and *Journeys in New Worlds: Early American Women's Narratives* (1990). He is general editor of Studies in American Autobiography, published by the University of Wisconsin Press, and associate editor of *a/b: Auto/Biography Studies*.

Margot Badran, an associate professor at Kuwait University, is a historian of the modern Middle East specializing in women's history. She is coeditor of *Opening the Gates: A Century of Arab Feminist Writing* and editor and translator of *Harem Years: The Memoirs of an Egyptian Feminist, Huda Sha'rawi*. Her numerous articles include "Competing Agenda: Feminists, Islam, and the State," in Deniz Kandiyoti, ed. *Women, Islam, and the State*. She is currently researching the role of women in the Kuwaiti resistance.

John Beverley is professor of Hispanic literature and a member of the Program in Cultural Studies at the University of Pittsburgh. His books include *Aspects of Gongora's "Soledades"* (1980), *Del Lazarillo al Sandinismo* (1987), and *Literature and Politics in the Central American Revolutions*. He has recently edited, with Hugo Achugar, a volume of essays on Latin American *testimonio, La voz del otro: Testimonio, subalternidad y verdad narrativa (1991)*.

Debra A. Castillo is associate professor of romance studies and comparative literature at Cornell University, where she specializes in contemporary Hispanic literature, women's studies, and postcolonial literary theory. She is author of *The Translated World: A Postmodern Tour of Libraries in Literature* (Florida State University Press, 1984), and *Talking Back: Strategies for a Latin American Feminist Literary Criticism* (forthcoming from Cornell University Press). She has published numerous essays on contemporary Latin American, Spanish, U.S. Hispanic, and British Commonwealth fiction. She is also editor of *Diacritics* and book review editor of *Letras femeninas*.

Suzanne Chester is currently a visiting lecturer in the Department of Foreign Languages and Literatures at North Carolina State University.

She received a B.A. in French and Spanish from University College Dublin, Ireland, and an M.A. in French literature from Louisiana State University. She has recently completed a Ph.D. dissertation titled "Dominance, Marginality and Subversion in French (Post) Colonial Discourse" at LSU. Her interests include feminist and cultural theory, postcolonial fiction and autobiography, and the twentieth-century French novel.

Carole Boyce Davies is an associate professor with joint appointments in English, African-American studies, and comparative literature at the State University of New York at Binghamton. She has an ongoing commitment to feminist criticism of African, Caribbean, and African-American literatures and to feminist theory from women of color. She has published widely in these fields and has edited two volumes of criticism: *Ngambika: Studies of Women in African Literature* (1986) and *Out of the Kumbla: Caribbean Women and Literature* (1990). Her contribution to this volume is from her manuscript in progress on black women's life stories.

Anne Goldman is a graduate student in English at the University of California, Berkeley, where she is finishing a dissertation on the problematics of culture and class in the autobiographies of American women. Her essay "'I Made the Ink': (Literary) Production and Reproduction in *Dessa Rose* and *Beloved*," was recently published in *Feminist Studies*.

Janice Gould received her B.A. in linguistics from the University of California at Berkeley. She also earned her M.A. at U.C. Berkeley in English, in 1987. She is currently enrolled as a doctoral student in the English Department at the University of New Mexico. Her field is American Indian literature. In 1989 she received an award from the National Endowment for the Arts for a manuscript of poetry. A book of her poetry titled *Beneath My Heart* was published in 1991 by Firebrand Books.

Janet Varner Gunn is currently living in Pittsburgh, where she is finishing a book on a West Bank refugee family and continuing work on Third World autobiography theory. Before her two years of work and study in the Middle East, she was associate professor of religious studies at the University of North Carolina at Greensboro.

Caren Kaplan is an assistant professor in the Department of English at Georgetown University. She is currently writing a book titled *Questions of Travel: Postmodernism and the Poetics of Displacement*. Her work has appeared in *Discourse, Inscriptions, Cultural Critique, a/b, Modern Fiction Studies,* and *Public Culture.*

Shirley Geok-lin Lim is professor of Asian American studies at the University of California, Santa Barbara. Recipient of the 1980 Commonwealth Poetry Prize, she has published three books of poetry, a collection of short stories, and articles on Asian American and Southeast Asian literature and on women's writing. She is co-editor of *The Forbidden Stitch: An Asian American Women's Anthology,* which received the 1990 American Book Award, and is editor or coeditor of three forthcoming volumes: *Approaches to Teaching Kingston's "The Woman Warrior"* (MLA), an anthology on contemporary global literature (Houghton Mifflin), and *Asian American Critical Essays* (Temple University Press).

Françoise Lionnet teaches French and comparative literature at Northwestern University. She is currently a senior Rockefeller Fellow at the Center for Advanced Feminist Studies at the University of Minnesota (1991–92), where she is working on a study of postcolonial women writers tentatively titled *Spiraling Tensions.* She is the author of *Autobiographical Voices: Race, Gender, Self-Portraiture* (Cornell, 1989) and is coediting a special double issue of *Yale French Studies* on exile and nomadism.

Kateryna Olijnyk Longley is a Ukrainian Australian who is a senior lecturer in English and comparative literature at Murdoch University in Perth, Western Australia. She is the coeditor of *Beckett's Later Fiction and Drama: Texts for Company* (1987) and *Striking Chords: Multicultural Literary Criticism* (forthcoming 1991), and she has published numerous articles on new forms of postcolonial writing in Australia and Canada, especially writing by women and by indigenous and immigrant people. She is currently the editor of *SPAN,* the journal of the South Pacific Association for Commonwealth Literature and Language Studies.

Nancy L. Paxton is associate professor of English at Northern Arizona University, where she teaches courses in Victorian literature, feminist theory, and women's writing. She has published widely on Victorian women writers and has recently completed *George Eliot and Herbert Spencer: Feminism, Evolutionism, and the Reconstruction of Gender* (Princeton University Press, 1991). Research for her current work on British autobiographies and novels about India has been supported by the Mary Ingraham Bunting Foundation at Radcliffe College, a Mellon Faculty Fellowship at Harvard University, the Davis Humanities

Institute at the University of California at Davis, and the Fulbright Foundation.

Lee Quinby is an associate professor of English and American studies at Hobart and William Smith Colleges. Her publications include essays in *Signs, American Historical Review,* and *Panic Encyclopedia.* She is coeditor of *Feminism and Foucault: Reflections on Resistance* (1988) and author of *Freedom, Foucault, and the Subject of America* (1991).

Gita Rajan is an assistant professor at the University of New Orleans. She has published articles on colonial/postcolonial discourse, feminist theory, and Victorian literature. She is currently revising her manuscript *Ecriture Féminine as Autobiography in Walter Pater.*

Claudine Raynaud is associate professor of English and American literature at the University François Rabelais in Tours and visiting lecturer at the University of Paris X, Nanterre. She has taught French at the University of Liverpool, the University of Birmingham, Northwestern University, and women's studies and English literature at Oberlin College and the University of Michigan. She received a doctorate from the University Paul Valéry, Montpellier, and a Ph.D. from the University of Michigan, Ann Arbor. She has published on Marvell, Joyce, Milton, and Lowry and is currently working on a book-length study of black women writers' autobiographies.

Greg Sarris is an assistant professor of English at the University of California, Los Angeles. His articles and essays have appeared in many journals and magazines.

Sidonie Smith is professor of English and comparative literature at the State University of New York at Binghamton. She is the author of *Where I'm Bound: Patterns of Slavery and Freedom in Black American Autobiography* (1974) and *A Poetics of Women's Autobiography: Marginality and the Fictions of Self-Representation* (1987). She has just completed a book on twentieth-century women's autobiographical practice titled *Subjectivity, Identity, and the Body.* Her recent essays include "Self, Subject, and Resistance: Marginalities and Twentieth-Century Autobiographical Practice" (1990), "Construing Truths in Lying Mouths: Truthtelling in Women's Autobiography" (1990), and "The Autobiographical Manifesto: Identities, Temporalities, Politics" (1991).

Julia Watson is associate professor of humanities at the University of Montana and has also taught at Hobart and William Smith Colleges.

She has written essays, published and forthcoming, on aspects of women's autobiography and feminist theory, as well as on Montaigne and on twentieth-century German literature and film; she has also published translations from German. In 1991 she chaired the executive committee of the Division on Life Writing of the Modern Language Association. She is on the editorial board of *a/b: Auto/biography Studies* and gives talks on life writing to diverse groups for the Montana Committee for the Humanities.

Index

Compiled by Suzanne Sherman Aboulfadl

6–7; location of, xxviii; male, ordering imperative in, 13; of marginalized
people, 299–300; versus memoirs,
299; in Mexico, 244; Middle Eastern,
290 n.17; mimetic potential of, xix;
in nonindividualistic cultures, 371–
72; nontraditional forms of, xviii; and
out-law genres, xxvii, 115–38; as personal mythology, 321; postcolonial,
321–22; power relationships in, 299;
as process and product of decolonization, xxi; as sexual self-decolonization, 145; specific locations of, xvi;
spiritual, 409 n.37; as survival literature, 75, 76; versus *testimonio*, 96,
103; *testimonio* as "politically
correct" alternative to, 106; as therapy, 161–62; Third World, 65–87;
versus mainstream Western autobiography, 77; the unspeakable in, 139–
41; Western cultural values in, 371–
72; Western practice of, xvii–xviii; as
white male genre, 371; by women of
color, 322; working class, 91–92. *See
also* life stories
"Autobiography: An Anatomy and a Taxonomy" (Olney), 7
*Autobiography: Essays Theoretical and
Critical* (Olney), 117
*Autobiography: Toward a Poetics of
Experience* (Gunn), 75
Autobiography of Alice B. Toklas, The
(Stein), 149
Autobiography of a Runaway Slave
(Barnet), 93, 105
Autobiography of Malcolm X, The
(Haley), 4
autoethnography: autobiography as, 35;
Cliff's narratives as, 334; in culinary
memoirs, 169–95
automythology, in *My Story* (Das), 353–
54
*Aventuras, desaventuras, y sueños de
Adonis García: El vampiro de la
Colonia Roma, Las* (Zapata), 105
Avi-ram, Amitai, 168 n.33
Al-Ayyam (Husain), 275

Babur, memoirs of, 118
Badran, Margot, xxvi, 270–93

Bakhtin, Mikhail, 347, 363
Baldwin, James, 165 n.3
Balfour Declaration, 72
Ballestier, Caroline, 392
Baluch, Akhtar, 121
Balún-Canán (Castellanos), 245–66; crit-
ical reaction to, 247–48; doubled story-
teller in, 250, 257; negation in, 256–
60; silence of the oppressed in, 253–
60
Barber, Karin, 16
Barker, Francis, 388–89
Barnet, Miguel, 93, 105
Barrage contre le pacifique, Un (Duras),
436
Barrios de Chungara, Domitila, 121. *See
also Let Me Speak!*
Barthes, Roland, 322, 448
Basila, Nazik, 275
Bate, Barbara, 14–15
*Behind the Scenes; Or, Thirty Years a
Slave, and Four Years in the White
House* (Keckley), 227–28, 231–38
Behn, Aphra, 346
Bell, Diane, 372–73, 380
Benjamin, Anne, 4, 8, 9
Benson, Mary, 9
Benstock, Shari, 13, 300
Bentinck, William, 393
Benveniste, Emile, 444
Beverley, John, xxvi–xxvii, 91–114, 123
Bhabha, Homi, 206; identity in differ-
ence, 217 n.12
Bildungsroman, xx, 103; subjectivity in,
96
Biografía de un cimarrón (Barnet), 93
biography, romantic, 93
biomythography, 128–30, 322; of Audre
Lorde, 153–54, 156
bisexuality, 144
Black, Tom, 416, 417–18
Black Sisters, Speak Out (Thiam), 5, 14
Blixen, Blor, 414, 416
Blixen, Karen, 423. *See also* Dinesen,
Isak
"Blood" (Das), 355
Bloom, Harold, 56
body, female. *See* disembodiment;
female embodiment; women's bodies
Boktor, Amir, 274